Accounting for Managers

Interpreting Accounting Information for Decision-Making

Canadian Edition

Paul M. Collier

Previously at Monash University, Melbourne, Australia

Sandy M. Kizan

Athabasca University (AU)

With contributions by

Eckhard Schumann

University of Toronto at Mississauga

WILEY

Library and Archives Canada Cataloguing in Publication
Collier, Paul M.
    Accounting for managers : interpreting accounting information for
decision-making / Paul M. Collier and Sandy M. Kizan. — Canadian ed.

Includes index.
ISBN 978-1-118-03796-6

    1. Managerial accounting--Textbooks. I. Kizan, Sandy M.
(Sandy Margaret), 1965- II. Title.

HF5657.4.C64 2012   658.15'11   C2012-907087-4

Production Credits

Vice President & Publisher:	Veronica Visentin
Acquisitions Editor:	Zoë Craig
Marketing Manager:	Anita Osborne
Editorial Manager:	Karen Staudinger
Production Manager:	Tegan Wallace
Developmental Editor:	Theresa Fitzgerald
Media Editor:	Channade Fenandoe
Production Coordinator:	Lynda Jess
Permissions Coordinator:	Luisa Begani
Cover & Interior Design:	Joanna Vieira
Typesetting:	Aptara
Cover Image:	© Barrett & MacKay/All
Canada Photos/Corbis	

Printing and binding: RR Donnelley
Printed and bound in the United States.
2 3 4 5 CC 19 18 17 16

John Wiley & Sons Canada, Ltd.
6045 Freemont Blvd.
Mississauga, Ontario L5R 4J3

Visit our website at: www.wiley.ca

ABOUT THE AUTHORS

Sandy Kizan is an Academic Expert in the Faculty of Business at Athabasca University (AU). She has taught introductory through advanced management accounting at AU since 2006. Sandy is a certified management accountant (CMA), holds a masters degree in business (MBA) and is a member of the Society of Management Accountants of Alberta and the Institute of Management Accountants in the US. Sandy has authored several courses for the undergraduate program at Athabasca University including *Strategic and Competitive Analysis* and *Decision Analysis*, both focusing on developing a student's understanding of management accounting tools and techniques. Sandy's professional background includes nine years' experience as a senior business analyst for the oil and gas industry specializing in business development and the creation, operation and management of two small businesses.

Sandy is excited to have adapted this textbook for a Canadian audience. She believes the decision-based focus of the book provides a practical approach for non-accounting managers to learn the key tools and techniques in management accounting. Sandy seeks to help students develop a richer and more substantive understanding of how accounting is used in practice.

Sandy lives with her husband and two daughters in the mountains of southern Alberta where she enjoys skiing, running, and gardening, and aims to achieve balance between her dedication to teaching and learning and her passion for her family.

Dr. Paul Collier PhD (Warwick), B.Bus. (NSWIT), M.Comm. (NSW), Grad.Dip. Ed. (UTS), CPA (Aust.) was until recently Professor of Accounting at Monash University in Melbourne, Australia. He was until 2006 a senior lecturer at Aston Business School in Aston University, Birmingham, UK. Paul is currently consulting to a number of business organizations and undertaking casual postgraduate teaching and management training.

Paul has worked in senior financial and general management roles in the UK and Australia. He was chief financial officer and company secretary, and subsequently general manager (operations), for one of Australia's largest printing companies before moving to the UK in 1993. He has been a board member and chair of the audit committee of a non-profit-distributing housing association with assets of £200 million, and a board member and chair of the finance and resources committee of a public health service with annual expenditure of $350 million.

The book uses material developed by the author based on his experience as a practitioner, in his teaching at Aston and Monash, and in delivering financial training to non-financial managers in diverse industries over many years. Paul's research interests are in the use of management accounting and non-financial performance information in decision making, and the behavioural aspects of management accounting and management control systems. He has published a large number of articles in academic journals and has been an examiner for CPA Australia and the Chartered Institute of Management Accountants.

PREFACE

The Canadian edition of this textbook builds on the success of the original textbook that was published in the United Kingdom. While most of the topics from the original textbook are relevant to Canadian readers, this book has been adapted to include materials, examples, and case studies with a Canadian focus. Part I provides a discussion of financial accounting, with particular focus on international financial reporting standards and practices. Part II concentrates on management accounting information for planning, decision making, and control, while Part III provides the supporting information including relevant readings that demonstrate some current research and literature in management accounting.

RATIONALE FOR THE BOOK

This book was motivated by a need for a "decision-focused" accounting textbook for both MBA and undergraduate programs. As accounting has increasingly become decentred from the accounting department in organizations, line managers in all functional areas of business are expected to be able to prepare budgets, develop business cases for capital investment, and exercise cost control to ensure that profit targets are achieved. Managers are also expected to be able to analyze and interpret accounting information so that marketing, operations, and human resource decisions are made in the light of an understanding of the financial implications of those decisions.

Most accounting textbooks are *accounting centric*, with chapters typically covering accounting techniques rather than the types of decisions made by non-financial managers. The emphasis in those books, many of which are designed for people whose career aspirations are to become accountants, is on *doing* accounting rather than *using* accounting. This book has been written for the vast majority of postgraduate students and practising managers who do not want to become professional accountants. The book therefore has a *practitioner-manager orientation*.

The title of the book, *Accounting for Managers: Interpreting Accounting Information for Decision Making*, emphasizes the focus on accounting to meet the needs of managers. The material contained in the book stresses the interpretation (rather than the construction) of accounting information as well as a critical (rather than unthinking) acceptance of the underlying assumptions behind accounting. It is suitable for postgraduate and undergraduate students who are undertaking courses in accounting that do not lead to professional accreditation, and to practising non-financial managers who need a better understanding of the role of accounting in their organizations.

While there tends to be a strong focus in many accounting books on manufacturing organizations, the growth of service businesses and the knowledge economy has created a need for materials related to these areas. This book uses examples, case studies, and questions that are equally balanced between the needs of organizations in manufacturing, retail, and services.

This book also introduces the reader to some of the journal literature that is either fundamental to the role of accounting or is "path breaking." The book is not intended to be deeply theoretical, but rather provides research and additional readings which allow readers to explore the concept in question in a deeper manner.

Finally, the examples in this book emphasize *critical understanding and questioning* of the accounting numbers and of the underlying assumptions behind those numbers, and the need to supplement accounting reports with non-financial performance measures and broader perspectives than satisfying shareholder wealth alone.

OUTLINE OF THE BOOK

The book is arranged in three parts. The first part describes the context and role of financial account-ing and provides theoretical frameworks that relate to using accounting in practice. Part I also dis-cusses financial accounting practices and the analysis and interpretation of accounting information.

The second part of the book shows the reader how accounting information is used in decision making, planning, and control. In this second part the accounting tools and techniques are explained, illustrated by straightforward examples. Case studies also help draw out the concepts. The end-of-chapter case studies help in developing the ability to interpret and analyze financial informa-tion produced by an accountant for use by non-accounting managers in decision making.

The questions at the end of each chapter are presented in two parts. The first questions are mul-tiple choice and are simple, theory-reinforcing questions. Readers should use these questions as a guide to assess whether they understand the chapter materials. The answer key to these self-test questions is found at the end of the book. The second set of questions are more complex problems that require students to apply the tools to a business problem or situation. These problems rely on knowledge gained from reading the current and preceding chapters. Attempting the problems will help the reader to understand how accounting information can be used by non-accounting manag-ers in their decision-making processes.

The third part of the textbook provides materials that support the concepts taught throughout the book. Five readings from the accounting literature cover a broad spectrum of topics and support many of the important concepts in the book. They present five different yet complementary perspec-tives on accounting in organizations. The third part also contains an extensive glossary of account-ing terms. The use of blue colour in the text highlights that the meaning of the term is outlined in the glossary.

INSTRUCTOR'S RESOURCES

The **Instructor's Solutions Manual** is available on the Instructor's website and permits instructors to select, collate, and print solutions to the specific set of chapter problems that have been assigned as homework.

The **PowerPoint Presentations** are editable so instructors can modify the content to suit their own preferences.

Acknowledgments

I would like to thank Paul Collier, who developed the original concept for this book, for his inspira-tion and dedication in developing this book. I would also like to thank Eckhard Schumann who shared his expertise in financial accounting in adapting Chapters 2, 3, 4, and 5 for a Canadian audience.

I would like to acknowledge the following individuals who reviewed this textbook and provided their suggestions and ideas for improving the book.

Sam Alagurajah, George Brown College

Talal Al-Hayale, University of Windsor

Carmel Branston, Wilfrid Laurier University

François Brouard, Carleton University

Gillian Bubb, University of the Fraser Valley

Lynn Carty, University of Guelph

Denise Cook, Durham College

Gail Czember, Northern Alberta Institute of Technology

Robert Ducharme, University of Waterloo

Maureen Fizzell, Simon Fraser University

Howard Leaman, University of Guelph

Donna Losell, University of Toronto

Janet Morrill, University of Manitoba

Jim Power, Dalhousie University

Patti Proulx, Carleton University

Pamela Quon, Athabasca University

Naqi Sayed, Lakehead University

Glenn Skubbeltrang, Brock University

Ruth Ann Strickland, University of Western Ontario

Jane Wilson, Royal Roads University

Betty Wong, Athabasca University

Nancy Zowkewych, Centennial College

Thank you also to the Ancillary Authors and Technical Checkers, including. Ilene Gilborn, Mount Royal University, Robert Ducharme, University of Waterloo, and Jerry Zdril, MacEwan University.

Finally I would like to thank all of the people at John Wiley and Sons, Canada Ltd who helped develop this First Canadian Edition: Veronica Visentin, Zoe Craig, Anita Osborne, Theresa Fitzgerald, and Luisa Begani.

CONTENTS

PART I

Context of Accounting

Part I describes the context and role of accounting, both financial and managerial, in organizations and provides theoretical frameworks on which accounting is based. It is hoped that this will offer a foundation for readers' understanding that accounting is more than a technical subject and has practical applications for all organizations, both not-for-profit and profit. These first chapters provide the student with a foundation of financial accounting knowledge based on *International Financial Reporting Standards* (IFRS). A foundation of financial accounting is essential for understanding the tools of management accounting, on which the remainder of the book is focused.

Chapter 1 provides an introduction to accounting and an overview of both managerial and financial accounting. The chapter outlines some examples of management accounting methods in practice as well as an overview of current trends in management accounting that are influencing planning, decision making, and control within organizations.

Chapter 2 outlines the context in which management accounting operates: adding shareholder value through strategic planning, as well as company regulation and corporate governance that underlie the functioning of business organizations.

Chapter 3 describes how transactions are recorded by accounting systems and reported in the financial statements and the principles that underlie the preparation and presentation of financial statements. The chapter also outlines how accounting information is collected, stored, and controlled.

Chapter 4 takes a closer look at financial statements. Students are introduced to *International Financial Reporting Standards* (IFRS) and the *Conceptual Framework for Financial Reporting*. The principles of accrual accounting and depreciation are covered. The chapter also discusses management's responsibility for the financial statements.

Chapter 5 focuses on interpreting financial reports. Emphasis is placed on analyzing financial information in terms of profitability, liquidity, leveraging, efficiency, and shareholder return. The chapter also introduces students to alternative reporting information.

CHAPTER 1

Introduction to Accounting

LEARNING OBJECTIVES

After reading this chapter, you should be able to answer the following questions:

- In what way does accounting support accountability within companies?

- What are the key functions of accounting?

- How is management accounting different from financial accounting?

- How is financial and management accounting information used within organizations?

- What are some examples of practical applications of accounting by companies?

- What are some key developments in the role of accounting that are influencing planning, decision making, and control within organizations?

This chapter introduces financial and management accounting and explains the differences between these two types of accounting practices and the importance of both in today's multidivisional, multiproduct organizations. Also discussed are recent developments that have influenced the role of managers in relation to the use of financial and non-financial information for the purposes of planning, decision making, and control.

Accounting, Accountability, and Stewardship

Businesses exist to provide goods or services to customers in exchange for a financial reward. Public-sector and not-for-profit organizations also provide services, although their funding comes not from customers but from a government or charitable donations, and the objective of their work is to provide a service rather than to receive a financial reward. While this book is primarily concerned with profit-oriented businesses, most of the principles we will discuss are equally applicable to the public and not-for-profit sectors.

Business is not about accounting. It is about markets, people, and operations (the delivery of products or services), although accounting is implicated in all decisions related to these because it is the financial representation of business activity. The purpose of accounting can be summed up as the "process of identifying, measuring, and communicating economic information to permit informed judgments and decisions by users of the information" (American Accounting Association, 1966). This is an important definition for the following reasons:

- **It recognizes that accounting is a process.** The accounting process is concerned with capturing business events, recording their financial effects, summarizing and reporting the results of those effects, and interpreting those results.

- **It is concerned with economic information.** While economic information is predominantly financial, it can also include non-financial information, such as records of labour hours, machine hours, and other non-financial factors that impact the economic value of an enterprise.

- **Its purpose is to support "informed judgments and decisions by users."** This emphasizes both the usefulness of accounting information in making decisions and the broad spectrum of users of that information. While the book's primary concern is the use of accounting information for decision making, it takes a stakeholder perspective. Users of accounting information include all those who may have an interest in the survival, profitability, and growth of a business: shareholders, employees, customers, suppliers, financiers, governments, and society as a whole.

Accounting is a collection of systems and processes used to record, report, and interpret business transactions. It provides a way to demonstrate to stakeholders (owners, governments, investors, suppliers, customers, employees, etc.) that managers have acted in their best interests. This represents the notion of accountability—whereby a manager provides assurances to stakeholders through the process of accounting. Accounting is also important due to the stewardship function of managers—businesses are entrusted to the care of managers. Stewardship becomes an important concept in today's organizations because in all but very small businesses, the owners of the businesses are not the same as the managers. Consider Research In Motion (RIM), which was founded in 1984 by Mike Lazaridis and Douglas Fregin. RIM became a publically traded company in 1997 and as of February 26, 2011, had 522.8 million shares outstanding (Research In Motion, 2011). The management (or stewards) of RIM are accountable to each shareholder of the company and are entrusted with the responsibility of managing the company in the best interests of all stakeholders. This separation of ownership from control makes accounting, accountability, and stewardship particularly important.

Accounting is traditionally seen as fulfilling three functions:

1. Scorekeeping: Capturing, recording, summarizing, and reporting financial performance.

2. Attention directing: Drawing the attention of managers to, and assisting in the interpretation of, business performance, particularly in terms of the comparison between actual and planned performance.

3. Problem solving: Identifying the best choice from a range of alternative actions.

Scorekeeping is primarily regarded as a function of **financial accounting**, where financial reports are prepared to provide information to external and internal users. Attention directing and problem solving are seen more as **management accounting** activities that take place through three interrelated functions, all part of the role of both non-financial (marketing, operations, human resources, etc.) and financial managers:

- **Planning:** Using financial information to help establish goals and strategies to achieve those goals. This many include the formulation of a budget to communicate the plans and goals to the organization.

- **Decision making:** Using financial information to make decisions consistent with those goals and strategies. For example, this may include using accounting tools such as cost–volume–profit analysis (discussed in Chapter 8) to help decide on a product mix.

- **Control:** Using financial information to maintain performance as close as possible to plan, or using the information to modify the plan itself. This may include variance analysis and flexible budgets (both discussed in Chapter 15) and performance measurement (discussed in Chapter 13).

The functions of planning, decision making, and control have become increasingly important in today's businesses due to the prevalence of decentralized organization structures, where much of the planning, decision making, and control is at a business-unit level. Managers need financial and non-financial information to help them develop and implement strategies; make decisions about products, services, prices, and costs; and ensure that plans are put into action and goals are achieved.

The Role of Financial Accounting

Financial accounting is a very important practice in today's organizations due to the need for accountability within companies where management is separate from ownership and the need for equitable methods of reporting between companies for income tax and investing purposes. Financial accounting is regulated in Canada by generally accepted accounting principles (GAAP) outlined by the *International Financial Reporting Standards* (IFRS) as developed by the International Accounting Standards Board (IASB) and the rulings published in the *Income Tax Act*. Chapter 4 discusses the IFRS in more detail.

Financial accounting is focused on the recording of accounting transactions (transactions that involve economic events) in the financial system of an organization, with the end result being the formal financial statements of an enterprise. All Canadian companies must adhere to specific guidelines when recording transactions and reporting financial results. For example, companies must report income when earned, not when the money is received. If, for instance, a legal firm prepared a will for a customer in December but did not bill the client until January, the firm would still need to report the income as earned in December.

Similarly, companies must record expenses when incurred, not when the money is paid. If the same legal firm paid an employee wages to prepare the will in December but did not pay the employee until January, the firm still reports the wage expense in December. This ensures that companies match expenses with the incomes earned in a given period. It also ensures that companies do not defer incomes to future years. The basic principles of financial accounting are discussed further in Chapter 3.

The reason that financial transactions and reports are prepared according to the IFRS is to provide accountability to stakeholders and to provide a comparable and fair financial platform for different companies within Canada and worldwide. Financial standards create a fair way by which to assess organizations for both tax and investing purposes. An investor, for example, can look at two companies in a similar industry and compare their profitably to help make investment decisions. The fact that both companies use similar accounting standards ensures that the investor is comparing apples to apples and not apples to oranges. If standards were not used, an investor would have a very difficult time comparing the value of different companies on the stock market. In addition, tax-evasion practices would possibly run rampant. For instance, if a company was not required to report income until it was received, they might try to defer income from one year to the next year by asking customers to pay them after their year-end.

The role of the financial accountant, therefore, is to ensure that financial transactions and reports are prepared in accordance with regulations, to provide accountability to the stakeholders of a company, and to create an equitable and fair basis for assessing business performance. A financial accountant is concerned primarily with external reporting—reports that are prepared for shareholders, tax authorities, and other stakeholders. The report shown in Exhibit 1.1 is a WestJet statement of comprehensive income that would have been prepared according to standards set by the IFRS. The statement of comprehensive income is discussed further in Chapter 4.

Exhibit 1.1 WestJet Consolidated Statement of Earnings

Consolidated Statement of Earnings

(Stated in thousands of Canadian dollars, except per share data)

(Unaudited)

	Notes	Three Months Ended June 30		Six Months Ended June 30	
		2011	2010	2011	2010
Revenues:					
Guest		675,844	559,054	1,364,432	1,118,779
Other		66,444	52,630	150,278	112,197
		742,288	611,684	1,514,710	1,230,976
Expenses:					
Aircraft fuel		230,577	164,450	449,540	324,504
Airport operations		99,064	92,736	208,215	193,775
Flight operations and navigational charges		86,468	82,391	170,565	161,443
Sales and distribution		61,823	57,329	138,645	123,768
Marketing, general, and administration		54,486	48,139	102,302	97,958
Depreciation and amortization		43,508	42,677	86,815	85,298
Aircraft leasing		41,624	35,397	82,337	69,655
Inflight		34,316	31,404	67,815	61,734
Maintenance		34,505	27,080	65,127	56,352
Employee profit share		4,577	3,898	12,169	6,213
		690,948	585,501	1,383,530	1,180,700

(continued)

Exhibit 1.1 WestJet Consolidated Statement of Earnings (*continued*)

Earnings from operations		51,340	26,183	131,180	50,276
Non-operating income (expense):					
Finance income		3,808	2,065	7,739	3,772
Finance costs		(15,585)	(17,902)	(31,783)	(36,363)
Gain on foreign exchange		639	3,431	2,138	1,312
Gain on disposal of property and equipment		16	612	9	606
Gain (loss) on derivatives	10	(4,159)	(558)	(6,416)	74
		(15,281)	(12,352)	(28,313)	(30,599)
Earnings before income tax		36,059	13,831	102,867	19,677
Income tax expense:					
Current		603	370	1,184	732
Deferred		9,854	6,628	27,832	9,747
		10,457	6,998	29,016	10,479
Net earnings		25,602	6,833	73,851	9,198
Earnings per share:	9				
Basic		0.18	0.05	0.52	0.06
Diluted		0.18	0.05	0.52	0.06

The accompanying notes are an integral part of the condensed consolidated interim financial statements.

Source: WestJet. (2011). *Media and investor relations: Quarterly reports.* Retrieved from www.westjet.com/guest/en/media-investors/quarterly-reports.shtml.

The Role of Management Accounting

Management accounting differs from financial accounting in that it focuses on the needs of internal users of information and is not restricted by accounting principles or regulations. Management accounting became important following the Industrial Revolution, as companies became more operationally complex. Prior to the Industrial Revolution, companies were very uncomplicated. They used labour to produce a very simple line of products and had a small management group, often the owners of the company, overseeing the entire operation. The Industrial Revolution brought with it larger, more complex companies that were characterized by multiple product lines, automation, and large-scale operations. The complexity of diversified and decentralized organizations created a need for better internal controls and more accurate information for decision making.

There was also an increase in the number of public companies, which led to the separation of ownership from control. This caused increased attention to what was called *cost accounting* (the forerunner of *management accounting*) in order to determine cost and exercise control by absent owners over their managers. These early cost accountants were typically situated in factories and tended to know how the business ran, so they were able to advise non-financial managers in relation to operational decisions. Cost accounting was concerned with determining the cost of an object, whether it was a product, an activity, a division of the organization, or a market segment.

The new corporate structures that developed in the 20th century—multidivisional organizations, conglomerates, and multinationals—placed increased demands on accounting. These demands included divisional performance evaluation and budgeting. In their acclaimed book, *Relevance Lost*, Johnson and Kaplan (1987) traced the development of management accounting from its origins in the Industrial Revolution, supporting process-type industries such as textile and steel conversion, transportation, and distribution. These systems were concerned with evaluating the efficiency of internal processes rather than measuring organizational profitability. Johnson and Kaplan also described how the early manufacturing firms attempted to improve performance via economies of scale by reducing unit cost through increasing the volume of output.

As the product range expanded and businesses sought economies of scope through producing two or more products in a single facility, there was an increased need for better information about how the mix of products could improve total profits. This need resulted in the development of management accounting as we know it today.

One of the earliest writers on management accounting described "different costs for different purposes" (Clark, 1923). This theme was developed by one of the earliest texts on management accounting (Vatter, 1950). Vatter distinguished the information needs of managers from those of external shareholders and emphasized that it was preferable to get less-precise data to managers quickly rather than complete information too late to influence decision making.

Johnson and Kaplan (1987) described how

. . . a management accounting system must provide timely and accurate information to facilitate efforts to control costs, to measure and improve productivity, and to devise improved production processes. The management accounting system must also report accurate product costs so that pricing decisions, introduction of new products, abandonment of obsolete products, and response to rival products can be made. (p. 4)

Core Activities of Management Accounting

Partly as a result of the stimulus of *Relevance Lost*, but perhaps more as a consequence of rapidly changing business conditions, management accounting has moved beyond its traditional concern with costing to incorporate wider issues of performance measurement, quality management, customer focus, and other areas of management control. Management accounting practices involve a variety of planning, decision making, and control processes within organizations. The Certified Management Accountants (CMA) Canada (2011) website defines the core activities of management accounting as

1. *Cost management,* which encompasses managing and controlling costs within an organization. For example, comparing actual results to planned or budgeted amounts is one way a company can exert control over their costs.

2. *Strategic performance measurement,* which involves measuring the performance of business units and teams and how performance relates back to the overall strategies of the company. Tools such as the balanced scorecard (to be discussed in Chapters 6 and 13) are often used by companies to measure performance.

3. *Process management* entails assessing the processes within a company to identify areas for improvement. For example, cost improvements have been achieved through tools such as kaizen costing, whereby a company focuses on making small improvements to its production processes that will create large cost improvements for the company overall (kaizen costing is discussed further in Chapter 16).

4. *Risk management,* since assessing risk is an important part of a manager's job. Any decision made by a company is accompanied by a degree of risk, but there are many risk-management tools that can help companies to assess these risks. Chapter 12 discusses various tools for risk management.

5. *Connecting company strategy with operations and anticipating customer and supplier needs,* for which many tools are used in the management accounting field. For example, in Chapters 6 and 13 we will discuss the balanced scorecard and how it links strategy to operational plans. In Chapter 9 we will discuss the value chain and how to best manage relationships with customers and suppliers.

6. *Looking to the future to provide real-world strategic direction, business management, and leadership,* because many of the activities performed under the realm of management accounting are future-focused. For example, managers may want to perform a "what if" analysis (discussed in Chapter 8) to see what might occur if they change a particular aspect of the business.

Each of these core areas of management accounting will be discussed in this textbook.

Trends in Management Accounting

In addition to the preceding core activities, many new trends in management accounting have become evident over the last decade or two. The following is a list of recent trends that are important in the field of cost accounting:

- Value-based management
- Non-financial performance-measurement systems
- Quality management
- Environmental accounting
- Activity-based management
- Strategic management accounting
- Lean accounting

Value-based management is more fully described in Chapter 2, but it is, in brief, concerned with improving the value of the business to its shareholders. Management accounting is implicated in this, as a fundamental role of non-financial managers is to make decisions that contribute to increasing the value of the business.

The limitations of accounting information, particularly as a lagging indicator of performance, have led to an increasing emphasis on **non-financial performance measures**. For instance, the popularity of the balanced scorecard, which includes both financial and non-financial performance indicators as means for evaluating divisional performance, has increased substantially in the last decade. Non-financial performance measures, described more fully in Chapters 3 and 13, are a major concern of both accountants and non-financial managers, as they tend to be leading indicators of the financial performance that will be reported at some future time.

Improving the quality of products and services is of major interest to managers in companies, since advances in production technology and the need to improve performance by reducing waste have led to **quality management** tools such as total quality management (TQM), just-in-time (JIT) inventory management, and continuous improvement processes such as Six Sigma. Quality management is discussed more fully in Chapter 9.

Greater attention to environmental issues has also led companies to a better understanding of the short-term and long-term consequences of **environmental accounting** issues, such as inefficient energy usage and pollution. Management accounting has a role to play in these issues, and non-financial managers need to understand the relationship between accounting and new management techniques. Environmental accounting is also discussed more fully in Chapter 9.

CASE IN POINT

Environmental Accounting at Toshiba

Environmental accounting—considering the costs and benefits to the environment—is a key tool used by Japanese-based Toshiba Corporation, which manufactures everything from air conditioners to X-ray machines.

"Our aim is to identify environmental management issues by evaluating and analyzing our activities so as to reduce environmental impacts at each phase from product development, to manufacturing, usage, and recycling, by means of environmental accounting," the company stated in a recent annual environmental report.

Toshiba's environmental accounting assumes four basic concepts. The first is the prevention of environmental risks, as in investment in structures such as dikes on factory grounds to prevent soil and groundwater contamination. Next is competitive advantage, such as positive public relations flowing from environmental projects. This is followed by internal benefits, such as reduced electricity and water costs. Lastly, Toshiba accounts for external benefits; for example, from customers' reduced power consumption with energy-efficient products such as televisions with adjustable picture quality that use less power.

Toshiba reported that its environmental costs rose by 1.7% in fiscal year 2010 to 55.2 billion yen (about [CDN] $726 million), while its environmental benefits decreased by 163% to −58.1 billion yen (about [CDN] −$765 million] compared with 2009. The company attributes most of the decrease to the expansion of its thermal power generation business, which "emits an extremely large amount of pollutants compared to other business segments." The company vowed to continue developing strategies to boost its environmental benefits "based on a careful analysis of environmental costs."

Sources: Toshiba Corporation. *Environmental report 2003* and *Environmental report 2011*.

Activity-based management is an approach that emphasizes how resources are used in the production of goods and services and the need to identify the drivers or causes of those costs in order to be able to budget for and control them more effectively. Activity-based approaches are introduced throughout Part III.

Strategic management accounting, which is described more fully in Chapter 16, is an attempt to shift the perspective of accountants and non-financial managers from inward-looking to outward-looking. They must recognize the need to look beyond the business, along the value chain, to its suppliers and customers, and beyond the current accounting period to product life cycles, and to seek ways of achieving and maintaining competitive advantage.

Lean accounting, a consequence of lean manufacturing, is a just-in-time philosophy supporting the elimination of wasteful accounting practices that contribute little to management decision making. Just-in-time inventory practices, discussed in Chapter 7, emphasize this philosophy.

As you can see, the role of management accounting is far reaching. The change from a narrow view of accountants as "bean counters" to one of them as more active participants in formulating and implementing business strategy, has been accompanied by a shift in the tasks of collecting, reporting, and analysing of routine financial information from accountants to non-financial line managers. This decentralization of accounting is evidenced by the delegation of responsibility for budgets and cost control to line managers, and it is the underlying reason that non-financial managers need a better understanding of accounting information and how that information can be used in decision making.

Management Accounting in Practice

Management accounting functions within organizations take many forms, and the activities related to management accounting are not necessarily performed by accountants. Managers and supervisors of production operations also must compile and analyze accounting data. Also, the owner of a small business must be familiar with accounting practices since it is unlikely that the business will hire an accountant to help manage and control its daily finances. For these reasons, it is important for managers of all types have a background and understanding of accounting information and how it can be analyzed to help make decisions that are relevant, timely, and cost effective.

The following excerpts describe two different managers who utilize accounting information on a daily basis to help run their business.

Bronwyn Lane—Owner and Operator of the Tin Can Restaurant

Bronwyn Lane owns and runs the Tin Can Restaurant, which has sales of approximately $2,000 per day. Bronwyn knows that the restaurant industry is characterized by high costs of food and labour and low overall profits. The average restaurant has a profit margin between 4% and 10%. Sales of $2,000 per day could mean a profit of only $80 for a day's work ($3,000 × 4% = $80). Due to this low margin, Bronwyn understands that she needs to keep a close eye on her finances to ensure that she can keep the restaurant afloat.

Each day, Bronwyn prints a report (shown in Exhibit 1.2) that provides her with statistics on her daily sales and customer information. Accounting information provided in the report includes average sales per customer, food cost percentages, cost of labour as compared to overall sales, and the percentage of breakfast, lunch, and dinner sales that make up the total sales for the day. This information helps Bronwyn plan staffing requirements for each period of the day to ensure that she is not overstaffed. It also provides her with information that can be used for strategic planning. For instance, due to low breakfast sales and higher labour costs for breakfasts, Bronwyn is planning to implement a buffet breakfast on Saturdays and Sundays to increase sales during this time period.

Exhibit 1.2 Sales Statistics for the Tin Can Restaurant

	Sales	% of Total Sales	# of Orders	Average Order	Food Cost	Food Cost Percentage of Sales	Labour Cost	Labour Percentage of Sales	Profit after Food and Labour
Labour v. Sales for December 12, 2012									
Breakfast	$ 325	13%	39	$ 8.33	$112.50	35%	$185.00	57%	$ 27.50
Lunch	858	35%	68	12.62	322.50	38%	207.00	24%	328.50
Dinner	1,285	52%	47	27.34	528.45	41%	282.00	22%	474.55
Total Sales	$2,468	100%	154		$963.45	39%	$674.00	27%	$830.55

Bronwyn also utilizes accounting information to prepare standardized recipes for each item on the menu. Standardized recipes outline the quantities and specific cost of each menu item (see Exhibit 1.3). This helps her price her products so that she achieves a good profit margin on each item sold.

(continued)

Exhibit 1.3 Standard Menu Costing

Menu Item: Pecan Chicken Curry				
Ingredient	Qty	Unit	Cost per Unit	Extended Cost
Chicken	0.3750	kg	$6.85	$2.57
White onion	0.5000	whole	0.75	0.38
Garlic cloves	0.5000	whole	0.11	0.06
Ginger	3.7500	mg	0.01	0.04
Tomatoes	0.7500	whole	0.35	0.26
Salt	3.7500	mg	0.005	0.02
Curry powder	3.7500	mg	0.005	0.02
Cayenne pepper	3.7500	mg	0.005	0.02
Pecans	50.0000	g	0.025	1.25
Yogurt	50.0000	mL	0.015	0.75
Fresh cilantro	37.5000	mL	0.005	0.19
Total cost				$5.56
Mark-up				65%
Menu price				$9.17

Although Bronwyn is not an accountant, she must be able to utilize accounting information to help her run her business. Being able to compile and analyze accounting information enables Bronwyn to ensure her restaurant is profitable.

Jim Chen—Production Manager for Luna Belle Fitness Clothing

Jim Chen manages the production operations for Luna Belle Fitness Clothing, a mid-sized fitness clothing company operating out of a warehouse in Saskatoon. He has approximately 52 employees who cut, sew, and package clothing that is sold to various athletic retail stores across Canada.

Last year, Jim became concerned about the warehouse's large storage facility for fabric and other materials used in the production of Luna Belle's clothing. The storage area was taking up 30% of the warehouse, space which could be used to make more clothing. Demand was increasing for the company's products and he was concerned that Luna Belle might not be able to meet that demand in the upcoming year, which he felt could cause the company to lose $145,000 in total profits per year. Jim was also concerned about the costs of obsolescence, as fabrics change frequently in the fitness market.

Jim was able to compile the following accounting information showing the total cost of the storage facility for the year (see Exhibit 1.4).

(continued)

Exhibit 1.4 **Cost of Luna Belle Storage Area**

Luna Belle Fitness Cost of Storage per Year			
	Total Cost	**Portion of Facility Used for Storage**	**Storage-related Costs**
Heating	$ 36,000	30%	$10,800
Electricity	42,000	30%	12,600
Facility rent	84,000	30%	25,200
Total cost of storage area	$162,000		$48,600

In addition to the cost of maintaining the storage area, Jim estimated that approximately $57,400 in waste and spoilage occurs each year due to the obsolescence of fabrics. If you consider both this loss and the lost profits of $145,000 that could be earned if the storage space was used to make clothing, Exhibit 1.5 more accurately reflects the true cost of the storage area.

Exhibit 1.5 **True Cost of Luna Belle Storage Area**

Luna Belle Fitness True Cost of Storage per Year			
	Total Cost	**Portion of Facility Used for Storage**	**Storage-related Cost**
Heating	$ 36,000	30%	$ 10,800
Electricity	42,000	30%	12,600
Facility rent	84,000	30%	25,200
Total cost of storage area	$162,000		48,600
Waste and spoilage			57,400
Lost profits			145,000
Total cost of storage			$251,000

After analyzing this data, it seemed to Jim that the true costs of maintaining the large storage facility were too high. He researched ways to reduce the storage area and found many articles on just-in-time (JIT) inventory management. In a just-in-time inventory management system (discussed more fully in Chapter 7), inventory of raw materials are received by the warehouse just in time to be used in the production process, rather than keeping large supplies of the material in inventory.

In order to facilitate this process, Jim purchased a computer system that tracks orders from customers and then schedules production based on these orders. The system also orders materials from suppliers based on production needs. This is considered a *pull system of production*, where customer orders are first received and then production is scheduled to meet this demand. This is the opposite of a *push production process*, where production is based on an expected level of demand. The just-in-time production system used by Luna Belle is depicted in Exhibit 1.6.

(continued)

Exhibit 1.6 JIT Production at Luna Belle

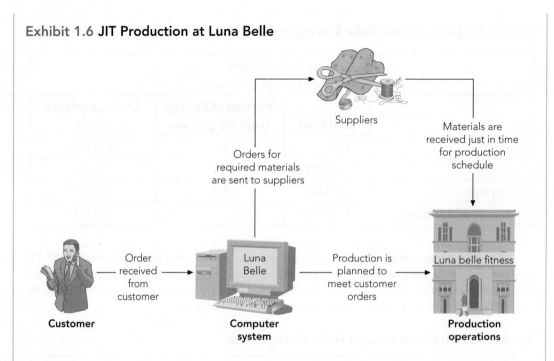

This new system has saved the company money in terms of storage costs and obsolescence. It has also freed up capacity so that Luna Belle can make more clothing. By understanding cost information, Jim was able to calculate the true cost of having a large storage facility in the company warehouse. Having this information helped Jim make the important decision to move to a JIT production environment.

CONCLUSION

This book is designed to help managers understand the tools and techniques of accounting and their role in the planning, controlling, and decision-making processes within an organization. Accounting information is both financial and non-financial. Although most readers think of accounting information as anything that is expressed in financial terms, it also includes non-financial information that can be measured and controlled within an organization. Management accounting is concerned not only with the management of costs but also with the management of other non-financial factors, such as quality, customer loyalty, and employee motivation.

KEY TERMS

Accountability, 4

Accounting, 4

Activity-based management, 10

Attention directing, 4

Control, 5

Decision making, 5

Environmental accounting, 9

Financial accounting, 5

Lean accounting, 10

Management accounting, 5

Non-financial performance measures, 9

Planning, 5

Problem solving, 4

Quality management, 9

Scorekeeping, 4

Stewardship, 4

Strategic management accounting, 10

Value-based management, 9

■ SELF-TEST QUESTIONS

S1.1 Which of the following is NOT a key characteristic of financial accounting?

a. Primary focus on external reporting

b. Developed to ensure accountability to stakeholders

c. Founded primarily in regulation

d. Initially developed in response the Industrial Revolution

S1.2 Which of the following best describes the main difference between management accounting and financial accounting?

a. Management accounting is focused on non-financial factors, whereas financial accounting is focused on financial factors.

b. Management accounting is primarily concerned with external stakeholders, such as shareholders and investors.

c. Management accounting is focused on internal users of information and is concerned with information used for planning, decision making, and control.

d. Management accounting is based solely on cost control within organizations.

S1.3 Why are stewardship and accountability interrelated?

a. Accountability would not be necessary without stewardship.

b. Accountability is important since owners are separate from the management of most companies.

c. Part of the role of a steward is to be accountable to the owners of a company.

d. Stewardship and accountability are separate concepts and are not interrelated.

e. Both (b) and (c).

S1.4 Why has accountability become so important in today's organizations?

a. After the Industrial Revolution, companies began producing multiple product lines, utilizing more complex processes.

b. There is a separation of management from ownership in most companies today.

c. The Canada Revenue Agency requires specific guidelines to be followed by all for-profit companies.

d. Many owners of businesses just don't trust their managers.

S1.5 Which of the following are recent trends in management accounting?

a. The use of non-financial measures of performance

b. The use of methods to help determine the cost of environmental practices

c. Reducing waste in the workplace and focusing on quality

d. Focusing on how organizations use resources and assigning costs accordingly

e. All of the above.

S1.6 Which of the following changes in the business environment increased the importance of management accounting?

a. The Industrial Revolution resulted in economies of scale.

b. The complexity of product lines decreased the need for efficiency in production.

c. The increased complexity of production processes increased the need for better information for decision making.

d. The increase in global competition drove costs down considerably.

S1.7 The Industrial Revolution resulted in growth of industries and, as a result of this growth, which of the following occurred?

a. The separation of ownership and control.

b. New organizational forms became common due to remotely located managers who made decisions on behalf of absent owners.

c. Many new cost accounting processes were developed to assist with creating economies of scale.

d. All of the above.

S1.8 The functions of management accounting do not include which of the following (according to Certified Management Accountants [CMA] Canada)?

a. Cost management

b. Strategic performance measurement

c. Auditing of financial statements

d. Risk management and assurance services

e. Looking to the future to provide real-world strategic direction, business management, and leadership

S1.9 The main functions of management accounting are planning, decision making, and control. Which of the following activities best describes the planning function?

a. Mark Smith, the president of ABC Industries, analyzed cost data for ABC's Toronto plant and determined that increasing costs were due to increases in material costs.

b. Anna Choy developed a 2012 budget for her division.

c. Noriyasu Tanaka, the financial officer for Great Homes Inc., prepared a variance report that compared actual costs to the budgeted costs for the year.

d. Amandeep Singh compared the costs of two different methods of producing Product A: an automated method and a more labour-intensive method. Based on the information, Amandeep chose the automated method because it resulted in substantial cost savings.

■ PROBLEMS

P1.1 *(Changing Accounting Practices)* Prior to the Industrial Revolution, single-product industries and high labour costs were the norm. After the Industrial Revolution, business changed dramatically. Single-product manufacturing companies that relied on human labour were replaced with multiproduct companies that relied on automated processes. Accounting methods also had to change. For instance, budgeting became very important as a control mechanism in decentralized departments.

You could say that today we are experiencing a new type of revolution—the Information Age—and that accounting techniques and practices must also change to reflect this new business environment. Summarize some of the key changes in business practices that have occurred due to the Information Age. What changes to accounting practices have been made or need to be made to support these changes?

P1.2 *(Role of Management Accounting)* Explain how the Industrial Revolution increased the need for management accounting information. What do you think would happen if management accounting was not practised within companies?

P1.3 *(Purposes of Accounting Information)* Accounting information (both financial and non-financial) can be used for a variety of purposes. Identify the most likely purpose for the following information (i.e., will it be used for scorekeeping, problem solving, or decision making?).

a. Bohdan prepared the financial statements for the Coil Division of TRS Industries.

b. Carol prepared an analysis of the variances between actual and budgeted results for her department.

c. Abdul explained why the Finishing Department of Tree Town Clothing Company did not meet its production expectations.

d. Cost accountant John Wong prepared a comparative report for the manager of Carlyle Industries on two different production methods for the company's factory.

e. A budget report for the Maintenance Department was prepared.

f. The financial statements for Havoc Manufacturing were made available online.

P1.4 *(Purposes of Accounting Information)* Accounting information (both financial and non-financial) can be used for a variety of purposes. Identify the most likely purpose for the following information (i.e., will it be used for scorekeeping, problem solving, or decision making):

a. A bank statement was prepared for a client at RBC.

b. The sales by division were reported for Apple Computers.

c. Natiq prepared a scrap report for the Production Department at the Chrysler plant in Brampton, Ontario.

d. Marita analyzed the effect of changing over to an automated production system in her plant.

e. Dominique prepared a five-year projection for expansion of her business into the Asian market.

f. Various measures were developed to help assess the business performance of Gifted Golf Warehouse.

P1.5 *(Purpose of Accounting Information)* Accounting information can be used for the purposes of planning, decision making, or control. For instance, a financial statement such as a statement of comprehensive income can be used to help decide which product lines are profitable for planning purposes. A financial statement can also be used to complete a ratio analysis. Ratio analysis (i.e., comparing financial values from one period on a company's financial statement to the next period, or from one company's financial statements to another company's) can assist with management control. For each type of information listed below, describe whether this information can be used for planning, decision making, and/or control.

a. A report of the costs for each product produced by the company over the past three years

b. A report showing sales for the last three quarters

c. An experience-curve study where labour hours have been plotted against the number of units produced to track whether labour hours have decreased with increased production volumes

d. A variance report showing the variances in actual product costs from budgeted costs

e. A three-year projection developed for the hat division of clothing company; the projection includes introduction of a new product line

f. A monthly report showing the spoilage costs for the brick division of Buildings Inc.

g. A performance report for the Cartoon Factory that compares actual performance to expected performance

h. A study of customer satisfaction ratings

P1.6 *(Changes to Accounting Methods)* Gulag Industries made a number of changes to its accounting system in 2012, which resulted in significant changes to the way the company costs its products. The company adopted new techniques for quality control (including business process re-engineering) and new allocation methods for costing (including activity-based costing). None of the changes the company made to its accounting systems needed to be reported to external stakeholders.

a. What might have motivated Gulag to change its accounting system?

b. Why was it not necessary to report these changes to external stakeholders?

P1.7 *(Stewardship and Accountability)* The owner of Touring Inc., Mei Chang, is concerned about the financial management of her company. When she started up Touring Inc., a company that provides bus tours in Banff, Alberta, she hired Peter Rosen to manage the company. Chang is not highly involved in the operations of her business since she is located in Toronto, Ontario. She has entrusted the management of Touring Inc. to Rosen. Chang recently received financial statements prepared by Rosen for the year ended 2012. She noticed that sales were quite high but that net income was very low. For instance, in July 2012, total sales were $6,800 but reported profits were only $600. Chang is worried that Rosen is not being honest. What action should Chang take to ease her mind?

P1.8 *(Non-Financial Measures of Performance)* Caro Company, a multidivisional company, has had a tough year. Because of a slowdown in the economy, Caro has experienced a 25% decline in overall profitability. The company managers are currently developing a performance-measurement process to help identify areas where the company needs to improve. Aldo Amatto, the company CEO, particularly wants to be able to identify financial indicators, such as changes in net income and gross margin, as well as return on investment. He also wants to track performance measures to ensure that the company is reaching its cost-reduction targets. Melinda Jenkins, a management accountant, feels that Caro Company also needs to focus on non-financial performance measures. Is Melinda correct? Why?

REFERENCES

American Accounting Association. (1966). *A statement of basic accounting theory.* Sarasota, FL: American Accounting Association.

Certified Management Accountants (CMA) Canada. (2011). *What is a CMA?* Retrieved from www.cma-canada.org/index.cfm?ci_id=4442&la_id=1.

Clark, J. M. (1923). *Studies in the economics of overhead costs.* Chicago, IL: University of Chicago Press.

Johnson, H. T., & Kaplan, R. S. (1987). *Relevance lost: The rise and fall of management accounting.* Boston, MA: Harvard Business School Press.

Research In Motion. (2011). *Investor FAQ.* Retrieved from www.rim.com/investors/faqs.

Vatter, W. J. (1950). *Managerial accounting.* New York, NY: Prentice Hall.

CHAPTER 2

Accounting and Its Relationship to Shareholder Value and Corporate Governance

LEARNING OBJECTIVES

After reading this chapter, you should be able to answer the following questions:

- What is the relationship between capital markets and product markets?

- What is value-based management and how does it relate to accounting?

- What is economic value added (EVA) and why is it important to management?

- What is the relationship between strategy, shareholder value, and accounting?

- What is corporate governance and what are the basic principles of corporate governance in Canada?

This chapter develops the theme that was identified in Chapter 1 as being important to business understanding: the separation of ownership from control and its importance for accounting information. This separation of ownership and control led to the emergence of capital markets and value-based management, the subject of this chapter. Several tools for measuring shareholder value are also described. The link between shareholder value, strategy, and accounting is then discussed.

This chapter also introduces the regulation of companies as it applies to accounting, and provides an overview of corporate governance and the responsibilities of directors, auditors, and the audit committee. Furthermore, it touches on risk and internal control. The chapter concludes with a critical perspective that questions the focus on shareholders alone.

Capital and Product Markets

Since the 17th century, companies (or corporations) have been formed by shareholders in order to consolidate resources and invest in opportunities. Shareholders have *limited liability,* through which their personal liability in the event of business failure is limited to their investment in shares. Shareholders appoint directors to manage the business, who in turn employ managers.

Shareholders have few direct rights in relation to the conduct of the business. Their main powers are to elect the directors and appoint the auditors in an annual general meeting of shareholders. They are also entitled to an annual report containing details of the company's financial performance (see Chapter 5).

One of the oldest companies in the world is a Canadian company—the Hudson's Bay Company, which was formed in 1670. It was originally known as "The Governor and Company of Adventurers of England Trading into Hudson's Bay."

Companies can be classified as either private companies or public companies. A private company has only a few shareholders and its shares are traded privately. A public company normally has many shareholders and its shares are traded publicly. The market in which investors buy and sell the shares of public companies is called the **capital market**, which is normally associated with a stock exchange. Companies obtain funds raised from shareholders (**equity**) and borrowings from financiers (**debt**). Both of these constitute the **capital employed** in the business.

The **cost of capital** represents the cost incurred by the organization to fund all of its investments, comprising the cost of equity and the cost of debt weighted by the mix of debt and equity. The cost of debt is **interest**, which is the price charged by the lender. The cost of equity is partly **dividend** and partly capital growth, because most shareholders expect both regular income from profits (the dividend) and an increase in the value of their shares over time in the capital market. Thus, the different costs of each form of capital, weighted by the proportions of different forms of debt and equity, constitute the **weighted average cost of capital**. The management of the business relationship with capital markets is called *financial management* or *corporate finance*.

Companies use their capital to invest in technologies, people, and materials in order to make, buy, and sell products or services to customers. This is called the **product market**. The focus of shareholder wealth, according to Rappaport (1998), is to obtain funds at competitive rates from capital markets and invest those funds to exploit imperfections in product markets. When this takes place, shareholder wealth is increased through dividends and increases in the share price. The 1990s saw a growing concern with the role of accounting in improving shareholder wealth.

The relationship between capital markets and product markets is shown in Exhibit 2.1.

Value-Based Management

Since the mid-1980s, more and more emphasis has been placed on increasing the value of a business to its shareholders. Traditionally, business performance has been measured through accounting ratios such as return on capital employed (ROC), return on investment (ROI), earnings per share

Exhibit 2.1 **Capital and Product Market Structure and Interaction**

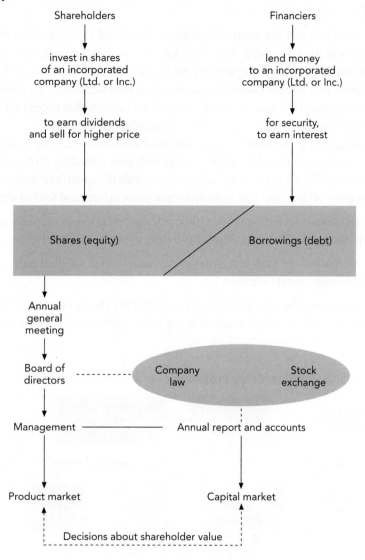

(EPS), and so on (which are described in Chapter 5). However, it has been argued that these are historical rather than current measures, and they vary between companies as a result of different accounting treatments.

Value-based management (VBM) emphasizes shareholder value, on the assumption that this is the primary goal of every business. VBM approaches include total shareholder return, market value added, shareholder value added, and economic value added. A number of different approaches to value-based management exist, including the following:

- **Total shareholder return (TSR)**, which compares the dividends received by shareholders and the increase in the share price with the original shareholder investment, expressing the TSR as a percentage of the initial investment.

- **Market value added (MVA)**, which is the difference between total market capitalization (number of shares issued times share price plus the market value of debt) and the total capital invested in the business by debt and equity providers. This is a measure of the value generated by managers for shareholders.

Rappaport (1998) coined the term *shareholder value added (SVA)* to refer to the increase in shareholder value over time. He defined shareholder value as the economic value of an investment, which can be calculated by using the cost of capital to discount forecast future cash flows (which he called *free cash flows*) into present values (discounted cash flow techniques are described in detail in Chapter 12). The business must generate profits in product markets that exceed the cost of capital in the capital market for value to be created (if not, shareholder value is eroded).

Rappaport developed a shareholder value network (see Exhibit 2.2). Through this diagram, he identified seven drivers of shareholder value: sales growth rate, operating profit margin, income tax rate, working capital investment, fixed capital investment, cost of capital, and forecast duration. Managers make three types of decisions that influence these value drivers and lead to shareholder value:

1. **Operating decisions**—including product mix, pricing, promotion, and customer service, which are then reflected in the sales growth rate, operating profit margin, and income tax rate.

2. **Investment decisions**—in both inventory and capacity, which are then reflected in both working capital and fixed capital investment.

3. **Financing decisions**—the mix of debt and equity and the choice of financial instrument determine the cost of capital, which is assessed by capital markets in terms of business risk.

Exhibit 2.2 **The Shareholder Value Network**

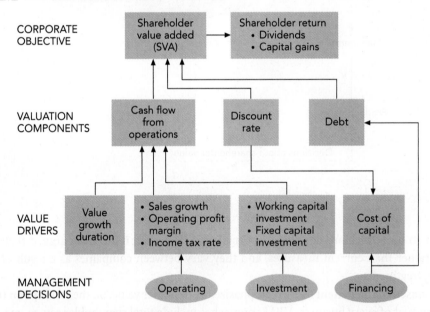

The value growth duration is the estimated number of years over which the return from investments is expected to exceed the cost of capital.

The seven value drivers determine the cash flow from operations, the level of debt, and the cost of capital, all of which determine shareholder value. A detrimental consequence of the emphasis on shareholder value is that it has led to a continued focus on short-term financial performance at the expense of longer-term strategy.

Economic value added (EVA) is a financial performance measure developed by consultants Stern Stewart & Co. It claims to capture the economic profit of a business that leads to shareholder value creation. In simple terms, EVA is net operating profit after deducting a charge to cover the opportunity cost of the capital invested in the business (when by taking one course of action you lose the opportunity to undertake an alternative course). EVA's "economic profit" is the amount by which earnings exceed (or fall short of) the minimum rate of return that shareholders and financiers could get by investing in other securities with a comparable risk (visit Stern Stewart's website at www.sternstewart.com).

The EVA formula is

$$\textbf{EVA = Modified after-tax operating profit}$$
$$\textbf{− (Modified total capital × Weighted average cost of capital)}$$

Modified after-tax operating profit is modified in the sense that it "capitalizes" or shows certain expenditures that are normally shown as expenses when incurred as intangible assets instead, and writes these expenditures off over the time period they are deemed to provide benefit to the company. Examples of such expenditures are employee training, research and development, and advertising.

Modified total capital includes fixed assets, working capital, and the capitalized intangible assets mentioned above.

Weighted average cost of capital reflects the weighted average cost of borrowed funds (debt) and funds provided by the owners of the company (equity).

EVA accepts the assumption that the primary financial objective of any business is to maximize the wealth of its shareholders. The value of the business depends on the extent to which investors expect future profits to be greater or lower than the cost of capital. Returns over and above the cost of capital increase shareholder wealth, while returns below the cost of capital erode shareholder wealth.

One of the advantages of using EVA as a financial performance measurement is that it capitalizes some of the most important discretionary expenditures managers might cut if they aim for maximum short-term profit. These include advertising, employee training, and research and development costs, all expenditures that have a more long-term return horizon.

Stern Stewart argues that managers understand this measure because it is based on operating profits. By introducing a notional charge based on assets held by the business, managers (whether at corporate or divisional level) manage those assets as well as the profit generated.

The increase in shareholder value is reflected in compensation strategies for managers, whose goals, argues Stern Stewart, are aligned to increasing shareholder wealth through bonus and share option schemes that are paid over a period of time to ensure consistent future performance.

EVA also has its critics. For example, the calculation of EVA allows up to 164 adjustments to reported accounting profits in order to remove distortions caused by arbitrary accounting rules and estimates the risk-adjusted cost of capital, both of which can be argued as subjective, although Stern Stewart claims that most organizations need only about a dozen of these. EVA adjustments can also be manipulated by managers.

EVA still reflects primarily a summary of past transactions, while, ideally, economic value added should reflect changes in future cash flow potential. Therefore, EVA is considered to be a poor indicator of value for companies that create value through future growth. Also, EVA can be expensive to implement as it sometimes requires a considerable amount of consultants' time and significant management investment and training.

Shareholder (or strategic) value analysis emphasizes the processes by which shareholder value is achieved. In practice, the pursuit of shareholder value (or economic value added) can be achieved through the introduction of new or redesigned products and services, the management of costs, the development of performance measurement systems, and improved decision making. This form of value analysis compares cost with the value to the customer. Consequently, improving shareholder value is inextricably linked with both strategy and accounting.

Shareholder Value, Strategy, and Accounting

This book treats accounting as part of the broader business context of strategy, marketing, operations, and human resources. The focus of accounting in business organizations is shareholder value—increasing the value of the business to its shareholders—through dividends from profits and/or through capital growth. Strategy both influences and is influenced by shareholder value. Strategy is reflected in the functional business areas of marketing, operations, and human resources, through the actions the business wants to take to achieve, maintain, and improve competitive advantage. The relationship among these elements is shown in Exhibit 2.3.

Exhibit 2.3 Shareholder Value, Strategy, and Accounting

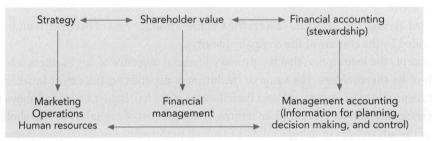

Financial management (which is beyond the scope of this book) is concerned with raising funds from shareholders or financiers to provide the capital that the business needs to produce and sell goods and services. Financial accounting represents the stewardship function, which is that managers are accountable to those with a financial interest in the business and produce financial reports to satisfy that accountability (Chapters 4 and 5).

Management accounting provides the information for planning, decision making, and control (Chapters 8 to 16). Therefore, the main content of this book is about the interaction among the functional areas of marketing, operations, and human resources—driven by strategy—and how accounting provides a set of tools and techniques to assist functional managers. Management accounting both influences and is influenced by the functional areas and by business strategy.

The importance of strategy for management accounting and the information it provides is that a strategic perspective involves taking a longer-term view about the business than is usually provided by traditional accounting reports. Management accounting comprises a set of tools and techniques to support planning, decision making, and control in business organizations.

Accounting is—or at least should be—integrated with business strategy. However, these same accounting tools and techniques can be used to help evaluate the performance of customers, suppliers, and competitors in order to improve competitive advantage. This is called *strategic management accounting*, which is described in Chapter 16.

Accounting should also extend beyond a narrow concern with financial measurement and encompass non-financial performance measurement, a subject of steadily increasing importance for those managers who are responsible for achieving performance targets, as well as for accountants (performance measurement is also described in Chapter 6).

Strategy is concerned with long-term direction, achieving and maintaining competitive advantage, identifying the scope and boundaries of the organization, and matching the activities of the organization to its environment. Strategy is also about building on resources and competencies to create new opportunities, and to take advantage of those opportunities and manage change within the organization. There is also a link between strategy and operational decisions in order to turn strategy formulation into strategy implementation (for a fuller description, see, for example, Johnson and Scholes, 2006).

An economic perspective is added by Grant (1998), who saw the value created by firms distributed among customers, suppliers, and equity risk-takers. In order to provide this value, business firms establish profit as the single dominant objective. The purpose of strategy is "to pursue profit over the long term" (p. 34). Strategy is thus linked to performance by setting performance targets (both financial and non-financial) for the business as a whole and for individual business units, and then measuring performance against those targets (this is the subject of Chapter 6).

Company Regulation and Corporate Governance

THE REGULATION OF COMPANIES

In Canada, an organization can incorporate under federal, provincial, or territorial law. The legislation that governs companies registered federally is called the *Canada Business Corporations Act* (CBCA). If a company is incorporated provincially, it will fall under one of the provincial corporation acts, such as the *British Columbia Business Corporations Act* or the *Ontario Corporations Act*. Whether a company decides to incorporate on the federal or provincial level depends on the scope of the company's business. A company that operates countrywide will probably incorporate federally, while a company that operates solely in one province or territory will probably incorporate in that province or territory. The differences between the different federal and provincial/territorial acts are minor and technical in nature and fall beyond the scope of this book. The remainder of this chapter will refer to the CBCA.

The CBCA sets out the effects of incorporation; that is, the "limited liability" of shareholders for any unpaid portion of their shares. In most cases, issued shares are fully paid and therefore shareholders have no liability beyond this in the event of a company's failure. The CBCA also sets out the need for companies to have a constitution, formally known as the *Articles of Incorporation*. Each company has a share capital, enabling ownership to be divided over many shareholders.

Shareholders appoint directors to manage the company on their behalf. Those directors have various duties; for example, they can authorize the company to borrow money. The directors must keep accounting records and produce financial reports in a specified format. If the company makes a profit, the directors may recommend that a dividend be paid out of the profit. An auditor must be appointed to report annually to shareholders of all public companies. Shareholders have no management rights. However, shareholders receive an annual report (see Chapter 5) containing the financial statements, and an annual general meeting of shareholders must be held that elects directors, ratifies the dividend (if any), appoints auditors, and so on.

CORPORATE GOVERNANCE

Corporate governance is the system by which companies are directed and controlled. Boards of directors are responsible for the governance of their companies. The shareholders' role is to appoint the directors and auditors. The responsibilities of the board include setting the company's strategic goals, providing leadership to senior management, monitoring business performance, and reporting to shareholders. There are two models of corporate governance:

1. Shareholder value (as discussed earlier in this chapter)

2. The stakeholder model (described in more detail later in this chapter and in Chapter 5)

Each represents a different means by which the functioning of boards of directors and top management can be understood. In company law, there is no doubt that shareholders are in a privileged position compared with other stakeholders. Hence, corporate governance is founded on the shareholder value/agency model. However, other models of governance take a broader view; for example, that found in South Africa, where the *King Report on Governance for South Africa 2009* provides an integrated approach to corporate governance in the interest of all stakeholders, embracing social, environmental, and economic aspects of organizational activities. It therefore takes, to some extent at least, a broader stakeholder model of governance.

Over the last decade or so, a growing number of institutional investors have been starting to encourage greater disclosure of governance processes, emphasizing the quality and sustainability of earnings rather than short-term profits alone. Research has shown that an overwhelming majority of institutional investors are prepared to pay a significant premium for companies exhibiting high standards of corporate governance. The media has also increased its reporting of governance practices. The high-profile failures of companies, notably the press coverage given to Enron and World-Com, brought corporate governance to worldwide attention.

In the United States, the introduction of the *Sarbanes-Oxley Act* in 2002 (often referred to as SOX) was the legislative response to the financial and accounting scandals of Enron and WorldCom and misconduct at the accounting firm Arthur Andersen, Enron's auditor. The *Sarbanes-Oxley Act* introduced the requirement to disclose all material off-balance-sheet transactions. It also requires the certification of annual and quarterly financial reports by the chief executive and chief financial officer of all companies with U.S. securities registrations, with criminal penalties for knowingly making false certifications.

Canada has legislation similar to the *Sarbanes-Oxley Act*; for example, *Bill 198* in Ontario (sometimes referred to as C-SOX). Each province and territory has its own legislation, but these differ little across the country. Canadian legislation addresses mainly the same issues as the *Sarbanes-Oxley Act* for mainly the same reasons, since there have been notable corporate failures in Canada, too, such as those of Nortel and Livent.

In the United Kingdom, the *UK Corporate Governance Code* (formerly known as the *Combined Code*) has applied for reporting years since 2003. The United Kingdom has also seen its share of corporate failures, including the Maxwell Communication Corporation, the Bank of Credit & Commerce International, Polly Peck International, and Marconi PLC. Similar high-profile failures have occurred in most countries. The resulting increased attention to corporate governance has been global.

The emergence of this emphasis on corporate governance can therefore be traced to

- An enforcement exercise in relation to past misdeeds

- Changing financial markets, including the rapid rise of institutional investors and their increasing desire to be more active investors

- The growth of pension savings in most countries and the dependence of an aging population on pensions and savings, which have been affected by declining confidence in stock markets

PRINCIPLES OF CORPORATE GOVERNANCE

The role of a company's board of directors is to provide entrepreneurial leadership of the company within a framework of prudent and effective controls that enables risk to be assessed and managed. The board should set the company's strategic aims and ensure that the necessary financial and human resources are in place for the company to meet its objectives and review management performance. The board should also set the company's values and standards and ensure that its obligations to its shareholders and others are understood and met.

The main principles of corporate governance found in the Canadian corporate governance legislation relate to manipulation of share prices, the roles and responsibilities of directors, accountability and audit, internal control, and disclosure of governance arrangements in annual reports.

In relation to the manipulation of share prices, Canadian legislation states that persons are prohibited from committing fraud that will mislead the public or create an artificial price for the company's shares. This includes false or misleading statements or omissions of facts that would have a significant effect on the company's share price.

CASE IN POINT

The Fall of Nortel

The board of directors plays a crucial role in overseeing company management on behalf of shareholders, as the case of Canadian-based Nortel Networks Corporation shows.

Nortel, once the world's largest supplier of telecommunications equipment, was rocked by accounting scandals starting in the first quarter of 2003, when the company posted a profit after losing money in the 2001 and 2002 dot-com bust. The profit report triggered bonuses totalling $19 million for the top 43 Nortel managers. Nortel's independent auditors were skeptical of this return to profitability, so the board of directors hired a law firm to investigate Nortel's accounting practices.

The law firm reported to the board that Nortel managers had a culture of meeting earnings targets—and thus achieving bonuses—by using accounting practices they "ought to have known were not in compliance" with accounting standards. The board required the managers to return their bonuses, and fired several of them. Nortel revised its financial statements from 2001 to mid-2003.

Nortel's accounting problems escalated, with various civil actions launched by regulators and shareholders who were upset that the accounting irregularities caused Nortel's share price to drop. The U.S. Securities and Exchange Commission, which regulates Nortel's shares trading in the United States, alleged that in the first quarter of 2003, instead of a $54 million profit, Nortel had a loss of $220 million.

The company restated its financial statements several more times. Its mounting costs to settle lawsuits and get its accounting house in order largely caused Nortel to file for bankruptcy in 2009, and its patents and other intellectual property were auctioned off for approximately (US)$7.7 billion.

Sources: Wahl, A. (2009), The good, the bad, and the ugly: Nortel Networks, *Canadian Business*, March 30, 2009; Bagnall, J. The beginning of the end: How an accounting scandal permanently weakened Nortel, *Ottawa Citizen*, November 2, 2009; *Nortel reports financial results for the fourth quarter and full year 2011*, Nortel news release, March 8, 2012.

RESPONSIBILITY OF DIRECTORS

Under governance legislation, the financial reports of a company are the responsibility of directors, not managers. Directors are responsible for keeping proper accounting records that disclose with reasonable accuracy the financial position of the company at any time, and to ensure that financial reports comply with generally accepted accounting principles (GAAP) (see Chapter 4 for more details). They are also responsible for safeguarding the company's assets and for taking reasonable steps to prevent and detect fraud.

Chief executive officers (CEOs) and chief financial officers (CFOs) are required to personally certify that the company's financial statements do not contain any material misrepresentations and that the financial statements and other financial information fairly present the corporation's financial condition.

In preparing the financial statements, directors must select suitable accounting policies and apply them consistently, make judgments and estimates that are reasonable and prudent, and prepare financial reports on a going concern basis unless it is inappropriate to presume that the company will continue in business (see Chapter 3 for a discussion of these principles).

Although in practice the performance of these functions will be delegated to a company's managers, the responsibility for them cannot be delegated by the board of directors.

AUDIT

An **audit** is a periodic examination of the accounting records of a company carried out by an independent auditor to ensure that

- Those records have been properly maintained.

- The financial statements that are drawn up from those records do not contain any material misrepresentations.

- The financial statements and other financial information fairly present the corporation's financial condition.

An audit includes examination, on a test basis, of evidence relevant to the amounts and disclosures in financial reports. It also includes an assessment of significant estimates and judgments made by directors in the preparation of financial reports, and whether accounting policies are appropriate, consistent, and adequately disclosed. Auditors carry out their audit in accordance with *Canadian Auditing Standards*, which are the *International Standards on Auditing* that have been adopted by the Auditing and Assurance Standards Board.

Each year, the auditors present a report to shareholders, giving their opinion as to whether the statements do or do not contain any material misrepresentations and that the financial statements and other financial information fairly present the company's financial condition and are properly prepared in accordance with generally accepted accounting principles (see Chapter 5).

Expressing an opinion on whether the financial statements are free of any material misrepresentations and fairly represent the company's financial condition in accordance to GAAP is the highest level of assurance an auditor can give regarding financial information. The auditor can also provide other forms of audit reports that either vary in the level of assurance they provide or in the type of information on which they are expressing an opinion. Some examples of these reports are

- **Review engagements**, where the intent of the report is to express negative assurance that nothing came to the auditor's attention that led the auditor to believe that the representations made by management would be misleading.

- **Agreed-on procedures**, where the auditor performs only audit procedures previously agreed on by the user of the audit report and the auditor. The level of assurance may vary depending on the audit procedures agreed on.

- **Compilation reports**, where the auditor assists management in preparation of the financial information. The auditor does not express an opinion or give assurance on the reasonableness of the financial information.

The auditor can also produce reports that give various levels of assurance on information other than financial statements based on GAAP, for example on financial statements based on another basis of accounting other than GAAP, compliance with contractual agreements or a prospectus.

AUDIT COMMITTEES

An audit committee is a committee of the board of directors to which the board delegates responsibility for oversight of the financial reporting process. The objectives of an audit committee are to

- Help directors meet their responsibilities, especially for accountability
- Provide better communication between directors and external auditors
- Enhance the external auditor's independence
- Increase the credibility and objectivity of financial reports
- Strengthen the role of the outside directors by facilitating in-depth discussions among directors on the committee, management, and external auditors

Risk, Internal Control of Financial Reporting, and Management Accounting

The benefits of applying good corporate governance are to reduce risk, stimulate performance, improve access to capital markets, enhance the marketability of products/services by creating confidence among stakeholders, improve leadership, and demonstrate transparency and accountability.

Risk can be defined as uncertain future events that could influence the achievement of the organization's strategic, operational, and financial objectives. Risk may be business or operational, arising from the normal course of business (such as loss of customers, failure of computer systems, poor-quality products), or it may be financial (arising from changes in interest rates, foreign currency exposure, poor credit control, and so on), environmental (arising from changes in external economic, social, or technological factors), or reputational.

Risk may be considered in relation to downside factors (bad things might happen) or upside factors (good things might not happen). This recognizes that taking risks is a necessary part of conducting business, with returns being the compensation. The U.S. 9/11 attacks also resulted in an increase in attention to risk.

The management of a company must evaluate the effectiveness of the company's internal control over financial reporting as of the end of a financial year. A company must file an internal control report separately but concurrently with the filing of its annual financial statements.

An internal control report must include the following:

- A statement of management's responsibility for establishing and maintaining adequate internal control over financial reporting for the company.

- A statement identifying the control framework used by management to evaluate the effectiveness of the company's internal control over financial reporting.

- Management's assessment of the effectiveness of the company's internal control over financial reporting as of the end of the company's financial year, including a statement as to whether the internal control over financial reporting is effective.

- Disclosure of any material weaknesses in the company's internal control over financial reporting identified by management.

- A statement that the participating audit firm which audited the company's annual financial statements has issued an internal control audit report.

- Disclosure of any limitations in management's assessment of the effectiveness of the company's internal control over financial reporting, extending into a joint venture or a variable interest entity in which the company has a material interest.

- Disclosure of any limitations in management's assessment of the effectiveness of the company's internal control over financial reporting, extending into a business that was acquired by the company during the financial year. A comprehensive approach to risk management ensures appropriate risk responses, monitoring and reporting processes, and the development of appropriate internal controls to guard against risk.

Internal control is the whole system of internal controls, financial and otherwise, established in order to provide reasonable assurance of effective and efficient operation, internal financial control, and compliance with laws and regulations. Although there are forms of control other than financial ones (see Chapter 6), internal financial controls are established to provide reasonable assurance of the safeguarding of assets against unauthorized use or disposition, the maintenance of proper accounting records, and the reliability of financial information used within the business or for publication.

Accounting controls are important in all organizations and include control over cash, debtors, inventory, creditors, the business infrastructure (non-current assets; see Chapter 5), loans, income, and expenses. Financial controls also exist over the costing of products and services (Chapters 8–11), capital investment decisions (Chapter 12), divisional performance evaluation (Chapter 13), and budgets and budgetary control (Chapters 14 and 15).

Management accounting is an important form of internal control and is the subject of Part III of this book, although the theoretical foundations are laid in Chapters 6 and 7.

A Critical Perspective

Shareholder value movement has historically overshadowed the wider accountability of business to other stakeholders. Shareholders' interests dominate business, and accountants occupy a privileged position as those who establish the rules and report business performance. This can be seen as a historical development (see Chapter 1).

Stakeholder theory looks beyond shareholders to those groups who influence, or are influenced by, the organization. Shareholders are not representative of society and stakes are held in the organization by employees, customers, suppliers, government, and the community. Stakeholder theory is concerned with how the power of stakeholders, with their competing interests, is managed by the organization in terms of its broader accountabilities. Although this chapter has been concerned with shareholder value and corporate governance, a critical approach questions this emphasis on the shareholder value/agency model.

Dermer (1988) suggested a broader view of organizations with interdependent but conflicting stakeholders, arguing

> Cognitive and/or political models view organizations as non-goal-oriented, noninstrumental social systems, enmeshed in broader socio-political contexts. (p. 29)

Dermer contrasted the presumption that management has the authority to act on behalf of the shareholders with a pluralistic governance model comprising four elements: leadership (management), citizenship (stakeholders), institutions (formal and informal patterns of relating), and ideologies (patterns of belief).

Given that accountability (as we saw in Chapter 1) is the duty to provide an explanation—an account—of the actions for which an organization is responsible, this implies a *social accounting* and a *right to information* by various stakeholder groups in a democracy (some of these broader reporting issues are discussed in Chapter 5).

The idea of strategy oriented toward achieving goals is also open to criticism. Mintzberg (1994) was critical of strategic planning because it is a "calculating style of management," resulting in strategies that are extrapolated from the past or copied from others. Rather, Mintzberg saw some strategy as deliberate but other strategy as an emergent process, which should lead to learning. He argued,

> Strategic planning often spoils strategic thinking, causing managers to confuse real vision with the manipulation of numbers. (p. 107)

The separation of management from control, as well as the pursuit of shareholder value, implies a particular goal-oriented, economic, and rational theory of management behaviour and organizational action. We will consider the theoretical assumptions behind this perspective in Chapters 5 and 6.

CONCLUSION

While Chapter 1 gave an introduction to accounting, its history, and the changing role of the management accountant, this chapter has provided the context in which the changing role of accounting and the accountant has taken shape. First, we considered the importance of capital markets and how they dictate the drive for shareholder value-based management through strategic planning.

We then discussed company regulation and corporate governance that underlie the functioning of business organizations. Capital markets and corporate governance provide the context in which management accounting provides information to the board and managers to aid their planning and decision making, as well as to ensure control. Finally, we concluded with a critical perspective that challenges shareholder value with a stakeholder view and raises concerns about strategy which will be developed in later chapters.

KEY TERMS

Audit, 30

Audit committee, 31

Capital employed, 22

Capital market, 22

Corporate governance, 28

Cost of capital, 22

Debt, 22

Dividend, 22

Economic value added (EVA^{TM}), 25

Equity, 22

Internal control, 32

Interest, 22

Product market, 22

Risk, 31

Shareholder (or strategic) value analysis, 25

Value-based management (VBM), 23

Weighted average cost of capital, 22

■ SELF-TEST QUESTIONS

S2.1 The responsibility to produce financial statements for a company belongs to the company's

a. Directors

b. Managers

c. Chief executive officer (CEO)

d. Chief financial officer (CFO)

S2.2 CEOs and CFOs are required to personally certify that the company's financial statements

a. Are true and correct

b. Do not contain any misrepresentations and that the financial statements and other financial information fairly present the company's financial condition

c. Do not contain any mistakes and that the financial statements and other financial information fairly present the company's profits

d. Account for all of the company's assets, liabilities, revenues, and expenses

S2.3 Canadian legislation states that persons are prohibited from

a. Owning shares in a company if they are also directors of the company

b. Committing fraud that will mislead the public or create an artificial price for the company's shares

c. Buying or selling more than 10% of a company's shares at any given time

d. Doing anything that will create interest in the company and make the share price increase or decrease significantly

S2.4 The main principles of corporate governance found in Canadian corporate governance legislation are in relation to the roles and responsibilities of

a. Directors, shareholders, and accountability

b. Shareholders, accountability, audit, and internal control

c. Directors, shareholders, auditors, and employees

d. Directors, accountability, audit, and internal control

S2.5 Shareholder value can refer to

a. The price a shareholder can get for his or her shares

b. Increasing the value of the business to its shareholders through dividends, from profits, and/or through capital growth

c. The fair value of the company's net assets and goodwill

d. All of the above

S2.6 Managers make three types of decisions that lead to shareholder value, namely

a. Operating, financing, and investment decisions

b. Operating, management, and financing decisions

c. Management, financing, and investment decisions

d. Operating, management, and investment decisions

■ PROBLEMS

P2.1 Explain the idea of value-based management and how shareholder value relates to the interaction between product and capital markets.

P2.2 Explain the key issues in corporate governance as they relate to accounting.

P2.3 What is shareholder (or strategic) value analysis and how is it carried out?

P2.4 What is an audit of financial statements?

P2.5 What are the objectives of an audit committee?

P2.6 Discuss the basic responsibilities of directors under Canadian governance legislation.

REFERENCES

Dermer, J. (1988). Control and organizational order. *Accounting, Organizations and Society, 13*(1), 25–36.

Grant, R. M. (1998). *Contemporary strategy analysis: Concepts, techniques, applications.* Oxford: Blackwell Publishers.

Johnson, G., and Scholes, K. (2006). *Exploring corporate strategy: Text and cases.* (6th ed.). London: FT/Prentice Hall.

Institute of Directors in South Africa. (September 1, 2009). *King Report on Governance for South Africa* (*King III Report and Code*). Parklands, South Africa.

Mintzberg, H. (1994). The fall and rise of strategic planning. *Harvard Business Review*, Jan.–Feb., 107–114.

Ontario Securities Commission. (1990). National Instrument 52–109: *Certification of disclosure in issuers' annual and interim filings.*

Ontario Securities Commission. (1990). National Instrument 52–111: *Reporting on internal control over financial reporting.*

Rappaport, A. (1998). *Creating shareholder value: A guide for managers and investors.* (Revised ed.). New York, NY: Free Press.

CHAPTER 3

Recording Financial Transactions and Accounting and Information Systems

LEARNING OBJECTIVES

After reading this chapter, you should be able to answer the following questions:

- How is a business event recorded in the financial statements?

- How are the four basic types of accounts presented in the financial statements?

- For common business transactions, what source documents are used, which accounts are influenced, and do these transactions lead to an increase or decrease in these accounts?

- What basic accounting principles underlie financial statements and how do these principles influence financial statements?

- How are accounting data collected, stored, and controlled by the information systems of an organization?

- What types of controls should be in place within organizations to ensure that financial information is accurate and secure?

In order to understand the accounting scorekeeping process, we need to understand how accounting captures information that is subsequently used for planning, decision making, and control purposes. This chapter describes how business events are recorded as transactions in an accounting system using the double-entry method that is the foundation of accounting. We introduce a simple form of the statement of comprehensive income and the statement of financial position, and explain the basic principles of accounting that underlie how financial statements are produced.

This chapter also introduces the notion of cost for decision making, and how cost may be interpreted in multiple ways. Finally, the chapter looks at accounting information systems, methods of accounting data collection, and internal controls for information systems.

Business Events, Transactions, and the Accounting System

For-profit businesses exist first and foremost to make a profit. They do this by buying or producing goods and services and selling those goods and services at a higher price than it cost to buy or produce those goods and services. Conducting business involves a number of *business events* such as buying equipment, purchasing goods and services, paying expenses, making sales, distributing goods and services, and so on. In accounting terms, each of these business events is a *transaction*. A **transaction** is the financial description of each business event.

Entities such as not-for-profit organizations and governments also conduct business and are parties to transactions in a similar way. They also record these transactions in accounting records and financial statements, although the detailed accounting rules and principles for these organizations are different from those applicable to for-profit businesses and are beyond the scope of this book.

It is important to recognize that transactions are a financial representation of the business event, measured in monetary terms. This is only one perspective on business events, albeit the one considered most important for accounting purposes. A broader view is that business events can also be recorded in non-financial terms, such as measures of product/service quality, speed of delivery, customer satisfaction, and so on. These non-financial performance measures (which are described in detail in Chapter 6) are important elements of business events that are not captured by financial transactions. This is a limitation of accounting as a tool of business decision making.

Each transaction is recorded on a **source document** that forms the basis for recording in a business's accounting system. Examples of source documents are invoices and cheques. The **accounting system** comprises a set of accounts that summarize the transactions that have been recorded on source documents and entered into the accounting system. **Accounts** can be considered as "buckets" within the accounting system, each containing similar transactions.

There are five basic types of accounts:

1. **Assets:** Things the business *owns*.

2. **Liabilities:** Debts the business *owes*.

3. **Income:** The *revenue* generated from the *sale* of goods or services.

4. **Expenses:** The *costs* incurred in *buying* or *producing* the goods and services.

5. **Shareholders' equity:** The *capital* invested by the shareholders and the *retained earnings*, the profit that is left in the business after all the expenses have been paid and any payments of dividends have been made to the shareholders.

These five types of accounts, or elements of financial statements, will be discussed in more detail in Chapter 4.

The main difference between these categories is that business profit is calculated as

$$\text{Profit} = \text{Income} - \text{Expenses}$$

while the shareholders' equity of the business is calculated as

$$\text{Equity} = \text{Assets} - \text{Liabilities}$$

Accumulated profits (or losses) from each year, less any dividends paid to the shareholders, become retained earnings (or deficits, in the case of accumulated losses). The retained earnings and the capital contributed by the shareholders are known as *shareholders' equity*.

As assets can either be bought with the capital contributed by the shareholders, from the retained earnings, or from borrowed funds, it follows that

$$\text{Assets} = \text{Equity} + \text{Liabilities}$$

Financial statements—the statement of comprehensive income, the statement of financial position, the statement of changes in equity, and the statement of cash flows (all explained in Chapter 4)—are produced from the information in the accounts in the accounting system. Exhibit 3.1 shows the process of recording and reporting transactions in an accounting system.

Exhibit 3.1 Business Events, Transactions, and the Accounting System

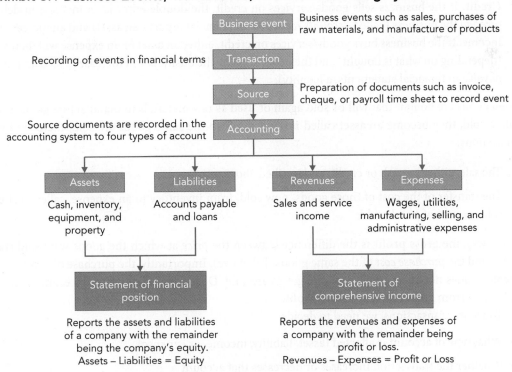

Business event	Business events such as sales, purchases of raw materials, and manufacture of products
Recording of events in financial terms → **Transaction**	
Source	Preparation of documents such as invoice, cheque, or payroll time sheet to record event
Source documents are recorded in the accounting system to four types of account → **Accounting**	

Assets — Cash, inventory, equipment, and property

Liabilities — Accounts payable and loans

Revenues — Sales and service income

Expenses — Wages, utilities, manufacturing, selling, and administrative expenses

Statement of financial position — Reports the assets and liabilities of a company with the remainder being the company's equity. Assets – Liabilities = Equity

Statement of comprehensive income — Reports the revenues and expenses of a company with the remainder being profit or loss. Revenues – Expenses = Profit or Loss

The Double Entry: Recording Transactions

Businesses use a system of accounting called *double entry*. Double entry means that every business transaction affects at least two accounts. Those accounts may *increase* or *decrease*. Accountants record the increases or decreases as debits or credits, where assets and expenses are increased by debiting the accounts and decreased by crediting the accounts. Revenue, liabilities, and share-holders' equity, on the other hand, are increased by crediting the accounts and decreased by debiting the accounts. (*Credit* in this case simply refers to the opposite of *debit*, as *plus* is the opposite of *minus*. It should not be confused with a *credit transaction*, which refers to paying in cash at a later date).

The double-entry system requires that, for each transaction, the debits must be equal to the credits. The following two equations will therefore always balance:

$$\text{Profit} = \text{Income} - \text{Expenses}$$

$$\text{Equity} = \text{Assets} - \text{Liabilities}$$

Transactions take place in one of two forms:

1. **Cash.** If the business sells goods/services for cash, the double entry is an increase in income and an increase in the bank account (an asset). If the business buys goods/services for cash, either an asset or an expense will increase (depending on what is bought) and the bank account will decrease.

2. **Credit.** If the business sells goods/services on credit, the double entry is an increase in debts owed *to* the business (called *accounts receivable* in financial reports, an asset) and an increase in income. If the business buys goods/services on credit, either an asset or an expense will increase (depending on what is bought) and the debts owed *by* the business will increase (called *accounts payable* in financial statements, a liability).

When goods are bought that will be sold again or used as raw materials to manufacture goods that will be sold, they become an asset called *inventory*. When the same goods are sold, there are two transactions:

a. The sale, either by cash or credit, as described above.

b. The transfer of the cost of those goods, now sold, from inventory to an expense, called cost of sales or cost of goods sold.

In this way, the gross profit is the difference between the *price* at which the goods were sold ([a] above) and the *purchase cost* of the same goods ([b] above). Importantly, the purchase of goods into inventory does not affect profit until the goods are sold. Deducting other costs, for example, rent, wages, etc., from gross profit, gives net profit.

To record transactions, we need to decide

- What type of account is affected (asset, liability, income, or expense)
- Whether the transaction increases or decreases that account

Some examples of business transactions and how the double entry affects the accounting system are shown in Exhibit 3.2.

Exhibit 3.2 Business Transactions and the Double Entry

Business Event	Transaction	Source Document	Account Affected	Type of Account	Increase or Decrease
Install new equipment for production	Buy equipment for cash: $25,000	Cheque	Equipment	Asset	Increase $25,000
			Cash	Asset	Decrease $25,000
Receive inventory of goods for resale	Purchase inventory on credit: $15,000	Invoice from supplier	Inventory	Asset	Increase $15,000
			Accounts Payable	Liability	Increase $15,000
Pay weekly wages	Pay wages: $3,000	Cheque	Wages	Expense	Increase $3,000
			Cash	Asset	Decrease $3,000
Sell goods to customer from inventory	Sell inventory on credit: $9,000	Invoice to customer	Accounts Receivable	Asset	Increase $9,000
			Sales	Income	Increase $9,000
Deliver goods from inventory	The goods that were sold for $9,000 cost $4,000 to buy	Goods delivery note	Cost of Sales	Expense	Increase $4,000
			Inventory	Asset	Decrease $4,000
Advertising	Pay $1,000 for advertising	Cheque	Advertising	Expense	Increase $1,000
			Cash	Asset	Decrease $1,000
Receive payment from customer for earlier sale on credit	Receive $4,000 from Accounts Receivable	Bank deposit	Cash	Asset	Increase $4,000
			Accounts Receivable	Asset	Decrease $4,000
Pay supplier for goods previously bought on credit	Pay $9,000 to Accounts Payable	Cheque	Cash	Asset	Decrease $9,000
			Accounts Payable	Liability	Decrease $9,000

The accounts are all contained in a **ledger**, which is simply a collection of all the different accounts for the business. The ledger would summarize the transactions for each account, as shown in Exhibit 3.3.

Exhibit 3.3 Summarizing Business Transactions in a Ledger

Account Transaction	Asset: Equipment	Asset: Inventory	Asset: Accounts Receivable	Asset: Cash	Liability: Accounts Payable	Income: Sales	Expenses
Buy equipment for cash: $25,000	+25,000			−25,000			
Purchase inventory on credit: $15,000		+15,000			+15,000		
Pay wages: $3,000				−3,000			+3,000
Sell inventory on credit: $9,000			+9,000			+9,000	
The goods that were sold for $9,000 cost $4,000 to buy		−4,000					+4,000
Pay advertising: $1,000				−1,000			+1,000
Receive $4,000 from Accounts Receivable			−4,000	+4,000			
Pay $9,000 to Accounts Payable				−9,000	−9,000		
Total of transactions for this period	+25,000	+11,000	+5,000	−34,000	+6,000	+9,000	+8,000

In the example shown in Exhibit 3.3, there would be a separate account for each type of expense (wages, cost of sales, advertising) but for ease of presentation, these accounts have been placed in a single column. The ledger is the source of the financial reports that present the performance of the business. However, the ledger would also contain the balance of each account brought forward from the previous period. In our simple example, assume that the business commenced with $50,000 in the bank account that had been contributed by the owner (the owner's *equity* or *capital*). Exhibit 3.4 shows the effect of the opening balances.

Exhibit 3.4 Summarizing Business Transactions with Opening Balances in a Ledger

Account	Capital	Asset: Equipment	Asset: Inventory	Asset: Accounts Receivable	Asset: Cash	Liability: Accounts Payable	Income: Sales	Expenses
Investment by owner	+50,000				+50,000			
Total of transactions for this period		+25,000	+11,000	+5,000	−34,000	+6,000	+9,000	+8,000
Totals of each account at end of period	+50,000	+25,000	+11,000	+5,000	+16,000	+6,000	+9,000	+8,000

Extracting Financial Information from the Accounting System

To produce financial reports we need to separate the accounts for income and expenses from those for assets and liabilities. Carrying on with the example introduced in the preceding section, we would produce a **statement of comprehensive income** based on the income and expenses, as shown in Exhibit 3.5.

Exhibit 3.5 Statement of Comprehensive Income

Income		$9,000
Less cost of goods sold		4,000
Gross profit		$5,000
Wages	$3,000	
Advertising	1,000	4,000
Net profit		$1,000

The **statement of financial position** lists the assets and liabilities of the business, as shown in Exhibit 3.6. In this case, the statement is in the less-commonly used horizontal format.

Exhibit 3.6 Statement of Financial Position: Horizontal Format

Assets		Liabilities	
Equipment	$25,000	Accounts payable	$ 6,000
Inventory	11,000	**Equity**	
Accounts receivable	5,000	Owner's original investment	$50,000
Bank	16,000	Plus profit for period	1,000
Total assets	$57,000	Total equity	$51,000
		Total liabilities plus equity	$57,000

The statement of financial position must *balance*; that is, assets must be equal to liabilities plus owners' equity. The double-entry system records the profit earned by the business as an addition to the owner's investment in the business:

$$\text{Assets} = \text{Liabilities} + \text{Equity}$$

This is called the *accounting equation*. However, a more common presentation of the statement of financial position is in a vertical format, as shown in Exhibit 3.7.

Exhibit 3.7 Statement of Financial Position: Vertical Format

Assets	
Equipment	$25,000
Inventory	11,000
Accounts receivable	5,000
Cash	16,000
Total assets	$57,000
Liabilities	
Accounts payable	$ 6,000
Equity	
Total original investment	$50,000
Plus profit for period	1,000
Total equity	$51,000
Total liabilities and equity	$57,000

The accounting equation can therefore be restated as

Equity ($51,000) = Assets ($57,000) − Liabilities ($6,000)

There are some important points to note about the above example:

1. The purchase of equipment of $25,000 has not affected profit (although we will consider depreciation in Chapter 4).

2. Profit is not the same as cash flow. Although there has been a profit of $1,000, the bank balance has decreased by $34,000 (from $50,000 to $16,000).

3. Most of the cash has gone into the new equipment ($25,000), but some has gone into working capital (this is covered in Chapter 5).

An example of a statement of financial position shown in a vertical format follows in Exhibit 3.8.

Exhibit 3.8 Air Canada, 2011 Consolidated Statement of Financial Position

(Canadian dollars in millions)		December 31 2011	December 31 2010	January 1 2010
ASSETS				
Current				
Cash and cash equivalents	Note 3P	$ 848	$ 1,090	$ 1,115
Short-term investments	Note 3Q	1,251	1,102	292
Total cash, cash equivalents, and short-term investments		2,099	2,192	1,407
Restricted cash	Note 3R	76	80	78
Accounts receivable		712	641	701
Aircraft fuel inventory		92	67	63
Spare parts and supplies inventory	Note 3S	93	88	64
Prepaid expenses and other current assets		255	279	338
Total current assets		3,327	3,347	2,651
Property and equipment	Note 5	5,088	5,629	6,287
Intangible assets	Note 6	312	317	329
Goodwill	Note 7	311	311	311
Deposits and other assets	Note 8	595	549	547
Total assets		**$ 9,633**	**$10,153**	**$10,125**
LIABILITIES				
Current				
Accounts payable and accrued liabilities		$ 1,175	$ 1,182	$ 1,246
Advance ticket sales		1,554	1,375	1,288

(continued)

Exhibit 3.8 Air Canada, 2011 Consolidated Statement of Financial Position (*continued*)

Current portion of long-term debt and finance leases	Note 9	424	567	468
Total current liabilities		3,153	3,124	3,002
Long-term debt and finance leases	Note 9	3,906	4,028	4,313
Pension and other benefit liabilities	Note 10	5,563	3,328	3,940
Maintenance provisions	Note 11	548	493	461
Other long-term liabilities	Note 12	469	468	429
Total liabilities		**13,639**	**11,441**	**12,145**
EQUITY				
Shareholders' equity				
Share capital	Note 14	840	846	844
Contributed surplus		58	54	53
Deficit		(4,983)	(2,334)	(2,881)
Accumulated other comprehensive loss	Note 18	—	—	(184)
Total shareholders' equity		(4,085)	(1,434)	(2,168)
Non-controlling interests		79	146	148
Total equity		(4,006)	(1,288)	(2,020)
Total liabilities and equity		**$ 9,633**	**$ 10,153**	**$ 10,125**

The accompanying notes are an integral part of the consolidated financial statements.

The distinction between profit, cash flow, and capital investment—the purchase of assets—is a crucial one for accounting. Whether a payment is treated as an expense (which affects profit) or as a statement of financial position item (**capitalize** the expense, therefore not affecting profit) is important, as it can have a significant impact on profit, which is one of the main measures of business performance. Chapter 4 discusses this distinction in more detail.

Both the statement of comprehensive income and the statement of financial position are described in more detail in Chapter 4. In financial reporting, as this chapter and Chapters 4 and 5 will show, there are strict requirements for the content and presentation of these financial reports. One of these requirements is that the financial statements (produced from the ledger accounts) be based on line items. **Line items** are the generic types of assets, liabilities, income, and expenses that are common to all businesses. This is an important requirement, as all businesses are required to report their expenses using the same accounts, such as rent, salaries, advertising, interest costs, and so on. While this may not appear to be significant, it does cause a problem when a business is trying to make decisions based on cost information, because cost information is needed for products and services, rather than for line items.

Basic Principles of Accounting

For financial statements to be useful and informative to a large and diverse group of users, it is important that all financial statements adhere to a standardized set of rules or principles that are accepted by the broadest group of users. These rules or principles are referred to as **generally accepted** accounting principles (GAAP). The most commonly used GAAP standards globally are the *International Financial Reporting Standards* (IFRS). These will be discussed in more detail in Chapter 4.

Basic principles or conventions have been created over many years and form the basis on which financial information is reported. These principles include

- Business entity
- Accounting period
- Accrual principle
- Matching principle
- Monetary unit of measurement
- Cost and other measuring alternatives
- Going concern
- Consistency

Each is dealt with in turn.

BUSINESS ENTITY

Business entity refers to the principle of treating distinctive legal entities, including people, separately for accounting purposes. Because the business and its owners are separate entities, financial reports are produced for the business, independent of the owners. This is particularly important for owner-managed businesses, where the personal finances of the owner must be separated from the business finances. The problem caused by the entity principle is that complex organizational structures are not always clearly identifiable as an "entity" (see the Enron Case in Point feature).

CASE IN POINT

Hiding the Truth Behind "Special-Purpose Entities"?

In December 2001, U.S. energy trader Enron collapsed. It was the largest bankruptcy in U.S. history. Even though the United States was believed by many to be the most regulated financial market in the world, it was evident from Enron's collapse that investors were not properly informed about the significance of off-balance-sheet transactions. Enron had taken out large loans that were created through special-purpose entities, so they were not treated as liabilities in its financial reports.

U.S. accounting rules may have contributed to this situation, in that they are concerned with the strict legal ownership of investment vehicles rather than with their control. There were some indications that Enron may have actively lobbied against changing the treatment in U.S. financial reporting of special-purpose entities used in off-balance-sheet financing. As a consequence of the failure of Enron and WorldCom (see the Case in Point feature on WorldCom later in this chapter), the United States introduced the *Sarbanes-Oxley Act* to address many of the criticisms of reporting and auditing practices.

Enron's former chief executive Kenneth Lay died in 2006 before he could stand trial. The former chief financial officer Andrew Fastow was sentenced in late 2006 to six years in prison for stealing from Enron and devising schemes to deceive investors about the company's true financial condition. Lawyers have to date won settlements totalling (US)$7.3 billion from banks including JPMorgan Chase, Bank of America, and Citigroup.

CASE IN POINT

Accounting Periods Fraudulently Manipulated

An organization's accounting period is crucial to shareholders, lenders, and other stakeholders, since they need to know how a company is faring at a given point in time. All transactions have to be accounted for in one period or another. But accounting periods can be manipulated fraudulently for personal gain, as the case of an Irish banker shows.

It is alleged that the Anglo Irish Bank loaned €179 million to some of its directors, including €87 million to its chair, Seán FitzPatrick, without shareholders' approval. FitzPatrick admitted that over a period of eight years, to hide these loans, he temporarily shifted the loans at every year-end to another lender, so the loans never appeared on his bank's annual financial statements. It is said that the loans were discovered by Ireland's financial regulator when it examined the books of the other lender. The regulator said while it seemed nothing illegal took place, these practices were "not appropriate" and it urged the Anglo Irish Bank to disclose the loans in its next annual report. FitzPatrick and Anglo Irish's chief executive resigned after the loans scandal broke.

Loans made to directors must be approved by shareholders and must be disclosed in a company's financial statements—specifically, in the statement of financial position and notes to the financial statements.

Sources: Aldrick, P., Anglo Irish chairman Sean FitzPatrick resigns over "inappropriate" loan, *The Telegraph*, December 19, 2008; Anglo Irish Bank chief quits after hiding €87m loans, *Belfast Telegraph*; Sean Farrell: Anglo Irish Bank chiefs quit amid loans scandal, *The Independent*, December 20, 2008.

ACCOUNTING PERIOD

Financial information is normally produced for a financial year but can sometimes be produced for a month or a quarter. The **accounting period** is arbitrary and is not necessarily related to business cycles. Many businesses end their **financial year** at the end of a calendar year, while others choose another time period.

The business cycle is more important than the calendar year, which after all is nothing more than the time it takes for the earth to revolve around the sun. If we consider the early history of accounting, merchant ships did not produce monthly accounting reports. They reported to the ships' owners at the end of the business cycle, when the goods they had traded were all sold and profits could be calculated meaningfully. In today's environment, where trade happens faster and business cycles tend to be shorter, all businesses report at least annually. Public companies are required to report their results on a quarterly basis as well as on an annual basis.

ACCRUAL ACCOUNTING

Accrual accounting dictates that income is recognized when it is earned and expenses when they are incurred, rather than on a cash basis. For example, utilities expense for January belongs to the expenses for January and should affect January's profit, even though the bill might not be paid until February. The accrual method of accounting provides a more meaningful picture of the financial performance of a business from year to year. The accrual principle will be discussed in more detail in Chapter 4.

MATCHING PRINCIPLE

Closely related to the accrual principle is the **matching principle**. This principle is based on the fact that profit equals income less expenses. It is important for users of financial statements to know what

CASE IN POINT

"Accounting Improprieties of Unprecedented Magnitude"

WorldCom filed for bankruptcy protection in June 2002, after using accounting tricks to conceal a deteriorating financial condition and to inflate profits. It was one of the biggest corporate frauds in history, largely a result of treating operating expenses as capital expenditures. This meant that expenses that were supposed to have been recognized in the current year were added to assets and only recognized in following years through depreciation. WorldCom (now renamed MCI) admitted in March 2004 that the total amount by which it had misled investors over the previous 10 years was almost (US)$75 billion and that it had reduced its stated pre-tax profits for 2001 and 2002 by that amount.

Former WorldCom chief executive Bernie Ebbers resigned in April 2002 amid questions about (US)$366 million in personal loans from the company and a federal probe of its accounting practices. Ebbers was subsequently charged with conspiracy to commit securities fraud and filing misleading data with the Securities and Exchange Commission (SEC). Scott Sullivan, former chief financial officer, pleaded guilty to three criminal charges.

The SEC said that WorldCom had committed "accounting improprieties of unprecedented magnitude"—proof, it said, of the need for reform in the regulation of corporate accounting.

---

the profit for a specific accounting period is. To calculate the profit for a specific period, the income earned for that period has to be matched with the expenses which produced that income. In other words, we first determine how much revenue was earned during a specific period and then we determine the expenses that were incurred to earn that revenue. The profit for the period is thus the revenue for the period less the expenses incurred to earn that revenue.

The concept of cost of goods sold introduced earlier in this chapter illustrates the matching principle. If inventory bought and paid for in Year 1 is sold in Year 2, the cost of that inventory is included in the statement of comprehensive income in Year 2 to reflect the profit made in Year 2. This is done by not including that inventory purchase as an expense in Year 1, but rather by showing it as an asset in Year 1 and including it in cost of goods sold (an expense) in Year 2.

However, the matching principle has its disadvantage. The preparation of accounting reports requires certain assumptions to be made about the recognition of income and expenses. One of the criticisms made of many companies is that they attempt to "smooth" their reported performance to satisfy the expectations of stock market analysts in order to maintain shareholder value. This practice has become known as *earnings management* and is achieved by showing income or expenses that belong in one period in another period.

This has been particularly difficult in the telecom industry, where income that should have been spread over several years has been recorded earlier, or where an expenditure has been treated as an asset in order to improve reported profits. When this latter practice was disclosed, it was a significant cause of the difficulties faced by WorldCom (see the Case in Point feature on WorldCom).

MONETARY UNIT OF MEASUREMENT

Despite the importance of market, human, technological, and environmental factors, accounting records transactions and reports information in financial terms; that is, in some monetary value, like the Canadian dollar. This provides a limited although important perspective on business performance.

COST AND OTHER MEASURING ALTERNATIVES

What is the value of an asset? At what amount should it be shown in the statement of financial position? At what amount should we show an expense in the statement of comprehensive income? The answers to these questions depend on how we decide to value or cost the items. One option is to value an asset at the amount paid for it when it was bought, less depreciation (see Chapter 4). This is known as the *historic cost*. Alternatives are to show it at market (realizable) value or at current (replacement) cost. The historic cost may be unrelated to market or replacement value. GAAP specifies which assets should be shown at historic cost and which at market or replacement value.

Keep in mind that the statement of financial position does not attempt to represent the value of the business, and the owner's capital is merely a calculated figure rather than a valuation of the business. The statement of financial position excludes assets that have not been purchased by a business but have been built up over time, such as customer goodwill, brand names, and so on. The *market-to-book ratio* (MBR) is the market value of the business divided by the original capital invested. Major service-based companies such as Microsoft, which have enormous goodwill and intellectual property but a low asset base, have high MBRs because the stock market takes account of information that is not reflected in accounting reports.

GOING CONCERN

The financial reports are prepared on the basis that the business will continue in operation for the foreseeable future, and is therefore known as a **going concern**. Many businesses have failed soon after their financial statements have been prepared on a going concern basis, making the asset values in the statement of financial position impossible to realize. As asset values after the liquidation of a business are unlikely to equal historic cost, the continued operation of a business is an important assumption. The going concern principle is a significant limitation of financial statements, as the Carrington Printers case study in Chapter 5 reveals.

CONSISTENCY

The application of accounting standards and principles should be consistent from one year to the next. This is known as the consistency principle. When those principles vary, the effect on profits must be reported separately. However, some businesses have tended to change their rules, even with disclosure, in order to improve their reported performance, explaining the change as a once-only event.

The eight principles that we have just discussed are elaborated on in the *International Financial Reporting Standards* (IFRS) and the *Framework for the Preparation and Presentation of Financial Statements*, both of which are described in Chapter 4.

One of the most important pieces of financial information for line managers is cost, which forms the basis for most of the chapters in Part III. While this is largely outside the scope of financial reporting, it is worth introducing here, as the calculation of cost is influenced in large part by accounting principles and the requirements of financial reporting. However, the cost that is calculated for financial reporting purposes may have limited decision usefulness.

Cost Terms and Concepts: The Limitations of Financial Accounting

Cost can be defined as "a resource sacrificed or foregone to achieve a specific objective" (Horngren et al., 2009, p. 27).

Accountants define costs in monetary terms, and while we will focus on monetary costs, readers should recognize that there are not only financial measures of performance but also human, social, and environmental costs. For example, making employees redundant causes family problems (a human cost) and transfers to society the obligation to pay unemployment benefits (a social cost). Pollution causes long-term environmental costs that are also transferred to society. These are as important as (and perhaps more important than) financial costs, but they are not recorded by accounting systems (see Chapter 5 for further discussion). The exclusion of human, social, and environmental costs is a significant limitation of accounting.

For planning, decision making, and control purposes, cost is typically defined in relation to a *cost object*, which is anything for which a measurement of costs is required. While the cost object is often an *output*—a product or service—it may also be a resource (an *input* to the production process), a *process* of converting resources into outputs, or an *area of responsibility* (a department or cost centre) within the organization. Examples of inputs are materials, labour, rent, marketing expenses, and so on. These are line items, which were discussed previously. Examples of processes are purchasing, customer order processing, order fulfillment, dispatch, and so on. Departments or cost centres may include Purchasing, Production, Marketing, Accounting, and so on. Other cost objects are possible when we want to consider profitability; for example, the cost of dealing with specific customers is important for customer profitability analysis.

Businesses typically report in relation to line items (the resource inputs) and responsibility centres (departments or cost centres). This means that decisions requiring cost information on business processes and product/service outputs are difficult, because most accounting systems (except activity-based systems, as will be described in Chapter 11) do not provide adequate information about those cost objects. Reports on the profitability of each product, each customer, or each business unit are rarely able to be produced from the traditional financial accounting system and must be determined through management accounting processes that use, but are not incorporated within, financial accounting systems.

Businesses might adopt a system of management accounting to provide this kind of information for management purposes, but rarely will this second system reconcile with the external financial reports, because the management information system may not follow the same accounting principles described in this chapter and in Chapter 4. Therefore, the requirement to produce financial reports based on line items rather than on more meaningful cost objects (customers, processes, and so on) is a second limitation of accounting as a tool of decision making.

The notion of cost is also problematic because we need to decide how cost is to be defined. If, as Horngren and his colleagues defined it, cost is a resource sacrificed or foregone, then one of the questions we must ask is whether that definition implies a cash cost or an opportunity cost. A **cash cost** is the amount of cash expended (a valuable resource), whereas an **opportunity cost** is the lost opportunity of not doing something, which may be the loss of time, the loss of a customer, or the diminution in the value of an asset (such as machinery), all equally valuable resources.

If it is the cash cost, is it the *historical* (past) cost or the *future* cost with which we should be concerned? For example, is the cost of an employee

- The historical cash cost of salaries and benefits, training, recruitment, and so on already paid?

- The future cash cost of salaries and benefits to be paid?

- The lost opportunity cost of what we could have done with the money had we not employed that person; for instance, the benefits that could have resulted from expenditure of the same money on items such as advertising, computer equipment, external consulting services?

Wilson and Chua (1988) quoted the economist Jevons, writing in 1871, that past costs were irrelevant to decisions about the future because they are "gone and lost forever." We call these past costs *sunk costs*. The problematic nature of calculating costs may have been the source of the comment by Clark (1923) that there were "different costs for different purposes."

This, then, is our third limitation of accounting: What do we mean by *cost* and how do we calculate it? The concept of cost will be discussed thoroughly throughout this book.

The criticism of accounting numbers is that they are *lagging* indicators of performance. Chapter 6 considers non-financial measures of performance that are more likely to present *leading* indicators of performance. An emphasis on financial numbers tends to overlook the important issues of customer satisfaction, product/service quality, innovation, and employee morale, which have a major impact on business performance.

Accounting and Information Systems

An information system is a system that collects and communicates information within an organization. Information is different from data. **Data** are the raw forms of information that must be synthesized and summarized into something that is useful and meaningful to a decision maker. This synthesized and purposeful data is **information**. While data comprise a set of raw facts, information is usable. For example, sales data can be summarized and analyzed by customer and/or product or service in a monthly sales analysis report and thereby becomes meaningful management information that can then be used for decision making.

Organizations typically have an **information system strategy** (ISS) that follows the organizational business strategy and determines the long-term information requirements of the business. The ISS strategy provides an "umbrella" for different information technologies to help ensure that appropriate information is acquired, retained, shared, and available for use in strategy implementation. The ISS strategy can be distinguished from the **information technology strategy** (ITS), which defines the specific technological systems that are required to satisfy the information needs of the organization, including the hardware, software, and operating systems. The third element is the **information management strategy** (IMS), which is concerned with ensuring that the necessary information is being provided to users. This includes databases, data warehousing, and reporting systems. Exhibit 3.9 illustrates how the information infrastructure of an organization might operate.

Information is an essential management tool, but it needs to be relevant, timely, accurate, complete, concise, and understandable. The benefits of quality information that meets these criteria may include improved decision making, superior customer service, high product/service quality, productivity gains, and reduced staffing. However, the collection, processing, analysis, and reporting of information constitute an expensive process (e.g., the cost of hardware, software development, and staff time), and organizations need to ensure that the value of the information obtained is greater than the cost of providing that information.

An accounting information system is one that uses technology to capture, store, process, and report accounting information. However, in this chapter and from a management accounting perspective, we consider accounting to be only one, albeit important, component of information systems.

METHODS OF ACCOUNTING DATA COLLECTION

Most accounting data collection in organizations takes place as a by-product of transaction recording through computer systems, which have automated tasks that were carried out before computers by manual processing of documents and entries into journals and ledgers.

Exhibit 3.9 Information Systems Infrastructure

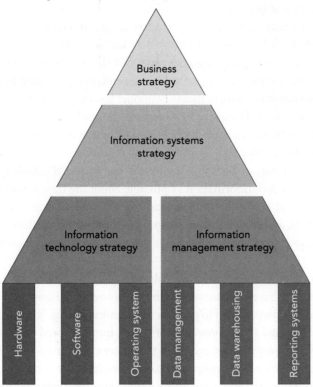

Computer systems have automated tasks substantially, with multiple aspects of a transaction being carried out simultaneously. For example, credit sales typically incorporate the entire process of delivering goods or services by producing an accompanying delivery receipt, reducing the inventory balances on hand, producing an invoice, updating the accounts receivable records to show the amount owed by customers, producing a sales analysis by customer/product, and calculating the margin on the sale by deducting the cost of goods sold. This information is transferred into the general ledger where, along with all other similar transactions, it is summarized and reported as sales and gross profit. Similar processes exist in relation to payments to suppliers and the collection of money owed by customers.

Retailers make extensive use of electronic point-of-sale (POS) technology, which uses bar-code scanning to reduce inventory levels on hand, price goods, calculate margins, and print a cash register receipt for the customer. Over a time period (day, week, or month), the outputs from such a system include reports on business volume (number of customers, number of items sold, and so on), sales analysis, product profitability, and inventory re-order requirements.

Additional benefits of POS systems include information about peak sales times during each day, products that may need to be discounted, sales locations that may need to be expanded, and so on. The use of electronic funds transfer at point of sale means that customers do not have to pay cash (which is expensive for retailers to deal with due to security requirements) but can automatically transfer funds from their bank account (or credit card) to the retailer's bank account, thereby eliminating further transactions.

The increase in e-commerce for business-to-consumer sales (B2C) means that for many products and services, purchasing on the Internet enables customers to carry out the data processing previously carried out by a retailer's own employees. Companies such as Amazon save costs by not needing expensive retail premises or staff taking customer orders. Customers order and pay online. All the retailer has to do is ship the goods.

For business-to-business (B2B) activities, electronic data interchange (EDI) enables suppliers' and customers' systems to be linked by a common data format, so that purchase orders raised by the customer are automatically converted into sales orders on the supplier's system. For example, in the automotive industry, orders from the major vehicle assemblers are placed to suppliers using EDI. EDI systems enable the buyer to confirm that the supplier has the inventory on hand without having to contact a sales representative. The use of EDI enables automatic generation of invoices by the supplier, tracing of deliveries by the logistics supplier and receipt of goods by the purchaser, ultimately leading to payment to the supplier.

An important part of data collection is collecting the financial details of a transaction. Also important is capturing as much information as possible about the transaction from a non-financial perspective. An example of this is the information collected from customers through retail credit cards, store loyalty cards, and frequent flyer programs. These allow retailers to maintain a detailed database of their customers' purchasing habits, enabling promotional campaigns targeting specific customers.

Due to technology, businesses are now able to use technologies to accumulate extensive customer information databases. Customer databases have enabled businesses to know their customers intimately, but companies need to use this information wisely. "Corporate knowledge of the customer is ostensibly related to the provision of better, more tailored customer service. But customer information systems are increasingly used to segment customers into identifiable groups, to calculate the financial value of each group, and to selectively target some groups whilst excluding others" (Boyce, 2002). Organizations need to be careful not to create exclusionary practices that could be viewed as unethical. Also, companies need to be careful in their practices of sharing information about their customers with outside parties. Privacy policies should be clearly indicated on a company website.

Companies also collect information about their suppliers. For example, in the automotive industry, the large vehicle assemblers collect vast quantities of information about their suppliers' costs: the cost of labour, the cost of manufacturing equipment and its capacity, and the cost of raw materials such as steel. Much of this information is publicly available, but retaining it in an organization's information system supports subsequent negotiations between the automotive assembler's purchasing department and the supplier's sales staff. By using this information, buyers can check the reasonableness of supplier prices for component parts, as buyers can perform their own checks on what it should cost to produce the same components.

Of course, the more that is expected of an information system, the more data have to be collected, stored, and reported. Accounting is one type rather than the only type of information that is collected. In Chapter 6, we will see that information is often collected for balanced scorecard-type performance measurement systems that report information about customers, business processes, and innovation to supplement financial performance measures. Therefore, organizations need to capture information from their marketing, purchasing, production, distribution, and human resource activities. Information about key factors such as customer satisfaction, cycle times (from order to delivery), quality, waste, and on-time delivery need to be part of an information system and reported together with financial information.

TYPES OF INFORMATION SYSTEMS

Various types of information systems are used in accounting. **Transaction processing systems** are a product of financial accounting activities in which data are collected about each business transaction. For example, data are collected related to customer orders, sales, purchases, stock movements, payments, and receipts. Transaction processing reports are important for control and audit purposes.

Information management systems often include both financial and non-financial information and typically are more oriented to supporting management decisions. For example, displays of key performance data with graphical representations are becoming increasingly common. Traffic lights (red/yellow/green) draw attention to those aspects of performance that are meeting target (green), those that are in need of urgent attention (red), and those that need attention because they are borderline (yellow). However, these systems do not integrate accounting, manufacturing, and distribution systems.

An **enterprise resource planning (ERP)** system helps to integrate data flow and access to information over the whole range of a company's activities. ERP systems typically capture transaction data for accounting purposes, together with operational, customer, and supplier data, which are then made available through data warehouses against which custom-designed reports can be produced.

ERP systems take a holistic approach to data collection and reporting. The system data can be used to update performance measures in a balanced scorecard system and for activity-based costing, shareholder value, strategic planning, customer relationship management, and supply chain management. In this chapter, we will use the term *enterprise resource planning* (ERP) systems to refer to information systems that are not limited to accounting but integrate different functional areas of the business and take a business process perspective. Examples of these systems include SAP and Oracle.

INTERNAL CONTROLS FOR INFORMATION SYSTEMS

As organizations increasingly rely on their information systems, information system controls are essential to ensure the security of data and the reliability of information. There are four main types of controls in relation to information systems:

1. **Security controls** prevent unauthorized access, modification, or destruction of stored data. Recruitment, training, and supervision need to be in place to ensure the competence of those responsible for programming and data entry. Personnel controls include the separation of duties within departments and the separation of data processing between departments. Access controls provide security over unauthorized access to data. The most common form of access security is through password authorization. Software controls also ensure that the software used by the organization is authorized.

2. **Application controls** are designed for each individual application, such as payroll, accounting, and inventory control. The aim of application controls is to prevent, detect, and correct transaction processing errors. Input controls are designed to detect and prevent errors during transaction data entry to ensure that data entered are complete and accurate. Processing controls ensure that processing has occurred according to the organization's requirements and that no transactions have been omitted or processed incorrectly. Output controls ensure that input and processing activities have been carried out and that the information produced is reliable and distributed to users.

3. **Network controls** have arisen in response to the growth of distributed processing and e-commerce and the need for protection against hacking, viruses, and online theft. A firewall comprises a combination of hardware and software located between the company's private network (intranet) and the public network. Data encryption can be used to convert data into a non-readable format before transmission and then re-convert it after transmission.

4. **Contingency controls** are relied on if security or integrity controls fail. There must be a back-up facility where information is kept and a contingency plan to restore business operations as quickly as possible (for instance, a business continuity or disaster recovery plan).

CONCLUSION

This chapter has described how an accounting system captures, records, summarizes, and reports financial information using the double-entry system of recording financial transactions in accounts. It has introduced in simple terms the statement of comprehensive income and statement of financial position, which are dealt with in more detail in Chapters 4 and 5.

This chapter has also identified the principles underlying the accounting process. The limitations of financial accounting for managerial decision making are highlighted through the introduction to the concept of cost, which as we will see throughout Part III is crucial for decision making. Lastly, the accounting and information systems that need to be in place to record the accounting transactions in a complete, accurate, and secure way has been highlighted.

KEY TERMS

Accounting period, 48
Accounting system, 38
Accounts, 38
Accrual accounting, 48
Application controls, 55
Assets, 38
Business entity, 47
Capitalize, 46
Cash cost, 51
Contingency controls, 56
Cost, 50
Cost of sales or cost of goods sold, 40
Data, 52
Double entry, 40
Enterprise resource planning (ERP), 55
Expenses, 38
Financial statements, 39
Financial year, 48
Generally accepted accounting principles (GAAP), 46–47
Going concern, 50

Gross profit, 40
Income, 38
Information, 52
Information management strategy (IMS), 52
Information system strategy (ISS), 52
Information technology strategy (ITS), 52
Ledger, 42
Liabilities, 38
Line items, 46
Matching principle, 48
Net profit, 40
Network controls, 55
Opportunity cost, 51
Security controls, 55
Shareholders' equity, 38
Source document, 38
Statement of comprehensive income, 43
Statement of financial position, 44
Transaction, 38
Transaction processing systems, 54

■ SELF-TEST QUESTIONS

S3.1 Which one of the following equations is not correct?

a. Income − Expenses = Profit

b. Asset − Liabilities = Equity

   c. Income + Assets = Equity

   d. Assets = Equity + Liabilities

S3.2 A transaction to record the sale of merchandise for profit on credit would have the following effect:

   a. Increase sales and decrease inventory

   b. Increase profit and increase sales

   c. Increase accounts receivable and increase sales

   d. All of the above

S3.3 A transaction to record the purchase of merchandise for cash would have the following effect:

   a. Increase in expenses and assets

   b. Increase in expenses and liabilities

   c. Increase in expenses and decrease in assets

   d. Total assets will not change

S3.4 A transaction to record the purchase of an asset on credit would involve

   a. Increasing assets and increasing expenses

   b. Increasing assets and decreasing profit

   c. Increasing assets and increasing accounts payable

   d. Decreasing assets and increasing accounts payable

S3.5 A retail business had cash of $15,000 and inventory of $70,000 on hand on January 1. On January 7, it sold half of the inventory on credit for $50,000 and collected half of this amount on January 26. The financial statements of the business would show

   a. Profit of $15,000 and cash of $40,000

   b. Profit of $15,000 and cash of $65,000

   c. Profit of $50,000 and cash of $65,000

   d. Loss of $20,000 and cash of $40,000

S3.6 A business person starts a retail company by contributing $100,000 cash. The company then buys inventory for $90,000, has sales of $150,000, cost of goods sold of $80,000, salaries of $30,000, rental of $12,000, advertising expenses of $8,000, and equipment purchases of $40,000. All of the transactions, except the purchase of equipment, are for cash. The financial statements of the company would show

   a. Profit of $20,000, cash of $30,000, and equity of $100,000

   b. Profit of $20,000, cash of $110,000, and equity of $120,000

   c. Profit of $10,000, cash of $110,000, and equity of $120,000

   d. Loss of $70,000, cash of $110,000, and equity of $30,000

S3.7 A company has income of $200,000 and expenses of $175,000 for the year. At the end of the year, it has assets of $600,000 and liabilities of $500,000. Equity at the end of the year is

a. $25,000

b. $75,000

c. $100,000

d. $125,000

S3.8 An accounting system comprises accounts that can be grouped into

a. Income, expenses, and profit

b. Statement of financial position, profit, and cash flow

c. Assets, liabilities, income, and expenses

d. Profit, capital, assets, and cash flow

S3.9 A transaction to record the sale of goods on credit would involve a double entry for the sales value to the following accounts:

a. Increase sales and reduce inventory

b. Increase sales and increase inventory

c. Increase accounts payable and increase sales

d. Increase accounts receivable and increase sales

S3.10 A *new* retail business has sales of $100,000, cost of goods sold of $35,000, salaries of $15,000, rental of $4,000, and advertising of $8,000. All of the income and expenses have been paid out of the owner's initial capital of $25,000. In addition, the business paid cash of $30,000 for inventory (which remains unsold) and purchased equipment on credit for $20,000. The financial statements of the business would show

a. Profit of $38,000, cash of $13,000, and shareholders' equity of $25,000

b. Profit of $38,000, cash of $33,000, and shareholders' equity of $63,000

c. Profit of $65,000, cash of $3,000, and shareholders' equity of $38,000

d. Profit of $63,000, cash of $33,000, and shareholders' equity of $38,000

S3.11 A statement of financial position shows liabilities of $125,000 and assets of $240,000. The statement of comprehensive income shows income of $80,000 and expenses of $35,000. Capital is

a. $45,000

b. $115,000

c. $160,000

d. $365,000

S3.12 A transaction to record the purchase of assets on credit would involve

a. Increasing assets and reducing accounts payable

b. Reducing assets and reducing accounts payable

c. Increasing accounts payable and increasing assets

d. Increasing accounts payable and reducing assets

■ PROBLEMS

P3.1 *(Effect of Transactions on Accounting Equation)* For each of the following transactions, identify whether there is an increase or decrease in profit, cash flow, assets, or liabilities.

Transaction	Profit	Cash Flow	Assets (excluding cash)	Liabilities
Owner contributes cash				
Buys equipment on credit				
Buys inventory on credit				
Takes out a loan from the bank				
Sells goods on credit				
Pays cash for expenses				
Pays cash to suppliers				
Receives cash from customers				
Depreciates equipment				

P3.2 *(Conceptual Framework)* Explain what is meant by the following terms:

a. Business entity

b. Accrual principle

c. Matching principle

d. Going concern

e. Consistency

P3.3 *(Costs)* Explain what is meant by the following cost terms:

a. Social cost

b. Opportunity cost

c. Sunk cost

d. Cash cost

P3.4 *(Internal Control for Information Systems)* Name and briefly describe the four main categories of internal control for information systems.

P3.5 *(Effect of Transactions on Accounting Equation)* The general ledger of Colourful Corporation, a paint store, had the following balances in its general ledger on May 31, 2012:

Cash	$8,500
Accounts Receivable	$1,400
Inventory	$22,050
Equipment	$2,500
Accounts Payable	$9,600
Common Shares	$10,000
Retained Earnings	$14,850

The following transactions occurred during June 2012:

1. Collected all, but $800 of the accounts receivable outstanding on May 31.
2. Sold paint that costs $20,500 to customers for $34,000. Of these sales, 80% was for cash and 20% was on credit.
3. Paid the accounts payable outstanding on May 31.
4. Bought paint from a supplier for $18,300, half on credit and half for cash.
5. Paid rent for June of $2,200.
6. Sent out a statement reminding a customer that he still owed $800 from May.
7. Purchased additional equipment for $3,000 with money borrowed from the bank.
8. Took out an advertisement in the local paper for $150. The company will pay for it in July.
9. Paid salaries and wages of $5,500.
10. Paid utilities for June of $550.
11. Paid dividends of $1,000 cash to the owner of the company.

Prepare a Statement of Comprehensive Income for June 2012 and Statement of Financial Position at June 30, 2012.

P3.6 *(Calculation of Profit and shareholders' equity)* The balances below are shown in alphabetical order in a professional service firm's ledger at the end of a financial year.

Calculate

a. The profit for the year

b. The shareholders' equity at the end of the year

Advertising	$15,000
Bank	5,000
Shareholder's equity at the beginning of the year	71,000
Accounts payable	11,000
Accounts receivable	12,000
Fixed assets	100,000
Income	135,000
Rent	10,000
Salaries	75,000

REFERENCES

Boyce, G. (2002). *Beyond privacy: The ethics of customer information systems*. Retrieved from
http://proceedings.informingscience.org/IS2002Proceedings/papers/Boyce230Beyon.pdf.

Canadian Institute of Chartered Accountants (2012). *The CICA standards and guidance collection* (electronic version). Toronto: CICA.

Clark, J. M. (1923). *Studies in the economics of overhead costs*. Chicago, IL: University of Chicago Press.

Horngren, C. T., Datar, S. M., Foster, G., Rajan, M., and Ittner, C. (2009). *Cost accounting: A Managerial emphasis* (13 ed.). Upper Saddle River, NJ: Pearson Prentice Hall.

Wilson, R. M. S., and Chua, W. F. (1988). *Managerial accounting: Method and meaning*. London: VNR International.

Constructing Financial Reports: IFRS and the Framework of Accounting

LEARNING OBJECTIVES

After reading this chapter, you should be able to answer the following questions:

- What is management's basic responsibility regarding a company's financial statements?

- What parties are generally considered to be the external users of a company's financial statements?

- What are the objectives, elements, and qualitative characteristics of financial statements?

- How is accrual accounting applied in the recording of prepayments accruals, provisions, and depreciation?

The chapter begins with a discussion of the *International Financial Reporting Standards* (IFRS) and the *Conceptual Framework for Financial Reporting*; the latter sets out the concepts underlying the preparation and presentation of financial statements for external users. The chapter then introduces each of the principal financial statements: the statement of comprehensive income, the statement of financial position, the statement of changes in equity, and the statement of cash flows. It offers examples of the matching principle and accrual accounting, which emphasizes prepayments and accruals and other common accounting treatments, such as depreciation. The chapter concludes with a discussion of the limitations of accounting standards.

Accounting provides an explanation or report in financial terms about the transactions of an organization. Accounting enables managers to satisfy the *stakeholders* in the organization (owners, shareholders, government, financiers, suppliers, customers, employees, and so on) that they have acted in the best interests of stakeholders rather than in their own interests. Chapter 1 provided a more in-depth treatment of accountability.

These explanations are provided to stakeholders through financial statements or reports, often referred to as the company's *accounts*. The main financial reports are the statement of comprehensive income, the statement of financial position, the statement of cash flows, and the statement of changes in shareholders' equity. The first two of these were introduced briefly in Chapter 3.

Management's Responsibility for Fair Presentation

Canadian legislation often requires that organizations' financial statements present fairly the financial position, financial performance, and cash flows of an entity; be prepared according to generally accepted accounting principles (GAAP); and be audited or reviewed to ensure that this is the case. This means that the financial statements must comply with the principles set out in the Canadian Institute of Chartered Accountants' *CICA Handbook*. Part I of the *Handbook* consists of *International Financial Reporting Standards* (IFRS) and is applicable to public entities. (For companies listed on a provincial stock exchange such as the Toronto Stock Exchange, there are additional rules set by the provincial securities commissions.) Part II of the *Handbook* consists of *Accounting Standards for Private Enterprises* (ASPE) and applies to private companies (although they can choose to use Part I if they wish), while Part III applies to not-for-profit organizations. These "parts" are often referred to as the financial reporting framework, the basis upon which an entity must prepare its financial statements.

Private companies tend to have far fewer users, including current and potential shareholders, and those shareholders are normally closely involved with the business, so there is less reason to have detailed accounting information for these users. Private companies and not-for-profit organizations also usually have fewer resources to spend on accounting. For these reasons, Parts II and III of the *Handbook* require less-detailed information to be provided in the financial statements. For simplicity's sake, this book will focus on Part I, IFRS.

Laws or regulation may establish the responsibilities of management in relation to financial reporting. However, the extent of these responsibilities, or the way in which they are described, may differ across jurisdictions. Despite these differences, management is always responsible for the preparation of financial statements in accordance with the applicable financial reporting framework, and for their fair presentation. Furthermore, management is also responsible for such internal control as it determines is necessary to enable the preparation of financial statements that are free from material misstatement, whether due to fraud or error.

The United States has not yet adopted IFRS, but negotiations are taking place between the U.S. Financial Accounting Standards Board (FASB) and the International Accounting Standards Board (IASB) for some form of convergence. The United States currently requires companies to apply generally accepted accounting principles specific to the United States (or U.S. GAAP), which rely more on a rules-based approach rather than the principles-based approach in IFRS. Because Canada has adopted the IFRS, its accounting standards are principles based. The rules-based approach has been criticized following the failures of Enron and WorldCom.

CASE IN POINT

"It Was Like Riding a Tiger"

In one of the biggest accounting scandals to shake India, Satyam Computer Services—which served more than one-third of the Fortune 500 companies—grossly violated the principle of faithful representation in its financial statements. Its founder and chairman, Ramalinga Raju, resigned after admitting that he exaggerated the company's earnings and assets for several years. In the second quarter of 2008, some (US)$1 billion—more than 90%—of its reported cash and assets was fictitious. The statement of financial position overstated revenues by 20% and understated liabilities. After the announcement, the company's shares plunged more than 70% and the Indian rupee lost value.

Raju said he did not take any money from the company and the board of directors had no knowledge of the fraudulent statements. In his resignation letter, Raju said the problem began small but ballooned out of control. "What started as a marginal gap between actual operating profit and the one reflected in the books of accounts continued to grow over the years," he wrote. "It was like riding a tiger, not knowing how to get off without being eaten."

Sources: Timmons, H., & Wassener, B., Satyam chief admits huge fraud, *The New York Times*, January 8, 2009; Reuters, Satyam accounting scandal could be "India's Enron," *The Telegraph*, January 7, 2009; Kawamoto, D., Satyam chairman resigns amid accounting scandal, *CNet.com*, January 7, 2009.

International Financial Reporting Standards: An Overview

Accounting standards reflect the basic accounting principles that are generally accepted by the accounting profession (see Chapter 3) and that are an essential requirement for reporting financial information. Historically, each country had its own set of accounting standards. The move toward the harmonization of accounting standards among countries through the work of the International Financial Reporting Standards Foundation and the International Accounting Standards Board has been a consequence of the globalization of capital markets, with the consequent need for accounting rules that can be understood by international investors. The dominance of multinational corporations and the desire of companies to be listed on several stock exchanges have led to the need to rationalize different reporting practices in different countries.

The IFRS Foundation is an independent, not-for-profit, private-sector organization based in London, England. The IASB is the standard-setting arm of the IFRS Foundation that, according to the IFRS website, is responsible for developing "a single set of high-quality, understandable, enforceable and globally accepted international financial reporting standards." The IASB has 15 members, each with one vote. The members are practising auditors, preparers of financial statements, users of financial statements, and academics.

In addition to developing international financial reporting standards, the IFRS objectives are to promote the use and rigorous application of those standards, to take account of the financial reporting needs of emerging economies and small and medium-sized entities (SMEs), and to bring about convergence of national accounting standards and IFRSs to high-quality solutions. (IFRS Foundation and the IASB, 2011).

The *International Financial Reporting Standards* (IFRS) are published by the IASB. The predecessor of the IASB was the Board of the International Accounting Standards Committee, which published the *International Accounting Standards* (IAS). Today's *International Financial Reporting Standards* include both the newer IFRS and the older IAS, together with "Interpretations" issued under these standards. These interpretations provide guidance on how the standards should be applied under specific circumstances. A full list of the IFRS and ASPE can be found in the appendix to this chapter.

IFRS and ASPE set out recognition, measurement, presentation, and disclosure requirements dealing with transactions and events that are important in general-purpose financial statements, although some standards refer to specific industries. General-purpose financial statements are directed toward the common information needs of a wide range of users.

IFRS and ASPE are designed for profit-oriented entities. Part III of the *CICA Handbook* addresses issues specifically applicable to not-for-profit organizations. Apart from these specific issues, not-for-profit organizations apply ASPE. There are also separate accounting standards for the public sector or government.

The *Sarbanes-Oxley Act* of 2002 (see Chapter 2) is the main legislation affecting companies listed in the United States. While the United States has not yet adopted the IFRS, the U.S. FASB and the IASB have agreed in principle to develop a common conceptual framework.

Conceptual Framework for Financial Reporting

Financial statements are prepared and presented by many entities around the world. Although such financial statements may appear to be similar from country to country, there are differences that have probably been caused by a variety of social, economic, and legal circumstances and by each country having to consider the needs of different users of financial statements when setting national requirements.

These different circumstances have led to the use of a variety of definitions of the elements of financial statements, such as assets, liabilities, equity, income, and expenses. They have also resulted in the use of different criteria for the recognition of items in the financial statements and in different bases of measurement. The scope of the financial statements and the disclosures made in them have also been affected.

Part I of the *CICA Handbook* contains a document called the *Conceptual Framework for Financial Reporting*. The purpose of the *Conceptual Framework* is to narrow the differences outlined above by seeking to harmonize regulations, accounting standards, and procedures relating to the preparation and presentation of financial statements. While not part of the IFRS, the *Conceptual Framework* is used when an accounting policy is needed and there is no appropriate standard to choose. All IFRS are based on the *Conceptual Framework*. Where there is conflict between the requirements of a standard and the *Conceptual Framework*, the standard prevails. ASPE does not have a specific framework, but the same principles are contained in Section 1000 of Part II of the *Handbook*.

A complete set of financial reports includes

- Statement of financial position
- Statement of comprehensive income
- Statement of changes in shareholders' equity
- Statement of cash flows
- Notes to the financial statements

Information about financial position is primarily provided in the statement of financial position, and about performance over a period of time in a statement of comprehensive income. The statement of cash flows and the statement of changes in shareholders' equity provide information on how the shareholders' funds changed during a specific period, while the statement of cash flows shows how much cash flowed into and out of the company during a specific period. The notes to the financial statements contain explanatory notes and further details about the amounts in the financial statements.

The *Conceptual Framework* sets out the concepts underlying the preparation and presentation of financial reports for external users. Users are defined as existing and potential investors, lenders, and other creditors; however, financial statements can also be used by employees, customers, governments and their agents, and by the public in general. Importantly, management is not defined as a user in terms of financial reports. This is because management has the ability to determine the form and content of additional information to meet its needs. The reporting of information to meet the needs of management is beyond the scope of the *Conceptual Framework*. Part III of this book is concerned with the information needs of managers, although, as we will see in Chapter 5, the analysis and interpretation of performance trends and benchmarks through ratio analysis is important for managers in improving shareholder value.

The *Conceptual Framework* deals with

- The objectives of financial reporting
- The qualitative characteristics of useful financial information
- The definition, recognition, and measurement of the elements from which financial statements are constructed

We will consider each of these in turn.

OBJECTIVES OF FINANCIAL STATEMENTS

The objective of financial reporting is to provide financial information about the reporting entity that is helpful to the users in making decisions about providing resources to the entity (that is, "decision usefulness"). Those decisions involve buying, selling, or holding equity and debt instruments, and for providing or settling loans and other forms of credit. Many existing and potential investors, lenders, and other creditors cannot require that reporting entities provide information directly to them and must rely on financial statements for much of the financial information they need. Consequently, they are the primary users to whom financial statements are directed.

Financial statements are not designed to show the value of a reporting entity, but they provide information to help existing and potential investors, lenders, and other creditors to estimate its value. The financial statements also show the results of the stewardship or accountability of managers for the resources entrusted to them by shareholders.

QUALITATIVE CHARACTERISTICS OF FINANCIAL STATEMENTS

The underlying assumptions of financial reports are that they are prepared on an accruals basis and for the company as a going concern (see Chapter 3). There are also qualitative characteristics that make the information useful to users, such as the following:

1. **Relevance.** Information must be relevant to the decision-making needs of users. Relevant financial information can make a difference in the decisions made by users if it has predictive value, confirmatory value, or both.

Financial information has **predictive value** if it can be used to predict future outcomes, and it need not be a prediction or forecast to have predictive value. Financial information with predictive value is employed by users in making their own predictions. Financial information has **confirmatory value** if it provides feedback about (confirms or changes) previous evaluations. Information that has predictive value often also has confirmatory value. For example, the current year's revenue information can be compared to previous years' revenue predictions, and it can be used to predict the revenue of future years.

The relevance of information is affected by its nature and **materiality**. Information is material if its omission or misstatement could influence the economic decisions of users made on the basis of financial reports.

2. **Faithful representation.** To be useful and reliable, financial information must not only be relevant, but it must also faithfully represent the events that it purports to represent. Information is reliable when it is complete, neutral, and free from error.

   Complete refers to the fact that the financial statements include all necessary descriptions and explanations to make them useful for the user. *Neutral* means that the financial information is not slanted or manipulated to increase the probability that it will be received favourably or unfavourably. *Free from error* does not mean that the information is perfectly accurate in all respects. It means there are no errors or omissions in the information and the process used to produce it has been applied with no errors.

   To be represented faithfully, it is necessary that transactions are accounted for and presented in accordance with their substance and economic reality and not merely their legal form, which may be contrived (this is called *substance over form*; see the Case in Point feature in this chapter on Satyam Computer Services and the features in Chapter 3 on Enron and WorldCom).

3. **Comparability.** Users must be able to compare the financial reports of an entity through time and also able to compare the financial reports of different entities in order to evaluate their relative financial position, performance, and changes in financial position. Measurement and presentation must therefore be consistent throughout an entity and over time.

   It is important that users be informed of the accounting policies employed in the preparation of financial reports, any changes in those policies, and the effects of those changes. It is not appropriate for an entity to leave its accounting policies unchanged when more relevant and reliable alternatives exist, but corresponding information for the preceding period is essential for comparability.

4. **Verifiability.** Verifiability means that different knowledgeable and independent observers could reach consensus, although not necessarily a complete agreement, that a particular depiction is a faithful representation.

5. **Timeliness.** Timeliness means having information available to decision makers in time to be of value in influencing their decisions. Generally, older information is less useful, and it may lose its relevance and reliability if there is undue delay in reporting.

6. **Understandability.** Financial information is understandable if it is classified, characterized, and presented in a clear format. Users are assumed to have a reasonable knowledge of business, economic activities, and accounting and are assumed to analyze the information diligently.

ELEMENTS OF FINANCIAL STATEMENTS

Financial statements portray the financial effects of transactions by grouping them into broad classes according to their economic characteristics. These broad classes are **financial report elements**. The elements related to the measurement of financial position in the statement of financial position are assets, liabilities, and equity, and those related to the measurement of performance in the statement of comprehensive income are income and expenses. The *Conceptual Framework for Financial Reporting* defines these elements as follows:

Assets. An **asset** is a resource controlled by the entity as a result of past events and from which future economic benefits are expected to flow to the entity.

Liabilities. A **liability** is a present obligation of the entity arising from past events, the settlement of which is expected to result in an outflow from the entity of resources embodying economic benefits.

Equity. **Equity** is the residual interest of the shareholders in the assets of the entity after deducting all of its liabilities.

Income. Income is increases in economic benefits during the accounting period in the form of inflows or enhancements of assets or decreases of liabilities, other than those relating to contributions from shareholders, that result in increases in equity. Income is, in other words, the value of sales of goods or services produced by the business. The definition of income includes both revenue and gains. **Revenue** arises in the ordinary course of business (for example, sales, fees, interest, dividends, royalties, and rent). **Gains** represent other items, such as income from the disposal of non-current assets or revaluations of investments, and are usually disclosed separately in the financial reports.

Expenses. Expenses are decreases in economic benefits during the accounting period in the form of outflows or depletions of assets or incurrences of liabilities that result in decreases in equity, other than those relating to distributions to shareholders. Put simply, expenses are all of the costs incurred in buying, making, or providing goods or services, and all the marketing and selling, production, distribution, human resource, IT, financing, administration, and management costs involved in operating the business. The definition of expenses includes expenses that arise in the ordinary course of business (for example, salaries and advertising) as well as losses. **Losses** represent other items such as those resulting from disasters such as fire and flood, the disposal of non-current assets, or losses following from changes in foreign exchange rates. Losses are usually disclosed separately in the financial reports. The fact that an item meets the definition of an element as described above does not mean that it will necessarily be included or recognized in the financial statements.

Recognition is the process of incorporating into the statement of financial position or statement of comprehensive income an item that meets the definition of an element. Recognition involves depiction of an item in words and a monetary amount, and the inclusion of that figure in the statement of financial position or statement of comprehensive income totals. An item that meets the definition of an element should be recognized if both of the following are true:

1. It is probable that any future economic benefit associated with the item will flow to or from the entity.

2. The item has a cost or value that can be measured with reliability.

An item that has the characteristics of an element but does not meet these criteria for recognition may warrant disclosure in a note to the financial reports (see Chapter 5).

An asset is not recognized in the statement of financial position when expenditure has been incurred for which it is considered improbable that economic benefits will flow to the entity beyond the current accounting period. This should be treated as an expense (see the Case in Point feature on WorldCom in Chapter 3 for an example).

Measurement is the process of determining the monetary amounts at which the elements of the financial reports are to be recognized and carried in the statement of financial position and statement of comprehensive income. There are four bases of measurement:

1. Historical cost. Assets are recorded at the cash or fair value consideration given at the time of their acquisition.

2. Current cost. Assets are carried at the cash value that would have to be paid if the same or equivalent assets were acquired currently.

3. Realizable value. Assets are carried at the cash value that could currently be obtained by selling the assets.

4. Present value. Assets are carried at the present discounted value of the future net cash inflows that the assets are expected to generate (see Chapter 12 for a full explanation of present value).

Different elements of the financial statements are measured at different costs. Some common examples follow:

- Property, plant, and equipment are normally shown at historical cost, although they can sometimes be shown at a revaluation value.

- Accounts receivable and payable are shown at fair market value.

- Inventories are usually carried at the lower of cost and net realizable value (see Chapter 7).

- Marketable investments may be carried at market value.

- Non-current liabilities are normally shown at present value.

Reporting Profitability: The Statement of Comprehensive Income

Businesses exist to make a profit. Thus, as we saw in Chapter 3, the basic accounting concept is that

$$\textbf{Profit} = \textbf{Income} - \textbf{Expenses}$$

If expenses exceed income, the result is a loss.

The profit (or loss) of a business for a financial period is reported in a statement of comprehensive income. This will typically appear as in Exhibit 4.1.

Exhibit 4.1 Statement of Comprehensive Income

Sales	$2,000,000
Less: Cost of goods sold	1,500,000
Gross profit	$ 500,000
Less: Selling, administration expenses	400,000
Operating profit before interest and taxes	$ 100,000

However, business profitability is determined by the matching principle—*matching income earned with the expenses incurred in earning that income.*

As mentioned in Chapter 3, in both financial accounting and management accounting, we distinguish between gross profit and operating (or net) profit. Gross profit is the difference between the selling *price* and the purchase (or production) *cost* of the goods or services sold. Using a simple example, a retailer selling baked beans may buy each can for 50 cents and sell it for 80 cents. The gross profit is 30 cents per can.

$$\text{Gross profit} = \text{Sales} - \text{Cost of goods sold}$$

Gross margin is gross profit expressed as a percentage of sales. So in our baked beans example, the gross margin is 37.5% (30 cents/80 cents).

The cost of goods sold is the cost of one of the following:

- Providing a service
- Buying goods sold by a retailer
- Raw materials and production costs for a product manufacturer

However, not all the goods bought by a retailer or used in production will have been sold in the same period as the sales are made. The matching principle requires that the business adjusts for increases or decreases in *inventory*—goods bought or produced for resale but not yet sold (this is described in detail in Chapter 7). It is, therefore, the cost of goods *sold*, not the cost of goods *produced*, that is recorded as an expense in the statement of comprehensive income. Because the production and sale of services are simultaneous, the cost of services produced always equals the cost of services sold (there is no such thing as an inventory of services).

Expenses deducted from gross profit will include all of the other costs of the business, such as selling, administration, and finance; that is, costs not directly concerned with buying, making, or providing goods or services but supporting that activity. The same retailer may treat such items as the rent of the store, the salaries of employees, and distribution and computer costs as expenses in order to determine the **operating profit**.

$$\text{Operating profit} = \text{Gross profit} - \text{Expenses}$$

The operating profit is one of the most significant figures because it represents the profit generated from the ordinary operations of the business. It is also called *net profit,* **profit before interest and taxes (PBIT)**, or **earnings before interest and taxes (EBIT)**.

The distinction between cost of goods sold and expenses can vary between industries and organizations. A single store might treat only the product cost as the cost of goods sold, and salaries and rent as expenses. A large retail chain might include the salaries of staff and the store rental as cost of goods sold, with expenses covering the head office corporate costs. For any particular business, it is important to determine the demarcation between cost of goods sold and expenses.

From operating profit, a company must pay *interest* to its lenders, *income tax* to the government and a *dividend* to shareholders (for their share of the profits, as they—unlike lenders—do not receive an interest amount for their investment). The remaining profit is retained by the business as part of its *capital* (see Exhibit 4.2).

Exhibit 4.2 **Statement of Comprehensive Income (extended)**

CONSOLIDATED STATEMENT OF INCOME

(In thousands of Canadian dollars, except per share information)

	Fifty-two weeks ended	
	December 31, 2011	January 1, 2011
Sales	$ 668,589	$ 584,715
Cost of sales	516,659	447,542
Gross profit	151,930	137,173
Distribution expenses	35,021	30,027
Selling, general and administrative expenses	72,086	68,500
Business acquisition, integration and other expenses	11,275	875
Results from operating activities	33,548	37,771
Finance costs	5,983	5,165
Share of income of equity accounted investee (net of income tax)	53	(18)
Income before income taxes	27,512	32,624
Income taxes		
Current	5,692	6,380
Deferred	3,640	6,259
Total income taxes	9,332	12,639
Net income	$ 18,180	$ 19,985
PER SHARE EARNINGS		
Earnings per common share		
Basic	1.20	1.24
Diluted	1.19	1.23
Weighted average number of shares outstanding		
Basic	15,108,823	16,096,010
Diluted	15,340,963	16,243,780

See accompanying notes

The statement of comprehensive income can also stop at profit after taxes, or net profit. In such cases, the dividends paid and the balance of retained earnings are shown in the statement of changes in shareholders' equity. An example of a statement of comprehensive income from High Liner Foods is shown in Exhibit 4.3.

Exhibit 4.3 High Liner Foods, 2011 Consolidated Statement of Comprehensive Income

CONSOLIDATED STATEMENT OF COMPREHENSIVE INCOME

(In thousands of Canadian dollars)

		Fifty-two weeks ended
	December 31, 2011	January 1, 2011
Net income for the period	$18,180	$19,985
Other comprehensive income (loss), net of income tax (note 20)		
Gain on hedge of net investment in foreign operations	291	313
Gain (loss) on translation of net investment in foreign operations	1,872	(4,082)
	2,163	(3,769)
Effective portion of changes in fair value of cash flow hedges	1,211	(2,251)
Net change in fair value of cash flow hedges transferred to income	399	2,669
	1,610	418
Defined benefit plan actuarial losses	(1,076)	(1,727)
Other comprehensive income (loss), net of income tax	2,697	(5,078)
Total comprehensive income	$20,877	$14,907

See accompanying notes.

Reporting Financial Position: The Statement of Financial Position

Not all business transactions appear in the statement of comprehensive income. The second financial statement is the statement of financial position. This shows the financial position of the business—its assets, liabilities, and equity—at the *end* of a financial period.

Some business payments are to acquire assets in order to produce goods or services that are capable of satisfying customer needs. The statement of financial position has to distinguish between current and non-current assets. An entity must classify an asset as current when

- It expects to realize the asset, or intends to sell or consume it, in its normal operating cycle or within 12 months after the reporting period, whichever is the longest.

- It holds the asset primarily for the purpose of trading.

- The asset is cash or a cash equivalent.

Current assets include money in the bank, **accounts receivable** (sales to customers on credit, but unpaid), and **inventory** (goods bought or manufactured, but unsold). The word *current* in accounting means 12 months, so current assets are those that will change their form during the next year.

Non-current assets are all assets that are not current. By contrast, non-current assets do not normally change their form in the ordinary course of business; as infrastructure, they have a longer-term role. Physical form is not essential. Non-current assets are things that the business normally keeps for longer than one year and uses as part of its infrastructure. There are two types of non-current assets: tangible and intangible. *Tangible assets* comprise those physical assets that can be seen and touched, such as buildings, machinery, vehicles, and computers. These are generally referred to as *property, plant, and equipment. Intangible assets* comprise non-physical assets, such as customer goodwill or a business's intellectual property; for example its ownership of patents and trademarks.

Sometimes assets are acquired or expenses incurred without paying for them immediately. In doing so, the business incurs *liabilities*, debts that the business *owes*. **Current liabilities** include **accounts payable** (purchases from suppliers on credit, but unpaid), loans due to be repaid, and amounts due for taxes. Just as for assets, the word *current* means that the liabilities will be repaid within 12 months. Current liabilities also form part of working capital.

Working capital refers to the net current assets or liabilities; that is, current assets less current liabilities. This is an important number as it gives an indication of the current assets that will be left if all current liabilities have to be paid immediately (see Chapter 5).

Non-current liabilities include loans to finance the business that are repayable after 12 months, other amounts owing that are not current, and certain kinds of provisions (discussed later in this chapter). Equity (or capital) is the money invested by the owners in the business. As mentioned above, equity is increased by the retained profits of the business (the profit after paying interest, taxes, and dividends). In a company, capital or equity is often called *shareholders' equity* in the statement of financial position.

The statement of financial position will typically appear as in Exhibit 4.4. In this statement, equity (sometimes referred to as *net assets*) is the difference between total assets and total liabilities. This is called the *accounting equation*, which can be shown in a number of different ways:

$$\text{Net assets} = \text{Total assets} - \text{Total liabilities}$$
(as shown in a statement of financial position)

$$\text{Assets} = \text{Liabilities} + \text{Equity}$$

or

$$\text{Assets} - \text{Liabilities} = \text{Equity}$$

Importantly, the capital of the business does *not* represent the value of the business. It represents the funds initially invested by owners (or the shareholders in a company) plus the retained profits (after payment of taxes and dividends). In Exhibit 4.4, share capital represents the initial investment, and retained earnings include all of the retained profits since the business commenced. Importantly, it includes not only the current year's retained profit of $40,000 (Exhibit 4.2) but also all prior years' retained profit.

An example of a statement of financial position for Via Rail is shown in Exhibit 4.5.

Exhibit 4.4 Statement of Financial Position

Assets	
Non-current assets	
Property, plant and equipment	$1,150,000
Current assets	
Accounts receivables	300,000
Inventory	200,000
	500,000
Total assets	$1,650,000
Liabilities	
Non-current liabilities	
Long-term loans	$ 300,000
Current liabilities	
Accounts payables	300,000
Bank overdraft	50,000
	350,000
Total liabilities	$ 650,000
Equity	
Share capital	$ 900,000
Retained earnings	100,000
Total equity	$1,000,000
Total Liabilities and Equity	$1,650,000

Exhibit 4.5 Via Rail, 2011 Statement of Financial Position

Statement of Financial Position

As at (in thousands of canadian dollars)	December 31, 2011	December 31, 2010	January 1, 2010
CURRENT ASSETS			
Cash and cash equivalents	$ 13,253	$ 76,829	$ 4,596
Accounts receivable, trade	10,707	7,988	7,581
Prepaids, advances on contracts, and other receivables	11,147	14,414	10,467
Receivable from the Government of Canada	—	15,702	5,182
Derivative financial instruments (Note 20)	2,161	3,769	1,497
Materials (Note 8)	21,287	21,302	24,592
Asset Renewal Fund (Note 11)	24,022	15,295	25,295
	82,577	155,299	79,210

(continued)

Exhibit 4.5 Via Rail, 2011 Statement of Financial Position (*continued*)

NON-CURRENT ASSETS			
Property, plant, and equipment (Note 9)	814,876	729,932	673,433
Intangible assets (Note 10)	337,182	235,371	74,068
Asset Renewal Fund (Note 11)	9,881	25,645	23,120
Accrued benefit asset (Note 14)	186,937	159,081	152,655
Derivative financial instruments (Note 20)	64	880	1,578
	1,348,940	1,150,909	924,854
Total assets	**$1,431,517**	$1,306,208	$1,004,064
CURRENT LIABILITIES			
Accounts payable and accrued liabilities (Note 12)	$ 103,841	$ 135,952	$ 116,529
Provisions (Note 13)	18,050	16,342	13,718
Deferred government funding	6,148	51,000	—
Derivative financial instruments (Note 20)	1,057	996	6,699
Deferred revenues	26,734	25,546	24,129
	155,830	229,836	161,075
NON-CURRENT LIABILITIES			
Accrued benefit liability (Note 14)	35,425	33,055	31,930
Deferred corporate tax liabilities (Note 15)	—	404	—
Derivative financial instruments (Note 20)	116	205	354
Deferred investment tax credits	566	909	1,302
Other non-current liabilities	—	623	809
	36,107	35,196	34,485
DEFERRED CAPITAL FUNDING (Note 16)	1,143,800	965,546	745,951
SHAREHOLDER'S EQUITY			
Share capital (Note 17)	9,300	9,300	9,300
Retained earnings	86,480	66,330	53,253
	95,780	75,630	62,553
Total liabilities and shareholder's equity	**$1,431,517**	$1,306,208	$1,004,064

Commitments and Contingencies [Notes 18 and 23, respectively].
The notes are an integral part of the financial statements.

Accrual Accounting

An important principle that is particularly relevant to the interpretation of accounting reports is the matching principle. The matching (or accrual) principle recognizes income when it is *earned* and expenses when they are *incurred* (this is called *accrual accounting*), not when money is received or paid out (a method called *cash accounting*). **Accrual accounting** provides a more meaningful calculation of profit for a specific period, as revenues earned during the period are matched with the expenses that were incurred to generate the revenue, irrespective of whether the expenses have been paid. While cash is very important in business, the accruals method provides a more meaningful picture of the financial performance of a business from year to year.

Accrual accounting makes adjustments for

- **Prepayments.** Cash payments made in advance of when they are treated as an expense for profit purposes

- **Accruals.** Items treated as expenses for profit purposes even though no cash payment has yet been made

- **Provisions.** Estimates of possible liabilities that may arise, but where there is uncertainty as to timing or the amount of money involved

The matching principle requires that certain cash payments made in advance must be treated as *prepayments;* that is, payments made in advance of when they are treated as an expense for profit purposes. A good example of a prepayment is insurance, which is paid 12 months in advance. Assume that a business with a financial year ending March 31 pays its 12 months' insurance premium of $12,000 in advance, on January 1. At its year-end, the business will treat only $3,000 (3/12 of $12,000) as an expense and will treat the remaining $9,000 as a prepayment (a current asset in the statement of financial position).

Other expenses are **accrued**; that is, treated as expenses for profit purposes even though no cash payment has yet been made. A good example of an *accrual* is electricity, which like most utilities is paid (often quarterly) in arrears. If the same business usually receives its electricity bill in May (covering the period March to May), it will need to accrue an expense for the month of March, even if the bill has not yet been received. If the prior year's bill was $2,400 for the same quarter (allowing for seasonal fluctuations in usage), then the business will accrue $800 (1/3 of $2,400). The effect of prepayments and accruals on profit, the statement of financial position, and cash flow is shown in Exhibit 4.6.

Exhibit 4.6 Prepayments and Accruals

	Profit Effect	Statement of Financial Position	Cash Flow
Prepayment	Expense of $3,000	Prepayment (current asset) of $9,000	Cash outflow of $12,000
Accrual	Expense of $800	Accrual (current liability) of $800	No cash flow until quarterly bill received and paid

A further example of the matching principle is in the creation of provisions. *Provisions* are estimates of liabilities that may arise, but where there is uncertainty as to timing or the amount of money. An example of a possible future liability is a provision for warranty claims that may be payable on sales of products. The estimate will be based on the likely costs to be incurred in the future.

Other types of provisions cover reductions in asset values. The main examples are

- **Doubtful accounts (or bad debts).** Customers may experience difficulty in paying their accounts and a provision may be made, based on experience, that a proportion of debtors will never pay.

CASE IN POINT

Airlines Show Accrual Accounting in Action

A common example of accrual accounting in action is how airlines account for advance ticket sales. For example, when an airline such as Air Canada sells a ticket for a future flight, it doesn't recognize that sale as revenue until it provides the service by transporting the passenger. Until the flight happens, Air Canada considers the sale to be a current liability. That's because an airline ticket is a legal contract that the airline must honour by later incurring the expenses to provide the service. In other words, the airline hasn't actually earned the revenue until the flight happens. In the meantime, it has an obligation to the passenger that will lead to an outflow of resources in the future.

Immediately after the flight, the amount already collected from the passenger is transferred to revenue. That means that revenue is recognized at the same time as the airline incurs the expenses involved in making that flight. Not all advance sales become revenue due to refunds and exchanges, as not all tickets sold result in the passenger taking a particular flight.

As at December 31, 2011, Air Canada had $1,554 million in advance ticket sales liabilities.

Source: Air Canada, *2011 Annual Report*.

- **Inventory.** Some inventory may be obsolete but still held by the company. A provision reduces the value of the obsolete stock to its sale or scrap value (if any).

- **Depreciation.** Depreciation is a charge against profits, intended to write off the value of each non-current asset over its useful life.

Provisions for likely future liabilities (for example, warranty claims) are shown in the statement of financial position as liabilities, while provisions that reduce asset values (for example, doubtful debts, inventory, and depreciation) are shown as deductions from the cost of the asset.

Depreciation

Non-current assets are capitalized in the statement of financial position so that their purchase does not affect profit. They may be measured at their historical cost or revalued, also known as depreciated (see below). Depreciation is an expense that spreads the cost of the asset over its useful life. The following example illustrates the matching principle in relation to depreciation.

A non-current asset costs $100,000. It is expected to have a life of four years and resale or residual value of $20,000 at the end of that time. The depreciation charge is

$$\frac{\text{Asset cost} - \text{Resale value}}{\text{Expected life}} = \frac{100,000 - 20,000}{4} = 20,000 \text{ per year}$$

It is important to recognize that the cash outflow of $100,000 occurs when the asset is bought. The depreciation charge of $20,000 per annum is a non-cash expense each year. However, the value of the asset in the statement of financial position reduces each year as a result of the depreciation charge, as Exhibit 4.7 shows. The asset can be depreciated to a nil value in the statement of financial position even though it is still in use. If the asset is sold, any profit or loss on the sale is treated as a separate item in the statement of comprehensive income.

Exhibit 4.7 Statement of Financial Position: Effect of Depreciation Charges

	Original Asset Cost	Accumulated Depreciation	Net Value in Statement of Financial Position
End of Year 1	$100,000	$20,000	$80,000
End of Year 2	100,000	40,000	60,000
End of Year 3	100,000	60,000	40,000
End of Year 4	100,000	80,000	20,000
End of Year 5	100,000	100,000	Nil

Using historical costs results in a potentially misleading picture of the true value of non-current assets. Revaluation provides more relevant information to the user of the accounts than does the asset's historical cost. However, the usefulness of this information diminishes over time as the valuation ceases to reflect the current value of the asset. Under accounting standards, revaluation of tangible non-current assets can be applied only by public companies in certain circumstances, and revaluation remains optional. Land, however, is never depreciated. This is because land is considered to have an infinite useful life. The standards require that when a policy of revaluation is adopted, it must be applied to an entire class of assets (not individual assets) and the valuations must be kept up to date through regular independent valuations. This ensures consistency in the treatment of similar assets from year to year.

A type of depreciation used for intangible assets, such as patents or copyrights, is called **amortization**, which has the same meaning and is calculated in the same way as depreciation.

Certain investments and other assets may be valued at fair value. *Fair value* is a measure of market value, defined as the value that is determined by knowledgeable and willing buyers and sellers in arm's-length transactions. However, the dramatic falls in asset values following the U.S. subprime mortgage crisis of 2007–2008 have called fair value into question.

CASE IN POINT

Via Rail's Property, Plant, and Equipment Depreciation

Different types of property, plant, and equipment are depreciated at different rates. Via Rail Canada, for example, has more than $725 million worth of property, plant, and equipment, which it depreciates at various rates. It depreciates its tangible assets on a straight-line basis, meaning that an equal amount is depreciated in each year of an asset's estimated useful life, minus its residual value at the end of its life. Its trains (also known as *rolling stock*), for example, are depreciated over time periods of between 12 and 30 years; maintenance buildings, over 25 years; stations and facilities, over 20 years; owned infrastructure, over 5 to 40 years; machinery and equipment, over 4 to 15 years; and computer hardware, over 3 to 7 years. In 2010, Via's depreciation expense of property, plant, and equipment totalled $51.4 million.

Source: Via Rail Canada, *2010 Annual Report*.

In reporting profits, some companies show the profit before depreciation (or amortization) is deducted, because it can be a substantial cost, but one that does not result in any cash flow. A variation of EBIT (see earlier in this chapter) is **earnings before interest, taxes, depreciation, and amortization (EBITDA)**.

Specific IFRS Accounting Treatments

The full list of IFRS and their predecessor IAS is contained in the appendix to this chapter. Many relate to specific accounting treatments or specific industries that are beyond the scope of this book. However, some important standards are given here:

- IAS 1, *Presentation of Financial Statements* requires that an entity whose financial reports comply with IFRS must make an explicit and unreserved statement of compliance in the notes to the financial reports. The impact of changed accounting policies must also be shown in the financial reports.

- IFRS 2, *Share-Based Payment*: Companies have increasingly used grants of shares through share options and share ownership plans for employees. Previously, these were not reflected in financial reports until such time as the option was exercised. There has been much criticism of this accounting treatment by shareholders. The IFRS now requires an entity to reflect in its statement of comprehensive income the effects of share-based payment transactions based on the fair value of the equity instruments granted, measured at the date of the grant. Concern has been expressed that some companies may limit their share options in view of this change in accounting treatment.

- IAS 2, *Inventory*: Inventory is valued at the lower of cost and net realizable value (that is, sales proceeds less costs of sale). The cost of inventory includes all costs of purchase, costs of conversion, and other costs incurred in bringing the inventory to its present location and condition. Costs of purchase include import duties and transport, less any discounts or rebates. Accounting for inventory is covered in detail in Chapter 7. Costs of conversion include direct labour and a systematic allocation of fixed and variable production overheads (this is covered in detail in Chapters 11 to 13).

- IAS 11, *Construction Contracts*: How profits are generated over long-term constructions is covered in Chapter 7.

- IAS 16, *Property, Plant, & Equipment*: Assets are valued at cost less accumulated depreciation (explained above).

- IAS 17, *Leases* requires accounting for most finance leases as though they were owned and depreciated by the lessee.

- IAS 36, *Impairment of Assets*: *Impairment* refers to the reduction in value of an intangible asset such as goodwill.

- IAS 37, *Provisions, Contingent Liabilities, and Contingent Assets*: A provision is a liability of uncertain timing or amount. Examples include warranty obligations and retail policies for refunds. The amount recognized as a provision is the best estimate of the expenditure required to settle the obligation.

- IAS 38, *Intangible Assets*: Internally generated goodwill, brands, customer lists, and so on are not recognized as assets. Intangible assets arise when they are purchased.

There are also standards relating to accounting for hedging and changes in foreign exchange (IAS 21) and financial instruments (IAS 39), but these are outside the scope of this book.

Reporting Cash Flow:
The Statement of Cash Flows

The third financial statement is the statement of cash flows, which shows the movement in cash for the business during a financial period. It includes

- Cash flow from operations
- Interest receipts and payments
- Income taxes paid
- Capital expenditure (that is, the purchase of new non-current assets)
- Dividends paid to shareholders
- New borrowings or repayment of borrowings

The cash flow from operations differs from the operating profit because of

- Depreciation, which as a non-cash expense is added back to profit (since operating profit is the result *after* depreciation is deducted)
- Increases (or decreases) in working capital (for example, trade receivables, inventory, prepayments, trade payables, and accruals), which reduce (or increase) available cash

An example of a statement of cash flows is shown in Exhibit 4.8, and Exhibit 4.9 shows Shoppers Drug Mart's statement of cash flows.

Exhibit 4.8 Statement of Cash Flows

Cash flows from operating activities	
Operating profit	$100,000
Depreciation	20,000
Changes in inventories	(10,000)
Changes in accounts receivables	(15,000)
Changes in accounts payables	20,000
Cash generated from operations	115,000
Income tax paid	(12,000)
Net cash flows from operating activities	$103,000
Cash flows from investing activities	
Purchase of plant & equipment	$(100,000)
Cash flows from financing activities	
Additional borrowing	$ 50,000
Interest paid	(16,000)
Dividends paid	(25,000)
Net cash flows from financing activities	$ 9,000

(continued)

Exhibit 4.8 Statement of Cash Flows (*continued*)

Net increase in cash	12,000
Cash balance—beginning of the year	4,000
Cash balance—end of the year	16,000

Note: Taxation and dividends are not the same as the amounts shown in the statement of comprehensive income earlier in this chapter because of timing differences between when those items are treated as expenses and when the cash payment is made, which is normally after the end of the financial year.

Exhibit 4.9 Shoppers Drug Mart, 2011 Statement of Cash Flow

Consolidated Statements of Cash Flows

For the 52 weeks ended December 31, 2011
and January 1, 2011

(in thousands of Canadian dollars)	Note	2011	2010[1]
Cash flows from operating activities			
Net earnings		$ 613,934	$ 591,851
Adjustments for:			
Depreciation and amortization	13, 15, 17	296,464	278,421
Finance expenses	12	64,038	60,633
Loss on sale or disposal of property and equipment, including impairments	15, 17	2,015	3,880
Share-based payment transactions	26	(1,210)	1,592
Recognition and reversal of provisions, net	22	9,218	12,160
Other long-term liabilities	23	296	18,491
Income tax expense	14	232,933	244,838
		1,217,688	1,211,866
Net change in non-cash working capital balances	27	32,166	(34,824)
Provisions used	22	(9,907)	(9,817)
Interest paid		(63,853)	(62,916)
Income taxes paid		(202,256)	(276,108)
Net cash from operating activities		973,838	828,201
Cash flows from investing activities			
Proceeds from disposition of property and equipment and investment property		55,459	60,538
Business acquisitions	8	(10,496)	(11,779)
Deposits		105	1,534

(continued)

Exhibit 4.9 Shoppers Drug Mart, 2011 Statement of Cash Flow (*continued*)

Acquisitions or development of property and equipment	15	**(341,868)**	(415,094)
Acquisition or development of intangible assets	17	**(53,836)**	(56,625)
Other assets		**1,464**	(3,249)
Net cash used in investing activities		**(349,172)**	(424,675)
Cash flows from financing activities			
Repurchase of own shares	24	**(206,779)**	—
Proceeds from exercise of share options	26	**1,220**	491
Repayment of share-purchase loans	24	**7**	33
Repayment of bank indebtedness, net	19	**(36,714)**	(61,319)
Repayment of commercial paper, net	19	**(128,000)**	(133,000)
Revolving term debt, net	20	**152**	(1,298)
Payment of transaction costs for debt refinancing	20	**(575)**	(2,792)
Repayment of financing lease obligations	23	**(2,173)**	(1,436)
Associate interest		**13,887**	9,277
Dividends paid	24	**(211,479)**	(193,519)
Net cash used in financing activities		**(570,454)**	(383,563)
Net increase in cash		**54,212**	19,963
Cash, beginning of the year		**64,354**	44,391
Cash, end of the year		**$ 118,566**	$ 64,354

[1] In preparing its 2010 comparative information, the Company has adjusted amounts reported previously in financial statements prepared in accordance with previous Canadian GAAP. See Note 30 to these consolidated financial statements for an explanation of the transition to IFRS.

The accompanying notes are an integral part of these consolidated financial statements.

A Critical Perspective on Accounting Standards

Various criticisms of accounting standards have been expressed, including the following:

- New and amended standards are continually being introduced.

- Standards don't consider practical implementation issues; for example, the impact of pension fund accounting (IAS 19) and accounting for inventory options (IFRS 2), and the strong for and against arguments in relation to those particular standards.

- International standards do not yet include the United States.

- The complexity of standards means that they are unlikely to be understood by anyone other than professional accountants, and their effect may be ignored by inventory market analysts and be confusing to lay investors.

- Lobbying may influence the development of standards (there is evidence from the United States of lobbyists for Enron attempting to influence standard-setters).

- It has been argued that standards are a remedy for creative accounting, but there is evidence that standards are likely to lead to more creative endeavours.

- Standards have a narrow accounting focus rather than being inclusive of non-financial performance and broader accountability issues, such as social and environmental reporting (see Chapter 5 for a discussion of these issues).

CONCLUSION

This chapter has covered the main financial reports: statement of comprehensive income, statement of financial position, and statement of cash flows. It has introduced the *International Financial Reporting Standards* (IFRS) and the *Conceptual Framework for Financial Reporting.* The principles of accrual accounting and depreciation have also been covered. The chapter concluded with a brief critique of accounting standards.

In the next chapter, we introduce the tools and techniques that are used to interpret financial reports and consider some alternative theoretical perspectives.

KEY TERMS

Accounting Standards for Private Enterprises (ASPE), 64

Accounts payable, 74

Accounts receivable, 74

Accrual accounting, 77

Accruals, 77

Accrued, 77

Amortization, 79

Asset, 69

Comparability, 68

Conceptual Framework for Financial Reporting, 66

Confirmatory value, 68

Current assets, 74

Current liabilities, 74

Current cost, 70

Depreciation, 78

Earnings before interest and taxes (EBIT), 71

Earnings before interest, taxes, depreciation and amortization (EBITDA), 80

Equity, 69

Faithful representation, 67

Financial report elements, 69

Gains, 69

Gross margin, 71

Historical cost, 70

International Financial Reporting Standards (IFRS), 64

Inventory, 74

Liability, 69

Losses, 69

Materiality, 68

Measurement, 70

Non-current assets, 74

Non-current liabilities, 74

Operating profit, 71

Predictive value, 68

Prepayments, 77

Present value, 70

Profit before interest and taxes (PBIT), 71

Provisions, 77

Realizable value, 70

Recognition, 69

Relevance, 67

Revenue, 69

Timeliness, 68

Understandability, 68

Verifiability, 68

Working capital, 74

■ SELF-TEST QUESTIONS

S4.1 Which of the following is *not* a qualitative characteristic of financial reporting?

a. Understandability

b. Accuracy

c. Relevance

d. Faithful representation

S4.2 Which one of the following statements is true?

a. *Free of error* means financial statements have to be 100% accurate.

b. Financial statements are prepared under the assumption that users have no knowledge of business or accounting.

c. Transactions are accounted for and presented in accordance with their legal form rather than their substance and economic reality.

d. Users must be able to compare the financial reports of an entity through time and be able to compare the financial reports of different entities in order to evaluate their relative financial position, performance, and changes in financial position.

S4.3 The cost of sales is

a. The cost of providing a service

b. The cost of buying goods sold by a retailer

c. The cost of production for a manufacturer

d. All of the above

S4.4 Operating profit is the same as

a. Operating profit

b. EBIT (Earnings before interest and taxes)

c. PBIT (Profit before interest and taxes)

d. All of the above

S4.5 Inventory is an example of a

a. Fixed asset

b. Current asset

c. Current liability

d. Long-term debt

S4.6 Assets minus liabilities equal

a. Net assets

b. Shareholders' equity

c. Capital contributed plus retained earnings

d. All of the above

S4.7 If a business has fixed assets of $750,000, working capital of $150,000, and long-term debt of $300,000, its shareholders' equity can be calculated as

a. $1,200,000

b. $1,050,000

c. $900,000

d. $600,000

S4.8 A business has agreed to undertake an advertising campaign that will cost $240,000 and will be carried out equally over the financial year, beginning January 1. Half of the annual cost is to be paid six-monthly in advance on the first days of January and July. At March 31 the financial statements would show

a. An expense of $120,000 and an accrual of $120,000

b. An expense of $60,000 and a prepayment of $60,000

c. An expense of $120,000 and a prepayment of $120,000

d. An expense of $60,000 and an accrual of $60,000

S4.9 Virko Inc. buys a new computer system for $180,000 on January 1. It expects the system to last for four years. If the company's financial year is from January 1 to December 31, the value of the computer system in Virko's statement of financial position at December 31 of the same year will be

a. $180,000

b. $135,000

c. $90,000

d. $45,000

S4.10 Thomas Investments has an operating profit for the year of $185,000. An examination of the statement of comprehensive income and statement of financial position shows that depreciation was $65,000, taxation was $40,000, new capital investment was $100,000, and repayment of borrowings was $65,000. The change in cash over the period was

a. An increase of $45,000

b. A decrease of $85,000

c. A decrease of $20,000

d. An increase of $120,000

S4.11 The amounts shown as taxation and dividends in the statement of comprehensive income and statement of cash flows are

a. Always the same

b. Can never be the same

c. Different because they are prepayments

d. Different because of the timing of cash outflows

◼ PROBLEMS

P4.1 A company has sales of $100,000, salaries expense of $30,000, utilities expense of $2,000, and cost of sales of $60,000. Calculate the following:

a. Gross profit

b. Gross profit margin

c. Net profit

d. Net profit margin

P4.2 *(Users of Financial Statements)* Explain (with reasons) whether managers are included as users of financial statements.

P4.3 *(Management's Responsibility)* Describe the responsibility that management has regarding the preparation and presentation of financial statements.

P4.4 **(CICA Handbook)** The accounting section of the *CICA Handbook* consists of three parts. Explain which parts apply to which type of entity.

P4.5 **(Conceptual Framework)** Explain the purpose of the *Conceptual Framework for Financial Reporting*.

P4.6 **(Conceptual Framework)** Explain what is meant by the following financial information terms:

a. Confirmative value

b. Predictive value

c. Materiality

P4.7 *(Recording of Transactions)* Kazam Services begins the month with capital of $200,000 and the following assets and liabilities:

Assets		Liabilities	
Property, plant, and equipment	$500,000	Bank overdraft	$ 35,000
Accounts receivable	$125,000	Accounts payable	$ 90,000
		Long-term loan	$300,000

The following transactions took place in the accounting records of the business during the past month:

- Took out long-term loan for new building: $150,000
- Received from debtors: $45,000
- Paid to creditors: $30,000
- Invoiced customers for services carried out: $70,000
- Paid salaries: $15,000
- Paid various office expenses: $5,000

In addition, depreciation of $20,000 was provided for the period.

a. Produce a schedule of transactions under appropriate headings for each account.

b. Total each account and produce a statement of comprehensive income and statement of financial position.

P4.8 *(Statement of Financial Position)* Beaupre Ltee has property, plant, and equipment of $250,000, current assets of $125,000, non-current liabilities of $125,000, and accounts payable within 12 months of $75,000.

a. What is the working capital?

b. What are the total assets of the company?

c. What is the shareholders' equity?

P4.9 *(Statement of Comprehensive Income)* Disanity Corporation's statement of comprehensive income shows the following:

	2012	2011
Sales	$1,250,000	$1,175,000
Cost of goods sold	787,000	715,000
Selling and administrative expenses	324,000	323,000

Based on these figures, which of the following statements is true?

a. Sales, cost of goods sold, and expenses have all increased; therefore, profit, gross margin, and operating margin have all increased.

b. The operating profit has increased due to sales growth, higher gross margins, and similar expenses.

c. Although the operating profit has decreased, the operating margin has increased as a result of sales growth and an increase in gross profit.

d. The operating profit has decreased due to lower gross margins and higher expenses, despite sales growth.

e. Although the operating profit has increased, the operating margin has decreased as a result of a reduction in the gross margin and higher expenses, despite sales growth.

P4.10 *(Accrual Accounting)* What is the impact of the following prepayment, accrual, and provision transactions on profit, the statement of financial position, and the statement of cash flows?

a. A business has 24 motor vehicles that it leases in return for a monthly payment, excluding insurance. The company's financial year is April 1–March 31, but the annual insurance premium of $400 per vehicle for the calendar year January–December is due for payment on December 31.

b. A business budgets for energy costs of $6,000 per annum over its financial year January 1–December 31. Bills for usage are sent each quarter on the last day of February, May, August, and November. Historically, 70% of the annual energy cost is spent during the autumn and winter (September–February).

c. A business with a financial year of April 1–March 31 purchases a new computer network server for $12,000 on June 30. The business depreciates computer hardware at the rate of 20% of cost per annum, beginning the month following purchase.

P4.11 *(Effect of Transactions on Financial Statements)* Indicate how the following transactions will be accounted for in the statement of comprehensive income and the statement of financial position for a company with a fiscal year-end of December 31, 2012:

a. The company receives an invoice on October 1, 2012, for rent for the period November 1, 2012, to April 30, 2013, and pays the invoice on October 20, 2012.

b. The company buys a machine on June 1 for $28,000. The machine is expected to be used for six years and has an estimated residual value of $4,000.

c. The company's accounts receivable balance is $150,000. It has not created a provision for bad debt in the past as customers have always paid their outstanding accounts. On December 20, 2012, the company learns that one of its customers who owes the company $22,000, has filed for bankruptcy and they will probably not receive any of the money owed.

P4.12 *(Statement of Comprehensive Income)* Rosi Inc. imports high-end wooden furniture from overseas and sells it to furniture stores. The following are amounts extracted from the company's general ledger for January 2012:

Administrative salaries	$ 5,000
Commission paid to sales people	2,100
Depreciation of office furniture and equipment	2,500
Dividends paid	5,000
Income tax expense	12,000
Interest paid	800
Inventory of furniture for sale—January 1	12,000
Inventory of furniture for sale—January 31	56,000
Office rent and utilities	3,100
Purchase of furniture for sale	178,000
Sales	200,000

Prepare the company's statement of comprehensive income for January 2012.

P4.13 *(Sale of an Asset)* A business sells a non-current asset for less than its statement of financial position value. Under IFRS, how will the difference between the asset value in the statement of financial position and the amount received on the sale of the asset be disclosed in the statement of comprehensive income?

P4.14 *(Sale of an Asset)* A business sells a non-current asset for more than its statement of financial position value. Under IFRS, how will the difference between the asset value in the statement of financial position and the amount received on the sale of the asset be disclosed in the statement of comprehensive income?

P4.15 *(Sale of Depreciable Asset)* A company bought a machine on July 1, 2009, for $50,000. At that date, it was estimated to have a useful life of five years and a residual value of $5,000 at the end of its useful life. On December 31, 2012, the company sold the machine for $25,000. How will this sale be accounted for in the company's financial statements?

REFERENCES

Canadian Institute of Chartered Accountants (2012). *The CICA standards and guidance collection* (electronic version). Toronto: CICA.

IFRS Foundation and the IASB website (2011): www.ifrs.org.

CHAPTER 4 APPENDIX: IFRS AS AT JANUARY 1, 2013

IFRS 1 First-time adoption of *International Financial Reporting Standards*

IFRS 2 Share-based payment

IFRS 3 Business combinations

IFRS 4 Insurance contracts

IFRS 5 Non-current assets held for sale and discontinued operations

IFRS 6 Exploration for and evaluation of mineral resources

IFRS 7 Financial instruments: Disclosures

IFRS 8 Operating segments

IFRS 10 Consolidated financial statements

IFRS 11 Joint arrangements

IFRS 12 Disclosure of interest in other entities

IFRS 13 Fair value measurement

IAS 1 Presentation of financial statements

IAS 2 Inventories

IAS 7 Statement of cash flows

IAS 8 Accounting policies, changes in accounting estimates and errors

IAS 10 Events after the reporting period

IAS 11 Construction contracts

IAS 12 Income taxes

IAS 16 Property, plant, and equipment

IAS 17 Leases

IAS 18 Revenue

IAS 19 Employee benefits

IAS 20 Accounting for government grants and disclosure of government assistance

IAS 21 The effects of changes in foreign exchange rates

IAS 23 Borrowing costs

IAS 24 Related party disclosures

IAS 26 Accounting and reporting by retirement benefit plans

IAS 27 Consolidated and separate financial statements

IAS 28 Investments in associates

IAS 29 Financial reporting in hyperinflationary economies

IAS 32 Financial instruments: Presentation

IAS 33 Earnings per share

IAS 34 Interim financial reporting

IAS 36 Impairment of assets

IAS 37 Provisions, contingent liabilities, and contingent assets

IAS 38 Intangible assets

IAS 39 Financial instruments: Recognition and measurement

IAS 40 Investment property

IAS 41 Agriculture

CHAPTER 5

Interpreting Financial Reports and Alternative Perspectives

LEARNING OBJECTIVES

After reading this chapter, you should be able to answer the following questions:

- What information is typically disclosed in a public company's annual report?

- What is the Management's Discussion and Analysis (MD&A) and what information is normally disclosed in an MD&A?

- How are a company's profitability, liquidity, leveraging, activity/efficiency, and shareholder return calculated and then analyzed?

- What is meant by intellectual capital and institutional theory, and how can these two perspectives be used as alternatives to financial reporting.

- How can corporate social and environmental reporting be used to supplement financial reporting?

This chapter begins with an overview of a company's annual report and the Management's Analysis and Discussion (MD&A) section, and shows how ratio analysis can be used to interpret financial reports. This interpretation covers profitability, liquidity (cash flow), leveraging (borrowings), activity/efficiency, and shareholder return. We also look at working capital management in detail.

Two case studies demonstrate how ratios can be used to look "behind the numbers" contained in financial reports. The chapter concludes with several alternative theoretical perspectives on financial reporting, including corporate social and environmental reporting.

Annual Reports

International Financial Reporting Standards (IFRS) require all public companies to prepare financial statements. Although *Accounting Standards for Private Companies* (ASPE) do not explicitly require private companies to prepare financial statements, they are normally required to do so for taxation or financing purposes or due to shareholder agreements. Financial statements are an important part of a company's annual report, which must be available to all shareholders of the company.

The annual report for a public company listed on a stock exchange typically contains

- A financial summary—the key financial information.

- A list of the main advisers to the company, such as legal advisers, bankers, and auditors.

- The reports of the chairman/president/chief executive officer, directors, and/or chief financial officer. These reports provide a useful summary of the key factors affecting the company's performance over the past year and its prospects for the future. It is important to read this information as it provides a background to the financial reports, in particular the company's products/services and major market segments. The user must read between the lines of this report, since one intention of the annual report is to paint a realistic yet "glossy" picture of the business. However, as competitors will also read the annual report, the company must take care not to disclose more than is necessary.

- The statutory reports (i.e., those required by the *Canada Business Corporations Act*) by the directors and auditors. These will contain a summary of financial performance, major policies, strategies and activities, details about the board of directors, and statements about corporate governance, internal control, and the responsibility of the board for the financial reports.

- The audit report, defining the auditors' responsibilities; an opinion as to whether the financial represents fairly, in all material aspects, the organization's financial position, financial performance, and cash flows in accordance with GAAP (see Chapter 4); and the basis on which that opinion has been formed.

- The financial reports: statement of comprehensive income, statement of financial position, and statement of cash flows. Where consolidated figures are provided, these should be used, as they are the total figures for a group of companies that comprise an entire business.

- Notes to the financial reports, which provide detailed explanations of items in the financial reports and usually run to many pages. As well as a breakdown of many of the figures contained in the statement of comprehensive income, statement of financial position, and statement of cash, the notes will include details such as the major accounting policies adopted, directors' remuneration, depreciation of assets, investments, taxation, share capital, capital expenditure contracted for, pension liabilities, lease liabilities, subsidiaries, events occurring after the end of the reporting period (end of the financial year), and so on.

- A five-year summary of key financial information.

Management's Discussion and Analysis

Public companies in Canada are required to include an operating and financial review as part of their annual financial reports. This review is generally known as the Management's Discussion and Analysis (MD&A). The MD&A is intended to be forward looking, providing details of strategy for shareholders and a broader group of stakeholders to complement and supplement financial reports, including key performance indicators (KPIs; see "Balanced Scorecard" in Chapter 6).

The Canadian Performance Reporting (CPR) Board published a guideline for MD&A entitled *Management's Discussion and Analysis: Guidance on Preparation and Disclosure*. The International Accounting Standards Board (IASB) published a similar guide: *IFRS Practice Statement: Management Commentary* in 2010. The guidelines are voluntary statements meant to indicate "best practice" principles for listed companies.

Although the particular focus of the MD&A will depend on the facts and circumstances of the entity, according to the IASB (2010), the MD&A should include information that is essential to an understanding of

- The nature of the business
- Management's objectives and its strategies for meeting those objectives
- The entity's most significant resources, risks, and relationships
- The results of operations and prospects
- The critical performance measures and indicators that management uses to evaluate the entity's performance against stated objectives

Ratio Analysis

The statement of comprehensive income, statement of financial position, and statement of cash flows can be studied using ratios. *Ratios* are typically two numbers, with one being expressed as a percentage of the other. Ratio analysis can be used to help interpret *trends* in performance from year to year by *benchmarking* to industry averages or to the performance of individual competitors or against a predetermined *target*. Ratio analysis can be used to interpret performance against five criteria:

1. The rate of profitability
2. Liquidity; that is, cash flow
3. Leveraging (also known as *gearing*); that is, the proportion of borrowings to shareholders' investment
4. How efficiently assets are utilized
5. The return to shareholders

Different definitions can be used for each ratio, but it is important that whatever ratios are used, they are meaningful to the business and applied consistently.

The most common ratios are discussed in the following sections. The calculations refer to the example statement of comprehensive income and statement of financial position in Chapter 4, repeated in Exhibits 5.1, 5.2, and 5.3. Ratios may be calculated on the end-of-year statement of financial position figures (as has been done in the examples that follow) or on the basis of the average of

Exhibit 5.1 **Statement of Comprehensive Income**

Sales	$2,000,000
Less: Cost of sales	1,500,000
Gross profit	500,000
Less: Selling, administration, and finance expenses	400,000
Operating profit before interest and taxes	$ 100,000

Exhibit 5.2 Statement of Comprehensive Income (Extended)

Operating profit before interest and taxes	$100,000
Less: Interest	16,000
Profit before taxes	**84,000**
Less: Income taxes	14,000
Profit after taxes	**70,000**
Less: Dividend	30,000
Retained profit	$ 40,000

Exhibit 5.3 Statement of Financial Position

Assets	
Non-current assets	
Property, plant and equipment	$1,150,000
Current assets	
Accounts receivable	300,000
Inventory	200,000
	500,000
Total assets	$1,650,000
Liabilities	
Non-current liabilities	
Long-term loans	$ 300,000
Current liabilities	
Accounts payable	300,000
Bank overdraft	50,000
	350,000
Total liabilities	$ 650,000
Net assets	$1,000,000
Equity	
Share capital	$ 900,000
Retained earnings	100,000
Total equity	$1,000,000

statement of financial position figures over two years. However, different analysts and credit agencies use different definitions of these ratios, as do different textbooks. Whichever definition of the ratio is chosen, it is important to apply it consistently.

Ratios are nearly always expressed as a percentage (by multiplying the answer by 100). In the following examples, amounts shown are thousands of dollars.

Profitability

RETURN ON (SHAREHOLDERS') INVESTMENT (ROI)

Return on investment (ROI) is a performance measure used to evaluate the efficiency of an investment or to compare the efficiency of a number of different investments. It is a very popular ratio because of its simplicity and versatility. An investment should be undertaken only if it has a positive ROI; if there is more than one investment opportunity, the one with the highest ROI should be undertaken.

$$\frac{\text{Net profit after taxes}}{\text{Shareholders' equity}} = \frac{70}{1,000} = 7\%$$

RETURN ON CAPITAL EMPLOYED (ROCE)

Return on capital employed (ROCE) measures a company's efficiency at allocating the funds provided by shareholders and long-term financing to profitable investments. The return on invested capital measure gives a sense of how well a company is using its money to generate returns.

$$\frac{\text{Operating profit before interest and taxes}}{\text{Shareholders' equity} + \text{Long-term debt}} = \frac{100}{1,000 + 300} = 7.7\%$$

OPERATING MARGIN (OR OPERATING PROFIT/SALES)

Operating margin is a measurement of the proportion of a company's revenue that is left after paying for variable costs, such as direct wages and raw materials. The higher the operating margin, the higher the likelihood that the company will be able to pay its fixed costs, such as interest on debt.

$$\frac{\text{Operating profit before interest and taxes}}{\text{Sales}} = \frac{100}{2,000} = 5\%$$

GROSS MARGIN (OR GROSS PROFIT/SALES)

The gross margin is the percentage of total sales revenue that a company retains after incurring the direct costs associated with producing the goods and services sold by a company. The higher the percentage, the more money the company has to cover its other operating costs and obligations.

$$\frac{\text{Gross profit}}{\text{Sales}} = \frac{500}{2,000} = 25\%$$

OPERATING EXPENSES/SALES

$$\frac{\text{Operating expenses}}{\text{Sales}} = \frac{400}{2,000} = 20\%$$

Each of the profitability ratios provides a different method of interpreting profitability. Satisfactory business performance requires an adequate return on shareholders' equity and total capital employed in the business (the total of the investment by shareholders and lenders).

Profit must also be achieved as a percentage of sales, which ideally should itself grow year by year. The operating profit and gross profit margins emphasize different elements of business performance, as does the proportion (and growth) of operating expenses in relation to sales.

SALES GROWTH

A further method of interpreting performance is sales growth, which is simply

$$\frac{\text{Sales in Year 2} - \text{Sales in Year 1}}{\text{Sales in Year 1}}$$

Hence, if the sales in the previous year had been $1,800,000 (not shown in the example), the sales growth would be

$$\frac{2,000 - 1,800}{1,800} = \frac{200}{1,800} = 11.1\%$$

Businesses and investors like to see increasing profitability but also increasing sales, which are an important measure of the long-term sustainability of profits.

Liquidity

WORKING CAPITAL RATIO

The working capital ratio is a measure of a company's short-term financial health. A ratio of 100% or more means a company has enough current assets, such as cash or assets that it can turn into cash, over its operating cycle to pay off its current debt.

$$\frac{\text{Current assets}}{\text{Current liabilities}} = \frac{500}{350} = 143\%$$

ACID TEST (OR QUICK RATIO)

The acid test, also known as the *quick ratio*, is an indicator that measures whether a company has enough current assets to cover its immediate liabilities without selling inventory.

$$\frac{\text{Current assets} - \text{Inventory}}{\text{Current liabilities}} = \frac{500 - 200}{350} = 86\%$$

A business that has an acid test result of less than 100% may experience difficulty in paying its debts as they fall due. On the other hand, a company with too high a working capital ratio may not be utilizing its assets effectively and may be missing important investment opportunities.

Accounts receivable is sometimes also deducted from current assets in a stricter version of the acid test. The rule of thumb is often that anything which the company does not totally control is deducted. With accounts receivable, someone else has to decide to pay the company. With inventory, someone else has to decide to buy it. Therefore, only cash and cash equivalents are included in the stricter version of the acid test. Cash and cash equivalents are easy to control and are at the discretion of the company.

Leveraging

DEGREE OF OPERATING LEVERAGE OR GEARING RATIO

The degree of operating ratio indicates the percentage of all funds available to a company that are borrowed funds.

$$\frac{\text{Long-term debt}}{\text{Shareholders' equity} + \text{Long-term debt}} = \frac{300}{1,000 + 300} = 23.1\%$$

INTEREST COVER RATIO

The **interest cover ratio** gives an indication of the company's ability to pay interest on borrowed funds.

$$\frac{\text{Profit before interest and taxes}}{\text{Interest payable}} = \frac{100}{16} = 6.25 \text{ times}$$

The higher the degree of operating leverage, the higher the risk of not repaying debt and interest. The lower the interest cover, the more pressure there is on profits to fund interest charges. However, because external funds are being used, the *rate of profit* earned by shareholders is higher. The relationship between risk and return is an important feature of interpreting business performance. Consider the example in Exhibit 5.4 of risk and return for a business whose capital employed is derived from different mixes of debt and equity.

While in the Exhibit 5.4 example the return on capital employed is a constant 20% (an operating profit of $20,000 on capital employed of $100,000), the return on shareholders' equity increases as debt replaces equity. This improvement to the return to shareholders carries a risk, which increases as the proportion of profits taken by the interest charge increases (and is reflected in the interest cover ratio). If profits decrease, substantially more risks are carried by the highly leveraged business.

Exhibit 5.4 **Risk and Return: Effect of Different Debt/Equity Mix**

	100% equity	50% equity 50% debt	10% equity 90% debt
Capital employed	$100,000	$100,000	$100,000
Equity	100,000	50,000	10,000
Debt	0	50,000	90,000
Operating profit before interest and taxes	20,000	20,000	20,000
Interest at 10% on debt	0	5,000	9,000
Profit after interest	20,000	15,000	11,000
Taxes at 30%	6,000	4,500	3,300
Profit after taxes	$14,000	$ 10,500	$ 7,700
Return on investment	14%	21%	77%

Activity/Efficiency

ASSET TURNOVER

$$\frac{\text{Sales}}{\text{Total assets}} = \frac{2,000}{1,150 + 500} = 121\%$$

The **asset turnover ratio** is a measure of how efficiently assets are utilized to generate sales. The principal purpose of investment in assets is the generation of sales.

Working Capital

The management of working capital is a crucial element of cash flow management. Working capital is the difference between current assets and current liabilities. In practical terms, we are primarily concerned with inventory and accounts receivable (debtors), although prepayments are a further element of current assets. Current liabilities comprise accounts payable (creditors) and accruals. The other element of working capital is cash and cash equivalents, representing either surplus cash (a current asset) or short-term borrowing through a bank overdraft facility (a current liability).

The working capital cycle is shown in Exhibit 5.5. Money tied up in receivables and inventory puts pressure on the firm either to reduce the level of that investment or to seek additional borrowings. Alternatively, cash surpluses can be invested to generate additional income through interest earned.

Exhibit 5.5 **The Working Capital Cycle**

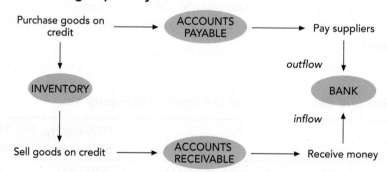

Managing working capital is essential for success, as the ability to avoid a cash crisis and pay debts as they fall due depends on managing

- Receivables, through effective credit approval, invoicing, and collection activity
- Inventory, through effective ordering, storage, and identification of inventory
- Payables, by negotiation of trade terms and through taking advantage of prompt-payment discounts
- Cash, by effective forecasting, short-term borrowing, and/or investment of surplus cash where possible

Ratios to determine the efficiency of the management of working capital and methods for managing and monitoring receivables, inventory, and payables are described in the following sections.

Managing Accounts Receivable

The main measure of how effectively accounts receivable (debtors) are managed is the number of days' sales outstanding. **Days' sales outstanding** is

$$\frac{\text{Accounts receivable}}{\text{Average daily sales}}$$

The business has sales of $2 million and receivables of $300,000. Average daily sales are $5,479 ($2 million/365). There are therefore 54.75 average days' sales outstanding ($300,000/$5,479). The target number of days' sales outstanding will be a function of the industry, the credit terms offered by the firm, and its efficiency in both credit approval and collection activity. The aim of receivables management is to reduce days' sales outstanding over time and to minimize bad debts.

Acceptance policies will aim to determine the creditworthiness of new customers before sales are made. This can be achieved by checking trade and bank references, searching company accounts, and consulting a credit reference agency for any adverse reports. Credit limits can be set for each customer.

Collection policies should ensure that invoices and statements are issued quickly and accurately, that any queries are investigated as soon as they are identified, and that continual follow-up (by telephone and mail) of late-paying customers should take place. Discounts may be offered for settlement within credit terms.

Bad debts may occur because a customer's business fails. For this reason, firms establish a provision (see Chapter 4) to cover the likelihood of customers not being able to pay their debts.

Managing Inventory

The main measure of how effectively inventory is managed is the inventory turnover. **Inventory turnover** is

$$\frac{\text{Cost of sales}}{\text{Inventory}}$$

In the example, cost of sales is $1.5 million and inventory is $200,000. The inventory turnover is therefore 7.5 ($1,500,000/$200,000). This means that inventory turns over 7.5 times per year, or on average every 49 days (365/7.5). Sound management of inventory requires an accurate and up-to-date inventory control system.

Often in inventory control the *Pareto principle* (also called the *80/20 rule*) applies. This recognizes that a small proportion (often about 20%) of the number of inventory items accounts for a relatively large proportion (say 80%) of the total value. In inventory control, ABC analysis takes the approach that, rather than attempt to manage all inventory items equally, efforts should be made to prioritize the "A" items which account for most value, then "B" items, and then, only if time permits, the many smaller-value "C" items.

Some businesses adopt the **just-in-time** (JIT) strategy to minimize inventory holding, treating any inventory as a wasted resource. JIT requires sophisticated production planning, inventory control, and supply chain management so that inventory is received only as it is required for production or sale.

Inventory may be written off because of inventory losses, obsolescence, or damage. For this reason, firms establish a provision to cover the likelihood of writing off part of the value of inventory.

Managing Accounts Payable

Just as it is important to collect accounts receivable from customers, it is also essential to ensure that suppliers are paid within their credit terms. As for accounts receivable, the main measure of how effectively accounts payable (creditors) are managed is the number of days' purchases outstanding. **Days' purchases outstanding** are

$$\frac{\text{Accounts payable}}{\text{Average daily purchases}}$$

The business has cost of sales (usually its main credit purchases, as many expenses, such as salaries or rent, are not on credit) of $1.5 million and accounts payable of $300,000. Average daily purchases are $4,110 ($1.5 million/365). There are therefore 73 average days' purchases outstanding ($300,000/$4,110).

The number of days' purchases outstanding will reflect credit terms offered by the supplier, any discounts that may be obtained for prompt payment, and the collection action taken by the supplier. Failure to pay accounts payable may result in the loss or stoppage of supply, which can then affect the ability of a business to satisfy its customers' orders. The average payment time for accounts payable has to be disclosed in a company's annual report to shareholders.

The final group of ratios comprises measures used by shareholders in evaluation of investment performance.

Shareholder Return

For these ratios we need some additional information:

Number of shares issued	100,000
Market value of shares	$2.50

DIVIDEND PER SHARE

Dividend per share gives an indication of how much money a shareholder will receive for each share held.

$$\frac{\text{Dividends paid}}{\text{Number of shares}} = \frac{\$30,000}{100,000} = \$0.30 \text{ per share}$$

DIVIDEND PAYOUT RATIO

Dividend payout ratio measures how much of available net income was paid out to shareholders in the form of a dividend. Together with dividend per share, it is an indication of the size of the dividend paid.

$$\frac{\text{Dividends paid}}{\text{Profit after taxes}} = \frac{\$30,000}{\$70,000} = 43\%$$

DIVIDEND YIELD

Dividend yield is a ratio that shows how much a company pays out in dividends each year relative to its share price. It is a way to measure how much cash return an investor is getting for each dollar invested in a company's shares.

$$\frac{\text{Dividends paid per share}}{\text{Market value per share}} = \frac{\$0.30}{\$2.50} = 12\%$$

EARNINGS PER SHARE (EPS)

Earnings per share (EPS) calculates the part of the company's profit that is attributed to each individual share. EPS is a good indicator of a company's profitability, and is a very important metric to look at when evaluating a certain share.

$$\frac{\text{Profit after taxes}}{\text{Number of shares}} = \frac{\$70,000}{100,000} = \$0.70 \text{ per share}$$

PRICE/EARNINGS (P/E) RATIO

The price/earnings (P/E) ratio compares the share price of the company to its earnings per share.

$$\frac{\text{Market value per share}}{\text{Earnings per share}} = \frac{\$2.50}{\$0.70} = 3.57 \text{ times}$$

The shareholder ratios are measures of returns to shareholders on their investment in the business. The dividend and earnings ratios reflect the annual return to shareholders, while the P/E ratio measures the number of years over which the investment in shares will be recovered through earnings. Note that because share issues can take place during the year, the number of shares needs to be weighted. Companies are required to calculate this weighting in a particular way and show their earnings per share as part of the statement of comprehensive income.

Interpreting Financial Information Using Ratios

The interpretation of any ratio depends on the industry. In particular, the ratio needs to be interpreted as a trend over time, or as a comparison to industry averages or competitor ratios or predetermined targets. These comparisons help determine whether performance is improving and where further improvement may be necessary. Based on the understanding of the business context and competitive conditions, and the information provided by ratio analysis, users of financial reports can make judgments about the pattern of past performance and prospects for a company and its financial strength. Importantly, ratio analysis can be undertaken not only in relation to the manager's own organization, but also in relation to the financial reports of competitors, customers, and suppliers. However, the annual report in general and the operating and financial review in particular provide important contextual information with which to interpret ratios.

Broadly speaking, businesses seek

- Increasing rates of profit on shareholders' equity, capital employed, and sales
- Adequate **liquidity** (a ratio of current assets to liabilities of not less than 100%) to ensure that debts can be paid as they fall due, but not an excessive rate to suggest that funds are inefficiently used
- A level of debt commensurate with the business risk taken
- High efficiency as a result of maximizing sales from the business's investments
- A satisfactory return on the investment made by shareholders

When considering the movement in a ratio over two or more years, it is important to look at possible causes for the movement. This knowledge can be acquired by understanding that either the numerator (the top number in the ratio) or the denominator (the bottom number in the ratio) or both can influence the change. Some of the possible explanations behind changes in ratios are described in the following sections.

PROFITABILITY

Improvements in the returns on shareholders' investments (ROI) and capital employed (ROCE) may be either because profits have increased and/or because the capital used to generate those profits has altered. When businesses are taken over by others, one way of improving ROI or ROCE is to increase profits by reducing costs (often as a result of economies of scale), but another is to maintain profits while reducing assets and repaying debt.

Improvements in operating profitability as a proportion of sales (profit before interest and taxes (PBIT) or earnings before interest and taxes (EBIT)) are the result of profitability growing at a faster rate than sales growth, a result of either a higher gross margin or lower expenses. Note that sales growth may result in a higher profit but not necessarily in a higher rate of profit as a percentage of sales.

Improvement in the rate of gross profit may be the result of higher selling prices, lower cost of sales, or changes in the mix of product/services sold or different market segments in which they are sold, which may reflect differential profitability. Naturally, the opposite explanations hold true for deterioration in profitability.

LIQUIDITY

Improvements in the working capital and acid test ratios are the result of changing the balance between current assets and current liabilities. As the working capital cycle in Exhibit 5.5 showed, money changes form between receivables, inventory, bank, and payables. Borrowing over the long term in order to fund current assets will improve this ratio, as will profits that generate cash flow. By contrast, using liquid funds to repay long-term loans or incurring losses will reduce the working capital used to repay creditors.

LEVERAGING

The **degree of operating leverage** reflects the balance between long-term debt and shareholders' equity. It changes as a result of changes in either shareholders' equity (more shares may be issued), increasing debt, or repayments of debt. As debt increases in proportion to shareholders' equity, the degree of operating leverage will increase.

CASE IN POINT

Leverage at Lehman Brothers

Leading up to its spectacular collapse in 2008, U.S. investment bank Lehman Brothers used some accounting manoeuvres to improve how its leverage, or borrowings, appeared on its books. It was required by its own lenders to maintain a certain cap on leverage. According to a report by an examiner after the bank went bankrupt, Lehman Brothers temporarily shifted billions in assets to hide its mounting debt and its dependence on leverage, which played a large role in the firm's demise. Using a process it called "Repo 105," the bank "sold" some of its assets just before the end of a quarter to reduce its leverage ratio on its financial statements. Then, after the quarter, it would borrow cash and buy back the assets for 5% less than it sold them for. Essentially, it paid 5% interest on the temporary loan.

While a British law firm deemed Lehman's Repo 105 to be an acceptable practice at the time, New York State later filed charges against the company, alleging that it deliberately misled investors. The charges were still before the courts when this textbook went to press.

Sources: De la Merced, M., & Ross Sorkin, A., Report details how Lehman hid its woes, *The New York Times*, March 11, 2010; Robertson, D., & Frean, A., British law firm cleared way for Lehman cover-up, *The Times*, March 12, 2010; Craig, S., & Spector, M., Repos played a key role in Lehman's demise, *The Wall Street Journal*, March 13, 2010; Henning, P., In Lehman's demise, a dwindling chance of charges, *The New York Times*, March 15, 2011.

Interest cover may increase as a result of higher profits or lower debt (and reduce as a result of lower profits or higher debt), but even with constant debt, changes in the interest rate paid will also influence this ratio.

ACTIVITY/EFFICIENCY

Asset turnover improves either because sales increase or the total assets used decrease, a similar situation to that described above for ROCE. The efficiency with which accounts receivable are collected, inventory is managed, and accounts payable paid is also an important measure.

SHAREHOLDER RETURN

Decisions made by directors influence both the dividend per share and the dividend payout ratio. Directors decide on dividends on the basis of the proportion of profits they want to distribute and the capital needed to be retained in the business to fund growth. Often, shareholder value considerations will dictate the level of dividends, which businesses do not like to reduce on a per share basis. This is sometimes at the cost of retaining fewer profits and then having to borrow additional funds to support growth strategies. However, the number of shares issued also affects this ratio, as share issues will result in a lower dividend *per share* unless the total dividend is increased. As companies have little influence over their share price—which is a result of market expectations as much as past performance—dividend yield, while influenced by the dividend paid per share, is more readily influenced by changes in the market price of the shares.

Earnings per share are influenced, as is profitability, by the profit but also (like dividends) by the number of shares issued. As for the dividend yield, the price/earnings ratio is often more a result of changes in the share price than of the profits reflected in the earnings per share. Explanations for changes in ratios are illustrated in the following case study.

CASE STUDY 5.1: HIGH LINER FOODS INCORPORATED

High Liner Foods is a leading North American processor and marketer of prepared, value-added frozen seafood. The company's branded products are sold throughout the United States, Canada, and Mexico under the High Liner, FisherBoy, Mirabel, Sea Cuisine, and Royal Sea labels, and are available in most grocery and big-box stores. High Liner Foods also sells its products under High Liner, FPI, Mirabel, Viking, Icelandic Seafood, Samband of Iceland, Seastar, and Seaside brands to restaurants and institutions, and is a major supplier of private-label seafood products to North American food retailers and food service distributors.

The information in Exhibits 5.6 and 5.7 has been extracted from the company's annual report for the year ended December 31, 2011. The full annual report, including Management's Discussion and Analysis (MD&A) and the financial statements, is available on the High Liner website.

The weighted average number of common shares issued was 15,108,823 and 16,096,010 in 2011 and 2010, respectively. High Liner Foods' share price was $16.25 on January 1, 2011, and $16.35 on December 31, 2011, the year-end dates. The company also paid dividends of $5,891,000 and $5,238,000 in 2011 and 2010, respectively.

When calculating and interpreting ratios, it is important to know and understand the company, the industry it operates in, and the larger, current economic environment. The following pertinent facts were retrieved from the company's annual report:

- High Liner Foods Inc. acquired a rival company, Icelandic USA, on December 19, 2011. It acquired the assets for a purchase price of (US)$232.7 million paid in cash, excluding seasonal working capital of (US)$14 million, and financed with new long-term debt of (US)$250 million.

- Cost of raw materials increased significantly during the year.

- There was some economic uncertainty in North America in 2010 and 2011. Unemployment was high and consumers and customers were putting pressure on High Liner to keep prices low. However, food is a staple, so demand for the company's products remained fairly stable.

Although ratios can be calculated without reference to the MD&A, the MD&A and notes to the financial statements give important information and perspective, making inferences from the ratios much more meaningful.

Ratios for profitability are shown in Exhibit 5.8, which shows that as at December 31, 2011, investors had invested $161.5 million in the company in the form of common shares bought and retained earnings in the company. Return on shareholders' equity indicates that shareholders earned a return of 11.3% in 2011 on this investment, compared to 13.6% in 2010. This return may seem very favourable compared to interest rates on other investments at the time, but keep in mind that most investors would actually have had a much lower return. For example, an investor who paid $16.25 per share on January 1, 2011, would have received a return of about 7.4% ($18,180,000/15,108,823 × $16.25 shares).

Return on capital employed fell from 15.6% to 6.4%, which at first might seem like a very negative indicator. The decrease, however, is largely due to the fact that the company borrowed nearly $250 million in 2011 to finance the acquisition of Icelandic USA. Because the acquisition did not take place until December 19, 2011, the acquisition had no significant effect on the company's net income in 2011, but management believes that Icelandic USA will contribute significantly to net income in future years.

This just illustrates the importance of reading a company's annual report and understanding the context of the ratios before trying to interpret them. Notice that the calculation of return on capital employed includes both short-term and long-term debt. The short-term debt is the portion of the debt that is repayable within one year.

Even though sales increased by 14.3%, gross margins fell slightly due to the pressure put on the company by customers to reduce prices in light of the economic climate, as well as due to increases in the cost of raw materials. This also partly explains the decrease in operating margins. Another contribution to the decrease in operating margins is the cost associated with acquiring Icelandic USA, which is included in operating expenses.

Ratios for liquidity are shown in Exhibit 5.9. Even though the working capital ratio has declined in 2011 from 163.2% to 151.1%, High Liner is still in a healthy situation. Notice that both the numerator and denominator have nearly doubled in 2011 compared to 2010. That is largely due to the fact that the current assets and current liabilities of Icelandic USA are included in the 2011 numbers. The acid test ratio has also declined from 47.7% to 40.6%. Because a wholesaler such as

Exhibit 5.6 **Statement of Income for High Liner Foods Inc. ($thousands)**
(modified from the original)

	2011	2010
Sales	$668,589	$584,715
Cost of sales	516,659	447,542
Gross profit	151,930	137,173
Distribution expenses	35,021	30,027
Selling, general, and admin. expenses	72,086	68,500
Other operating expenses	11,275	875
Income from operating activities	33,548	37,771
Finance costs	6,036	5,147
Income before income taxes	27,512	32,624
Income taxes	9,332	12,639
Net income	$ 18,180	$ 19,985

Exhibit 5.7 **Statement of Financial Position for High Liner Foods Inc.**
($thousands) (modified from the original)

	December 31, 2011	January 1, 2011
Assets		
Current assets:		
Cash and cash equivalents	$ 3,260	$ 598
Accounts receivables	84,920	50,452
Income tax receivables	3,557	701
Other financial assets	1,346	890
Inventories	261,330	131,980
Prepaid expenses	3,019	1,889
Total current assets	$357,432	$186,510
Non-current assets:		
Property, plant, and equipment	99,933	67,269
Intangible assets	103,109	31,239
Goodwill	126,787	39,819
Other non-current assets	3,274	3,465
Total non-current assets	333,103	141,792
Total assets	$690,535	$328,302

(continued)

Exhibit 5.7 Statement of Financial Position for High Liner Foods Inc.
(modified from the original) (*continued*)

Liabilities and Shareholders' Equity		
Current liabilities:		
Bank loans and short-term debt	$124,587	$ 48,123
Accounts payable and accrued liabilities	110,021	62,949
Income tax payable	1,990	3,230
Total current liabilities	236,598	114,302
Non-current liabilities:		
Long-term debt	240,037	47,164
Deferred income taxes	41,099	9,895
Employee future benefits	11,274	9,630
Total liabilities	$529,008	$180,991
Shareholders' equity:		
Common shares	78,067	78,326
Retained earnings	83,460	68,985
Total shareholders' equity	161,527	147,311
Total liabilities and shareholders' equity	$690,535	$328,302

Exhibit 5.8 Profitability Ratios

	2011	2010
Return on shareholders' investments (ROI)	$\dfrac{18,180}{161,527}$ = 11.3%	$\dfrac{19,985}{147,311}$ = 13.6%
Return on capital employed (ROCE)	$\dfrac{33,548}{(161,527 + 240,037 + 124,587)}$ = 6.4%	$\dfrac{37,771}{(147,311 + 47,164 + 48,123)}$ = 15.6%
Operating margin	$\dfrac{33,548}{668,589}$ = 5.0%	$\dfrac{37,771}{584,715}$ = 6.5%
Gross margin	$\dfrac{151,930}{668,589}$ = 22.7%	$\dfrac{137,173}{584,715}$ = 23.5%
Operating expenses over sales	$\dfrac{(35,021 + 72,086 + 11,275)}{668,589}$ = 17.7%	$\dfrac{30,027 + 68,500 + 875}{584,715}$ = 17.0%
Sales growth	$\dfrac{(668,589 - 584,715)}{584,715}$ = 14.3%	

Exhibit 5.9 **Liquidity Ratios**

	2011	2010
Working capital	$\dfrac{357{,}432}{236{,}598}$	$\dfrac{186{,}510}{114{,}302}$
	$= 151.1\%$	$= 163.2\%$
Working capital excluding debt	$\dfrac{357{,}432}{(110{,}021 + 1{,}990)}$	$\dfrac{186{,}510}{(62{,}949 + 3{,}230)}$
	$= 319.1\%$	$= 281.8\%$
Acid test	$\dfrac{(357{,}432 - 261{,}330)}{236{,}598}$	$\dfrac{(186{,}510 - 131{,}980)}{114{,}302}$
	$= 40.6\%$	$= 47.7\%$
Acid test excluding debt	$\dfrac{(357{,}432 - 261{,}330)}{(110{,}021 + 1{,}990)}$	$\dfrac{(186{,}510 - 131{,}980)}{(62{,}949 + 3{,}230)}$
	$= 85.8\%$	$= 82.4\%$

High Liner Foods will always have significant amounts of inventory, it is expected that acid test ratios will be much lower than working capital ratios.

Although inventory has doubled from 2010, short-term debt has increased by significantly more (2.6 times). This is, again, due to the financing of the acquisition of Icelandic USA through debt. If short-term debt is excluded, both the working capital and acid test ratios improved in 2011.

As shown in Exhibit 5.10, at the end of 2010, 39.3% of the funds employed in the company were borrowed. This increased to 69.3% by the end of 2011, again due to the fact that the company took on significant debt during that year to finance the Icelandic USA acquisition.

Interest cover was not calculated because interest payable was not shown as a separate number in the financial statements.

The ratios for activity/efficiency are shown in Exhibit 5.11. Asset and inventory turnover have both decreased significantly. Even though this may seem alarming at first, this is again due to the fact that the

Icelandic USA assets were added to the company very late in the year and have not had a chance to generate sales for the company. It will be more meaningful to compare 2012 ratios with 2010 ratios next year to see the effect of the Icelandic USA acquisition.

Days' sales outstanding has increased from 31.5 days to 46.4 days. Note 9 to the financial statements breaks accounts receivable down to trade accounts receivable and other accounts receivable. As trade accounts relate specifically to sales, it is more meaningful to use this number, rather than the total accounts receivable. Recalculating days' sales outstanding based on trade accounts receivable shows an increase from 29.1 days to 42.9 days. This is again probably due to the accounts receivable acquired from Icelandic USA.

High Liner Foods sells mostly to retailers, the catering industry, and restaurants on a 30-day payment basis. Note 9 to the financial statements reveals that 95% of the accounts receivable at December 31, 2011, were less than 30 days old. This compares to 93% in 2010 and 89% in 2009. This confirms that the company collects on nearly all of its sales within about 30 days.

Exhibit 5.10 **Degree of Operating Leverage**

	2011	2010
Degree of operating leverage	$\dfrac{124{,}587 + 240{,}037}{(124{,}587 + 240{,}037 + 161{,}527)}$	$\dfrac{48{,}123 + 47{,}164}{(48{,}123 + 47{,}164 + 47{,}311)}$
	$= 69.3\%$	$= 39.3\%$

Exhibit 5.11 **Activity/Efficiency Ratios**

	2011	2010
Asset turnover	668,589	584,715
	690,535	328,302
	= 0.97 times	= 1.78 times
Days' sales outstanding	84,920	50,452
	(668,589 / 365)	(584,715 / 365)
	= 46.4 days	= 31.5 days
Inventory turnover	516,659	447,542
	261,330	131,980
	= 2.0 times	= 3.4 times
Days' purchases outstanding	86,286	43,770
	(643,382 / 365)	(460,028 / 365)
	= 49.0 days	= 34.7 days

Neither purchases of inventory nor trade accounts payable are disclosed in the face of the financial statements, but both numbers can be calculated using the information in Notes 8 and 10. Using this information, we can calculate days' purchases outstanding. Days' purchases outstanding increased from 34.7 days in 2010 to 49.0 days in 2011, again probably due to the inclusion of Icelandic USA's inventory and trade accounts payable. Just like trade accounts receivable, the norm for the industry is around 30 days, so this ratio can be expected to return to around 30 days in 2012 once the effect of the Icelandic USA acquisition has been absorbed.

The shareholders' return ratios are shown in Exhibit 5.12. Both dividends per share and earnings per share are available from High Liner's annual report. A closer look at the MD&A reveals that the company has steadily increased its quarterly dividend from 7.5 cents per share in 2010 to 10.0 cents per share by the fourth quarter of 2011. The company made the following disclosure in the MD&A regarding its dividend policy:

> The dividend policy reflects our confidence in our growth strategy, together with significant improvements on our balance sheet since divesting our fishing assets.

The dividend yield is an effective interest rate and therefore fluctuates in line with both the dividend per share and the share price. As the dividend per share increased, while the share price stayed roughly consistent, the dividend yield increased moderately from 2.0% to 2.4%. The price/earnings ratio remained roughly unchanged.

As was indicated earlier, it is important to understand the underlying factors relating to the company, industry, and broader economic condition to be able to interpret the ratios in a meaningful way. The management of the company more than anyone else has detailed knowledge about the company that most users of the financial statements don't have. It is therefore insightful to look at the ratios calculated by the management and discussed in the MD&A.

Exhibit 5.13 was extracted from High Liner's MD&A and contains five ratios that management believes are important indicators of success for a company, together with benchmarks that management has set to compare the ratios to.

An explanation of the calculation and a discussion of each ratio follow. Notice that the company uses non-standard formulas to calculate some of the ratios. This is due to the fact that High Liner, as will other companies, will probably have some unique circumstances from year to year which will make it difficult to calculate meaningful ratios that can be compared over time and across the industry, without adjusting for those circumstances. In the case of High Liner Foods, for example, the acquisition of Icelandic USA means that the company incurred some one-time acquisition costs that are included in the company's statement of income, but that make comparison from year to year difficult if the numbers are not adjusted to eliminate this one-time cost.

Exhibit 5.12 Shareholders' Return Ratios

	2011	2010
Dividend per share	5,891,000	5,238,000
	15,108,823	16,096,010
	= $0.39	= $0.33
Dividend payout ratio	5,891	5,238
	18,180	19,985
	= 32%	= 26%
Dividend yield	0.39	0.33
	$16.35	$16.25
	= 2.4%	= 2.0%
Earnings per share (EPS)	18,180,000	19,985,000
	15,108,823	16,096,010
	= $1.20	= $1.24
Price/earnings ratio	16.35	16.25
	1.20	1.24
	= 13.59	= 13.09

Exhibit 5.13

	Benchmark	2011 Actual
Returns		
– On assets managed	15.0%	14.7%
– On equity	14.0%	17.5%
Profitability:		
– Trailing 12-month EBIT as a percentage of net sales	6.0%	6.7%
Financial strength		
– Interest-bearing debt to trailing 12-month EBITDA* (not to exceed)	3.0 times	4.4 times
Inventory management		
– Inventory turnovers	4.2 times	3.7 times

*Earnings before interest, taxes, depreciation, and amortization.

While the company's own calculations are more accurate, the important thing to remember about calculating and interpreting ratios is to be consistent: Choose the formula that you think is most reliable and apply the same principle from year to year.

Return on Assets Managed (ROAM)

Return on assets managed (ROAM) is calculated as follows: Adjusted EBITDA (as defined on page 71) minus depreciation and amortization equals earnings before interest and taxes (EBIT) divided by average assets managed. "Assets managed" include all assets, excluding employee future benefits and deferred income taxes less accounts payable. Average assets managed is calculated using the average net assets managed for each of the preceding 13-month periods.

In 2011, High Liner's return on assets managed was 14.7%, lower than the company's benchmark by

0.3 percentage points. Adjusted EBITDA in 2011 increased by $7.5 million over 2010; however, the Icelandic USA average assets managed for one month were included, while income for only a few days was included. Excluding the assets and income of Icelandic USA, ROAM was 15.6%.

Return on Equity (ROE)

Return on equity (ROE) is calculated as follows: net income (excluding after-tax business acquisition, integration costs, and other income or expenses) divided by average common equity. Average common equity is calculated using common equity for each of the preceding 13-month periods.

Return on equity in 2011 was 17.5%. Income, excluding the business acquisition, integration costs, and other income or expenses, increased in 2011 and average debt levels were higher, both contributing to a higher ROE in 2011. Increased borrowing for the Icelandic USA acquisition in December 2011 is expected to increase average leverage and return in equity for 2012. Excluding the Icelandic USA acquisition, ROE in 2011 was unchanged at 17.5%.

Trailing 12-Month Earnings before Interest and Taxes

Trailing 12-month earnings before interest and taxes as a percentage of net sales is calculated as follows: all earnings before interest and taxes (excluding business acquisition, integration costs, and other income or expenses) divided by sales, as disclosed on the consolidated statement of income.

The trailing 12-month EBIT as a percentage of net sales revenue was 6.7%. This ratio was a slight improvement over the previous year due to the Viking acquisition (an acquisition completed in 2010), as margins at Viking were higher on value-added products, and as High Liner continued to improve its performance from operations.

Interest-Bearing Debt to Trailing 12-Month Earnings before Interest, Taxes, Depreciation, and Amortization

Interest-bearing debt to trailing 12-month EBITDA is calculated as follows: interest-bearing debt (i.e., bank loans plus current and long-term portions of long-term debt and capital lease obligations) divided by adjusted EBITDA. High Liner made the following note regarding EBITDA:

> Adjusted EBITDA is earnings before interest, taxes, depreciation and amortization, business acquisition, integration and other expense as disclosed on the consolidated statements of

income. Management believes that this is a useful performance measure as it approximates cash generated from operations, before capital expenditures and changes in working capital, and excludes non-operating items. Adjusted EBITDA also assists comparison among companies as it eliminates the differences in earnings due to how a company is financed. Adjusted EBITDA does not have a standardized meaning prescribed by generally accepted accounting principles and therefore may not be comparable to similar measures presented by others. Our definition of adjusted EBITDA follows the October 2008 general principles and guidance for reporting EBITDA issued by the Canadian Institute of Chartered Accountants (CICA).

Interest-bearing debt to trailing 12-month adjusted EBITDA was 4.4 times on a pro forma basis to include the income of the Icelandic USA acquisition, based on the interest-bearing debt at the end of fiscal 2011. This was higher than the previous year because debt increased in December 2011 due to the Icelandic USA acquisition. On a pro forma basis, including the historical EBITDA and near-term synergies expected from the Icelandic USA acquisition, the ratio was 3.7 times. High Liner stated its intention to bring the interest-bearing debt to 12-month EBITDA ratio to its target of 3.0 times as soon as possible.

Inventory Turnovers

Inventory turnovers are calculated as follows: cost of sales for the year divided by average inventory available for sale or use as of the end of each month of the year. It includes raw material, finished goods, packaging, and ingredients, but excludes maintenance parts and inventory in transit and in inspection.

High Liner inventory turnovers occurred 3.7 times in 2011. The target in 2010 was 5.0 times. Because many of the company's products come from various parts of the world, the resulting lead time is long. The company's commitment to ensuring that it meets customer service requirements results in an inventory level that is higher than ideal. Given this dynamic, the company changed the benchmark target in 2011 to 4.2 times to reflect what it thinks is achievable in the current business environment. This is a more realistic target for inventory turnovers given the long supply chain and seasonality for the company's products.

Source: High Liner Foods Incorporated *2011 Annual Report*. Retrieved from www.highlinerfoods.com/en/home/investorinformation/annualreports.aspx.

CASE STUDY 5.2: CARRINGTON PRINTERS—AN ACCOUNTING CRITIQUE

Carrington Printers was a privately owned, 100-year-old British printing company employing about 100 people and operating out of its own premises in a medium-sized town. Although the company was heavily in debt and had been operating at a small loss for the past three years, it had a fairly strong statement of financial position and a good customer base spread over a wide geographic area. Carrington's simplified statement of financial position is shown in Exhibit 5.14. Note that the statement of financial position is in a different format and uses slightly different terminology than we have used in this chapter. This is because accounting standards change and the presentation of financial reports can alter. In this example, the original published format has been retained (it is important that users can apply the principles to different styles of presentation).

The nature of the printing industry at the time the accounts were prepared was that there was excess production capacity and, over the previous year, a price war had been fought between competitors in order to retain existing customers and win new ones. The effect of this had been that selling prices (and consequently profit margins) had fallen throughout the industry. Carrington's plant and equipment were, in the main, quite old and not suited to some of the work that it was acquiring. Consequently, some work was being produced inefficiently, with a detrimental impact on profit margins. Before the end of the year, the sales director had left the company and had influenced many of Carrington's customers, with whom he had established a good relationship, to move to his new employer. Over several months, Carrington's sales began to drop significantly.

Lost sales and deteriorating margins on some of the business affected cash flow. Printing companies typically carry a large inventory of paper in a range of

Exhibit 5.14 Carrington Printers' Statement of Financial Position (in British pounds)

Fixed assets	
Land and buildings at cost less depreciation	£1,000,000
Plant and equipment at cost less depreciation	450,000
	1,450,000
Current assets	
Accounts receivable	500,000
Inventory	450,000
	950,000
Less creditors due within one year	
Accounts payable	850,000
Bank overdraft	250,000
	1,100,000
Net current liabilities	150,000
Total assets less current liabilities	1,300,000
Less payables due after one year	750,000
Total net assets	£ 550,000
Capital and reserves	
Common shares	100,000
Net profit	450,000
Shareholders' equity	£ 550,000

weights, sizes, and colours, while customers often take up to 60 days to pay their accounts. Because payment of taxes and employees takes priority, suppliers are often the last group to be paid. The major suppliers are paper merchants, who stop supplies when their customers do not pay on time. The consequence of Carrington's cash flow difficulties was that suppliers limited the supply of paper which the company needed to satisfy customer orders.

None of these events was reflected in the financial reports, and the auditors, largely unaware of changing market conditions, had little understanding of the gradual detrimental impact on Carrington that had taken place at the time of the audit. Although aware of the tightening cash flow experienced by the company, the auditors signed the accounts, satisfied that the business could be treated as a going concern.

As a result of the problems identified above, Carrington approached its bankers for additional loans. However, the bankers declined, believing that existing loans had reached the maximum percentage of asset values against which they were prepared to lend. The company attempted a sale and leaseback of its land and buildings (through which a purchaser pays a market price for the property, with Carrington becoming a tenant on a long-term lease). However, investors interested in the property were not satisfied that Carrington was a viable tenant and the property could not be sold on that basis.

Cash flow pressures continued, and the shareholders were approached to contribute additional capital. They were unable to do so, and six months after the statement of financial position was produced, the company collapsed and was placed into receivership and subsequently liquidation by its bankers.

The liquidators found, as is common in failed companies, that the values in the statement of financial position were substantially higher than the amount for which the assets could be sold:

- Land and buildings were sold for far less than an independent valuation had suggested, as the property would now be vacant.

- Plant and machinery were almost worthless given their age and condition and the excess capacity in the industry at the time.

- Substantial amounts were being written off accounts receivable as bad debts. Customers often refused to pay accounts, giving spurious reasons, and it was often not worthwhile for the liquidator to pursue collection action through the courts.

- Inventory was discovered to be largely worthless. Substantial inventories of paper had been held for long periods with little likelihood of ever being used and other printers were unwilling to pay more than a fraction of the cost for this paper.

As the bank had collateral over most of Carrington's assets, there were virtually no funds to pay the unsecured creditors after the bank loans were repaid.

This case raises some important issues about the value of audited financial reports:

1. The importance of understanding the context of the business; that is, how its market conditions and its mix of products or services are changing over time, and how well (or in this case, badly) the business is able to adapt to these changes.

2. The preparation of financial reports assumes a going concern, but the circumstances facing a business can change quickly and the statement of financial position can become a meaningless document.

3. The auditors rely on information from the directors about significant risks affecting the company. The Carrington directors did not intentionally deceive the auditors but genuinely believed that the business could be turned around and made profitable by winning back customers. They also believed that the large inventory would satisfy future customer orders. The directors also genuinely thought that the property could be sold in order to eliminate debt. This was unquestioned by the auditors.

Alternative Theoretical Perspectives on Financial Reports

Agency theory is the traditional theoretical perspective on which financial reporting is based. In this section, we consider some alternative perspectives: intellectual capital and institutional theory. We also introduce corporate, social, and environmental reporting.

INTELLECTUAL CAPITAL

The **intellectual capital** of a company refers to the collective abilities of the company's management, employees, and systems to add value to the company. Edvinsson and Malone (1997) defined intellectual capital as "the hidden dynamic factors that underlie the visible company" (p. 11). Stewart (1997) defined intellectual capital as "formalized, captured and leveraged knowledge" (p. 68). Intellectual capital is of particular interest to accountants in increasingly knowledge-based economies, in which the limitations of traditional financial reports erode their value as a tool supporting meaningful decision making (Guthrie, 2001). Three dimensions of intellectual capital have been identified in the literature: human (developing and leveraging individual knowledge and skills), organizational (internal structures, systems, and procedures), and customer (loyalty, brand, image, and so on). The disclosure of information about intellectual capital as an extension to financial reporting has been proposed by various accounting academics. The most publicized example is the *Skandia Navigator* (see Edvinsson and Malone, 1997).

While most businesses espouse a commitment to employees and the value of their knowledge, as well as to some form of social or environmental responsibility, this is often merely rhetoric, a façade to appease the interest groups of stakeholders. The *institutional* setting of organizations provides another perspective from which to view accounting and reporting.

INSTITUTIONAL THEORY

Institutional theory studies the process by which structures such as rules, regulations, schemas, and norms are formed. Institutional theory is valuable because it locates the organization within its historical and contextual setting. It is predicated on the need for legitimation and on isomorphic processes. Scott (1995) describes *legitimation* as the result of organizations being dependent, to a greater or lesser extent, on support from the environment for their survival and continued operation. Organizations need the support of government institutions that regulate their operations (and few organizations are not regulated in some form or other). Organizations are also dependent on the acquisition of resources (for example, labour, finance, technology) for their purposes. If an organization is not legitimated, it may incur sanctions of a legal, economic, or social nature.

The second significant aspect of institutional power is the operation of *isomorphism*, the tendency for different organizations to adopt similar characteristics. DiMaggio and Powell (1983) identified three forms of isomorphism: coercive, as a result of political influence and the need to gain legitimacy; mimetic, following from standard responses to uncertainty; and normative, associated with professionalization. They held that isomorphic tendencies between organizations were a result of wider belief systems and cultural frames of reference. Processes of education, interorganizational movement of personnel, and professionalization emphasize these belief systems and cultural values at an institutional level, and facilitate the mimetic processes that result in organizations imitating each other. Isomorphic tendencies exist because "organizations compete not just for resources and customers, but for political power and institutional legitimacy, for social as well as economic fitness" (DiMaggio and Powell, p. 150).

These legitimating and isomorphic processes become taken for granted by organizations as they strive to satisfy the demands of external regulators, resource suppliers, and professional groups. These taken-for-granted processes themselves become institutionalized in the systems and processes—including accounting and reporting—adopted by organizations. Meyer (1994) argued that accounting arises "in response to the demands made by powerful elements in the environment on which organizations are dependent" (p. 122).

Institutional investors (insurance companies, mutual funds, and pension funds, although this is not the only meaning of "institution") own a significant percentage of Canadian listed companies. Institutional ownership has grown significantly over the last few decades at the expense of individual ownership. One of the issues arising from this changing pattern of share ownership has been institutional investor activism, or rather the lack of it. This is beginning to change, and some institutional investors are becoming more active in holding boards more accountable for their performance. This has been at least in part a response to the failures of large corporations such as Enron and WorldCom and the increased importance given to corporate governance (see Chapter 2).

Corporate Social and Environmental Reporting

The concern with stakeholders rather than shareholders (introduced in Chapter 2) began in the 1970s and is generally associated with the publication in 1975 of *The Corporate Report*, a publication by the Accounting Standards Steering Committee (now known as simply the Accounting Standards Committee). Accounting academics began to question profit as the sole measure of business performance and suggested a wider social responsibility for business and a more *social accounting*.

Stakeholder theory (Chapter 2) argues that managers should serve the interests of anyone with a stake in the organization (that is, anyone who is affected by the organization). Stakeholders include shareholders but also encompass employees, suppliers, customers, government, and the communities in which the firm operates. Managers need to strike an appropriate balance between these interests when directing the firm's activities so that one stakeholder group is not satisfied to the detriment of others. Much of the argument behind stakeholder theory is that the economic pressure to satisfy only shareholders is short-term thinking and that organizations need to ensure their survival and success in the long term by satisfying other stakeholders as well—this is called *sustainability* (discussed in detail in the next section). A concern with stakeholders beyond shareholders has led to a wider view about the content of annual reports.

Concepts of *corporate social accounting* and *socially responsible accounting*—most recently, corporate social and environmental reporting (CSR)—attempt to highlight the impact of organizations on society. Jones (1995) suggests three reasons for this:

1. A moral imperative that business organizations were insufficiently aware of the social consequences of their activities.

2. External pressure from government and pressure groups, and the demand by some institutional investors for ethical investments. This was linked to the role of accounting in demonstrating how well organizations were fulfilling their *social contract*, the implied contract between an organization and society.

3. Change taking place within organizations as a result of such factors as education and professionalization.

However, there has been little support for broader social accounting because accountants and managers have generally regarded themselves as the agents of owners. Social reporting could be seen as undermining both the power of shareholders and the foundation of the capitalist economic system. There are also technical difficulties associated with social reporting, as well as a dominant belief among business leaders that government and not business has the responsibility to determine what is reported.

During the 1980s and 1990s, environmental accounting (see for example Gray, Owen, & Adams, 1996) focused on responsibility for the natural environment and in particular on sustainability as a result of concerns about ozone depletion, the greenhouse effect, and global warming. These concerns were associated with the growth of pressure groups, such as Greenpeace and Friends of the Earth. Part of the appeal of environmental accounting was that issues of energy efficiency, recycling, and reduction in packaging had cost-saving potential, and therefore profits and social responsibility came to be seen as not necessarily mutually exclusive.

Zadek (1998) argued that social and ethical accounting, auditing, and reporting together provide one of the few practical mechanisms for companies to integrate new patterns of civil accountability and governance with a business success model focused on stakeholders and core non-financial as well as financial values. Socially responsible businesses

> . . . find the spaces in the pipeline between investors and consumers where some choice in behaviour is possible . . . [and] a far more ambitious agenda of shifting the basic boundaries by raising public awareness towards social and environmental agendas, and supporting the emergence of new forms of investors that take non-financial criteria into account. (p. 1439)

SUSTAINABILITY AND THE "TRIPLE BOTTOM LINE"

The best-known definition of **sustainability** comes from the UN's *Report of the World Commission on Environment and Development: Our Common Future* (also known as *The Brundtland Report*), published in 1987, which defines sustainable development as that which "meets the needs of the present without compromising the ability of future generations to meet their own needs." In other words, sustainability is a condition in which the demands placed on the environment by people and business organizations can be met without reducing the capacity of the environment to provide for future generations. Some of the major sustainability issues are population, climate change, ecology, and energy use.

An example is global warming, generally accepted to be a consequence of poor use of technology and short-term management thinking. Reducing pollution and harmful carbon emissions through better technology will almost always lower cost or raise product value in the long term, which will offset the cost of compliance with environmental standards, although doing so may require innovation. Carbon trading may be an advantage in forcing companies to address their levels of emissions.

The term **triple bottom line** is attributed to John Elkington and his consultancy firm SustainAbility, and it describes new types of markets and innovative business approaches that are needed to achieve success. The originators believe not only that profitable business must be socially and environmentally responsible, but further, that social and environmental innovation is key to the new market opportunities of the future. In its broadest sense, the triple bottom line captures the spectrum of values that organizations must embrace: economic, environmental, and social. In practical terms, triple bottom line accounting means expanding the traditional company reporting framework to take into account not just financial outcomes but also environmental and social performance.

Global Reporting Initiative

The **Global Reporting Initiative** (GRI) is a multi-stakeholder non-profit organization that works toward a sustainable global economy by providing sustainability reporting guidance through its *Sustainability Reporting Guidelines*. These guidelines are for voluntary use by organizations to measure and report economic, environmental, social, and governance dimensions of their activities, products, and services. The GRI incorporates the active participation of representatives from business, accountancy, investment, environmental, human rights, research, and labour organizations around the world. Started in 1997, GRI became independent in 2002 and has strategic partnerships with the United Nations Environment Programme, the UN Global Compact, the Organisation for Economic Co-operation and Development, the International Organization for Standardization, and many others.

In broad terms, the GRI *Sustainability Reporting Guidelines* (Version 3.1 was released in 2011) recommend specific information related to environmental, social, and economic performance. They are structured around a CEO statement; key environmental, social, and economic indicators; a profile of the reporting entity; descriptions of relevant policies and management systems; stakeholder relationships; management performance; operational performance; product performance; and a sustainability overview.

The GRI has developed a set of core performance measures or metrics intended to be applicable to all business enterprises, sets of sector-specific metrics for specific types of enterprises, and a uniform format for reporting information integral to a company's sustainability performance. The indicators are categorized as economic, environmental, social, human rights, and workplace.

For the GRI ambition to be realized, companies need to do three things:

1. Describe factors that are genuinely about the health of the business and its relationship with various stakeholders.

2. Cover all the different aspects of how the business has significant impacts on society.

3. Include measures of performance, not just management process.

CONCLUSION

This chapter has provided the context for the annual report and MD&A and explained and illustrated the ratios for analyzing financial information in terms of profitability, liquidity, leveraging, efficiency, and shareholder return. We have looked in detail at interpreting these ratios, and the chapter has identified some of the limitations of financial statement analysis.

KEY TERMS

■ SELF-TEST QUESTIONS

S5.1 Tubular Steel has 1 million shares issued that have a market price of $5.00 each. After-tax profits are $350,000 and the dividend paid is 25 cents per share.

a. Dividend payout ratio is 71.4%

b. Earnings per share are 35 cents

c. Price/earnings ratio is 14.3

d. All of the above

S5.2 When considering the working capital ratio for a company with inventory, the acid test ratio will

a. Always be better

b. Always be worse

c. Always be the same

d. May be better or worse

S5.3 If ROCE declines from 12% to 10% from one year to the next and shareholders' equity has remained constant, it is most likely because

a. PBIT is higher and/or long-term debt is lower

b. PBIT is lower and/or long-term debt is lower

c. PBIT is lower and/or long-term debt is higher

d. PBIT is higher and/or long-term debt is higher

S5.4 Sales have increased since the previous year and the gross-profit-to-sales ratio has increased but the operating-profit-to-sales ratio has fallen. This is most likely because

a. Expenses have increased

b. Taxes are higher

c. Selling price is lower

d. Cost of sales has not been effectively controlled

S5.5 Risk is highest when

a. Degree of operating leverage is lower and interest cover ratio is lower.

b. Degree of operating leverage is higher and the interest cover ratio is higher.

c. Degree of operating leverage is lower and interest cover ratio is higher.

d. Degree of operating leverage is higher and the interest cover ratio is lower.

S5.6 The asset turnover ratio represents

a. How long assets are kept before they are sold

b. The efficiency of use of assets to generate sales

c. New capital expenditure

d. The period over which assets are depreciated

S5.7 Brigand Ltd. has 2 million shares issued with a market price of $2.50 each. The company wants to pay a dividend of 60% of its after-tax profits of $1,750,000. The dividend yield would be

a. 60%

b. 52.5%

c. 25%

d. 21%

S5.8 Brulé Ltee's statement of comprehensive income shows the following:

	2012	2011
Sales	$1,250,000	$1,175,000
Cost of sales	787,000	715,000
Selling & admin. expenses	324,000	323,000

Based on these figures, which one of the following statements is true?

a. Sales, cost of sales, and selling and administration expenses have all increased, therefore operating profit, gross margin, and operating margin have all increased.

b. Although the operating profit has decreased, the operating margin has increased as a result of sales growth and an increase in gross profit.

c. The operating profit has decreased due to lower gross margins and higher expenses, despite sales growth.

d. Although the operating profit has increased, the operating margin has decreased as a result of a reduction in the gross margin and higher expenses, despite sales growth.

S5.9 The term *triple bottom line* refers to disclosing which information?

a. Financial, economic, and social

b. Assets, liabilities, and shareholders' equity

c. Names of owners, directors, and employees

d. Revenues, expenses, and profits

S5.10 Sustainability reporting refers to a company reporting on

a. Its ability to continue making profits in the future

b. Its ability to obtain financing for future development

c. The social and environmental impact of its operations

d. The value it created for its shareholders

S5.11 Compared to the previous year, a company's profits increased while its share price decreased. The company paid more dividends than the previous year. The number of shares issued remained unchanged. Which one of the following statements is true?

a. Dividends per share decreased

b. P/E ratio increased

c. EPS decreased

d. Dividend yield increased

S5.12 Generally speaking, a company would strive for which of the following?

a. Increase in rates of profit on shareholders' equity, capital employed, and sales

b. Increase in dividend EPS and P/E

c. Increase in return on assets, inventory turnover, and accounts receivable turnover

d. All of the above

■ PROBLEMS

P5.1 *(Calculation of Ratios)* The financial statements of Voyager Productions Ltd. are shown below:

Voyager Productions Ltd.
Statement of Comprehensive Income for the Year Ended December 31 (in $millions)

	2012	2011
Turnover	$141.1	$138.4
Cost of sales	−58.9	−54.9
Gross profit	82.2	83.5
Selling & administrative costs	−55.0	−54.0
Operating profit	27.2	29.5
Interest payable	−6.1	−7.5
Profit before taxes	21.1	22.0
Tax on profit	−7.3	−5.7
Profit after taxes	13.8	16.3
Dividends	−8.0	−8.0
Retained profit	$5.8	$8.3

Voyager Productions Ltd.
Statement of Financial Position as at December 31 (in $millions)

	2012	2011
Non-current assets		
Tangible assets	$266.7	$265.3
Current assets		
Inventory	5.3	5.8
Accounts receivable	15.7	20.9
Other receivables & prepayments	2.4	2.0
Bank	4.9	6.3
	28.3	35.0
Total Assets	295.0	300.3

(continued)

Voyager Productions Ltd.
Statement of Financial Position as at December 31 (in $millions) *(continued)*

Non-current liabilities		
Long-term loans	96.7	146.1
Current liabilities		
Accounts payable	66.8	27.6
Total Liabilities	163.5	173.7
Net Assets	$131.5	$126.6
Equity		
Share capital	81.9	82.8
Retained earnings	49.6	43.8
Shareholders' Funds	$131.5	$126.6

Calculate the following ratios:

a. Return on investment (ROI)

b. Return on capital employed (ROCE)

c. Operating margin

d. Gross margin

e. Sales growth

f. Working capital to sales

g. Degree of operating leverage

h. Asset turnover

P5.2 *(Interpretation of Ratios)* Jupiter Services has produced some financial ratios for the past two years. Use the ratios that have already been calculated to draw some conclusions about Jupiter's

a. Profitability

b. Liquidity

c. Leveraging

d. Efficiency

Jupiter Services: Ratios

	Current Year	Previous Year
Return on (shareholders') investment (ROI)		
$\dfrac{\text{Net profit after taxes}}{\text{Shareholders' equity}}$	$\dfrac{193.4}{2,610.1} = 7.4\%$	$\dfrac{251.9}{2,547.0} = 9.9\%$
Return on capital employed (ROCE)		
$\dfrac{\text{Net profit before interest and taxes}}{\text{Shareholders' equity + Long-term debt}}$	$\dfrac{367.3}{2,610.1 + 1,770} = 8.4\%$	$\dfrac{394.7}{2,547 + 1,537.7} = 9.7\%$

(continued)

Jupiter Services: Ratios (*continued*)

Net profit/sales

$$\frac{\text{Net profit before interest and taxes}}{\text{Sales}} \qquad \frac{367.3}{1,681.6} = 21.8\% \qquad \frac{394.7}{1,566.6} = 25.2\%$$

Working capital

$$\frac{\text{Current assets}}{\text{Current liabilities}} \qquad \frac{613.3}{1,444} = 42.5\% \qquad \frac{475.3}{1,089.2} = 43.6\%$$

Degree of operating leverage

$$\frac{\text{Long-term debt}}{\text{Shareholders' equity + Long-term debt}} \quad \frac{1,770}{2,610.1 + 1,770} = 40.4\% \quad \frac{1,537.7}{2,547 + 1,537.7} = 37.6\%$$

	Current Year	**Previous Year**

Interest cover

$$\frac{\text{Profit before interest and taxes}}{\text{Interest payable}} \qquad \frac{367.3}{161.1} = 2.28 \qquad \frac{394.7}{120.7} = 3.27$$

Accounts receivable collections

$$\frac{\text{Accounts receivable}}{\text{Average daily sales}} \qquad \frac{414.7}{1,681.6/365 = 4.607} = 90 \qquad \frac{353.8}{1,566.6/365 = 4.292} = 82.4$$

Asset turnover

$$\frac{\text{Sales}}{\text{Total assets}} \qquad \frac{1,681.6}{5,304.5 + 613.3} = 28.4\% \qquad \frac{1,566.6}{4,794.6 + 475.3} = 29.7\%$$

P5.3 *(Calculation of Ratios)* Jones and Calenti Retail Stationery sells its products to other businesses. It has provided the following information:

Sales	$1,200,000
Cost of sales	450,000
Inventory at end of year	200,000
Accounts receivable at end of year	200,000
Accounts payable at end of year	100,000

Using 250 days as the number of days the business is open, calculate

a. Days' sales outstanding

b. Inventory turnover

c. Days' purchases outstanding

P5.4 *(Sales Growth)* The five-year financial statements of Raj Inc. show the following sales figures:

	2012	**2011**	**2010**	**2009**	**2008**
Sales (in $millions)	$155	$144	$132	$130	$120

Calculate the sales growth figures for each year.

P5.5 *(Overhead-to-Sales Ratio)*

Raj Inc. Statement of Comprehensive Income, 2012 (in $millions)

Sales	$155
Cost of sales	45
Gross profit	110
Selling, administration expenses	65
Operating profit before interest and taxes	45
Interest	10
Profit before taxes	35
Taxes	7
Profit after taxes	$28

Calculate the overhead-to-sales ratio.

P5.6 *(Interpretation of Financial Statements and Ratios)* Equinox Services Inc. provides a range of business consultancy services. Its financial statements for the last two years are given in Exhibit 5.15.

Exhibit 5.15 Equinox Services Inc. Statement of Comprehensive Income (in $thousands)

	2012	2011
Income	$34,000	$29,000
Less expenses	16,500	13,000
Operating profit before interest	17,500	16,000
Less interest expense	4,000	2,700
Profit before taxes	13,500	13,300
Tax expense	5,400	5,320
Net profit after taxes	8,100	7,980
Less dividends paid	4,000	3,750
Retained profits	$4,100	$4,230
Number of shares issued	10,000,000	10,000,000
Earnings per share	$0.81	$0.80
Dividend per share	0.40	0.38
Market price of shares	8.55	10.20

Equinox Services Inc. Statement of Financial Position (in $thousands)

Non-current assets		
Property, plant, & equipment	$21,933	$17,990
Current assets		
Accounts receivable	7,080	4,750
Bank	377	1,250

(continued)

Exhibit 5.15 Equinox Services Inc. Statement of Financial Position (in $thousands) (continued)

	7,457	6,000
Total assets	$29,390	$23,990
Non-current liabilities		
Long-term loans	2,750	2,000
Current liabilities		
Accounts payable	4,300	3,750
Total liabilities	7,050	5,750
Shareholders' equity		
Share capital	10,000	10,000
Retained earnings	12,340	8,240
	22,340	18,240
Total liabilities and shareholders' equity	$29,390	$23,990

An analyst has produced the following ratio analysis (Exhibit 5.16) and has asked you to comment on any aspects that you think are important.

Exhibit 5.16 Equinox Services Inc. Ratio Analysis

	2012	2011
Sales growth	17.2%	
Expense growth	26.9%	
Profit growth	9.4%	
Interest cover	4.4	5.9
PBIT/sales	39.7%	45.9%
ROCE	53.8%	65.7%
ROI	36.3%	43.8%
Dividend payout	49.4%	47.0%
Dividend yield	4.7%	3.7%
P/E ratio	10.56	12.78
Asset efficiency	1.2	1.2
Days' sales outstanding	76.0	59.8
Working capital	1.7	1.6
Degree of operating leverage	11.0%	9.9%

P5.7 *(Analysis of Revenues and Expenses)* Cosy Homes Inc.'s Statement of Comprehensive Income shows the following:

	2012	2011
Sales	$1,250,000	$1,175,000
Cost of sales	787,000	715,000
Selling & admin. expenses	324,000	323,000

Based on these figures, which one of the following statements is true?

a. Sales, cost of sales, and selling and administration expenses have all increased, therefore operating profit, gross margin, and operating margin have all increased.

b. Although the operating profit has decreased, the operating margin has increased as a result of sales growth and an increase in gross profit.

c. The operating profit has decreased due to lower gross margins and higher expenses, despite sales growth.

d. Although the operating profit has increased, the operating margin has decreased as a result of a reduction in the gross margin and higher expenses, despite sales growth.

The following information relates to problems 5.8 and 5.9

Acorn Services Inc. has produced the following information:

Acorn Services Inc.
Statement of Comprehensive Income for the Year Ended March 31 (in $thousands)

	2012	2011
Revenue	$227,138	$227,778
Operating profit	54,094	38,507
Profit on ordinary activities before taxation	54,616	38,205

Acorn Services Inc.
Statement of Financial Position for the Year Ended March 31 (in $thousands)

	2012	2011
Non-current assets		
Property, plant and equipment	$88,720	$77,934
Current assets		
Accounts receivable	134,860	107,612
Cash at bank	90	4,205
	134,950	111,817
Total assets	223,670	189,751
Non-current liabilities		
Long-term loans	2,088	12,264
Current liabilities		
Accounts payable	127,799	94,301
Total liabilities	129,887	106,565
Net assets	93,783	83,186
Shareholders' equity	$93,783	$83,186

P5.8 *(Return on Capital Employed)* Using the above information for Acorn Services Inc., the return on capital employed

a. Has improved from 40.3% to 56.4%

b. Has worsened from 56.4% to 40.3%

c. Has improved from 46.3% to 57.6%

d. Has worsened from 57.6% to 40.3%

P5.9 *(Liquidity and Leveraging Ratios)* In reviewing liquidity and leveraging ratios for Acorn Services Inc., we can say that

a. Long-term debt has increased as a proportion of total capital employed, and liquidity has improved due to the decrease in current liabilities.

b. Long-term debt has decreased as a proportion of total capital employed, and liquidity has declined due to the increase in current liabilities.

c. Long-term debt has increased as a proportion of total capital employed, and liquidity has worsened due to the increase in current liabilities.

d. Long-term debt has decreased as a proportion of total capital employed, and liquidity has improved due to the decrease in current liabilities.

P5.10 *(Calculation of Ratios)* Fortune Stationers is open 250 days each year and last year achieved sales of $9 million with a gross profit of 60% of sales. At the end of the year, Fortune's statement of financial position showed

Accounts receivable	$1,200,000
Inventory	450,000
Accounts payable	1,400,000

Calculate (a) the days' sales outstanding, (b) inventory turnover, (c) days' inventory held, and (d) days' purchases outstanding.

P5.11 *(Calculation and Interpretation of Ratios)* Rockford Inc. is a retail chain with 160 stores and 14,000 employees. Its financial statements for 2012 are shown below:

Rockford Inc.
Statement of Comprehensive Income (in $millions)

	2012	2011
Turnover	$1,021.5	$847.4
Cost of sales	−855.3	−710.4
Gross profit	166.2	137.0
Administrative expenses	−47.9	−29.1
Operating profit	118.3	107.9
Net interest payable	−0.9	−0.3
Profit on ordinary activities before taxes	117.4	107.6
Taxes	−30.7	−33.5
Profit on ordinary activities after taxes	86.7	74.1
Dividends	−33.3	−29.3
Profit retained for the period	$53.4	$44.8

Additional information:

Earnings per share	21.3¢	18.4¢
440 million shares were issued at 10¢ each:		
Market value of shares	$1.50	$1.40

Rockford Inc.
Statement of Financial Position (in $millions)

	2012	2011
Non-current assets		
Goodwill	$37.3	$32.3
Property, plant, & equipment	167.6	132.3
Investments	22.5	25.7
	227.4	190.3
Current assets		
Inventory	135.0	105.3
Accounts receivable	22.5	20.8
Cash at bank	16.2	17.8
	173.7	143.9
Total assets	401.1	334.2
Non-current liabilities		
Long-term loans	14.8	13.4
Provision for deferred taxes	9.5	7.6
	24.3	21.0
Current liabilities		
Accounts payable	159.8	149.6
Total liabilities	184.1	170.6
Net assets	$217.0	$163.6
Equity		
Share capital	44.0	44.0
Retained earnings	173.0	119.6
Shareholders' equity	$217.0	$163.6

Calculate sufficient ratios for both 2012 and 2011 to demonstrate the changes in profitability, liquidity, efficiency, leveraging, and shareholder return of Rockford, and comment on the most important changes between 2012 and 2011.

P5.12 *(Interpretation of Ratios)* Ratunga Inc. manufactures and sells office furniture to business customers. It is listed on a stock exchange. A ratio analysis of its statement of comprehensive income and statement of financial position over the last four years has identified the following trends:

	2012	2011	2010	2009
Sales growth	10.0%	8.5%	8.0%	7.0%
Return on investment (ROI)	5.0%	4.8%	4.5%	4.1%
Return on capital employed (ROCE)	4.0%	4.5%	5.0%	5.3%
Operating profit/sales	6.0%	6.3%	6.5%	6.7%

(continued)

(continued)

Gross profit/sales	28.0%	27.0%	26.5%	25.0%
Working capital	104.0%	108.0%	111.0%	112.0%
Acid test (quick ratio)	68.0%	72.0%	73.0%	77.0%
Degree of operating leverage	65.0%	62.0%	60.0%	56.0%
Interest cover	1.7	1.9	2.1	2.3
Asset turnover	108.0%	105.0%	99.0%	94.0%
Days' sales outstanding	61.0	58.0	55.0	57.0
Inventory turnover	15.0	13.0	13.0	12.0
Days' purchases outstanding	72.0	68.0	64.0	61.0
Dividend per share	10c	10c	10c	10c
Dividend payout ratio	65.0%	60.0%	58.0%	58.0%
Dividend yield	4.0%	3.8%	3.5%	3.2%
Price/earnings ratio	9.6	8.5	8.2	7.7

a. Explain how ratio analysis can be used to interpret business performance, with an emphasis on the different types of ratios that can be used.

b. Use the above ratios to explain the strengths and weaknesses of the financial performance of Ratunga Inc. over the last four years.

The following information relates to problems 5.13 through 5.15

Below is some information from the financial records of Cleereen Co.:

Accounts payable	$ 18,000
Accounts receivable	20,000
Bank overdraft	5,500
Inventory	45,000
Property, plant, and equipment	150,000
Sales	236,500

P5.13 *(Working Capital Ratio)* Cleereen's working capital ratio is

a. 0.85

b. 2.77

c. 3.92

d. 9.15

P5.14 *(Acid Ratio)* Cleereen's acid ratio is

a. 0.85

b. 1.42

c. 2.77

d. 3.92

P5.15 *(Asset Turnover)* Cleereen's asset turnover is

a. 90.9%

b. 110.0%

    c. 157.3%

    d. 121.3%

P5.16 *(Debt versus Equity)* Give two reasons why a company might prefer to take on long-term debt rather than issue more shares.

P5.17 *(Debt versus Equity)* Give two reasons why a company might prefer to issue more shares rather than take on long-term debt.

P5.18 *(MD&A)* List the most important issues that should be addressed in the MD&A.

REFERENCES

Canadian Institute of Chartered Accountants. (2009). The Canadian Performance Reporting (CPR) Board, *Management's Discussion and Analysis: Guidance on preparation and disclosure.* Toronto: CICA.

DiMaggio, P. J., and Powell, W. W. (1983). The iron cage revisited: Institutional isomorphism and collective rationality in organizational fields. *American Sociological Review, 48,* 147–160.

Edvinsson, L., and Malone, M. S. (1997). *Intellectual capital.* London: Piatkus.

Gray, R. H., Owen, D. L., and Adams, C. (1996). *Accounting and accountability: Changes and challenges in corporate social and environmental reporting.* London: Prentice Hall.

Guthrie, J. (2001). The management, measurement and the reporting of intellectual capital. *Journal of Intellectual Capital, 2*(1), 27–41.

International Accounting Standards Board. (2010). *IFRS practice statement: Management commentary—A framework for presentation.* London: IASB.

Jones, T. C. (1995). *Accounting and the enterprise: A social analysis.* London: Routledge.

Meyer, J. W. (1994). Social environments and organizational accounting. In W. R. Scott and J. W. Meyer (eds.), *Institutional environments and organizations: Structural complexity and individuality.* Thousand Oaks, CA: Sage.

Scott, W. R. (1995). *Institutions and organizations.* Thousand Oaks, CA: Sage.

Stewart, T. A. (1997). *Intellectual capital: The new wealth of organizations.* London: Nicholas Brealey Publishing.

Zadek, S. (1998). Balancing performance, ethics, and accountability. *Journal of Business Ethics, 17*(13), 1421–1441.

PART II

Using Accounting Information for Decision Making, Planning, and Control

Part I was concerned with the rules of financial reporting and interpreting financial reports. Financial reporting tends to have an external focus, such as providing scorekeeping or attention-directing information to stakeholders. Part II shows the reader how accounting information is used by managers within a company. While an analysis of financial reports is useful, particularly for external interested parties (shareholders, bankers, and the government), the information is of limited use to the internal management of the business for the following reasons:

- It is aggregated to the corporate level, whereas managers require information at the business-unit level.

- It is aggregated to annual figures, whereas managers require timely information, usually at not less than monthly intervals.

- It is aggregated to headline figures, whereas managers require information in much greater detail.

- It does not provide a comparison of plan to actual figures to provide a gauge on progress towards achieving business goals.

Consequently, the chapters in Part II are concerned with management accounting: the production of accounting information for use by managers. This information is disaggregated (to business-unit level), more regular (typically, monthly), and is more detailed for management decision making, planning, and control. In addition, it is not regulated by accounting standards. This means that an organization's method of management accounting can be developed to meet its particular needs, which may be different than other companies, even in the same industry.

Chapter **6** explores management control and how management accounting information is utilized to maintain control in companies. Non-financial performance measurement, and the balanced scorecard method in particular, is discussed.

Chapter **7** is concerned with accounting for inventory, which is a crucial link between financial accounting and management accounting.

Chapters **8, 9,** and **10** consider the accounting techniques that are of value in marketing, operations, and human resource decisions, respectively.

Chapter **11** explores some key terms used in the practice of management accounting and evaluates methods for allocating the overheads within companies.

Chapter **12** focuses on strategic decisions, such as capital investment decisions, and

Chapter **13** on divisional performance measurement.

Chapter **14** covers the subject of budgeting, and

Chapter **15** discusses budgetary control.

Chapter **16** introduces the reader to more recent developments through the topic of strategic management accounting.

CHAPTER 6

Management Control

LEARNING OBJECTIVES

After reading this chapter, you should be able to answer the following questions:

- How does management control fit into the strategic planning process?

- What are the key aspects of a management control system?

- What is the difference between a feedforward and a feedback control system?

- Why are non-financial measures of performance important in a control system?

- What is a balanced scorecard (BSC) and what types of measures are included in the four perspectives of the BSC?

- How can an organization extend the concept of management control to include process improvements?

Management accounting needs to be understood as part of the broader context of management control systems. In this chapter, we describe the theoretical background of management control and management accounting and the most recent developments: non-financial performance measurement and developments: non-financial performance measurement and the balanced scorecard.

Management Control and Strategic Planning

Anthony (1965) defined management control as

> . . . the process by which managers assure that resources are obtained and used effectively and efficiently in the accomplishment of the organization's objectives.

Today, **management control** is considered as part of the broader process of the strategic planning process, and it involves measuring financial and non-financial performances to ensure that both of these types of performances meet expectations. Exhibit 6.1 illustrates the process of strategic planning within an organization and how management control fits into this overall process. The evaluation and control process is tightly tied to the strategic planning process. Feedback from the control process will impact strategy formulation and the overall objectives of a company.

Exhibit 6.1 The Strategic Planning Process

Mission Statement Development. In this step, the company defines its broad vision. For example, according to the Tim Hortons website, the company's mission is to

> . . . deliver superior quality products and services for our guests and communities through leadership, innovation and partnerships. Our vision is to be the quality leader in everything we do.

This statement suggests that the control system at Tim Hortons relates strongly to quality control and innovation.

Internal and External Review. In this step, the organization looks at both the internal and external environments in which it operates in order to determine where the company's strategic advantages might be best utilized. In terms of analyzing the internal environment, the company might prepare a value chain analysis in which it would look at the activities that are performed within the company in delivering a product/service to its customers to identify strengths and weaknesses in the value chain. (Value chain analysis is discussed further in Chapter 9.) This step might also include an external assessment of the industry, in which the company would look at social, technological, economic, environmental, and political factors that might impact the industry. This helps a company identify opportunities and threats that may impact its overall strategies.

Strategy Development. In this process, an organization clearly defines its strategy based on its overall mission and the internal and external environments in which it operates. Strategy development is also impacted by the management control process. For example, if a company's particular product line is underperforming, the company might need to adjust its strategies.

Implementation of Strategy. Implementing a strategy is the company putting its plans into action. The specific plans and objectives are implemented by the divisions and employees of the company to help achieve the overall strategy.

Management Control. This involves the development of a management control system that can be used to ensure that the specific objectives of the organization are being achieved. This may impact all other steps in the strategic planning process. Tools for management control will be discussed throughout this and subsequent chapters.

Management Control Systems

Management control systems have been described in terms of strategic plans, long-range plans, annual operating budgets, periodic statistical reports, performance appraisals, and policies and procedures (Daft & Macintosh, 1984); in terms of personnel, action, and results controls (Merchant, 1998); and in terms of objectives, strategies, plans, target-setting incentive and reward structures, and information feedback loops (Otley, 1999).

In this chapter, we are concerned with management control as a system (a collection of interrelated mechanisms) of rules. Management control is made up of both planning and control systems. Planning systems are concerned with feedforward control, which ensures that the inputs into a process meet predesigned standards and helps to ensure that errors in the process do not occur. For instance, quality control standards are a form of feedforward control that from the outset help prevent substandard products from being produced. Exhibit 6.2 illustrates feedforward control systems that might be in place in a company's product design and manufacturing processes.

Exhibit 6.2 Examples of Feedback and Feedforward Controls

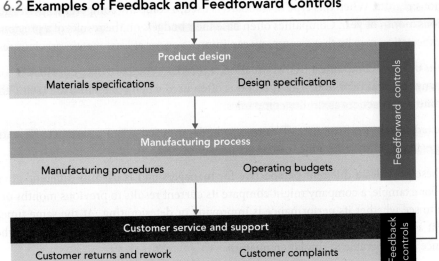

Control systems, on the other hand, are concerned with **feedback (diagnostic) control**, where an error is identified with a process and corrections are made to reduce the occurrence of this error. As shown in Exhibit 6.2, customer returns and complaints are examples of feedback control. When a product does not meet customer expectations, they will return the product and it may need to be reworked (repaired to its original specifications) or replaced, which might indicate to the company that there is a problem with product specifications or quality management.

Feedforward is the process of determining whether strategies are likely to achieve target results that are consistent with organizational goals. Feedforward controls include established policies and procedures, budgets, and operational plans. **Feedback** is the retrospective process of measuring performance, comparing it with the plan, and taking corrective action. The two systems need to be integrated as a management control system since they share common targets—the need for corrective action to be reflected either in goal adjustment, changed behaviour, and/or the allocation or utilization of resources.

We can consider the management planning and control systems as a single system in which both feedback and feedforward are concerned with reducing the performance gap. Downs (1966) defined the performance gap as "the difference in utility [that an individual] perceives between the actual and the satisfactory level of performance" (p. 169). According to Downs, the larger the gap, the greater the motivation to undertake actions to increase controls.

According to Anthony and Govindarajan (2000), every control system has at least four elements:

1. A detector or sensor that measures what is happening

2. An assessor that determines the significance of what is happening by comparing it with a standard or expectation

3. An effector (feedback) that alters behaviour if the assessor indicates the need to do so

4. A communication network that transmits information between the other elements

For example, Ely Enterprises makes jams and jellies used by commercial food manufacturers. Ely makes 3,000 kg of jams and jellies on a given day. To be acceptable, a container of jam or jelly leaving Ely's factory must contain between 998 and 1,002 grams of product. A scale is used to weigh each product that is produced by the factory. Any products that are over or under this standard are taken off the production line and disposed of.

There are three types of standards against which performance can be compared:

1. **Previous results:** When this type of standard is used, a company compares its performance to a previous month or year. Companies often base their budgets on the results of a previous period. The expectation may be that a company can improve on, or at least match, previous results.

2. **Results of other companies:** In this situation, a company compares its performance to that of a company that is similar to it. This method is often used when companies are trying to achieve the same best practices as similar companies.

3. **Expected future performance:** Future standards are used when a company is anticipating changes in its performance due to changes in its processes.

Each of these provides a different perspective for managers and is used in different situations or contexts. For example, a company might compare its current results to previous months or years of operation to see whether its performance is improving or deteriorating. At the same time, a company might also compare its results to other companies in its industry to understand whether its performance is comparable to similar companies.

Measurement of Non-Financial Factors and Intangible Assets

When measuring performance, it is important that companies use a combination of financial and non-financial measures. The limitations of financial measures were identified most clearly by Johnson and Kaplan (1987), who argued that most companies focused excessively on short-term financial performance. A focus on purely financial measurements may result in decisions that can lower the long-term profitability of a company.

Canada Post, for instance, tracks many non-financial indicators as well as financial indicators in its performance evaluation process. The key performance indicators that are tracked by Canada Post are customer value, delivery service, and employee engagement, all critical aspects of providing strong service and achieving customer value (Canada Post, 2011). Johnson and Kaplan (1987) suggest that by focusing only on financial measures, a company may be encouraged to eliminate costs such as those associated with research and development, promotion, customer relations, and quality improvement in order to boost short-term profitability. Elimination of these costs may improve short-term performance, but in the long run will have a detrimental effect on the company.

Johnson and Kaplan (1987) further emphasized the importance of non-financial indicators, stating

> Short-term financial measures will have to be replaced by a variety of non-financial indicators that provide better targets and predictors for the firm's long-term profitability goals, signifying this as a return to the operations-based measures that were the origin of management accounting systems. (p. 259)

This focus on non-financial measures also emphasizes the importance of intangible assets within a company. Intangible assets are those assets that cannot be measured financially; that is, they are difficult to assign a value to. In a company's financial accounting system, intangible assets (other than goodwill and research and development—see Chapter 4) are not reported as assets of the organization. These assets include things such as employee knowledge and skills, company reputation, commitment to skill development and training, talent at innovating, dedication to quality, employee dedication, and customer loyalty. Companies recognize that these intangibles, more so than financial indicators, provide a better indication of long-term profitability and success, but in the past it has been difficult to value these assets or to assess them in a company's management control system.

Kaplan and Norton (2007) suggest that during the early 20th century, competitive advantage was achieved through effective management of tangible assets such as property, plant, and equipment. However, this changed once we entered the 21st century. Today, intangible assets have become a key resource and source of competitive advantage for most organizations. At the extreme end of this spectrum, there are companies that are based mainly on an intangible asset base, such as information. For example, consider Google and its strengths in programming, information collection and management, and innovation—all intangible assets. In today's business environment, companies are not made entirely of physical assets but rather are rich in information, people, and knowledge.

To support the belief that intangible assets are important to company value, Kaplan and Norton (2007) compiled the book values and the market values of industrial companies in 1982 and compared these values to the book values and market values at the end of the 20th century. Surprisingly, they found a large drop in the book value percentage of total market value. In 1982, the book values equalled 62% of the market values, but by 1999 this had dropped to less than 20% of companies' market values. The difference in values, Kaplan and Norton suggest, is due to the value of intangible

CASE IN POINT

Measuring Google's Intangible Assets

How much does Google Inc. own? In its 2010 fiscal year, the Internet technology giant had more than (US)$57.8 billion in assets. Of that, the company reported nearly $35 billion in cash and cash equivalents, along with investments in marketable securities—all of which are relatively easy to measure.

But among its assets, Google reported only $1 billion in intangible assets, even though intangible assets are largely what technology companies are made of. That's because intangible assets are difficult to measure financially.

While Google did not specify in its 2010 annual report what those intangible assets consist of, it is certainly brimming with such assets, including intellectual property such as technology patents, trademarks, domain names, and copyrights, along with business processes. These intangibles include assets that Google has developed itself, such as the Android mobile operating system, and those it purchased from competitors that it acquired, such as the YouTube video site.

Perhaps an even more valuable intangible asset is the knowledge and expertise of Google's founders, Larry Page and Sergey Brin, along with executive chairman Eric Schmidt and other skilled personnel. "If we were to lose the services of Larry, Sergey, Eric, or other members of our senior management team, we may not be able to execute our business strategy," the company identifies as a key risk in its 2010 annual report. "We rely on highly skilled personnel and, if we are unable to retain or motivate key personnel, hire qualified personnel, or maintain our corporate culture, we may not be able to grow effectively."

Sources: Google Inc. *Annual Report 2010*; Caruso, D., The real value of intangibles. *strategy+business*, *52*, Autumn 2008.

assets that are not reported on the financial statements of a company but are reflected in the market value of the company. This supports the idea that the value of a company is no longer determined by its physical assets. Rather, intangible assets need to be considered as a critical part of strategic advantage and success in today's company.

Although managers will continue to ask questions about profitability, the increasing importance of intangible assets means that other questions are also important, such as

- How innovative and creative are we?

- Are our employees empowered?

- Do we have a skilful workforce?

- Do we have a good reputation in our marketplace?

- Have we improved our quality?

Management accounting is therefore becoming more concerned with intangibles and non-financial performance measures, and various tools have been developed that consider this change in focus. For example, the balanced scorecard creates a platform where the importance of intangible assets becomes visible and measurable.

BALANCED SCORECARD

The development of the balanced scorecard (Kaplan and Norton, 1992, 1993, 1996, 2001) has received extensive coverage in the business press. It presents four different perspectives and complements traditional financial indicators with measures of performance for customers, internal processes, and innovation/improvement. These measures are grounded in an organization's strategic objectives and competitive demands. The balanced scorecard is shown in Exhibit 6.3.

Exhibit 6.3 **Translating Vision and Strategy: Four Perspectives**

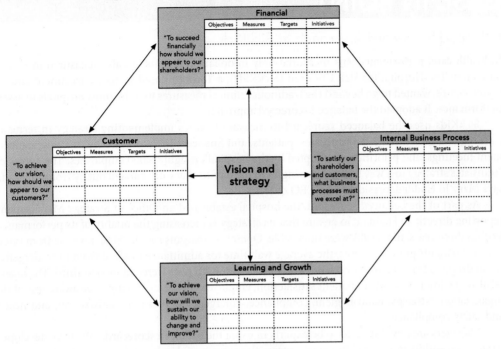

Source: Reprinted by permission of *Harvard Business Review*. From "Using the balanced scorecard as a strategic management system" by R. S. Kaplan and D. P. Norton, January–February 1996. Copyright 1996, Harvard Business School Publishing Corporation; all rights reserved.

The balanced scorecard (BSC) provides the ability to link a company's long-term strategy with its short-term actions. Essentially, every measure on the BSC should collectively help the organization achieve its long-term strategies.

As shown in Exhibit 6.3, there are four perspectives of the BSC:

- The financial perspective represents the financial measures that an organization identifies as important to monitor in achievement of their strategy. This may include sales targets, cost-reduction targets, and other financial measures that help indicate achievement of strategy.

- The customer perspective is focused on the customer. Most organizations recognize the importance of the customer and their perception the company and products. This perspective often includes measurement of customer satisfaction and the tracking of change in market share and of customer complaints.

- The internal business process perspective focuses on the internal operations of the company. It involves looking at the activities performed by a firm and determining specific measures which will help to ensure that the company is delivering customer value and long-term profitability. Measures in this perspective may relate to quality management, operational efficiency, and creating competitive advantage.

- The learning and growth perspective focuses on the intangible resources within a company, such as employee knowledge, information management, and a culture of innovation. Measurements in this perspective may relate to employee training, employee satisfaction, and investment in technology.

CASE IN POINT

Balanced Scorecard Approach at SickKids

In health care, performance isn't measured only in dollars and cents, it's also measured in patient outcomes. The Hospital for Sick Children (SickKids), a Toronto-based pediatric treatment and research centre, wanted to go beyond the traditional clinical measures used by most hospitals to assess performance. It adopted the balanced scorecard approach.

SickKids uses the balanced scorecard to measure how it's implementing strategy in terms of learning and growth, internal processes, patients, and finances. The scorecard helps guide management meetings, and priorities are adopted by the hospital's roughly 8,000 employees. The approach "translates strategy in a way that is meaningful to the day-to-day work carried out by frontline staff," says Mary Jo Haddad, president and CEO of SickKids.

As part of the balanced scorecard, the hospital established an Office of Strategy Management, reporting directly to Haddad, to ensure that its strategy is increasing the quality of its performance. Within three years, the results were noticeable. Operating margins rose by 80%, revenue from international patients grew five times, the average wait time for admittance to a bed from the emergency room dropped from 9.6 to 6.1 hours, and wait times for MRI tests were cut by one-third. The hospital also saw improvements in patient satisfaction, employee engagement, employee awareness of the organization's strategy, hand-hygiene compliance, emergency department satisfaction, and health and safety compliance.

Managers are now expected to be experts in using the balanced scorecard. "We have developed strategy execution as a core competency across the enterprise that has helped us achieve an execution premium," says Haddad.

Sources: Palladium Group, *Palladium Balanced Scorecard Hall of Fame for Executing Strategy inducts eight performance leaders at the 2010 Palladium Americas Summit in La Jolla, California*, news release, November 10, 2010; The Hospital for Sick Children, *SickKids named performance leader*, news release, November 10, 2010; Smith, A., Mainland, J., & Blais, I., Managing strategy to enhance care for children, *Healthcare Quarterly*, *14*, Special Issue, October 2011, pp. 21–26.

Management Control versus Organizational Improvement

To compete in today's global economy, manufacturers have had to move toward higher-quality products, shorter cycle times, smaller batch sizes, greater variety in product mix, and cost reductions. The development of new manufacturing philosophies such as computer integrated manufacturing (CIM), flexible manufacturing systems (FMS), just-in-time (JIT), optimized production technology (OPT), and total quality management (TQM) has shifted the balance from financial to non-financial performance measurement. However, Sinclair and Zairi (1995b) argued that performance measurement has been dominated by management control systems that are focused on control rather than improvement. They saw management accounting and financial performance as a limiting constraint rather than as a tool for managing continuous improvement.

Brignall and Ballantine (1996) described the concept and history of **multidimensional performance measurement** (PM):

> PM systems are part of an attempt to give management accounting a more strategic, outward-looking focus, incorporating non-financial, competitor-centred and customer-focused information into the search for a sustainable competitive advantage in services. (p. 27)

Otley (1999) concluded that performance *management* (which he contrasted with performance *measurement*) goes beyond the boundaries of traditional management accounting. It could be achieved by accountants having a better understanding of the operational activities of the business and building this understanding into control systems design, connecting control systems with business strategy, and focusing on the external environment within which the business operates.

One avenue that may address the need for a more holistic approach to performance management is provided by enterprise resource planning (ERP) (see Chapter 3). ERP is an information system that supports the strategic management process, and aims to overcome the difficulties of integrating information from diverse systems. It is based on the concept of a data warehouse holding large amounts of data that can be accessed by a range of analytical tools, such as balanced scorecard-type measures, benchmarking, or shareholder value measures. The end result is argued to be faster and to improve managerial decision making throughout the organization, using information captured from both inside and outside the organization. The weakness of the ERP approach is its cost, as it is a systems-based solution that requires integration of data typically held in many systems, often in different formats with overlapping and ambiguous connections.

Conclusion

In this chapter, we have identified management accounting as part of a broader management control system that is driven by goals and strategy. We have also expanded the notion of management control to incorporate non-financial performance measurement.

Management accounting should be understood in this broader context of management control. Emmanuel, Otley, and Merchant (1990) believed that management accounting is important because it represents "one of the few integrative mechanisms capable of summarizing the effect of an organization's actions in quantitative terms" (p. 4). Because management information can be expressed in monetary terms, it can be aggregated across time and diverse organizational units and provides a means of integrating activities.

In this chapter, we have discussed the importance of management control in an organization and how it fits within the strategic planning process. We reviewed the different types of controls, including feedback and feedforward systems, and emphasized the importance of non-financial control and management of intangible assets. Management control should be seen not only as a way to monitor a company's resources but also as a way to encourage improvement to the overall business processes.

KEY TERMS

Balanced scorecard, 136

Customer perspective, 137

Enterprise resource planning (ERP), 139

Environmental scanning, 132

Evaluation and control, 133

Feedback, 134

Feedback (diagnostic) control, 134

Feedforward, 134

Feedforward control, 133

Financial perspective, 137

Intangible assets, 135

Internal business process perspective, 137

Learning and growth perspective, 137

Management control, 132

Management control systems, 133

Mission statement and objectives, 132

Multidimensional performance
 measurement, 138

Strategy formulation, 133

Strategy implementation, 133

CASE STUDY 6.1: BALANCED SCORECARD AT CRANFELD OFFICE EQUIPMENT

Consider Cranfeld Office Equipment, manufacturer of four different office chairs: Models A1, A2, B1, and D1. The A1, A2, and B1 models are standard office chairs, designed to provide comfort and style at a relatively low price. The D1 is a more expensive model that was developed only after extensive office ergonomic research.

The D1 model was developed after Don Alpert, the marketing manager, conducted a customer survey that indicated customers were asking for a better-quality chair due to posture-related problems, like back pain. He felt that there was a substantial market for this better-quality product. In the same survey, customers also reported that they were not happy with the quality of the A1, A2, and B1 chair models. Problems with loose parts, poor workmanship, and faulty materials were reported.

In the past, Cranfeld has sourced materials and parts from the most cost-effective suppliers. The company has also worked to speed up production efficiency and has increased its overall assembly-line efficiency. However, the survey strongly indicated that the company needed to improve the quality of its products if it wanted to retain its current customers, get new customers, and vastly improve its company image.

Overall, Cranfeld has been experiencing declining profits due to increased international competition, with Cranfeld's competitors offering better-quality products. Its competitors are also better at managing costs, so Don and company president Sally Lee feel that they must also focus on cost control.

During 2012, Cranfeld established the following company goals and objectives:

Cost Control
- Develop stronger relationships with suppliers and implement just-in-time ordering where possible.
- Maintain a profit margin of 25% on all sales.
- Achieve a 5% cost reduction on manufactured products through just-in-time inventory management.

Sales
- Sell $100,000 worth of D1 chairs in 2013.
- Increase sales of A1, A2, and B1 chairs by 15% in 2013 over 2012.

Quality
- Buy better-quality products from suppliers.
- Lower warranty and repair costs by 50% in 2013.
- Reduce quality costs by 40% from 2012.
- Improve the quality of A1, A2, and B1 chairs.
- Improve customers' perception of the quality of the company's product.

Other
- Implement training programs for all employees to increase product quality and customer service focus.
- Increase employee satisfaction and retention.
- Explore customer requirements more closely and identify new products or desirable modifications of existing lines.
- Develop a good reputation over the long term as a manufacturer of quality office chairs.

Develop a BSC for Cranfeld that will help the company achieve its plans for 2013.

Solution
A BSC has been set up for Cranfeld Office Equipment that is aimed at improving sales, quality, customer focus, and employee satisfaction. The BSC shown on page 141 identifies measures that will help Cranfeld to achieve these goals.

Cranfeld Office Equipment Balanced Scorecard

Perspective	Objective	Metrics
Financial	Maintain profit margin of 25% on sales	✓ Profit margin percentage
	Sell $100,000 worth of D1 chairs	✓ Total sales of D1 x sales price
	Increase sales of A1, A2, and B1 by 15%	✓ (2013 Sales – 2012 Sales) / 2012 Sales
	Reduce quality costs	✓ Rework costs per hour ✓ Value of scrapped units ✓ Inspection costs as a percentage of total costs
	Lower warranty and repair costs	✓ Warranty costs per hour
Customer	Increase market awareness of quality	✓ Customer survey related to quality
	Increase sales	✓ (2013 Sales – 2012 Sales) / 2012 Sales ✓ Change in number of customers
	Customer satisfaction	✓ # of customer complaints as a percentage of total customer sales ✓ % customer satisfaction rating
	Customer focus	✓ # of customer focus initiatives (i.e., research projects, customer surveys)
Internal business process	Reduce quality costs	✓ % of defective units shipped ✓ % scrap ✓ Number of units reworked ✓ Hours of preventative equipment maintenance
	Increase focus on quality	✓ # of quality initiatives implemented ✓ % of suppliers ranked as high quality
	Implement just-in-time inventory management	✓ # of suppliers providing JIT delivery ✓ # of materials utilizing JIT processes
	Increase customer focus	✓ # of product design changes made due to customer requirements
Learning and growth	Increase focus on quality	✓ # of employees taking quality control training
	Increase in innovation	✓ # of employees taking customer service training
	Employee satisfaction and retention	✓ Employee satisfaction rating ✓ # of employee initiatives received by management ✓ # of employee initiatives implemented

The Perspective column also contains a strategy map diagram with the following linked ovals:

- Financial: Increase profits ← Increase revenues, Lower costs
- Customer: More customers ← Improve preception of quality, Best prices
- Internal business process: Improve quality, Improve production processes ← Increase focus on quality and customers
- Learning and growth: Increase employee satisfaction, Increase employee knowledge

■ SELF-TEST QUESTIONS

S6.1 Management control encompasses which of the following activities?

a. Creating goals, strategies, and policies for an organization

b. Implementing strategies

c. Managing the performance of individual tasks within an organization

d. Using resources effectively and efficiently in the accomplishment of the organization's objectives

e. All of the above

S6.2 _____ is used by an organization to assess the internal and external environments.

a. Environmental scanning

b. Environmental management

c. Evaluation and control

d. Internal and external assessments

S6.3 Which of the following items would NOT be part of a management control system?

a. Budgets

b. Plans and objectives

c. Policies and procedures

d. Incentives and reward structures

e. Published financial statements

S6.4 Which of the following is an example of a feedback system?

a. A flashing engine warning symbol on the dashboard of a car

b. An employee manual outlining the steps to assemble an electronic toy

c. Standard recipes used by a restaurant

d. An employee training program

S6.5 Feedforward control systems can be characterized by

a. Predesigned standards

b. A process where errors are identified and actions are taken to correct the errors

c. Involvement of management in employees' decisions

d. Changing policies and procedures as a response to changes in the business environment

S6.6 Intangible assets would NOT include

a. Organizational culture

b. Employee skills and knowledge

c. Equipment owned by the business

d. Goodwill

S6.7 Which of the following tools translates an organization's strategy into a number of performance measures (both financial and non-financial)?

a. Balanced scorecard

b. Operations budget

c. Mission and objectives

d. Environmental analysis

e. Value chain analysis

S6.8 Carol's Cupcakes would like to report a measure of profitability on her BSC. Under which perspective should she include this measure?

a. Customer perspective

b. Internal business process perspective

c. Financial perspective

d. Learning and growth perspective

S6.9 Andrew Finning, the CFO for New Bank, wants to measure the increase in the number of loan applications on the bank's BSC. In which perspective should this measure be included?

a. Customer perspective

b. Internal business process perspective

c. Financial perspective

d. Learning and growth perspective

S6.10 Manufacturing cycle time is a measure that could be included under which perspective?

a. Customer perspective

b. Internal business process perspective

c. Financial perspective

d. Learning and growth perspective

S6.11 One of the objectives of the learning and growth perspective is

a. Increasing customer satisfaction

b. Increasing market share

c. Improving knowledge of employees

d. Lowering costs of manufacture

S6.12 A more holistic approach to performance management that supports the strategic management process and aims to overcome the difficulties of integrating information from diverse systems is called

a. Agency theory

b. Enterprise resource management

c. Feedforward control

d. Environmental scanning

■ PROBLEMS

P6.1 *(Management Control Systems)* Ethan Coleman, the president and CEO of High-Tech Inc., recently stated:

> We are in the business of innovation! If we don't innovate and encourage creative thinking in our employees, we are doomed. Why should I encourage my staff to develop budgets and standards? This will limit their creativity. Budgets, performance measures and cost control are for traditional manufacturing organizations—not for high-tech industries.

Do you agree with what Ethan says? Do you think it is important to have a management control system in high-tech companies?

P6.2 *(Types of Control Systems)* Identify if each of the following is a control system. Why or why not?

a. The employees of Hadden Industries respect their employer and always try to make a high-quality product.

b. Benjamin Quarin always checks the work of his employees before he allows them to send it to Shipping.

c. The quality control manager for Gulam Clothing Corporation checks every 5 out of 100 shirts to ensure that they meet the company's pre-set standards. Any faulty shirts are sent back to manufacturing to be redone.

d. Adam Grant must make 100 toasters each day to receive his incentive compensation at Kitchen Inc.

e. Celia, the owner of Celia's Fine Meats, asks her staff to package only food products that they would take home to their own families.

f. The supervisor at Holiday Trailers Inc. signs the sales order for every RV sold off the lot.

P6.3 *(Feedback and Feedforward Control)* The following discussion took place between Harold Adams, the Garcia Industries plant supervisor, and Serena Garcia, the company president:

Harold: "Serena, I think we have some very good standards here at Garcia Industries."

Serena: "Yes, Harold, I agree with you but I'm concerned that our standards might not be enough. Currently, we adjust our production process if a product is not within the standards that are set for each product, but some products must be slipping through the inspection process. We have had an increase in customer complaints in the last quarter. A substantial increase!"

Harold: "Well I don't think it has anything to do with our quality assurance inspectors. Aaron and John are both very experienced and I am sure that they have not let any products pass inspection that do not meet our standards."

Serena: "What do you think is causing the complaints then?"

Harold: "I think that customers are now expecting more from our products. Global Inc., our key competitor, has been improving its quality. Maybe customers expect the same from us."

Serena: "We need to think of some controls we can put in place to ensure that we reduce these customer complaints, Harold. I would like to you meet with Jacqueline Gauthier, our management accountant, this week and between the two of you I would like a list of controls that we can implement at our plant to increase the quality of the products we are selling."

Harold: "That sounds like a good plan, Serena. I'll get back to you early next week with my report."

Prepare a list of controls including both feedback and feedforward controls that Harold and Serena could utilize to help manage quality at Garcia Industries.

P6.4 *(Control Systems)* According to Anthony and Govindarajan (2000), every control system has at least four elements:

1. A detector or sensor that measures what is happening
2. An assessor that determines the significance of what is happening by comparing it with a standard or expectation
3. An effector (feedback) that alters behaviour if the assessor indicates the need to do so
4. A communication network that transmits information between the other elements

   For the following scenarios, identify how each of the four elements might occur:

   a. A quality control system at a plant that manufactures peanut butter

   b. The product design control system for a computer manufacturer

   c. The customer service control system at a telephone company

P6.5 *(Intangible Assets)* Robert Kaplan and David Norton (2004) state that "intangible assets almost never create value by themselves." The value of intangible assets is strong only if the intangible assets support the strategy the company is pursuing. For example, consider McDonald's, which pursues a low-cost strategy. Staff training and knowledge related to process improvements (such as just-in-time [JIT] inventory management and total quality management [TQM]) will be valuable for a company like McDonald's, since this intangible resource supports the overall strategy of cost leadership.

Describe an example of an intangible asset that might be valuable to each of the following companies:

a. Dell Computers

b. Lululemon Athletica (a high-quality athletic clothing company)

c. Canadian Tire

d. Walmart

e. Tim Hortons

f. Research In Motion

P6.6 *(Balanced Scorecard)* Goodall Corporation makes a wireless computer keyboard called the Blackbird. The following information was compiled for 2010 and 2011.

	2010	2011
Number of keyboards sold	28,000	29,500
Plastic used (kilograms)	14,000	15,100
Direct materials costs per kilogram	$7	$10
Manufacturing capacity	35,000	35,000
Spoilage	18%	25%
Total manufacturing costs	$495,000	$585,000
Total customer service costs	$152,000	$161,650
Number of customers	608	610
Cost per customer	$250	$265

Due to increases in direct materials costs, Goodall is concerned that the profitability of its Black-bird line is decreasing. The company would like to reduce manufacturing costs and also reduce the amount of materials that are spoiled in a given year. Goodall also wants to grow its customer base more rapidly, as the industry market size for wireless keyboards increased over 25% from 2010 to 2011, but its results did not reflect this growth.

Identify three measures that you could use to help the company achieve its plans in each of the BSC perspectives.

P6.7 *(Balanced Scorecard)* Rose Oil Cosmetics plans to grow its company by offering a new line of anti-aging products that are superior and uniquely different than their competitor's product. Rose Oil knows that it needs to invest heavily in R&D and innovative methods to ensure that it can achieve its goal.

Identify two key elements that you would expect to see included in the balanced scorecard for each of the perspectives (financial, customer, internal business, and learning and growth) for Rose Oil.

P6.8 *(Balanced Scorecard)* Mandy's Magic Cleaners manufacturers cleaning products for the restaurant industry, including industrial strength degreasers and dishwasher products. Her products have an average sales price of $40 per litre. The following information relates to her sales for 2011 and 2012.

	2011	2012
Litres of cleaner sold	8,500	10,600
Chemical purchases	$37,000	$58,500
Manufacturing capacity	15,000	15,000
Spoilage (percentage)	8%	7.3%
Total manufacturing costs	$102,000	$183,500
Number of products	14	25

During 2012, Mandy began selling 11 new products. Some of the new products required specialized equipment and she had to invest in new machinery in order to produce these lines. She is concerned that overall manufacturing costs have increased dramatically over 2011 and she is not sure if her investment in the new machinery was worth it. She realizes it may take some time for her new products to gain market share. Overall, Mandy wants to expand her company to be more diverse and offer products that her competitors do not provide.

Identify three measures that you could use to help the company achieve its plans in each of the BSC perspectives.

P6.9 *(Financial and Non-Financial Measures)* Phone-Tech manufactures cellphones that utilize a touch-screen platform. Part of its overall strategy is to provide a high-quality phone that customers NEVER return for warranty repair. The company wants to be able to measure its quality performance by using both financial and non-financial measures of quality.

a. List the merits of both financial and non-financial performance measures. Can one exist without the other?

b. Describe both financial and non-financial measures that Phone-Tech could utilize to help it ensure that it is meeting its quality standards.

P6.10 *(Performance Management)* No-One-Home is a security system provider in western Canada. Over the years, the company has implemented many management techniques (such as flexible budgeting, just-in-time inventory management, and value chain analysis) that have increased its level of customer service and quality. Last year, the CFO of No-One-Home mentioned that he felt that the company has a good handle on management control but that it has not gone far enough in terms of improving its processes. The president asked the CFO to present some ideas for how to take this next step of improving performance.

List some ideas that No-One-Home could implement to increase its focus on performance improvement.

REFERENCES

Anthony, R. N. (1965). *Planning and control systems: A framework for analysis.* Boston, MA: Harvard Business School Press.

Anthony, R. N., & Govindarajan, V. (2000). *Management control systems* (10th international ed.). New York, NY: McGraw-Hill Irwin.

Brignall, S., & Ballantine, J. (1996). Performance measurement in service businesses revisited. *International Journal of Service Industry Management, 7*(1), 6–31.

Canada Post. (2011). 2010 *Annual Report.* Retrieved from www.canadapost.ca/cpo/mc/assets/pdf/aboutus/annualreport/2010_annual_report_en.pdf.

Daft, R. L., & Macintosh, N. B. (1984). The nature and use of formal control systems for management control and strategy implementation. *Journal of Management, 10* (1), 43–66.

Downs, A. (1966). *Inside bureaucracy.* Boston, MA: Little, Brown.

Emmanuel, C., Otley, D., & Merchant, K. (1990). *Accounting for management control* (2nd ed.). London: Chapman & Hall.

Johnson, H. T., & Kaplan, R. S. (1987). *Relevance lost: The rise and fall of management accounting.* Boston, MA: Harvard Business School Press.

Kaplan, R. S., & Norton, D. P. (1992). The balanced scorecard—Measures that drive performance. *Harvard Business Review,* January–February, 71–79.

Kaplan, R. S., & Norton, D. P. (1993). Putting the balanced scorecard to work. *Harvard Business Review,* September–October, 134–147.

Kaplan, R. S., & Norton, D. P. (1996). Using the balanced scorecard as a strategic management system. *Harvard Business Review,* January–February, 75–85.

Kaplan, R. S., & Norton, D. P. (2001). *The strategy-focused organization: How balanced scorecard companies thrive in the new business environment.* Boston, MA: Harvard Business School Press.

Kaplan, R. S., & Norton, D. P. (2004). Measuring the strategic readiness of intangible assets. *Harvard Business Review,* February 2004.

Kaplan, R., & Norton, D. P. (2007). Transforming the balanced scorecard from performance measurement to strategic measurement: Part 1. In S. Young (Ed.), *Readings in management accounting* (5th ed., pp. 199–209). New Jersey: Pearson Prentice Hall.

Merchant, K. A. (1998). *Modern management control systems: Text and cases.* Upper Saddle River, NJ: Prentice-Hall.

Otley, D. (1999). Performance management: A framework for management control systems research. *Management Accounting Research,* 10, 363–382.

Sinclair, D., & Zairi, M. (1995b). Effective process management through performance measurement. *Business Process Re-engineering and Management Journal,* 1(1), 75–88.

Tim Hortons. *Frequently asked questions.* Retrieved from www.timhortons.com/ca/en/about/faq.html.

CHAPTER 7

Inventory Management

LEARNING OBJECTIVES

After reading this chapter, you should be able to answer the following questions:

- How are inventories presented on a company's financial statements?

- How does the flow of inventory costs differ between a manufacturing and a merchandising company?

- What are the various methods used to value inventory? How are these methods applied in practice?

- What are the benefits and challenges of just-in-time (JIT) inventory management?

- Why are inventory management practices important in controlling costs of inventory?

This chapter begins with an explanation of inventory as it relates to financial reports for both merchandising and manufacturing enterprises. It then looks at the alternative methods of inventory valuation, including job costing, process costing, and costing of inventory for services. The chapter also looks at just-in-time (JIT) inventory practices and long-term contract costing. It concludes by looking at inventory management and control.

Introduction to Inventory

Inventory is the term used for goods bought or manufactured for resale but as yet unsold. Inventory enables the timing difference between production capacity and customer demand to be smoothed. In other words, maintaining inventories ensures that a company has product on hand when it is ordered by customers.

The cost of inventory includes all costs of purchase, conversion (i.e., manufacture), and those incurred in bringing the inventory to its present location and condition. Costs of purchase include the cost of the purchased inventories plus import duties and transportation, less any rebates or discounts. Costs of conversion include direct labour and an allocation of both fixed and variable production overheads (overheads are covered in greater detail in Chapter 11).

The matching principle (see Chapter 3) requires a business to adjust for changes in inventory in its statement of comprehensive income and statement of financial position. On a company's statement of comprehensive income, the cost of inventories is recorded as "Cost of goods sold" and on the statement of financial position, it is reported under current assets as "Inventory." For instance, if the inventory of merchandise on hand at the end of the year decreased from the balance at the beginning of the year, an expense must be recognized on the statement of comprehensive income that reflects the sale of this merchandise (Cost of goods sold expense) and the new balance of inventory at year-end must be reflected on the statement of financial position.

Inventory for a Merchandising Company

For a merchandising company, inventory is the cost of goods bought for resale. Companies maintain one inventory account called **merchandise inventory** on the statement of financial position. The cost of goods sold for a merchandising company is calculated as shown in Exhibit 7.1.

Exhibit 7.1 Cost of Goods Sold: Merchandising Company

Opening inventory (at beginning of period)	$12,000
Plus purchases	32,000
Inventory available for sale	$44,000
Less closing inventory (at end of period)	10,000
Cost of goods sold	$34,000

The values reflected on the cost of goods sold statement would be presented on both the statement of financial position and statement of comprehensive income for the company as shown in Exhibit 7.2.

Exhibit 7.2 Statement of Comprehensive Income and Statement of Financial Position: Merchandising Company

Statement of Comprehensive Income	
Sales	$85,000
Less cost of goods sold	**34,000**
Gross profit	$51,000
Less selling and administrative expenses	28,000
Operating profit	$23,000
Statement of Financial Position	
Assets	
Cash	$25,000
Accounts receivable	12,000

(*continued*)

Inventory	**10,000**
Equipment (net of depreciation)	35,000
Total assets	$82,000
Liabilities and Shareholders' Equity	
Accounts payable	$22,000
Salaries payable	15,000
Total liabilities	$37,000
Shareholders' equity	45,000
Total liabilities and shareholders' equity	$82,000

Inventory for a Manufacturing Company

For a manufacturing company, there are three different types of inventory:

1. Raw materials
2. Work in process
3. Finished goods

Manufacturing firms purchase raw materials (unprocessed goods) and undertake the *conversion process* through the application of labour, machinery, and know-how to manufacture finished goods. The finished goods are then available to be sold to customers. Work in process consists of goods that have begun the conversion process but have not yet been completed. For example, a clothing manufacturer would have a raw materials inventory of fabric, thread, and buttons on hand. The manufacturer would likely also have partially completed clothing at the end of an accounting period (work-in-process inventory) and fully completed clothing that is ready for sale (finished goods inventory).

In order to value inventories, a manufacturing company must track all of the costs of manufacturing its goods. These costs will include raw materials, direct labour costs (costs of hourly workers), and manufacturing overhead, such as rent, utilities, indirect materials, depreciation, and salaries of plant supervisors. In order to track these costs, a company will prepare a statement called the *cost of goods manufactured*. The cost of goods manufactured statement is calculated for a manufacturing company as shown in Exhibit 7.3:

Exhibit 7.3 Cost of Goods Manufactured: Manufacturing Company

Direct material:		
Raw material inventory at beginning of period	$ 50,000	
Purchases of raw materials	150,000	
Raw material available for use	$200,000	
Less raw material inventory at the end of period	40,000	
Raw material used in production		$160,000
Direct labour		330,000
Manufacturing overhead:		
Factory rent	$ 50,000	
Depreciation on plant and equipment	30,000	

(continued)

Exhibit 7.3 Cost of Goods Manufactured: Manufacturing Company (*continued*)

Light and power	10,000	
Salaries and wages of indirect labour	60,000	$150,000
Total manufacturing costs		$640,000
Add work-in-process inventory at beginning of period		100,000
		$740,000
Less work-in-process inventory at end of period		60,000
Cost of goods manufactured		$680,000

Next, the cost of goods is calculated similarly to that of a merchandising company. The main difference is that *purchases* are replaced by *cost of goods manufactured* as shown in Exhibit 7.4.

Exhibit 7.4 Cost of Goods Sold Statement: Manufacturing Company

Finished goods inventory at beginning of period	$160,000
Cost of goods manufactured	680,000
Goods available for sale	$840,000
Less finished goods inventory at end of period	120,000
Cost of goods sold	$720,000

The reporting of cost of goods sold expense is similar to that of a merchandising company, while the statement of financial position of a manufacturing company differs from that of a merchandising company in that three levels of inventory are reported. Exhibit 7.5 shows the format of both the statement of comprehensive income and the statement of financial position for a manufacturing company.

Exhibit 7.5 Statement of Comprehensive Income and Statement of Financial Position: Manufacturing Company

Statement of Comprehensive Income	
Sales	$1,000,000
Less cost of goods sold	720,000
Gross profit	$ 280,000
Less selling and administrative expenses	150,000
Operating profit	$ 130,000
Statement of Financial Position	
Assets	
Cash	$ 35,000
Accounts receivable	172,000
Inventory	220,000
Property, plant, and equipment (net of depreciation)	580,000
Total assets	$1,007,000

(*continued*)

Liabilities and shareholders' equity	
Accounts payable	$ 242,000
Salaries payable	255,000
Total liabilities	$ 497,000
Shareholders' equity	510,000
Total liabilities and shareholders' equity	$1,007,000

Included in the notes to the financial statements would be a breakdown of the valuation of inventory in the current assets section of the statement of financial position. This would show the following:

Inventory raw materials	$ 40,000
Inventory work in process	60,000
Inventory finished goods	120,000
Total	$220,000

Flow of Costs

Exhibits 7.6 and 7.7 show the flow of costs from purchasing to sales for a merchandising organization (Exhibit 7.6) and a manufacturing organization (Exhibit 7.7).

Exhibit 7.6 The Flow of Costs in Purchasing

	Inventory finished goods	Cost of sales
Purchases ⟶	Increases inventory	
Sales ⟶	Decreases inventory ⟶	Increases cost of sales

Exhibit 7.7 The Flow of Costs in Manufacturing

	Inventory raw materials	Inventory work in progress	Inventory finished goods	Cost of sales
Purchases ⟶	Increases inventory			
Issued to production ⟶	Decreases inventory ⟶	Increases inventory		
Production labour ⟶		Increases inventory		
Production overhead ⟶		Increases inventory		
Completed production ⟶		Decreases inventory ⟶	Increases inventory	
Sales of finished goods ⟶			Decreases inventory ⟶	Increases cost of sales

Valuation of Inventory

Inventory valuation is important because the determination of the cost of inventory affects both the cost of goods sold in the statement of comprehensive income and the inventory valuation in the statement of financial position. The value that companies assign to inventory on both the statement of comprehensive income and the statement of financial position must be the lower of cost or net realizable value (NRV) according to the *International Financial Reporting Standards* (IFRS). Cost represents the cost of acquiring or manufacturing the inventory, while (NRV) is the value at which the inventory could be sold on the open market, less costs of disposal, such as shipping or reclamation. In most cases, cost is less than NRV due to inflation.

Methods of Inventory Valuation in Merchandising Firms

In merchandising firms, inventory is purchased for resale. How the inventory is valued depends on whether the inventory is purchased individually or in bulk. When inventory is purchased individually, the purchase cost is used to value the inventory and the cost of goods sold when the inventory is sold. For example, a used motor vehicle purchased by a dealer for $8,000 would be valued in inventory as $8,000. When it is sold, cost of goods sold of $8,000 will be reported on the company's statement of comprehensive income.

However, if inventory items are similar and cannot be differentiated (which would be the case for most goods bought in bulk), costs are assigned by using either the weighted average cost or first-in, first-out (FIFO) methods.

WEIGHTED AVERAGE METHOD FOR MERCHANDISING COMPANIES

Under the weighted average method, the cost of each item is determined from the weighted average of the cost of similar items at the beginning of a period and the cost of similar items purchased or produced during the period.

For example, Jasmine Industries purchases exotic spices that are resold to specialty food stores. During March, batches of spice were purchased on three separate occasions:

Date	Units	Unit Price	Total Cost
March 4	5,000	$1.20	$ 6,000
March 16	2,000	$1.25	2,500
March 27	3,000	$1.27	3,810
	10,000		$12,310

During March, Jasmine had sales of 6,000 units. In order to value inventory and cost of goods sold using the weighted average method, Jasmine would need to calculate a weighted average cost for all units purchased during the month. The weighted average cost is $12,310/10,000 or $1.231 per unit. The cost of goods sold is, therefore, 6,000 at $1.231 = $7,386. The value of inventory is 4,000 at $1.231 = $4,924 (ending inventory is 10,000 units less 6,000 sold).

FIRST-IN, FIRST-OUT METHOD FOR MERCHANDISING COMPANIES

The first-in, first-out (FIFO) method assumes that items of inventory purchased or produced first are sold first, so that those remaining in inventory are those most recently purchased or produced.

Using the same information as in the previous example, we can calculate the cost of 6,000 units sold and the value of inventory using the FIFO method. Under FIFO, the 6,000 units sold come first from the original 5,000 purchased, and the balance of 1,000 from the second purchase of 2,000 units. The cost of goods sold is therefore

$$
\begin{array}{rl}
& 5{,}000 \; @ \; \$1.20 = \$6{,}000 \\
\text{and} & 1{,}000 \; @ \; \$1.25 = \underline{1{,}250} \\
\text{Total} & \phantom{1{,}000 @ \$1.25 = } \$7{,}250
\end{array}
$$

The remaining inventory is the last purchased; that is, 1,000 from the second purchase of 2,000 and 3,000 from the third purchase. The value of inventory is therefore

$$
\begin{array}{rl}
& 1{,}000 \; @ \; \$1.25 = \$1{,}250 \\
\text{and} & 3{,}000 \; @ \; \$1.27 = \underline{3{,}810} \\
\text{Total} & \phantom{1{,}000 @ \$1.27 = } \$5{,}060
\end{array}
$$

Note that, depending on the method used, the cost of goods sold (and therefore profit) differs. If the 6,000 units were sold at a price of $2.00

- Under weighted average, the gross profit would be $4,614 ($12,000 − $7,386)
- Under FIFO, the gross profit would be $4,750 ($12,000 − $7,250)

NET REALIZABLE VALUE

Net realizable value (NRV) is the potential proceeds of sale of inventory, less any costs of disposal (such as transport, reclamation, cleaning, and so on). When the net realizable value is less than the original cost of the inventory, this value should be used for inventory valuation. As mentioned earlier, this is a requirement of the IFRS (*International Accounting Standard 2*).

NVR is normally higher than cost, but there are circumstances when an inventory's NRV is less than the original cost. This might happen if an inventory item has become obsolete or if a significant market shift in price has occurred. Both are common occurrences in industries in which technology is changing rapidly (such as those involving, for example, computers, cellphones, and digital media players).

A key principle of accounting is *conservatism*, which requires that if an item can be reported using more than one method of costing, the costing method that creates the lowest net income should be used. As a result, if the NRV is lower than the recorded cost, the inventory item should be recorded at NRV.

Methods of Costing Inventory in Manufacturing

In manufacturing companies, there are different types of manufacturing that utilize different methods of inventory costing:

- *Custom:* Where unique, custom products are produced singly; for example, a building. In this case, the company would use job order costing to value inventory.

- *Batch*: Where a quantity of the same goods are produced at the same time (often called a *production run*); for example, textbooks. In this case, a company would also use job order costing.

- *Continuous*: Where products are produced in a continuous production process; for example, oil and chemicals, and soft drinks. For continuous production, a company uses process costing.

JOB ORDER COSTING

For custom and batch manufacture, costs are collected through a job order costing system that accumulates the cost of raw materials as they are issued to each job (either a custom product or a batch of products), plus the cost of time spent by different categories of labour. To each of these costs, overhead is allocated to cover the fixed and variable manufacturing overheads that are not included in materials or labour (overhead will be explained in Chapter 11). When a custom product is completed, the accumulated cost of materials, labour, and overhead is the cost of that custom product. For each batch, the total job cost is divided by the number of units produced (e.g., the number of copies of a textbook) to give a cost per unit (e.g., a cost per textbook).

Consider Helo Ltd., a manufacturer of helicopter components, which it produces in batches of 100. Each batch of 100 components requires the following:

- 500 kg of rolled and formed steel

- 15 direct labour hours at $125/hour

- allocated overhead (at completion) of $2,000

During July, Helo purchased 1,000 kg of steel at a cost of $12 per kg. Using 1,000 kg of steel, the company fully finished 100 components and partially completed another 100 units. In total, 15 labour hours were incurred to produce the fully completed components, and 7 labour hours were incurred to produce the partially completed units. By month-end, the company had sold 60 of the completed components for $130 each.

To calculate costs, Helo first needs to calculate the value of work in process at month-end. The partially completed components (work in process) are valued as follows:

Materials: Steel—500 kg @ $12/kg	$6,000
Labour: 7 hours @ $125	875
Total work in process	$6,875

Next, Helo needs to value the competed components to assign these costs to cost of goods sold and finished goods inventory. The value of completed components will be

Materials: Steel—500 kg @ $12/kg	$6,000
Labour: 15 hours @ $125	1,875
Overhead	2,000
Total job cost	$9,875
Cost per component	$98.75 ($9,875/100)

The cost of goods sold for the 60 components sold is $5,925 (60 @ $98.75). The sales income is $7,800 (60 @ $130) and the gross profit is $1,875 ($7,800 –$5,925). The inventory of finished goods is $3,950 (40 @ $98.75).

PROCESS COSTING

For continuous manufacture a process costing system is used (under which costs are collected over a period of time) together with a measure of the volume of production. At the end of the accounting period, the total costs are divided by the volume produced (equivalent units) to give a cost per unit of volume. In process costing, equivalent units are the number of fully completed units in production.

In a process costing environment, at the end of an accounting period, there are units that are finished (fully completed) and units in process (work-in-process [WIP] inventory). Equivalent units measure the fully completed units by multiplying the number of units in the work-in-process inventory by their percentage of completion. This amount is added to the finished units to determine the equivalent units. For instance, if a soft drink manufacturer had 50,000 bottles of beverages completed and 10,000 bottles in process that were 25% complete at the end of the accounting period, the equivalent units would be 52,500 (50,000 + 10,000 × 25%).

Consider Kazoo Company, which produces oils on a process basis. The data in Exhibit 7.8 relate to production during the month of February. According to these data, 7,000 units in the work-in-process inventory were 55% completed in January. Costs of $12,000 for direct materials and $30,000 for conversion (labour costs and overhead) were carried forward from January for these units. During February, the company started 12,000 units and spent $140,000 in direct materials and $80,000 in conversion costs. At the end of February, 4,000 units in the work-in-process inventory were 75% complete.

Exhibit 7.8 **Kazoo Company: Production Data for February**

	Units	Direct Materials Costs	Conversion Costs	% of Completion
Opening WIP inventory (from January)	7,000	$ 70,000	$30,000	55%
Units started in February	12,000	$140,000	$80,000	
Ending WIP inventory (end of February)	4,000			75%

Either the weighted average method or the first-in, first-out (FIFO) method can be used to calculate inventory costs for process costing. Under both methods, it is necessary to complete three steps:

1. Determine the number of units completed.
2. Calculate the equivalent units in work in process and the cost per equivalent unit.
3. Assign the cost to finished goods and ending WIP inventory.

Note: In process costing examples, materials are usually assumed to be added at the beginning of the process, but in practice, you would need to determine the stage at which they are added. Conversion costs are added uniformly throughout the process. Exhibit 7.9 shows the calculations.

WEIGHTED AVERAGE METHOD

The weighted average method calculates the value of inventory based on an average cost of units in inventory. If the Kazoo Company used the weighted average method, the company would prepare the inventory calculation shown in Exhibit 7.9.

Exhibit 7.9 Weighted Average Process Costing

Step 1. Calculation of units completed

	Units
Opening WIP inventory	7,000
Units started	12,000
Units to account for	19,000
Closing WIP inventory	4,000
Completed units	15,000

Step 2. Calculation of equivalent units and cost per unit

	Opening WIP Inventory	Cost for Month	Total	Completed Units	Ending WIP Inventory Equivalent Units	Total Equivalent Units	Cost per Equivalent Unit[1]
Material	$ 70,000	$140,000	$210,000	15,000	4,000	19,000	$11.053
Conversion	30,000	80,000	110,000	15,000	3,000[2]	18,000	6.111
Total	$100,000	$220,000	$320,000				$17.164

Step 3. Assignment of costs

Work in process:

Materials 4000 @ $11.053	$ 44,212
Conversion 3,000 @ $6.111	18,333
Total work in process	$ 62,545

Finished goods:

15,000 units $17.164	$257,460
Total costs	$320,005

Notes

[1]Total cost divided by total equivalent units.

[2]4,000 units, 75% complete at end of month = 3,000 equivalent units.

*difference of $5 in total costs is due to rounding.

FIFO METHOD

If a FIFO method of costing and inventory valuation is used, a variation of this calculation is necessary. The main difference between the FIFO and weighted average methods is the treatment of beginning WIP inventory costs. The beginning WIP inventory is assumed to be completed first, but those costs are not averaged into a rate per equivalent unit as is done in the weighted average method. Using the same information as used for the weighted average method, Exhibit 7.10 depicts the FIFO process.

Exhibit 7.10 FIFO Process Costing

Step 1. Calculation of units completed

	Units
Opening WIP inventory	7,000
Units started	12,000
Units to account for	19,000
Closing WIP inventory	4,000
Completed	15,000

Step 2. Calculation of equivalent units and cost per unit

	Opening WIP Inventory[1]	Cost for Month	Beginning WIP Inventory Units Completed This Period[2]	Started and Completed Units[3]	Ending WIP Inventory Equivalent Units	Total Equivalent Units for This Period	Cost per Equivalent Unit[5]
Material	n/a[1]	$140,000	0	8,000	4,000	12,000	$11.6667
Conversion	n/a[1]	80,000	3,150	8,000	3,000[4]	14,150	5.6537
Total	$100,000	$220,000					$17.3207

Step 3. Assignment of costs

Work in process:

Materials 4,000 @ $11.6667	$ 46,667
Conversion 3,000 @ $5.6537	16,961
Total work in process	$ 63,628

Finished Goods:

From beginning WIP inventory:	
Beginning WIP already completed	$100,000
Beginning WIP finished this period (3,150 @ $5.6537)	17,809
Units started and completed this period 8,000 units @ $17.3207	138,564
Total finished goods	$ 256,373
Total costs	$ 320,001*

*There is a small rounding difference between the total costs assigned of $320,001 and the actual beginning WIP costs of $100,000 plus the costs for the month of $320,000, a total of $262,000.

Notes

[1]Beginning WIP inventory costs are not included in the rate per equivalent units under FIFO.

[2]Direct materials = 0 (all direct materials were added last period at the beginning of the process). Conversion = 7,000 units × (100% − 55% complete at start of month) = 3,150 equivalent units; 45% of the units were completed this period.

[3]Started and completed units = Total units completed less beginning inventory; Started and completed = 15,000 − 7,000 = 8,000 units.

[4]4,000 units, 75% complete at end of month = 3,000 equivalent units.

[5]Total cost added this period divided by total equivalent unit.

The FIFO method is more complex than the weighted average method but provides a more accurate measure of how inventory costs flow through a production system. In most cases, older inventories are used first in the production system and the FIFO reflects this usage of older materials first.

Valuation of Inventory for Service Companies

While inventory might be thought of as relating only to manufacturers and retailers, professional service firms also have inventories. Accountants and lawyers are examples of firms with large work-in-process inventories, covering work carried out on behalf of clients but not yet invoiced. For example, Petersen Accountants have been conducting ABC Limited's audit. At month-end, 15 partner hours and 60 audit hours have been allocated to ABC's work, which has not been invoiced. The hourly cost rates used by Petersen are $200/hour for partners and $80/hour for managers.

The calculation of the work in process for Petersen at month-end is

15 partner hours @ $200	$ 3,000
60 audit hours @ $80	4,800
Total	$ 7,800

JUST-IN-TIME INVENTORY MANAGEMENT

With just-in-time (JIT) inventory management, a company attempts to maintain minimal inventories (as close to zero as possible) to reduce inventory carrying costs, such as storage and materials handling costs, and to reduce the cost of obsolescence. The following are some of the key characteristics of a JIT system.

1. **Pull process**. Production is driven by customer demand. In a pure JIT system, finished inventories are not required because products are produced as demanded. This is different from a push system, where finished goods are produced based on expected demand levels, not on actual sales orders.

2. **Coordination with suppliers**. A JIT system requires a strong coordination of purchasing and production processes. Constant communication with suppliers is a necessity for a JIT system since a supplier must deliver materials when they are needed in the production process.

3. **Smaller and more frequent orders**. A JIT system is normally characterized by smaller, more frequent orders from suppliers, which reduces the inventories of raw materials.

4. **Flexible capacity and customizable product**. Production processes are flexible, with short setup times and the ability to customize products. Employees are trained in multiple processes.

5. **Focus on quality**. Quality tends to increase in a JIT environment because employees are more skilled and the focus is on customer expectations.

CASE IN POINT

Reducing Spoilage at McDonald's

Few industries are as time-sensitive as the fast-food industry. That's one reason why restaurant chains have been embracing just-in-time (JIT) inventory management to reduce the spoilage of food, the cost of which has been rising in recent years.

McDonald's Corporation used to cook up batches of hamburgers and keep them warm under heat lamps. Whatever didn't sell within about half an hour was simply thrown away. To compensate for this loss, the restaurant had to raise menu prices to absorb high inventory carrying costs.

The chain abandoned this "push" system of inventory management in favour of a "pull" system, where each burger is cooked when the customer orders it. Improved technology, including a fast bun toaster, enables the restaurant to provide made-to-order food with little spoilage to an average of 64 million customers worldwide each day. This is crucial, since the company expected the price it pays for food commodities to increase in 2012 by up to 5.5% in the United States and as much as 3.5% in Europe. However, Louis Payette, national media relations manager for McDonald's Canada, noted that "economic conditions and suppliers are different in Canada." He said, "McDonald's Restaurants of Canada management believes the company is well positioned to mitigate the impact of economic pressures that other countries are experiencing," adding, "the Canadian operation has a sophisticated menu that no single food item dominates."

JIT has not only helped McDonald's control food costs, but it has also improved customer satisfaction, since the restaurants can offer fresher food and accommodate special orders without delays or panic. JIT also helps manage inventory during periods of high demand, since the restaurants won't run out of pre-made burgers in peak periods.

McDonald's credits its rapid inventory turnover as one way that it manages inflationary cost increases effectively.

Sources: Atkinson, C., McDonald's, A guide to the benefits of JIT, *Inventory Management Review*, November 8, 2005; McDonald's Corporation, *2010 Annual Report*; McDonald's Corporation, McDonald's positioned for continued growth under the plan to win, news release, November 10, 2011; McDonald's planning price increases outside Canada, *Restaurant News*, January 2012.

A JIT system has a number of advantages over traditional inventory systems, including the following.

- **Cost savings**. A company will save a considerable amount in carrying costs in a JIT environment. A reduction in storage facilities and materials handling will result from a strong coordination with suppliers. Also, obsolescence of older inventories is decreased. Companies may experience an increase in ordering costs, such as shipping and administrative costs, but this is normally offset considerably by cost savings.

- **Improved customer and employee satisfaction**. Customer satisfaction is expected to improve with shorter lead times, improved quality, and customization of products. Also, improved employee satisfaction is often an outcome of a JIT system due to greater variety in work and delegation of responsibility.

- **Improved quality**. Quality improvement is a hallmark of the JIT environment. Materials that come into the production process must be of a very high quality as there is no storage of spare raw materials and parts. Also, employees tend to be more skilful because they are trained on more than one task. Employees need to be adaptable and are expected to solve problems at their own workstations.

However, a JIT system does face some important challenges:

- **Inability to predict demand**. JIT is based on the premise that demand will drive production. This requires that a company have a good idea of when it will need the materials it is ordering. Sometimes, demand is not easy to predict and, if demand expectations are not well defined, a JIT system can hurt customer relationships. For example, if a company underestimates demand, it might have stockouts since it is not carrying extra finished goods, resulting in negative customer reactions and loss of sales to a competitor.

- **Strong reliance on suppliers**. A JIT system requires that delivery of materials and goods occur at specified times; this may need to be coordinated to the minute. Not receiving a part on time can result in down time in the factory, which can cost the company money in terms of labour and overhead. This was a very large problem after the tsunami in Japan in 2010. Because of the closure of Japanese suppliers, Toyota was forced to temporarily shut down all of its North American plants due to shortages of parts (Hollbrock, 2011). In this case, if the company had carried inventories of parts, it might have been able to continue production during this catastrophe.

CASE IN POINT

JIT at Harley-Davidson

Harley-Davidson (H-D) has been a well-known manufacturer of motorcycles for over 100 years. However, in the 1980s, H-D was struggling as a company, facing challenges competing with its low-cost Japanese counterparts (Honda, Yamaha, Suzuki, and Kawasaki). During this period, H-D utilized excessive inventories to help smooth production inefficiencies.

In 1981 and 1982, Harley-Davidson reported losses of over $60 million dollars. The company was close to shutting down operations and it knew that it had to change its practices in order to regain control of its operations. During this time period, H-D management devoted themselves to studying Toyota's JIT system (JIT was originally developed by the Toyota Motor Company). H-D then implemented a JIT system based on the Toyota model that was characterized by small work teams (generally 8 to 15 people per team), full employee involvement, a strong supplier selection process, and a complex computerized inventory system. As a result of the JIT implementation, H-D was able to reduce inventories by 75% and increase productivity overall.

This business practice has helped Harley-Davidson thrive as a company. In 2008, H-D reported net income of over $654 million dollars.

Sources: Grant, R. M., *Case Eight: Harley-Davidson, Inc.*, February 2004. Available at www.blackwellpublishing.com/grant/docs/08Harley.pdf; Wilson, J., Real-life examples of successful JIT systems, *Bright Hub*, May 18, 2010. Available at www.brighthub.com/office/project-management/articles/71540.aspx.

Backflush Costing

The introduction by many manufacturing companies of just-in-time supply has resulted in a significant reduction in inventories, so inventory valuation becomes less relevant. JIT systems often use a costing system called backflush costing to reduce the number of transactions that are necessary to record inventory purchases and transfers.

Under traditional costing approaches, each material transaction is recorded separately. Rather than tracking each movement of materials, in backflush costing, the output from the production process determines (based on the *expected* usage and cost of materials) the amount of materials to be transferred from raw materials to finished goods. Importantly, under backflush costing, there is no separate accounting for work in process. The timing of the recording of costs is based on a *trigger point.*

In its simplest version, backflush costing transfers the cost of materials from suppliers, along with conversion costs, to finished goods inventory when production of finished goods is complete (the trigger point). In a modified version, trigger points occur when raw materials are purchased and when finished goods are completed. The modified version is shown in Exhibit 7.11.

Exhibit 7.11 The Flow of Costs in Backflush Costing

	Inventory raw materials	Inventory finished goods	Cost of sales
Purchases ——————▶	Increases inventory		
Complete production ——▶	Decreases inventory ——▶	Increases inventory	
Conversion costs ——————————————————▶		Increases inventory	
Sales of finished goods ——————————————▶		Decreases inventory ——▶	Increases cost of sales

For example, New Tech Corporation produces e-readers in a just-in-time manufacturing environment. The company records all purchases of raw materials (such as electrical components, memory cards, and plastic casings) when the materials are received in the factory from the suppliers. When an e-reader is completed, all costs accumulated for the product are compiled and recorded to finished goods inventory. The company maintains no work-in-process inventory accounts since most of its product is produced when demanded by customers.

Long-Term Contract Costing

Long-term contract costing is a method of job costing that applies to large units which are produced over long periods of time; for example construction projects. Because of the length of time the contract takes to complete, it is necessary to apportion the profit over several accounting periods. Although the goods that are the subject of the contract have not been delivered, the IFRS (*International Accounting Standard 11*) requires that revenue and costs be allocated over the period in which the contract takes place (e.g., the construction period).

The **percentage of completion method** is the most common costing method to be applied to long-term contracts. Under this method, revenues and gross profit are recognized in the applicable periods of production, not when production has been completed. The costs incurred in reaching the relevant stage of completion are then matched with income. However, when the outcome of a contract is not known with reasonable certainty, no profit should be estimated, although losses should be recognized as soon as they are foreseen.

Long-term contracts frequently allow for progress payments to be made by a customer at various stages of completion. For construction contracts, there will typically be an architect's certificate to support the stage of completion. Contracts may also include a *retention value*, a proportion of the total contract price that is retained by the customer and not paid until a specified period after the end of the contract.

Consider Macro Builders Ltd., which has entered into a two-year contract to construct a building. The contract price is $1.2 million, with an expected cost of construction of $1 million. After one year, the following costs have been incurred:

Material delivered to site	$500,000
Salaries and wages paid	130,000
Overhead costs	170,000

The architect certifies the value of work completed to the contractual stage for a progress payment as $600,000. Macro estimates that it will cost $250,000 to complete the contract over and above the costs already incurred.

Exhibit 7.12 shows the calculations for anticipated profit on the contract and the amount of profit that can be considered to have been earned to date.

Exhibit 7.12 Anticipated Profit and Profit to Date

Costs of construction:	
Material delivered to site	$ 500,000
Salaries and wages paid	130,000
Overhead costs	170,000
	$ 800,000
Less work not certified	200,000
Cost of work certified	$ 600,000
Anticipated profit:	
Cost of work certified	$ 600,000
Work not certified	200,000
Estimated cost to complete	250,000
	$1,050,000
Contract price	1,200,000
Anticipated profit	$ 150,000
Expected cost of construction	$1,000,000
Percentage complete ($600,000/$1,000,000)	60%
Profit to date (60% × $150,000)	$ 90,000

Inventory Management

The objective of inventory management is to optimize the levels of inventory in a company to reduce costs associated with ordering and carrying inventories while at the same time ensuring there is enough inventory on hand to meet consumer demand.

Three main costs are associated with ordering and carrying inventory:

1. **Ordering costs.** Ordering costs are the costs associated with ordering inventory, including those to prepare and pay for purchase orders and those associated with receiving and inspecting goods that are delivered to the factory.

2. **Carrying costs.** Costs related to storing inventories such as depreciation, utilities, insurance, and materials handling are called carrying costs. These costs also include the cost of obsolescence and spoilage.

3. **Stockout costs.** Stockout costs occur when a company cannot meet its customers' demands. To rectify a stockout, companies will pay a premium for special orders to suppliers. A company may also experience lost sales due to a stockout. In this case, the sales price less variable costs for the order is an opportunity cost of the stockout.

ECONOMIC ORDER QUANTITY AND LEAD TIMES

In order to optimize inventory levels within a company, managers often utilize a tool called economic order quantity (EOQ) to help them determine the levels of inventory that will reduce costs while meeting demand. EOQ is calculated using the following formula:

$$EOQ = \sqrt{\frac{2DO}{C}}$$

where

   D = Demand for a given period
   O = Ordering costs
   C = Carrying costs

For example, Billy Hogs, located in Long Beach, Vancouver Island, produces a touring bike that is a cross between a mountain and a road bike. The company currently has a demand of 2,500 bikes per year. Tires for the bikes are ordered each month. Monthly demand for bikes is generally stable due to the temperate climate. Ordering costs (shipping-related costs) per purchase order are $100 while carrying costs (including insurance, materials handling, breakage, and facility costs) are $4 per tire. The manager of Billy Hogs, Frank Wu, is wondering whether the company can reduce costs by optimizing the size and frequency of its tire purchase orders. He applied the EOQ formula to determine the optimal order size:

$$EOQ = \sqrt{\frac{2DO}{C}}$$

$$EOQ = \sqrt{\frac{2 \times 5,000 \times \$100}{\$4}}$$

$$EOQ = \sqrt{\frac{\$1,000,000}{\$4}}$$

$$EOQ = \sqrt{\$250,000}$$

$$EOQ = 500 \text{ tires}$$

*Demand for tires will be 5,000 (2,500 bikes per year multiplied by 2 tires).

This would suggest that Billy Hogs should place 10 tire orders per year (5,000 tires demanded/ 500 tires in order = 10 orders per year) to optimize costs.

The company must also consider, however, that stockout costs could occur if only 10 orders are placed per year. Billy Hogs may want to ensure that it has an appropriate lead time (the time between when an order is placed with a supplier and when it is needed) and an appropriate safety stock (an amount of extra stock that is kept on hand to cover any unexpected increases in demand).

CONCLUSION

In this chapter, we have looked at several methods of calculating the value of inventory and cost of goods sold and how inventories are reported on the financial statements for a company. We have also looked at the two main methods of costing inventories, job costing and process costing, as well as a method of long-term contract costing. Finally, we explored the benefits and challenges of using just-in-time (JIT) inventory management practices and discussed how economic order quantity can be used to optimize inventory costs.

KEY TERMS

Backflush costing, 162

Carrying costs, 165

Economic order quantity (EOQ), 165

Equivalent units, 157

First-in, first-out (FIFO) method, 154

Finished goods, 151

Inventory management, 164

Job order costing, 156

Just-in-time (JIT) inventory management, 160

Lead time, 165

Merchandise inventory, 150

Net realizable value (NRV), 155

Ordering costs, 164

Percentage of completion method, 163

Process costing, 157

Raw materials, 151

Safety stock, 165

Stockout costs, 165

Weighted average method, 154

Work in process, 151

■ SELF-TEST QUESTIONS

S7.1 Opening inventory for a month is $25,000 and closing inventory for the same month is $30,000. Cost of goods sold for that month is $35,000. Purchases for the month are

a. $20,000

b. $30,000

c. $40,000

d. $50,000

S7.2 Goods that are completed in the production process of a manufacturing business

a. Increase work-in-process inventory and decrease finished goods inventory

b. Decrease work-in-process inventory and increase finished goods inventory

c. Decrease work-in-process inventory and decrease finished goods inventory

d. Decrease finished goods inventory and increase cost of goods sold

S7.3 In a retail organization, sales

a. Increase inventory and increase cost of goods sold

b. Increase inventory and decrease cost of goods sold

c. Decrease inventory and decrease cost of goods sold

d. Decrease inventory and increase cost of goods sold

S7.4 National Retail Stores has identified the following data from its accounting records for the year ended December 31: Sales, $1,100,000; purchases, $650,000; and general and administrative expenses, $275,000. It had an opening inventory of $150,000 and a closing inventory of $200,000. Based on this information, the gross profit and operating profit/loss is

a. A gross profit of $450,000 and an operating profit of $185,000

b. A gross profit of $500,000 and an operating profit of $225,000

c. A gross profit of $400,000 and an operating profit of $125,000

d. A gross profit of $500,000 and an operating loss of $185,000

S7.5 Backflush costing does not account for

a. Raw materials inventory

b. Work-in-process inventory

c. Finished goods inventory

d. Cost of goods sold

S7.6 The key advantage of a just-in-time inventory management system is

a. The reduction in carrying costs

b. Improved relationships with suppliers

c. Greater employee satisfaction

d. All of the above

S7.7 An item of inventory is purchased for $1,500. The sales price was $2,000, but as the item has now been replaced by a new model, it can only be sold for a discounted price of $1,350. The scrap value of the item is $1,100. To sell or scrap the inventory will involve transport costs of $100. The value of the inventory for statement of financial position purposes is

a. $1,500

b. $1,350

c. $1,250

d. $1,000

The following information relates to questions S7.8 and S7.9

Purchases made during the month:

Feb 10   6,000 @ $2
Feb 20   3,000 @ $2.20
Feb 28   2,000 @ $2.30

S7.8 The cost of 8,000 units sold in the month and the value of ending inventory using the weighted average method are

a. $16,873; $6,327

b. $16,400; $6,800

c. $17,000; $7,000

d. $52,000; $19,500

S7.9 The cost of 8,000 units sold in the month and the value of ending inventory using the FIFO method are

a. $16,400; $6,800

b. $16,873; $6,327

c. $52,000; $19,500

d. $18,400; $6,900

S7.10 Bluesky Limited's Assembly Department had 20,000 units in its WIP inventory on March 1, 2012. Direct materials are added at the beginning of the assembly process. An additional 60,000 units were started during March, and 15,000 units were in the WIP inventory on March 31, 2012. The units in the WIP inventory on March 31 were 30% complete with respect to conversion.

Costs incurred in the Assembly Department for March 2012 were as follows:

	WIP March 1	**Costs Incurred in March**
Direct material	$62,000	$192,000
Conversion	$25,000	$85,150

Using the weighted average method of process costing, the cost of goods completed and transferred to finished goods inventory during March *and* the cost of work-in-process inventory on March 31, 2012, are

a. $277,150; $87,000

b. $309,400; $54,757

c. $295,872; $20,483

d. $295,872; $68,278

S7.11 Jerry's Engineering has a three-year contract to construct a large piece of capital equipment for its client. The contract price is $4 million. At the end of the first financial year of the project, material, labour, and overheads charged to the job totalled $850,000. Jerry estimates that a further $2.65 million will be required to complete the job. An independent evaluation has certified the value of the work completed as $850,000, which the client has paid under the contract as a progress payment.

The profit that Jerry can recognize as having been earned in the current year is

a. $500,000

b. $331,250

c. $121,500

d. None of the above

S7.12 Kurt's Kitchen orders 1,000 packages of ketchup per month to meet customer demand. Kurt used all of the ketchup packages in the given month. The ketchup ordering cost is $50 per order, while the ketchup carrying cost is $0.02 per package. Kurt wonders if he can optimize the number of orders of ketchup he places in a given year. The EOQ for ketchup is

a. 7,746

b. 2,236

c. 480

d. 155

S7.13 The following information has been recorded for Model B manufactured by JKL Enterprises:

Annual ordering costs	$4,000
Annual carrying costs	$6,000
Average inventory level of Model B	300
Orders per year	40
Average daily demand	36
Working days per year	250

The EOQ for Model B is

a. 1,639

b. 300

c. 110

d. None of the above

■ PROBLEMS

P7.1 *(Cost of Goods Manufactured and Cost of Goods Sold)* Gabriel's Guacamole manufactures guacamole in one-litre tubs for the restaurant industry. The following information relates to Gabriel's manufacturing operations for the month of May.

Inventory Account	May 1 Balance	May 31 Balance
Raw materials	$25,000	$45,000
Work in process	$52,000	$15,000
Finished goods	$32,000	$58,000

During May, Gabriel's also incurred the following costs:

Raw materials purchases	$68,000
Direct labour (rate of $10/hour)	$98,000
Manufacturing overhead per labour hour	$7.50

Calculate the cost of goods manufactured and the cost of goods sold for Gabriel's Guacamole for the end of May.

P7.2 *(Cost of Goods Manufactured and Cost of Goods Sold)* Goodman Products has the following balances for its accounts for the quarter ending March 31:

Direct manufacturing labour	$150,000
Direct materials used	120,000
Depreciation of manufacturing equipment	80,000
Depreciation of computer equipment	41,000
Plant utilities	38,000
Property taxes on building	5,500
Miscellaneous plant overhead	46,000
Finished goods inventory	165,000
General office expenses	98,000
Marketing costs	22,000
Work-in-process inventory	65,000

At the beginning of the quarter (January 1), the following balances for inventories were reported:

Work-in-process inventory	$46,000
Finished goods inventory	$192,000

Prepare a cost of goods manufactured schedule and a cost of goods sold schedule for the quarter.

P7.3 *(Statement of Comprehensive Income Presentation)* Acme Fireworks had sales in June of $350,000 for its stores in Hamilton, Vancouver, and Calgary. The beginning merchandise inventories for June and July were $120,000 and $135,000, respectively. June purchases totalled $220,000. All sales are on account (terms 2/15, net 30 days) and 50% is collected in the month of the sale and 50% is collected in the following month. As a result, one-half of all sales discounts are taken. May sales totalled $285,000, while July sales were $385,000. Additional information for June is as follows:

Supplies used	$1,000,000
Salaries and benefits	1,500,000
Maintenance	45,000
Amortization	9,000
Utilities	35,000

Prepare a statement of comprehensive income for the company for the month of June.

P7.4 *(Cost of Goods Manufactured and Statement of Comprehensive Income Presentation)* The following transactions relate to Mammoth Product Company for the year ended December 31, 2012:

Transaction	Revenue/Expense
Sales revenue	$900,000
Purchases of raw materials	250,000
Direct factory labour	450,000
Factory rental	75,000
Depreciation of plant and equipment	50,000
Factory light and power	25,000
Salaries and wages of factory labour	100,000
Selling and administrative expenses	75,000
Opening inventory January 1	
Finished goods	150,000
Work in process	300,000
Raw materials	100,000
Closing inventory December 31	
Finished goods	250,000
Work in process	400,000
Raw materials	150,000

Prepare the following:

a. Cost of goods manufactured statement

b. Cost of goods sold statement

c. Statement of comprehensive income

Calculate the value of inventory to be shown in the statement of financial position.

P7.5 *(Cost of Goods Manufactured and Statement of Comprehensive Income Presentation)* The following information is taken from the records of Harry Jingle Pens for September:

Purchases of direct materials	$ 8,000,000
Sales	32,000,000
Selling and administrative costs	3,800,000
Direct manufacturing labour	5,500,000
Rent	3,000,000
Utilities	1,500,000
Advertising	800,000
Purchases of indirect materials	500,000
Purchases of office supplies	200,000

The following balances were recorded in its inventory accounts:

	September 1	September 30
Direct materials	$ 4,800,000	$ 1,960,000
Indirect materials	420,000	720,000
Work in Progress	3,850,000	4,700,000
Office supplies	110,000	120,000
Finished Goods	6,800,000	4,200,000

Prepare a schedule of cost of goods manufactured and a statement of comprehensive income for the month of September.

P7.6 *(Process Costing)* The Micron Corporation produces semiconductor chips that are used by the computer industry. The direct materials are added at the beginning of the production process, while conversion costs are added uniformly throughout the production process. During the month of June, there was no beginning inventory. Direct materials cost for the month totalled $650,000 and conversion costs totalled $1,895,000. During June, a total of 490,000 chips were started and 290,000 chips were completed. The ending inventory was 75% complete as to conversion costs.

1. What is the total manufacturing cost per chip for June?
2. Determine the costs that would be assigned to
   a. Finished goods inventory
   b. Ending work-in-process inventory

P7.7 *(Process Costing: Weighted Average)* Arnold's Custom Log Beds manufactures log beds in a production line. Direct materials are added at the beginning of the production process. Conversion costs are consumed evenly throughout production. The following information pertains to the month of April:

Work in process, beginning inventory:	85 units
Direct materials (100% complete)	
Conversion costs (45% complete)	
Units started during April	125 units
Work in process, ending inventory:	60 units
Direct materials (100% complete)	
Conversion costs (65% complete)	
Costs added in April:	
Direct materials	$38,000
Conversion costs	$28,000

Work in process, beginning inventory:

Direct materials	$24,000
Conversion costs	$19,500

Determine the value of the finished goods during April and the value of the ending work-in-process inventory for April if Arnold's used the weighted average method of process costing.

P7.8 *(Process Costing: FIFO Method)* Red Coffee Company packages coffee beans for use in restaurants and coffee shops. Direct materials are added at the end of the process. The following data were presented for September:

Work in process, beginning inventory	85,000 units
Direct materials (0% complete)	
Conversion costs (90% complete)	
Started during current period	300,000 units
Completed and transferred out	350,000 units
Work in process, ending inventory	
Direct materials (0% complete)	
Conversion costs (65% complete)	

The following were costs reported by Red Coffee Company:

Beginning WIP inventory:	
Direct materials	$85,000
Conversion costs	$15,000
Added in September:	
Direct materials	$320,000
Conversion costs	$85,000

Determine the value of the finished goods inventory and the ending inventory for the month of September using the FIFO method of process costing.

P7.9 *(Process Costing: Weighted Average and FIFO Method)* Green Machine is a company that makes ride-on mowers for home use. The company utilizes an assembly-line manufacturing system to make the mowers. The company uses process costing as it does not keep track of each individual mower's costs. Materials are added at the beginning of the process and conversion costs are uniformly incurred. At the beginning of September, the beginning work-in-process inventory was 75% complete and at the end of the month it was 50% complete. The following information pertains to the month of September:

Beginning work-in-process inventory	1,200 mowers
Units started	2,000 mowers
Units placed in finished goods	2,800 mowers
Conversion costs added in September	$250,000
Cost of direct materials for September	$800,000
Beginning work-in-process costs include	
Materials	$450,000
Conversion	$180,000

Determine the cost of units completed in September using the FIFO and the weighted average methods of process costing.

P7.10 (*Process Costing: Weighted Average*) Massive Mining Co. refines iron ore for export markets. The following data relates to the company's mine for the month of April:

25,000 units of work in process existed on April 1, the costs for which were as follows:

Direct materials	$18,500
Conversion	$36,750

Production of 35,000 units commenced during April. The costs incurred during the month for refining were as follows:

Direct material	$300,000
Conversion	$230,000

The closing work in process on April 30 was 15,000 units. Materials were added at the beginning of the refining process and conversion was one-third complete at month end.

1. Calculate the cost per equivalent unit for the month of April using the weighted average method of process costing.

2. Calculate the value of work in process and the value of completed inventory transferred to finished goods during the month.

P7.11 (*Job Costing*) The job cost records for Azzizi Company for the month of June show the following information:

Job No.	Date Finished	Date Sold	Job Cost at June 30
101	June 10	June 25	$10,500
102	June 21	June 25	8,900
103	July 6	July 10	13,600
104	June 29	July 1	8,800
105	July 9	July 15	14,000

1. Determine the value of the work-in-process inventory for June 30 and the finished goods for June 30.

2. What is the value of the cost of goods sold for June?

P7.12 (*Job Costing*) Schell, Pickings, and Matthews is a law firm that focuses on environmental law. It employs ten lawyers and three partners. During the last year, each lawyer and partner charged 1,500 billable hours to clients. Lawyer salaries for the current year are $1,800,000 in total and partner salaries averaged $375,000 per partner. Other costs including administrative support, computer services, and legal assistance are charged at a rate of 50% of direct wages. For a recent client, the company billed 50 hours of lawyer time and 10 hours of partner time. What is the cost of the client? If the firm charges a rate of 200% of cost to its clients, what will be the fee charged to the client?

P7.13 (*Job Costing*) The Big Table Co. produced a batch of 20 tables during June on Job 2487. The following materials were issued to Job 2487:

	Units	Units Cost
Plastic	100	$12
Timber	70	20
Metal	15	35

Twenty hours of labour were charged to the job. The labour cost is $20 per hour. Overhead is charged to jobs on the basis of $20 per labour hour. After Job 2487 was completed and placed into finished goods inventory, 15 tables were sold at a unit price of $450.

Calculate:

1. The total job cost and the cost per table

2. The cost of goods sold

3. The value of inventory

4. The gross profit for the tables that were sold

P7.14 *(Job Costing)* Fisher Ltd. manufactures custom furniture and uses a job costing system. On January 1, 2012, there were no balances in work-in-process or finished goods inventories. The following events occurred in January 2012:

1. The company began two jobs: Job A101 (comprising 40 tables) and Job B202 (comprising 60 chairs).

2. 400 square metres of timber were purchased at a total cost of $5,800.

3. 80 litres of glue were purchased at a cost of $6 per litre.

4. The following materials were issued during the month:

    Issue 1: Job A101—200 square metres of timber

    Issue 2: Job B202—150 square metres of timber

    Issue 3: 20 litres of glue to be used on each job

5. The following number of direct labour hours were spent on the two jobs:

    Job A101: 200 direct labour hours

    Job B202: 100 direct labour hour

    Actual direct labour cost per hour was $30.

6. Overhead should be charged to each job on the basis of $25 per direct labour hour.

7. Job A101 was completed and 30 tables from the job were sold for a total price of $15,000. Job B202 was unfinished at month-end.

    a. Calculate the inventory value at month-end of

    • Raw materials

    • Work in process

    • Finished goods

    b. Calculate the cost of goods sold and gross profit for the month.

P7.15 *(Determining the Appropriate Type of Costing)* For each of the following companies, identify whether it would use a process or job costing system.

a) Lawyer's office

b) Oil and gas company

c) Newspaper

d) Catering company

e) Textbook publisher

f) Cellphone manufacturer

g) Doll manufacturer

h) Luxury car manufacturer

i) Soft drink producer

j) Accountant's office

k) Engineering firm

l) Automotive garage

m) Peanut butter factory

P7.16 (Long Term Contracts) Smiley Homes recently purchased a large piece of land and has begun construction of ten new homes, which are anticipated to cost a total of $280,000 each to manufacture. At the end of Year 1, Smiley Homes has incurred the following costs:

Land purchase	$1,200,000
Materials	500,000
Salaries and wages	750,000
Overhead	250,000

The homes will be sold for $450,000 each. At the end of Year 1, $1,300,000 of certified work was completed. What profit will be reported in Year 1 for the project?

P7.17 (Long-Term Contract Pricing) The Children's Hospital has hired Fared Construction as the contractor to build the new cancer wing for the hospital. The project, earning Fared Construction $52,000,000 in revenues, is expected to extend over four years and cost $47,500,000. At the end of Year 1, Fared Construction has spent the following on construction:

Materials	$ 6,500,000
Labour	3,600,000
Overhead	2,800,000
Total	12,900,000

A progress payment of $15,000,000 was paid to Fared Construction at the end of Year 1.

How much will Fared Construction report on their income tax for Year 1, using the percentage of completion method?

P7.18 (Economic Order Quantity) Houston Publishing purchases paper by the ream for the production of textbooks for colleges and universities. One ream of paper is equivalent to approximately 500 pages of paper. The publisher normally purchases 4,000 reams of paper a year. The paper is ordered in quantities of 400 reams, approximately 10 times per year. The carrying cost of one ream of paper is $5, while the ordering cost is $35 per order.

a. What is the economic order quantity of reams of paper?

b. What are the overall cost savings if the company changes from an order size of 400 reams to the economic order size?

P7.19 (Economic Order Quantity) A cellphone manufacturer orders batteries in lot sizes of 15,000 batteries. Each phone manufactured by the company requires one battery. The annual demand for cellphones is 250,000 phones. The ordering cost for the batteries is $2,500 per order, and the annual carrying cost is $0.50 per battery.

a. What is the economic order quantity of batteries?

b. What are the annual cost savings if the company changes from an order size of 15,000 batteries to the economic order size?

c. One supplier offers a discount of $0.20 per unit off the purchase price of orders in lots of 75,000 units or more. What impact would this have on the EOQ, and should the order size be changed?

P7.20 (*Economic Order Quantity*) UltraFit Organic Foods orders many of its grocery items in lot sizes of 50 units. Average demand for organic coffee is 20,000 one-kilogram bags per year. Ordering cost is $12.50 per order, with an average purchasing price of $8. Annual inventory carrying cost is $1.50 per one-kilogram bag of coffee.

a. What is the economic order quantity for coffee?

b. What are the annual cost savings if the shop orders the economic order quantity as opposed to the 50-unit lots?

c. If the coffee beans have a shelf life of only 90 days, what is the optimal order size?

REFERENCES

Hollbrock, E. In the wake of the quake: A supply chain unlinked. *Risk Management Magazine*, May 1, 2011.

CHAPTER 8

Marketing Decisions

LEARNING OBJECTIVES

After reading this chapter, you should be able to answer the following questions:

■ Why is it important to understand cost behaviour in pricing and marketing decisions?

■ How can cost–volume–profit (CVP) analysis be used to help answer "what if" questions related to sales volume and pricing?

■ How is cost information used in setting prices?

■ How can a company determine an optimal price for its products by considering demand volumes?

■ What costs must a company include when setting a price for a one-time special order?

■ How does a company determine a minimum transfer price between intercompany divisions?

◢ What cost information needs to be considered when a company is in the process of deciding to keep or drop a product line?

This chapter considers the use of accounting information in making marketing decisions. It begins with an overview of some of the key elements of marketing theory and introduces cost behaviour: the distinction between fixed and variable costs. Decisions involving the relationship between price and volume are covered through the technique of cost–volume–profit (CVP) analysis. Different approaches to pricing are covered, including cost-plus, target rate of return, market, special order and transfer pricing. The chapter concludes by looking at the process of making decisions to keep or drop a product line.

Marketing Strategy

Marketing is the business function that aims to understand customer needs and satisfy those needs more effectively than competitors. Marketing can be accomplished through a focus on selling products and services or through building lasting relationships with customers (customer relationship management).

Marketing textbooks emphasize the importance of adding value through marketing activity. Adding value differentiates products/services from those of competitors and enables a price to be charged that equates to the benefits obtained by the customer. However, for any business to achieve profitability, customers must be prepared to pay more for the product/service benefit than the cost of providing that benefit.

The sales mix is the mix of products/services offered by the business, where each item may be aimed at satisfying different customer needs. Businesses develop marketing strategies to meet the needs of their customers in different *market segments*, each of which can be defined by its unique characteristics. These segments may yield different prices and incur different costs as customers demand more or less of different products/services.

A focus on customer relationship management emphasizes the profits that can be derived from a satisfied customer base over the long run. Loyal customers are considered assets to a business: They tend to buy more regularly, spend more, and are often willing to pay premium prices (Doyle, 1998). This is an element of business goodwill, part of the "intellectual capital" that is not reported in financial statements (see Chapter 5).

Marketing textbooks typically introduce marketing strategy as a combination of the 4 Ps: product, price, place, and promotion. The marketing strategy for a business will encompass decisions about product/service mix, customer mix, market segmentation, value and cost drivers, pricing, and distribution channels. Each element of marketing strategy implies an understanding of accounting, which can help to answer questions such as

- What is the volume of products/services that we need to sell to maintain profitability?
- What sales mix will optimize our profitability?
- What alternative approaches to pricing can we adopt?
- How can we ensure we earn a profit over our costs?
- Should we keep or drop product lines that are underperforming?

This chapter is concerned with answering these questions and focuses on how accounting information is used to help a company make decisions related to sales mix, pricing, and product/service offerings.

Cost Behaviour

Marketing decisions cannot be made without a knowledge of the costs of the business and the impact that marketing strategy has on operations and business profitability. Profitability for marketing decisions is the difference between *revenue*—the income earned from the sale of products/services—and cost. Often, understanding the costs associated with producing a product or service can be the largest challenge to overcome in ensuring that a company is profitable.

For many business decisions, it is helpful to distinguish between how costs behave; that is, whether they are fixed or variable. Fixed costs are those that do not change with increases in business activity (such as rent). This is not to say that fixed costs never change (obviously rents do increase in accordance with the terms of a lease), but there is no connection between cost and the volume of activity. Exhibit 8.1 is a simple graph representing a fixed cost function. As this graph depicts, as the number of units increases, the costs remain the same. By contrast, **variable costs** do increase or decrease in proportion to an increase or decrease in business activity, so that as a business produces more units of a good or service, the business incurs proportionately more costs.

Exhibit 8.1 **Fixed Cost Function**

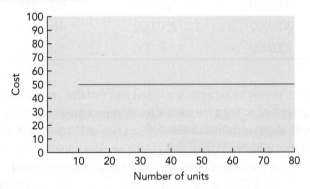

Exhibit 8.2 demonstrates a variable cost function, where costs increase in proportion to increases in the number of units. For example, advertising is a fixed cost because there is no direct relationship between spending on advertising and generating revenue (although we may wish there was). However, sales commission is a variable cost because the more a business sells, the more commission it pays out.

Exhibit 8.2 **Variable Cost Function**

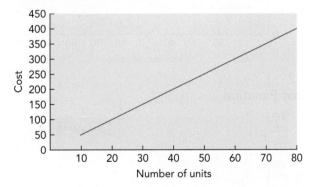

A simple example shows the impact of fixed and variable cost behaviour on total and average cost. XYZ Limited has the capacity to produce between 10,000 and 30,000 units of a product each period. Its fixed costs are $200,000. Variable costs are $10 per unit. In this example, shown in Exhibit 8.3, even if the business produces no units, costs are still $200,000 because fixed costs are independent of volume. Total costs increase as the business incurs variable costs of $10 for each unit produced. However, the average cost declines with the increase in volume because the fixed cost is spread over more units. **Average cost** is the total of both fixed and variable costs divided by the total number of units produced.

Exhibit 8.3 Cost Behaviour: Fixed and Variable Costs

Activity (number of units sold)	Fixed Costs ($200,000)	Variable Costs ($10 per unit)	Total Cost	Average Cost (per unit)
10,000	$200,000	$100,000	$300,000	$30.00
15,000	200,000	150,000	350,000	23.33
20,000	200,000	200,000	400,000	20.00
25,000	200,000	250,000	450,000	18.00
30,000	200,000	300,000	500,000	16.67

Not all costs are quite as easy to separate into fixed and variable components. Step costs are constant within a particular level of activity, but can increase when activity reaches a critical level. This can happen, for example, with changes from a single-shift to a two-shift operation, which requires not only additional variable costs but additional fixed costs (such as extra supervision). A step cost function is shown in Exhibit 8.4. Mixed costs have both fixed and variable components. A simple example is a telephone bill, which will have a fixed component (telephone network access) and a variable component (long-distance calls). Maintenance of motor vehicles can be both time-based (the fixed component) and kilometre-based (the variable component). A mixed cost function is shown in Exhibit 8.5.

Exhibit 8.4 Step Cost Function

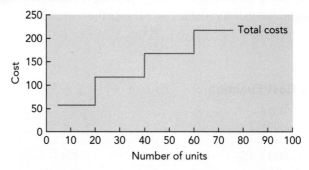

Exhibit 8.5 Mixed Cost Function

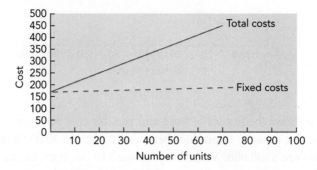

The marginal cost is the cost of producing one extra unit. As shown in Exhibit 8.3, to increase volume from 10,000 to 15,000 units, a marginal cost of $50,000 is incurred (which in this case is 5,000 additional units at a variable cost of $10 each). However, marginal costs may include a fixed cost element (in the case of semi-fixed costs).

Cost–Volume–Profit Analysis

A method for understanding the relationship between revenue, cost, and sales volume is cost–volume–profit analysis, or CVP analysis. CVP analysis is concerned with understanding the relationship between changes in activity (the number of units sold) and changes in selling prices and costs (both fixed and variable). Typical questions that CVP analysis may help with are

- What is the likely effect on profits of changes in selling price or the volume of activity?

- If we incur additional costs, what changes should we make to our selling price or to the volume that we need to sell?

CVP analysis is used by accountants in a relatively simple way. While most businesses sell a wide range of products/services at many different prices (e.g., quantity discounts), accountants assume a constant product/service mix and average selling prices per unit within a relevant range. The relevant range is the volume of activity within which the business expects to be operating over the short term, typically the current or next accounting period, and the business will usually have had experience in operating at this level of output.

Operating profit is the difference between revenue and costs (both fixed and variable). This relationship can be shown in the following formula:

Operating profit = Revenue − (Fixed costs + Variable costs)
Operating profit = (Units sold × Selling price) − [Fixed costs + (Units sold × Unit variable cost)]

In mathematical terms, this is

$$P = Sx - (F + Vx)$$

where

P = Operating profit
x = Number of units sold
S = Selling price per unit
F = Total fixed costs
V = Variable cost per unit

Using the example of XYZ Limited, a selling price of $20 for 25,000 units would yield a net profit of

$P = (\$20 \times 25{,}000) - [\$200{,}000 + (\$10 \times 25{,}000)]$
$P = \$500{,}000 - \$450{,}000$
$P = \$50{,}000$

CVP analysis is a very valuable tool because it enables a company to perform a sensitivity analysis or "what if" analysis. Sensitivity analysis is an approach to understanding how changes in one variable (such as price) affect other variables (such as volume). This is important because revenues and costs cannot be predicted with certainty, and there is always a range of possible outcomes; that is, different mixes of price, volume, and cost.

Using sensitivity analysis, a business might ask questions such as, what is the selling price (S) required for a profit (P) of $150,000 on sales of 25,000 units? To calculate this, we enter the data we know into the formula and solve for the missing figure (in this case, price):

$\$150{,}000 = S \times 25{,}000 - [\$200{,}000 + (\$10 \times 25{,}000)]$
$150{,}000 = \$25{,}000S - \$450{,}000$
$S = \$600{,}000/25{,}000$
$S = \$24 \text{ per unit}$

When we use CVP analysis, we are often working with contribution margin rather than operating profit (as you will see shortly). **Contribution margin (CM)** is calculated by deducting the variable costs from the revenues for a product or service. For example, if XYZ Limited had sales of $500,000 and variable costs of $250,000, the contribution margin would be $250,000 ($500,000 less $250,000). The **contribution margin ratio** is the contribution margin divided by the revenues. In the case of XYZ Limited, the contribution margin ratio is 50% ($250,000/$500,000). The contribution margin ratio can be interpreted as the percentage of each sales dollar that is available to cover fixed costs and profit.

One of the key aspects of contribution margin is that it always changes in direct proportion to sales. In the case of XYZ Limited, the CM ratio is 50% ($500,000), which applies to any level of sales because the ratio of contribution to selling price remains constant within the relevant range. Therefore, if XYZ had sales of $1,000,000, for instance, its contribution margin would be $500,000 (50% of sales).

The **breakeven point** is the point at which total costs equal total revenue; that is, where there is neither a profit nor a loss. How many units have to be sold for the business to break even? This question can be answered by using simple algebra to solve the above operating profit equation for x (the number of units) where P (operating profit) is 0, as follows:

$$P = Sx - (F + Vx)$$
$$\$0 = Sx - (F + Vx)$$
$$\$0 = \$20x - (\$200,000 + \$10x)$$
$$x = \$200,000/\$10$$
$$x = 20,000 \text{ units}$$

From the above formula, we can derive a simpler formula for breakeven:

$$\text{Breakeven in units} = \text{Fixed costs}/(\text{Selling price per unit} - \text{Variable cost per unit})$$
$$= F/(S - V)$$
$$= \$200,000/(20 - 10)$$
$$= 20,000 \text{ units}$$

But rather than using $(S - V)$ as the denominator, we can simplify by using unit contribution margin (UCM), as UCM is equal to sales less variable costs. Therefore, the above formula for breakeven in units could also be expressed as follows:

$$\text{Breakeven in units} = F/UCM$$
$$= \$200,000/\$10$$
$$= 20,000 \text{ units}$$

The breakeven point can also be expressed in total sales dollars. To determine the breakeven level of sales in dollars, a modification to the formula for breakeven in units is made by substituting the unit contribution margin for the contribution margin ratio (CM ratio). For this example, the CM ratio is equal to 50% ($10/$20).

$$\text{Breakeven in sales \$} = F/CM \text{ ratio}$$
$$= \$200,000/50\%$$
$$= \$400,000$$

This is equivalent to the breakeven units of 20,000 at a $20 selling price per unit (20,000 units × $20 = $400,000).

Businesses establish profit targets, and a variation to the above formulas can be used to calculate the number of units that need to be sold to generate a target operating profit:

$$\text{Sales (in units) for profit of \$150,000} = \text{(F + Target profit)/UCM}$$
$$= (\$200,000 + \$150,000)/\$10$$
$$= \$350,000/\$10$$
$$= 35,000 \text{ units}$$

$$\text{Sales (in dollars) for profit of \$150,000} = \text{(F + Target profit)/CM ratio}$$
$$= (\$200,000 + \$150,000)/50\%$$
$$= \$350,000/50\%$$
$$= \$700,000$$

If the business has a maximum capacity of 25,000 units, the limit of its relevant range, this profitability may not be achievable and the cost structure of the business reflected in the CVP relationship would have to be revised.

CVP can be understood through a graphical representation. A CVP graph incorporating the data from the discussion above and on the previous page is shown in Exhibit 8.6. In this CVP diagram, the vertical axis represents money (both revenue and cost) and the horizontal axis represents volume (the number of units sold). Fixed costs are constant, as increases in volume do not influence total fixed costs within the relevant range. Total costs are the sum of variable and fixed costs and begin above zero because, even with zero level of activity, fixed costs are still incurred. Total revenue starts at nil and increases with the volume sold. As fixed costs remain constant, profit per unit will vary at different levels of activity. The point at which the total cost line intersects the total revenue line is the breakeven point.

Exhibit 8.6 **Breakeven Chart for XYZ Limited**

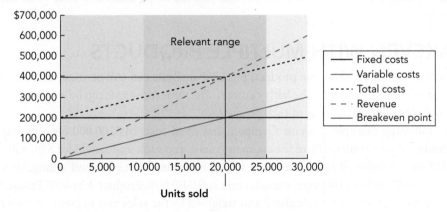

The breakeven point is shown by the vertical lines and can be read as the revenue required ($400,000) to sell a given volume (20,000 units) at a selling price of $20 per unit. The area of profit is found to the right of the breakeven point, between total revenue and total cost. The area of loss is found to the left of the breakeven point, between total cost and total revenue. Note, however, that outside the relevant range of between 10,000 and 25,000 units, cost behaviour may be different so that the CVP diagram might have to be redrawn.

The **margin of safety** is a measure of the difference between the anticipated and breakeven levels of activity. It is expressed as a percentage:

$$\text{Margin of safety (\%)} = \frac{\text{Expected sales} - \text{Breakeven sales}}{\text{Expected sales}} \times 100$$

Using the same example, the margin of safety, assuming anticipated sales of 25,000 units, is

$$\frac{25,000 - 20,000}{25,000} \times 100 = 20\%$$

The lower the margin of safety, the higher the risks, as sales do not have to fall much before reaching the breakeven point. Conversely, there is less risk when businesses operate with higher margins of safety.

Whereas the breakeven graph shows the breakeven point, the *profit–volume graph* shows the profit or loss at different levels of activity. For the same example, the profit–volume graph is shown in Exhibit 8.7. Profit is shown on the vertical axis and volume on the horizontal axis.

Exhibit 8.7 Profit–Volume Graph for XYZ Limited

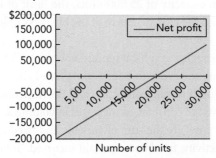

At any level of output the net profit (or loss) can be seen. This example shows the breakeven point of 20,000 units and the small margin of safety at the anticipated sales level of 25,000 units, which can be compared to the risk of substantial loss following from any level of activity below 20,000 units.

BREAKEVEN WITH MULTIPLE PRODUCTS

Most businesses sell more than one product, but CVP analysis can still be used in these instances, although the sales mix does need to be fairly constant. The same technique can be applied by weighting the sales and contribution margins of each product.

In the following example, Ardente Company has fixed costs of $200,000 for a period. In that period, Product A constitutes 60% of the company's sales and each unit is sold for $30, with variable costs of $12 each. Product B represents the other 40% of sales, with each unit selling for $15, with variable costs of $7 each. In this case, the sales mix is 60/40: 60% Product A to 40% Product B.

The contribution per unit is calculated and weighted by the sales mix to give a breakeven number of units. Exhibit 8.8 shows the calculation of the breakeven point. In this example, the breakeven is 14,286 units, but this number represents combined sales of Products A and B. The sales mix (60/40) is applied again to derive the number of breakeven units for each of Products A and B. The accuracy of the result can be seen by calculating the total contribution margin for the breakeven level of sales for each unit that is equal to fixed costs.

Importantly, if 14,286 units are sold but more units of Product A are sold and fewer of Product B (that is, their sales mix is different from the 60/40 split), the business will earn a higher total contribution because the contribution per unit from Product A is higher than that for Product B. The opposite is also true: If the mix changes and more of Product B is sold than anticipated, even though 14,286 units are sold in total, breakeven will not be reached. Hence, while this method is useful, it does rely on close monitoring of the sales mix itself. The marketing department needs to clearly define the sales mix in order for a breakeven analysis to be meaningful.

Exhibit 8.8 **Breakeven with Multiple Products**

	Product A: 60% Sales Mix	**Product B: 40% Sales Mix**
Selling price	$30	$15
Variable costs	$12	$7
Contribution margin (CM) per unit	$18 60% × $18 = $10.80	$8 40% × $8 = $3.20
Weighted average CM	$10.80 + $3.20 = $14	
Breakeven	$200,000/$14 = 14,285.7 or 14,286 units	
Units by product to breakeven	14,286 × 0.6 = 8,572	14,286 × 0.4 = 5,714
Sales	8,572 @ $30 = $257,160	5,714 @ $15 = $85,710
Variable costs	8,572 @ $12 = 102,864	5,714 @ $7 = 39,998
Contribution margin	$154,296	$45,712
Total contribution margin	$154,296 + $45,712 = $200,008*	

*Rounding difference

OPERATING LEVERAGE

Operating leverage refers to the mix of fixed and variable costs in a business. A high operating leverage means that there are high fixed costs, low variable costs, and a high contribution margin per unit sold.

Assume that two companies sell the same number of products at the same price and make the same profit. However, the mix of fixed and variable costs is different between the two companies. Exhibit 8.9 shows an example.

Exhibit 8.9 **Fixed and Variable Costs**

	Company A		**Company B**	
Sales	200,000 units @ $1.50	$300,000	200,000 units @ $1.50	$300,000
Variable costs	$0.90 per unit	$180,000	$0.30 per unit	$60,000
Contribution margin	$0.60 per unit	$120,000	$1.20 per unit	$240,000
Fixed costs		$100,000		$220,000
Operating income		$20,000		$20,000
Breakeven point in units	$100,000/$0.60	166,667 units	$220,000/$1.20	183,333 units
CM ratio	$0.60/$1.50	40%	$1.20/$1.50	80%
Breakeven point in sales	$100,000/40%	$250,000	$220,000/80%	$275,000

These companies have the same operating income but very different breakeven levels. Exhibit 8.9 shows that Company B has a higher operating leverage and, therefore, a higher level of risk. This leads to a higher breakeven point, as more units must be sold to achieve breakeven. However, as shown in Exhibit 8.10, since Company B also has a higher contribution margin per unit, once it has passed the breakeven point and recovered its fixed costs, it will generate profits faster for each additional unit sold because its contribution margin per unit sold is higher than that for Company A. At 175,000 units sold, Company B will experience a loss, whereas at a level of 250,000 units sold, Company B will make a substantial profit over Company A. Company B can potentially make a higher return but, because of its higher fixed costs, also faces a higher risk if the breakeven point is not reached. In times of uncertainly, it is best to have a highly variable structure until uncertainties can be reduced.

Exhibit 8.10 Demonstration of Operating Leverage

Volume produced/sold	175,000	200,000	225,000	250,000
Company A				
Sales	$262,500	$300,000	$337,500	$375,000
Variable costs	157,500	180,000	202,500	225,000
CM	105,000	120,000	135,000	150,000
Fixed costs	100,000	100,000	100,000	100,000
Operating income (loss)	$ 5,000	$ 20,000	$ 35,000	$ 50,000
Company B				
Sales	$262,500	$300,000	$337,500	$375,000
Variable costs	52,500	60,000	67,500	75,000
CM	210,000	240,000	270,000	300,000
Fixed costs	220,000	220,000	220,000	220,000
Operating income (loss)	$(10,000)	$ 20,000	$ 50,000	$ 80,000

Certain industries are considered to be highly leveraged, such as industries that require a large investment in capital assets or in research and development. Highly leveraged industries include telecommunications, pharmaceuticals, software development, and airlines. Companies that have low leverage include merchandisers that have most of their investment in goods to be resold, and manufacturers that rely on labour and manual assembly lines to produce a product. Manufacturers that are highly automated are more leveraged due to the large investment required for machinery and equipment.

ASSUMPTIONS OF CVP ANALYSIS

Despite the advantages presented by CVP analysis, we do need to make some significant assumptions for the analysis to work. The notion of cost can be very complex. When we use CVP analysis, we often oversimplify the concept of cost by making the following assumptions:

- Costs can be clearly segregated between fixed and variable, although in practice, many costs are step costs and mixed costs. For example, we often assume that direct labour costs are variable. However, these costs can be fixed in the short term through time scheduling.

- The behaviour of costs is linear. We assume that as volume increases, costs will either stay the same (i.e., fixed costs) or will increase in direct proportion to units produced or levels of services provided (i.e., variable costs). However, costs are constantly changing due to inflation and market conditions. Consider fuel costs, which can change daily.

- Changes in costs occur only because of changes in the number of units sold or the level of service provided. We assume that the reason costs increase is that there has been a change in production (or service) levels. However, other factors can also impact the costs of an organization, such as inflation, supply versus demand, import and export regulations, and competition.

- A single product/service or a product/service mix remains constant. We often assume a set sales mix (i.e., for every unit of Product A sold, we sell 2 units of Product B). In practice, product/service mix can vary significantly, and different product/services may have different cost structures, prices, and contribution margins.

- CVP analysis applies only to the relevant range. This may limit our analysis as decisions may be made in the current period to move outside this range and the analysis will need to be adjusted accordingly.

- CVP analysis has a short-term focus and cannot really be used as a long-term planning tool.

Despite the limitations due to these assumptions, CVP analysis is a useful tool in making decisions about pricing and volume, based on an understanding of the cost structure of the business. How, then, do firms make decisions about what price to charge?

Alternative Approaches to Pricing

Many companies use one of the following strategies for pricing their products.

- Cost-plus pricing
- Target rate of return pricing
- Market-based pricing

A discussion of each of these approaches follows.

COST-PLUS PRICING

Accounting information may be used in pricing decisions, particularly when a firm is a market leader (or **price-maker**) or when a company offers a unique product or service that has no direct competition. In these cases, firms may adopt **cost-plus pricing** in which a margin is added to the total product/service cost to establish the selling price. In many organizations, however, prices are set by market leaders, and competition requires that prices follow the market; that is, the firms are **price-takers**. Nevertheless, even in those cases, an understanding of cost helps management make decisions about what products/services to produce, how many to provide, and whether the price that exists in the market warrants the business risk involved in any decision to sell in that market. An understanding of the firm's cost information is essential for developing a marketing strategy.

In the long term, the prices at which a business sells its goods/services must cover all of its costs; otherwise, the business will incur losses and may not survive. For every product/service, the full cost must be calculated, to which the desired profit margin is added. **Full cost** includes an allocation to each product/service of all the costs of the business, including producing, marketing, distributing, selling, finance, and administration costs. The calculation of full cost is discussed further in Chapter 11.

Consider a company that sells small kitchen appliances. The company has just developed a new product that can be used to cook pasta in half the regular time. There are no competitors in the current marketplace making a similar product. Since there is no established market price for this product, the company has decided to use cost-plus pricing to ensure that it receives a return over and above its costs. The following costs are related specifically to the pasta machine:

Direct materials	$15 per machine
Direct labour	$20 per machine
Variable overhead	$12 per machine
Fixed overhead	$250,000 per year
Selling costs	$5 per machine

The company plans to produce and sell 20,000 machines in a year. The company also incurs the following business costs that are not specifically related to its product lines:

Administration	$150,000 per year
Plant depreciation	$75,000 per year

A portion of the above costs is allocated to each of its product lines based on the product line's share of the factory space. The pasta machine will take up approximately 500 m^2 of the 3,000 m^2 factory. The selling price that will be charged for each pasta machine will represent a 40% mark-up on total costs.

The total cost for each machine and the expected selling price is presented in Exhibit 8.11. As shown in this exhibit, the **mark-up** is the percentage added to the cost that represents the profit that will be earned. The actual mark-up used may be based on a ratio such as return on sales (as in this example), which is likely to be arbitrary, or on a target return on investment. The **profit margin** is the percentage of the selling price that is profit. In this case, the profit margin is 28.57% ($26.55/$92.93).

Exhibit 8.11 Cost-Plus Pricing Example

	Total	Per Machine	Calculations
Direct materials		$15.00	
Direct labour		20.00	
Variable overhead		12.00	
Fixed overhead	$250,000.00	12.50	$250,000/20,000 units = $12.50 per machine
Selling costs		5.00	
Administration	150,000.00	1.25	$150,000 × 500/3000 m^2 = $25,000
			$25,000/20,000 units = $1.25 per machine
Plant depreciation	75,000.00	0.63	$75,000 × 500/3000 m^2 = $12,500
Total costs		$66.38	$12,500/20,000 units = $0.625 per machine
Mark-up		$26.55	40% × $66.38
Selling price		$92.93	

TARGET RATE OF RETURN PRICING

Target rate of return pricing estimates the fixed and working capital investment required for the business, and takes into account the need to generate an adequate return on that investment to satisfy shareholders. Apply this in the case of the previous example. If the investment required for the new pasta machine is $1,000,000 and the company would like to earn a 20% return on investment, the desired profit is $200,000 ($1,000,000 at 20%). Assuming a volume of 20,000 units, each unit would need to generate a profit of $10 ($200,000/20,000 units). If the total cost was $66.38, the selling price would be $76.38. This represents a 15% mark-up on cost and a 13% profit margin on selling price.

Target rate of return pricing is likely to lead to pricing decisions that are more closely linked to shareholder value than to adding an arbitrary margin to total cost. However, in a competitive marketplace, it is unlikely that a company would use target rate of return pricing because the market price for the product would prevail.

MARKET PRICING

In a competitive environment (where numerous companies are selling similar products), a company is unlikely to use a cost-plus or target rate of return pricing strategy. In this case, the company will more likely be a price-taker and thus base its pricing on the competitive market price—**market pricing**—adjusted to take into account quality, product features, and extended services that may be offered with the product.

Although it is unlikely that all companies' pricing will be exactly the same in a given market, the pricing strategies are often similar. For example, consider the coffee industry. A company like Tim Hortons will not price its products much higher than its competitors, like McDonalds or Dunkin' Donuts. Similarly, a premium coffee provider like Starbucks will price its products similarly to Second Cup. There may be minor differences between pricing due to differences in product features and service levels, but the prices will be in the same ballpark.

Determining the Optimum Selling Price

While cost-plus pricing is useful, it ignores the relationship between price and demand in a competitive business environment. The sensitivity of demand to changes in price is reflected in the *price elasticity of demand*. **Elastic demand** exists when a price increase leads to a significant fall in demand, because customers are highly sensitive to changes in price and may switch to substitute products. For example, the cost of air travel can be highly elastic and when WestJet entered the airline industry, there was a significant customer shift to this low-cost carrier. **Inelastic demand** exists where small price increases/decreases cause only a small change in demand, because customers value the product more than the price or because no substitute is available. An example would be gasoline. We need gas to run our vehicles and although more and more companies are developing "green" substitutes for gasoline, we remain highly dependent on this product.

The **optimum selling price** is the point at which profit is maximized. To ascertain the optimum selling price, a business must understand cost behaviour in terms of its variability and have some ability, via market research, to predict likely changes in volume as prices increase or decrease.

Let's consider an example. Appleco Ltd. is able to estimate the likely increase in demand as the selling price falls. For each level of activity, we can calculate the revenue, variable costs, and total contribution margin. Our findings are shown in Exhibit 8.12.

Exhibit 8.12 Appleco Ltd.: Contribution at Different Activity Levels

Selling Price per Unit	Volume Expected at Given Selling Price (units)	Revenue (Selling price × Volume) (a)	Variable Costs (@ $10 per unit) (b)	Contribution Margin (a) – (b)
$40	10,000	$400,000	$100,000	$300,000
35	15,000	525,000	150,000	375,000
30	20,000	600,000	200,000	400,000
25	25,000	625,000	250,000	375,000
20	30,000	600,000	300,000	300,000

To maximize sales revenue, Appleco needs to sell 25,000 units at $25 each, with total revenue being $625,000. However, taking into account the price–volume relationship and variable costs shows that the business will *maximize its contribution* toward fixed costs and profit with an optimum selling price of $30. At $30 per unit, the contribution margin is $400,000, which is higher than a contribution margin of $375,000 at a price of $25 per unit.

The selling price with the highest contribution margin will always result in the highest profit, as the fixed costs will be unchanged at each level of activity within the relevant range. Although businesses often seek to *increase* sales revenue, in the end they need to focus on *maximizing* contribution margin and, therefore, profitability. This issue is often the cause of conflict between marketing and finance staff in organizations.

CASE IN POINT

Determining the Optimum Price of Popcorn

You've probably at some time used popcorn to fuel late-night study sessions or movie marathons. How much did you pay for it?

If you bought large jars of popping corn or multiple microwave popcorn bags at a big-box store like Walmart or Costco, you likely saved money by buying in bulk. Those retailers did, too, as they negotiated bulk discounts from suppliers and passed the savings on to customers. With razor-thin contribution margins, Walmart and Costco promise everyday low pricing on all items, relying on massive volumes for their profit, to make up for the lower prices.

If you bought a regular-sized jar of popping corn or one bag of microwave popcorn in a supermarket, you will have paid regular price or maybe bought it on sale. Supermarkets tend to use promotional pricing, pricing regular items higher than big-box stores do but putting certain items on sale every week to draw customers in.

Which is the optimum pricing strategy? A recent U.S. study found that supermarkets which used regular pricing plus promotional pricing yielded an average of $6.2 million more in revenues per store each year than supermarkets that used everyday low pricing.

And what if you bought popcorn ready made at the movies? You likely paid a handsome premium. Movie theatres charge more for popcorn in order to keep ticket prices lower, which drives up ticket volume. Sales of popcorn, soft drinks, and other concession items account for about 40% of theatres' profits. While they have to share box office receipts with movie distributors, theatres can keep all of the concession revenue for themselves.

Sources: Rigoglioso, M., Everyday low pricing may not be the best strategy for supermarkets, *Stanford Graduate School of Business News,* December 2011; Rigoglioso, M., Why does movie popcorn cost so much? *Stanford Graduate School of Business News,* December 2009.

Special Pricing Decisions

Special pricing decisions occur when a company has some available capacity or downtime with which to process an order that is outside its normal operations. These are usually **one-time special orders** at a price below the price that the product usually sells for in the market. In the long term, all the costs of the business must be covered by the selling price if the business is to be profitable. However, in the short term, spare capacity may lead to decisions to accept orders from customers at less than the full cost. As fixed costs remain constant irrespective of volume, the selling price must cover the variable costs of a special order in order for it to make a positive contribution to recovering some of the fixed costs of the business, therefore creating a greater profit (or lower loss).

Using the figures from the previous example, assume that Appleco adopted a marketing strategy to sell at a price of $30, but only 17,000 units were sold in the given year. The business profitability was calculated as follows:

Revenue	17,000 units @ $30	$510,000
Variable costs	17,000 units @ $10	170,000
Contribution margin		340,000
Fixed costs		200,000
Operating profit		$140,000

Accepting an order of 3,000 units at $12 each will increase profits by $6,000 (3,000 at a selling price of $12 less variable costs of $10) because fixed costs will remain unchanged. The business profitability will then be

Revenue	17,000 units @ $30	$510,000
	3,000 units @ $12	36,000
Total revenue		546,000
Variable costs	20,000 units @ $10	200,000
Contribution margin		346,000
Fixed costs		200,000
Net profit		$146,000

Consequently, provided that the business can sell a product at a price that at least covers variable costs, the business will be better off in the short term.

A special pricing offer can also help a company that is experiencing a loss. A business can minimize its losses by selling at a price that covers variable costs but not full costs. Consider the previous example for Appleco Ltd., but in this case, only 9,500 units are sold, which is below the breakeven point:

Revenue	9,500 units @ $30	$285,000
Variable costs	9,500 units @ $10	95,000
Contribution margin		190,000
Fixed costs		200,000
Operating loss		$(10,000)

If an order of 3,000 units at $15 is accepted, the loss will be reduced by $15,000:

Revenue	9,500 units @ $30	$285,000
	3,000 units @ $15	45,000
Total revenue		330,000
Variable costs	12,500 units @ $10	125,000
Contribution margin		205,000
Fixed costs		200,000
Operating profit		$5,000

To accept a special order at a price well below full cost, the business must have spare capacity that has no alternative use, and the fixed costs must be unavoidable in the short term. In addition, consideration must be given to the following long-term marketing implications:

1. The future selling price may be affected by accepting a special order if competitors adopt similar pricing tactics.

2. Customers who receive or become aware of a special selling price may expect a similar low price in the future.

3. Accepting this order may prevent the firm from accepting a more profitable order at a higher price if one subsequently comes along.

TRANSFER PRICING

Transfer pricing is concerned with the price at which goods or services are sold between business units in the same company, rather than with the price at which sales are made to external customers. Transfer pricing is used in companies that have a decentralized organizational structure, and it can help management monitor the profitability of each of its divisions. Divisions that transfer products or services to other divisions of the same company are deemed to have sold their products and services to the receiving division. Transfer prices may be based on

- The market price to external customers
- The marginal cost of making the product
- The full cost of producing the goods or services, including fixed and variable costs but excluding any profit margin
- The full cost of the goods or services plus a mark-up
- A negotiated price

When a company is setting a transfer price, it needs to consider opportunity costs. Opportunity costs are the additional income that could be earned on the sales if they were made to an external party or if the resources (i.e., machinery, labour, and plant) were used for another purpose. The general guideline for setting a transfer price is that the minimum transfer price must equal the incremental costs of producing the goods or services plus any opportunity cost.

Minimum transfer price = Incremental costs + Opportunity costs

An important issue in establishing a transfer price is the motivational effect that this may have on managers of both the buying and selling business units, who may prefer to buy and sell on the open market. However, in an increasingly globalized business world, manufacturing, assembly, and selling operations may take place in different countries. In these cases, transfer prices are often set to ensure that reported profits are earned in countries where lower corporation tax is payable, to maximize the after-tax earnings of the multinational corporation. The impact of transfer pricing on motivation and performance is discussed in more detail in Chapter 13.

CASE IN POINT

Transfer Pricing at GlaxoSmithKline

Multinational companies commonly use transfer pricing to move revenues to jurisdictions with lower tax rates. But many countries, including Canada, have strict laws on transfer pricing to protect government tax revenues. Canadian legislation requires that all transactions between related parties—business units of a parent company—be carried out under arm's-length terms.

The global pharmaceutical company GlaxoSmithKline Inc. (GSK Canada) was the subject of Canada's first major transfer pricing court case. GSK Canada had a supply agreement with a related party based in Switzerland, Adechsa S.A., to pay between $1,512 and $1,651 per kilogram for ranitidine, a key ingredient in the over-the-counter heartburn medication Zantac. The drug was manufactured by a related party in Singapore.

GSK Canada's transfer pricing policy allowed the manufacturer to earn approximately 90% in gross profits, Adechsa was required to earn at least 4% in profit, and GSK Canada earned about 60% profit on Zantac sales.

The Tax Court of Canada required GSK Canada to increase its income by almost $51.5 million for three tax years. The court found that generic drug producers paid arm's-length suppliers between only $194 and $304 per kilogram of ranitidine. The court stated that GSK Canada could have reasonably paid Adechsa the highest price per kilogram that generic pharmaceutical companies did.

At the time of writing, this case was under appeal and was still before the courts.

In each of the 2009 and 2010 fiscal years, the Canada Revenue Agency reassessed more than 1,000 transfer pricing files, totalling nearly $1.5 billion in reassessments.

Sources: PricewaterhouseCoopers, *International Transfer Pricing 2011*, Chicago, 2010; Barette, F., Hanly, K., & Yip, K., Glaxo-SmithKline transfer pricing case heads to Supreme Court, Fasken Martineau, *Bulletin: Taxation*, March 25, 2011; KPMG, GlaxoSmithKline Inc.: Taxpayer wins but at what price? *TaxNewsFlash—Canada*, August 5, 2010.

Decisions to Keep or Drop a Product Line

Companies often need to make decisions regarding expanding or contracting product lines based on the relative profitability of those segments. These are important decisions, but the methods by which costs are allocated over each segment must be understood before informed decision making can take place.

As we will see in Chapter 11, major assumptions are involved in how costs are allocated within a business. However, for the purposes of the present chapter, we will separate fixed costs into unavoidable businesswide costs and avoidable segment-specific costs. **Unavoidable costs** are often allocated by an arbitrary method to each business unit or market segment, although these costs are able to be influenced only at the corporate level. **Avoidable costs** are identifiable with and are able to be influenced by decisions made at the business-unit level.

As this chapter has already shown, provided that the selling price exceeds variable costs, the sales of products/services contribute toward covering fixed costs and toward profitability. This position is confused when financial reports include an allocation of unavoidable businesswide costs, and those reports need to be analyzed more carefully.

Consider an example. BC Accounting prepares tax returns on behalf of clients. The clients are grouped into three market segments: business (where BC Accounting also carries out accounting services), business tax only (where the firm completes only the tax return), and personal returns. BC Accounting thinks that personal returns may be unprofitable, and a partner has produced the data in Exhibit 8.13.

Exhibit 8.13 Profitability of BC Accounting Business Segments

	Business (accounting services)	Business (tax only)	Personal	Total
Revenue	$120,000	$50,000	$30,000	$200,000
Variable costs	50,000	22,000	18,000	90,000
Contribution margin	70,000	28,000	12,000	110,000
Avoidable fixed costs for administrative support	20,000	10,000	5,000	35,000
Contribution to overhead	50,000	18,000	7,000	75,000
Unavoidable fixed business expenses (rent, partner salaries, etc.);	30,000	12,500	7,500	50,000
allocated as a percentage of revenue	(60%)	(25%)	(15%)	
Profit	$20,000	$5,500	$(500)	$25,000

As the example in Exhibit 8.13 shows, despite the loss made by the personal tax returns market segment, these clients contributed $7,000 toward the unavoidable overhead. If this segment was discontinued, the profit of the practice would fall by $7,000 to $18,000. This is because, even though the fixed costs for administrative support would be saved if the segment was discontinued, all of the unavoidable costs of $50,000 would continue.

Case Study 8.2 also demonstrates the relevant revenues and costs that must be considered prior to dropping a product line.

CONCLUSION

This chapter has introduced various cost concepts, including cost behaviour, cost–volume–profit analysis, alternative approaches to pricing, optimizing prices, special order decisions, and the issues that must be considered when deciding to keep or drop a product line. Marketing decisions need to be made with a good understanding of costs and cost behaviour. Marketing and finance managers must work together to provide a collaborative approach to pricing and pricing decisions as well as product/service mix decisions.

KEY TERMS

CASE STUDY 8.1: LATEX DIVISION OF HARMON PAINTS

Harmon Paints recently established a new division in the company—the Latex Division. The Latex Division will produce latex paint for use by Harmon's Commercial Paint Division to make a high-quality line of latex-based paints used on commercial buildings. The Latex Division is expected to sell 100,000 litres of latex to the Commercial Paint Division on a yearly basis. The cost to manufacture one litre of latex paint is as follows:

Direct materials	$1.00
Direct labour	0.80
Factory overhead	2.40 (related specifically to the Latex Division)
Total costs	$4.20

The Commercial Paint Division would like a transfer price of $4.20 per litre, as this will cover the Latex Division's costs. However, the company has also been approached by McGill Traffic Paint, which would like to purchase an annual amount of 100,000 litres of paint at a price of $5.50 per litre. What is the minimum transfer price for the internal transfer if

a. The Latex Division has a capacity of 100,000 litres per year?

b. The Latex Division has a capacity of 200,000 litres per year?

   If the Latex Division has a capacity of only 100,000 litres per year, the concept of an opportunity cost comes into play, since the division could sell its paint to McGill at a higher price than the internal price. This means that the opportunity cost of the lost revenue on a sale to McGill must be considered when setting the transfer price:

$$\text{Opportunity cost} = \$5.50 - \$4.20$$
$$= \$1.30 \text{ per litre}$$
$$\text{Minimum transfer price} = \text{Incremental costs} + \text{Opportunity cost}$$
$$\text{Minimum transfer price} = \$4.20 + \$1.30$$
$$= \$5.50 \text{ per litre}$$

A transfer price of $5.50 per litre should be set on transfers to the Commercial Paint Division. If the Commercial Paint Division has an outside source of paint that charges less than $5.50, it could potentially use this outside source (as long as the paint quality is acceptable). The Latex Division could then sell to McGill, which will result in an optimization of profits for the company.

   If the Latex Division has a capacity of 200,000 litres, the division can satisfy both the Commercial Paint Division and McGill, so there is no lost opportunity cost. Therefore, the minimum transfer price will be

$$\text{Minimum transfer price} = \text{Incremental costs} + \text{Opportunity costs}$$
$$\text{Minimum transfer price} = \$4.20 + \$0$$
$$= \$4.20 \text{ per litre}$$

However, the Latex division could include a mark-up on the $4.20 transfer price to the Commercial Paint Division, so that it could also report a profit on the internal transaction.

CASE STUDY 8.2: RETAIL STORES COMPANY—CVP ANALYSIS

Retail Stores Company has three product lines: clothing, electrical, and toys. The profitability of each line is reported below in Exhibit 8.14.

Variable costs are based on a percentage of sales. The contribution margin ratio, assuming a constant sales mix, is 70.6% ($600,000/$850,000). The company's breakeven point in sales is calculated as

$$\text{Breakeven in sales \$} = (\$255,000 + \$280,000)/0.706$$
$$= \$758,000$$

Current sales of $850,000 represent a margin of safety of

$$\text{Margin of safety} = \frac{(\text{Expected sales} - \text{Breakeven sales})}{\text{Expected sales}} \times 100\%$$

$$\text{Margin of safety} = \frac{(\$850,000 - \$758,000)}{\$850,000} \times 100\%$$

$$\text{Margin of safety} = 10.8\%$$

Management is considering dropping the toys segment due to its reported loss after deducting avoidable segment-specific fixed costs and unavoidable businesswide costs, which are allocated as a percentage of sales revenue. However, an understanding of cost behaviour helps to identify that each segment is making a positive contribution to businesswide costs after deducting the segment-specific fixed costs, as the modification to the reported profits in Exhibit 8.15 demonstrates.

Based on the figures in Exhibit 8.15, despite the toys segment making a loss, it makes a positive contribution of $30,000 to allocated businesswide costs. If this segment was discontinued, total profit would fall by $30,000, as Exhibit 8.16 shows.

Total profit falls because the loss of the contribution by the toys segment to businesswide costs and profits amounts to $30,000 after deducting avoidable segment-specific fixed costs. The businesswide costs of $255,000 are reallocated over the two remaining business segments in proportion to sales revenue, which, in turn, makes the electrical segment appear only marginally profitable.

Exhibit 8.14 **Retail Stores Company: Analysis of Trading Results**

	Clothing	Electrical	Toys	Total
Sales	$400,000	$300,000	$150,000	$850,000
Variable costs	25%	30%	40%	
	$100,000	$ 90,000	$ 60,000	$250,000
Contribution margin	300,000	210,000	90,000	600,000
Segment-specific fixed costs	120,000	100,000	60,000	280,000
Allocated businesswide costs (as a % of sales revenue)	120,000	90,000	45,000	255,000
Profit/(loss)	$ 60,000	$ 20,000	$ (15,000)	$ 65,000

Exhibit 8.15 Retail Stores Company: Contribution by Business Segment

	Clothing	Electrical	Toys	Total
Sales	$400,000	$300,000	$150,000	$850,000
Variable costs	25%	30%	40%	
	$100,000	$ 90,000	$ 60,000	$250,000
Contribution margin	300,000	210,000	90,000	600,000
Segment-specific fixed costs	120,000	100,000	60,000	280,000
Segment contribution to businesswide costs and profits	180,000	110,000	30,000	320,000
Allocated businesswide costs (as a % of sales revenue)	120,000	90,000	45,000	255,000
Profit/(loss)	$ 60,000	$ 20,000	$ (15,000)	$ 65,000

Exhibit 8.16 Retail Stores Company: Effect of Closure of Toys Segment

	Clothing	Electrical	Toys	Total
Sales	$400,000	$300,000		$700,000
Variable costs	25%	30%		
	$100,000	$ 90,000		$190,000
Contribution margin	300,000	210,000		510,000
Segment-specific fixed costs	120,000	100,000		220,000
Segment contribution to businesswide costs and profits	180,000	110,000		290,000
Allocated businesswide costs (as a % of sales revenue)	146,000	109,000		255,000
Profit/(loss)	$ 34,000	$ 1,000		$ 35,000

CASE STUDY 8.3: SUPERTECH—USING ACCOUNTING INFORMATION TO WIN SALES

One of Global Enterprises' target customers is Super-Tech, a high-technology company that makes semiconductors for advanced manufacturing capabilities. SuperTech has grown rapidly and its sales are $35 million per year. Variable costs consume about 60% of sales, and fixed selling, distribution, and administrative expenses are about $10 million, leaving a profit of $4 million. The challenge facing SuperTech is to continue to grow while maintaining profitability. It plans to achieve this by continuing to re-engineer its production processes to reduce the lead time between order and delivery and improve the yield from its production by improving quality.

Global sees SuperTech as a major customer for its services. However, Global operates in a highly price-competitive industry, and it is unwilling to reduce its pricing because it has a premium brand image and believes that it should be able to use its customer knowledge, including published financial information, to increase sales and justify the prices being charged. Global believes that its services can contribute to SuperTech's strategy of reducing lead time and improving yield.

Global has been able to ascertain the following information from the published accounts of SuperTech:

- SuperTech's cost of goods sold last year was $21.6 million and its inventory was $17.5 million. This is because the equipment made by SuperTech is highly technical and requires long production lead times.

- Employment-related costs for the 250 employees were $8 million, 25% of the total business costs of $31 million.

- The company has outstanding loans of $14.5 million and interest costs last year were $787,000.

We need to make a number of assumptions about the business, but these are acceptable in order to estimate the kind of savings that Global's services might make possible for SuperTech.

We can calculate the company's cost of production, assuming 240 working days per year, as $90,000 per day ($21.6 million/240). Given the low number of employees and the knowledge that many of these are employed in non-production roles, the vast majority (over 80%) of production costs are believed to be material costs. Using the inventory turnover ratio (see Chapter 5), we can calculate that the inventory turns over 1.23 times each year ($21.6 million/$17.5 million). This is means that inventory is held in stock for 195 days (240 days/1.23) which is equivalent to 81% of working days (195/240).

Global's services will increase the production costs because of its premium pricing, and they expect the price differential to be $250,000 per year. However, these services will generate savings for SuperTech. First, the service will reduce the lead time in manufacture by 10 days. The company's interest cost of $787,000 is 5.4% of its borrowings of $14.5 million. This is a very rough estimate, as borrowings increased during the year and the company most likely had different interest rates in operation. However, it is useful as a guide. If Global's services can reduce SuperTech's lead time by 10 days, the level of inventory will be reduced by $900,000 ($90,000 per day × 10), which can be used to reduce debt, resulting in an interest saving of $48,600 ($900,000 @ 5.4%).

Second, Global also believes that its services will increase the yield from existing production through the higher quality achieved. Global estimates that this yield improvement will lower the cost of goods sold from 60% to 59%. This 1% saving on sales of $35 million is equivalent to $350,000 per year.

Global's business proposal (which, of course, needs to demonstrate how these gains can be achieved from a technical perspective) can contain the following financial justification:

Savings per Year

Interest savings on reduced lead time	$ 48,600
Yield improvements	350,000
Total savings	398,600
Additional cost of Global's services	250,000
Net saving per year	$148,600

This is equivalent to an increase of 3.7% in the net profit (after interest) to SuperTech.

■ SELF-TEST QUESTIONS

S8.1 Mayo Manufacturing had the following activity levels and costs for the last two months:

	November	December
Activity level in units	5,000	10,000
Variable costs	$10,000	?
Fixed costs	30,000	?
Mixed costs	20,000	?
Total costs	$60,000	$75,000

Assuming both activity levels are within the relevant range, what are the variable costs, fixed costs, and mixed costs for December?

a. $20,000, $30,000, and $25,000

b. $10,000, $60,000, and $5,000

c. $10,000, $30,000, and $35,000

d. $30,000, $60,000, and $10,00

S8.2 At Goldfish Enterprises, the costs for 15,000 hours of consultant services are $345,000 and the costs for 7,000 hours are $185,000. What are the variable costs per unit for Goldfish?

a. $20.00

b. $23.00

c. $26.43

d. $10.67

The following data relate to questions S8.3 and S8.4:

Midlands Products estimates the costs of one unit of a product as

Direct materials	40 kg @ $2.50 per kg
Direct labour	7 hours machining @ $12 per hour
	4 hours finishing @ $7 per hour

Variable production overhead is applied at a rate of $5 per direct labour hour
Fixed production overhead is $1,000,000, based on a production volume of 12,500 units

S8.3 What is the variable cost of producing one unit?

a. $100

b. $202

c. $267

d. $265

S8.4 What is the total production cost for one unit?

a. $106.50

b. $297.00

c. $347.00

d. $267.00

S8.5 Corporate Document Service incurs variable costs of $7 every time a document is processed. The company also has fixed costs of $100,000 per month. The selling price for each service is $25. By how much does the average cost change between processing 10,000 and 20,000 documents?

a. $17

b. $12

c. $5

d. $7

S8.6 Relay Co. makes baseballs. It can make 300,000 baseballs a year at a variable cost of $750,000 and a fixed cost of $450,000. Relay predicts that next year it will sell 240,000 baseballs at the normal price of $5 per baseball. In addition, a special order has been placed for 60,000 baseballs to be sold at a 40% discount. What will be Relay Co.'s total operating profit if the special order is accepted in addition to the planned sales at full price?

a. $180,000

b. $30,000

c. $0

d. $210,000

S8.7 Yorkstar plans for a profit of $40,000 and expects to sell 20,000 units. Variable cost is $8 per unit and total fixed costs are $100,000. Calculate the selling price per unit.

a. $2

b. $15

c. $7

d. $20

S8.8 Ryanna's Flowershop sells her flower arrangements for an average price of $30 per bunch, with an average cost of $20. Her fixed costs are $66,000 per year. How many flower arrangements must Ryanna sell in a year to break even?

a. 6,600

b. 2,200

c. 3,300

d. 5,000

S8.9 Jasper Technology Consultants have fixed costs of $450,000 per year. There are 10,000 hours billed on average per year. If variable costs are $35 per hour, calculate the breakeven charge rate per hour.

a. $35

b. $45

c. $10

d. $80

S8.10 Hong Long Ltd. has a product that is sold for $75; variable costs are $30 and fixed costs are $1,000 per month. Calculate how many products must be sold to obtain a profit of $10,000 per year.

a. 267

b. 244

c. 489

d. 147

S8.11 Victory Sales Co. predicts its selling price to be $20 per unit. Estimated costs include: direct materials, $8 per unit; direct labour, $5 per unit; and fixed overhead, $7,000. Calculate the number of units to be sold to generate a profit of $5,000.

a. 1,714

b. 583

c. 1,000

d. 800

S8.12 John Richards Inc. has a cost per unit of $10 and an annual volume of sales of 18,000 units. If a $200,000 investment is required and the target rate of return is 12%, calculate the target mark-up per unit.

a. $11.11

b. $1.33

c. $11.33

d. $1.20

S8.13 Hall Company produces 1,000,000 widgets per year and has a total plant capacity of 1,200,000 widgets. Based on making 1,000,000 widgets a year, the revenues and costs for one widget are

Revenue	$23.00
Direct materials	5.00
Direct labour	2.50
Variable overhead	2.00
Fixed overhead	10.00
Total cost	$19.50

The company was approached by a key customer to provide 200,000 widgets at a reduced price. What is the minimum price the company could accept on this special order?

a. $9.50

b. $19.50

c. $23.00

d. None of the above

S8.14 Gigantic Motors has just developed a new SUV—the Rage. The costs associated with making the Rage include

Direct materials	$13,400
Direct labour	$15,000
Variable overhead	$ 5,000
Fixed overhead	$ 8,000

What is its prospective selling price, using cost-plus pricing, if the company wants a mark-up of 15%?

a. $52,850

b. $38,410

c. $41,400

d. $47,610

S8.15 Division A sells tomato paste internally to Division B, which, in turn, makes tomato sauce that is sold for $3 per jar. The costs to manufacture tomato paste are $2.50 per kg. Approximately 250 grams of paste are used to make each jar of tomato sauce. Division B incurs an additional $0.80 cost per jar to make tomato sauce. If Division A has no other customer to which it can sell the tomato paste, what is the minimum transfer price that Division A should charge Division B per kilogram?

a. $3.00

b. $2.50

c. $1.25

d. $2.05

■ PROBLEMS

P8.1 *(Cost Classification)* The table below shows cost items for Gobblers Restaurant. Classify each of the items as a variable, fixed, mixed, or step cost and explain your reasoning.

Cost	Variable	Fixed	Mixed	Step
Food				
Napkins				
Tablecloths				
Server wages				
Kitchen manager salary				
Electricity				
Rent				
Depreciation on kitchen equipment				
Telephone				
Oil for deep fryer				
Internet service				

P8.2 *(Optimum Selling Price)* Luffer Enterprises estimates the following demand for its services at different selling prices. All demand is within Luffer's relevant range. Variable costs are $15 per unit and fixed costs are $10,000.

Price ($)	Quantity
26	1,075
27	1,000
28	925
29	850
30	775

a. Calculate the level of sales that will generate the highest profit.

b. If fixed costs increased by 5% at volumes of 900 units or over, how would this change your answer to (a)?

P8.3 *(Pricing Decision)* Godfrey Associates adopts a target rate of return pricing system for its services and expects a target rate of return of 25% on an investment of $750,000. Its labour costs are $25 per hour and other variable costs are $4 per hour. The company anticipates charging 20,000 hours per year to clients and has fixed overheads of $250,000.

a. Calculate Godfrey's target selling price per hour.

b. Assume Godfrey operates in a competitive market where the average market price is $50 per hour. What price should Godfrey charge per hour? Is this price feasible with its current cost structure?

c. Assume the competitive market price is still $50 per hour, if Godfrey was able to charge 30,000 hours per year, how would this impact its profitability?

P8.4 *(Optimum Selling Price)* The marketing department of Giggo Hotels has estimated the number of hotel rooms (it has a capacity of 200) that could be sold at different price levels. This information is shown below:

Number of Rooms Sold	Price per Room per Night
120	$ 90
100	105
80	135
60	155
50	175

Giggo has estimated its variable costs at $25 per room per night. It also incurs costs of $10 per room per night for utilities, depreciation, and security, regardless of the occupancy rate.

a. Calculate the occupancy rate that Giggo needs in order to maximize its profits.

b. What occupancy rate does Giggo need to break even if its price was set at $125 and fixed costs were $15,000?

P8.5 *(Keep or Drop a Division)* The Cook Co. has two divisions, Eastern and Western. The divisions have the following revenue and expenses:

	Eastern	Western
Sales	$550,000	$500,000
Variable costs	275,000	200,000
Divisional fixed costs	180,000	150,000
Allocated corporate costs	170,000	135,000

The management of Cook is considering the closure of the Eastern Division sales office. If the Eastern Division was closed, the fixed costs associated with this division could be avoided but allocated corporate costs would continue.

a. Calculate the effect on Cook's operating profit before and after the closure. Should the Eastern Division be closed? Show calculations.

b. The manager of Cook believes that if the Eastern Division is closed, the Western Division will have an increase of $200,000 in sales. If this prediction proved true, should the company close the Eastern Division? Show calculations.

P8.6 *(CVP Analysis)* Jacobean Creek Corporation has provided the following data for last year:

Sales	5,000 units
Sales price	$80 per unit
Variable cost	$55 per unit
Fixed cost	$25,000

For the current year, Jacobean Creek believes that although sales volume will remain constant, the contribution margin per unit can be increased by 20% and total fixed cost can be reduced by 10%.

a. Calculate the operating profit for last year and the current year.

b. What is the increase in profit between the two years?

P8.7 *(Keep or Drop a Product Line)* Travesty Stores are considering deleting its porcelain product due to losses being experienced. Travesty's summary profit report shows the following:

	Cutlery	Glassware	Porcelain	Total
Sales	$30,000	$35,000	$10,000	$75,000
Variable costs	15,000	20,000	7,000	42,000
Avoidable product-related fixed costs	5,000	7,500	2,500	15,000
Allocated corporate fixed costs	5,000	5,833	1,667	12,500
Operating profit	$ 5,000	$ (1,667)	$(1,167)	$ 5,500

a. What allocation basis is the company using to allocate the corporate fixed costs?

b. What is the effect on Travesty's operating profit if it drops the porcelain product line?

c. If the allocated corporate fixed costs could be decreased by 25% overall, would this change the decision in (a)? Show calculations.

P8.8 *(Optimal Selling Price)* Webster Products Group has conducted a major market survey of its likely product sales of automotive accessories for the next year. The survey has produced the range of price/quantity combinations shown in the following table:

Price per Unit	Quantity
$250	33,750
300	30,500
350	27,250
400	24,000
450	20,750
500	17,500
550	14,250
600	11,000

Webster's maximum production capacity is 30,000 units and the relevant range of production is 12,000 to 30,000 units. Within the relevant range, fixed costs are $4.5 million per period and variable costs are $85 per unit. Webster's marketing manager has established an upper and lower price range of $250 and $600, respectively, with possible price increments of $50 within that range.

a. Calculate the possible price/quantity combinations within the relevant range of production and the permissible pricing range, and determine the optimum level of sales that will maximize profitability.

b. What will be Webster's net profit for that optimum price/quantity combination?

c. What is the number of units that must be sold at the optimum selling price to achieve Webster's target profit of $3.5 million?

P8.9 *(Breakeven Analysis, Operating Leverage)* Matthew Hall Elementary School is planning a fundraiser to raise money to buy sports equipment. It is researching two fundraising ideas: chocolates and muffin mix. The details for each fundraiser are as follows:

Box of Chocolates

Size	500 g
Cost per box	$2.00 per box
Fixed costs	$600.00
Selling price	$6.00 per box

Muffin Mix

Size	1 kg bucket
Cost per bucket	$11.00 per bucket
Fixed costs	$200.00
Selling price	$15.00 per bucket

a. Calculate the breakeven volume for each fundraiser.

b. Which fundraiser would you suggest that the school stage? Why? What other factors, other than breakeven volume, should be considered in the school's decision?

c. How does the concept of operating leverage come into play in this decision?

P8.10 *(CVP Analysis)* Clinical Services imports and sells surgical instrument kits to hospitals at a price of $150 per kit. The cost of each kit is $85. Average sales per month are 1,000 kits, which results in the following profit:

Sales 1,000 @ $150	$150,000
Cost of goods sold 1,000 @ $85	85,000
Gross profit	65,000
Fixed costs	50,000
Net profit	$15,000

The national Hospital Purchasing Authority is negotiating with Clinical Services to reduce its selling price by 20%, promising to buy at least 1,200 kits per month. Should Clinical Services accept this offer? If so, why? If not, what would be your suggestion in order for Clinical Services to maintain its current level of profitability?

P8.11 *(Product Mix Decisions)* Unfocused Books is a discount retail bookshop that has three departments: fiction, non-fiction, and children's books. Sales and variable cost of goods sold for each department are shown below. In addition, each department has its own fixed costs for staffing and takes a one-third share of rental and management costs for the bookstore as a whole.

	Fiction	Non-Fiction	Children's
Sales	$250,000	$100,000	$75,000
Variable cost of goods sold	45%	50%	55%
Departmental costs	$50,000	$35,000	$35,000
Shared fixed costs	$30,000	$30,000	$30,000

What is the profitability of Unfocused Books' three departments and what recommendations would you make to the owners?

P8.12 *(Breakeven Analysis, Optimal Pricing with Capacity Constraints)* Greentown Industries sells its transport services at a range of prices to five different customer groups. The company has fixed costs of $150,000 per year. The average variable costs for each transport service, irrespective of customer group, are $7 per service. The table below shows the prices charged to each customer group and the quantity of transport services that are currently sold at that price.

Customer Group	Selling Price	Quantity
Multinational	$19	13,000
Corporate	$20	12,500
Small business	$21	12,000
Government	$22	11,000
Private	$23	10,000

a. If the average selling price is $21, calculate the breakeven point in dollars and volume, and draw a rough sketch of a cost–volume–profit (CVP) graph that shows the relationships between the elements of CVP.

b. Ignoring any market demand or capacity limitations, calculate the optimum selling price for Greentown Industries, and identify which customer group is most profitable.

c. Assume that the maximum market demand for each customer group is 20,000 transport services at the same price as currently charged (see the table above). Also assume that Greentown's capacity limitation is 60,000 transport services. Based on the calculation of optimum selling prices in (b) above but with the capacity and demand assumptions taken into consideration, calculate the maximum profit that Greentown can earn and the customer mix and quantity by which that profit can be achieved.

P8.13 *(Keep or Drop a Product Line)* General Consultants Ltd. has four divisions, whose summary profit reports are shown below (in thousands of dollars):

	IT	Finance	Strategy	M&A	Total
Income	$1,200	$1,700	$ 900	$1,500	$5,300
Variable staff costs	600	900	350	600	2,450
Contribution margin	600	800	550	900	2,850
Fixed costs	471	885	804	490	2,650
Operating profit/(loss)	$ 129	$ (85)	$(254)	$ 410	$ 200

The senior partners are considering whether to continue with the Finance and Strategy consulting activities, as these have consistently been loss makers. The chief accountant has advised the senior partners that businesswide costs, which are included in fixed costs, total $1,200,000. Businesswide costs will continue irrespective of the closure of any division. Those costs are allocated to the four divisions in proportion to their income. The remaining fixed costs in each division are attributable to that division and cover the cost of staff whose expertise means that they can work only in that division. If a division is closed, these fixed costs would be avoidable.

a. Present the financial information in a more meaningful form, showing the contribution each division makes to total profitability.

b. Advise the senior partners as to
1. which, if any, divisions should be closed
2. the likely profit, assuming constant sales, if those divisions were closed

c. By presenting the financial information in a different form, explain the consequences to remaining divisional profitability if any division is closed.

P8.14 *(One-Time Special Order)* Borgus Computer Monitors makes flat-screen computer monitors to sell to major computer manufacturers. Borgus was approached by Green Systems, a new customer, to fill a one-time special order for 1,000 monitors. The following information relates to the normal pricing for computer monitors at Borgus:

Direct materials	$ 17
Direct labour	20
Variable manufacturing costs	18
Fixed manufacturing costs	25
Total manufacturing costs	80
Mark-up (40%)	32
Targeted selling price	$112

Borgus currently has excess capacity that can be used to fill this special order. Green Systems, however, wants the plastic on the monitor to be green, which will cost an additional $5 per unit.

a. What is the minimum acceptable price for this one-time-only special order?

b. What other factors must Borgus consider before accepting this order?

c. If Borgus was currently operating at capacity, what is the minimum price it can accept for this order?

P8.15 *(Transfer Pricing, Special Orders)* The India Company manufactures handmade Persian rugs. Within the India Company, there are two divisions: the Dye Division makes dyes and colours the wool, while the Weaving Division hand weaves each rug. The dyed wool can be sold to outside companies for a price of $20 per kilogram. The finished rugs sell for $1,000 each, and 10 kg of wool are used to make each rug. The following information relates to operations of the India Company for 2011:

Number of rugs sold in 2011	2,000
Wool sold to external parties	30,000 kg
Wool sold internally to Weaving Division	20,000 kg
Capacity of Dye Division	60,000 kg
Dye Division: Direct material costs	$4 per kg
Dye Division: Direct labour costs	$1 per kg

Weaving Division: Direct material costs	$50 per rug
Weaving Division: Direct labour costs	$300 per rug
Fixed costs	$600,000

a. Calculate the operating income for each division and for the company as a whole. Use market value as the transfer price.

b. If a special order of 20,000 kg of dyed wool was received from an external party during the year at a price of $15 per kg, should the company accept this order?

c. What other factors need to be considered, outside of profits?

P8.16 *(Transfer Pricing)* The Oak Company is made up of two divisions: the Cutting Division cuts oak to the desired lengths and the Assembly Division uses the oak to manufacture tables. During its first year of operation, the Cutting Division cut 500 cords of oak at a cost of $50,000. This division transferred all of this production to the Assembly Division, which processed the oak into tables for an additional cost of $45 per table. (Note: There are approximately 1,500 board feet in one cord and each table uses approximately 75 board feet). The finished tables are sold by the assembly division for $80 per table.

a. Determine the operating income for each division and for the company as a whole if the transfer price from Cutting to Assembly is $100 per cord.

b. Determine the operating income for each division and for company as a whole if the Cutting Division uses a cost plus 20% transfer price on wood sold to Assembly.

c. What price would the Cutting Division manager prefer: the transfer price in (a) or (b)?

d. In this situation, what are the advantages of using a market-based price? A cost-based price?

REFERENCES

Doyle, P. (1998). *Marketing management and strategy* (2nd ed.). London: Prentice Hall Europe.

CHAPTER 9

Operating Decisions

LEARNING OBJECTIVES

After reading this chapter, you should be able to answer the following questions:

- How is the operations function in manufacturing companies different from the operations function in service companies?

- Why is it important to calculate the cost of unused capacity? How is this information used in decision making?

- How can a company maximize profitability by altering the product mix and improving bottleneck operations?

- How does the analysis of relevant costs in operating decisions improve decision making?

- Why is it important to monitor and control the costs of quality and environmental costs within companies?

This chapter introduces the operations function in companies, and contrasts the different operating decisions faced by manufacturing businesses and service businesses. Operational decisions, such as capacity utilization, the cost of spare capacity, and the product/service mix under capacity constraints are considered. The relevant costs in decisions related to making or buying components in manufacturing, equipment replacement, and the use of direct materials are examined. The cost of quality and environmental management accounting are also introduced.

The Operations Function

Operations is the business function that produces the goods and services to satisfy customer demand. This function, interpreted broadly, includes all aspects of purchasing, manufacturing, and distribution. While purchasing and distribution may be common to all industries, manufacturing is relevant to only a manufacturing business. There will also be different emphases for different types of businesses, such as distribution for a retail business and the separation of "front office" (or customer related) functions from "back office" (or support) functions for a financial institution.

Irrespective of whether the business is in manufacturing, retailing, or services, we can consider **operations** to be the all-encompassing processes that *produce* the goods or services which satisfy customer demand. In simple terms, operations is concerned with the conversion process between resources (materials, facilities, equipment, and people) and the products/services that are sold to customers. The operations function depends on factors such as quality, efficiency, capacity utilization, and environmental considerations. Each of these has cost implications, and the lower the cost of producing goods and services, the lower the price to the customer. Lower prices tend to increase volume, leading to economies of scale and increased profits (as we saw in Chapter 8).

A useful analytical tool for understanding the conversion process is Michael Porter's **value chain** (1985), shown in Exhibit 9.1. According to Porter, every business is

> . . . a collection of activities that are performed to design, produce, market, deliver, and support its product. . . . A firm's value chain and the way it performs individual activities are a reflection of its history, its strategy, its approach to implementing its strategy, and the underlying economics of the activities themselves. (Porter, 1985, p. 36)

Exhibit 9.1 **Porter's Value Chain**

Source: Reprinted from Porter, M. E. (1985). *Competitive advantage: creating and sustaining superior performance.* ©1985, 1998 by M. E. Porter. All rights reserved.

Porter separates business activities into primary and support activities. Primary activities start with the *upstream activities* of research, development, product design, and sourcing (which Porter calls "inbound logistics"). Support activities include the production ("operations") and distribution ("outbound logistics") functions and the *downstream activities* of marketing and after-sales customer service.

Porter argues that profits and costs should be assigned to the value chain in order to calculate the profitability of each activity in the chain. If an activity costs more than the value it provides, it is considered a non-value-added activity and should be modified (i.e., cost-reduction efforts should be initiated) or eliminated from the value chain altogether.

In many organizations, accounting systems can get in the way of analyzing the costs of each activity in the value chain. Accounting systems categorize costs through line items (see Chapter 3), such as salaries and wages, electricity expenses, and facility rent, rather than in terms of value activities that are technologically and strategically distinct. This "may obscure the underlying activities a firm performs" (Porter, 1985). Porter developed the notion of cost drivers, which he defined as the structural factors that influence the cost of an activity and are "more or less" under the control of the business. He proposed that the cost drivers of each value activity be analyzed to enable comparisons with competitor value chains. This would result in the relative cost position of the business being improved by better control of the cost drivers or by reconfiguring the value chain, while maintaining a differentiated product. This is an approach that is supported by strategic management accounting (see Chapter 16).

The value chain as a collection of interrelated business processes is a useful concept in understanding businesses that produce either goods or services. However, we can extend the idea of the value chain by considering the industry value chain or set of connections between suppliers, the organization, distribution channels, and customers. Exhibit 9.2 demonstrates the concept of the industry value chain.

Exhibit 9.2 Industry Value Chain

Strategically managing a company's industry value chain would mean that the company would focus not only on creating value with its own activities but also on creating relationships between business partners and working together to reduce costs and increase efficiencies in the movement of goods and information. Through linking these various stakeholders in the industry value chain, a company will gain strategic advantage over its competitors.

CASE IN POINT

The Automotive Industry Value Chain

The value chain in the automotive industry is complex and relies on solid relationships and connections among automakers and the other firms in the chain.

The chain begins at the design stage. Automakers such as Toyota and General Motors design vehicles based on the latest consumer trends and needs. The automakers then source raw materials from suppliers of steel, rubber, plastic, and other materials needed to make components. "First tier" large parts suppliers such as General Electric and Canadian-based Magna International make parts that are incorporated into the vehicle, such as seats and interiors, while "second tier" smaller suppliers sell components for parts to the first-tier suppliers. Still other suppliers, such as Cooper Tire, make vehicle replacement parts. The components are then assembled by the automakers. To reduce inventory carrying costs, more automakers are having parts delivered to factories on a just-in-time (JIT) basis (see Chapter 7 for a discussion of JIT practices). Many parts suppliers are located close to assembly plants.

The automakers spend large budgets on marketing their products. The last link in the industry value chain is distribution and sales. Most vehicles are delivered to dealerships for sales to consumers.

While there are no Canadian-owned automobile manufacturers, global firms have many assembly plants in Canada and many second-tier parts suppliers are based in Canada. The automotive industry is considered Canada's most important manufacturing and export sector, accounting for almost one-third of the value of the country's manufactured exports.

Sources: Duke University, Department of Sociology, Professor Gary Gereffi's Research Team I report, 2007, *Global value chain*, available at www.duke.edu/web/soc142/team1/valuechain.html; Sturgeon, T., Van Biesebroeck, J., & Gereffi, G., The North American automotive value chain: Canada's role and prospects, *International Journal of Technological Learning, Innovation and Development*, 2(1/2), 2009, pp. 25–52.

Managing Operations: Manufacturing

A distinguishing feature between a manufacturing organization and a service organization is the need to carry inventories. This topic was covered in detail in Chapter 7. Inventory enables the timing difference between production capacity and customer demand to be smoothed. This is, of course, not possible in the supply of services.

As was discussed in Chapter 7, manufacturing firms purchase raw materials (unprocessed goods) and undertake the conversion process through the application of labour, machinery, and know-how to manufacture finished goods. The finished goods are then available to be sold to customers.

The three main types of manufacturing include custom, batch, and continuous manufacturing (discussed in Chapter 7). In a manufacturing business, the materials are identified by a materials requisition record, which is a list of all the components that go to make up the completed project, and a labour time record, which is a list of the labour hours for the conversion process. In relation to the cost of materials and labour, overhead is allocated to cover the manufacturing costs that are not included in either the materials requisition or the time record (this will be discussed in more detail in Chapter 11).

The manufacturing process and its relationship to accounting can be seen in Exhibit 9.3. When a custom product is completed, the accumulated cost of materials, labour, and overhead is the cost of that custom product. For a batch, the total job cost is divided by the number of units produced to determine a cost per unit. In process costing, which is used for continuous manufacturing, at the end of the accounting period, the total costs are divided by the volume produced to give a cost per unit of volume. The actual cost per unit can be compared to the budget or standard cost per unit. Any variation needs to be investigated and corrective action taken (we explain this in Chapter 15).

Exhibit 9.3 The Manufacturing Process and Its Relationship to Accounting

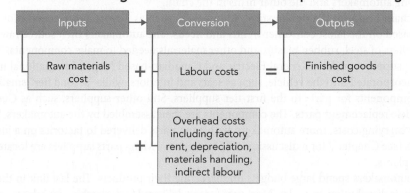

The distinction between custom and batch manufacturing is not always clear. Some products are produced on an assembly line as a batch of similar units but with some customization, since technology allows each unit to be unique. For example, motor vehicles are assembled as "batches of one," since technology facilitates the sequencing of different specifications for each vehicle along a common production line. Within the same model, different colours, transmissions (manual or automatic), steering (right-hand or left-hand drive), and other customized features can be accommodated.

Any manufacturing operation involves a number of sequential activities that need to be scheduled so that materials arrive at the appropriate time at the correct stage of production and labour is available to carry out the required process. Organizations that aim to have materials arrive in production without holding buffer inventories are said to operate a just-in-time (JIT) manufacturing system (discussed in Chapter 7).

Most manufacturing processes require an element of *set-up* time, during which equipment settings are made to meet the specifications of the next production run (a custom product or batch). These settings may be made by manual labour or by computer. Investments in computer and robotics technology have changed the shape of manufacturing industry. These investments involve substantial costs that need to be justified by an increased volume of production or by efficiencies that reduce production costs.

Managing Operations: Services

Fitzgerald et al. (1991) emphasized the importance of the growing service sector and identified four key differences between products and services: intangibility, heterogeneity, simultaneity, and perishability. Services are *intangible* rather than physical and are often delivered in a "bundle"; customers may value the various aspects of the service differently. Services involving high labour content are *heterogeneous*; that is, there may be little consistency in the service. The production and consumption of services are *simultaneous*, so that services cannot be inspected before they are delivered. Services are also *perishable*, so that, unlike physical goods, there can be no inventory of services that have been provided but remain unsold.

Fitzgerald et al. also identified three different service types. *Professional services* are "front office," people-based services involving discretion and the customization of services to meet customer needs so that the process is more important than the service itself. Examples include lawyers, accountants, and management consultants. *Mass services* involve limited contact time with staff and little customization. Examples of mass services are rail transport, airports, and retailing. The third type of service is the *service shop*, a mixture of the other two extremes with emphasis on customer service. Examples of service shops are banks and hotels.

Fitzgerald et al. emphasize how cost traceability differs between each of these service types. Their research found that many service companies do not try to cost individual services accurately for either price-setting or profitability analysis, with the exception of time-recording practices of professional service firms. According to Fitzgerald et al., in mass services and service shops there are

> . . . multiple, heterogeneous and joint, inseparable services, compounded by the fact that individual customers may consume different mixes of services and may take different routes through the service process. (p. 24)

Note that, in describing operations, we will use the term *production* to refer to both goods and services and use *manufacturing* where raw materials are converted into finished goods.

Accounting information has an important part to play in operational decisions for both manufacturing and service companies. Typical questions that may arise include the following:

- What is the cost of spare capacity?
- What product/service mix should be produced when there are capacity constraints?
- What are the costs that are relevant for operational decisions?

This chapter considers each of these in turn.

Accounting for the Cost of Spare Capacity

Production resources (material, facilities/equipment, and people) allocated to the process of supplying goods and services provide a capacity. The utilization of that capacity is a crucial performance driver for businesses, as the investment in capacity often involves substantial outlays of funds which need to be recovered by utilizing that capacity fully in the production of products/services. Capacity may also be a limitation for the production and distribution of goods and services where market demand exceeds capacity.

A weakness of traditional accounting is that it equates the cost of *using* resources with the cost of *supplying* resources. However, often the cost of resources supplied is not equal to the resources used, with the difference being unused capacity:

Cost of resources supplied − Cost of resources used = Cost of unused capacity

Consider a company that has ten staff members, each costing $30,000 per year, who provide banking services, where the cost driver (the cause of the activity) is the number of banking transactions. Assuming that each member of staff can process 2,000 transactions per year, the cost of resources supplied is $300,000 *(10 × $30,000)* and the capacity number of transactions is 20,000 (10 × 2,000). The standard cost per transaction would be $15 ($300,000/20,000 transactions).

If, in fact, 18,000 transactions were carried out during the year, the cost of resources used would be $270,000 (18,000 @ $15) and the cost of unused capacity would be $30,000 (2,000 @ $15, or $300,000 resources supplied − $270,000 resources used). Traditional accounting systems do not recognize this value of unused capacity—it is simply buried in the expenses of the organization and not specifically recognized as unused capacity cost.

Although there can be no carry forward of an "inventory" of unused capacity in a service delivery function, management information is more meaningful if the standard cost is maintained at $15 and the cost of spare capacity is identified separately. Management action can then be taken to reduce the cost of spare capacity to zero, either by increasing the volume or by business or by reducing the capacity (i.e., the number of staff).

Capacity Utilization and Product Mix

When demand exceeds the capacity of the business to produce goods or deliver services as a result of scarce resources (whether that is space, equipment, materials, or staff), the scarce resource is the limiting factor. That is, the scarce resource will limit the number of units of each product or service that the company can produce and therefore sell. A business will want to maximize its profitability by selecting the optimum product/service mix. The product/service mix is the mix of products or services sold by the business, each of which may have a different selling price and cost. Therefore, when demand exceeds capacity, it is necessary to rank the products/services with the highest contribution margin per unit of the limiting factor (i.e., the scarce resource). For example, Beaufort Accessories makes three parts (F, G, and H) for automobiles, each with a different selling price and variable costs, and each requiring a different number of machine hours, which are shown in Exhibit 9.4. However, Beaufort has an overall capacity limitation of 10,000 machine hours.

The first step is to identify the ranking of the products by calculating the contribution margin per unit of the limiting factor (machine hours, in this case) for each product. This is shown in Exhibit 9.5.

Exhibit 9.4 **Beaufort Accessories: Cost Information**

	Part F	Part G	Part H
Selling price per unit	$150	$200	$225
Direct material cost per unit	$50	$80	$40
Direct labour cost per unit	$50	$60	$125
Contribution margin per unit	$50	$60	$60
Machine hours per unit	2	4	5
Estimated sales demand (units)	2,000	2,000	2,000
Required machine hours based on estimated demand	4,000	8,000	10,000

Exhibit 9.5 **Beaufort Accessories: Product Ranking Based on Contribution Margin per Machine Hour**

	Part F	Part G	Part H
Contribution margin per unit	$50	$60	$60
Machine hours per unit	2	4	5
Contribution per machine hour	$25	$15	$12
Ranking (preference)	1	2	3

Although both Part G and Part H have higher contributions per unit, the contribution per machine hour (the unit of limited capacity) is higher for Part F. Profitability will be maximized by using the limited capacity to produce as many Part Fs as can be sold, followed by Part Gs. Based on this ranking, the available production capacity can be allocated as follows:

Production	Contribution
2,000 of Part F @ 2 hours = 4,000 hours	2,000 @ $50 per unit = $100,000
Based on the capacity limitation of 10,000 hours, 6,000 hours remain, so Beaufort can produce three-quarters of the demand for Part G (6,000 hours available/8,000 hours to meet demand) equivalent to 1,500 units of Part G (¾ of 2,000 units).	
1,500 of Part G @ 4 hours = 6,000 hours	1,500 @ $60 per unit = $90,000
Maximum contribution	$190,000
There is no available capacity for Part H	

In this case, based solely on the capacity analysis, the company will use all of its machine hours to produce Parts F and G as there is no remaining capacity to produce Part H. This decision, of course, will need to be made considering other factors such as the following:

- Will demand for Parts F and G decline as a result of the company not producing Part H? Will customers seek a new supplier that can provide all parts?

- Do the products have any interdependencies? Will customers wanting to purchase Part F also need to purchase Part H?

As with most cost-analysis tools, an analysis of capacity constraints must be accompanied by a thorough review of other non-financial factors that may impact product demand.

Theory of Constraints

A different approach to limited capacity that focuses on the existence of bottlenecks in production and the need to maximize volume through the bottleneck (throughput) is the **Theory of Constraints** (ToC). Within the Theory of Constraints, only three aspects of performance are considered important: throughput contribution, operating expenses, and inventory. **Throughput contribution** is defined as sales revenue less the cost of direct materials:

$$\text{Throughput contribution} = \text{Sales} - \text{Direct materials}$$

All costs, other than direct materials, are considered fixed and independent of sales volume. Supporters of this view argue that direct materials are really the only true variable cost of a business. This assumption is often accurate when a company is committed to set production schedules and therefore to set employee schedules.

The Theory of Constraints suggests that a company can increase profitability and maximize throughput contribution by reducing the effect of bottleneck resources. **Bottleneck resources** are those resources that limit the amount of product or service a company can provide. Common bottleneck resources are machine hours, labour hours, and storage capacity. We also recognize that there is little point in maximizing non-bottleneck resources if this does not lead to increased throughput of a bottleneck that is not addressed. For example, if the available machine capacity is limiting the number of products the factory can produce, there is no point in hiring additional staff to operate the machines.

Applying the Theory of Constraints to the Beaufort Accessories example and assuming that machine hours are the bottleneck resource, Exhibit 9.6 shows the throughput ranking. Under the Theory of Constraints, Part F retains the highest ranking, but Part H has a higher return per unit of the bottleneck resource than Part G after deducting only the variable cost of materials. This is a different ranking than provided by the previous method, which used the contribution after deducting *all* variable costs. The difference is due to the treatment of variable costs other than materials. In this case, it is assumed in throughput costing that the cost of labour is fixed and will not vary with the number of units produced in the short term.

Exhibit 9.6 Beaufort Accessories: Product Ranking Based on Throughput

	Part F	Part G	Part H
Selling price per unit	$150	$200	$225
Variable material cost per unit	$50	$80	$40
Throughput contribution per unit	$100	$120	$185
Machine hours per unit	2	4	5
Return per machine hour	$50	$30	$37
Ranking (preference)	1	3	2

Using the Theory of Constraints, Beaufort would focus its efforts on maximizing the number of machine hours available, since this is the bottleneck in the production process. Beaufort may consider purchasing an additional machine to produce the parts or modifying the machines so that they provide more capacity.

Operating Decisions: Relevant Costs

Operating decisions imply an understanding of costs, but not necessarily the costs that are defined by accountants. We have already seen in Chapter 8 the distinction between avoidable and unavoidable costs. This brings us to the notion of **relevant costs**—the costs that are relevant to a particular decision. Relevant costs are the *future, incremental cash flows* that result from a decision. Relevant costs specifically do not include **sunk costs**—that is, costs that were incurred in the past—because nothing we do can change those earlier decisions. Relevant costs are avoidable costs because, by taking a particular decision, we can avoid the cost. Unavoidable costs are not relevant because, irrespective of what our decision is, we will still incur the cost. Relevant costs may, however, be opportunity costs. An **opportunity cost** is not a cost that is paid out in cash. It is the loss of a future cash flow that takes place as a result of making a particular decision.

MAKE VERSUS BUY

A concern with subcontracting or outsourcing has dominated business in recent years as the cost of providing goods and services in-house is increasingly compared to the cost of purchasing goods on the open market. The **make-versus-buy decision** should be based on which alternative is less costly on a relevant cost basis; that is, taking into account only future, incremental cash flows. Generally, with a make-versus-buy decision, the relevant costs that must be considered are shown in Exhibit 9.7.

Exhibit 9.7 Relevant Costs of Make v. Buy Decisions

Make v. Buy: Relevant Costs
• Purchase cost of component or product
• Variable costs of producing the component or product
• Fixed costs that are avoidable

For example, the costs of in-house production of a computer processing service that averages 10,000 transactions per month are calculated as $25,000 per month. This cost is composed of $0.50 per transaction for stationery and $2 per transaction for labour. In addition, there is a $10,000 charge from head office as the share of the depreciation charge for equipment. An independent computer company has offered a fixed price of $20,000 per month to provide this same service.

Based on this information, stationery and labour costs are variable costs that are both avoidable if processing is outsourced. The depreciation charge is likely to be a fixed cost to the business irrespective of the outsourcing decision. It is therefore unavoidable. The fixed outsourcing cost will be incurred only if outsourcing takes place.

The total costs for each alternative can be compared as shown in Exhibit 9.8. The $10,000 share of depreciation costs is not relevant as it is unavoidable. The relevant costs for this decision are therefore those shown in Exhibit 9.9.

Exhibit 9.8 **Total Costs: Make v. Buy**

	Cost to Make	Cost to Buy
Stationery		
10,000 @ $0.50	$5,000	
Labour		
10,000 @ $2	20,000	
Share of depreciation costs	10,000	$10,000
Outsourcing cost		20,000
Total relevant cost	$35,000	$30,000

Exhibit 9.9 **Relevant Cost: Make v. Buy, Simplified**

	Relevant Cost to Make	Relevant Cost to Buy
Stationery		
10,000 @ $0.50	$5,000	
Labour		
10,000 @ $2	20,000	
Outsourcing cost		$20,000
Total relevant cost	$25,000	$20,000

Based on relevant costs, a $5,000 per month saving would be realized by outsourcing the computer processing service.

As you can see with the above example, you only need to include relevant costs in the analysis of a make versus buy decision. Irrelevant costs (in this case deprecation) complicate the analysis and can be excluded.

EQUIPMENT REPLACEMENT

A further example of the use of relevant costs is in the decision to replace plant and equipment. Once again, the concern is with future incremental cash flows, not with historical or sunk costs or with non-cash expenses such as depreciation. The relevant costs for an equipment replacement decision are shown in Exhibit 9.10.

Exhibit 9.10 **Relevant Costs of Equipment Replacement Decisions**

- Purchase price of new equipment
- Trade-in value of old equipment
- Change in operating costs per year
- Change in income per year

For example, Miramar Hotel Company replaced its kitchen one year ago at a cost of $120,000. The kitchen was to be depreciated over five years, although it will still be operational after that time. The hotel manager wants to expand the dining facility and needs a larger kitchen with additional capacity. A new kitchen will cost $150,000, but the kitchen equipment supplier is prepared to offer $25,000 as a trade-in for the old kitchen. The new kitchen will ensure that the dining facility earns additional income of $25,000 for each of the next five years.

The existing kitchen incurs operating costs of $40,000 per year. Due to labour-saving technology, operating costs, even with additional diners, will fall to $30,000 per year if the new kitchen is bought. These figures are shown in Exhibit 9.11. On a relevant cost basis, the difference between retaining the old kitchen and buying the new kitchen is a saving of $50,000 cash flow over five years. On this basis, it makes sense to buy the new kitchen.

Exhibit 9.11 Relevant Costs: Equipment Replacement

	Retain Old Kitchen	Buy New Kitchen
Purchase price of new kitchen		−$150,000
Trade-in value of old equipment		+$25,000
Operating costs		
$40,000/yr. × 5 years	−$200,000	
$30,000/yr. × 5 years		−$150,000
Additional income from dining of		
$25,000/yr. × 5 years		+$125,000
Total relevant cost	−$200,000	−$150,000

Before making a decision, Miramar must take into account that the original kitchen cost has been written down to $96,000 (a cost of $120,000 less one year's depreciation at 20% or $24,000). The original capital cost is a sunk cost and is therefore irrelevant to a future decision. The loss on sale of $71,000 ($96,000 written down value − $25,000 trade-in) will affect the hotel's reported profit for the given year and may impact income taxes paid. For this example, however, we are not considering tax implications and therefore this loss on sale of the equipment cost is not a future incremental cash flow and is therefore irrelevant to the decision.

However, a conflict of interest might be created in this scenario: The company will show a significant (non-cash) financial loss in the year in which the old kitchen is written off, which will have a negative impact on the overall profitability of the company as per the reported financial statements. This may impact the performance evaluation of the manager who makes this decision. Decisions that extend over a number of years, like the equipment replacement decisions, are also impacted by inflation. The time value of money with regards to capital expenditure decisions are explained in more detail in Chapter 12.

RELEVANT COST OF MATERIALS

As the definition of *relevant cost* is the *future incremental cash flow*, it follows that the relevant cost of direct materials is not the historical (or sunk) cost but the replacement price of the materials. Therefore, it is irrelevant whether those materials are held in inventory, unless such materials have only scrap value or an alternative use, in which case the relevant cost is the opportunity cost of the foregone alternative. The cost of using materials can be summarized as follows:

- If the material is purchased specifically, the relevant cost is the purchase price.

- If the material is already in inventory and is used regularly, the relevant cost is the purchase price (i.e., the replacement price).

- If there is a surplus of the material in inventory as a result of previous overbuying, the relevant cost is the opportunity cost, which may be its scrap value or its value in any alternative use.

Let's consider an example. Stanford Ceramics Ltd. has been approached by a customer who wants to place a special order and is willing to pay $16,000. The order requires the materials shown in Exhibit 9.12.

Exhibit 9.12 Materials Requirements

Material	Total Kilograms Required	Kilograms in Inventory	Original Purchase Price/Kg	Scrap Value/Kg	Current Purchase Price/Kg
A	750	0	—	—	$6.00
B	1, 000	600	$3.50	$2.50	5.00
C	500	400	3.00	2.50	4.00
D	300	500	4.00	6.00	9.00

Material A would have to be purchased specifically for this order. Material B is used regularly, and any inventory used for this order would have to be replaced. Material C is surplus to requirements and has no alternative use. Material D is also surplus to requirements, but can be used as a substitute for Material E. Material E, although not required for this order, is in regular use and currently costs $8.00 per kg, but is not in inventory. The relevant material costs are shown in Exhibit 9.13.

Exhibit 9.13 Relevant Cost of Materials

Material		Relevant Cost
A	750 @ $6 (replacement price)	$4,500
B	1,000 @ $5 (replacement price)	5,000
C	400 @ $2.50 (opportunity cost of scrap value)	1,000
	100 @ $4 (replacement price)	400
D	300 @ $8 (substitute for material E)	2,400
Total relevant material cost		13,300
Proceeds of sale		16,000
Incremental gain		$2,700

As a result of the above, Stanford Ceramics would accept the special order because the additional income exceeds the relevant cost of materials. In the case of Material A, the material is purchased at the current purchase price. For Material B, even though some inventory is held at a lower cost price, it is used regularly and has to be replaced at the current purchase price. For Material C, the 400 kg in inventory has no other value than scrap, which is the opportunity cost of using it in this order. The 100 kg of Material C not in inventory has to be purchased at the current replacement price. For Material D, the opportunity cost is either the scrap value or the saving made by using Material D as a substitute for Material E. As the substitution value is higher, this is what Stanford would do in the absence of this particular order. Therefore, the opportunity cost of Material D is the loss of the ability to substitute for Material E.

Quality Management and Control

One aspect of operational management that deserves particular attention is quality management and control. The importance of quality is often overlooked by managers but can significantly impact the profitability of an organization. If a company continually makes a poor-quality product, it will lose customers and will also incur costs that are unnecessary—costs of quality. For example, the costs of repairing faulty products that have been sold and of honouring warranties for poor-quality products can be significant.

Recognizing the cost of quality and reducing these overall costs can be critical within a company. **Costs of quality** can be classified into four categories:

1. **Prevention costs** include design, engineering, and training costs incurred to ensure that a product meets specifications.

2. **Appraisal costs** include inspection costs and testing costs incurred to identify products that do not meet specifications.

3. **Internal failure costs** are the costs of rework, spoilage, and repairs that occur prior to the product being sent to the customer.

4. **External failure costs** include the costs of warranties, repairs, legal claims, and customer service after the product has been sent to or bought by the customer.

Identifying the cost of quality is important to the continuous improvement process, as substantial improvements to business performance can be achieved by investing in prevention and appraisal, thereby avoiding the much larger costs usually associated with failure.

Let's consider an example. Bigalow Industries reported the quality costs shown in Exhibit 9.14 for the years ended 2010 and 2011 (expressed in thousands of dollars). The overall costs of quality were much lower in 2011 than in 2010. During 2011, the company spent more on prevention, which resulted in a large reduction in failure costs and the overall costs of quality. In addition to the reported costs of quality, a company needs to be aware that costs of quality can extend beyond these reported costs and that an opportunity cost of lost sales can occur if customers receive substandard products. As such, Bigalow's decrease in external failure costs could potentially mean that fewer defective units are being delivered and, therefore, the company will experience less opportunity costs due to lost sales.

Exhibit 9.14 Quality Costs at Bigalow Industries ($thousands)

Type of Quality Cost	2010	2011
Prevention costs	$50	$150
Appraisal costs	138	145
Internal failure costs	625	325
External failure costs	890	275
Total quality cost	$1,703	$895

Many different quality improvement methods are used by companies to reduce the costs of quality. **Total quality management** (TQM) encompasses design, purchasing, operations, distribution, marketing, and administration. TQM involves comprehensive measurement systems, often developed from statistical process control, and aims to improve performance and efficiencies by improving quality.

Continuous improvement is perhaps the most common form of total quality management. This is a systematic approach to quality management that focuses on customers, re-engineers business processes, and ensures that all employees are committed to quality. Standardization of processes ensures consistency, which may be documented in a quality management system such

CASE IN POINT

Six Sigma at Honeywell Federal Manufacturing & Technologies

Honeywell Federal Manufacturing & Technologies is a U.S.-based defence contractor, making weapons components and systems, along with custom electrical components. It adopted a version of Six Sigma called the Six Sigma Plus Continuous Improvement Model.

The model ensures that the company integrates customer and business requirements into all design and manufacturing projects. All employees have been trained in Six Sigma Plus. Honeywell collects and evaluates internal and external performance feedback from customers, suppliers, and collaborators. Teams are launched to systematically improve business systems and work processes where the feedback shows room for improvement. The teams are led by senior leaders.

The model's results are significant. Using this approach, Honeywell has cut costs by between $23.5 million and $27 million each year. It has improved energy conservation by at least 20% each year. Supply chain savings went from $2 million in 2007 to a whopping $65 million in 2009.

The continuous improvement model has resulted in a business culture focusing on making and keeping commitments to customers. For at least four years running, overall customer satisfaction with Honeywell has been at or above 95%, compared with an industry average of 78 to 85%.

If the company does well, so do the staff. Honeywell's salaried employees have their compensation and promotional opportunities tied to the results of the Six Sigma model.

Sources: Brousell, D. R. Top of their game (Honeywell's Federal Manufacturing & Technologies subsidiary wins the [2010] Baldrige Award for operational excellence and quality), *Managing Automation*, February 9, 2011; National Institute of Standards and Technology, *Malcolm Baldrige National Quality Award, Honeywell Federal Manufacturing & Technologies: 2009 award recipient.*

as the International Organization for Standardization's *ISO 9000*, a set of standards that represent an international consensus on good quality management practices. Continuous improvement goes beyond processes to encompass employee remuneration strategies, management information systems, and budgetary systems.

The Six Sigma approach, developed by Motorola, is a measure of standard deviation; that is, how tightly clustered observations are around a mean (the average). Six Sigma aims to improve quality by removing defects and the causes of defects. Six Sigma is a customer-oriented approach to managing quality, with customer requirements defining quality improvement goals. Balanced scorecard-type measures (see Chapter 6) are often used in Six Sigma, which is well developed as a management tool in high-technology manufacturing organizations.

Not only is non-financial performance measurement crucial in TQM, but accounting has a significant role to play because of its ability to record and report the cost of quality and how cost influences, and is influenced by, continuous improvement in production processes.

Environmental Cost Management

Of increasing importance to organizations are costs relating to environmental protection and the costs of remedying problems caused during the production process. Environmental costs involve recognition of the importance of corporate social responsibility. By environment we mean any aspects of land, water, and air pollution, as well as waste treatment.

The *ISO 14000* is a series of international standards on environmental management. It provides a framework for the development of both the system and the supporting audit program, and specifies a framework of control for an environmental management system against which an organization can be certified by a third party.

While Chapter 5 considered the external financial reporting of environmental issues, in management accounting we are concerned with recognizing costs for internal decision making. We call this environmental management accounting, but the principles of measuring environmental costs are similar to those for measuring quality costs in total quality management. Environmental management accounting is concerned with collecting, measuring, and reporting costs about the environmental impact of an organization's activities. These costs can be broken down into four types:

1. **Prevention costs** incurred to avoid environmental damage. This could include the cost of equipment to reduce pollution, and the training of employees.

2. **Measurement costs** incurred to determine the extent of the organization's environmental impact. This could include testing, monitoring, and external certification.

CASE IN POINT

Harvard Study Details Coal's True Costs

CHARLESTON, W.Va. — Fully accounting for coal's costs in environmental and public health damage would triple the cost of coal-generated electricity and make less-polluting fuels more competitive, according to a new study by Harvard University researchers.

The study, by the Harvard Medical School's Center for Health and the Global Environment, is scheduled to be published in the *Annals* of the New York Academy of Sciences. Researchers tried to take a broader look at the full cost of coal, following its life cycle from mining and processing, to transportation and burning. They estimated that coal is costing the U.S. between $174 billion and $523 billion a year.

"Coal carries a heavy burden," the researchers said in a summary of their detailed publication.

"Energy is essential to our daily lives, and for the past century and a half we have depended on fossil fuels to produce it," they said. "But, from extraction to combustion, coal, oil and natural gas have multiple health, environmental and economic impacts that are proving costly for society."

The researchers put their "best" estimates of costs from coal's annual air pollution at $188 billion and costs from its contributions to global warming at $62 billion.

Researchers also examined deaths from coal-mining accidents and the $74 billion a year cost in early deaths that other studies by West Virginia University have said appear to be linked to pollution from coal-mining sites. They also looked at economic subsidies for coal, deaths from coal-hauling railroad accidents, and a host of other impacts.

The study was funded in part by the Rockefeller Family Foundation, and was being promoted by a news release issued by the group Greenpeace.

"The public is unfairly paying for the impacts of coal use," said Dr. Paul Epstein, associate director of the Harvard center.

"Accounting for these 'hidden costs' doubles to triples the price of electricity from coal per kWh, making wind, solar, and other renewable very economically competitive," Epstein said. "Policy-makers need to evaluate current energy options with these types of impacts in mind. Our reliance on fossil fuels is proving costly for society, negatively impacting our wallets and our quality of life."

Source: Ward, K., Jr. Harvard study details coal's true costs. *The Charleston Gazette*, February 16, 2011. Retrieved from http://sundaygazettemail.com/News/Business/201102161070. Reprinted with permission.

- **Internal failure costs**, where remedial action has to be taken; for example, cleaning up spillages or leakages, or employee health and safety-related damages.
- **External failure costs**, including penalties incurred for environmental damage.

As countries begin to develop emissions trading schemes to reduce greenhouse gas emissions, environmental accounting is likely to increase in importance, not only in relation to the external reporting and audit requirements, but also in how organizations take environment-related costs into consideration in their decision making.

Waste recycling is an area that can lead to cost savings and revenue generation. For example, in one newsprint recycling company, power is generated as a by-product of the recycling process and excess power is sold to nearby customers. The company treats the water it uses in the recycling process before returning it to the river system. In the longer term, if paper is recycled, the amount of waste going to landfill is reduced and less timber needs to be taken from forests.

For most organizations, continuous environmental improvement, similar to that of continuous quality improvement, is likely to result from an investment in preventive measures and measurement to enable corrective action, rather than in after-the-event remedying of failures. Failure can involve substantial costs, both financial and reputational. Consider BP and the oil catastrophe in the Gulf of Mexico that occurred in April 2010. BP expects the spill to cost in excess of US$39 billion (Forbes, 2011). Further, this tragedy has negatively impacted the reputation of BP and has created major concerns related to offshore drilling's impact on the planet.

CONCLUSION

Operational decisions are critical in satisfying customer demand. Optimizing production capacity for products or services using relevant costs for decision making and understanding the long-term impact of production design and continuous improvement are both necessary to improve business performance. These techniques can be applied to other organizations in the value chain (suppliers and customers) and to competitors in order to improve competitive advantage.

KEY TERMS

Bottleneck resources, 218

Continuous improvement, 223

Costs of quality, 223

Environmental management accounting, 225

Industry value chain, 213

Make-versus-buy decision, 219

Operations, 212

Opportunity cost, 219

Relevant costs, 219

Scarce resources, 216

Six Sigma, 224

Sunk costs, 219

Theory of Constraints, 218

Throughput contribution, 218

Total quality management, 223

Value chain, 212

CASE STUDY 9.1: QUALITY PRINTING COMPANY— PRICING FOR CAPACITY UTILIZATION

Quality Printing Company (QPC) manufactures high-quality, multicolour printed brochures and stationery. Historically, orders were for long-run, high-volume printing, but over recent years, the sales mix has changed to shorter runs of greater variety. This is reflected in a larger number of orders but a lower average order size. However, expenses have increased in order to process the increased orders, resulting in an increase in sales but a decline in profitability. During the last year, QPC had virtually no spare production capacity to increase its sales but needed to improve profitability. The trend in business performance is shown in Exhibit 9.15.

An analysis of these figures shows that while sales have increased steadily, profits have declined as a result of a lower gross margin (materials and other costs have increased as a percentage of sales). QPC noticed that the change in sales mix has led not only to

a higher material content, and therefore to more working capital, but also to higher costs in manufacturing, selling, and administration, since employment had increased to support the larger number of smaller orders. An analysis of the data in Exhibit 9.15 is shown in Exhibit 9.16.

A throughput contribution approach that calculates the sales less cost of materials and relates this to the production capacity utilization shows how the contribution per hour of capacity has declined. This is shown in Exhibit 9.17.

As a result of the analysis in Exhibit 9.17, QPC initiated a pricing strategy that emphasized the throughput contribution per hour in pricing decisions. For each product sold by QPC, a throughput contribution per hour was determined. Target contribution margins were set in order to force price increases and alter the sales mix to restore profitability.

Exhibit 9.15 Quality Printing Co.: Business Performance Trends

	Last Year	One Year Ago	Two Years Ago
Sales	$2,255,000	$2,125,000	$2,000,000
Variable production costs:			
Materials	1,260,000	1,105,000	980,000
Labour	250,000	225,000	205,000
Other production costs	328,000	312,000	295,000
Total variable costs	1,838,000	1,642,000	1,480,000
Contribution margin	417,000	483,000	520,000
Fixed selling and administration expenses	325,000	285,000	250,000
Net profit	$ 92,000	$ 198,000	$ 270,000
Production capacity utilization (hours)	12,100	11,200	10,500

Exhibit 9.16 Quality Printing Co.: Analysis of Business Performance (% of sales)

	Last Year	One Year Ago	Two Years Ago
Sales growth	6.1%	6.3%	
Net profit	4.1	9.3	13.5%
Contribution margin	18.5	22.7	26.0
Materials	55.9	52.0	49.0
Labour and other costs	25.6	25.3	25.0
Fixed selling and administration expenses	14.4	13.4	12.5

Exhibit 9.17 **Quality Printing Co.: Throughput Contribution**

	Last Year	One Year Ago	Two Years Ago
Throughput contribution margin	$995,000	$1,020,000	$1,020,000
Production hours	12,100	11,200	10,500
Throughput contribution per hour	$82	$91	$97

CASE STUDY 9.2: VEHICLE PARTS CO.—THE EFFECT OF EQUIPMENT REPLACEMENT ON COSTS AND PRICES

Vehicle Parts Company (VPC) is a privately owned manufacturer of components and a first-tier supplier to several major motor vehicle assemblers. VPC has a long history and substantial machinery that was designed for long-run, high-volume parts. The nature of the machinery meant that long set-up times were needed to make the machines ready for the small production runs. The old equipment kept breaking down and quality was poor. As a result of these problems, about 35% of VPC's production was delivered late. Consequently, there was a gradual loss of production volume as customers sought more reliable suppliers. Demand was unlikely to increase in the short term because of delivery performance. However, as the current machinery had been fully written off, the company incurred no depreciation expense. As a result, its reported profits were quite high.

The market now demands more flexibility, with short production runs of parts to meet the assemblers' just-in-time (JIT) requirements. New computer-numerically controlled (CNC) equipment was bought in order to satisfy customer demand and provide the ability to grow sales volume. While the new CNC equipment substantially reduced set-up times, the significant depreciation charge increased the product cost and made the manufactured parts less profitable. The marketing manager believes that the depreciation cost should be discounted, as, otherwise, the business would lose sales by retaining the existing mark-up on cost. VPC's accountant argued that depreciation is a cost that must be included in the cost of the product, and prepared the summary in Exhibit 9.18.

Exhibit 9.18 **Vehicle Parts Company: Comparison of Costs and Selling Prices for Existing and New CNC Machine**

	Existing Machine	New CNC Machine
Original cost	$250,000	$1,000,000
Depreciation at 20% per year	Fully written off	$200,000
Available hours (2 shifts)	1,920	1,920
Set-up time	35%	5%
Running time	65%	95%
Available running hours	1,248	1,824
Hours per part	0.5	0.35
Production capacity (number of parts)	2,496	5,211
Market demand		2,500
Depreciation cost per part (New machine = $200,000/2,500)	$ 0	$ 80
Material cost per part	$ 75	$ 75
Labour and other costs per part	$ 30	$ 20
Total cost per part	$105	$175
Mark-up 50%	$ 53	$ 88
Selling price	$158	$263
Maximum selling price		$158
Effective markdown on cost		−10%

If the capital investment was not made, volume would decline as a result of quality and delivery performance. If existing prices were maintained, reported profitability would decline by $175,000 per year ($175 − $105 = $70 per part × 2,500 parts). If prices were increased to cover the depreciation cost, volume would fall further and profitability would decline.

This presents a challenge for the company. There is little choice but to make the capital investment if the business is to survive. However, unless market demand increases, there is little likelihood of an adequate return on investment being achieved. VPC believes that, under a life-cycle approach, volume will increase and returns will be generated once quality and delivery performance have improved with the new equipment. On a relevant cost basis, once the capital investment decision has been made, depreciation could be ignored as it did not incur any future, incremental cash flow.

This case is a good example of how accounting makes visible certain aspects of organizations and changes the way managers view events.

CASE STUDY 9.3: ALOHA INDUSTRIES— MAKE v. BUY CASE

Aloha Industries expects to sell 10,000 sailboards this year. Currently, Aloha manufactures the sails for its sailboards. The company reported the following costs for making 10,000 sails.

Cost	Per Unit Cost	Total Cost (10,000 units)
Direct materials	$80	$ 800,000
Direct labour	60	600,000
Variable overhead	10	100,000
Other fixed costs		55,000
Facility rent		154,000
Allocated head office costs		85,000
Total cost		$1,794,000

Aloha has received an offer from Ocean Sails to provide 10,000 sails per year for $160 each. After analyzing the costs for producing sails, Aloha Industries has determined that the facility rent and allocated head office costs will not change if the company accepts the offer from Ocean Sails. The other fixed costs will be reduced to $25,000 if the offer is accepted.

Aloha has considered that if it purchases sails from Ocean Sails, it may be able to use the existing space in the factory to make 5,000 board bags—bags that are used to carry windsurfing gear. These bags can be sold for $150 each and will cost $35 in direct materials, $40 in direct labour, and $10 in variable overhead, and they will incur the same other fixed costs as Aloha currently incurs in making sails.

In order to decide on whether to accept this offer from Ocean Sails, Aloha identified the relevant costs for making and buying the sails as shown in Exhibit 9.19.

Exhibit 9.19 **Relevant Cost of Making v. Buying Sails**

	Relevant Cost to Make Sails		Relevant Cost to Buy Sails	
	Per Unit	Total	Per Unit	Total
Purchase price			$160	$1,600,000
Direct materials	$80	$800,000		
Direct labour	60	600,000		
Variable overhead	10	100,000		
Other fixed costs		55,000		25,000
Total relevant costs	$150	$1,555,000		$1,625,000

If the company did not consider using the freed space to make board bags and based its decision solely on discontinuing making the sails and buying them from Ocean Sails, Aloha would not accept this offer because the costs to buy exceed the costs of making the sails. However, Aloha must consider the additional profits that will occur if it uses the freed space to make board bags. The relevant cost data of using the freed space is presented in Exhibit 9.20.

If Aloha uses the freed space to make board bags, the other fixed costs become irrelevant as they will be $55,000 for both scenarios. The additional sales, direct materials, direct labour, and variable overhead costs that are included under the buy decision are based on sales of 5,000 bags. If the company decides to purchase the sails externally and use the existing space to make board bags, it will improve its overall profitability by $225,000 ($1,500,000 less $1,275,000).

Exhibit 9.20 Relevant Cost of Making Sails v. Buying Sails/Making Board Bags

	Relevant Cost to Make Sails		Relevant Cost to Buy Sails and Use Space to Make Bags	
	Per Unit	Total	Per Unit	Total
Purchase price			$160	$1,600,000
Incremental sales			150	(750,000)
Direct materials	$80	$800,000	35	175,000
Direct labour	60	600,000	40	200,000
Variable overhead	10	100,000	10	50,000
Total relevant costs	$150	$1,500,000		$1,275,000

■ SELF-TEST QUESTIONS

S9.1 Maxitank makes four products. The following information relates to each product:

	Product R	**Product S**	**Product T**	**Product U**
Selling price	$12	$20	$25	$8
Direct materials	$ 4	$11	$15	$4
Direct labour hours	2	4	5	2
Machine hours	4	3	5	1.5

Maxitank's sales are limited by the machine capacity of the factory, which is the company's bottleneck. Which product should be produced first in order to maximize the throughput generated from the limited capacity?

a. Product R

b. Product S

c. Product T

d. Product U

S9.2 Nathan Eldridge is a lawyer whose services are in very high demand. He currently has five clients seeking his services but only 80 hours of available time. He has provided the following estimates for each of his clients:

Client	A	B	C	D	E
Revenue	$5,000	$7,500	$10,000	$3,000	$3,500
Costs	$2,000	$3,500	$6,000	$1,000	$1,000
Estimated hours	15	25	30	5	10

How should Nathan spend his time? Rank the jobs in order of highest return per hour.

a. D, E, A, B, C

b. E, D, A, C, B

c. C, B, A, E, D

d. D, C, A, E, B

S9.3 Which one of the following items is NOT relevant in a make-or-buy decision?

a. Variable costs of producing each unit

b. Cost to purchase each unit from outside supplier

c. Possible revenues earned from using space for another purpose

d. Fixed costs of the factory that will not change whether the units are made or purchased

e. Capacity of plant

S9.4 A call centre can process 100,000 calls per month for a cost of $250,000. During one month, the number of calls processed was 85,000. During that month, the cost of unused capacity was

a. $25,000

b. $37,500

c. $21,250

d. $15,000

S9.5 Sunny Enterprises makes a component that is used in the assembly of radios, the company's main product. For the component, the variable costs per unit are $18. Razor Edge Products wants to sell Sunny 10,000 units of the component for $22 per unit. Sunny will be able to avoid $30,000 in fixed overhead costs if it chooses to purchase the component externally. What is the cost or benefit of purchasing the component from Razor Edge?

a. $10,000 benefit

b. $10,000 cost

c. $40,000 cost

d. $70,000 cost

S9.6 Pawistik Corporation makes computer screens that are used in the assembly of laptops which Pawistik sells to the general public. The costs per screen are as follows:

Direct materials	$12.00
Direct labour	15.00
Variable overhead	15.00
Fixed overhead	22.00

Computer Accessories Inc. has offered to sell Pawistik 50,000 of the screens for $45 each. If Pawistik accepts this offer, the company will be able to eliminate $200,000 in fixed manufacturing overhead costs. What is the cost or benefit of purchasing from Computer Accessories?

a. $50,000 benefit

b. $750,000 cost

c. $150,000 cost

d. $200,000 benefit

S9.7 Halls Medical Labs makes medical examining tables for hospitals. The current equipment used to manufacture the tables has a book value of $250,000. Halls is considering replacing the existing equipment because it will increase the company's production capacity by 500 tables per year. Currently, Halls is operating at full capacity and is not able meet all of the demand for its tables. The cost of the new equipment is $500,000 and the manufacturer will provide a $45,000 trade-in for the old equipment. The tables sell for $2,000 each and have variable costs of $500 each. What is the cost or benefit of purchasing the new equipment if they expect to recoup the cost in one year?

a. $455,000 cost

b. $45,000 benefit

c. $295,000 benefit

d. $545,000 benefit

S9.8 Barb's Fine Bakery is considering purchasing a new truck for the business. Barb's existing truck is a gas guzzler, and with increases in the costs of fuel, she feels she may be able to save a great deal of money if she bought a new hybrid truck. Both the old and new trucks are expected to last five years. The following information relates to both the new and the old truck:

	Old Delivery Truck	New Delivery Truck
Original cost	$45,000	$60,000
Market value	15,000	60,000
Annual operating costs	10,000	5,000

What is the cost or benefit of purchasing the new truck?

a. $40,000 cost

b. $45,000 cost

c. $10,000 benefit

d. $20,000 cost

S9.9 The goal of the Theory of Constraints and throughput accounting is to maximize production capacity in bottlenecks by a ranking of products that have

a. The highest selling price

b. The highest rate of contribution as a percentage of sales

c. The highest contribution (of sales less variable costs) per hour of bottleneck capacity

d. The highest throughput contribution (of sales less cost of materials) per hour of bottleneck capacity

S9.10 Warranty costs are an example of

a. Internal failure costs

b. External failure costs

c. Prevention costs

d. Appraisal costs

S9.11 Quality training is an example of

a. Internal failure costs

b. External failure costs

c. Prevention costs

d. Appraisal costs

S9.12 Which of the following is NOT an example of an internal failure cost?

a. Scrap

b. Reworking of products

c. Supplier scrap and rework

d. Returned product

■ PROBLEMS

P9.1 *(Decisions under Capacity Constraints)* Harrison Products' capacity is 20,000 units of Product J per year. A summary of operating results for last year is as follows:

Sales (12,000 units @ $100)	$1,200,000
Variable costs	588,000
Contribution margin	612,000
Fixed costs	245,000
Net operating income	$367,000

A foreign distributor has offered to buy a guaranteed 8,000 units of Product J at $95 per unit next year. Harrison expects its regular sales next year to be 15,000 units.

a. If Harrison accepts this offer and foregoes some of its expected sales to ensure that it does not exceed capacity, what would be the total operating profit next year, assuming that total fixed costs increase by $100,000?

b. If Harrison can use the extra capacity not needed for its regular sales of 15,000 of Product J to produce 5,000 of Product K, which can be sold for $125 each with a variable cost of $45 and additional fixed costs of $80,000, should Harrison produce the new product, accept the offer from the foreign distributor, or just produce the regular 15,000 units of Product J per year?

P9.2 *(Relevant Cost of Materials)* Universal Conglomerates has a new product that requires 150 kg of material (Y876), which is in continual use within the firm. There are 100 kg of Y876 in inventory, at a cost $11.00/kg. The replacement value is $12.50/kg and the scrap value is $2.00/kg.

a. Calculate the relevant cost of the material to be used in the new product.

b. How would the relevant cost of materials change if there is an excess of inventory of this material?

P9.3 *(Product Mix Decisions under Capacity Constraints)* Magnificent Products makes three products: Macro, Mezzo, and Micro. The following information has been provided in relation to each product:

	Macro	Mezzo	Micro
Budgeted sales units	10,000	7,500	5,000
Selling price per unit	$12	$16	$18
Direct materials	$ 3	$ 6	$ 1
Direct labour	$ 3	$ 1	$ 3
Machine hours per unit	3	3	5

a. If the company has a limited production capacity, preventing all of its budgeted sales from being produced, how should Magnificent rank its products for manufacture in order to maximize profitability?

b. If the production operation at Magnificent has a set production schedule for the next two months, which means that employees' work schedules are fixed regardless of the sales mix or production volumes, how will this change your recommended product mix?

P9.4 *(Product Mix)* The Ontario Toy Car Company makes two types of tin toy cars: the sedan and the SUV. These tin cars have become a fad among many children and adults. Both cars are made on the same machine but use a slightly different process. In normal operating circumstances, the machine has a capacity of 360 machine hours per month to make both types of cars. The following information relates to the two types of car:

	Sedan	SUV
Cars made per hour	10	8
Selling price	$28	$35
Direct materials	$ 9	$12
Direct labour	$ 5	$ 7
Variable overhead per car	$ 8	$ 9
Annual fixed manufacturing costs	$75,000 in total	

a. Since these cars are so popular, the Ontario Toy Car Company believes that demand will exceed its supply for the next two years. What is the optimal product mix that maximizes net income for Ontario Toy Cars?

b. Assume that the sedan is not quite as popular as the SUV. The company believes that it can sell no more than 1000 sedans per month. Does this change the optimal production mix? How?

c. What other factors will the company want to consider before committing to a particular product mix?

P9.5 *(Capacity Utilization)* HiTek Industries spends $20,000 per year on Component A. NewIdea Co. has a product that can be used instead of Component A, and it would cost HiTek $30,000 per year, compared to HiTek's current costs for Component A of $20,000 per year. NewIdea believes that it can justify the additional price through productivity improvements.

NewIdea's sales representative visits HiTek and is able to determine that HiTek has a maximum capacity of 25,000 units per year. The sales price is $100 per unit and the contribution margin is 30%. HiTek has currently been experiencing a 7.5% scrap rate and a 7.5% downtime rate. NewIdea's product is expected to reduce scrap to 5% and downtime to 5%.

a. Produce a financial justification that will support NewIdea's proposal, assuming that NewIdea's products will reduce the downtime and waste to the target levels.

b. If you received such a proposal from NewIdea, what would you want to be sure of before accepting it?

P9.6 *(Capacity Utilization)* Maximus Company has met all production requirements for the current month and has an opportunity to produce additional units of product with its excess capacity. Unit selling prices and unit costs for three models of one of its product lines are as follows:

	Plain Model	Regular Model	Super Model
Selling price	$30.00	$32.50	$40.00
Direct material	9.00	10.00	9.50
Direct labour (@ $5 per hour)	5.00	7.50	10.00
Variable overhead	4.00	6.00	8.00
Fixed overhead	8.00	7.50	7.50

Variable overhead is applied on the basis of direct-labour dollars, while fixed overhead is applied on the basis of machine hours. There is sufficient demand for the additional production of any model of the product line.

a. If Maximus Company has excess machine capacity and can add more labour as needed (i.e., neither machine capacity nor labour is a constraint), which product is the most attractive to produce? Provide calculations and reasons to support your answer.

b. If Maximus Company has excess machine capacity but a limited amount of labour time available, to which product or products should the excess production capacity be devoted? Provide calculations and reasons to support your answer.

P9.7 *(Product Mix Decision)* Process Solutions provides a computer-based document processing service. The accountant has produced the following analysis.

	Standard	**Modified**	**Advanced**
Sales quantity	1,000	1,100	1,200
Selling price	$5	$5	$6
Sales revenue	$5,000	$5,500	$7,200
Labour hours	100	120	160
Labour cost @ $20/hour	$2,000	$2,400	$3,200
Contribution margin	$3,000	$3,100	$4,000
Contribution margin per unit sold	$3	$2.82	$3.33

The sales manager, whose team is paid a commission on sales revenue, prefers to sell the higher priced Advanced service. This is also the preferred service for the accountant, although not for the same reason. The accountant argues that the Advanced service is better because of the higher contribution margin per unit sold. The operations manager argues that the advanced service consumes more labour hours than the Standard or Modified services and as labour availability limits his ability to process work, this should also be taken into account. The operations manager prefers the Standard or Modified service, as these provide greater ability to use his capacity more flexibly.

The general manager has asked for your advice in relation to this disagreement within the management team. What advice would you give her?

P9.8 *(Product Mix Decisions)* Swift Airlines has a daily return flight from Saskatoon, Saskatchewan, to Calgary, Alberta. The aircraft for the flight has a capacity of 120 passengers. Swift sells its tickets at a range of prices. Its business plan works on the basis of the following mix of ticket prices for each day's flight:

Business	30 @ $300	$9,000
Economy regular	40 @ $200	$8,000
Advance purchase	20 @ $120	$2,400
Seven-day purchase	20 @ $65	$1,300
Standby	10 @ $30	$300
Revenue	120 tickets	$21,000

Swift's head office accounting department has calculated its costs per flight as follows:

Cost per passenger (additional fuel, insurance, baggage handling, etc.)	$25 per passenger × 120 tickets sold = $3,000
Flight costs (aircraft lease, flight and cabin crew, airport and landing charges, etc.)	$7,500 per flight
Route costs (support needed for each destination)	$2,000 (based on one-half of the daily cost of $4,000—balance charged to return flight)
Business overhead	$3,000 (allocation of head office overhead)
Total	$15,500

This results in a budgeted profit of $5,500 per flight, assuming that all seats are sold at the budgeted price. The head office accountant for western Canada routes has advised the route manager for Calgary that while the Saskatoon–Calgary inbound leg is breaking even, losses are being made on the Calgary–Saskatoon outbound leg. If profits cannot be generated, the route may need to be closed, with the aircraft and crew being assigned to another route. The route manager for Calgary has extracted recent sales figures, a typical flight having the following sales mix:

Business	18 @ $300	$5,400
Economy regular	28 @ $200	$5,600
Advance purchase	16 @ $120	$1,920
Seven-day purchase	15 @ $65	$ 975
Standby	10 @ $30	$ 300
Revenue	87 tickets	$14,195

The route manager has calculated a loss on each outbound flight of $1,305. She believes that there is a market for 48-hour ticket purchases if a new fare of $40 is introduced, as this would be $5 less than the price charged by a competitor for the same ticket. She estimates that she could sell 15 seats per flight on this basis. This would not affect either the seven-day purchase or standby fares, which are usually oversubscribed. The additional revenue of $600 (15 @ $40) would cover almost half of the loss. The route manager has prepared a report for her manager asking that the new fare be approved and allowing her three months to prove that the new tickets could be sold.

Comment on the route manager's proposal.

P9.9 *(New Equipment Decision)* Harry's Pizzeria currently uses a gas pizza oven to cook pizzas. Harry was approached by a sales representative from Superior Restaurant Supplies, who offered a new wood-burning pizza oven from Italy that will be cheaper to operate and may increase the sales at the restaurant due to overall demand for "authentic wood-fired" pizzas. Harry has compiled the following information about the two types of ovens:

	Current Oven	**Wood-Burning Oven**
Original cost	$10,000	$45,000
Accumulated depreciation	$ 3,000	–
Current salvage value	$ 5,000	–
Remaining life	10 years	10 years
Annual operating expenses	$ 5,000	$ 2,000
Expected increase in sales		$ 7,000
Disposal value in 10 years	$ 2,000	$ 5,000

a. What costs are relevant to this decision?

b. What costs are not relevant?

c. What is the overall cost or benefit of replacing the oven over the next 10 years?

d. Are there other factors that need to be considered before Harry makes a decision?

P9.10 *(Make or Buy Decision)* Easy Meals makes meals for airlines. Currently, Easy Meals provides 150,000 meals a year for $6 per meal. Variable costs for each meal include $0.75 in packaging, $2.00 in food costs, and $1.00 in labour costs. The overall fixed costs for the company are $250,000 per year.

To date, Easy Meals has been manufacturing the food trays on which the food is packaged. However, Easy Meals has approached Tara Products to supply food trays because the company believes that it may be able to cut costs considerably if it does not manufacture the trays in-house. Easy Meals must order 175,000 trays per year at a cost of $0.65 per tray. Fixed costs for the factory will not change, however, and the company does not have any use for the idle facilities if it does purchase the trays outside.

a. Should Easy Meals make or buy the trays?

b. If the company could rent out for $10,000 per year the idle space that was previously used to make trays, would the decision to make or buy the trays change?

P9.11 *(Make or Buy Decision)* Power Skateboards sold 15,000 skateboards during 2011, but the company expects to sell 20,000 skateboards in 2012. The company is proud that all components of its skateboards are made in-house. Overall, Power Skateboards is known by the boarding community as a quality skateboard manufacturer. During 2011, the company incurred the following costs to manufacture the skateboard wheels:

Direct materials	$2 per wheel
Direct labour	$1 per wheel
Variable overhead	$0.50 per wheel
Set-up costs	$2,000 per batch
Quality control	$250 per batch
Depreciation	$10,000 per year

Power Skateboards received an offer from an outside supplier of skateboard wheels to supply wheels at a cost of $4.50 per wheel.

Additional information: Depreciation costs relate to the manufacturing plant where the skateboards are made. A percentage share of total depreciation is assigned to manufacturing wheels based on the Wheel Division's share of the physical space in the plant. The set-up and quality control costs are based on each batch of wheels that is manufactured; at this time, Power Skateboards manufactures 5,000 wheels in each batch. Both set-up and quality control costs will be avoided if the outside supplier sells the wheels to Power Skateboards.

a. Assume that the company purchases the wheels from the outside supplier and the plant where the wheels are manufactured remains idle. If this is the case, what is the financial benefit or cost of purchasing the wheels outside?

b. Assume that the company will be able to use the idle facilities to provide custom painting on the skateboard decks if the wheels are purchased outside. Power Skateboards anticipates that

5,000 skateboards per year will feature custom painting, for a total price of $25 per board and at variable costs of $18 per board. What is the financial benefit or cost of purchasing the wheels outside but using the idle space to provide a custom painting service?

c. What other non-financial factors should be considered before Power Skateboards decides to outsource skateboard wheels?

P9.12 *(Make or Buy Decision)* Cowboy Construction Company employs a full-time driver and pays the costs for a vehicle to deliver paperwork between each of its building sites. Select Couriers has offered to make these deliveries to the same standard of service for a fixed sum of $2,000 per month. Cowboy's annual costs are currently as follows:

Salary and costs of driver	$18,800
Depreciation of vehicle	2,500
Registration, insurance, & servicing	1,000
Fuel	3,000
Total	$25,300

If Cowboy uses Select Couriers, it will sell the vehicle for $2,000 and the driver's employment will be terminated without any severance payment.

a. What are the relevant costs involved in this decision?

b. Should Cowboy subcontract its delivery requirements to Select?

c. What other considerations are there in making this decision?

P9.13 *(Theory of Constraints)* Jolly Inc. makes men's work shirts in two divisions: cutting and assembly. The Cutting Department is highly automated and the Assembly Department uses manual labour to sew the shirts. The Assembly Department is limited by the number of labour-hours available. The company has had to slow down the cutting process so that the sewers do not become overwhelmed by the amount of cut fabric entering the Assembly Department. Further, demand has increased to 10,000 shirts per month and management is considering adding another sewer to the Assembly Department or having the existing sewers work overtime 1.5 hours per day at an overtime rate of one and half times their regular pay. The cost of each sewer is $12 per hour, averaging 8 hours per day and 20 days per month. Currently, the company has 5 sewers and makes 10 shirts per day.

a. What is the total production that the company could make in a month if it hired a new sewer?

b. What is the total production that the company could make in a month if it had the staff work an additional 1.5 hours per day?

c. What is the overall cost difference between hiring a new sewer and having employees work extra time? Should the company hire a new sewer or pay existing sewers overtime to provide the capacity needed?

d. What other factors would need to be considered when deciding which approach to take?

P9.14 *(Costs of Quality)* CompuTrain creates instructional DVDs that provide instruction on various software applications. Maya Sloan, the company president, just received a report of the company's quality costs and was surprised to see a dramatic decline in prevention costs as a percentage of total sales over the last two years. Maya was happy to see this decrease in quality costs.

Is Maya correct in thinking this is a good thing? What negative outcomes may occur from this decrease in prevention costs?

P9.15 *(Cost of Quality and Environmental Costing)* The Ceramic Coffee House has been experiencing declining sales over the last two quarters and has noticed a reduction in the number of customers. Gupta Sanjay, the store owner, recently negotiated a new supply contract with Bargain Beans. He has been able to purchase his coffee beans for a 20% discount over his last supplier.

a. Discuss the implications of using a cheaper coffee bean. Be specific as to how this will impact costs of quality.

b. What environmental costs might a coffee house need to consider? What are some suggestions to reduce its overall environmental costs?

REFERENCES

Fitzgerald, L., Johnston, R., Brignall, S., Silvestro, R., & Voss, C. (1991). *Performance measurement in service businesses*. London: Chartered Institute of Management Accountants.

Forbes (online). (April 3, 2011). *BP rising from deepwater horizon abyss but not free yet*. Retrieved from http://blogs.forbes.com/greatspeculations/2011/03/04/bp-rising-from-deepwater-horizon-abyss-but-not-free-yet.

Porter, M. E. (1985). *Competitive advantage: Creating and sustaining superior performance*. New York, NY: Free Press.

CHAPTER 10

Human Resource Decisions

LEARNING OBJECTIVES

After reading this chapter, you should be able to answer the following questions:

- Which costs should be included in the cost of labour of an organization?

- Why is it not necessarily correct to assume that labour costs associated with the production of a good or service are variable?

- Which relevant labour costs should be included in decision making?

- What are options for reducing labour costs, other than layoffs? What are the costs associated with redundancy programs?

- How can an organization measure the effectiveness of human capital?

This chapter discusses the importance of human resources (HR) within an organization and explores the challenges of measuring the value of these resources. It explains the components of labour costs and how those costs are applied to the production of goods or services. The relevant cost of labour for decision-making purposes is explained. The measurement of human capital beyond cost is also discussed within the context of the balanced scorecard.

Human Resources and Accounting

Personnel management—or human resources, as it is more commonly called—is a function concerned with job design; recruitment, training, and motivation; performance appraisal; industrial relations, employee participation, and teamwork; remuneration; redundancy; health and safety; and employment policies and practices. It is through human resources—that is, people—that the production of goods and services takes place.

Historically, as Chapter 1 suggested, employment costs were a large element of the cost of manufacture. Today, even with the shift to service industries, people costs have tended to decline in proportion to total costs, a consequence of computer technology. Yet in spite of this decline in human resource costs, the management of human resources within organizations has become increasingly important in today's service-focused organizations.

Management of human resources extends far beyond just control of costs. The people in an organization provide a degree of competitive advantage that is critical for today's companies. Customer service, collaboration, communication, and relationships are all words that describe the "human" aspect of business. Often these human-related functions provide a company with a unique or distinctive advantage. An example is Hatch Ltd., an Ontario-based engineering firm that was rated one of Canada's best employers by *Maclean's* magazine (Warnica, 2011). As a 100% employee-owned company, Hatch has been able to keep employees happy by empowering them to make their own decisions about their work. John Pearson, the company's global managing director, stated, "When you take these clever people and you unleash them in this environment, you get the absolute best out of them" (Warnica, 2011). We must consider, therefore, that decisions related to human resources have behaviour implications in addition to cost implications.

Many non-accounting readers often ask why the statement of financial position of a business does not show the value of its human assets (what the HR literature refers to as *human resource* or *intellectual capital accounting*). Many people would argue that the knowledge, skills, and abilities of people are key resources of a company. However, it is very difficult to quantify the value of an employee. Accounting practices are conservative; the values of assets in a business are based on quantifiable measures. Since the value of people to the business is in the application of their knowledge, skills, and abilities, these intangible attributes are very difficult to value and are, therefore, not included in the financial records of a business. People are recruited, trained, and developed, then motivated to accomplish tasks for which they are appraised and rewarded. People may leave the business for personal reasons or be made redundant when there is a business downturn. In accounting terms, people are treated as *labour*, a resource that is consumed—therefore, an expense rather than an asset—either *directly* in producing goods or services or *indirectly* as a business overhead. Intellectually, we know that human resources are truly an asset but the conservatism of accounting prevents human capital as being reported as such.

The Cost of Labour

We begin our discussion of human resource management with a discussion of costs. In the most simplistic sense, the **cost of labour** is the salary or wage paid to the employee, plus any benefits. The **benefits** consist of the non-salary or wage costs that follow from the payment of salaries or wages. In Canada, benefits include the Canada Pension Plan (CPP) and Employment Insurance (EI) contributions. A total of 4.95% of an employee's wage is withheld for CPP to be remitted to the government and 1.8% is withheld for EI. Employers must match the employee's CPP contributions by 1.0 times and EI contributions by 1.4 times. This means that an employer must pay 4.95% and 2.52% of an employee's wages in CPP and EI contributions, respectively, to the federal government.

The **total employment cost** may also include other forms of remuneration, such as bonuses, profit shares, and non-cash remuneration, such as stock options, health benefits such as dental and medical insurance, pension contributions, expense allowances, and business-provided motor vehicles.

A less visible but important element of the cost of labour are the periods during which employees are paid but do not work—public holidays, annual leave, and sick leave. The rules and rates related to vacation pay in Canada vary in different parts of the country. A second aspect of this cost of labour is the time when people are at work but are unproductive, such as when they are on scheduled breaks and during equipment downtimes. These unproductive times all increase the cost of labour in relation to the volume of production. For instance, the following example shows how the employment cost can be higher than we expect when we consider downtime. We have assumed the employee is paid 8% vacation pay in the area in which the employee works.

Salary		$30,000
Benefits:		
CPP (1.0 × 4.95%)	$1,485	
EI (1.4 × 1.8%)	756	
Vacation pay (8% × $30,000)	2,400	
Total benefits		4,641
Total salary cost		$34,641
Non-Salary Benefits:		
Cost of motor vehicle	4,000	
Expense allowance	500	4,500
Total employment cost		$39,141

Assuming a 5-day workweek, 20 days of holiday leave, 5 days of sick leave and 8 public holidays per year, the actual days at work (the production capacity) can be calculated as

Working days 52 × 5		260
Less:		
Annual leave	20	
Sick leave	5	
Public holidays	8	33
Actual days at work		227

The total employment cost per working day for this employee is therefore $172.43 ($39,141/227 days). Assuming that the employee works eight hours per day and is productive for 80% of the time at work, then the cost per hour worked is $26.94($172.43/[8 × 80%]).

As a company, we may first consider that the employee's cost is much lower than $26.94 per hour. We would likely calculate the cost per hour as $30,000 per year for a 40-hour week, which is a cost of $14.42 per hour ($30,000/52/40). However, this is not really the true cost to the employer. The total employment costs including benefits and unproductive time almost doubles this value. What is $14.42 per hour as a wage to the employee is actually a cost of $26.94 to the employer.

The calculation of the cost of labour is shown in Exhibit 10.1.

Exhibit 10.1 The Cost of Labour

Cost	Time
Salaries and wages + Benefits + Non-salary benefits (motor vehicles, expenses, etc.) = Total employment cost	Working days − Annual leave, sick leave, public holidays, etc. = Actual days at work × At-work hours × Productivity = Actual hours worked

$$\frac{\text{Total employment cost}}{\text{Actual hours worked}} = \textbf{Labour cost per hour}$$

We can also express the labour cost as a cost per unit of production. In companies that manufacture a product or provide a service, the labour cost to make each unit of product or to provide each service transaction is a direct cost that is important in determining the cost of production of the product or service. Assuming that the above example relates to an employee of a company which manufactures a product, and that in productive hours the employee completes four units of a product, the *direct labour cost per unit of production* is $6.74 ($26.94/4). If the above example related to a service company and the service employee processes five transactions per hour, the *direct labour cost per unit of production* (a transaction is still a unit of production) is $5.39 ($26.94/5).

In the longer term, a business may also want to take an even broader view of the total cost of employment. Many costs are incurred over and above the salary, wages, and benefits paid to employees. A longer-term approach to the total cost of employment may include recruitment and training costs as additional costs of employment.

Variability in Labour

Accountants have historically considered labour that is consumed in producing goods or services as a variable cost. That is, it is a cost that varies with the number of units produced or the volume of service provided. Many companies express labour costs associated with production (such as the labour cost for assembly-line workers or labour associated with providing a service) as a cost per unit of product made or service provided. In a car manufacturing plant, for example, the cost of the assembly workers on the production line is often expressed as a labour cost per car. In 2008, the cost of labour to make a car at General Motors was approximately $69 per hour for 30 hours, a total of $2,070 per car (Selley, 2008). Similarly, an insurance company might calculate the cost of labour required to prepare different types of policies. This concept of labour as a cost per service provided or per product produced is commonly used across many industries.

However, the true variability of labour is much more complex than this seems. The employees of an insurance company, for example, will not always process the same number of policies each month. The cost of the labour (i.e., the salaries and benefits of the insurance employees), however, will be the same each month. Since the cost of the employee does not change with different levels of output, the cost is not truly variable. Nor is it feasible to hire and fire staff as service volumes change. A company makes a decision about the number of staff it will employ based on a longer-term perspective, not considering short-term fluctuations in volume. Furthermore, changing legislation, the influence of trade unions, and human resource policies have meant that in the very short term all labour takes on the appearance of a fixed cost—a cost that will remain constant regardless of production or service levels.

Most companies cannot change their labour costs dramatically over the short term. For instance, consider a company that manufactures televisions. In one week, the company produces 1,000 TVs with a production workforce of 30 employees. If the production schedule in Week 2 decreases to 800 TVs due to a decline in demand, it is unlikely that the company will see a reduction in employee wages.

Laying off staff for a short-term reduction in production is not cost-effective or easy to do—it takes time, and legislation governs layoff procedures. Furthermore, many organizations hire employees on a salary not a wage basis. This means that whether the employees produce 200 or 2,000 TVs in a given week, the staffing costs remain the same. Consequently, many businesses today account for labour related to production of products or services as a fixed cost. As a result, many companies are moving to the method of throughput costing (as was discussed in Chapter 9), which reports only the cost of direct materials as a variable cost and reports labour as fixed expense to the company.

Relevant Cost of Labour

Decisions related to labour costs must be based on relevance. As we saw in Chapter 9, a relevant cost is the cost that will change if a particular decision is made. If a cost will change with a particular decision, it is relevant. If a cost does not change, it is not relevant. Decision making is not concerned with the past, thus historical (or *sunk*) costs are irrelevant. The **relevant cost of labour** is therefore the future, incremental cash flow that will result from making a particular decision. This may include an **opportunity cost**; that is, the loss from an opportunity foregone. For example, if a plant is operating at full capacity, the relevant cost of accepting an order above the capacity volumes could be the additional labour costs (such as overtime) that may have to be incurred by producing above capacity. The opportunity cost could be the loss of income from a particular order and the wider potential loss of customer goodwill if the company is already operating at capacity and cannot exceed these limits.

Relevant costs may change over time and with changing circumstances. This is particularly so with the cost of labour. When there is spare capacity and surplus labour that will be paid whether or not a particular decision is made, the labour cost is irrelevant to the decision. When casual labour must be used or overtime incurred, a decision to exceed capacity causes costs to increase; the labour cost is then relevant. When labour is scarce and the company is working at full capacity, labour has to be diverted from alternative work involving an opportunity cost, so the opportunity loss is relevant.

For example, Brown & Co. is a small management consulting firm that has been offered a market research project for a client. The estimated workloads and labour costs for the project are

	Hours	Hourly Labour Cost
Partners	120	$60
Managers	350	$45
Support staff	150	$20

There is, at present, a shortage of work for partners, but this is a temporary situation. This means that partners will not need to work any additional overtime to accept this project. Managers, however, are fully utilized and if they are used on this project, other clients will have to be turned away, which will involve a loss of revenue from these clients of $100 per hour since the company charges out the managers' hours at $100 per hour. Support staff is hired on a contract basis, and in order to accept this project, the company will need to hire new staff for the full 150 hours. Fixed costs are $100,000 per year.

The relevant cost of labour to be used when considering this project can be calculated by considering the future, incremental cash flows:

Partners	120 hours—irrelevant as partners currently have a shortage of work	Nil
Managers	350 hours @ $100—the opportunity cost of lost revenue from clients turned away	$35,000
Support staff	150 hours @ $20 cost	3,000
Relevant cost of labour		$38,000

The above approach is different from a non-relevant costing approach. A non-relevant costing approach would have identified the cost of labour as

	Hours	Hourly Labour Cost	Total Labour Cost
Partners	120	$60	$ 7,200
Managers	350	45	15,750
Support staff	150	20	3,000
Variable cost of labour			$25,950

The relevant cost approach is more accurate, as it identifies the future, incremental cash flows associated with acceptance of the order. This ignores the cost of partners as there is no future, incremental cash flow. The cost of managers is the opportunity cost—the lost revenue from the work to be turned away. The support staff cost is due to the need to employ more temporary staff. Fixed costs are irrelevant as they will occur regardless of whether the company takes on this project.

Outsourcing Labour Costs

Chapter 9 introduced outsourcing as a business strategy used to reduce the cost of labour and increase capacity utilization in the form of a make or buy decision. In recent years, outsourcing to developing countries has become a common practice in large corporations due to cost advantages. Countries where outsourcing services are prevalent include India, China, Brazil, and Pakistan. In developing countries, the cost of labour can be very low. For example, although Chinese factory workers' wages have increased in recent years, they are still only a fraction of North American factory workers' wages. It is anticipated that by 2015, Chinese factory workers will make $4.41 per hour as compared to $26.06 per hour for an average American factory worker (Kumar, 2011). This saving can be a considerable motivator for companies who are looking to save costs.

Whether the current labour costs can be avoided if the company chooses to outsource will depend on a number of factors. One factor that must be considered is the length of the decision. If the decision to outsource is a long-term one where a company will discontinue the outsourced operations, the cost of labour will be avoidable as they will likely lay off staff. However, if a company wants to utilize an outside provider on a short-term basis, labour costs may not be avoidable. Also, the company must consider whether the employees who perform the service will be made redundant when the project is finished or whether they will be moved to another part of the company, in which case the cost of labour will still occur.

For example, Hart Industries is considering outsourcing its production of packing materials for its products to SmartBox Inc., which will charge $3.50 per box to manufacture 10,000 boxes each year. Currently, Hart incurs $1.50 in direct material costs and $2.50 in direct labour costs for each box manufactured. If Hart chooses to use SmartBox and is able to lay off the labour force in the material-packing department, the relevant costs of the decision will be as shown in Exhibit 10.2.

Exhibit 10.2 Make v. Buy: Relevant Costs with Avoidable Labour Costs

	Relevant Cost to Make	Relevant Cost to Buy
Materials	$15,000	
Labour	25,000	
Outsourcing cost		$35,000
Total relevant cost	$40,000	$35,000

Outsourcing would save the company $5,000 per year or $0.50 per box. However, Hart Industries is also considering relocating 50% of the existing material-packaging staff to the warehouse to manage the shipments of the packaged materials from SmartBox. In this case, only 50% of the labour costs will be avoidable. The relevant costs of this decision are presented in Exhibit 10.3.

Exhibit 10.3 Make v. Buy: Relevant Costs with Unavoidable Labour Costs

	Relevant Cost to Make	Relevant Cost to Buy
Material	$15,000	
Labour	25,000	$12,500
Outsourcing cost		35,000
Total relevant cost	$40,000	$47,500

If labour costs cannot be avoided in the short run, labour is no longer a relevant cost, as it is incurred irrespective of the decision to outsource. In this case, it would be more costly to outsource the service unless the under-utilized employees could be used for tasks that generated a contribution of at least $7,500 ($47,500 − $40,000). This example shows how it is important in any calculation of relevant costs to be sure about which costs are avoidable and which costs are unavoidable.

Of course, other non-financial factors must be considered when an organization is deciding to outsource a service:

- **Quality.** Can the outsourcing company provide the same quality or better? In Chapter 9 we discussed the costs of quality. These costs can include lost sales and lost customer loyalty, not just warranty and repair costs.

- **Privacy and security.** Outsourcing a sensitive service can be a challenge. This is especially true for intellectual property, such as software development, particularly if the company is outsourcing to another county. Some countries do not have the same level of intellectual property protection as Canada.

- **Ethical issues.** There are many ethical issues surrounding outsourcing. Laying off staff and transferring functions to an outside firm may impact employee morale and weaken a company's culture. Outsourcing to developing countries entails even more ethical considerations. Companies must consider the impact this will have on their existing employees, who cannot compete with employees who are paid a fraction of their wage. On the other side of the coin, what are the implications of exploiting cheap labour? It needs to evaluate whether moving its business to a developing country will stimulate the economy. The company must also consider the implications for the outsourcing county if it pulls its business out of the country at a later date.

- **Importance.** Many companies have chosen to outsource support services, such as accounting, human resources, customer support, or technical support to other companies. The idea is that support services do not represent a key competency (i.e., a function that creates a competitive advantage) of an organization and outsourcing non-core functions can help the organization to focus on its primary activities, such as production and sales. However, history has shown us that this is not always the case, and often effective support services (especially those services related to the customer) can have a tremendous effect on competitive advantage. Careful assessment is necessary to determine whether outsourcing might result in a loss of control of an activity that is directly important to customers.

Cost of Redundancy

Unfortunately, one of the first business responses to a downturn in profits is to make staff redundant. Some costs of redundancy are very obvious, such as severance payments, legal fees, and outplacement service fees. There are also less tangible costs, such as a loss of employee knowledge, skills, and experience, as well as costs related to low morale on the part of other employees and a decline in employee efficiency. In addition, usually when a layoff occurs, the work still remains, which can create additional stress for the existing employees. This can result in a large cost related to sick leave, poor productivity, and employee turnover.

Deciding to lay off staff as a short-term solution to reduce labour costs is not always the best response. A company might want to first consider cost-improvement initiatives such as activity-based costing (this will be discussed in Chapter 11), cost of quality improvements (see Chapter 9), and improvements to capacity utilization (see Chapter 9) before considering staff reductions. If the company is determined to decrease staffing costs, it can also look at alternatives to across-the-board layoffs, such as reduced work weeks, job sharing, voluntary severance programs, and un-paid leaves. Often, the employees of a company can surprise management with creative solutions for reducing costs.

CASE IN POINT

No Layoffs at Hypertherm

At the height of the recession in 2009, U.S. manufacturer Hypertherm's production workforce was 20% larger than needed. Yet the company did not lay off a single employee. In fact, it has not issued a pink slip in its 40-year history. As a maker of advanced metal-cutting systems used in shipbuilding and automotive repair, Hypertherm needs a skilled workforce with institutional knowledge—one that it wants to stand by through thick and thin. So when orders fall in one area, employees are cross-trained and reassigned to a busier section or given other duties.

The privately held company has also eliminated overtime, reduced its temporary staff, and brought some outsourced work back in-house in order to keep its permanent staff working during leaner periods. In the recession of the early 1980s, Hypertherm reduced the workweek to four days to keep jobs but reduce payroll costs. Company CEO Dick Couch says the firm has a "social contract" with employees: They keep their jobs but they give the company their all. "Once you have a highly skilled workforce, the last thing you want to do is lay them off," Couch says. "This isn't altruism. It's good business."

Sources: Tuna, C., Some firms cut costs without resorting to layoffs, *The Wall Street Journal*, December 15, 2008; Greenberg, J., Battered company says "No" to job cuts, *NPR*, November 9, 2009; Duggan, K., Hypertherm: Lean leverage to compete globally from New Hampshire, *Association for Manufacturing Excellence* website at www.ame.org, March 15, 2012.

Measuring Human Capital

The value of human resources is tied to the knowledge, skills, attitudes, and abilities of the people within a company. Some important questions we should ask about our human resources include

1. How knowledgeable is our workforce?

2. Do our employees have skills that are superior to those of our competitors' employees?

3. Do our employees feel empowered to do their work to the best of their ability?

4. Is our level of customer service strong?

5. Are our employees compensated appropriately?

Most of these questions are not measured on the financial statements of a company, as we discussed previously. Although these questions are somewhat subjective, most organizations recognize the importance of their human resources and realize that effective management of human resources can be a source of competitive advantage.

How do we go about answering these questions? How can we set up a measurement process that helps us control the effectiveness of our human resources? The balanced scorecard (discussed in Chapter 6) is an important tool that can be used to help measure and manage human resources. Specific metrics can be established that help to measure employee skills, knowledge, attitudes, empowerment, learning, and dedication. Exhibit 10.4 demonstrates metrics that could be used to measure and control human resources and intellectual capital within a company,

Exhibit 10.4 Human Capital Metrics Using the Balanced Scorecard

Measure	Objective
Employee satisfaction rating	To measure the extent to which employees are satisfied in their jobs.
Retention rate = (Total employees − Employees leaving the company)/Total employees	To identify the level of employee satisfaction within the company and the degree to which employees favour the company over competitors' companies.
Training cost factor = Total training costs/ Number of employees	To measure the degree to which employees are provided with training and new-skill development.
Employee productivity = Number of units or services provided/Total number of employees	To measure the level of productivity and efficiency of employees.
Percentage of employees generating new ideas = Number of new ideas/Total number of employees	To measure employee innovation and empowerment.
Average customer service response times	To measure employees' ability to serve customers in a timely manner.
Customer satisfaction rating related to customer support activities	To measure the value generated by employees in customer support roles.
Salary index = Average wage/Industry wage	To measure the level of compensation of employees as compared to industry norms.

CASE IN POINT

Employee Engagement at Scotiabank

In a service industry, keeping employees satisfied is critical to customer service, innovation, and retention. That's why Scotiabank surveys its 75,000 employees in Canada and more than 55 countries around the world to measure their level of employee engagement: "The passion and commitment employees have for their job, coworkers and organization that influences them to go the 'extra mile.'" The annual survey, in place since 1992, asks employees to rate their confidence in the organization's future, corporate responsibility, and manager effectiveness, among other things.

Its 2011 survey revealed an overall employee satisfaction level of 85%, compared with the 81% norm among global financial services organizations—putting Scotiabank in the top 10% of benchmarked financial services companies worldwide. Among the things it does to help create a culture where employees feel engaged, Scotiabank strongly encourages employees to volunteer in their local communities by matching funds raised by employee teams and donating money to community organizations in which individual employees have been active volunteers. It also has a recognition program called *Scotia Applause* in which employees can nominate colleagues for a job well done.

"Employee engagement is an integral part of the profitability cycle," says Cory Garlough, vice-president, Global Employment Strategies. "By focusing on maintaining and even increasing engagement, we know there will be a positive impact on customer satisfaction and on our revenues."

Sources: Scotiabank, *2011 Scotiabank corporate social responsibility report*; Crawford, N., & Mathers, T., In good times and bad, *Benefits Canada*, January 1, 2010; *Providing a forum for employees*. Retrieved from www.scotiabank.com/ca/en/0,,419,00.html.

CONCLUSION

This chapter outlined the relevant costs that should be included in computing the cost of labour and explored how relevancy is important in any human resource decisions. Specific issues related to human resources, including the variability of labour and the costs of redundancy, were also discussed. The chapter concluded with a discussion on measuring human capital within an organization.

KEY TERMS

Benefits, 242

Cost of labour, 242

Costs of redundancy, 248

Human resources, 241

Opportunity cost, 245

Personnel management, 241

Relevant cost of labour, 245

Total employment cost, 242

CASE STUDY 10.1: THE DATABASE MANAGEMENT COMPANY—LABOUR COSTS AND UNUSED CAPACITY

The Database Management Company (DMC) is a call centre within a multinational company that has built a sophisticated database to hold consumer buying preferences. DMC contracts with large retail organizations to provide access to its database, charging a fixed monthly fee plus a fee for each transaction (i.e., each time a retail company accesses and requests information from the database). DMC estimates transaction volume based on past experience and recruits employees accordingly, to ensure that it is able to satisfy its customers' demands without delay.

Employees have a mix of permanent and temporary contracts. Labour costs are separated into variable elements (transaction-processing costs, which can be directly attributable to specific contracts) and fixed elements (administration and supervision). DMC also incurs fixed costs for building occupancy (a charge made by the parent company based on floor area occupied) and the lease of computer equipment.

DMC's budget (based on anticipated activity levels and standard costs) is shown in Exhibit 10.5. As a result of declining retail sales, the demand for consumer information has fallen. However, because of uncertainty at DMC about how long this downturn will last, the company has been able to reduce its variable labour cost by ending the contracts of only a small number of temporary staff. DMC's actual results for the same period are shown in Exhibit 10.6.

Exhibit 10.5 DMC Budget

	Contract 1	Contract 2	Contract 3	Total
Budgeted number of transactions	10,000	15,000	25,000	50,000
Fee per transaction	$5	$4	$3.50	
Budgeted transaction income	$50,000	$60,000	$87,500	$197,500
Fixed monthly fee	5,000	7,500	12,000	24,500
Total budgeted income	55,000	67,500	99,500	222,000
Variable labour costs	16,000	24,000	40,000	80,000
Contribution margin	39,000	43,500	59,500	142,000
Fixed labour costs	11,000	13,000	15,000	39,000
Occupancy costs	15,000	17,500	22,000	54,500
Computer costs	7,000	8,000	9,000	24,000
Budgeted net profit	$6,000	$5,000	$13,500	$24,500

Exhibit 10.6 DMC Actual Results

	Contract 1	Contract 2	Contract 3	Total
Budgeted number of transactions	9,000	10,500	22,000	41,500
Fee per transaction	$5	$4	$3.50	
Budgeted transaction income	$45,000	$42,000	$77,000	$164,000
Fixed monthly fee	5,000	7,500	12,000	24,500
Total budgeted income	50,000	49,500	89,000	188,500
Variable labour costs	15,300	17,850	37,400	70,550
Contribution margin	34,700	31,650	51,600	117,950
Fixed labour costs	11,000	13,000	15,000	39,000
Occupancy costs	15,000	17,500	22,000	54,500
Computer costs	7,000	8,000	9,000	24,000
Budgeted net profit	$1,700	$(6,850)	$5,600	$450

How can DMC'S poor performance compared with its budget be interpreted?

DMC's income has fallen across the board because of the reduced number of transactions on all of its contracts. Because it has been unable to alter its variable labour cost significantly in the short term, the contribution margin toward fixed costs and profits has fallen. Therefore, although the business treats labour costs as variable, in practice they are fixed costs, especially in the short term. The fixed salary and non-salary costs are constant despite the fall in transaction volume, so profitability has been eroded. DMC cannot alter its floor space allocation from the parent company or its computer lease costs, despite having spare capacity.

What information can be provided to help in making a decision about cost reductions?

Calculating the variance (or difference) between the budget and actual income and variable costs shows how the difference between budget and actual profit of $24,050 ($24,500 − $450) is represented by a fall in income of $33,500, offset by a reduction in variable labour costs of $9,450. This is shown in Exhibit 10.7. Therefore, the fall in income does not result in an equal fall in variable labour costs.

Calculating the cost of unused capacity identifies the profit decline more clearly, as can be seen in Exhibit 10.8.

Of the gap between the budget and actual profit, $13,600 is accounted for by the cost of unused capacity in variable labour. This gap has been offset to some extent by the reduction in variable labour costs of $9,450. There is still the capability to reduce variable costs to meet the actual transaction volume, as Exhibit 10.9 shows.

Exhibit 10.7 DMC Loss of Contribution

	Contract 1	Contract 2	Contract 3	Total
Income reduction from budget	$5,000	$18,000	$10,500	$33,500
Variable labour costs reduction	700	6,150	2,600	9,450
Contribution reduction	$4,300	$11,850	$7,900	$24,050

Exhibit 10.8 DMC Cost of Unused Capacity

	Contract 1	Contract 2	Contract 3	Total
Budgeted variable labour costs	$16,000	$24,000	$40,000	$80,000
Budgeted number of transactions	10,000	15,000	25,000	50,000
Budgeted cost per transaction	$1.60	$1.60	$1.60	
Actual number of transactions	9,000	10,500	22,000	41,500
Standard variable labour cost[1]	$14,400	$16,800	$35,200	$66,400
Cost of unused capacity (budgeted variable labour cost less standard variable labour cost)	$1,600	$7,200	$4,800	$13,600

[1]The actual number of transactions multiplied by the budgeted variable labour cost per transaction.

Exhibit 10.9 DMC Variable Costs

	Contract 1	Contract 2	Contract 3	Total
Actual variable labour costs	$15,300	$17,850	$37,400	$70,550
Standard variable labour costs	14,400	16,800	35,200	66,400
Difference	$900	$1,050	$2,200	$4,150

What conclusions can be drawn from this information? It is clear that DMC either has to increase its income or reduce its costs in order to reach its profitability targets. The company has a significant cost of unused capacity. However, it can reduce this unused capacity only on the basis of sound market evidence; otherwise, it may be constraining its ability to provide services to its customers in future, which may in turn result in a greater loss of income. DMC needs to renegotiate its prices and volumes with its customers.

CASE STUDY 10.2: TABAK SALES—THE COST OF LOSING A CUSTOMER

Tabak Sales employs a number of sales representatives, each costing the business $40,000 per year. This figure includes salary, benefits, and motor vehicle expenses. Sales representatives also earn a commission of 1% on the orders placed by their customers. On average, each sales representative looks after 100 customers, and each year customers place an average of five orders, with an average order size of $2,500. Therefore, each representative generates sales of

$$100 \times 5 \times \$2,500 = \$1,250,000$$

and earns a commission of 1%, amounting to $12,500.

However, Tabak has suffered from a loss to competitors of about 10% of its customer base each year. Consequently, only about 70% of each sales representative's time is spent with existing customers; the other 30% is spent on obtaining new customers. Each representative needs to find 10 new customers each year. The business wants to undertake a campaign to prevent the loss of customers and has asked for a calculation of the cost of each lost customer.

A first step is to calculate the cost of the different functions carried out by each sales representative:

$$\text{Account maintenance costs} = \frac{(\text{Annual salary} \times 70\% \text{ of time})}{\text{Number of existing customers}}$$
$$= \$40,000 \times 70\%$$
$$= \$28,000 \text{ per year}$$
$$= \$28,000/90 \text{ existing customers*}$$
$$= \$311 \text{ per existing customer}$$

*Note: Existing customers = 100 customers − 10% loss of customers to competition ($100 × 90% = 90 existing customers).

$$\text{New customer costs} = \frac{(\text{Annual salary} \times 30\% \text{ of time})}{\text{Number of new customers}}$$
$$= \$40,000 \times 30\% = \$12,000$$
$$= \$12,000/10 \text{ new customers per year}$$
$$= \$1,200 \text{ per new customer}$$

The cash cost of obtaining a new customer is $1,200. However, the opportunity cost provides a more meaningful cost. If there was no lost business and sales representatives could spend all of their time with existing customers, each representative could look after 142 customers (100 × 100/70) in the same amount of time.

If each of the 142 customers placed an average of five orders with an average order size of $2,500, each representative could generate an income of $1,775,000 and earn a commission of $17,750. The opportunity cost is the company's lost opportunity to generate the extra income of $525,000 ($1,775,000 − $1,250,000), and the opportunity cost to the representative personally is the lost opportunity to earn extra income of $5,250 (commission of $17,750 − $12,500).

For this reason, businesses sometimes adopt a strategy of splitting their sales force into those representatives who are good at new account prospecting and those who are better at account maintenance.

■ SELF-TEST QUESTIONS

S10.1 A consultant is paid a salary of $40,000 per year. Her employer's share of CPP is 4.95% and of EI is 2.52%. Assuming that the consultant works 230 days per year and is productive for 75% of that time, her daily cost rate to the company is closest to

a. $173

b. $187

c. $249

d. $140

S10.2 Grant & McKenzie is a firm of financial advisers that needs to calculate an hourly rate to charge customers for its services.

The average salary cost for its advisers is $50,000. The employer's share of CPP and EI is paid to the government as 4.95% and 2.52%, respectively. Each adviser has a four-week annual holiday and there are 10 days per year when the firm closes for holidays. Each adviser is expected to do 25 chargeable hours of work per week for clients; the remainder of the 40-hour week is spent on administrative work.

What hourly rate (to the nearest hour) would cover the cost of each financial adviser?

a. $46.72

b. $29.20

c. $43.78

d. $41.33

Use the following information to answer questions S10.3 and S10.4:

Local Bank does not know how much of its salaries related to cheque processing are fixed and how much are variable. However, total costs have been estimated at $750,000 for processing of 1,000,000 transactions and $850,000 for processing of 1,200,000 transactions.

S10.3 What are the variable costs per transaction?

a. $0.71

b. $0.75

c. $0.50

d. $2.00

S10.4 What are the fixed costs?

a. $40,000

b. $250,000

c. $0

d. $200,000

S10.5 A company has 5 employees who have a cost of $100 per day each but currently have no work to do; this situation is expected to last for the next two weeks. The company is considering accepting a special order that will take 5 employees one week each, commencing immediately. The work will require supervision, equivalent to 10% of the variable labour time, but all of the supervisors are very busy. Supervision costs are normally $200 per day but additional supervision will involve overtime at the rate of $300 per day. The relevant cost for the order is

a. $750

b. $1,250

c. $3,000

d. $3,250

S10.6 A call centre department incurs wage costs of $100,000 per year for staff to make 25,000 sales calls each year. At the end of the year, management reports disclose that the actual number of calls made is 23,000. The cost of spare capacity can be calculated as

a. $2,000

b. $8,000

c. $8,050

d. $8,750

S10.7 Cirrus Company has calculated that the cost to make a component is made up of materials, $120; variable labour, $60; variable overhead, $30; and fixed overhead, $25. Another company has offered to make the component for $140.

If Cirrus has spare capacity and wants to retain its skilled labour force, what is the benefit of making or buying the component?

a. $40 benefit to buy the component

b. $10 benefit to buy the component

c. $20 benefit to make the component

d. $10 benefit to make the component

S10.8 Zipper Ltd. incurs the following costs to provide each "Special Delivery Service" for its customers:

Variable labour	$25
Variable vehicle costs (fuel, etc.)	$10
Fixed vehicle costs	$18
Administrative support (overtime cost)	$ 5

Zipper is considering outsourcing the service and wants to determine the relevant cost of each Special Delivery Service, assuming that its variable labour could be made redundant at no cost to the business and vehicles could be sold at statement of financial position values. The unavoidable cost for each Special Delivery Service is

a. $35

b. $28

c. $10

d. $5

S10.9 Bromide Partners provides three services: accounting, auditing, and tax services. The total business overhead of $650,000 has been divided into two cost pools, as shown below:

Partners $200,000
Juniors $450,000

The hours spent by each type of staff are as shown below:

	Accounting	Auditing	Tax Services	Total
Partner hours	150	250	400	800
Junior hours	1,200	2,800	1,000	5,000

What is the total cost of providing audit services?

a. $314,500

b. $341,810

c. $722,500

d. $650,000

■ PROBLEMS

P10.1 (*Outsourcing Decision*) Cardinal Co. needs 20,000 units of a certain part to use in one of its products. The following information is available.

Cost to Cardinal to make each part:

Materials	$ 4
Variable labour	16
Variable manufacturing overhead	8
Fixed manufacturing overhead	10
Total	$38

The cost to outsource the production of the part to Oriole Co. is $36. If Cardinal buys the part from Oriole instead of making it, Cardinal would have no use for the spare capacity. Additionally, 60% of the fixed manufacturing overhead would continue regardless of what decision is made. Cardinal decides that labour is an avoidable cost for the purposes of this decision.

By comparing the relevant costs, decide whether to make or buy the 20,000 parts.

P10.2 (*Outsourcing Decision*) Bendix Ltd. is considering the alternatives of either outsourcing component VX-1 to an outside supplier or producing the component itself. Production costs to Bendix are estimated as follows:

Labour	$ 200
Materials	600
Variable overhead	100
Fixed overhead	300
Total	$1,200

An outside supplier, Cosmo PLC, has quoted a price of $1,000 for each VX-1 for an order of 100 of these components. However, if Bendix accepts the quote from Cosmo, the company will need to give three months' notice of redundancy to staff.

a. Calculate the relevant costs of the alternative choices (show your work) and make a recommendation to management about which choice to accept.

b. How would your recommendation differ if Bendix employees were on temporary contracts with no notice period?

c. Explain the significance of an inventory valuation of $1,300 for the VX-1 at the end of the last accounting period.

P10.3 *(Relevant Costs of Labour)* Call Centre Services (CCS) operates two divisions: a call centre that answers incoming customer service calls on behalf of its clients and a telemarketing operation that makes outgoing sales calls to seek new business for its clients. Each CCS operator can handle on average about 6,000 calls per year.

Although staff are allocated to one division or the other, when there is a high volume of incoming calls, sales staff from the telemarketing division assist customer service staff in the call centre division. This is a result of a current recruitment "freeze."

The finance department has produced the information shown below.

	Call Centre	Telemarketing	Total
Number of calls	70,000	25,000	
Fee per call	$5	$10	
Revenue	350,000	250,000	$600,000
Less expenses			
Staff costs: 10 @ $15,000 per year; 5 @ $22,000 per year	150,000	110,000	260,000
Lease costs equipment (shared 50/50)	20,000	20,000	40,000
Rent (shared in proportion to staffing: 2/3, 1/3)	80,000	40,000	120,000
Telephone call charges	—	20,000	20,000
Total expenses	250,000	190,000	440,000
Operating profit	$100,000	$60,000	$160,000

What conclusions can you draw about the performance of each of the two divisions?

P10.4 *(Balanced Scorecard)* Abby Gale Services understands the importance of hiring qualified staff to help run its credit-counselling company. Abby Gale is developing a balanced scorecard to help determine the effectiveness of its human resource management practices. Management at Abby Gale is particularly concerned about whether its employees are delivering customer value.

Develop 10 metrics that could be used on the balanced scorecard of Abby Gale Services to help ensure that its employees are delivering customer value.

P10.5 *(Relevant Costs of Labour)* Magic Solutions Consultants (MSC) wants to bid for a market research project. The cost estimates on which MSC will base its bid are shown below:

- 200 hours of work in initial data collection and preparation of research questionnaire
- 100 hours can be provided by existing staff who are not currently utilized—their total employment cost is $22 per hour
- 100 hours will have to be provided by temporary staff at a cost of $15 per hour

- MSC's in-house, existing database resources will be utilized to provide data for the project. The research data that will be used was purchased some months previously at a cost of $2,500. The data have never been used before and are unlikely to be used again. An additional updated report will, however, have to be purchased at a cost of $500.

- Printing and postage of questionnaires will cost $1,000.

- The in-house computer processing facility will process returned questionnaires. The computer facility charges $2,000 for each survey it processes internally.

- The consultancy will have to purchase a specialist software package to undertake the sophisticated statistical analysis required. The software will cost $1,750 and training costs of $500 will be incurred for employees to learn how to use the package. The package may be used again in the future.

- A manager will be involved in the detailed planning, design, and logistics for the research. The manager's time has been costed at 14 days @ $500 or $7,000, but he is very busy and will have to be remunerated through overtime at an additional cost of $3,500 in order for him to carry out other work that he is committed to complete.

- A partner will supervise the entire project. An estimate of her time has been costed at $1,500, but the consultancy will not incur any additional costs for the project.

a. Calculate the cost for the market research project based on the full costs for the project.

b. Calculate the relevant cost of the market research project.

c. What are the standard costs identified in this case? What are the marginal or variable costs identified in this case? Explain why there is a difference between the costs calculated in (a) and (b).

P10.6 *(Variability of Labour)* Coté Freres Ltee. manufactures high-technology products for the computer industry. Coté's accountant has produced the following profit report showing statistics for each of its three main customers for last year.

	Franklin Industries	Engineering Partners	Zeta Inc.	Other Customers	Total
Sales	$1,000,000	$1,500,000	$2,000,000	$1,500,000	$6,000,000
Cost of materials	250,000	600,000	750,000	750,000	2,350,000
Cost of labour	300,000	200,000	300,000	75,000	875,000
Gross profit	450,000	700,000	950,000	675,000	2,775,000
Corporate overheads:					
Allocated as 30% of sales	300,000	450,000	600,000	450,000	
Rental					250,000
Depreciation					350,000
Non-production salaries					600,000
Selling expenses					350,000
Administration					250,000
Operating profit	$ 150,000	$ 250,000	$ 350,000	$ 225,000	$ 975,000

Coté is operating at almost full capacity, but wants to improve its profitability further. The accountant has reported that, based on the above figures, Franklin Industries is the least-profitable customer and has recommended that prices be increased. If this is not possible, the accountant has suggested that Coté discontinue selling to Franklin and try to obtain more profitable business from Engineering Partners and Zeta.

Labour is the most significant limitation on capacity. The employees are highly specialized and difficult to replace. Consequently, Coté does all it can to keep its workforce even when there are seasonal downturns in business. The company charges $100 per hour for all labour, which is readily transferable between each of the customer products.

Comment on the accountant's recommendations. Do you agree or not? Show your work.

P10.7 *(Cost of Labour)* Sly & Partners is a city law firm with 12 partners and 30 associates. Charge-out rates are based on the following calculations:

	Partners	Associates
Total employment costs	$1,000,000	$1,350,000
Target chargeable hours	16,000	60,000
Hourly labour cost (rounded)	$62.50	$22.50
Total cost per hour (Add 100% to cover fixed costs as these are 100% of total employment costs)	$124	$44
Charge-out rate (Add 50% profit margin on total cost base of firm)	$186	$66

At year-end, the partners consider the profit report which shows the following:

	Budget	Actual
Revenue	$6,936,000	$6,036,000
Employment costs	2,350,000	2,250,000
Other fixed costs	2,350,000	2,300,000
Net profit	$2,236,000	$1,486,000

Due to a shortage of work, only 14,000 partner hours and 52,000 associate hours have been billed. To offset this reduction in revenues, the firm was able to reduce expected employment costs by $100,000 ($2,350,000 less $2,250,000) since three associates left the firm and their positions were left vacant.

Provide some explanations for the profit shortfall.

P10.8 *(Labour Efficiency)* The Recruitment Department of a major company has 13 staff members: a manager, seven recruiters, and five administrators. The department is continually exceeding its budget for expenses, particularly in relation to overtime payments. There have been some complaints against the department for poor recruitment decisions and the time taken to fill vacant positions.

After holidays, training, and non-recruitment activity, each recruiter has an average of 170 days to carry out recruitment activity, working 7 hours per day. An analysis of business processes has revealed that the average time spent by recruiters is 18 hours on each vacancy. An average of 45 vacancies per month require recruitment action, although there are seasonal fluctuations in this workload.

What steps could the department take to overcome its difficulties?

P10.9 *(Relevant Costs of Labour)* Harris Construction Ltd. has been asked to tender for a job to build and install a large customized shed. Harris's estimator has calculated the following costs associated with satisfying the tender:

- *Variable labour* to build the shed in the factory: 25 hours. The cost of staff is $30 per hour, including all payroll-related costs; however, Harris has insufficient work at the moment to keep its employees busy.

- *Delivery/installation:* 4 hours. This will have to be subcontracted at $50 per hour.

- *Supervision:* Harris always charges 20% of the direct labour in the factory as the cost of supervision. This is an allocation of the costs of the factory manager, storeman, and administration staff.

- *Materials:*

  ○ The timber needed for the shed is regularly used in the factory. Sufficient timber is held in stock to build the shed. The cost of the timber from the stock records is $1,000, but it will cost $1,100 to replace at current prices.

  ○ The shed also needs a metal frame. A suitable frame was purchased 2 years ago for $750 but has never been used. A supplier who saw the frame last week offered Harris $500 for it.

  ○ Indirect materials (paint, fixings, etc.) will cost about $100.

- *Overhead:* Harris uses a simple method of fixed overhead allocation, charging $250 for every job produced by the factory.

- *Other costs:* Because the customer requires quality certificates for everything it buys, Harris will need to have the completed shed inspected by a registered inspector at a cost of $175.

a. Calculate both the total product cost (using standard accounting practices) and the relevant cost for this custom job.

b. What is the lowest price at which the tender should be submitted, assuming that Harris Construction wants to make a profit of $200? What will be the impact of such a price on profits reported in the management profits report? What are the opportunity costs of not undertaking this job?

c. Would the lowest price change if Harris's employees were fully employed with other projects and Harris would need to hire additional staff to handle the job at the same rate as existing employees? Why?

REFERENCES

Kumar, V. (2011). A better stimulus idea: Training new factory workers. *CNNMoney.* Retrieved from http://finance.fortune.cnn.com/2011/05/18/a-better-stimulus-idea-training-new-factory-workers.

Selley, C. (2008). The car industry crash, by the numbers. *Macleans.ca.* Retrieved from www2.macleans.ca/2008/11/21/the-car-industry-crash-by-the-numbers.

Warnica, R. (2011). Best employers: They're happy and they know it. *Macleans.ca.* Retrieved from www2.macleans.ca/2011/10/21/they%e2%80%99re-happy-and-they-know-it/#more-220660.

CHAPTER 11

Accounting Decisions

LEARNING OBJECTIVES

After reading this chapter, you should be able to answer the following questions:

- How do I distinguish between various types of costs, including product, period, direct, indirect, prime, conversion, and overhead costs?

- What risks are present when arbitrary methods of overhead allocation are used?

- How does activity-based costing create more accurate product costs?

- What is the difference between absorption and variable costing?

- What are two methods of writing off an overallocation or underallocation of overhead?

This chapter explains how accountants classify costs and how they differentiate product and period costs, and direct and indirect costs. The chapter highlights the overhead allocation problem: how to accurately allocate indirect costs to products/services. In doing so, it contrasts traditional with activity-based costing. This chapter also discusses the difference between absorption costing and variable costing methods, and concludes with a discussion of the assignment of overallocation and underallocation of overhead.

Cost Classification

PRODUCT AND PERIOD COSTS

The first categorization of costs made by accountants is between period and product costs. **Period costs** relate to the accounting period (year, month) in which a cost was incurred. **Product costs** relate to the cost of goods or services produced. This distinction is particularly important to the link between management accounting and financial accounting, because the calculation of profit is based on the separation of product and period costs. As discussed in Chapter 4, operating profit is determined as follows:

$$\text{Revenues} - \text{Cost of goods sold} = \text{Gross profit}$$
$$- \text{S\&A and other period costs} = \text{Operating profit}$$

Gross profit is the amount of income remaining after the costs of producing a product or providing a service are covered. Period costs, such as selling and administrative expenses, are deducted from gross profit to determine operating profit.

The **cost of goods sold** can be one of the following:

- the cost of providing a service

- the cost of buying goods sold by a retailer

- the cost of raw materials and production costs to produce a finished good

Expenses, such as selling and administrative expenses, are the period costs, as they relate more to a period of time than to the production of a product or services. Period costs also include all of the other business costs that are not directly related to buying, making, or providing goods or services but that do support the business activity.

Cost of goods sold is the cost of the product or service that is sold in the period. If some inventory is not sold, the cost associated with the unsold product is recorded as inventory on the statement of financial position of the company. To calculate the cost of goods sold, therefore, we need to take into account the change in inventory. As we saw in Chapter 7, inventory is the value of goods purchased or manufactured that have not yet been sold. Therefore, for a retailer

$$\text{Cost of goods sold} = \text{Opening inventory} + \text{Purchases} - \text{Closing inventory}$$

and for a manufacturer,

$$\text{Cost of goods sold} = \text{Opening inventory} + \text{Cost of production} - \text{Closing inventory}$$

For a service provider, there can be no inventory of services provided but not sold, as the production and consumption of services take place simultaneously, so

$$\text{Cost of sales} = \text{Cost of providing the services that are sold}$$

The cost of goods sold can be shown on the statement of comprehensive income for a company as depicted in Exhibit 11.1.

Exhibit 11.1 Calculation of Operating Profit

Sales		$1,000,000
Less cost of goods sold		
Opening inventory	$250,000	
Plus purchases (or cost of production)	300,000	
Inventory available for sale	550,000	
Less closing inventory	200,000	
Cost of sales		$ 350,000
Gross profit		650,000
Less period costs		400,000
Operating profit		**$250,000**

DIRECT AND INDIRECT COSTS

Production costs (the cost of producing goods or services) may be classified as direct or indirect. Direct costs are readily traceable to particular products/services. For example, the cost of wheels used in the production of a skateboard is a direct cost because it can be traced directly to each skateboard made. Indirect costs are necessary to produce a product/service but cannot readily be traced to particular products/services. Indirect costs are often referred to as overhead costs. For example, the cost for heating the factory where the skateboards are made is not directly traceable to each skateboard that is produced.

Because direct costs are readily traceable, they are generally considered to be variable costs because such costs increase or decrease with the volume of production. Indirect costs may be variable (such as electricity) or fixed (such as rent).

Direct materials are traceable to particular products, and for a manufacturer include the materials bought and used in the manufacture of each unit produced. These direct material costs are clearly identifiable from a materials requisition record: a detailed list of all the materials used in a particular job (see Exhibit 11.2).

Materials of little value that are used in production (such as screws, adhesives, and cleaning materials) do not appear on the materials requisition record because the cost of recording their use would be higher than the value achieved. These are still costs of production, but because

Exhibit 11.2 Source Documents for Cost of Goods Sold

Job Cost Record	
Job #	458-789
Customer Name	JCT Fishing Supplies
Date Started	22-Jun-11
Date Completed	28-Jun-11

Date Received	Materials Requisition #	Part Description	Part #	Quantity	Cost per Unit	Total Cost
22-Jun-11	12548	Boat Kit	125-85	1	$2,580	$2,580
24-Jun-11	12555	Red Paint	584-7	5	25	125
26-Jun-11	12568	Motor Assembly	12548	1	3,500	3,500
28-Jun-11	12579	Rudder Assembly	15789	1	1,500	1,500
28-Jun-11	12800	Component Kit	19785	1	590	590
Total						$8,295

Direct Labour						
Time Period	Employee Time Record #	Employee #	Employee	Hours	Rate	Total Cost
Jun 20–24	458	6769	Harold Chang	27	$22	$ 594
Jun 27–Jul 1	475	6769	Harold Chang	32	22	704
Total				59		$1,298

(continued)

Exhibit 11.2 Source Documents for Cost of Goods Sold (*Continued*)

Manufacturing Overhead

Date	Allocation Basis	Units Used	Rate	Total Cost
27-Jun-11	Direct Labour Hours	59	$5	$295
Total				$295

TOTAL JOB COST				**$9,888**

Materials Requisition Record

		Materials Requisition #	12548
		Job #	458-789
		Date	22-Jun-11

Part #	Part Description	Quantity	Unit Cost	Total
125-85	Boat Kit	1	$2,580	$2,580
Issued by:	Mark Jones	Date:	22-Jun-11	
Received by:	Harold Chang	Date:	22-Jun-11	

Employee Time Record

Employee Time Record #	458
Name	Harold Chang
Employee #	6769
Hourly Rate	22
Week of	Jun 20-24

Job #	SU	M	T	W	TH	F	SA	Total Hours
458-789		7.00	6.50	7.50	6.00			27.00
458-790		1.00	1.50	0.5	2.00	8.00		13.00

they are not traced to particular products, they are considered to be indirect materials and are included in overhead. Overhead is assigned to a job based on an allocation basis, such as direct labour hours used on the job or another cost driver. Both direct materials and an allocation of indirect materials are recorded for a job on the job cost record, a detailed list of all costs for a particular job (see Exhibit 11.2).

While the cost of materials will usually apply only to retail or manufacturing businesses, the cost of labour applies across all business sectors. Direct labour is the labour directly involved in the conversion process of raw materials to finished goods. It is traceable to particular products or services via the employee time record, a detailed list of the time an employee has spent on each job in a factory. The direct labour totals are then recorded in the job cost report (see Exhibit 11.2).

In a service business, direct labour is provided by the employees who supply the service that is sold. In a call centre, for example, the cost of the employees making and receiving calls is a direct cost. Other labour costs cannot be traced directly to the services provided, such as supervision, quality control, health and safety, cleaning, and maintenance. These are still costs of providing a service, but because they cannot be traced to a particular service, they are indirect labour costs.

Other costs are incurred that may be direct or indirect. For example, in a manufacturing business, the depreciation of machines (a fixed cost) used to make products may be a direct cost if each machine is used for a single product, or an indirect cost if the machine is used to make many products. The electricity used in production (a variable cost) may be a direct cost if it is metered to particular products, or indirect if it applies to a range of products. A royalty paid per unit of a product/service produced or sold will be a direct cost. The cost of rental of premises, typically relating to the whole business, will be an indirect cost.

OTHER COST TERMS

Prime cost is an umbrella term that refers to the total of all direct costs. Prime costs include the total of direct materials and direct labour. *Production overhead* is the total of all indirect material, indirect labour, and other indirect costs; that is, all production costs other than direct costs. This distinction applies equally to the production of goods and services. *Conversion costs* are the production costs, other than direct materials, used to make a product or provide a service. Conversion costs include direct labour and production overhead.

Distinguishing between materials, labour, and overhead costs as direct or indirect is *contingent* on the type of product/service and the particular production process used in the organization. There are no strict rules, as the classification of costs depends on the circumstances of each business and the decisions made by the accountants in that business. Consequently, unlike financial accounting, there is far greater variety between businesses—even in the same industry—in how costs are treated for management accounting purposes.

Calculating Product/Service Costs

The costs of a product or service are made up of all costs that are incurred to produce the product or provide a service (i.e., the cost of goods sold). As direct costs by definition are traceable, these direct costs of a product or service are usually easily identified and reasonably accurate. However, indirect costs, which by their nature cannot be traced to products/services, must in some way be *allocated* over products/services in order to calculate the product or service's full cost. *Overhead allocation* is the process of spreading production overhead (i.e., those overhead costs that cannot be traced directly to products/services) equitably over the volume of production.

Exhibit 11.3 illustrates the assignment of costs to a job for the Willow Company. One job in the company, Job 100, incurred a total of $95,000 in direct labour costs and $45,000 in direct materials costs. The indirect costs for the company, however, cannot be assigned directly to the job. The Willow Company therefore uses a cost-allocation base of direct labour hours to allocate these costs to each job. For this, the company uses a company-wide overhead rate—that is, an overhead rate calculated using the total of the overhead costs for the company, divided by the total of the allocation base for the overhead. Willow incurred a total of 340,000 direct labour hours in the year and a total of $1,700,000 in indirect costs—a cost-allocation rate of $5 per direct labour hour ($1,700,000/340,000). Job 100 involved 7,000 direct labour hours, which means the company assigned $35,000 in overhead to the job (7,000 × $5).

Exhibit 11.3 Costs Allocated to Job 100 Using Company-wide Overhead Rate

Direct labour
$95,000

Direct materials
$45,000

Cost for job 100
$175,000

Indirect costs allocated
7,000 DLH × $5 =
$35,000

Indirect costs total:
$1,700,000

Allocation base: DLH
340,000 DLH = $5 per DLH

The method used to allocate indirect costs is a significant issue for businesses that produce a range of products/services using multiple production processes. As shown above, the most common form of overhead allocation employed by accountants has been to allocate overhead costs to products/services using a company-wide overhead rate that is based on total direct labour hours. However, this may not always accurately reflect the resources consumed in production. For example, processes may be resource intensive in terms of space, machinery, people, or working capital. Some processes may be labour intensive, while others may use differing degrees of technology.

To improve the accuracy of the overhead allocation, companies often move from a company-wide overhead rate to a divisional-based overhead rate. A **divisional-based overhead rate** calculates the overhead for each division within the company and then uses an allocation base to assign the divisional overhead to jobs. Assume that the Willow Company processed its jobs through two divisions: assembly and finishing. The total overhead costs for each department were $1,000,000 and $700,000, for assembly and finishing, respectively. The company used 250,000 direct labour hours (DLH) in assembly and 90,000 direct labour hours in finishing. For Job 100, the company used 6,000 DLH in assembly and 1,000 labour hours in finishing. The revised overhead allocation is shown in Exhibit 11.4.

Exhibit 11.4 Costs Allocated to Job 100 Using Divisional-Based Overhead Rates

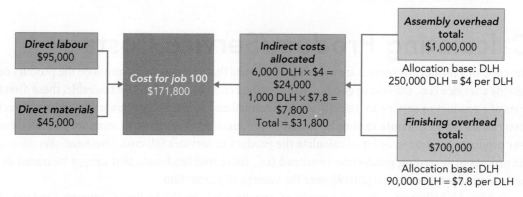

Direct labour
$95,000

Direct materials
$45,000

Cost for job 100
$171,800

Indirect costs allocated
6,000 DLH × $4 =
$24,000
1,000 DLH × $7.8 =
$7,800
Total = $31,800

Assembly overhead total:
$1,000,000

Allocation base: DLH
250,000 DLH = $4 per DLH

Finishing overhead total:
$700,000

Allocation base: DLH
90,000 DLH = $7.8 per DLH

As a result of refining the overhead-allocation process, the company has assigned $3,200 less in overhead to this job. This could be significant if the company is using job costs as a basis for charging-out to clients.

As a result of different resource consumption, the allocation process, if not carefully designed, may lead to overhead costs being arbitrarily allocated across different products/services, which can lead to misleading information about product/service profitability. It can also result in an incorrect valuation of inventory and, hence, reported profitability. The next section explores how activity-based costing can help an organization avoid arbitrary cost allocations.

ACTIVITY-BASED COSTING

In 1987, Johnson and Kaplan recognized the limitations of traditional overhead-allocation methods:

> Costs are distributed to products by simplistic and arbitrary measures, usually direct-labor based, that do not represent the demands made by each product on the firm's resources . . . the methods systematically bias and distort costs of individual products . . . [and] usually lead to enormous cross subsidies across products. (p. 2)

Even today, this fact is still true, as organizations continue to use arbitrary methods of indirect cost allocation such as direct labour hours. Poor decisions can result from inaccurate product costing. For example, inaccurate costing can result in acquiring capital assets to support a failing product, underpricing or overpricing a product, deciding on an unprofitable product mix to be sold by the company, and establishing budgets that are not feasible. These types of poor decisions can result in lowered profitability through non-optimal product mixes, poor demand for a product due to over-pricing, and the inability to compete in a cost-effective manner in the global marketplace.

Activity-based costing (ABC) is a method of allocating indirect costs (overhead costs) in a more direct manner to provide a more accurate cost of products or services. ABC uses *cost pools* to accumulate the indirect costs of significant business activities and then assigns the costs from the cost pools to products based on *cost drivers*, which measure each product's demand for activities.

Cost pools accumulate the indirect cost of business processes, irrespective of the organizational structure of the business. For example, a purchasing cost pool can be the result of work taking place in many different departments. A store clerk may identify the need to restock a product. This will often lead to a purchase requisition, which must be approved by a manager before being passed to the Purchasing Department. Purchasing staff will have negotiated with suppliers in relation to quality, price, and delivery and will generally have approved suppliers and terms. A purchase order will be created. The supplier will deliver the goods against the purchase order and the goods will be received into the store. The paperwork will be passed to the Accounting Department to be matched to the supplier invoice, and a cheque will be produced and posted. This business process of purchasing inventory cuts across several departments. ABC collects the purchasing costs in all of the departments into a cost pool.

A cost driver is then identified. The cost driver is the most significant cause of the activity. In the purchasing example, the cause of purchasing costs is often due to the number of purchase orders processed. Cost drivers enable the cost of activities to be assigned from cost pools to cost objects. Rates are calculated for each cost driver, and overhead costs are allocated to products/services on the basis of the cost driver rates.

There are no rules about which cost pools and cost drivers should be used, as this will be contingent on the circumstances of each business and the choices made by its accountants. The following are examples of cost pools and drivers:

Cost Pool	Cost Driver
Purchasing	Number of purchase orders
Material handling	Number of set-ups (i.e., batches)
Scheduling	Number of production orders
Equipment maintenance	Machine hours
Indirect materials	Number of products made

A rate will be calculated for each cost driver (e.g., for each purchase order or set-up) and costs will be assigned to each product based on how many purchase orders and set-ups the product has required. The more purchase orders and set-ups a product requires, the higher the overhead cost allocated to it. ABC does not mean that direct labour hours or machine hours or the number of units produced are ignored. When these are the significant cause of activities for particular cost pools, they are used as the cost drivers for those cost pools.

In order to identify a cost driver, it can be helpful to categorize costs as follows:

- **Unit-level activities** are performed each time a unit is produced; for example, direct labour, direct materials, and variable manufacturing costs, such as electricity. Unit-level activities consume resources in proportion to the number of units produced. If a company produces books, then the cost of paper, ink, and binding, and the labour of printers, are unit-level activities. If the company produces twice as many books, unit-level activities will be doubled. These costs are normally considered to be direct costs, since they can be assigned directly to a unit of production. ABC is not required to allocate direct costs.

- **Batch-related activities** are performed each time a batch of goods is produced; for example, a machine set-up. The cost of batch-related activities varies with the number of batches, but is fixed irrespective of the number of units produced within the batch. Using our book example, the cost of preparing the printing machines (e.g., changing the ink and changing the paper) is fixed, irrespective of how many books are printed in that batch, but it is variable in relation to the number of batches that are printed.

CASE IN POINT

Activity-Based Costing at Pratt & Whitney Canada

After spending some $400 million a year on research and development of airplane engines, Pratt & Whitney Canada needs to ensure that the products it develops have costs properly allocated so it can thrive in the competitive global aerospace market. That's why the Montreal-based company, with more than 6,200 employees at manufacturing facilities in five provinces, moved from traditional costing to activity-based costing.

Using traditional costing, Pratt & Whitney Canada would allocate overhead to each component based on time spent in a machine, among other things. So if a washer used the same number of machine hours as an engine case, each would be allocated the same amount of overhead, even though the actual cost to produce those items was very different.

So the company adopted ABC software, which calculates precisely how many resources an item requires through the entire production process, including materials, machine usage, and energy use. In some cases, the traditional costs were off by 100% or more. For example, using ABC, the company's costing team found that the cost of the sandblasting process varied widely, based not on the number of hours of machine use, but on materials consumed—the amount and size of beads used in sandblasting an item.

In addition to calculating the exact cost to produce each product, the ABC software is also able to show which machines are used to capacity and which are underutilized, so managers can decide where to shift production to best meet demand. After all, the cost of production bottlenecks (and potential lost sales) and unused capacity must be factored into decision making.

Sources: 3C Software, *Success Story*, Object technology opens new costing horizons for Pratt & Whitney Canada, retrieved from www.3csoftware.com/clients/success-stories/success-story-pratt-whitney; *Pratt & Whitney Canada to invest $1 billion in research & development over five years*, company news release, December 13, 2010.

- **Product-sustaining activities** enable the production and sale of multiple products/services; for example, maintaining product specifications, after-sales support, and product design and development. The cost of these activities increases with the number of products, irrespective of the number of batches or the number of units produced. For each differently titled book published, there is a cost incurred in dealing with the author, obtaining copyright approval, typesetting the text, and so on. No matter how many batches of the book are printed, these costs are fixed. Nevertheless, the cost is variable depending on the number of books that are published.

- **Customer-sustaining activities** support individual customers or groups of customers; for example, different costs may apply to supporting retail—that is, end-user—customers compared with resellers. In the book example, particular costs are associated with promoting a textbook to academics in the hope that it will be adopted by schools as required reading. Fiction books may be promoted through advertising and in-store displays. Customer-related costs are often driven by the number of customers.

- **Facility-sustaining activities** support the entire business and are common to all products/services. Examples of these costs include senior management and administrative staff compensation, building rent, and depreciation. ABC cost drivers for facility-sustaining costs can vary from square metres of floor space for plant depreciation costs to number of employees for senior management costs.

To illustrate ABC, the following overhead costs were accumulated for Grey Owl Company:

Purchasing	$ 40,000
Scheduling	60,000
Materials handling	25,000
Inspection	10,000
Total	$135,000

For each of the above activities and costs, the company identified the following drivers that directly impact the level of these indirect costs:

Purchasing	Number of purchase orders
Scheduling	Number of production orders
Materials handling	Number of set-ups
Inspection	Number of inspection hours

The cost per activity is the cost pool divided by the cost drivers, as shown in Exhibit 11.5.

Exhibit 11.5 **Calculation of Cost per Activity**

Overhead Cost	Total Cost	Cost Driver	Cost per Activity
Purchasing	$40,000	4000	$10
Scheduling	60,000	100	600
Materials handling	25,000	200	125
Inspection	10,000	250	40

If the company produced two products, the overhead costs are then assigned to each product based on each product's share of the cost driver volume, as shown in Exhibit 11.6.

Exhibit 11.6 Allocation of Overhead to Products

Overhead Cost (per driver)	Product A		Product B		Total Overhead Costs Allocated
	Driver Volume	Total Cost	Driver Volume	Total Cost	
Purchasing ($10)	2000	$20,000	2000	$20,000	$40,000
Scheduling ($600)	25	15,000	75	45,000	60,000
Materials handling ($125)	90	11,250	110	13,750	25,000
Inspection ($40)	150	6,000	100	4,000	10,000
Total Overhead		$52,250		$82,750	$135,000

We can then calculate the overhead cost per product/service by dividing the total overhead costs assigned to each product by the quantity of products/services produced. This is shown in Exhibit 11.7.

Exhibit 11.7 Overhead per Product Based on ABC

	Product A	Product B
Total overhead	$52,250.00	$82,750.00
Quantity produced	350	100
Per product	$ 149.29	$ 827.50

The total of direct costs is not affected by the method of overhead allocation—it will be the same under both a traditional approach and ABC. The total cost of each product is calculated by adding the direct materials and direct labour costs to the overhead allocation calculated using ABC, as shown in Exhibit 11.8.

Exhibit 11.8 Total Product Cost under ABC

	Direct Materials	Direct Labour	Manufacturing Overhead	Total Cost per Product
Product A	$150	$100	$149.29	$ 399.29
Product B	$175	$ 55	$827.50	$1,057.50

Assume that prior to the ABC adoption, Grey Owl Company used a company-wide overhead rate, using direct labour hours to allocate overhead costs. The company had a total of 2,000 labour hours—1,500 hours for Product A and 500 hours for Product B. This would mean that each labour hour worked could be assigned $67.50 per labour hour worked ($135,000/2000 = $67.50). The total product costs under the company's traditional method are shown in Exhibit 11.9 and the difference between the two methods is shown in Exhibit 11.10.

Exhibit 11.9 Total Product Cost under Traditional Approach

	Direct Materials	Direct Labour	Manufacturing Overhead	Total Cost per Product
Product A	$150	$100	$289.29*	$539.29
Product B	$175	$55	$337.50**	$567.50

*Product A = $67.50 × 1,500 hours = $101,250/350 units = $289.29
**Product B = $67.50 × 500 hours = $33,750/100 units = $337.50

Exhibit 11.10 Difference between Traditional Approach and ABC

	Product A	Product B
Total cost under traditional costing	$539.29	$ 567.50
Total cost using activity-based costing	$399.29	$1,057.50
Difference	$140.00	$ (490.00)

The difference between traditional costing allocation and ABC can be significant. In this case, under the traditional approach, Product A was subsidizing Product B by absorbing a large portion of Product B's overhead costs. After looking at this more closely, the company noted that Product A is much more labour-intensive and is a standardized product that has fewer set-ups and requires less inspection hours per unit. Product B, on the other hand, is produced in a more complex process, with more components requiring more machine changeovers and a greater degree of inspection. If the company continued assigning overhead costs to each product based on labour hours, they could be under-pricing Product B or choosing a less-than-optimal mix of Products A and B.

Although this is an extreme example, significant differences can result from the adoption of an activity-based approach to overhead allocation. Overheads allocated using direct labour hours under traditional costing do not reflect the actual causes for overhead costs being incurred. Cross-subsidization, as in this case, can be hidden in situations where a business sells a mixture of high-volume and low-volume products or services.

The ABC method is preferred because the allocation of costs is based on *cause-and-effect* relationships, while the traditional approach is based on an *arbitrary* allocation of overhead costs. However, ABC can be costly to implement because of the need to analyze business processes in detail, to collect costs in cost pools, and to identify cost drivers and measure the extent to which individual products/services consume resources. For this reason, ABC is not for all companies. A company needs to assess the costs versus benefits prior to implementing an ABC system.

ABSORPTION AND VARIABLE COSTING

Variable costing is a method of reporting in which only variable costs are treated as inventoriable—that is, costs that are assigned, in some way, to each product made by the company. Direct materials, direct labour, and variable overhead costs are assigned to each product made during the period. However, fixed overhead costs are treated as period expenses—that is, they are expensed in the period in which they occur. They are not assigned to each product that is made and sold.

Absorption costing, on the other hand, is a system where all production overhead costs (fixed and variable) are inventoriable. Variable costs (such as direct materials, direct labour, and variable overhead) are assigned directly to each unit made, similar to variable costing. Fixed overhead costs, however, are assigned to each product/service based on an allocation base. The fixed production overhead for a company is estimated and divided by the allocation base to calculate a budgeted overhead rate for the company. Each and every product that is made at the plant is then assigned fixed production overhead costs based on this budgeted overhead rate.

The budgeted fixed overhead rate is

$$\text{Fixed overhead rate} = \frac{\text{Estimated fixed overhead expenditure for the period}}{\text{Estimated activity for the period}}$$

For example, a business with budgeted fixed overhead costs of $100,000 and an activity level of 40,000 units of production would have a company-wide budgeted overhead rate of $2.5 per unit ($100,000/40,000).

Absorption costing is used for external financial reporting. Section 3031 of the *CICA Handbook* states that "the cost of inventories shall comprise all costs of purchase, costs of conversion, and other costs incurred in bringing the inventories to their present location and condition" (Canadian Institute of Chartered Accountants). The *Handbook* further indicates that fixed overhead must be allocated to inventories based on the normal production capacity of the production facility. This practice of including fixed overhead costs as an inventoriable item is also found in IFRS standards. Variable costing, on the other hand, is not approved for external reporting but is often used by companies for internal reporting.

Let's compare the two methods. Consider the data in Exhibit 11.11 for Novelties Galore Warehouse Inc. Exhibit 11.12 shows the income reported using both variable and absorption costing.

Exhibit 11.11 **Data for Novelties Galore Warehouse**

Beginning inventory (units)	0
Units produced	5,800
Units sold	5,000
Sales	$110 per unit
Direct materials cost	$18 per unit
Variable conversion costs	$15 per unit
Fixed manufacturing costs	$145,000
Fixed selling and administrative costs	$62,000
Variable selling costs	$5 per unit

Under variable costing, the full $145,000 in fixed manufacturing costs is expensed in the year. Under absorption costing, this cost is treated as an inventoriable cost and the 800 remaining units in inventory are assigned a portion of the fixed costs. This results in a higher income under absorption costing, since some fixed manufacturing costs are carried forward to the next year when the inventory is sold.

A key issue with absorption costing is the potential risk that a manager may be inclined to build up inventories to increase reported income each year. A manager who increases production to build up inventories can move some of the production overhead costs from one period to the next. Managers may be inclined to do this if they are paid a bonus on their divisional profits.

A major risk with this approach is that the next year, inventories must be built up again to move any new fixed manufacturing costs to the following year and so on. This can result in an extremely high buildup of inventories that will cost the company a great deal in terms of storage, inventory

Exhibit 11.12 **Income Reported Using Variable and Absorption Costing**

Variable Costing		Absorption Costing	
Sales	$550,000	Sales	$550,000
Cost of goods sold		Cost of goods sold	
Beginning inventory	$0	Beginning inventory	$0
Materials	104,400	Materials	104,400
Conversion costs	87,000	Conversion costs	87,000
Less ending inventory[1]	26,400	Fixed manufacturing	145,000
Cost of goods sold	$165,000	Less ending inventory[2]	46,400
Variable selling costs	$25,000	Cost of goods sold	$290,000
Contribution margin	$360,000	Gross margin	$260,000
Fixed manufacturing	145,000	Variable selling costs	25,000
Fixed S&A costs	62,000	Fixed S&A costs	62,000
Net income	$153,000	Net income	$173,000

[1]5,800 − 5,000 = 800 units in ending inventory × ($18 direct materials + $15 conversion costs) = $26,400

[2]Fixed manufacturing rate = $145,000/5,800 = $25 per unit produced

5,800 − 5,000 = 800 units in ending inventory × ($18 direct materials + $15 conversion costs + $25 fixed manufacturing costs) = $46,400

handling, and obsolescence costs. For this reason, the use of variable costing for internal performance evaluation is recommended.

OVERALLOCATION OR UNDERALLOCATION OF OVERHEAD

When a rate for fixed manufacturing costs is developed by the company, it is based on budgeted costs and the budgeted level of activity. This is due to the fact that the overhead rate is normally established prior to the production year, enabling the company's accounting systems to systematically assign the overhead costs to each product produced in a production period. At the end of the year, however, when actual cost and actual activity volumes are known, there is definitely going to be a difference between the actual overhead and the budgeted overhead that was allocated throughout the period. The result is an underallocation or overallocation of overhead.

For example, assume that the Novelties Galore Warehouse budgeted fixed manufacturing overhead cost was $150,000, based on an estimated 5,000 units of production. The example in Exhibit 11.12 is based on actual values, but in normal practice the overhead rate will be a budgeted value. This will result in an overhead rate of $30 per tree (per unit). If absorption costing was used, the following fixed manufacturing costs would be recorded throughout the year:

Fixed manufacturing rate = $30/tree
Number of actual units produced = 5,800
Total fixed manufacturing costs allocated = $174,000 ($30 × 5800)

Since the actual fixed manufacturing costs were only $145,000 (as shown in Exhibit 11.12), this resulted in an overallocation of fixed overhead costs of $29,000.

In order to adjust the records of the company, there are two approaches that can be used: assignment of overallocation or underallocation to cost of goods sold, or prorate overallocation or underallocation to cost of goods sold, work in progress inventory, and finished goods inventory.

Option 1: Assignment of over- or underallocation to cost of goods sold

Often, for simplicity's sake, the company will record the over- or underallocation to cost of goods sold. In the case of Novelties Galore Warehouse, the cost of goods sold (COGS) reported on the statement of comprehensive income would be decreased by $29,000, as shown in Exhibit 11.13.

Exhibit 11.13 Statement of Comprehensive Income Showing Overallocation of Overhead Recorded to COGS

Sales	$550,000
Cost of goods sold	
Beginning inventory	$0
Materials	104,400
Conversion costs	87,000
Fixed manufacturing	174,000
Less ending inventory[*1]	50,400
COGS	$315,000
Adjustment for overallocation of overhead	29,000
Adjusted COGS	$286,000
Gross margin	$264,000
Variable selling costs	25,000
Fixed selling and admin costs	62,000
Net income	$177,000

[1]Fixed manufacturing rate = $150,000/5000 = $30 per unit produced
5800 − 5000 = 800 units in ending inventory × ($18 direct materials + $15 conversion costs + $30 fixed manufacturing costs) = $50,400

Option 2: Prorate over- or underallocation to cost of goods sold, work in progress inventory, and finished goods inventory

The problem when the over- or underallocation is recorded to cost of goods sold is that this does not reflect true inventoriable costs. In the normal course of operations, there will be some units of production that are sold, some that are sitting in the ending inventory but are not sold (finished goods inventory), and some partially completed in the work in progress (WIP) inventory. Since fixed manufacturing costs are inventoriable costs, the over- or underallocation should really be assigned to all three product categories (COGS, WIP inventory, and finished goods inventory). This method assigns the over- or underallocation of overhead to each of the three categories based on their value at the end of the accounting period.

Assume that the values of each product-related account are as follows:

Finished goods inventory	$ 35,000
Cost of goods sold	315,000 (based on the absorption costing method from Exhibit 11.13)
WIP inventory	57,000
Total	$407,000

The $29,000 overallocation of overhead will be assigned based on the prorated amount of the total product-related balances as shown in Exhibit 11.14.

Exhibit 11.14 Overallocation of Overhead Assigned to COGS and to Finished Goods and WIP Inventories

Category	Percentage	Assigned Overallocation
Finished goods	$35,000/$407,000 = 8.6%	$2,494
Cost of goods sold	$315,000/$407,000 = 77.4%	22,446
WIP inventory	$57,000/$407,000 = 14%	4,060
Total	100%	$29,000

In this case, the adjustment to COGS will be shown on the statement of comprehensive income and the adjustments to both finished goods and work in progress inventories will be shown on the statement of financial position, as shown in Exhibit 11.15 and Exhibit 11.16.

Exhibit 11.15 Statement of Comprehensive Income Showing Proration of Overallocation of Overhead Recorded to COGS

Sales	$550,000
Cost of goods sold	
Beginning inventory	$0
Materials	104,400
Conversion costs	87,000
Fixed manufacturing	174,000
Less ending inventory[*1]	50,400
COGS	$315,000
Adjustment for overallocation of overhead	$22,446
Adjusted COGS	$292,554
Gross margin	$257,446
Selling and admin costs	62,000
Net income	$195,446

[1]Fixed manufactruing rate = $150,000/5000 = $30 per unit produced
5800 − 5000 = 800 units in ending inventory × ($18 direct materials + $15 conversion costs + $30 fixed manufacturing costs) = $50,400

Exhibit 11.16 Adjusted Balances of Inventory Accounts after Proration of Overallocation of Overhead

Finished goods inventory	$35,000
Adjustment for overallocation of overhead	2,494
Adjusted finished goods inventory	$32,506
Work in progress inventory	$57,000
Adjustment for overallocation of overhead	$4,060
Adjusted work in progress inventory	$52,940

CONCLUSION

Understanding product and service costing is important for all decisions related to pricing, product or service mix, production planning and budgeting. Understanding the components of product cost is critical in cost management and control. With the shift in most western economies to service industries and high-technology manufacturing, overheads have increased as a proportion of total business costs. This chapter has shown the importance to decision making of the methods used by accountants to allocate overheads to products/services. Understanding the methods used, and their limitations, is essential if informed decisions are to be made by accountants and by non-financial managers.

KEY TERMS

Absorption costing, 271

Activity-based costing (ABC), 267

Company-wide overhead rate, 265

Cost driver, 267

Cost of goods sold, 262

Cost pools, 267

Direct costs, 263

Direct labour, 264

Direct materials, 263

Divisional-based overhead rate, 266

Employee time record, 264

Gross profit, 262

Indirect costs, 263

Indirect labour, 265

Indirect materials, 264

Job cost record, 264

Materials requisition record, 263

Overhead costs, 263

Period costs, 261

Product costs, 261

Variable costing, 271

CASE STUDY 11.1: **ABC AT SMITH COMPONENTS**

Smith Components has four product lines: A1, A2, A3, and B1. The A1, A2, and A3 products are produced using an automated system. The only employee involvement is at the end of the process when the product is packaged and sealed. B1, on the other hand, is highly labour-intensive, requiring hands-on assembly throughout the production process.

Smith has always used a traditional method of assigning overhead costs to all products, using machine hours. During 2011, the total overhead costs for Smith were $245,000, with a total of 10,000 machine hours. The company used an overhead rate of

Overhead rate = $245,000/10,000
= $24.50 per machine hour

During 2011, the $245,000 in overhead cost was assigned to each product based on machine hours as shown in Exhibit 11.17.

The profitability by product for 2011 was calculated as shown in Exhibit 11.18. Based on the calculations in Exhibit 11.18, it seems that the B1 component is providing the most profit for the company. Scott Lee, the management accountant at Smith, just attended

a seminar on activity-based costing. He arranged a meeting with the plant manager, Ariel Marks, and described how ABC may result in more accurate product costing. He mentioned that he felt the use of machine hours might not be appropriately assigning overhead costs due to the fact that Component B1 used very few machine hours. Ariel asked Scott to complete an activity-based costing analysis for the company.

Scott first identified the various overhead cost pools that made up the total overhead costs for the company, and the cost drivers that he felt most accurately impacted changes in the overhead costs (see Exhibit 11.19). Next, as shown in Exhibit 11.20, Scott determined the cost driver volume for each component manufactured by the company. He then determined a cost driver rate for each overhead cost, as shown in Exhibit 11.21. Finally, he assigned the overhead costs to each component, using the cost driver rates shown in Exhibit 11.21 and the cost driver volumes shown in Exhibit 11.22. Scott then restated operating profit using the overhead based on ABC in Exhibit 11.23.

Exhibit 11.17 **Overhead Assignment**

Component	Machine Hours	Overhead Costs
A1	2,700	$66,150
A2	3,250	79,625
A3	3,800	93,100
B1	250	6,125
Total machine hours	10,000	$245,000

Exhibit 11.18 **Profitability Using the Traditional Approach**

	A1	A3	A3	B1	Total
Sales in units	27,000	28,000	30,000	10,000	95,000
Sales	$135,000	$168,000	$210,000	$140,000	$653,000
Direct materials	54,000	67,200	84,000	49,000	254,200
Direct labour	13,500	16,800	21,000	42,000	93,300
Contribution margin	$67,500	$84,000	$105,000	$49,000	$305,500
Overhead	66,150	79,625	93,100	6,125	245,000
Operating profit	$1,350	$4,375	$11,900	$42,875	$60,500

Exhibit 11.19 **Overhead Costs and Cost Drivers**

Overhead Cost		Cost Driver
Materials handling	$28,000	Number of parts
Machine setup	85,000	Number of batches
Machine maintenance	25,000	Number of machine hours
Inspection costs	20,000	Inspection hours
Administration costs	35,000	Number of direct manufacturing labour hours
R&D	52,000	R&D hours
Total	$245,000	

Exhibit 11.20 **Cost Driver Volumes**

Component	Number of Parts	Number of Batches	Machine Hours	Inspection Hours	Direct-Labour Hours	R&D Hours
A1	50	5	2,700	12	500	150
A2	55	7	3,250	18	750	350
A3	57	12	3,800	15	950	175
B1	62	18	250	35	4,500	850
Total	224	42	10,000	80	6,700	1,525

Exhibit 11.21 **Cost Driver Rates**

Component	Cost Driver	Cost $	Cost Driver Volume	Cost Driver Rate
Materials handling	No. of parts	$28,000	224	$125.00
Machine setup	No. of batches	85,000	42	$2023.81
Machine maintenance	Machine hours	25,000	10,000	$2.50
Inspection costs	Inspection hours	20,000	80	$250.00
Administration costs	Direct labour hours	35,000	6,700	$5.22
R&D	R&D hours	52,000	1,525	$34.10
Total		$245,000		

Exhibit 11.22 **Assignment of Overhead Costs Using ABC**

Product	Materials Handling	Machine Set Up	Machine Maintenance	Inspection Costs	Admin Costs	R&D Costs	Total
A1	$6,250	$10,119	$6,750	$3,000	$2,612	$5,115	$33,846
A2	6,875	14,167	8,125	4,500	3,918	11,934	49,519
A3	7,125	24,286	9,500	3,750	4,963	5,967	55,591
B1	7,750	36,429	625	8,750	23,507	28,984	106,045
	$28,000	$85,001	$25,000	$20,000	$35,000	$52,000	$245,001

*The above values may be slightly different than your calculator due to the rounding of the activity rates.

Exhibit 11.23 **Operating Profit Using ABC**

	A1	A3	A3	B1	Total
Sales in units	27,000	28,000	30,000	10,000	95,000
Sales	$135,000	$168,000	$210,000	$140,000	$653,000
Direct materials	54,000	67,200	84,000	49,000	254,200
Direct labour	13,500	16,800	21,000	42,000	93,300
Contribution margin	$ 67,500	$84,000	$105,000	$49,000	$305,500
Overhead	33,846	49,519	55,591	106,045	$245,001
Operating profit	$33,654	$34,481	$49,409	$(57,045)	$60,501

Ariel was surprised by the results shown in Exhibit 11.23. Using the traditional costing system, the A1, A2, and A3 products are subsidizing the B1 product. The B1 product was not as profitable as it seemed at first. She asked Scott to revise the existing overhead allocation method to the ABC method, to ensure that they have the right costs when making product mix decisions. Ariel also took steps to increase the sales price of B1 to ensure that an acceptable profit is achieved.

CASE STUDY 11.2: HUB CELLULAR COMMUNICATIONS— ABSORPTION v. VARIABLE COSTING

Hub Cellular, which manufactures a variety of cellphones, opened its offices in 2009. The Elite Division of Hub Cellular, which produces a high-end cellphone, reported the operating profit for the last three years shown in Exhibit 11.24.

Danny Quentin, the manager of the Elite Division, is paid a yearly bonus of 5% of operating profit if his profitability increases by more than 12% each year. During 2010 and 2011, Quentin received substantial bonuses due to strong increases in profitability.

Elli Fitzgerald, the company president, was concerned, however, about the size of inventory reported on the Elite Division's statement of comprehensive income. Inventories have increased from $322,500 in 2009 to $1,548,000 in 2011. Cellphone technologies have short lifespans and she is concerned that the obsolescence costs for the company will be extreme. She asked Mohammed Houda, the head of accounting, to look into this concern. Houda mentioned to Fitzgerald that they should be using a variable costing statement of comprehensive income for performance evaluation, and he restated the statement of comprehensive incomes for 2009 through 2011 for the Elite Division, as shown in Exhibit 11.25.

Houda suggested that Quentin might have been purposely building up inventories in order to carry forward fixed manufacturing costs from one period to the next. By doing this, he was able to make his profitability much higher to ensure he would receive his bonus.

Fitzgerald was shocked that the income for a division could be manipulated in such as manner. She took necessary actions to discipline Quentin. She also changed the performance evaluation process at Hub to base performance assessment on variable costing techniques, and to incorporate inventory management into the performance-assessment process. This was an important lesson for the company regarding the behaviour implications of accounting methods.

Exhibit 11.24 Absorption Costing Statement of Comprehensive Income for 2009, 2010, and 2011

	2009	2010	2011
Sales	$4,625,000	$5,250,000	$5,625,000
Cost of goods sold:			
Opening inventory	$ –	$322,500	$838,500
Cost of goods manufactured			
Direct materials ($10 per unit)	420,000	500,000	560,000
Direct labour ($8.50 per unit)	357,000	425,000	476,000
Variable OH ($6 per unit)	252,000	300,000	336,000
Fixed overhead ($40 per unit)[1]	1,680,000	2,000,000	2,240,000
Total COGM	$2,709,000	$3,547,500	$4,450,500
Less: ending inventory [*2]	322,500	838,500	1,548,000
Cost of goods sold	2,386,500	2,709,000	2,902,500
Gross profit	$2,238,500	$2,541,000	$2,722,500
Selling and admin expenses	1,500,000	1,650,000	1,700,000
Operating profit	$738,500	$891,000	$1,022,500
Percentage increase over previous year		**20.65%**	**14.76%**

[1] The fixed manufacturing costs for each year and the rate for fixed MOH is as follows:

Fixed manufacturing overhead	$1,680,000	$2,000,000	$2,240,000
Production volume	42,000	50,000	56,000
Rate	40	40	40

[*2] The ending inventories for each year are as follows:

Opening Inventory	0	5,000	13,000
Produced	42,000	50,000	56,000
Sold	37,000	42,000	45,000
Ending Inventory (Opening + Produced − Sold)	5,000	13,000	24,000
Total Cost per Unit	$64.50	$64.50	$64.50
Value of Ending Inventory	$322,500	$838,500	$1,548,000

Total Cost per Unit = $10 (direct materials) + $8.50 (direct labour) + $6 (variable overhead) + $40 (fixed overhead)
        = $64.50

Exhibit 11.25 **Variable Costing Statement of Comprehensive Income for 2009, 2010, and 2011**

	2009	2010	2011
Sales	$4,625,000	$5,250,000	$5,625,000
Cost of goods sold:			
Opening inventory	$ 0	$122,500	$318,500
Cost of goods manufactured			
Direct materials ($10 per unit)	420,000	500,000	560,000
Direct labour ($8.50 per unit)	357,000	425,000	476,000
Variable OH ($6 per unit)	252,000	300,000	336,000
Total COGM	$1,029,000	$1,347,500	$1,690,500
Less: ending inventory [1]	122,500	318,500	588,000
Cost of goods sold	906,500	1,029,000	1,102,500
Gross profit	$3,718,500	$4,221,000	$4,522,500
Fixed manufacturing overhead	1,680,000	2,000,000	2,240,000
Selling and admin expenses	1,500,000	1,650,000	1,700,000
Operating profit	$538,500	$571,000	$582,500
Percentage increase over previous year		**6.04%**	**2.01%**

[1] The ending inventories for each year are as follows:

Opening Inventory	0	5,000	13,000
Produced	42,000	50,000	56,000
Sold	37,000	42,000	45,000
Ending Inventory (Opening + Produced - Sold)	5,000	13,000	24,000
Total Cost per Unit	$24.50	$24.50	$24.50
Value of Ending Inventory	$122,500	$318,500	$ 588,000

Total Cost per Unit = $10 (direct materials) + $8.50 (direct labour) +
$6 (variable overhead) = $24.50

■ SELF-TEST QUESTIONS

S11.1 The accounting records of Turner Industries, a manufacturer of flash drives, shows the following costs for the year ended December 31, 2011.

Direct materials	$700,000
Direct labour	220,000
Indirect materials	100,000
Indirect labour	135,000
Variable overhead	220,000
Fixed overhead	325,000
Variable selling costs	100,000
Fixed S&A costs	185,000

The amount of prime costs incurred in 2011 were

a. 920,000

b. $1,140,000

c. $1,240,000

d. $765,000

S11.2 Use the following costs per unit to identify the total product cost and conversion cost per unit:

	$ per unit
Direct materials	12
Indirect materials	6
Direct labour	24
Indirect labour	8
Other variable overhead costs	10
Variable selling expense	5
Fixed production overhead	12
Fixed S&A expense	8

	Product Cost	**Conversion Cost**
a.	$72	$54
b.	$46	$34
c.	$46	$46
d.	$58	$34

S11.3 Intelco, a professional services firm, has overhead costs of $500,000. It operates three divisions, and an accountant's estimate of the overhead allocation per division is 50% for Division 1, 30% for Division 2, and 20% for Division 3. The divisions respectively bill 4,000, 2,000, and 3,000 hours. What is the overhead rate for Division 2?

a. $75

b. $56

c. $17

d. $63

S11.4 BCF Ltd. manufactures a product known as a Grunge. Direct material and labour costs for each Grunge are $300 and $150, respectively. To produce a Grunge requires 20 labour hours: 10 hours in machining, 7 hours in assembly, and 3 hours in finishing. Information for each department is as follows:

	Machining	Assembly	Finishing
Overhead costs	$120,000	$80,000	$30,000
Labour hours	20,000	10,000	10,000

What is the product cost of a Grunge using departmental overhead rates?

a. $455.75

b. $467.00

c. $450.00

d. $575.00

S11.5 Engineering Products produces Product GH1, which incurs costs of $150 for direct materials and $75 for direct labour per unit. The company has estimated its production overhead and direct labour hours for a period as

	Dept. A	Dept. B	Dept. C
Overhead	$150,000	$200,000	$125,000
Direct labour hours	5,000	10,000	5,000

Each unit of Product GH1 is produced using 10 hours in Dept. A, 12 hours in Dept. B, and 5 hours in Dept. C. Calculate the cost of one unit of GH1 using a company-wide overhead rate to the nearest dollar.

a. $300

b. $620

c. $866

d. $225

S11.6 Haridan Co. uses activity-based costing. The company has two products, A and B. The annual production and sales of Products A and B are 8,000 units and 6,000 units, respectively. There are three activity cost pools, with estimated total cost and expected activity as follows:

Activity Cost Pool	Estimated Cost	Expected Activity		
		Product A	Product B	Total
Activity 1	$20,000	100	400	500
Activity 2	37,000	800	200	1,000
Activity 3	91,200	800	3,000	3,800

What is the overhead cost per unit for Product A under activity-based costing?

a. $18.53

b. $5.94

c. $6.60

d. $21.46

S11.7 Elandem Ltd. produces 20,000 units of Product L and 20,000 units of Product M. Under activity-based costing, $120,000 of costs are purchasing-related. Each period, 240 purchase orders are produced and the number of orders used by each product is as follows:

	Product L	Product M
Number of orders	80	160

What is the per-unit activity-based cost of purchasing for Products L and M, respectively?

a. $2; $4

b. $3; $3

c. $500 each

d. $6; $4

S11.8 Heated Tools Ltd. uses activity-based costing. It has identified three cost pools and their drivers as follows:

	Purchasing	Quality Control	Dispatch
Driver	Purchase orders	Stores issues	Deliveries
Cost pool	$60,000	$40,000	$30,000
Driver quantity	12,000	4,000	2,000

What is the cost driver rate for quality control?

a. $10

b. $4

c. $15

d. $5

S11.9 Gyro Industries makes hub caps for the car industry. Direct materials are $12 per unit, while direct labour is $2.00 per unit. Variable overhead is $0.50 per unit and fixed overhead is $500,000 per year. Gyro produces 100,000 hub caps per year. 80,000 hub caps were sold this year.

What is the cost per hub cap under absorption costing?

a. $20.75

b. $14.00

c. $14.50

d. $19.50

Use the following to answer questions S11.10 and S11.11.

Ariana Corp. makes pencils. The actual and budgeted overhead for the year was $350,000. The company produced 5,000,000 pencils during the year and sold 4,760,000 pencils. The cost per batch of 1,000 pencils is as follows:

Direct materials	$20
Direct labour	$10
Variable overhead	$5

S11.10 What is the cost per batch of pencils if absorption costing is used?

a. $35

b. $105

c. $109

d. $45

S11.11 What is the cost per batch of pencils if variable costing is used?

a. $45

b. $105

c. $35

d. $109

S11.12 Andy's Office Warehouse makes office chairs. The following information was reported for the year ended 2011.

Total sales	$2,300,000
Direct materials	$20 per chair
Direct labour	$25 per chair
Variable overhead	$18 per chair
Fixed overhead	$665,000
Selling and admin. costs	$124,000
Total production	19,000
Sales	18,400

The operating profit for 2011 using absorption costing would be

a. $372,800

b. $351,800

c. $314,000

d. $360,800

■ PROBLEMS

P11.1 *(Determination of Overhead Rate)* Wolf Creek Industries produces custom uniforms. The company uses machine hours to allocate manufacturing overhead costs to jobs. The following yearly information was compiled for Wolf Creek:

Direct materials	$245,000
Direct labour	$325,000
Manufacturing overhead	$454,000
Machine hours	45,000

During the year, Wolf Creek completed a job for Carston College's cheerleading team; details are as follows:

Direct materials cost per uniform	$35
Direct labour cost per uniform	$38
Total machine hours per uniform	3.5
Total number of uniforms sold	65

a. What is the manufacturing overhead rate used by Wolf Creek?

b. What is the cost of making one uniform for Carston College?

c. What is the total cost of the Carston College job?

P11.2 (Divisional Overhead Rates) Phil Manufacturing uses divisional cost driver rates to apply manufacturing overhead costs to products. Manufacturing overhead costs are allocated on the basis of machine hours in the Cutting Department and on the basis of labour costs in the Assembly Department. The following budgeted values were provided for the upcoming year:

	Cutting	Assembly
Machine hours	100,000	2,000
Direct labour cost	$150,000	$750,000
Manufacturing overhead costs	$350,000	$562,500

The job cost record for Job 33456 shows the following:

	Cutting	Assembly
Machine hours	1,250	50
Direct materials cost	$1,500	$2,100
Direct labour cost	$ 450	$2,700

a. Compute the manufacturing overhead allocation rate for each department.

b. Compute the total cost of Job 33456.

c. Why does Phil's Manufacturing use two different rates for overhead?

P11.3 (Activity-Based Costing) Cooper's Components uses an activity-based costing system for its product costing. For the last quarter, the following data relate to costs, output volume, and cost drivers:

Total Overhead Costs	$
Machinery (driven by machine hours)	172,000
Set-ups (driven by production runs)	66,000
Materials handling (driven by store orders)	45,000
Total overhead	283,000

Product	A	B	C
Production and sales	4,000 units	3,000 units	2,000 units
Number of production runs	12	5	8
Number of stores orders	12	6	4
	per unit	per unit	per unit
Direct costs	$25	$35	$15
Machine hours	5	2	3
Direct labour hours	4	2	4

a. What is the total overhead cost assigned to each product?

b. What is the overhead cost per unit for each product?

c. What is the total cost per unit for each product?

P11.4 *(Activity-Based Costing)* Samuelson uses activity-based costing. The company manufactures two products, X and Y. The annual production and sales of Products X Y are 3,000 and 2,000 units, respectively. There are three activity cost pools, with estimated total cost and expected activity as follows:

Cost Pool	Estimated Cost	Expected Activity		
		X	Y	Total
Activity 1	$12,000	300	500	800
Activity 2	15,000	100	400	500
Activity 3	32,000	400	1,200	1,600
Total costs	$59,000			

a. Calculate the overhead cost per unit of Products X and Y under activity-based costing.

b. Samuelson wants to contrast its overhead allocation with that under the traditional costing method it previously used. Samuelson previously charged its overhead costs of $59,000 to products in proportion to machine hours. Each unit of X and Y consumed five machine hours in production. Calculate the overhead cost per unit of Products X and Y under the traditional method of overhead allocation.

P11.5 *(Contrasting Traditional and ABC Costing)* Brixton Industries makes three products: widgets, gadgets, and helios. The following budget information relates to Brixton for next year.

	Widgets	Gadgets	Helios
Sales and production (units)	50,000	40,000	30,000
Selling price (per unit)	$45	$95	$73
Direct labour and materials (per unit)	$32	$84	$65
Machine hours per unit in Machining Dept.	2	5	4
Direct labour hours per unit in Assembly Dept.	7	3	2

Overhead is allocated to production departments as follows:

- Machining Department at $1.20 per machine hour

- Assembly Department at $0.825 per direct labour hour

However, you have determined that the overheads could be reanalyzed into cost pools as shown below:

Cost pool	Cost ($)	Cost Driver	Quantity
Machining services	357,000	Machine hours	420,000
Assembly services	318,000	Direct labour hours	530,000
Set-up	26,000	Set-ups	520
Order processing	156,000	Customer orders	32,000
Purchasing	84,000	Supplier orders	11,200

You have also been provided with the following estimates for the current accounting period.

	Widgets	**Gadgets**	**Helios**
Number of set-ups	120	200	200
Customer orders	8,000	8,000	16,000
Supplier orders	3,000	4,000	4,200

a. Prepare a report showing profitability for each product for the next year using the traditional overhead allocation method.

b. Prepare a report showing profitability for each product using activity-based costing.

c. Explain the differences between the products' profitability using traditional and activity-based costing.

P11.6 *(ABC Costing)* Database Design does just what its name indicates: It provides a database design service for its clients. The cost of designing a database can be broken down into three elements:

1. **Designing the database.** The amount of work is based on the accuracy of the customer's specifications and how much time is spent with the customer to understand those specifications.

2. **Writing program code.** This is a function of the number of (input) screens, file records, and (output) reports, all of which are determined in the design phase.

3. **Testing.** This is also a function of the number of (input) screens, file records, and (output) reports.

Database Design has budgeted for staff and staff-related costs for each of the following:

Design Dept.	6 staff @ $30,000
Programming Dept.	4 staff @ $25,000
Testing Dept.	2 staff @ $20,000
Manager	1 person @ $45,000

Apart from for staff members, the main budget costs are for accommodation (rental and utilities), which costs $100,000 per year; lease costs of computer equipment of $25,000 per year; and travel costs of $10,000.

Accommodation and computer lease costs are primarily attributable to programming and testing staff while travel costs are attributable wholly to design staff. The manager's costs are split equally among the three functions.

Direct costs and overhead costs are to be allocated on an activity-costing basis, using the following estimates as cost drivers:

	Driver
Design	1,000 design days
Programming & Testing	10,000 screens, records, and reports

a. Calculate the total budgeted costs for the company.

b. Calculate the cost driver rates for each activity.

c. Estimate the cost for a job requiring 15 days of design and 150 screens, records, and reports.

P11.7 (*Contrasting Traditional and ABC Costing*) Zammit Engineering manufactures a number of components that are sold to the electronics industry. Most of the manufacturing processes are common to the products, and the direct costs (raw materials and labour) are relatively small in relation to the overhead costs, a consequence of the investment in sophisticated technology to mass-produce large numbers of items.

Zammit Engineering has divided its product range into four product groups: liggles, kicklets, zonnets, and carusos. Each product group is manufactured across three departments: Design, Machining, and Assembly. While design and assembly are labour-intensive, machining is capital-intensive.

Overhead costs have been estimated for each of the cost centres as follows:

	Design	**Machining**	**Assembly & Distribution**
Overhead costs)	$150,000	$250,000	$200,000

The number of direct labour hours (DLH) available for each department for the same period has been estimated as follows:

	Design	**Machining**	**Assembly & Distribution**
Direct labour hours	10,000 DLH	12,500 DLH	20,000 DLH

The four product groups require direct labour hours in each of the departments as follows:

	Design DLH	**Machining DLH**	**Assembly & Distribution DLH**	**Total DLH**
Liggles	2,000	1,500	10,000	13,500
Kicklets	3,000	1,000	5,000	9,000
Zonnets	3,000	7,000	2,000	12,000
Carusos	2,000	3,000	3,000	8,000

The Accounting Department recently carried out an activity-based costing exercise that has determined the following cost pool and cost driver information for the business:

Cost pool	**$**	**Cost driver**	**No. of drivers**
Order entry	100,000	Customer orders	5,000
Production	350,000	Production orders	2,000
Delivery	150,000	Delivery orders	5,000

Analysis has also shown the number of cost drivers associated with each product:

	Customer Orders	**Production Orders**	**Delivery Orders**
Liggles	1,500	500	1,000
Kicklets	500	1,000	1,000
Zonnets	1,000	250	1,000
Carusos	2,000	250	2,000

a. Calculate the overhead per direct labour hour using a departmental rate.

b. Calculate the total overhead cost allocated to each of the four product groups using the departmental rate.

  c. Calculate the costs per cost driver under activity-based costing.

  d. Calculate the total overhead cost allocated to each of the four product groups using activity-based costing.

  e. Comment on the approaches to costing and the differences between your answers to (b) and (d) above.

P11.8 *(Absorption and Variable Costing)* Clear Auto Glass sold 3,500 windshields in 2011 and produced a total of 4,000 windshields. Total costs incurred for the year included the following:

Direct materials	$450,000
Direct labour	300,000
Variable manufacturing overhead	150,000
Variable selling expenses	175,000
Fixed administrative expenses	200,000
Fixed manufacturing overhead	350,000

In January 2011, the beginning inventory of windshields was zero.

  a. Compute the ending finished goods inventory under both absorption and variable costing.

  b. Compute the cost of goods sold under both absorption and variable costing

P11.9 *(Absorption and Variable Costing)* Burchell Products sells a product for $25. Unit-level manufacturing costs for each unit are as follows:

- Direct materials, $5.00

- Direct manufacturing labour, $4.50

- Variable manufacturing overhead, $3.25

Marketing expenses are $1.50 per unit plus $35,000 per year. Total fixed manufacturing overhead costs are $60,000 per year. The current production level is 25,000 units per year and the company is budgeting for the sale of 22,000 units in the next year.

  a. Prepare a budgeted statement of comprehensive income for the year using variable costing.

  b. Prepare a budgeted statement of comprehensive income for the year using absorption costing.

P11.10 *(Absorption and Variable Costing)* Blue Mountain sells plastic tubes used in underground sprinkler systems. The company had a total finished goods inventory of 5,000 units on hand at the end of 2011. During 2011, variable manufacturing costs for one tube were $15, while fixed manufacturing costs were $35 per tube. The variable administrative costs related to one tube were $8, and fixed selling and administrative costs per tube were $20. During the year, Blue Mountain sold 25,000 units.

  a. If Blue Mountain used absorption costing, rather than variable costing, would its income be higher or lower?

  b. What would be the difference in reported profits?

P11.11 *(Absorption and Variable Costing)* Miri Sato was hired as the new manager of the Box Division of GRC Enterprises two years ago. During the last two years, sales have increased substantially and Sato has been pleased. She was excited to receive her bonus this year as she anticipated that her profits would have increased by the required 20%. However, the accountant just stopped by with the new financial statements for this year and Sato was shocked to see that her profits fell, even though her sales had increased substantially. Sato will not, therefore, receive her bonus.

The following report was shown to Sato and shows the profits for the last two years:

	Year 1	Year 2
Production (units)	5,000	2,000
Sales (units)	3,000	4,000
Sales ($650 per unit)	$1,950,000	$2,600,000
Cost of goods sold:		
Direct materials ($125/unit)	375,000	500,000
Direct labour ($110/unit)	330,000	440,000
Variable overhead ($60/unit)	180,000	240,000
Fixed overhead*	450,000	$1,050,000
Cost of goods sold	$1,335,000	$2,230,000
Profit	$615,000	$370,000

*During Year 1, the fixed manufacturing overhead rate per unit was determined to be $150, whereas in Year 2, it was $375 per unit based on production volumes as follows:

Overhead rate (Year 1) = $750,000/5,000 = $150
Overhead rate (Year 2) = $750,000/2,000 = $375

a. Why did Sato not receive her bonus?

b. Prepare a variable costing statement of comprehensive income for Years 1 and 2. Would Sato receive a bonus if variable costing was used?

c. Which method of statement of comprehensive income should be used to evaluate Sato's performance and why?

P11.12 *(Overallocated/Underallocated Overhead)* Bob's Bicycles manufactures high-quality trail bikes. The company has two divisions: Painting and Assembly. Painting is fully automated, as each bike part is run through a paint-spraying machine. Assembly, on the other hand, is highly labour-intensive, as most of the bike parts are assembled by hand. The company allocates overhead costs for the Painting Department based on machine hours and allocates overhead for the Assembly Department based on labour hours. The following are the budgeted overheads and estimated cost drivers for 2012 by department:

	Painting	Assembly
Overhead costs	$400,000	$175,000
Estimated DLH	2,500	30,000
Estimated machine hours	45,000	3,125

a. During 2012, Job 445 required the following labour and machine hours:

	Painting	Assembly
Actual DLH	20	300
Actual machine hours	475	18

How much overhead would be assigned to this job?

b. How much was overhead under- or overallocated if the actual overhead costs incurred during 2012 were $625,000, and the actual machine hours for painting were 47,500, and the actual labour hours for assembly were 33,000?

P11.13 *(Over-/Underallocated Overhead)* Good Vibes Products manufactures external drives for computers. The company has two production departments. Overhead in Department 1 is allocated based on 10,000 machine hours and overhead in Department 2 is allocated based on 6,000 direct labour hours. The budgeted manufacturing overhead for July, 2011, was $58,000 and $54,000 for Departments 1 and 2, respectively. During July, the company completed a number of jobs, one of which (Job 110) incurred the following costs:

	Department 1	**Department 2**
Direct materials used	$12,500	$ 5,100
Direct manufacturing labour	15,000	35,500
Indirect manufacturing labour	800	2,600
Equipment depreciation	2,900	1,500
Utilities	1,450	950

Job 110 incurred 800 machine hours in Department 1 and 1,000 labour hours in Department 2. The company uses a budgeted department overhead rate in allocating overhead to jobs.

a. What is the budgeted manufacturing overhead rate for Department 1?

b. What is the budgeted manufacturing overhead rate for Department 2?

c. What is the total cost of Job 110 using allocated overhead rates?

d. What is the over- or underallocated overhead for Job 110?

e. Explain why Good Vibes uses different overhead bases for Departments 1 and 2.

P11.14 *(Over-/Underallocated Overhead)* Overhead is usually allocated to production using a predetermined overhead rate based on an appropriate cost driver. The amount of overhead allocated to jobs is seldom the same as the actual amount of overhead cost incurred, resulting in over- or underallocated overhead. What is the benefit of allocating overhead to jobs based on a predetermined overhead rate? Why not simply assign overhead based on actual overhead costs?

REFERENCES

Canadian Institute of Chartered Accountants. *CICA Handbook—Accounting*.

Johnson, H. T., and Kaplan, R. S. (1987). *Relevance lost: The rise and fall of management accounting*. Boston, MA: Harvard Business School Press.

CHAPTER 12

Strategic Investment Decisions

LEARNING OBJECTIVES

After reading this chapter, you should be able to answer the following questions:

■ How are investment decisions impacted by the overall strategy of a company?

■ How can the accounting rate of return (ARR) and payback methods be used to evaluate an investment decision?

■ Why is the time value of money important to consider when looking at long-term investment decisions?

■ How can both discounted cash flow methods (the net present value [NPV] method and the internal rate of return [IRR] method) be applied to evaluate investment decisions?

■ Which method provides the most accurate assessment of an investment: ARR, payback, NPV, or IRR?

■ What qualitative factors should be considered when making investment decisions?

■ What risks are associated with investment decisions and how can these risks be mitigated?

In this chapter, we will explore capital investment decisions and the tools used to evaluate those decisions. We will look at the key methods of investment evaluation: accounting rate of return, payback, and discounted cash flow techniques, including net present value and internal rate of return. We will also discuss qualitative factors that must be considered in investment decisions and risk mitigation strategies that can be used with investment decisions.

Strategy Planning and Investments

The difficulty for businesses in the 21st century is that they must continually adapt to technological and market changes, making long-term strategy problematic. Nevertheless, strategy is crucial in enabling a business to be proactive in increasingly competitive and turbulent business conditions. The absence of strategy can lead to reactivity and a steady erosion of market share.

Porter (1980) identified three "generic strategies" for competitive advantage: cost leadership, differentiation, and focus. **Cost leadership** requires efficiency, tight cost control, and the avoidance of unprofitable work. Companies that pursue a low-cost strategy must achieve lower costs than their competitors to be successful. Walmart is a company that has mastered this strategy by creating economies of scale and efficiencies in all of its business processes. **Differentiation** can be achieved through brand image, technology, or a unique distribution channel. These factors insulate against price competition because of brand loyalty and lower customer sensitivity to pricing differences. Starbucks, for instance, differentiates itself from other competitors by providing a strong brand, high quality, and strong customer service. A **focus** strategy emphasizes servicing a particular market segment (whether customer, territory, or product/service) better than competitors that may be competing more broadly. Lululemon is an example of a company that focuses on a particular market—in this case, the fitness market.

However, the formulation of strategy is frequently divorced from the annual budgeting cycle, because organizations produce strategic planning documents separately from their annual budgets. Consequently, the issue of translating strategy formulation into implementation requires that resource allocations follow strategy.

Chapter 6 introduced the balanced scorecard that links overall strategy to individual business unit objectives and emphasizes an organization that is focused on strategy by linking financial performance with non-financial measures. Non-financial measures in the balanced scorecard capture how well the organization is meeting the targets established in its strategy. In addition to a balanced scorecard, budgetary allocations and incentives need to be consistent with strategy, while reflecting the importance of continual learning and improvement.

One of the most important elements of strategy implementation is capital investment decision making, because investment decisions provide the physical and human infrastructure through which businesses produce and sell goods and services. Choices of investment will be driven by a company's competitive strategy. A company that has a strategy of differentiation will need to ask whether a particular capital asset will provide differentiation in the marketplace. Companies that are pursuing a cost leadership strategy will want to invest in capital assets that help reduce costs per unit. For example, automation of assembly lines or production facilities can result in economies of scale and more efficient work processes.

Investment decisions are continually being assessed by companies, due to changes in market conditions and competitor actions. For example, at the end of the 20th century, McDonald's restaurants were focused on efficiency and standardized products. Hamburgers, for example, were prepared in batches, each made the same way, and stored under heat lamps to keep them warm. However, this method of preparing hamburgers soon became outdated as consumers came to expect customized sandwiches and freshly made products, even from fast-food restaurants. This problem was solved by McDonald's when it developed the "made-for-you" system that was characterized by partially prepped food which was assembled when ordered by the customer. Key to this new system was a new investment—an 11-second toaster that enabled workers to assemble a hamburger in a very short period of time (Canedy, 1998). The investment in the made-for-you system cost approximately $25,000 to $85,000 per store ($180 million corporate-wide) but it was critical to maintaining a competitive edge in the ever changing fast-food marketplace (Johnson, Pike, & Warren, 2004).

CASE IN POINT .

Robots Reduce Labour Costs at Foxconn

Reducing labour costs has long been a cost leadership strategy in manufacturing. China's low-cost labour pool has attracted manufacturers from around the globe, but wages are rising as the supply of workers is dwindling. This is leading more Chinese factories to use robots for repetitive, low-skill tasks. China is poised to become the world's top market for industrial robots, surpassing the long-time leader, Japan. Several industries in China are using automation on assembly lines, including makers of cars, metal, rubber, plastics, food and beverages, and pharmaceuticals.

But it's in the electronics field that the use of robots is set to explode. Foxconn, the largest contract manufacturer in the world, makes parts for Apple products such as iPhones and iPads. With a workforce in China of some 1.2 million, the company plans to use 1 million robots by 2015—more than three times the total number of robots in operation in all industries in Japan in 2012.

Foxconn is using the robots to reduce labour costs but also to increase quality and to help deal with a looming labour shortage. The company is also responding to criticism about its labour practices. Foxconn said that in 2012, it was already using 10,000 robots to perform routine operations, such as welding, spraying, and assembling. Analysts expect other Chinese manufacturers to follow.

"Workers can command higher wages and are less willing to settle for lower ones. You can no longer just double your workforce to double your output," said Alistair Thornton of IHS Global Insight.

Sources: Cochrane, L., Automation of Chinese factories takes off, Australian Broadcasting Corporation, *Correspondents Report*, April 22, 2012; Branigan, T., Taiwan iPhone manufacturer replaces Chinese Workers with robots, *The Guardian*, August 1, 2011; Global industrial robotics market to reach 204 thousand units by 2017, according to new report by Global Industry Analysts, Inc., *Global Industry Analysts news release*, February 27, 2012.

Investment Appraisal

Capital investment means spending money now in the hope of getting it back later through future cash flows. Capital acquisitions include long-term assets, such as plant and equipment or even other businesses. The process of evaluating or appraising potential capital investments is as follows:

- Generate ideas based on opportunities or by identifying solutions to problems while considering your overall competitive strategy.

- Research all relevant information.

- Consider possible alternatives.

- Evaluate the financial consequences of each alternative.

- Assess non-financial aspects of each alternative.

- Decide to proceed.

- Determine an implementation plan and implement the proposal.

- Control implementation by monitoring actual results compared to plan.

There are three main types of investment:

1. Purchasing new facilities for new products/services

2. Expanding capacity to meet demand

3. Replacing assets in order to reduce production costs or improve quality or service

These are inextricably linked to the implementation of business strategy. Most investment appraisals must consider factors, such as

- Will a capital investment improve profitability, both short and long term?

- What choice of capital investment will be most effective in terms of quality, customer value, and overall profitability?

- When is the best time to make a capital investment?

In this chapter, we will discuss three main methods of evaluating investments from a financial perspective: accounting rate of return (ARR), payback, and discounted cash flow (DCF). ARR is concerned with profits, whereas payback and DCF are concerned with cash flows from an investment. Investment appraisal requires an estimation of future incremental cash flows; that is, the additional cash flow (net of income less expenses) which will result from the investment, as well as the cash outflow for the initial investment. A cost that is excluded in cash flow analysis is that of depreciation and amortization, since these do not involve any cash flow. Cash flow is usually considered to be more important than accounting profit in investment appraisal because it is cash flow that drives shareholder value (see Chapter 2).

It is important to note the following:

- The financing decision is treated separately from the investment decision. So, even though there might not be an initial cash outflow for the investment (because it might be wholly financed), all investment appraisal techniques assume an initial cash outflow. If a decision is made to proceed, then the organization is faced with a separate decision about how best to finance the investment.

- The outflows are not just additional operating costs, as any new investment that generates sales growth is also likely to have an impact on working capital, since inventory, accounts receivables, and accounts payable are also likely to increase.

- Income tax is treated as a cash outflow because it is a consequence of the cash inflows from the new investment.

As we consider each method, let us assume three alternative investments. Exhibit 12.1 shows the estimated cash flows.

Exhibit 12.1 Cash Flows for Investment Alternatives

Year	Project 1	Project 2	Project 3
0 initial investment	$(100,000)	$(125,000)	$(200,000)
1 inflows	25,000	35,000	60,000
2 inflows	25,000	35,000	60,000
3 inflows	25,000	35,000	80,000
4 inflows	25,000	35,000	30,000
5 inflows	25,000	35,000	30,000

For simplicity, we assume that each of the cash flows occurs at the end of each year. Year 0 represents the beginning of the project, when the initial funds are paid out. If we add up the cash flows in the above exhibit, Project 1 returns $25,000 [(5 × $25,000) − $100,000], Project 2 returns a cash flow of $50,000 [(5 × $35,000) − $125,000], and Project 3 returns $60,000 [(2 × $60,000 + 1 × $80,000 + 2 × $30,000) − $200,000].

Accounting Rate of Return

The **accounting rate of return (ARR)** is the profit generated as a percentage of the investment. This is equivalent to the return on investment (ROI) that was introduced in Chapter 5, but relates specifically to a particular investment. The investment value for ARR is the depreciated value of the asset each year. The depreciated value each year, assuming a life of five years with no salvage value at the end of that time, is shown in Exhibit 12.2. The accounting rate of return varies annually, as Exhibit 12.3 shows for Project 1.

Exhibit 12.2 **Depreciated Value of Alternative Investments**

End of Year	Project 1*	Project 2*	Project 3*
1	$80,000	$100,000	$160,000
2	60,000	75,000	120,000
3	40,000	50,000	80,000
4	20,000	25,000	40,000
5	0	0	0

*Annual depreciation (the initial funds divided by 5 years):
Project 1 = $100,000/5 years = $20,000 per year
Project 2 = $125,000/5 years = $25,000 per year
Project 3 = $200,000/5 years =$40,000 per year

Exhibit 12.3 **ARR/ROI for Project 1**

Year	Cash Flow (a)	Depreciation (b)	Profit (a) − (b) = (c)	Investment (d)	ARR (c)/(d)
1	$25,000	$20,000	$5,000	$80,000	6.25%
2	25,000	20,000	5,000	60,000	8.3
3	25,000	20,000	5,000	40,000	12.5
4	25,000	20,000	5,000	20,000	25
5	25,000	20,000	5,000	0	
Total			$25,000		

We can also calculate an average accounting rate of return for the entire investment period. This would be calculated as the average annual return divided by the average investment, where the average annual return is the total profit for all years divided by the number of years. As we assume that depreciation is spread equally throughout the life of the asset, the average investment is half the initial investment; that is, halfway through its life,

$$\text{Average ARR} = \frac{\text{Total profits/Number of years}}{\text{Initial investment/2}}$$

The average ARR for Project 1 is

$$\text{Average ARR} = \frac{\$25,000/5}{\$100,000/2}$$

$$= 10\%$$

The accounting rate of return for Project 2 is shown in Exhibit 12.4.

Exhibit 12.4 ARR/ROI for Project 2

Year	Cash Flow	Depreciation	Profit	Investment	ARR
1	$35,000	$25,000	$10,000	$100,000	10%
2	35,000	25,000	10,000	75,000	13.3
3	35,000	25,000	10,000	50,000	20
4	35,000	25,000	10,000	25,000	40
5	35,000	25,000	10,000	0	

The average ARR for Project 2 is

$$\text{Average ARR} = \frac{\$50,000/5}{\$125,000/2}$$
$$= 16\%$$

The accounting rate of return for Project 3 is shown in Exhibit 12.5.

Exhibit 12.5 ARR/ROI for Project 3

Year	Cash Flow	Depreciation	Profit	Investment	ARR
1	$60,000	$40,000	$20,000	$160,000	13%
2	60,000	40,000	20,000	120,000	17
3	80,000	40,000	40,000	80,000	50
4	30,000	40,000	(10,000)	40,000	(25)
5	30,000	40,000	(10,000)	0	

The average ARR for Project 3 is

$$\text{Average ARR} = \frac{\$60,000/5}{\$200,000/2}$$
$$= 12\%$$

Project 3, in particular, has substantial fluctuations in ARR from year to year. Using the accounting rate of return, Project 2 shows the highest return. However, it does not take into account either the scale of the investment required or the timing of the cash flows. The next two methods we discuss—payback and discounted cash flow (DCF)—consider these factors in the analysis of a capital investment.

Payback Method

The **payback method** calculates how many years it will take, in cash terms, to recover the initial investment, on the assumption that the shorter the payback period, the better the investment. Based on the cash flows for each project,

- Project 1 takes four years to recover its $100,000 investment (4 @ $25,000).

- Project 2 has recovered $105,000 by the end of the third year (3 @ $35,000) and will take less than seven months (20/35 = 0.57 of 12 months) to recover its $125,000 investment. The payback is therefore 3.57 years.

- Project 3 recovers its investment of $200,000 by the end of the third year ($60,000 + $60,000 + $80,000 = $200,000).

Based on the payback method, Project 3 is preferred (followed by Projects 2 and 1, in that order) as it has the fastest payback. However, the payback method does not consider the time value of money or whether the investment earns a return above and beyond the costs of borrowing or financing. Only the DCF model, discussed next, provides analysis of the impact of time on an investment decision and utilizes a firm's cost of capital (i.e., its cost of debt and equity) as the basis for analysis.

Discounted Cash Flow Methods

Neither the accounting rate of return nor the payback method considers the **time value of money**; that is, that $1 is worth more now than in a year's time, because it can be invested now at a rate of interest that will increase its value. For example, $100 invested today at 10% interest is equivalent to $110 in a year's time. Conversely, receiving $100 in a year's time is not worth $100 today: Assuming the same rate of interest, that $100 is worth only $91 ($100/110%). The $91, invested at 10%, will be equivalent to $100 in a year's time.

The time value of money needs to be recognized in investment appraisals, because an investment decision may extend over many years. The third method of investment appraisal, therefore, involves **discounted cash flow (DCF)**; that is, it discounts the future cash flows to present values using a discount rate (or interest rate) that is usually the firm's cost of capital (the risk-adjusted cost of borrowing for the investment).

There are two discounted cash flow techniques: net present value and internal rate of return.

NET PRESENT VALUE METHOD

The **net present value (NPV) method** discounts future cash flows to their present value and compares the present value of future cash flows to the initial capital investment. The basic formula for present value of cash flows is

$$\text{Present value of cash flows} = \text{Cash flow} \times \text{Discount factor (based on number of years in the future and the cost of capital)}$$

Present value (PV) tables provide discount factors used to calculate the present value of cash flows. A **discount factor** relates to a specific cost of capital and time period; a future cash flow can be multiplied by a discount factor to determine its present value. There are two types of PV tables:

1. **PV of $1.** Exhibit 12.12 in this chapter's Appendix 12A provides the factors that determine the present value of $1 received in *n* years. For example, at the end of 3 years, using a cost of capital of 10%, the discount factor would be 0.751. This means that $1 received in 3 years' time is worth $0.751 today.

2. **PV of an annuity.** Exhibit 12.13 in this chapter's Appendix 12B shows the factors related to receiving an equal cash flow each year for *n* years. For example, if you received $1 every year for 10 years (at a cost of capital of 10%), this would be worth $6.145 today.

Usually, the discount factors are based on the company's cost of capital. The cost of capital represents the weighted average of the cost of debt and equity and takes into account the riskiness of a project. As the cost of borrowing has been taken into account, an investment makes sense if the NPV is positive.

Using the example from Exhibit 12.1, the NPV for Project 1 is shown in Exhibit 12.6. We have assumed for the purposes of this exercise that the company has determined their cost of capital to be 10%. As the net present value is negative, Project 1 should not be accepted, since the present value of future cash flows does not cover the initial investment.

Exhibit 12.6 NPV for Project 1

	Cash Flow	Discount Factor (10% for 5 years)*	Present Value
Annual cash inflow	$25,000	3.791	$94,775
Less: Initial investment	100,000	0	100,000
Net present value			$(5,225)

*See Exhibit 12.13 in this chapter's Appendix 12B.

The NPV for Project 2 is shown in Exhibit 12.7. Project 2 can be accepted because it has a positive net present value. However, we need to compare this with Project 3 to see if that alternative yields a higher net present value.

Exhibit 12.7 NPV for Project 2

	Cash Flow	Discount factor (10% for 5 years)*	Present Value
Annual cash inflow	$35,000	3.791	$132,685
Less: Initial investment	125,000		125,000
Net present value			$7,685

*See Exhibit 12.13 in this chapter's Appendix 12B.

The NPV for Project 3 is calculated differently from Projects 1 and 2. Since the cash flows each year are not equal, we cannot use the PV of an annuity table, since it can be used only with *equal* cash flows. This means that we need to use the PV of $1 table (Exhibit 12.12 in this chapter's Appendix A) and determine the PV of each year separately. We can then total the PVs for each year to determine the total PV of the cash flows. Exhibit 12.8 demonstrates this approach.

Exhibit 12.8 NPV for Project 3

Year	Cash Flow	Discount factor (10%)*	Present Value
1	$60,000	0.909	$54,540
2	60,000	0.826	49,560
3	80,000	0.751	60,080
4	30,000	0.683	20,490
5	30,000	0.621	18,630
Total			$203,300
Less: Initial investment			200,000
Net present value			$3,300

*See Exhibit 12.12 in this chapter's Appendix 12A.

Despite the faster payback for Project 3, the application of the net present value technique to the timing of the cash flows reveals that the net present value of Project 3 is lower than that for Project 2; therefore, Project 2, which also showed the highest accounting rate of return, is the recommended investment where DCF analysis is concerned.

The DCF analysis, however, is limited in that it bases the decision on a final NPV figure but does not consider the difference in the size of the initial investment. Another tool that can be used to rank projects with different NPVs is **cash value added** (CVA) or the **profitability index**, which is a ratio of the NPV to the initial capital investment:

$$\text{Cash value added} = \frac{\text{Net present value}}{\text{Initial investment}}$$

In the above example, Project 2 returns a CVA of 6.1% (7,685/125,000), while Project 3 returns a CVA of 1.65% (3,300/200,000). Clearly, Project 2 provides a better return on the initial investment. Companies often have a target CVA, such that, to be approved, a project must have a CVA of, say, 10% (i.e., the NPV is at least 10% of the initial capital investment).

SALVAGE VALUE

A modification to the above approach occurs when an investment has a residual or salvage value at the end of the investment period. Assets are often sold or traded in at the end of their productive lives and this value must be considered as part of the cash flow analysis for an investment. For example, assume a company is considering an investment of $175,000 for a new machine. It will return $40,000 in cash flows for 6 years and has a salvage value of $15,000 at the end of this period. The company's cost of capital is 12%. Exhibit 12.9 shows the calculation of NPV for this investment.

Exhibit 12.9 NPV with Salvage Value

	Cash Flow	Discount Factor (12%)	Present Value
Annual cash inflow	$40,000	4.111	$164,440
Salvage value	15,000	0.507	7,605
Less: Initial investment	175,000	0	175,000
Net present value			$2,955

In this case, both Exhibits 12.12 (Appendix A) and 12.13 (Appendix B) are used to determine NPV: Exhibit 12.12 to determine the discount factor for the annual cash flows received over 6 years and Exhibit 12.13 to determine the discount factor for the salvage value received one time at the end of Year 6. In this case, the investment returns a positive NPV and would be considered by the company.

The second DCF technique is the internal rate of return.

INTERNAL RATE OF RETURN METHOD

The **internal rate of return (IRR) method** determines the discount rate that produces a net present value of zero. There are two methods for determining IRR: the formula method and the trial and error method.

FORMULA METHOD. The formula method can be used only if there are equal cash flows each year and no salvage value for the investment. The following formula provides the discount factor for a particular investment:

$$\text{Discount factor} = \frac{\text{Initial investment}}{\text{Annual cash flow}}$$

For example, for Project 1 (refer back to Exhibit 12.1), the discount factor would be 4.00 ($100,000/$25,000). By looking up the 4.00 factor in Exhibit 12.12 in the row representing 5 years, we can see that the rate falls between 7% and 8%. In order to determine an "exact" percentage, the following formula can be used:

$$\text{IRR} = \text{Low rate} + \text{Proportion of difference in rates}$$

where the proportion of the difference would be determined as follows:

$$\text{Proportion} = \frac{(L - A)}{(L - H)}$$

where

L = The discount factor associated with the lowest interest rate. In the case of Project 1, this would be the discount factor associated with 7% for 5 years, or 4.1.

A = The actual discount factor for the project. In the case of Project 1, this is 4.00

H = The discount factor associated with the highest interest rate. In the case of Project 1, this would be the discount factor associated with 8% for 5 years, or 3.993.

For Project 1, the precise IRR would be calculated as follows:

$$\text{IRR} = 7\% + \frac{(4.1 - 4.00)}{(4.1 - 3.993)}$$
$$= 7\% + 0.935\%$$
$$= 7.935\%$$

For Project 2, the IRR would be determined as follows:

$$\text{Discount factor} = \frac{\$125,000}{\$35,000}$$
$$= 3.57$$

Looking up 3.57 in Exhibit 12.12, the rate is between 12% and 13%.

$$\text{IRR} = 12\% + \frac{(3.605 - 3.570)}{(3.605 - 3.517)}$$
$$= 12\% + 0.398\%$$
$$= 12.398\%$$

For Project 3, however, we cannot use this method since the cash flows are not equal each year. In this case, we need to use the trial and error method.

TRIAL AND ERROR METHOD. This method is used when the cash flows for an investment are unequal or when there is a salvage value at the end of the investment's life. It involves repeated calculations from the discount tables, on a trial-and-error basis, using different discount rates, until an NPV of 0 is reached.

For Project 3, we know that the project returns a positive NPV when a cost of capital of 10% is used. This means that the IRR must be higher than 10%. We, therefore, first try 11% and recalculate the NPV for Project 3 the same as we did in Exhibit 12.8, using 11%. As shown in Exhibit 12.10, 11% returns a negative NPV so, since 10% returns a positive NPV, we know the IRR must be between 10% and 11%.

IRR provides a useful method for comparing products because it presents the cash flows as an effective interest rate. The project with the highest internal rate of return would be preferred, provided that the rate exceeds the cost of capital (i.e., the borrowing cost). In this case, only Projects 2 and 3 exceed the cost of capital, but Project 3 provides the highest IRR and would be the preferred investment.

Exhibit 12.10 NPV for Project 3 at 11%

Year	Cash Flow	Discount Factor (11%)*	Present Value
1	$60,000	0.901	$54,060
2	60,000	0.812	48,720
3	80,000	0.731	58,480
4	30,000	0.659	19,770
5	30,000	0.593	17,790
Total			$198,820
Less: Initial investment			200,000
Net present value			$(1,180)

*See Exhibit 12.12 in this chapter's Appendix 12A.

Evaluation of Techniques

While the accounting rate of return method provides an average return on investment that enables a business to select the highest return, it ignores the timing of cash flows. Sometimes, when there are high short-term ROIs, managers prefer those investments, even though the longer-term impact is detrimental to the organization. This is because managers may be evaluated and rewarded on their short-term performance. Payback measures the number of years it will take to recover the capital investment, and while this takes timing into account, it ignores cash flows after the payback period. Both methods ignore the time value of money.

Discounted cash flow techniques take account of the time value of money and discounts future cash flows to their present value. This is a more reliable method of investment appraisal. However, for investment evaluation, while all projects with a positive net present value are beneficial, a business will usually select the project with the highest net present value, or in other words, the highest internal rate of return, sometimes using the initial cash investment (CVA) or the cost of capital as a benchmark for the return.

Because of rapid change in markets and increased demands for shareholder value, the use of discounted cash flow techniques has declined in many businesses. Rather, boards of directors typically set quite high "hurdle" rates for investing in new assets. These are commonly set in terms of payback periods of two to four years or ROI rates of 25% to 50%. This approach reduces the importance of discounted cash flow techniques. However, for larger investments for which returns are expected over many years, discounted cash flow techniques are still important. Investments in buildings and major plant items, mining exploration, and similar investing activities commonly use NPV and IRR as methods of capital investment appraisal.

All of the financial tools discussed in this chapter need to be considered in conjunction with non-financial factors. Investment decisions need to be based on more than just financial outcomes. Other factors, such as impact on employees and employee morale, changes in quality, likeliness of equipment breakdowns, levels of demand, changes in market conditions, and competitor strategies must be considered. Exhibit 12.11 shows both the quantitative and qualitative factors that can be considered in investment choices.

Shank (1996) used a case study to show how the conventional NPV approach was limited in high-technology situations as it did not capture the "richness" of the investment evaluation

Exhibit 12.11 **Factors Impacting Investment Decisions**

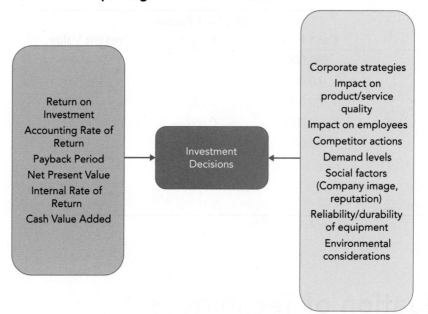

problem. Shank saw NPV more as a constraint than as a decision tool, because it was driven by how the investment proposal was framed. Shank argued that a strategic cost management approach (see Chapter 16 for a description of strategic management accounting) could apply value chain analysis, cost driver analysis, and competitive advantage analysis to achieve a better fit between investment decisions and business strategy implementation.

RISK MANAGEMENT IN INVESTMENT DECISIONS

Every investment decision comes with a degree of risk, and for investments that entail a substantial amount of money, that risk can be significant. Unexpected costs or outcomes can result after an investment is made. Risks come in many forms:

- **Financial loss.** A new investment can result in an expected financial loss if, for example, new equipment is not operating properly or if there are production delays due to the learning curve associated with the investment. Financial loss can also occur if the investment budget is exceeded, as is often in the case when building a new factory.

- **Unplanned quality issues.** An investment may result in changes to the quality of products or services. For example, although we would hope that new equipment would improve quality, the opposite effect could occur if the equipment is not used properly or if it is not installed correctly.

- **Negative impact on company's reputation.** If a new investment is controversial, such as an investment in a new oil or gas well in an environmentally sensitive area, a company's reputation can be impaired.

- **Strategic risks.** Risks can also be strategic in nature, such as an investment in a new product line that will change the company's direction. If a company is making an investment that will change its overall strategy, the company needs to fully assess the impact of this change on its employees, customers, suppliers, and internal business processes.

Whenever a company is faced with an investment decision, various actions, **risk mitigation strategies**, can be pursued to help minimize risk:

- **Risk transference**. In this strategy, the company transfers the risk of the investment. For example, the company can transfer the risk to the company from whom it purchases a piece of equipment by ensuring a warranty contract is in place covering the equipment for a specified amount of time. Or the company can transfer the risk to a building developer, in the case of a new factory or building development, by setting a fixed price on the contract. In either case, the company needs to be very clear about what the contract entails, including the level of quality and precise specifications of the project, as well as the responsibilities of each party involved.

- **Risk reduction**. Risks of an investment can also be reduced to an acceptable level by identifying all possible negative outcomes of the investment and reducing these outcomes through appropriate action. For example, if a business was considering a new type of equipment in its manufacturing process, it might research other companies that have implemented similar equipment and identify any problems these companies have had with the installation or operation. This may help the company identify changes to its current processes or factory layout that will make the equipment function more effectively. Or alternatively, it may prevent the company from making the investment in the first place.

- **Risk acceptance**. Sometimes, a particular investment is so critical to a company that it will accept most levels of risk. For example, a technology firm may accept the levels of risk and associated costs of new technology development to ensure that it is constantly innovating and developing new products. An organization may also accept risks that are known to be small and manageable. This may be an appropriate strategy if the investment is not substantial or if the risks are well understood.

CONCLUSION

In this chapter, we have introduced strategy and the role of investment appraisal in capital investment decisions. In particular, we have described the main methods of capital investment appraisal. Often, however, decisions are made subjectively and then justified after the event by the application of financial techniques. Despite the usefulness of these techniques, the assumption has been that future cash flows can be predicted with some accuracy. This is, however, one of the main difficulties in accounting. We also saw that most investment decisions will come with a degree of risk and companies must be aware of these and should identify ways to reduce them, especially if the invesetment is large or is of strategic importance.

KEY TERMS

Accounting rate of return (ARR) method, 297

Capital investment, 295

Cash value added, 301

Cost leadership, 294

Differentiation, 294

Discount factor, 299

Discounted cash flow (DCF), 299

Focus, 294

Internal rate of return (IRR) method, 301

Net present value (NPV) method, 299

Payback method, 298

Profitability index, 301

Risk mitigation strategies, 305

Salvage value, 301

Time value of money, 299

CASE STUDY 12.1: GOLIATH COMPANY— INVESTMENT EVALUATION

Goliath Company is considering investing in a project involving an initial cash outlay for an asset of $200,000. The asset is depreciated using straight-line deprecia- tion over five years. Goliath's cost of capital is 10%. The cash flows from the project are expected to be as follows:

Year	Inflow	Outflow
1	$ 75,000	$30,000
2	90,000	40,000
3	100,000	45,000
4	100,000	50,000
5	75,000	40,000

The company wants to consider the accounting rate of return, payback, and net present value as meth- ods of evaluating the proposal.

The depreciation expense is $40,000 per year. Net cash flows and profits are as follows:

Year	Inflow	Outflow	Net Cash Flow	Depreciation	Profit
1	$ 75,000	$30,000	$45,000	$40,000	$ 5,000
2	90,000	40,000	50,000	40,000	10,000
3	100,000	45,000	55,000	40,000	15,000
4	100,000	50,000	50,000	40,000	10,000
5	75,000	40,000	35,000	40,000	(5,000)
Total					$35,000

Return on investment:

	1	2	3	4	5
Investment	$160,000	$120,000	$80,000	$40,000	0
Profit	$5,000	$10,000	$15,000	$10,000	$(5,000)
ARR	3.125%	8.33%	18.75%	25%	—

Over the five years:

Profit $35/5 = $7 Investment $200/2 = $100

ARR 7/100 = 7%

Cumulative cash flows are as follows:

Year	Cash Flow	Cumulative
1	$45,000	$ 45,000
2	50,000	95,000
3	55,000	150,000
4	50,000	200,000

The payback period is the end of Year 4, when $200,000 of cash flows has been recovered.

Net present value of the cash flows is as follows:

Year	Cash Flow	Factor	Present Value
1	$45,000	0.9091	$40,910
2	50,000	0.8264	41,320
3	55,000	0.7513	41,321
4	50,000	0.6830	34,150
5	35,000	0.6209	21,731
Present value of net cash flows			$179,432
Cash outflow			(200,000)
Net present value			$(20,568)

Although the ARR is 7% and the payback is four years, the discounted cash flow shows that the net present value is negative. Therefore, the project should be rejected, as the returns are insufficient to recover the company's cost of capital.

■ SELF-TEST QUESTIONS

Use the following information to answer questions S12.1 and S12.2.

The Whitton Company has an opportunity to buy a computer now for $25,000 that will yield annual net cash inflows of $10,000 for the next three years, after which its resale value would be zero. Whitton's cost of capital is 16%.

S12.1 What is the net present value of the investment for the computer?

  a. $22,459

  b. $2,540

  c. $(2,540)

  d. $(5,000)

S12.2 What is the IRR for the investment?

  a. 9.7%

  b. 20.1%

  c. 11.5%

  d. 12.3%

S12.3 SmallCo, which has a cost of capital of 12%, is considering the following project:

Year	0	1	2	3
Cash flows of project	$(2,000)	$1,000	$800	$700

What is the NPV of the project?

  a. $2,029

  b. $500

  c. $29

  d. $700

S12.4 The projected net cash flows for three projects are (in $thousands):

Project	Year 0	Year 1	Year 2	Year 3	Year 4	Year 5
A	$(350)	$100	$200	$100	$100	$140
B	(350)	40	100	210	260	160
C	(350)	200	150	240	40	0

The payback period for each project (in years) is

	A	B	C
a.	3	3	2
b.	2.5	3	2
c.	3	2	3
d.	2.5	2	3

S12.5 The projected net cash flows for a project are (in $thousands):

Year	0	1	2	3	4	5
	$(350)	$40	$100	$210	$260	$160

Assuming the initial investment is depreciated over the life of the project, the accounting rate of return for the project is

a. 25%

b. 33%

c. 40%

d. 48%

S12.6 The projected net cash flows for an investment are (in $thousands):

Year	0	1	2	3	4	5
	$(850)	$130	$200	$300	$200	$150

The net present value of the investment, assuming a 7% cost of capital is

a. $801,000

b. $(801,000)

c. $49,500

d. $(49,500)

S12.7 The present values of cash flows for projects, each of which has an initial capital outlay of $350,000, are

Project A	$450,000
Project B	$400,000
Project C	$375,000

The cash value added (or profitability index) for each project suggests that the preferred project is

a. Project A

b. Project B

c. Project C

d. All projects are the same because the initial capital outlay is the same

S12.8 Rex Products has been considering the purchase of a new machine. The existing machine will operate for 4 more years and will then have a zero disposal value. If the machine is disposed of now, it may be sold for $60,000. The new machine costs $250,000 and will result in labour savings of $60,000 in additional cash inflows each year.

What is the net present value of the investment, assuming that the cost of capital is 10%? Would the company want to purchase the new machine?

a. $(200); no

b. $(59,800); no

c. $59,800; yes

d. $200; yes

S12.9 Pajama Company wants to purchase a new sewing machine that will have a useful life of 5 years. The investment is expected to generate annual cash inflows of $30,000. The cost of capital for the company is 12%. What is the maximum that the company would be willing to pay for the sewing machine?

a. $18,000

b. $108,150

c. $120,000

d. None of the above

S12.10 Wally's Plumbing provides commercial plumbing services to large factories. The company is looking at purchasing some new equipment that will have a useful life of 4 years. Information on the investment is as follows:

Initial investment:	
Asset	$90,000
Changes in annual cash flows	
Cash receipts	$60,000
Cash expenditures	$35,000
Salvage value equipment at end of 4 years	$10,000

In what range is the internal rate of return?

a. 8% and 9%

b. 9% and 10%

c. 7% and 8%

d. 10% and 11%

S12.11 Green Tea Corporation recently purchased a new tea processor for $320,900. The existing equipment had a remaining life of 10 years. The additional cash flows will be $50,000 per year from having the new machine. What is the internal rate of return?

a. 10%

b. 12%

c. 9%

d. 11%

S12.12 The following information was provided related to three machines that London Press is considering investing in:

	Machine A	Machine B	Machine C
Initial investment	$200,000	$250,000	$310,000
Annual cash inflows	$ 50,000	$ 65,000	$ 80,000
Useful lives	6 years	5 years	5 years

The cost of capital for the company is 12%. Which of the following decisions should the company make?

a. Purchase any of the three machines.

b. Purchase Machine C.

c. Purchase Machine A.

d. Do not purchase any machines.

e. Purchase Machine B.

PROBLEMS

P12.1 (Payback, ARR, and NPV) Brenda Blair is considering buying a Bobcat for her construction business; the machine costs $250,000. Purchasing the Bobcat will provide incremental cash flows of $51,000 per year for six years. The salvage value at the end of five years is expected to be nil. Brenda's cost of capital is 14%.

a. Should Brenda purchase the Bobcat?

b. Compute the payback period, accounting rate of return based on initial investment, and NPV for the investment in making your decision.

P12.2 (Payback, ARR, NPV) Greystone Hotel projects the cash flows for three alternative investment projects (in $thousands) as follows:

Project	Year 0	1	2	3	4	5
A	$(350)	$100	$200	$100	$100	$140
B	(350)	40	100	210	260	160
C	(350)	200	150	240	40	0

Depreciation is $70,000 per year for all three projects.
For each project, calculate

a. Payback period

b. Accounting rate of return (average)

c. Net present value (assuming a cost of capital of 9%)

1. Which (if any) project should be accepted?

2. Explain why.

P12.3 (CVA) Freddie Company has $5 million to invest this year. Three projects are available and all are divisible; that is, part of a project may be accepted and the cash flow returns will be pro rata. Details of the projects are as follows:

Project	1	2	3
Cash outlay ($M)	3.0	2.0	1.5
NPV ($M)	1.7	1.1	1.0

What is the ranking of the projects that should be accepted? Use CVA to help rank the projects.

P12.4 *(Payback, ARR, NPV)* Tropic Investments is considering a project involving an initial cash outlay for an asset of $200,000. The asset is depreciated over five years at 20% per year (based on the value of the investment at the beginning of each year). The cash flows from the project are expected to be as follows:

	Inflow	Outflow
Year 1	$ 75,000	$30,000
Year 2	90,000	40,000
Year 3	100,000	45,000
Year 4	100,000	50,000
Year 5	75,000	40,000

a. What is the payback period?

b. What is the return on investment (each year and average)?

c. Assuming a cost of capital of 10% and ignoring inflation, what is the net present value of the cash flows?

d. Should the project be accepted?

P12.5 *(Interpreting ARR, Payback, and NPV)* The Board of Grudgework Holdings has received a presentation supporting a $600,000 capital investment. The calculations for accounting rate of return, payback, and discounted cash flows are shown below.

Accounting Rate of Return	Year 0	Year 1	Year 2	Year 3	Year 4	Year 5
Initial investment	$600,000					
Depreciation @ 20%		$120,000	$120,000	$120,000	$120,000	$120,000
Book value at year-end		480,000	360,000	240,000	120,000	0
Cash flows		150,000	250,000	200,000	150,000	100,000
Profit		30,000	130,000	80,000	30,000	(20,000)
ARR		6.3%	36.1%	33.3%	25.0%	
Average profits	$ 50,000					
Average investment	300,000					
Average ARR	16.7%					

Payback	Year 0	Year 1	Year 2	Year 3	Year 4	Year 5
Initial investment	$(600,000)					
Cash flows		$150,000	$250,000	$200,000	$150,000	$100,000
Cumulative cash flow		150,000	400,000	600,000		
Payback				= 3 years		

Net Present Value	Year 0	Year 1	Year 2	Year 3	Year 4	Year 5
Cash flows	$(600,000)	$150,000	$250,000	$200,000	$150,000	$100,000
Net present value @ 8%	$90,303					

What issues would you draw to the attention of the board in considering these figures?

P12.6 *(NPV, Profitability Index, IRR)* Criterion Sales is considering three alternative investment proposals but can accept only one of these. The investments and cash flows are shown below:

Cash Flows	Year 0	Year 1	Year 2	Year 3	Year 4
Project A					
Cash inflows	$(150,000)	$50,000	$75,000	$75,000	$50,000
Project B					
Cash inflows	(200,000)	75,000	75,000	75,000	75,000
Project C					
Cash inflows	(300,000)	50,000	100,000	150,000	100,000

Compare for each alternative investment the

a. Net present value

b. Profitability index

c. Internal rate of return

Which of the three investment proposals would you prefer and why?

P12.7 *(NPV, IRR)* Cando Technologies is considering purchasing a networked computer system for $82,000. It will enable the company to generate $35,000 more in profit each year and will have a salvage value of $10,000 at the end of five years. The amortization on the computer system will be $14,400 per year.

a. If the company has a required rate of return of 12%, what is the net present value of the proposed investment?

b. What is the internal rate of return?

P12.8 *(NPV, Payback, ARR)* Mondao Computing is considering an investment of $2.3 million in new equipment. The predicted cash inflows and outflows are as shown below:

	Year 0	Year 1	Year 2	Year 3	Year 4	Year 5
Capital investment	$(2,300,000)					
Inflows		$800,000	$1,000,000	$1,200,000	$1,100,000	$900,000
Outflows		(300,000)	(250,000)	(300,000)	(400,000)	(500,000)

An alternative investment is for $2 million, the predicted cash inflows and outflows being as follows:

	Year 0	Year 1	Year 2	Year 3	Year 4	Year 5
Capital investment	$(2,000,000)					
Inflows		$700,000	$900,000	$1,100,000	$1,000,000	$800,000
Outflows		(300,000)	(250,000)	(300,000)	(400,000)	(500,000)

Mondao depreciates its equipment over five years and uses a cost of capital of 12%.

a. For each of the investment alternatives, calculate the

  1. Net present value

  2. Payback

  3. Accounting rate of return (on an average basis, not per year)

b. Recommend, with reasons, which of the investment proposals should be approved.

c. Compare and contrast net present value, payback, and accounting rate of return as methods of capital investment appraisal. What are the strengths and limitations of each method?

P12.9 *(Compare/Contrast NPV and IRR)* Glenda's High Fashion Boutique is looking for a new location for its store. Glenda wants to purchase a small building rather than leasing space in a mall, as she has done in previous years. Her realtor has shown her four possible locations and her accountant has compiled the following information about each of the locations:

	Location A	Location B	Location C	Location D
IRR	22%	16%	12%	15%
NPV	$25,000	$40,000	$30,000	$45,000

Glenda is bewildered by the fact that Location A has the highest IRR but the lowest NPV. She is confused as to which measure to use in order to assess each of the investments.

a. Explain to Glenda why Location A might have a higher IRR but lower NPV than the other two locations.

b. Which is a better indicator of future potential—IRR or NPV? Explain why.

c. What other factors should Glenda consider in order to make a good decision?

P12.10 *(Investment Choices)* Pilgrim Enterprises is planning to automate its factory and has sent out a request for proposals to various firms in the industry. Pilgrim received three bids on the project:

Bid 1	$3,500,000
Bid 2	$3,350,000
Bid 3	$3,625,000

Each of the bids meets the specifications required by Pilgrim. The annual savings from automating the plant are estimated to be $600,000 per year for ten years. Each bid will result in the same savings. The company's cost of capital is 10% and the company's policy is to make investments that exceed their cost of capital. Brian Wong, the plant manager, is not sure which firm's bid to accept since the bids are so close.

a. Do each of the bids exceed the Pilgrim's cost of capital?

b. If so, what other factors should Brian consider in making his decision?

REFERENCES

Canedy, D. (1998). McDonald's burger war salvo; Is 'made for you' the way folks want to have it? *The New York Times*. Retrieved from www.nytimes.com/1998/06/20/business/mcdonald-s-burger-war-salvo-is-made-for-you-the-way-folks-want-to-have-it.html?pagewanted=all&src=pm.

Johnson, E., Pyke, D., and Warren, A. (2004). Food fight: The day McDonald's blinked. Hanover, NH: Tuck School of Business at Dartmouth College. Retrieved from www.tuck.dartmouth.edu/cds-uploads/case-studies/pdf/1-0049.pdf.

Porter, M. E. (1980). *Competitive strategy: Techniques for analyzing industries and competitors*. New York, NY: Free Press.

Shank, J. K. (1996). Analyzing technology investments—From NPV to strategic cost management (SCM). *Management Accounting Research*, 7, 185–197.

APPENDIX A: PRESENT VALUE OF $1 TABLE

Exhibit 12.12 gives the present value of a single payment received n years in the future, discounted at an interest rate of r% per annum. For example, with a discount rate of 6%, a single payment of $100 in five years' time has a present value of $74.73 ($100 × 0.7473).

Exhibit 12.12 Present Value of $1 Factors

Present value interest factor of $1 per period at r% (discount rate) for n periods

Period	1%	2%	3%	4%	5%	6%	7%	8%	9%	10%	11%	12%	13%	14%	15%	16%	17%	18%	19%	20%
1	0.990	0.980	0.971	0.962	0.952	0.943	0.935	0.926	0.917	0.909	0.901	0.893	0.885	0.877	0.870	0.862	0.855	0.847	0.840	0.833
2	0.980	0.961	0.943	0.925	0.907	0.890	0.873	0.857	0.842	0.826	0.812	0.797	0.783	0.769	0.756	0.743	0.731	0.718	0.706	0.694
3	0.971	0.942	0.915	0.889	0.864	0.840	0.816	0.794	0.772	0.751	0.731	0.712	0.693	0.675	0.658	0.641	0.624	0.609	0.593	0.579
4	0.961	0.924	0.888	0.855	0.823	0.792	0.763	0.735	0.708	0.683	0.659	0.636	0.613	0.592	0.572	0.552	0.534	0.516	0.499	0.482
5	0.951	0.906	0.863	0.822	0.784	0.747	0.713	0.681	0.650	0.621	0.593	0.567	0.543	0.519	0.497	0.476	0.456	0.437	0.419	0.402
6	0.942	0.888	0.837	0.790	0.746	0.705	0.666	0.630	0.596	0.564	0.535	0.507	0.480	0.456	0.432	0.410	0.390	0.370	0.352	0.335
7	0.933	0.871	0.813	0.760	0.711	0.665	0.623	0.583	0.547	0.513	0.482	0.452	0.425	0.400	0.376	0.354	0.333	0.314	0.296	0.279
8	0.923	0.853	0.789	0.731	0.677	0.627	0.582	0.540	0.502	0.467	0.434	0.404	0.376	0.351	0.327	0.305	0.285	0.266	0.249	0.233
9	0.914	0.837	0.766	0.703	0.645	0.592	0.544	0.500	0.460	0.424	0.391	0.361	0.333	0.308	0.284	0.263	0.243	0.225	0.209	0.194
10	0.905	0.820	0.744	0.676	0.614	0.558	0.508	0.463	0.422	0.386	0.352	0.322	0.295	0.270	0.247	0.227	0.208	0.191	0.176	0.162
11	0.896	0.804	0.722	0.650	0.585	0.527	0.475	0.429	0.388	0.350	0.317	0.287	0.261	0.237	0.215	0.195	0.178	0.162	0.148	0.135
12	0.887	0.788	0.701	0.625	0.557	0.497	0.444	0.397	0.356	0.319	0.286	0.257	0.231	0.208	0.187	0.168	0.152	0.137	0.124	0.112
13	0.879	0.773	0.681	0.601	0.530	0.469	0.415	0.368	0.326	0.290	0.258	0.229	0.204	0.182	0.163	0.145	0.130	0.116	0.104	0.093
14	0.870	0.758	0.661	0.577	0.505	0.442	0.388	0.340	0.299	0.263	0.232	0.205	0.181	0.160	0.141	0.125	0.111	0.099	0.088	0.078
15	0.861	0.743	0.642	0.555	0.481	0.417	0.362	0.315	0.275	0.239	0.209	0.183	0.160	0.140	0.123	0.108	0.095	0.084	0.074	0.065
16	0.853	0.728	0.623	0.534	0.458	0.394	0.339	0.292	0.252	0.218	0.188	0.163	0.141	0.123	0.107	0.093	0.081	0.071	0.062	0.054
17	0.844	0.714	0.605	0.513	0.436	0.371	0.317	0.270	0.231	0.198	0.170	0.146	0.125	0.108	0.093	0.080	0.069	0.060	0.052	0.045
18	0.836	0.700	0.587	0.494	0.416	0.350	0.296	0.250	0.212	0.180	0.153	0.130	0.111	0.095	0.081	0.069	0.059	0.051	0.044	0.038

(continued)

Exhibit 12.12 Present Value of $1 Factors (continued)

19	0.828	0.686	0.570	0.475	0.396	0.331	0.277	0.232	0.194	0.164	0.138	0.116	0.098	0.083	0.070	0.060	0.051	0.043	0.037	0.031
20	0.820	0.673	0.554	0.456	0.377	0.312	0.258	0.215	0.178	0.149	0.124	0.104	0.087	0.073	0.061	0.051	0.043	0.037	0.031	0.026
25	0.780	0.610	0.478	0.375	0.295	0.233	0.184	0.146	0.116	0.092	0.074	0.059	0.047	0.038	0.030	0.024	0.020	0.016	0.013	0.010
30	0.742	0.552	0.412	0.308	0.231	0.174	0.131	0.099	0.075	0.057	0.044	0.033	0.026	0.020	0.015	0.012	0.009	0.007	0.005	0.004
35	0.706	0.500	0.355	0.253	0.181	0.130	0.094	0.068	0.049	0.036	0.026	0.019	0.014	0.010	0.008	0.006	0.004	0.003	0.002	0.002
40	0.672	0.453	0.307	0.208	0.142	0.097	0.067	0.046	0.032	0.022	0.015	0.011	0.008	0.005	0.004	0.003	0.002	0.001	0.001	0.001
50	0.608	0.372	0.228	0.141	0.087	0.054	0.034	0.021	0.013	0.009	0.005	0.003	0.002	0.001	0.001	0.001	0.000	0.000	0.000	0.000

APPENDIX B: PRESENT VALUE OF ANNUITY TABLE

Exhibit 12.13 gives the present value of an equal payment received each year for n years in the future, discounted at an interest rate of $r\%$ per annum. For example, with a discount rate of 6%, a payment of $100 received every year for five years' time has a present value of $421.20 ($100 $\times$ 4.212).

Exhibit 12.13 Present Value of Annuity Factors

Present value interest factor of an annuity of $1 per period at $r\%$ for n periods

Period	1%	2%	3%	4%	5%	6%	7%	8%	9%	10%	11%	12%	13%	14%	15%	16%	17%	18%	19%	20%
1	0.990	0.980	0.971	0.962	0.952	0.943	0.935	0.926	0.917	0.909	0.901	0.893	0.885	0.877	0.870	0.862	0.855	0.847	0.840	0.833
2	1.970	1.942	1.913	1.886	1.859	1.833	1.808	1.783	1.759	1.736	1.713	1.690	1.668	1.647	1.626	1.605	1.585	1.566	1.547	1.528
3	2.941	2.884	2.829	2.775	2.723	2.673	2.624	2.577	2.531	2.487	2.444	2.402	2.361	2.322	2.283	2.246	2.210	2.174	2.140	2.106
4	3.902	3.808	3.717	3.630	3.546	3.465	3.387	3.312	3.240	3.170	3.102	3.037	2.974	2.914	2.855	2.798	2.743	2.690	2.639	2.589
5	4.853	4.713	4.580	4.452	4.329	4.212	4.100	3.993	3.890	3.791	3.696	3.605	3.517	3.433	3.352	3.274	3.199	3.127	3.058	2.991
6	5.795	5.601	5.417	5.242	5.076	4.917	4.767	4.623	4.486	4.355	4.231	4.111	3.998	3.889	3.784	3.685	3.589	3.498	3.410	3.326
7	6.728	6.472	6.230	6.002	5.786	5.582	5.389	5.206	5.033	4.868	4.712	4.564	4.423	4.288	4.160	4.039	3.922	3.812	3.706	3.605
8	7.652	7.325	7.020	6.733	6.463	6.210	5.971	5.747	5.535	5.335	5.146	4.968	4.799	4.639	4.487	4.344	4.207	4.078	3.954	3.837
9	8.566	8.162	7.786	7.435	7.108	6.802	6.515	6.247	5.995	5.759	5.537	5.328	5.132	4.946	4.772	4.607	4.451	4.303	4.163	4.031
10	9.471	8.983	8.530	8.111	7.722	7.360	7.024	6.710	6.418	6.145	5.889	5.650	5.426	5.216	5.019	4.833	4.659	4.494	4.339	4.192
11	10.368	9.787	9.253	8.760	8.306	7.887	7.499	7.139	6.805	6.495	6.207	5.938	5.687	5.453	5.234	5.029	4.836	4.656	4.486	4.327
12	11.255	10.575	9.954	9.385	8.863	8.384	7.943	7.536	7.161	6.814	6.492	6.194	5.918	5.660	5.421	5.197	4.988	4.793	4.611	4.439
13	12.134	11.348	10.635	9.986	9.394	8.853	8.358	7.904	7.487	7.103	6.750	6.424	6.122	5.842	5.583	5.342	5.118	4.910	4.715	4.533
14	13.004	12.106	11.296	10.563	9.899	9.295	8.745	8.244	7.786	7.367	6.982	6.628	6.302	6.002	5.724	5.468	5.229	5.008	4.802	4.611
15	13.865	12.849	11.938	11.118	10.380	9.712	9.108	8.559	8.061	7.606	7.191	6.811	6.462	6.142	5.847	5.575	5.324	5.092	4.876	4.675
16	14.718	13.578	12.561	11.652	10.838	10.106	9.447	8.851	8.313	7.824	7.379	6.974	6.604	6.265	5.954	5.668	5.405	5.162	4.938	4.730
17	15.562	14.292	13.166	12.166	11.274	10.477	9.763	9.122	8.544	8.022	7.549	7.120	6.729	6.373	6.047	5.749	5.475	5.222	4.990	4.775
18	16.398	14.992	13.754	12.659	11.690	10.828	10.059	9.372	8.756	8.201	7.702	7.250	6.840	6.467	6.128	5.818	5.534	5.273	5.033	4.812

Exhibit 12.13 **Present Value of Annuity Factors** (*continued*)

19	17.226	15.678	14.324	13.134	12.085	11.158	10.336	9.604	8.950	8.365	7.839	7.366	6.938	6.550	6.198	5.877	5.584	5.316	5.070	4.843
20	18.046	16.351	14.877	13.590	12.462	11.470	10.594	9.818	9.129	8.514	7.963	7.469	7.025	6.623	6.259	5.929	5.628	5.353	5.101	4.870
25	22.023	19.523	17.413	15.622	14.094	12.783	11.654	10.675	9.823	9.077	8.422	7.843	7.330	6.873	6.464	6.097	5.766	5.467	5.195	4.948
30	25.808	22.396	19.600	17.292	15.372	13.765	12.409	11.258	10.274	9.427	8.694	8.055	7.496	7.003	6.566	6.177	5.829	5.517	5.235	4.979
35	29.409	24.999	21.487	18.665	16.374	14.498	12.948	11.655	10.567	9.644	8.855	8.176	7.586	7.070	6.617	6.215	5.858	5.539	5.251	4.992
40	32.835	27.355	23.115	19.793	17.159	15.046	13.332	11.925	10.757	9.779	8.951	8.244	7.634	7.105	6.642	6.233	5.871	5.548	5.258	4.997
50	39.196	31.424	25.730	21.482	18.256	15.762	13.801	12.233	10.962	9.915	9.042	8.304	7.675	7.133	6.661	6.246	5.880	5.554	5.262	4.999

CHAPTER 13

Performance Evaluation of Business Units

LEARNING OBJECTIVES

After reading this chapter, you should be able to answer the following questions:

- How has the change to multidivisional organizations impacted the way performance is evaluated within organizations?

- How can return on investment, residual income, and economic value added be used to assess the performance of company divisions?

- Should corporate-level costs be included in the evaluation of a business unit's performance?

- Why is it important to use more than just financial measures of performance?

- How can transfer pricing be used to help motivate managers of divisionalized organizations to work cost-effectively and competitively?

In today's business environment, we have seen a shift toward a decentralized, multidivisional business structure. The measurement and management of divisional (i.e., business unit) performance has, therefore, influenced the development of management accounting. This chapter introduces the structure of business organizations, with emphasis on the divisionalized structure and decentralized profit responsibility. This chapter also describes the methods by which the performance of divisions and their managers is evaluated, including non-financial measurements. We also consider controllability and transfer pricing within organizations.

Structure of Business Organizations

Organizations are typically considered to be one of three types:

1. **Private sector**, comprising businesses whose prime goal is profit.

2. **Public sector**, which is government funded through various kinds of taxation, and provides services for the public, such as health, education, and police services.

3. **Not-for-profit sector**, which provides a range of charitable or social services, funded by donations, lottery grants, and other fundraising activities.

The accounting described in this book is primarily concerned with private sector, for-profit businesses, although many of the concepts are equally applicable to the other two sectors.

Beyond the three basic types of organizational structures, organizations can be further structured to reflect the flow of activities and level of responsibilities in the company. Galbraith and Nathanson (1976) suggested that the choice of organizational form was the result of decisions concerning five design variables: task, people, structure, reward systems, and information and decision processes. These choices should be consistent with the firm's strategy; that is, there should be a "fit" or "congruence." For example, in a company based on innovation and new-product development, decision-making authority would probably be delegated to lower levels of the organization, and individuals would be rewarded for their ability to make decisions that contribute to innovation in the company. High-technology firms are examples of companies that encourage individual decision making. On the other hand, a company that has formalized processes designed to ensure a high degree of cost control may be more structured, where decisions are made at the top of the organization and tasks are well defined and standardized. Banking would be an example of a more formalized organization.

Businesses produce products/services through a variety of organizational forms, but predominantly through either a functional structure or a divisionalized structure. The **functional structure** locates decision making at the top of the corporate hierarchy, with functional responsibilities for marketing, operations, human resources, and finance allocated to departments, as shown in the typical organization chart in Exhibit 13.1.

Exhibit 13.1 Functional Organization Chart

In the functional structure, accounting provides a *staff* function to the *line* functions, simplified here as marketing and operations. **Staff functions** are those functions that indirectly support the primary operations of a company but do not provide a source of revenue. Accounting knowledge tends to be centralized in the accounting department, which collects, produces, analyzes, and reports accounting information on behalf of its internal departments.

Line functions are the company's primary functions that provide a source of revenue and support the company's primary objectives. Operations and marketing are both line functions in Exhibit 13.1. The functional structure may be suitable for smaller organizations with a narrow geographic spread and a limited product/service range, but it is not generally suitable for larger organizations. The downfall of the functional structure for large organizations is its inability to react quickly to a changing business environment.

Exhibit 13.2 **Divisional Organization Chart**

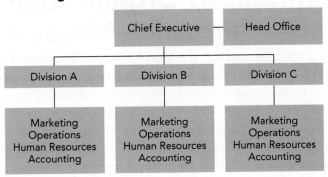

Most organizations today have a **divisional structure**, in which divisions are established for major elements of the business. These divisions may be based on geographic territories or different products/services, and each division will typically have responsibility for all of the functional areas: marketing, operations, human resources and accounting. A typical divisional structure is shown in Exhibit 13.2.

The managers of the divisions will perform a significant role in analyzing and interpreting the local financial information, typically supported by locally based accounting support staff. Accounting influences and is influenced by the structure adopted and the extent of managerial responsibility for business unit performance.

The advantage of the divisional structure is that while planning is centrally coordinated by the head office, the implementation of plans, decision making, and control is devolved to local managers, who should have a better understanding of their local operations.

The divisions are often referred to as *strategic business units* (SBUs) to describe their devolved responsibility for a segment of the business. These SBUs are also called *responsibility centres*. **Responsibility centres**, through their managers, are held responsible for achieving certain standards of performance. There are three types of responsibility centres for divisionalized businesses:

- **Cost centres.** In **cost centres**, managers are responsible for controlling costs within budget limits and are evaluated on the basis of how well they do this. A legal department of a large manufacturer would be an example of a cost centre. Since cost centres earn no revenue, managers are evaluated based on their ability to control costs.

- **Profit centres.** In **profit centres**, managers are responsible for sales performance, achieving gross margins, and controlling expenses; that is, for the "bottom-line" profit performance of the business unit. Managers are evaluated on their performance compared to budget in achieving or exceeding their profit target.

- **Investment centres.** With the decentralization of decisions in many organizations today, most divisions are **investment centres**. In investment centres, managers have profit responsibility, but also must make decisions regarding the amount of capital *invested* in their business unit, such as equipment purchases. Managers are evaluated based on a measure of the return on investment made by the investment centre.

Although organizations can have a combination of the various types of responsibility centres discussed above, we will focus most of this chapter on investment centres, as today's organization structure is characterized by divisionalized functions and delegation of decision-making authority.

The Decentralized Organization and Divisional Performance Measurement

Another way to look at organizational structure is on the basis of the degree of centralized decision-making authority. The **centralized business** is one in which most decisions are made at a head-office level, even though the business may be spread over a number of market segments and geographically diverse locations.

A **decentralized business** is characterized by the devolution of authority. Decentralized division managers are responsible for decision making and control at the business-unit level. Decentralization (also referred to as *divisionalization* in this chapter) allows managers to have autonomy over certain aspects of the business, but those managers are then accountable for the performance of their business units. In decentralized organizations, performance improvement is encouraged by assigning individual responsibility for divisional performance, typically linked to executive remuneration (bonuses, profit sharing, and share options).

Divisional performance measurements include both financial and non-financial performance measures. Financial reporting at the divisional level provides information for divisional managers in making decisions and enables top management to appraise the performance of divisional

CASE IN POINT

Enron's Accounting Sleight of Hand Led to Disaster

At energy company Enron Corporation, President and CEO Jeffrey Skilling used revenues, not profit, as the main measure of performance in his drive to be the "world's leading company." From 1996 to 2000, Enron's revenues ballooned from $13.3 billion to $100.8 billion, propelling it to the status of seventh-largest U.S. company in terms of revenues.

Executive compensation was tied to revenues—specifically, a deal's net present value rather than the actual cash flow it would generate—so divisional managers made riskier and riskier investments in creative ventures that didn't turn a profit. Among other things, Enron aggressively interpreted accounting rules, such as recording the entire value of its trades in energy futures as revenues rather than just the brokerage fees it earned on these transactions.

But what the company wasn't reporting transparently in its financial statements was that its liabilities were largely shifted off its books by special-purpose entities created by Enron. Through this accounting sleight of hand, it appeared to be more profitable than it was. As Enron's profitability declined as its investments went bust, its stock plunged from a high of $90 to less than $1 when it filed for bankruptcy in late 2001.

The company's performance management system focus on short-term earnings rather than long-term profit created a culture that was "dysfunctional" and "gladiator," say observers. "The obsessively compensation-driven culture encouraged high volume deal-making, often without regard to the quality of cash flow or profits, and getting accounting numbers booked as fast as possible to maintain the fragile underpinning of Enron's stock price, thus assuring that the deal-makers and executives would receive large cash bonuses and stock option exercise gains," write accounting researchers Bala G. Dharan and William R. Bufkins.

Sources: McEwen, W. J., Enron's misguided metrics, *Gallup Management Journal*, February 11, 2002; Lagace, M., Innovation corrupted: How managers can avoid another Enron, *Working Knowledge*, Harvard Business School, July 7, 2008; Dharan, B. G., & Bufkins, W. R., (2004), Red flags in Enron's reporting of revenues and key financial measures, in Nancy Rapoport and Bala G. Dharan (editors), *Enron: Corporate fiascos and their implications*, Foundation Press.

management. Divisional performance can be assessed through budgets and performance against budgets (these are the subjects of Chapters 14 and 15).

Divisions can also be assessed in terms of their ability to manage and earn income relative to their strategic investments. Evaluating divisional performance in comparison to a strategic investment is the subject of this chapter, and in it we will discuss three methods for evaluation of performance: return on investment, residual income, and economic value added.

Finally, divisions can be evaluated using non-financial measurements (also a topic of this chapter). Non-financial measurements, unlike financial measurements, are leading indicators of a division's success. Financial measurements are based on past performance (lagging indicators), whereas non-financial measurements evaluate a division's future potential, based on key success indicators, such as customer value, production efficiencies, and quality improvements.

Next, we will discuss three popular financial measurements (return on investment, residual income, and economic value added) to help assess a division's performance. Later in this chapter, we will discuss non-financial performance evaluation.

RETURN ON INVESTMENT

The relative success of managers can be judged by return on investment (ROI), which was introduced in Chapter 5. This is the rate of return achieved on capital employed for a division or business unit within the company. The formula for ROI is

$$\text{ROI} = \frac{\text{Operating profit}}{\text{Total assets}}$$

Operating profit for a division is normally based on before-tax operating income. Total assets, the denominator of the equation, is based on the book value of assets after depreciation. This means that divisions with older, more-depreciated assets could have a higher ROI than divisions with newer, less-depreciated assets. This is one of the key disadvantages of the ROI formula. If only ROI is used to evaluate a manager's performance, a manager may be inclined to hold on to older, less efficient assets to keep the ROI high. Managers may be tempted to invest in or divest investments to manipulate their overall ROI, especially if compensation is tied to divisional performance.

However, ROI remains a popular method of performance appraisal of investment centres as it includes revenues, costs, and investments—all key areas an investment centre manager is responsible for—in one measure. It is also simple to apply and easy to compare to a firm's cost of capital.

Interpreting the ROI is not always straightforward. Consider a company that has two divisions—Division A and Division B. The ROIs shown in Exhibit 13.3 were calculated for both divisions.

Division A has a better ROI than Division B but has a lower profit and a much lower asset base. Division B makes a higher profit in absolute terms but a lower return on the capital invested in the business. This could be due to the age of assets (i.e., Division A's assets may be highly depreciated) but it also could be due to the fact that Division A manages its assets better.

Exhibit 13.3 **ROI**

	Division A	Division B
Total assets (after depreciation)	$1,000,000	$2,000,000
Operating profit before tax	$ 200,000	$ 300,000
ROI	20%	15%

When using ROI as a performance assessment tool, a company often compares the division's ROI to the company's cost of capital. This gives the company an idea of whether the division is contributing a profit over and above the cost of financing the business. In this case, if we assumed the company had a 17.5% cost of capital, Division B's performance would not be considered to be very strong. Division A, on the other hand, would be earning a return above the cost of financing the business.

ROI does not really answer the question, "Which division is performing better?" This is why it is important to use more than just financial tools when assessing performance. A balanced scorecard approach to performance evaluation can help reward managers for innovation, production efficiency, and other measures that may not be captured by the ROI formula.

RESIDUAL INCOME

A different approach to evaluating performance is residual income, which takes into account a capital charge based on the cost of capital. **Residual income (RI)** is the profit remaining after deducting a portion of the capital invested that represents the cost of capital from the investment in the division. RI represents the amount of money left after the cost of financing a business is considered. RI is

$$\text{Residual income} = \text{Operating profit before tax} - \text{Capital charge}$$

The capital charge in the RI formula is based on the cost of capital for a company. Later in the chapter, we discuss how to calculate the weighted average cost of capital (WACC) for a company. Using the data in Exhibit 13.3 and assuming a cost of capital of 17.5% for the company, the residual income shown in Exhibit 13.4 were determined for Divisions A and B. Division A makes a satisfactory return but Division B does not. The aim of managers should be to maximize the residual income from the capital investments in their divisions.

Exhibit 13.4 Residual Income

	Division A	Division B
Capital invested	$1,000,000	$2,000,000
Operating profit	200,000	300,000
Less cost of capital at 17.5%	175,000	350,000
Residual income	25,000	(50,000)

Residual income is often considered a stronger measure than ROI because managers do not feel constrained to meet a percentage target. Rather, managers will make investments that have a return in excess of a firm's cost of capital, whereas if they used only ROI as a basis for evaluation, they might reject an investment if it lowers the division's overall ROI. For example, assume that Division A wants to invest in a new asset that costs $256,000 and would increase operating profit by $40,000. If ROI was used as a basis for performance evaluation, the new asset would change the division's ROI as shown in Exhibit 13.5.

Exhibit 13.5 ROI with New Asset

	Division A
Total assets (after depreciation)	$1,256,000
Operating profit before tax	$ 240,000
ROI	19.1%

Exhibit 13.6 **Residual Income with New Asset**

	Division A
Capital invested	$1,256,000
Operating profit	$240,000
Less cost of capital at 17.5%	$219,800
Residual income	$20,200

In this case, the manager of Division A might decide not to invest in the machine as it reduces the ROI, which is the basis of the manager's yearly bonus. However, if the division was evaluated based on residual income, the manager might choose to make the investment because it has a positive residual income and, therefore, contributes to the profitability of the division. The calculation of residual income is shown in Exhibit 13.6.

Using residual income as a basis for performance evaluation, the manager would choose to make the investment because it generates a return over and above the firm's cost of capital and contributes to true profit. Johnson and Kaplan (1987) believe that the residual income approach

> . . . overcame one of the dysfunctional aspects of the ROI measure in which managers could increase their reported ROI by rejecting investments that yielded returns in excess of their firm's (or division's) cost of capital, but that were below their current average ROI. (p. 165)

Economic value added (EVA), which we discuss next, is another approach that utilizes the same ideas as residual income but with more accuracy.

ECONOMIC VALUE ADDED

Economic value added (EVA) is a similar formula to residual income in that it deducts a percentage of the invested capital from income to determine the true earnings of a division. However, it has two key differences from residual income in terms of the specificity of the variables used in the formula:

1. It is calculated using after-tax earnings. EVA considers that tax is a cost of running a division and should be reflected in the evaluation of a division.

2. It deducts the current liabilities from total assets when determining the total invested capital for the division. It excludes assets that are funded through sources which are not part of the company's cost of capital. Current liabilities are subtracted from the value of total assets to recognize that current assets are financed through current liabilities.

The formula used for EVA is

$$\text{EVA} = \text{After-tax operating profit} - [(\text{Total assets} - \text{Current liabilities}) \times \text{WACC}]$$

WACC is determined as follows:

$$\text{WACC} = \left[d \times \left(\frac{\text{MVd}}{(\text{MVd} + \text{MVe})} \right) \right] + \left[e \times \left(\frac{\text{MVe}}{(\text{MVd} + \text{MVe})} \right) \right]$$

where

d is the cost of debt for the firm

e is the cost of equity for the firm

MVd is the market value of the firm's debt

MVe is the market value of the firm's equity

For example, Canada Goose Holdings uses both long-term debt and equity capital in order to raise funds. The long-term debt has a market value of $12 million and the equity has a market value of $15 million. The cost of debit is 10% and the cost of equity is 15%. The company reported total assets of $10,500,000 and an after-tax profit of $1,525,000. The current liabilities at the end of the period totalled $500,000.

To determine the EVA for Canada Goose Holdings, first the weighted average cost of capital (WACC) would be calculated as

$$\text{WACC} = \left[10\% \times \left(\frac{\$12,000,000}{(\$12,000,000 + \$15,000,000)} \right) \right] + \left[15\% \times \left(\frac{\$15,000,000}{(\$12,000,000 + \$15,000,000)} \right) \right]$$

$$\text{WACC} = 4.44\% + 8.33\%$$

$$\text{WACC} = 12.77\%$$

The EVA would be determined as shown in Exhibit 13.7.

Exhibit 13.7 EVA for Canada Goose Holdings

Total assets	$10,500,000
Less: Current liabilities	500,000
Invested capital	10,000,000
After-tax profits	1,525,000
Less WACC (12.77%)	1,277,000
EVA	248,000

Overall, the company had a return of $248,000 over and above its weighted average cost of capital.

Controllability

One of the limitations of operating profit as a measure of divisional performance is the inclusion of costs over which the divisional manager has no control. Corporate charges include head office costs related to administration, accounting, and depreciation of corporate assets. In financial reporting, the need for the company as a whole to make a profit demands that corporate costs be allocated to divisions so that these costs can be recovered in the prices charged. However, if a division's performance is evaluated based on profit after an allocation of corporate charges, a problem arises when a division's profit is not sufficient to cover the head office charge. Solomons (1965) argued that as long as corporate expenses are independent of divisional activity, allocating corporate costs to a division is irrelevant because a positive contribution by divisions will cover at least some of those costs. Allocating corporate charges to a division may be necessary for financial reporting but is not always desirable for performance evaluation purposes.

The example in Exhibit 13.8 shows the allocation of corporate charges to two divisions of the DFG Company. In this case, the D Division of DFG Company does not appear profitable. If, however, the division was closed, the full corporate costs would be assigned to the G Division, which would lower overall company profitability, as shown in Exhibit 13.9.

Exhibit 13.8 Corporate Charges Assigned to Divisions

	D Division	G Division	Total
Sales	$1,000,000	$3,000,000	$4,000,000
Less variable cost of goods sold	$300,000	$ 600,000	$ 900,000
Other variable expenses	100,000	400,000	500,000
Total variable costs	$400,000	$1,000,000	$1,400,000
Contribution margin	$600,000	$2,000,000	$2,600,000
Less controllable divisional overhead	250,000	450,000	700,000
Controllable profit	$350,000	$1,550,000	$1,900,000
Less non-controllable overhead	375,000	1,125,000	1,500,000
Operating profit	$(25,000)	$ 425,000	$ 400,000

Note: The total corporate-level costs are $1,500,000, allocated to each division based on its share of sales. D Division is assigned one-quarter of the total overhead or $375,000, while G Division is assigned three-quarters, or $1,125,000.

In the case shown in Exhibit 13.9, overall company profit will decrease by $350,000 ($400,000 − $50,000). The D Division provides a positive contribution before the allocation of non-controllable overhead, and its performance should be based on this fact.

While the business as a whole may consider the operating profit to be the most important figure, performance evaluation of managers can be carried out based only on the controllable profit. The **controllable profit** is the profit after deducting expenses that can be controlled by the divisional manager, but it ignores those expenses that are outside the divisional manager's control. What is controllable or non-controllable will depend on the circumstances of each organization.

Exhibit 13.9 Operating Profit with D Division Closed

	G Division
Sales	$3,000,000
Less variable cost of goods sold	$ 600,000
Other variable expenses	400,000
Total variable costs	$1,000,000
Contribution margin	$2,000,000
Less controllable divisional overhead	450,000
Controllable profit	$1,550,000
Less non-controllable overhead	1,500,000
Operating profit	$ 50,000

Non-Financial Performance Evaluation

Roberts and Scapens (1985) argued that in a divisionalized company there is distance between the division and the head office, such that "the context within which accounting information is gathered will typically be quite different from the context in which it is interpreted" (p. 452). This may result in manipulation of the appearance of accounting reports. Roberts and Scapens concluded:

> The image of an organization which is given through Accounts will be from a particular point of view, at a particular point in time and will be selective in its focus. Events, actions, etc., which are significant for the organization may be out of focus, or not in the picture at all . . . the image conveyed by the Accounts may misrepresent the actual flow of events and practices that it is intended to record. (p. 454).

The divisional form is a preferred organizational structure because it pushes responsibility and decision making down to the business-unit level. But at the same time, divisional performance can be difficult to evaluate from a financial perspective due to the potential manipulation of financial information. In a divisionalized company, performance is often tied to organizational goals through measures such as ROI, RI, and EVA. However, financial measures of performance are not enough if there is the potential that financial information has been manipulated or presented in a way that most favours the division. Further, a manager may be tempted to make non-optimal decisions (such as not invest in new machinery that may lower ROI) if a decision negatively impacts the division's financial measures of performance and, thus, his or her bonus. Accordingly, managers should also be evaluated based on their contribution to the development of strong customer and shareholder value through production efficiencies, customer service, quality, cost control, and innovation.

All of the performance evaluation tools discussed to this point have key limitations. ROI, RI, and EVA are based on historical financial information that could be manipulated. Also, these financial tools measure the effectiveness of only the tangible assets of the company—those assets shown on the statement of financial position. However, companies need to focus on more than their ability to manage their intangible assets. It is a company's intangible resources (such as people, knowledge, processes, and reputation) that provide a company with the ability to sustain competitive advantage and, thus, high customer and shareholder value.

"The ability of a company to mobilize and exploit its intangible or invisible assets has become far more decisive than investing in and managing physical, tangible assets" (Kaplan & Atkinson, 1998). Companies need to measure their ability to succeed in innovation, continuous improvement, learning, and customer service.

With the importance of intangible assets in creating shareholder value, companies are moving toward the balanced scorecard (BSC) approach to performance evaluation (discussed in Chapter 6 and explored more deeply in Reading A, "Using a Balanced Scorecard as a Strategic Management System" by Kaplan and Norton, 2007). A balanced score card can include measures of ROI, residual income, or EVA but also may include other measures that capture the effectiveness by which managers manage assets (both tangible and intangible), innovate, and build quality and efficiency in their divisions. A BSC for Hunter Homes is shown in Exhibit 13.10 and demonstrates how financial measures, such as ROI and EVA, can be supported by other measures, such as customer surveys, efficiency ratios, and inventory measures.

Exhibit 13.10 Balanced Scorecard for Hunter Homes

Perspective	Objective	Metrics
Financial	Profitability	ROI
		EVA
	Decrease product costs	Total manufacturing costs as a percentage of budget
	Increase sales	(2011 Sales − 2010 Sales)/2010 Sales
	Reduce quality costs	Rework costs per hour
	Decrease warranty costs	% of total products returned under warranty
Customer	Increase customer value	Customer survey related to value
	Increase customer base	Change in number of customers
	Customer satisfaction	Number of customer complaints received
		Customer satisfaction rating from survey
	Develop new customers	New customer contacts
Internal Business Process	Increasing customer value	% of value-added processes
		% of customer complaints resulting in product redesign
	Increase production efficiency	Production rate
		Inventory volumes
		% of suppliers providing JIT delivery
Innovation	Increase in innovation	Number of employees working on R&D activities
		Number of new-product introductions
	Employee involvement	Employee satisfaction rating
		Number of employee initiatives

Transfer Pricing

Transfer pricing was first introduced in Chapter 8. In this chapter, we again bring up this topic, as the choice of a transfer price can have a large impact on the performance and behaviours of managers in a divisionalized company. The intention of **transfer pricing** is to create an environment where managers are encouraged act competitively by controlling costs and managing capacity efficiently. If a supplying division is treated as a cost centre that is not responsible for earning a profit, its manager may not feel motivated to control costs. By using transfer prices between divisions, managers of the supplying division are encouraged to make a profit and, thus, to work efficiently and cost-effectively.

Managers of the purchasing division are also encouraged to work competitively. By having to pay a fee for intercompany transfers, they are encouraged to seek out the best input for their processes. It may be the decision of a purchasing division to purchase their inputs from an outside supplier if the internal supplier's prices are too high or the quality is too low.

For example, consider Hayer Company, which has two divisions. Division A can produce 10,000 units for $100,000. Any units produced over 10,000 will cost an additional $5 per unit. Division A sells its output to Division B at $13 per unit in order to show a satisfactory profit. Division B carries out further processing on the product. It can convert 10,000 units for a total cost of $300,000, with units above 10,000 costing $13 each. The prices that Division B can charge to customers will depend on the quantity it wants to sell. Market estimates of selling prices at different volumes (net of variable selling costs) are shown in Exhibit 13.11.

Exhibit 13.11 Demand Levels by Price

Volume	Price
10,000 units	$50 per unit
12,000 units	$46 per unit
15,000 units	$39 per unit

The financial results for each division at each level of activity are shown in Exhibit 13.12. Division A sees an increase in profit as volume increases and will want to increase production volume

Exhibit 13.12 Divisional Financial Results

Activity	10,000	12,000	15,000
Division A			
10,000 units	$100,000	$100,000	$100,000
2,000 units @ $5		10,000	
5,000 units @ $5			$25,000
Total cost	$100,000	$110,000	$125,000
Transfer price @ $13	130,000	156,000	195,000
Division profit	$30,000	$46,000	$70,000
Division B			
Transfer From Division A	$130,000	$156,000	$195,000
Conversion cost			
10,000 units	300,000	300,000	300,000
2,000 units @ $15		30,000	
5,000 units @ $15			$75,000
Total cost	$430,000	$486,000	$570,000
Selling price @	50	46	39
Sales revenue	$500,000	$552,000	$585,000
Division profit	$70,000	$66,000	$15,000
Company			
Sales revenue	$500,000	$552,000	$585,000
Division A cost	100,000	110,000	125,000
Division B cost	300,000	330,000	375,000
Company profit	$100,000	$112,000	$85,000

to 15,000 units. However, Division B sees a steady erosion of divisional profitability as volume increases and will seek to keep production limited to 10,000 units, at which point its maximum profit is $70,000.

The company's overall profitability is the highest at 12,000 units, and from a company-wide perspective, volume should be maintained at 12,000 units to maximize profits at $112,000. However, neither division will be satisfied with this result, as both will see it as a disadvantage in terms of divisional profits, by which divisional managers are evaluated.

For Division A, variable costs over 10,000 units are $5, but its transfer price is $13, so additional units contribute $8 each to divisional profitability. Division A's average costs reduce as volume increases, as Exhibit 13.13 shows.

Exhibit 13.13 Division A Costs

Number of Units	10,000	12,000	15,000
Division A total costs	$100,000	$110,000	$125,000
Average per unit	$ 10.00	$ 9.17	$ 8.33

However, Division B's variable costs over 10,000 units are $28 (transfer price of $13 plus conversion costs of $15). The reduction in average costs of $2.50 per unit is more than offset by the decrease in selling price (net of variable selling costs), as Exhibit 13.14 shows.

Exhibit 13.14 Division B Costs

	10,000	12,000	15,000
Division B total costs	$430,000	$486,000	$570,000
Average per unit	43.00	40.50	38.00
Reduction in average cost per unit		2.50	2.50
Reduction in selling price		4.00	7.00

Transfer prices between divisions can be established using several methods:

- **Market transfer price.** Using the market transfer price method, when products/services can be sold on the outside market, the market price is used. This is the easiest way to ensure that divisional decisions are compatible with corporate profit maximization. However, if there is no external market, particularly for an intermediate product—that is, one that requires additional processing before it can be sold—this method cannot be used.

- **Marginal cost-based transfer price.** In the marginal cost-based transfer price method, the transfer price is the additional (variable) cost incurred. In the above example, the transfer price would be $5, but Division A would have little motivation to produce additional volume if only incremental costs were covered.

- **Full-cost transfer price.** The full-cost transfer price would recover both fixed and variable costs. This has the same overhead allocation problem as identified in Chapter 11 and would have the same motivational problems as the marginal cost transfer price has.

- **Cost-plus transfer price.** The cost-plus transfer price provides a profit to each division, but has the problem identified in this example of leading to different management decisions in each division and at corporate level.

- **Negotiated transfer price.** The negotiated transfer price may take into account market conditions, marginal costs, and the need to motivate managers in each division. It tends to be the most practical solution to align the interests of divisions with the whole organization and to share the profits equitably between each division. In using this method, care must be taken to consider differential capital investments between divisions, so that both are treated equitably in terms of ROI or RI criteria.

In practice, many organizations adopt negotiated prices in order to avoid demotivating effects on different business units. For the Hayer Company, the best options would be to either use a market price if one can be established or a negotiated price where Division A sells at the units at $13 and Division B pays a different price at different volume levels.

CONCLUSION

In this chapter, we have described the divisionalized organization and how divisional performance can be evaluated using both financial and non-financial performance measures. We have also explored the controllability principle and challenges faced by transfer prices in vertically integrated companies. Organizations need to be aware of the behavioural implications of performance-evaluation measures, and should utilize a combination of measures to assess performance (both financial and non-financial) to ensure that actions by managers are in the best interests of the overall company.

KEY TERMS

Centralized business, 324

Controllable profit, 329

Cost centres, 323

Cost-plus transfer price, 334

Decentralized business, 324

Divisional structure, 323

Economic value added, 327

Full-cost transfer price, 333

Functional structure, 322

Investment centres, 323

Line functions, 322

Marginal cost based transfer price, 333

Market transfer price, 333

Negotiated transfer price, 334

Profit centres, 323

Residual income (RI), 326

Responsibility centres, 323

Staff functions, 322

Transfer pricing, 331

CASE STUDY 13.1: MAJESTIC SERVICES—DIVISIONAL PERFORMANCE MEASUREMENT

Majestic Services has two divisions, both of which have bid $1 million for projects that will generate significant cost savings. Majestic has a cost of capital of 15% and can invest in only one of the projects.

The current performance of each division is as follows:

	Division A	Division B
Current investment	$4 million	$20 million
Profit	$1 million	$2 million

Each division has estimated the additional controllable profit that will be generated from the $1 million investment. Division A estimates $200,000 and Division B estimates $130,000.

Each division also has an asset they would like to dispose of. Division A's asset currently makes a return on investment (ROI) of 19%, while Division B's asset makes an ROI of 12%. Majestic wants to use ROI and residual income techniques to determine which of the $1 million projects it should invest in, and whether either of the division's identified assets should be disposed of.

Using ROI, the two divisions can be compared as in Exhibit 13.15. While Division B is the larger division

and generates a higher profit in absolute terms, Division A achieves a higher return on investment.

Again using ROI, the impact of the additional investment can be seen in Exhibit 13.16, and the impact of the investment on the total divisional ROI is shown in Exhibit 13.17. Using ROI, Division A may not want its project to be approved, as the ROI of 20% is less than the current ROI of 25%.

The new investment would reduce Division A's ROI to 24%. However, Division B would want its project to be approved, as the ROI of 13% is higher than the current ROI of 10%. The effect would be to increase Division B's ROI slightly, to 10.14%. However, the divisional preference for Division B's investment over Division A's, because of the rewards attached to increasing ROI, are dysfunctional for Majestic. Majestic's corporate view would be to invest $1 million in Division A's project, because the ROI to the business as a whole would be 20% rather than 13%. The disposal of the asset can be considered even without knowing its value. If Division A currently obtains a 25% ROI, disposing of an asset with a return of only 19% will increase its average ROI. Division B would want to retain its asset because it generates an ROI of 12% and disposal would reduce its average ROI to

Exhibit 13.15 ROI on Original Investment

	Division A	Division B	Total
Current investment	$4,000,000	$2,000,000	$24,000,000
Current profit	$1,000,000	$2,000,000	$ 3,000,000
ROI	25%	10%	12.5%

Exhibit 13.16 ROI on Additional Investment

	Division A	Division B
Additional investment	$1,000,000	$1,000,000
Additional contribution	$ 200,000	$ 130,000
ROI on additional investment	20%	13%

Exhibit 13.17 New Divisional ROI after Additional Investment

	Division A	Division B
Additional investment	$5,000,000	$21,000,000
Additional contribution	$1,200,000	$ 2,130,000
ROI on additional investment	24%	10.14%

below the current 10%. Given a choice of retaining only one, Majestic would prefer to retain Division A's asset as it has a higher ROI.

The difficulty with ROI as a measure of performance is that it ignores both the difference in size between the two divisions and Majestic's cost of capital. These issues are addressed by the residual income method.

Using residual income, the divisional performance can be compared as in Exhibit 13.18. In this case, we can see that Division A is contributing to shareholder value as it generates a positive RI, while Division B is eroding shareholder value because the profit it generates is less than the cost of capital on the investment.

Using RI, the impact of the additional investment is shown in Exhibit 13.19. Under the residual income approach, Division A's project would be accepted (positive RI) while Division B's would be rejected (negative RI).

Similarly, for the asset disposal, Division A's asset would be retained (ROI of 19% exceeds cost of capital of 15%), while Division B's asset would be disposed of (ROI of 12% is less than cost of capital of 15%).

The main problem facing Majestic is that the larger of the two divisions (both in terms of investment and profits) is generating a negative residual income and, consequently, eroding shareholder value.

Exhibit 13.18 **RI on Original Investment**

	Division A	Division B
Current investment	$4,000,000	$20,000,000
Current profit	1,000,000	2,000,000
Cost of capital @ 15%	600,000	3,000,000
Residual income (Profit − Cost of capital)	$ 400,000	$ (1,000,000)

Exhibit 13.19 **RI on Additional Investment**

	Division A	Division B
Additional investment	$1,000,000	$1,000,000
Additional contribution	200,000	130,000
Less cost of capital @ 15%	150,000	150,000
Residual income	$ 50,000	$ (20,000)

■ SELF-TEST QUESTIONS

S13.1 The investment of $400,000 in a division returns a profit before interest of $25,000. However, head office charges a 5% cost of capital. The return on investment (%) and residual income ($) are

a. 6.25%; $20,000

b. 6.25%; $5,000

c. 5%; $25,000

d. 5%; $5,000

S13.2 The division of a multinational corporation shows sales of $2.1 million, variable cost of sales of $1.3 million, and divisional overheads of $600,000—60% of which is deemed controllable by the division and the other 40% is a head office allocation. The profit on which the divisional manager should be evaluated is

a. $800,000

b. $440,000

c. $360,000

d. $200,000

S13.3 Enrod Company has two divisions: Old and New. Its summary results are

	Old	New
Investment	$2,000,000	$5,000,000
Net profit	400,000	900,000

Enrod's cost of capital is 16%. What is the ROI and RI for Old Division?

a. 18%; $80,000

b. 20%; $100,000

c. 20%; $80,000

d. 18%; $100,000

S13.4 Abbygail Books has two divisions, Edmonton and Toronto, and their results for 2011 were as follows:

	Edmonton	Toronto
Sales	$5,500,000	$7,000,000
Cost of goods sold	2,000,000	2,500,000
S & A expenses	1,250,000	1,900,000
Operating income	2,250,000	2,600,000
Investment base (total assets)	8,200,000	8,700,000

The company's desired rate of return is 22%.

What are the respective return-on-investment ratios for the Edmonton and Toronto divisions?

a. 41%; 37%

b. 27%; 30%

c. 5%; 8%

d. None of the above

S13.5 During the past year, Labrador Retriever Kennels had a net income of $75,000. Its ROI was 12%. What was the value of the company's total assets?

a. $625,000

b. $9,000

c. $84,000

d. $650,000

S13.6 A company has total assets of $1,200,000, a required rate of return of 12%, and operating income for the year was $345,000. What is the company's residual income?

a. $303,600

b. $345,000

c. $144,000

d. $201,000

Use the following information to answer questions S13.7 and S13.8.
In a recent electrical storm, the Frizzle Company lost a portion of its accounting records. The IT manager at Frizzle was able to retrieve the following information:

Sales	$2,500,000
Net operating income	$1,500,000
Total assets	
Return on investment	0.25
Residual Income	

S13.7 What is the value of the total assets for the Frizzle Company?

a. $625,000

b. $375,000

c. $1,000,000

d. $6,000,000

S13.8 What is the residual income for the Frizzle Company if the firms cost of capital is 15%?

a. $600,000

b. $1,406,250

c. $1,443,750

d. $1,350,000

S13.9 JRT Enterprises has long-term debt with a market value of $2,000,000 and equity with a market value of $3,000,000. For the company, the cost of debt is 15%, while the cost of equity is 10%. The company's total assets are $800,000. During 2011, JRT reported after-tax profit of $550,000. Information related to the company's debt on its statement of financial position is shown below:

Liabilities	
Accounts payable	$ 50,000
Current portion of long-term loan	150,000
Total current liabilities	$ 200,000
Long-term debt	
Bank loan	1,850,000
Total long-term debt	1,850,000
Total liabilities	$ 2,050,000

What is the EVA for JRT Enterprises?

a. $478,000

b. $460,000

c. $472,000

d. $490,000

S13.10 A company's weighted average cost of capital was 10.4% in 2011. The company's market value for debt and equity are $400,000 and $600,000, respectively. The company's cost of equity is 12%. What is the company's cost of debt funding?

a. 10.4%

b. 12%

c. 8%

d. 9%

S13.11 The management of PaperPlus, a paperboard manufacturer, expects a return of 20% on investments. The company currently has total assets of $10,000,000, earns a contribution margin of 60% on sales, has variable costs of $3,000,000 and reports profits of $2,000,000. The manager is considering acquiring another factory, which will increase sales by 40% and will maintain a 60% contribution margin on sales. Fixed costs for the new factory will be $1,000,000. What is the maximum amount of investment the company should make in the new factory in order to meet its ROI expectation?

a. $2,800,000

b. $4,000,000

c. $15,000,000

d. None of the above

S13.12 The Component Division of TransCanada Industries provides components to the Elite Division in the production of grombets. It costs the Component Division a total of $5.50 per unit to manufacture the components, which they then sell to the Elite Division for $8 per unit, allowing for a profit. The Elite Division can purchase the component on the open market at $7.50. What transfer price should be charged between divisions and why?

a. $8; it allows for profit for the Component Division

b. $7.50; it encourages competitive behaviour and cost control in the Component Division and will help to ensure that the Elite Division purchases internally

c. $5.50; it is better to charge only the cost to manufacture, to ensure that the Elite Division is motivated to purchase internally

d. None of the above

■ PROBLEMS

P13.1 *(ROI and RI)* The Clarity Division of Mega Glass Company has an investment of $1,500,000 and currently generates a net profit of $112,500 per year. Clarity has proposed an additional investment of $1,000,000, which is expected to return an annual profit of $90,000. Mega Glass is concerned that Clarity is not recovering the group's cost of capital of 8%.

Use ROI and RI techniques to advise Mega Glass.

P13.2 *(RI)* Jakobs Ladder has capital employed of $10 million and currently earns an ROI of 15% per year. It can make an additional investment of $2 million for a five-year life. The average net profit from this investment would be 14% of the original investment. The division's cost of capital is 12%.

Calculate the residual income before and after the investment.

P13.3 *(ROI)* China Group has a division with capital employed of $10 million that currently earns an ROI of 15% per year. It can make an additional investment of $2 million for a five-year life, with no scrap value. The average net profit from this investment would be $280,000 per annum after depreciation. The division's cost of capital is 9%.

Calculate the ROI and residual income for the following:

a. Original investment

b. Additional investment

c. Total new level of investment

P13.4 *(ROI, RI)* A farm equipment company, with three divisions, shows the following results for 2011:

	Tractor Division	Mower Division	Harvester Division
Sales	$ 8,000,000	$ 9,000,000	$10,000,000
Contribution margin	2,000,000	2,500,000	3,500,000
Operating income	1,500,000	1,500,000	2,750,000
Investment base	12,000,000	14,000,000	16,000,000

The company's desired rate of return is 15%.

a. Compute each division's ROI.

b. Compute each division's residual income.

c. Rank each division by both ROI and residual income.

d. Which division had the best performance in 2001? Why?

P13.5 *(ROI, EVA)* Speed Boats Inc. has two divisions, Economy and Elite. The tax rate for the company is 40%. The following information pertains to the 2011 year:

	Economy	**Elite**
Revenues	$3,800,000	$2,500,000
Current liabilities	250,000	300,000
Total assets	1,800,000	1,100,000
Before-tax operating income	350,000	160,000
WACC	11.5%	11.5%

a. What is the ROI for each division?

b. What is the EVA for each division?

c. What other ratio could be used to evaluate each division?

P13.6 *(WACC and EVA)* Elsie Vinton Laboratories is evaluating the purchase of five new MRI machines for its labs at various locations in Vancouver for $9,000,000, which will increase the company's before-tax profit by $1.2 million per year. The company uses both long-term debt and equity capital to raise funds. The value of long-term debt held by the company is $15,200,000. Its equity market value is $21,345,000. The costs of debit and equity are 12% and 9%, respectively. Elsie Vinton reports total assets of $45,000,000 and before-tax profit of $8,325,000. The tax rate for Elsie Vinton is 32%. The current liabilities at the end of the period totalled $825,000.

Note: the new investment will not impact the company's WACC, current liabilities, or tax rate.

a. What is Elsie Vinton's EVA prior to the investment in the MRI machines?

b. How will the company's EVA change with the MRI investment?

c. Based on the EVA calculations, should Elsie Vinton pursue this investment?

P13.7 *(ROI, RI)* Managers at The Tea Company are currently working on the company's 2011 budget, which holds total assets of $3,500,000. For the 2011 year, The Tea Company is expecting its average selling price per box of tea to be $10 and its variable costs to be $3 per box. Total fixed costs are expected to be $200,000. The company's cost of capital is 12%.

a. How many boxes of tea need to be sold in 2011 to achieve a 15% ROI?

b. The manager for The Tea Company receives 15% of residual income. What is the manager's anticipated bonus for 2011, assuming that the company attains the 15% ROI.

P13.8 *(ROI, RI)* Brummy Limited consists of several investment centres. One investment centre, the Green Division, has a controllable investment of $750,000, and profits are expected to be $150,000 this year. An investment opportunity is offered to Green that will yield a profit of $15,000 from an additional investment of $100,000. Brummy accepts projects if the ROI exceeds the cost of capital, which is 12%.

a. Calculate Green's ROI currently, for the additional investment, and after the investment.

b. How will Green and Brummy view this investment opportunity?

c. Calculate the effect of the new investment opportunity on Green's residual income.

P13.9 *(ROI and RI)* Anston Industries is the manufacturing division of a large multinational. The divisional general manager is about to purchase new equipment for the manufacture of a new product. He can buy either the Compax or the Newpax equipment, each of which has the same capacity and an expected life of four years. Depreciation, the only non-cash expense, is expensed at an equal rate each year, with no salvage value. Each type of equipment has different capital costs and expected cash flows, as follows:

	Compax	Newpax
Initial capital investment	$6,400,000	$5,200,000
Net cash inflows (before tax)		
Year 1	$2,400,000	$2,600,000
Year 2	2,400,000	2,200,000
Year 3	2,400,000	1,500,000
Year 4	2,400,000	1,000,000
Net present value (at 16% per year)	$315,634	$189,615

The equipment will be installed and paid for at the end of the current year (Year 0) and the cash flows accrue at the end of each year. There is no scrap value for either piece of equipment. In calculating divisional returns, divisional assets are valued at net book value at the beginning of each year.

The multinational expects each division to achieve a minimum return before tax of 16%. Anston is just managing to achieve that target. Anything less than a 16% return would make the divisional general manager ineligible for his profit-sharing bonus.

a. Prepare return on investment (ROI) and residual income (RI) calculations for Compax and the Newpax for each year.

b. Suggest which equipment is preferred under each method.

c. Compare this with the NPV calculation.

P13.10 *(ROI and RI)* Magna Products has three divisions, A, B, and C. The current investments in and net profits earned by each division are as follows:

Division A

Investment	$1,000,000
Net profit	$75,000

Division B

Investment	$1,500,000
Net profit	$90,000

Division C

Investment	$2,000,000
Net profit	$150,000

Each division has put forward to the parent board a capital expenditure proposal for $500,000. Each expects to produce net profits of $40,000 from that investment. Magna's cost of capital is 7% per year.

Use ROI and RI calculations to

a. Evaluate the current performance of each division.

b. Evaluate which proposal the board should approve if finance limits the decision to a single proposal.

P13.11 *(ROI and NPV Evaluation)* Serendipity is an Internet service provider that has a major investment in computer and telecom equipment, which needs replacement on a regular basis. The company has recently evaluated a $5 million equipment-replacement program, which has an expected life of five years. The proposal is supported by the following data:

In $thousands	Year 0	1	2	3	4	5	6
Capital investment	$5,000						
Depreciation 20% per year		$1,000	$1,000	$1,000	$1,000	$1,000	
Asset value end of year Profit		4,000	3,000	2,000	1,000	0	
Additional income		1,500	2,000	2,500	2,500	2,500	
Additional expenses		(150)	(350)	(500)	2500	(500)	
Depreciation		(1,000)	(1,000)	(1,000)	(1,000)	(1,000)	
Profit		350	650	1,000	1,000	1,000	
Tax @ 35%		(105)	(195)	(300)	(300)	(300)	
Profit after tax		245	455	700	700	700	
ROI		6.1%	15.2%	35.0%	70.0%	n/a	
Cash flow							
Capital investment	(5,000)						
Cash receipts		1,500	2,000	2,500	2,500	2,500	
Additional expenses		(150)	(350)	(500)	(500)	(500)	
Tax @ 35%			(105)	(195)	(300)	(300)	(300)
Net cash flow	$(5,000)	$1,350	$1,545	$1,805	$1,700	$1,700	$(300)
Discount rate	8%						
Net present value	$1,225						

As the ROI and NPV look healthy, the investment proposal will be submitted to the board for approval. Prior to the above figures being submitted, what comments would you make?

P13.12 *(Transfer Pricing)* Paramount Homes provides rental properties for tenants. Repair services for the properties are provided by Paramount's subsidiary, Quicker Repair Co. Because virtually all of Quicker's sales are to Paramount and Paramount insists on prices that Quicker believes to be too low, Quicker is showing a loss in its management accounting reports. The latest report shows the following:

Sales	$1,000,000
Cost of sales	850,000
Gross profit (15%)	$150,000 (mark-up of 17.6%)
Overhead costs	120,000
Corporate costs recharged from parent	80,000
Net loss	−$50,000

Quicker believes that if it charged market prices for the repairs it undertakes, prices would be 20% higher. Paramount does not accept this argument, as it routinely market tests Quicker's prices to ensure that the prices it pays are realistic and competitive. However, Paramount does accept that Quicker has to bear a share of corporate overheads which its competitors would not incur, and so may be disadvantaged. Paramount has suggested that the appropriate mark-up is on the cost of sales plus total overhead expenses.

What would be the effect of these two alternatives on Quicker's reported profits and what might be the likely motivational effects? What suggestions would you make?

P13.13 *(Transfer Pricing)* Golf Holdings has two divisions: Alpha and Bravo. Alpha has a variable cost of sales of $11 per unit, which is its transfer price to Bravo. However, Alpha can sell its product on the open market for a variable selling cost of $17 per unit. It is unable to do so, however, as Bravo takes the entire product that Alpha can produce. Bravo uses the product it buys from Alpha as a raw material and adds its own cost of sales of $12. Bravo's market selling price is $45, although it incurs variable selling expenses of $10 per unit.

How does the transfer price influence the performance evaluation of Alpha and Bravo? What changes would you suggest?

P13.14 *(Transfer Pricing)* The Umber Company is a multidivisional company that manufactures toys. The Truck Division of the Umber Company has asked the Wheel Division to provide wheels that are required in the production of its toy monster trucks. Currently, the Wheel Division sells wheels only to outside customers for $4 per set of 4 wheels and is operating at capacity. The Truck Division, which is operating below capacity, wants to pay the Wheel Division $3 per set. The Wheel Division's variable costs per set are $2. The toy monster truck made by the Truck Division currently costs $15 to make, as follows:

Plastic parts	$ 6
Wheels (purchased outside)	4
Conversion costs	3
Fixed overhead	2
Total cost per monster truck	$15

The manager of Truck Division believes that the $3 price is fair since it covers the division's variable costs.

a. As manager of the Wheel Division, would you recommend that your division provide wheels to the Truck Division? If so, at what transfer price?

b. How would your decision change if you had excess capacity?

P13.15 *(Transfer Pricing)* Eva Petersen Professional Products has recently purchased a perfume factory that will be used to provide scents for its hair care products. The new factory has a capacity of 100,000 litres of scented oils per year. Last year, it sold 25,000 litres of scented oils at a price of $100 per litre. The Hair Care Division of Eva Peterson requires 80,000 litres of scented oil per year and, in the past, has been purchasing perfumes from external providers for $95 per litre. The management of Eva Petersen is trying to develop a transfer price between the perfume factory and the Hair Care Division. The costs to produce one litre of scented oils by the perfume factory are as follows:

Direct materials per litre	$35
Direct labour	20
Variable overhead	10
Fixed overhead	15
Total	$80

The manager of the Hair Care Division, therefore, feels that an $80 transfer price is appropriate to reflect the cost of making the scented oils. The perfume factory manager, however, suggests the price should be $100 per litre to reflect what the factory sells the product for on the open market. The perfume factory, under new ownership, is still planning to continue to sell product to outside markets.

a. Calculate the operating income for the perfume factory using a transfer price of $80.

b. How does the income change when using a transfer price of $100?

c. What transfer price(s) do you recommend and why?

P13.16 *(Transfer Pricing)* Maja and Mina are both divisions of Arbor Group. Both divisions trade on the open market but Maja also provides almost a quarter of its production output to Mina. Maja believes that Mina pays less than Maja could sell the product for on the open market. As evidence, Maja has calculated its cost of sales as 40% of external sales and 60% of intercompany sales.

The operating results of the company are shown below. The divisional managers are rewarded on the basis of achieving an ROI, provided that it is greater than the cost of capital of 12%. The higher the ROI over that base, the higher the divisional manager's performance bonus.

	Maja	Mina	Total
Total assets	$3,500,000	$6,500,000	$10,000,000
Sales revenue	1,200,000	2,400,000	3,600,000
Intercompany sales	350,000	−350,000	0
Variable costs	−690,000	−720,000	−1,400,000
Gross profit	860,000	1,330,000	2,190,000
Fixed selling & admin expense	−250,000	−300,000	−550,000
Operating profit before interest	610,000	1,030,000	1,640,000
Gross margin	71.7%	55.4%	60.8%
Return on investment	17.4%	15.8%	16.4%
Cost of capital @ 12%	420,000	780,000	1,200,000
Residual income	190,000	250,000	440,000

The management team of Mina has argued that it has been unfairly treated due to the transfer price from Maja. It has recalculated its performance (and that of Maja) based on a reduction in the transfer price by 20%. The revised figures produced by Mina's financial controller are shown below:

	Maja	Mina	Total
Total assets	$3,500,000	$6,500,000	$10,000,000
Sales revenue	1,200,000	2,400,000	3,600,000
Intercompany sales	280,000	−280,000	0
Variable costs	−690,000	−720,000	−1,410,000
Gross profit	790,000	1,400,000	2,190,000
Fixed selling & admin expense	−250,000	−300,000	−550,000
Operating profit before interest	540,000	1,100,000	1,640,000
Gross margin	65.8%	58.3%	60.8%
Return on investment	15.4%	16.9%	16.4%
Cost of capital @ 12%	420,000	780,000	1,200,000
Residual income	120,000	320,000	440,000

a. What are the strengths and weaknesses of Mina's argument?

b. What position would you take if you were on the management team of Maja?

c. How should Arbor Group resolve this issue?

REFERENCES

Galbraith, J. R. and Nathanson, D. A. (1976). *Strategy implementation: The role of structure and process*. St. Paul, MN: West Publishing Company.

Johnson, H. T., and Kaplan, R. S. (1987). *Relevance lost: The rise and fall of management accounting*. Boston, MA: Harvard Business School Press.

Kaplan, R. and Atkinson, A. (1998). *Advanced management accounting* (3rd ed). Upper Saddle River, NJ: Prentice Hall.

Roberts, J. and Scapens, R. (1985). Accounting systems and systems of accountability— Understanding accounting practices in their organizational contexts. *Accounting, Organizations and Society, 10*(4), 443–456.

Solomons, D. (1965). *Divisional performance: Measurement and control*. Homewood, IL: Richard D. Irwin.

CHAPTER 14

Budgeting

LEARNING OBJECTIVES

After reading this chapter, you should be able to answer the following questions:

■ What are the benefits of budgeting?

■ What types of budgets are used within organizations?

■ What are the main steps in the budgeting process?

■ How does the budgeting process for a manufacturing organization differ from the budgeting process for a service organization or a retail organization?

■ Why is it important to develop a cash budget?

■ What are the challenges faced when budgeting, and how can these challenges be overcome?

Anthony and Govindarajan (2000) described budgets as "an important tool for effective short-term planning and control" (p. 360). They saw strategic planning (see Chapter 6) as being focused on several years, contrasted to budgeting which focuses on a single year. Strategic planning "precedes budgeting and provides the framework within which the annual budget is developed. A budget is, in a sense, a one-year slice of the organization's strategic plan" (p. 361).

This chapter explores the process of budgeting for manufacturing, retail, and service organizations and considers the various types of budgets that might be developed.

What Is Budgeting?

A **budget** is a plan expressed in monetary terms that covers a future time period (typically a year). Budgets are based on a defined level of activity, either expected sales revenue (if market demand is the limiting factor) or capacity (if capacity is the limiting factor). While budgets are typically produced annually, **continuous budgets** add additional months to the end of the period so that there is always a 12-month budget for the business.

Budgeting provides the ability to

- Implement strategy by allocating resources in line with strategic goals
- Coordinate activities and assist in communication between different parts of the organization
- Motivate managers to achieve targets
- Provide a means to control activities
- Evaluate managerial performance

In establishing the budget allocation to specific profit centres, cost centres, or departments, there are four main methods of budgeting: incremental, priority-based, zero-based, and activity-based.

Incremental budgets take the previous year's budget as a base and add (or subtract) a percentage to determine this year's budget. The assumption is that the historical budget continues to reflect future organizational priorities and is rooted in some meaningful justification developed in the past.

Priority-based budgets allocate funds in line with strategy. If priorities change, budget allocations would follow those priorities, irrespective of the historical allocation. Priority-based budgets may be responsibility centre based, but are often associated with particular projects or programs.

Zero-based budgeting identifies the costs that are necessary to implement approved strategies and achieve goals, as if the budget holder was beginning with a new organizational unit, without any prior history. This method has the advantage of incorporating regular reviews of all of the activities that are carried out to see if they are still required, but with the disadvantage of the cost and time needed for such reviews. It is also very difficult to develop a budget while ignoring current resource allocations.

Activity-based budgeting is associated with activity-based costing (ABC) (see Chapter 11). ABC identifies *activities* that consume resources and uses the concept of *cost drivers* (essentially the causes of costs) to allocate costs to products or services according to how much of the resources of the firm they consume. Activity-based budgeting (ABB) bases a budget on the expected activities and cost drivers to meet sales (or capacity) projections.

Budgets might also be top down or bottom up. **Top–down budgets** begin with the sales forecast and, using the volume of sales, predict inventory levels, staffing, and production times within capacity limitations. For services, the top–down budget is based largely on capacity utilization and staffing levels needed to meet expected demand. In top–down budgeting, senior management establishes spending limits within which department managers must then establish their individual budgets. Senior managers set the revenue targets and spending limits that they believe are necessary to achieve profits which will satisfy shareholders. **Bottom–up budgets** are developed by the managers of each department based on current spending and approved plans, which are then aggregated to the corporate total.

Lack of employee involvement is a distinct disadvantage of top–down budgeting. Department managers may feel constrained by unrealistic budget objectives, and this can cause resentment and motivation issues. By contrast, the result of the bottom–up budget may be inadequate in terms of "bottom-line profitability, or unachievable as a result of either capacity limitations elsewhere in the business or market demand."

Consequently, most budgets are the result of a combination of top–down and bottom–up processes. By adopting both methods, budget holders are given the opportunity to bid for resources (in competition with other budget holders) within the constraints of the shareholder-value focus of the business.

The Budgeting Process

The typical **budget cycle**—the period each year over which budgets are prepared—will follow the sequence shown in Exhibit 14.1:

Exhibit 14.1 **The Budgeting Process**

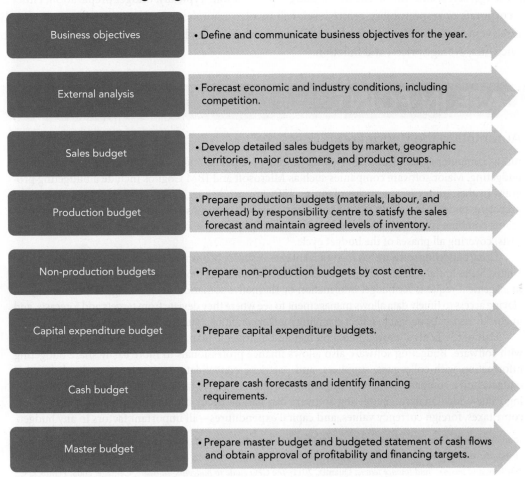

Business objectives	• Define and communicate business objectives for the year.
External analysis	• Forecast economic and industry conditions, including competition.
Sales budget	• Develop detailed sales budgets by market, geographic territories, major customers, and product groups.
Production budget	• Prepare production budgets (materials, labour, and overhead) by responsibility centre to satisfy the sales forecast and maintain agreed levels of inventory.
Non-production budgets	• Prepare non-production budgets by cost centre.
Capital expenditure budget	• Prepare capital expenditure budgets.
Cash budget	• Prepare cash forecasts and identify financing requirements.
Master budget	• Prepare master budget and budgeted statement of cash flows and obtain approval of profitability and financing targets.

The process of budgeting is largely based on making informed judgments about

- How businesswide strategies will affect the responsibility centre
- The level of demand placed on the business unit and the expected level of activity to satisfy internal and external customers
- The technology and processes used in the business unit to achieve desired productivity levels, based on past experience and anticipated improvements
- Any new initiatives or projects that are planned and require resources
- The historic spending patterns by the business unit

In preparing a budget, it is important to carry out a thorough investigation of current performance and business processes as well as of the external environment in which the business operates. The complexity of the budget will depend on a number of factors, such as

- knowledge of past performance
- understanding of market trends, seasonal factors, and competition
- whether the business is a price leader or a price follower
- understanding the drivers of business costs

How well these factors can be understood and modelled using a spreadsheet will depend on the knowledge, skills, and time available for budget preparation. Typically, budget preparation, either at the corporate or responsibility-centre level, will involve a number of subjective judgments of likely future events and customer demand, as well as a number of simplifying assumptions about product/service mix, average prices, and inflation.

CASE IN POINT

Automating the Budgeting Process

Just as computer spreadsheets revolutionized data processing, budgeting software is revolutionizing budgeting. Major software companies such as Microsoft and IBM Cognos include a budgeting program in their suites of enterprise planning software, while specialized vendors offer software for preparing budgets in certain industries or for certain company sizes. The more sophisticated programs combine historical data on sales and costs with business objectives and sales and cost forecasts, covering all phases of the budget cycle.

Using budgeting software has many advantages. A survey of business and finance professionals in the United States found that they are expected to recast their budgets more than quarterly, and to respond to management requests for budget information or alternative scenarios on an average of 12 times a year. Having access to timely data allows management to see where they deviate from targets and forecasts, and to quickly revise the budget to reflect changing market conditions, such as fluctuating commodity prices.

Half of the firms surveyed had a budget and a strategic plan, which are more easily integrated with software. Budgeting software also allows finance professionals to more easily share budgeting information with colleagues, suppliers, and partners; consolidate departmental and subsidiaries' budgets into a company-wide one; and automate administrative tasks that take them away from doing value-added analysis. Budgeting software can handle tricky calculations, such as projected income taxes, foreign currency values, and capital expenditures—all important factors in any budget.

Sources: *Quantix survey of business and finance professionals highlights serious challenges in budgeting, forecasting, and planning processes,* company news release, April 26, 2011; *2012 budgeting, forecasting, and planning survey: Insight into processes, solutions, and business and finance teams,* Quantix, 2011; *The CFO guide to budgeting software,* Centage, 2005; Pendock, C., Today's crystal ball is digital, *CA Magazine,* November 2000.

Budgeting for a Manufacturing Company

The budgeting for a manufacturing company normally starts with an estimate of sales. Let's consider a manufacturing company that sells lamps, Lighting Décor Ltd. The company has considered its operating goals and the external environment in which it operates, and has developed a sales budget for 2012 as shown in Exhibit 14.2.

Exhibit 14.2 Lighting Décor Ltd.: Sales Budget

Sales Budget
For the Year Ended December 31, 2012

Lamp Style	Units	Selling Price	Total Revenues
Table	10,000	$ 65	$ 650,000
Floor	2,000	125	250,000
Desk	5,000	35	175,000
Total	17,000		$ 1,075,000

The predicted unit sales are based on forecasts made by the company for 2012, using market information and previous sales data. The accuracy of the forecasted sales information is important, as it is the basis for all production budgets. When a manager is setting a sales forecast, the accuracy of the forecast can depend on more than just the data and information that the manager gathers internally and externally—it can also depend on a manager's motivation. For example, when a company evaluates a manager's performance based on achieving a particular volume of sales, a manager may feel inclined to underestimate sales for the budget. Use of **budgetary slack**—a deliberate underestimation of sales—is a common occurrence in businesses that use the budget as a means of evaluating performance. Companies need to be aware of this practice to ensure that their budgets are meaningful.

The next step is to develop a **production budget** based on the sales budget for the year. In developing the production budget shown in Exhibit 14.3, Lighting Décor Ltd. needed to consider its inventory needs in addition to forecasted sales. Inventory levels are estimated for this company based on potential demand fluctuations. For the purposes of its budget, Lighting Décor estimated the ending inventory requirements for 2012 as 15% of sales.

Exhibit 14.3 Lighting Décor Ltd.: Production Budget

Production Budget (in units)
For the Year Ended December 31, 2012

	Table	Floor	Desk	Total
Sales (from Exhibit 14.2)	10,000	2,000	5,000	17,000
Plus: Ending finished goods inventory (15% of sales)	1,500	300	750	2,550
Total required	11,500	2,300	5,750	19,550
Less: Beginning finished goods inventory* (given)	2,750	50	850	3,650
Production requirements	8,750	2,250	4,900	15,900

*Note: The beginning inventory levels are based on actual inventory volumes at the end of 2011.

Based on this production budget, Lighting Décor developed a direct materials purchases budget as shown in Exhibit 14.4, which calculates the quantity of direct materials the company will need to purchase during 2012. For this budget, Lighting Décor assumed that its direct materials ending inventory requirements are 10% of total direct materials used in 2012.

Exhibit 14.4 Lighting Décor Ltd.: Direct Materials Purchases Budget

Direct Materials Purchases Budget
For the Year Ended December 31, 2012 (in volumes)

	Table		Floor		Desk	
	Composite (kg)	Electrical Component (kit)	Composite (kg)	Electrical Component (kit)	Composite (kg)	Electrical Component (kit)
Direct materials per lamp	0.80	1.00	1.20	1.00	0.50	1.00
Total production planned	8,750	8,750	2,250	2,250	4,900	4,900
Total direct materials to be used	7,000	8,750	2,700	2,250	2,450	4,900
Plus: Ending inventory of direct materials	700	875	270	225	245	490
Total direct materials required	7,700	9,625	2,970	2,475	2,695	5,390
Less: Beginning direct materials inventory	2,500	1,000	500	550	400	650
Direct materials to purchase	5,200	8,625	2,470	1,925	2,295	4,740

Note: The beginning inventory levels for direct materials are based on actual inventory volumes at the end of the 2011 year.

Next, the company prepared the direct materials usage budget shown in Exhibit 14.5, which reports the values of direct materials that will be used during the year. The volumes in Exhibit 14.4 are multiplied by the material costs shown in Exhibit 14.5 to determine the values.

Exhibit 14.5 Lighting Décor Ltd.: Direct Materials Usage Budget

Direct Materials Usage Budget
For the Year Ended December 31, 2012 (in dollars)

	Table		Floor		Desk		
	Composite ($)	Electrical Component ($)	Composite ($)	Electrical Component ($)	Composite ($)	Electrical Component ($)	Total
Beginning direct materials	$45,000	$5,500	$7,250	$2,613	$4,400	$2,275	$67,038
Plus purchases of direct materials	98,800	51,750	37,050	9,625	27,540	18,960	243,725
Less ending direct materials	13,300	5,250	4,050	1,125	2,940	1,960	28,625
Direct materials used	$130,500	$52,000	$40,250	$11,113	$29,000	$19,275	$282,138

*Based on the following prices:

Beginning inventory prices	$18.00	$5.50	$14.50	$4.75	$11.00	$3.50
Prices for Current Year	$19.00	$6.00	$15.00	$5.00	$12.00	$4.00

Once the direct materials usage budget is complete, the company prepared budgets for direct labour and overhead, as shown in Exhibits 14.6 and 14.7. The overhead costs are based on last year's costs, adjusted for expected changes in cost rates for 2012.

Exhibit 14.6 **Lighting Décor Ltd.: Direct Labour Budget**

Direct Labour Budget
For the Year Ended December 31, 2012

	Table	Floor	Desk	Total
Units produced (from Exhibit 14.3)	8,750	2,250	4,900	
Direct labour hours per unit (given)	0.50	0.80	0.60	
Total direct labour hours	4,375	1,800	2,940	9,115
Hourly wage rate (given)	$20	$20	$20	
Total Direct Labour Costs	$87,500	$36,000	$58,800	$ 182,300

Exhibit 14.7 **Lighting Décor Ltd.: Overhead Budget**

Manufacturing Overhead Budget
For the Year Ended December 31, 2012 (in dollars)

Indirect materials and supplies	$ 50,000
Indirect labour	45,000
Supervisory salaries	90,000
Utilities	58,000
Depreciation	75,000
Plant maintenance	35,000
Total overhead	$353,000

After completing the manufacturing overhead budget, Lighting Décor was able to determine a manufacturing cost per lamp for each style of lamp it produces, as shown in Exhibit 14.8. Then, based on the other budgets, Lighting Décor developed a budgeted cost of goods manufactured as shown in Exhibit 14.9.

Lighting Décor also incurs non-manufacturing related costs in the sale of its lamps. The budget in Exhibit 14.10 was developed to estimate the costs related to product design, marketing, distribution, customer service, and general and administrative activities. Again, these costs are based on the 2011 expenses, adjusted for expected changes in sales volumes and rates for 2012.

Lighting Décor now has all of the required information to prepare a budgeted statement of comprehensive income for the year ended December 31, 2012, as shown in Exhibit 14.11.

Exhibit 14.8 Lighting Décor Ltd.: Budgeted Manufacturing Cost per Lamp
Total Production Cost Per Lamp (in dollars)

	Table	Floor	Desk
Composite materials *	$15.20	$18.00	$ 6.00
Electrical kits *	6.00	5.00	4.00
Direct labour **	10.00	16.00	12.00
Manufacturing overhead ***	19.36	30.98	23.24
Cost per lamp	$50.56	$69.98	$45.24

*Direct material price per input × volume of direct material per unit; for example,
$19 per kg of composite for table lamps × 0.80 kg per unit = $15.20 per lamp.

**Direct labour rate of $20 per hour × # of direct labour hours per unit; for example,
$20 per hour for table lamps × 0.50 hours per lamp = $10 per lamp.

***Allocated to each production line based on direct labour hours.

	Table	Floor	Desk	Total
Total direct labour hours	4,375	1,800	2,940	9,115
Share of Total DLH	48%	20%	32%	100%
Share of Overhead	$169,432	$69,709	$113,858	$353,000
Divided by units produced	8,750	2,250	4,900	15,900
Manufacturing Overhead Rate Per Unit	$19.36	$30.98	$23.24	

Exhibit 14.9 Lighting Décor Ltd.: Budgeted Cost of Goods Manufactured
Cost of Goods Manufactured
For the Year Ended December 31, 2012

Direct material inventory at beginning, Jan 1	$67,038		From Exhibit 14.5
Purchases of direct materials	243,725		From Exhibit 14.5
Direct material available for use	310,763		
Less direct material inventory, Dec 31	28,625		From Exhibit 14.5
Direct material used in production		$282,138	From Exhibit 14.5
Direct labour		182,300	From Exhibit 14.6
Manufacturing overhead		353,000	From Exhibit 14.7
Total manufacturing costs		$817,438	
Add work-in-process inventory, Jan 1* (given)		25,000	
		$842,438	
Less work-in-process inventory, Dec 31* (given)		50,000	
Cost of goods manufactured		$792,438	

*The work-in-process costs are provided by Lighting Décor's cost accounting system and not calculated as part of the budget process in this case.

Exhibit 14.10 **Lighting Décor Ltd.: Non-Production Budget**

Non-Production Budget
For the Year Ended December 31, 2012

Product design and development	$ 18,000
Selling and marketing	48,000
Distribution	22,000
Customer service	28,000
General and administrative	42,000
Total	$ 158,000

Exhibit 14.11 **Lighting Décor Ltd.: Budgeted Statement of Comprehensive Income**

Budgeted Statement of Comprehensive Income
For the Year Ended December 31, 2012

Sales	$1,075,000	From Exhibit 14.2
Cost of goods sold		
Beginning finished goods inventory* (given)	170,800	
Cost of goods manufactured	792,438	From Exhibit 14.9
Goods available for sale	$ 963,238	
Less: Finished goods inventory†	130,764	
Cost of goods sold	$ 832,474	
Other expenses:		
Product design and development	$ 18,000	
Selling and marketing	48,000	
Distribution	22,000	From Exhibit 14.10
Customer service	28,000	
General and administrative	42,000	
Total other expenses	$ 158,000	
Net income	$ 84,527	

*The beginning finished goods inventory is provided by Lighting Décor's cost accounting system from the previous period.

†The finished goods inventory is valued as the Number of units in finished goods × Average unit cost (Table lamp = 1,500 units × $50.56 per unit = $75,840; Floor lamp = 300 units × $69.98 = $20,994; Desk lamp = 750 units × $45.24 = $33,930; Total = $75,840 + $20,994 + $33,930 = $130,764).

Budgeting for a Retail Company

Budgets for a retail company are less complex than those for a manufacturing company since they maintain only one type of inventory: a merchandise inventory. Consider Retail News, a store that sells newspapers, magazines, and convenience items. Retail News is starting its second year of operation and needs to prepare a budget for the upcoming six months. Retail News maintains inventories at the end of each month equal to the next month's sales.

Exhibit 14.12 shows the monthly sales and cost data for the first six months in Year 1. It also shows how these values are expected to change during the first six months in Year 2.

Exhibit 14.12 Retail News: Year 1 Six-Month Sales and Cost Data and Expected Changes for Year 2

	Jan.	Feb.	Mar.	Apr.	May	June	Changes for Year 2
Sales	$8,333	$10,000	$12,500	$10,000	$9,167	$7,500	Increase by 20%
Cost of sales							
Beginning inventory	$3,333	$ 4,000	$ 5,000	$ 4,000	$3,667	$3,000	
Purchases	4,000	5,000	4,000	3,667	3,000	4,000	
Ending inventory	4,000	5,000	4,000	3,667	3,000	4,000	
Cost of sales	3,333	4,000	5,000	4,000	3,667	3,000	Remains unchanged as 40% of sales
Gross profit	$5,000	$ 6,000	$ 7,500	$ 6,000	$5,500	$4,500	
Less expenses							
Salaries and wages	$1,923.08	$ 1,923.08	$ 1,923.08	$ 2,115.38	$2,115.38	$2,115.38	Increase by 4%
Selling and distribution expenses (7.5%)	625	750	937.50	750	687.50	562.50	Remains unchanged at 7.5% of sales
Rent	1,000	1,000	1,000	1,000	1,000	1,000	Remains unchanged
Electricity and telephone	476.19	476.19	476.19	476.19	476.19	476.19	Increase by 5%
Insurance	510	510	510	510	510	510	Decrease by 2% due to new contract
Depreciation	500	500	500	500	500	500	Remains unchanged
Total expenses	$5,034.27	$ 5,159.27	$ 5, 346.77	$ 5,351.58	$5,289.08	$5,164.08	
Net profit (loss)	$ (34.27)	$ 840.73	$ 2,153.23	$ 648.42	$ 210.92	$ (664.08)	

Based on the data from Exhibit 14.12, Retail News has prepared a sales and cost budget for the first six months of Year 2, as shown in Exhibit 14.13.

Exhibit 14.13 Retail News: Year 2 Six-Month Sales and Cost Budget

	Jan.	Feb.	Mar.	Apr.	May	June	Total
Sales	$10,000	$12,000	$15,000	$12,000	$11,000	$9,000	$69,000
Cost of sales							
Beginning inventory	$4,000	$4,800	$6,000	$4,800	$4,400	$3,600	
Purchases	4,800	6,000	4,800	4,400	3,600	4,800	
Ending inventory	4,800	6,000	4,800	4,400	3,600	4,800	
Cost of sales	4,000	4,800	6,000	4,800	4,400	3,600	27,600
Gross profit	$6,000	$7,200	$9,000	$7,200	$6,600	$5,400	$41,400
Less expenses							
Salaries and wages	$2,000	$2,000	$2,000	$2,200	$2,200	$2,200	$12,600
Selling and distribution expenses	750	900	1,125	900	825	675	5,175
Rent	1,000	1,000	1,000	1,000	1,000	1,000	6,000
Electricity and telephone	500	500	500	500	500	500	3,000
Insurance	500	500	500	500	500	500	3,000
Depreciation	500	500	500	500	500	500	3,000
Total expenses	$5,250	$5,400	$5,625	$5,600	$5,525	$5,375	$32,775
Net profit	$750	$1,800	$3,375	$1,600	$1,075	$25	$8,625

Budgeting for a Service Industry

Budgets prepared for a service industry are based on service levels or capacity levels, depending on which is the constraining factor for the company. It is more simplified than a manufacturing budget because you often do not need to consider inventories. Exhibit 14.14 shows some statistics that the Superior Hotel has used for its budget for next year. Both last year's and the current year's figures are shown. For ease of presentation, the budget year has been divided into four quarters, and it is assumed that there are no inventories to consider.

The hotel capacity is limited to the number of rooms, but as is common in the industry, it rarely achieves full occupancy, although there are substantial variations both during the week and at peak times. The main income drivers are the number of rooms occupied, the price charged (which can vary significantly, depending on the number of vacant rooms), and the average amount spent per customer on dining, in the bar, and on business services.

The statistical information, together with estimations of direct costs (food and drink) and expenses, is based on experience and expected cost increases. The budget for the year for the Superior Hotel, based on these assumptions, is shown in Exhibit 14.15.

Exhibit 14.14 Superior Hotel: Service Budget Example—Budget Statistics

Superior Hotel Budget Statistics	Explanation	Last Year	Current Year	Q1 Jan.– Mar.	Q2 Apr.– June	Q3 July– Sept.	Q4 Oct.– Dec.	Next Year
Number of bedrooms		80	80	80	80	80	80	80
Days per year (per quarter)		365	365	90	91	92	92	365
Rooms available	Number of days × Number of rooms	29,200	29,200	7,200	7,280	7,360	7,360	29,200
Average occupancy rate	Historical	50%	50%	40%	45%	55%	60%	
Average number of rooms occupied	Number of rooms × Occupancy rate	14,600	14,600	2,880	3,276	4,048	4,416	14,620
Average room rate	Historical/ planned	$65.00	$70.00	$70.00	$72.00	$75.00	$75.00	
Average dining cost per customer	Historical/ planned	$25.00	$25.00	$25.00	$25.00	$25.00	$25.00	
Average bar cost per customer	Historical/ planned	$ 5.00	$ 5.00	$ 5.00	$ 5.00	$ 5.00	$ 5.00	
Average business services cost per customer	Historical/ planned	$ 2.00	$ 2.00	$ 2.00	$ 2.00	$ 2.00	$ 2.00	

Exhibit 14.15 Superior Hotel: Service Budget Example

Superior Hotel Budget Items	Explanation	Last Year	Current Year	Q1 Jan.–Mar.	Q2 Apr.–June	Q3 July–Sept.	Q4 Oct.–Dec.	Next Year
Rooms	Number of rooms × Room rate	$ 949,000	$1,022,000	$201,600	$235,872	$303,600	$331,200	$1,072,272
Dining	Number of rooms × Average cost	365,000	365,000	72,000	81,900	101,200	110,400	365,500
Bar	Number of rooms × Average cost	73,000	73,000	14,400	16,380	20,240	22,080	73,100
Business services	Number of rooms × Average cost	29,200	29,200	5,760	6,552	8,096	8,832	29,240
Total income		$1,416,200	$1,489,200	$293,760	$340,704	$433,136	$472,512	$1,540,112
Expenses:								
Direct costs								
Food cost of sales	35% of dining income	$ 127,750	$ 127,750	$ 25,200	$ 28,665	$ 35,420	$ 38,640	$ 127,925
Liquor cost of sales	40% of bar income	29,200	29,200	5,760	6,552	8,096	8,832	29,240
Total cost of sales		$ 156,950	$ 156,950	$ 30,960	$ 35,217	$ 43,516	$ 47,472	$ 157,165
Salaries and wages								
Hotel staff	Increases 3% per year	$ 212,000	$ 218,360	$ 56,228	$ 56,228	$ 56,228	$ 56,228	$ 224,911
Dining/bar staff	Increases 3% per year	75,000	77,250	19,892	19,892	19,892	19,892	79,568
Office staff	Increases 4% per year	35,000	36,400	9,464	9,464	9,464	9,464	37,856
Management	Increases 5% per year	50,000	52,500	13,781	13,781	13,781	13,781	55,125

(Continued)

Exhibit 14.15 *(Continued)*

Superior Hotel Budget Items	Explanation	Last Year	Current Year	Q1 Jan.–Mar.	Q2 Apr.–June	Q3 July–Sept.	Q4 Oct.–Dec.	Next Year
Electricity & water	Historical/estimate	12,000	14,000	4,000	4,000	4,000	4,000	16,000
Laundry	Historical/estimate	8,000	9,000	2,500	2,500	2,500	2,500	10,000
Cleaning	Historical/estimate	6,000	7,000	2,000	2,000	2,000	2,000	8,000
Repairs, maintenance	Historical/estimate	12,000	20,000	4,000	4,000	4,000	4,000	16,000
Advertising, promotion	Historical/estimate	10,000	12,000	3,000	3,000	3,000	3,000	12,000
Telephones	Historical/estimate	4,000	5,000	1,500	1,500	1,500	1,500	6,000
Supplies	Historical/estimate	5,000	5,000	1,500	1,500	1,500	1,500	6,000
Other expenses	Historical/estimate	6,000	7,000	2,000	2,000	2,000	2,000	8,000
Total expenditure		$ 591,950	$ 620,460	$150,825	$155,082	$163,381	$167,337	$ 636,624
Net profit before interest		$ 824,250	$ 868,740	$142,935	$185,622	$269,755	$305,175	$ 903,488

Cash Forecasting

Once a profit budget has been constructed, it is important to understand the impact on cash flow. The purpose of the **cash forecast** is to ensure that sufficient cash is available to meet the level of activity planned by the sales and production budgets, and to meet all of the other cash inflows and outflows of the business. Cash surpluses and deficiencies need to be identified in advance to ensure effective business financing decisions regarding, for instance, raising short-term financing or investing short-term surplus funds.

There is a difference between the amount a company reports as profit and the amount reported as cash in a given accounting period. Profits and expected cash proceeds are different, due to the different treatment of the following items for financial reporting.

Item	Impact On	
	Profits	**Cash**
Revenues	Revenues that are earned but not yet paid are reported as profit in a current period.	Revenues are reported as a cash inflow when paid. Cash proceeds can include revenues paid related to sales made in current and prior periods.
Expenses	Expenses reported on the income statement are expenses incurred but they may not yet be paid by the company.	Cash disbursements for a current period can include all cash payments for expenses incurred in current and prior periods.
Non-cash expenses	Non-cash expenses such as depreciation reduce reported profit earned in a given period.	Non-cash expenses do not impact cash balances.
Capital expenditures	Capital expenditures are capitalized and expensed over the life of an asset. Only a portion of a capital asset's cost will be expensed in the current period.	The cash balance will decrease by the amount of cash paid for capital expenditures in the current period. The entire value of the purchase, if made with cash, reduces the current period's cash balance.
Loans	A receipt or payment of a loan is not reflected in the determination of profit. The only portion of a loan payment that is shown as an expense for a company is loan interest.	Loan repayments decrease cash balances and new loans increase cash balances in the current period.

Let's look again at Retail News, which we discussed previously in the section on budgeting for a retail company.

Referring to the sales budget prepared for Retail News, as shown in Exhibit 14.13, consider that the company makes half of its sales in cash and half on credit to business customers, who typically pay their accounts in the month following the sales. Credit sales in December to customers who will pay during January amount to $3,500. Retail News' sales receipts budget is shown in Exhibit 14.16.

Exhibit 14.16 Retail News: Sales Receipts Budget

	Jan.	Feb.	Mar.	Apr.	May	June	Total
50% of sales received in cash	$5,000	$ 6,000	$ 7,500	$ 6,000	$ 5,500	$ 4,500	$34,500
50% of sales on credit: 30-day terms	3,500	5,000	6,000	7,500	6,000	5,500	33,500
Total receipts	$8,500	$11,000	$13,500	$13,500	$11,500	$10,000	$68,000

We also need to determine the purchases budget for Retail News, which requires inventory equal to one month's sales (at cost) at the end of each month. The inventory at the beginning of January is $4,000. The sales and cost of sales estimated for July are $12,000 and $4,800, respectively. The purchases budget is shown in Exhibit 14.17.

Exhibit 14.17 Retail News: Purchases Budget

	Jan.	Feb.	Mar.	Apr.	May	June	Total
Inventory at end of month	$4,800	$6,000	$4,800	$4,400	$3,600	$4,800	
Inventory at beginning of month	4,000	4,800	6,000	4,800	4,400	3,600	
Increase/decrease in inventory	$ 800	$1,200	$(1,200)	$(400)	$(800)	$1,200	
Sales during month (at cost)	4,000	4,800	6,000	4,800	4,400	3,600	
Total purchases	$4,800	$6,000	$4,800	$4,400	$3,600	$4,800	$28,400

Purchases are $28,400, compared with a cost of sales of $27,600, because inventory has increased by $800 (from $4,000 to $4,800). However, purchases are on credit and Retail News has arranged with its suppliers to pay on 60-day terms. Therefore, Retail News will pay for its November purchases ($3,800) in January and its December purchases ($3,500) in February. The cash purchases budget is shown in Exhibit 14.18.

Exhibit 14.18 Retail News: Cash Purchases Budget

	Jan.	Feb.	Mar.	Apr.	May	June	Total
Payments on 60-day terms	$3,800	$3,500	$4,800	$6,000	$4,800	$4,400	$27,300

We can now construct the cash forecast for Retail News using the sales receipts budget and the cash purchases budget. We also need to identify the timing of cash flows for all expenses. In this case, we determine that salaries and wages, selling and distribution costs, and rent are all paid monthly, as those expenses are incurred. Electricity and telephone are paid twice a year, in March and June. The annual insurance premium of $6,000 is paid in January. As we know, depreciation is not an expense that involves a cash flow.

The business also has a number of other cash payments that do not, however, affect profit. These "below-the-line" payments are

- Capital expenditure of $2,500 to be paid in March
- Income tax of $5,000 due in April
- $3,000 of dividends due to be paid in June
- Loan repayment of $1,000 due in February.

The Retail News opening bank balance is $2,500. The cash forecast in Exhibit 14.19 shows the total cash position.

Exhibit 14.19 Retail News: Cash Forecast

	Jan.	Feb.	Mar.	Apr.	May	June	Total
Sales receipts	$8,500	$11,000	$13,500	$13,500	$11,500	$10,000	$68,000
Cash purchases	3,800	3,500	4,800	6,000	4,800	4,400	27,300
Salaries and wages	2,000	2,000	2,000	2,200	2,200	2,200	12,600
Selling and distribution expenses	750	900	1,125	900	825	675	5,175
Rent	1,000	1,000	1,000	1,000	1,000	1,000	6,000
Electricity, telephone, etc.			1,500			1,500	3,000
Insurance	6000						6,000
Total payments	$13,550	$7,400	$10,425	$10,100	$8,825	$9,775	$60,075
Cash flow from operations	(5,050)	3,600	3,075	3,400	2,675	225	7,925
Capital expenditure			2,500				2,500
Income tax paid				5,000			5,000
Dividends paid						3,000	3,000
Loan repayments		1,000					1,000
Net cash flow	$(5,050)	$2,600	$575	$(1,600)	$2,675	$(2,775)	$(3,575)
Opening bank balance	2,500	(2,550)	50	625	(975)	1,700	
Closing bank balance	$(2,550)	$50	$625	$(975)	$1,700	$(1,075)	

In summary, the bank balance has reduced from an asset of $2,500 to a liability (bank overdraft) of $1,075 due to a net cash outflow of $3,575. The main issue here is that, in anticipation of the overdrawn position of the bank account in January, April, and June, Retail News needs to make arrangements with its bankers to increase its overdraft or obtain a line of credit to cover these fluctuations in cash flow.

Budgeting Challenges

Although the tools of budgeting and cash forecasting are well developed and made easier by the widespread use of spreadsheet software, there are many challenges to developing good budgets.

ACCURACY IN PREDICTIONS. First and foremost, one key difficulty with budgeting is in predicting the volume of sales for the business, especially the sales mix between different products or services and the timing of income and expenses. In order to predict this accurately, a manager would need the ability to see into the future. As it is, budgeted values are only estimates based on historical performance and expected outcomes. The likelihood of the actual results of the company meeting the budget are not high. Generally, managers strive to exceed budget expectations, which creates the potential for falsifying budget information.

MOTIVATIONAL PROBLEMS. When a budget is viewed by a company as an important tool used to control and monitor a division's performance, managers may be inclined to develop budgets that are easy to achieve. For instance, companies often set budget targets for their particular departments. If a department does not meet its target, the manager of the department possibly faces a poor performance evaluation and perhaps less compensation. Due to this impending threat, managers may include budgetary slack in their plans. During the year, they might also make decisions that might not be in the best interests of their departments in order to continue to meet budget targets.

LIMITING NATURE OF BUDGETS. Budgeting has also been criticized in recent years because it can disempower the workforce by constraining and limiting innovation and change and slowing the response to market developments. When employees are limited to working within a budget or encouraged to keep specific costs at a particular level, they may not take actions that could be beneficial for the company. For example, a manager might decide not to invest in research of a new method of production, as the research costs would not be covered by the budget. This could mean that the company could lose out on the opportunity to use new processes which might decrease overall costs in future periods—all because a budget requirement had to be met.

NEGATIVE REPUTATION OF BUDGETING. Budgeting is often viewed by employees as a necessary evil, and they groan at thoughts of the budgeting process. Budgeting is seen as a restrictive tool that does not help the company but rather encourages behaviours which may not be in its the best interests. If employees feel that they must lie about costs and revenues to ensure that they receive a favourable performance evaluation, the resulting budgets are useless.

So why bother? Has budgeting been given a bad reputation, for the wrong reasons? Budgeting, overall, allows an organization to plan for their needs in terms of suppliers, materials, employees, and space. Without a budget, a company will essentially fly by the seat of its pants.

It is when companies use budgeting as a control and performance-evaluation mechanism that the issues with budgeting come into play. If employees' compensation and evaluations are not tied to a master budget, employees may feel encouraged to report accurate information for the budgets (rather than building in slack) and they might even make decisions that exceed budgetary restrictions if these decisions are in the company's long-term best interests. Overall, it is the way that companies use budgeting within the organization which has created the negative reputation that budgeting has received.

CASE IN POINT

Forecasting Charities' Revenues

Forecasting revenues is difficult enough for companies, but it is especially challenging for non-profit organizations that rely on donations, corporate sponsorships, and government grants. During tough economic times, charities' revenues often fall, while the need for their services increases. It's difficult to predict what effects a recession will have on their budgets.

A survey of more than 100 charities in Ontario in the fall of 2009, while a recession was in full swing, found that almost two-thirds reported a decline in funding over the previous 12 months, 30% said corporate sponsorships had gone down, and 68% said that the fundraising climate was worse. Meanwhile, food banks across the province saw a 25% increase in demand, and one credit counselling agency saw its number of clients grow by 45%.

To respond to the recession, nearly nine in ten Ontario charities surveyed said they had developed plans or strategies, including taking a more conservative approach to budgeting. They were exploring new revenue streams by adding or increasing social enterprise ventures, such as thrift shops; drawing on their reserve funds to stay afloat; and exploring collaboration with similar or complementary charities to cut costs and pool resources. One food bank partnered with local farmers to donate leftover produce.

By 2010, the amount of giving across the country rebounded to its pre-recession level, as Canadians donated $10.6 billion to charities, similar to the amount reported in from Statistics Canada's previous survey in 2007. But charities still face a challenging climate in which to budget with any accuracy.

Sources: Tully, J., How to adapt to the "new normal" in the voluntary sector, *The Guardian* professional blog, May 14, 2012; Grant, T., Canadians continue to give to charity despite rocky economy: Statscan, *The Globe and Mail*, March 21, 2012; Cardozo, L. R., *In challenging times: How organizations have responded to the economic downfall*, Ontario Trillium Foundation, retrieved from www.trilliumfoundation.org/en/knowledgeSharingCentre/challenging_times.asp.

CONCLUSION

In this chapter, we have linked budgeting to the strategic planning process. We described various approaches to budgeting and the mechanics of the budgeting cycle. Through a series of examples, we explored budgeting for manufacturing, service, and retail organizations. We also introduced cash forecasting, and why it is important to budget cash needs to ensure a company has appropriate working capital available for short-term needs.

The assumptions behind budgets are important for planning purposes, but crucial when assessing how well a company is achieving its overall strategies and plans. This is the process of budgetary control, which is the subject of Chapter 15.

KEY TERMS

Activity-based budget, 348

Bottom–up budgets, 348

Budget, 348

Budget cycle, 349

Budgetary slack, 351

Cash forecast, 361

Continuous budgets, 348

Incremental budgets, 348

Priority-based budgets, 348

Production budget, 351

Top–down budgets, 348

Zero-based budgeting, 348

CASE STUDY 14.1: SPORTY STORES LTD.

Sporty Stores Ltd. is a large retail store selling a range of sportswear. It wants to develop a purchases budget for the next six-month period. Its anticipated sales levels and expenses for each of the next six months are shown in Exhibit 14.20.

Exhibit 14.20 Sporty Stores: Sales and Expenses ($thousands)

	Jan.	Feb.	Mar.	Apr.	May	June	Total
Sales	$75	$80	$85	$70	$65	$90	$465
Average cost of sales (40%)	30	32	34	28	26	36	186
Gross profit	$45	$48	$51	$42	$39	$54	$279
Less: Expenses							
Salaries	$10	$10	$10	$ 8	$ 7	$10	$ 55
Rent	15	15	15	15	15	15	90
Insurance	1	1	1	1	1	1	6
Depreciation on shop fittings	2	2	2	2	2	2	12
Advertising and promotion	8	8	8	9	9	8	50
Electricity, telephone, etc.	5	5	5	5	5	5	30
Total expenses	$41	$41	$41	$40	$39	$41	$243
Net profit	$ 4	$ 7	$10	$ 2	$ 0	$13	$ 36

Although there are several hundred different inventory items and the product mix fluctuates due to seasonal factors, Sporty Stores' budget is based on an average sales mix and applies an average cost of sales of 40%.

Sporty Stores carries six weeks' inventory; that is, sufficient inventory to cover six weeks' sales (at cost). At the end of each month, therefore, the inventory held by Sporty Stores will equal all of next month's cost of sales, plus half of the following month's cost of sales. In Exhibit 14.21, for example, the inventory required at the end of February ($48,000) is the cost of sales for March ($34,000), plus half the cost of sales for April ($14,000). In order to budget for the inventory for May and June, Sporty Stores needs to estimate its sales for July and August. As this is the peak selling time, the sales are estimated at $90,000 and $85,000, respectively. The cost of sales (based on 40%) is therefore $36,000 for July and $34,000 for August. Using these figures, the inventory required at the end of June ($53,000) is equal to the cost of sales for July ($36,000) and half the cost of sales for August ($17,000).

Sporty Stores inventory valuation on January 1 is $46,000. Purchases can be calculated as

Inventory required at end of month − Inventory at beginning of month
= Increase (or decrease) in inventory
+ Cost of sales for the current month

Exhibit 14.21 shows the calculation of total purchases.

Exhibit 14.21 Sporty Stores: Inventory ($thousands)

	Jan.	Feb.	Mar.	Apr.	May	June
Inventory required at end of month	$49	$48	$41	$44	$54	$53
Inventory at beginning of month	46	49	48	41	44	54
Increase/decrease in inventory	$ 3	$(1)	$(7)	$ 3	$10	$(1)
Sales during month (at cost)	30	32	34	28	26	36
Total purchases	$33	$31	$27	$31	$36	$35

CASE STUDY 14.2: TELCON MANUFACTURING

Telcon, a manufacturing firm, has prepared a budget for the next six months, as shown in Exhibit 14.22. The company wants to determine the total purchases of raw materials that will be required during the next six months based on its budget.

Exhibit 14.22 **Telcon Manufacturing: Budget ($thousands)**

	Jan.	Feb.	Mar.	Apr.	May	June	Total
Sales units	1,000	1,100	1,200	1,200	1,300	1,300	7,100
Expected selling price	$10	$10	$10	$10	$10	$11	
Revenue	$10,000	$11,000	$12,000	$12,000	$13,000	$14,300	$72,300
Cost of sales							
Direct materials @ $4 (2 kg @ $2)	$4,000	$4,400	$4,800	$4,800	$5,200	$5,200	$28,400
Direct labour @ $2.50	2,500	2,750	3,000	3,000	3,250	3,250	17,750
Variable overhead @ $1	1,000	1,100	1,200	1,200	1,300	1,300	7,100
Variable costs	$7,500	$8,250	$9,000	$9,000	$9,750	$9,750	$53,250
Contribution margin	$2,500	$2,750	$3,000	$3,000	$3,250	$4,550	$19,050
Total fixed costs	1,500	1,500	1,500	1,500	1,500	1,500	9,000
Net profit	$1,000	$1,250	$1,500	$1,500	$1,750	$3,050	$10,050

Telcon estimates its sales for July and August as 1,400 units per month. Its production budget is based on needing to maintain one month's inventory of finished goods; that is, the cost of sales for the following month. Its finished goods inventory at the beginning of January is 1,000 units. Exhibit 14.23 shows that the production required, $56,250, is greater than the cost of sales of $53,250 because of the need to produce an additional 400 units at a variable cost of $7.50; that is, an increase in inventory of $3,000.

Exhibit 14.23 **Telcon Manufacturing: Production Budget**

	Jan.	Feb.	Mar.	Apr.	May	June	Total
Variable costs per unit	$7.50	$7.50	$7.50	$7.50	$7.50	$7.50	$7.50
Inventory—end of month	1,100	1,200	1,200	1,300	1,300	1,400	
Inventory—beginning of month	1,000	1,100	1,200	1,200	1,300	1,300	
Increase in inventory	100	100	0	100	0	100	
Units to be sold	1,000	1,100	1,200	1,200	1,300	1,300	
Total units to be produced	1,100	1,200	1,200	1,300	1,300	1,400	
Units produced @ variable cost	$8,250	$9,000	$9,000	$9,750	$9,750	$10,500	$56,250
Production cost breakdown:							
Materials @ $4	4,400	4,800	4,800	5,200	5,200	5,600	30,000
Labour @ $2.50	2,750	3,000	3,000	3,250	3,250	3,500	18,750
Variable overhead @ $1	1,100	1,200	1,200	1,300	1,300	1,400	7,500
Total production cost	$8,250	$9,000	$9,000	$9,750	$9,750	$10,500	$56,250

However, in order to produce the finished goods, Telcon must also ensure that it has purchased sufficient raw materials. Again, it wants to have one month's inventory of raw materials (2 kg of the materials are required for each unit of finished goods). There are 2,000 units of raw materials at the beginning of January. Exhibit 14.24 shows the materials purchases budget.

Exhibit 14.24 **Telcon Manufacturing: Materials Purchases Budget**

	Jan.	Feb.	Mar.	Apr.	May	June	Total
Total units to be produced	1,100	1,200	1,200	1,300	1,300	1,400	
Total kg of materials (Units × 2 kg)	2,200	2,400	2,400	2,600	2,600	2,800	
Inventory units at end of month	2,400	2,400	2,600	2,600	2,800	2,800	
Inventory units at beginning of month	2,000	2,400	2,400	2,600	2,600	2,800	
Increase in inventory	400	0	200	0	200	0	
Total kg to be purchased	2,600	2,400	2,600	2,600	2,800	2,800	
Purchase cost @ $2/kg	$5,200	$4,800	$5,200	$5,200	$5,600	$5,600	$31,600

The purchases budget of $31,600 is more than the materials usage of $30,000 from the production budget because an additional 800 kg of materials is bought at $2 per kg (that is, $1,600), due to the need to increase the raw materials inventory.

■ SELF-TEST QUESTIONS

S14.1 A company's annual sales budget is for 120,000 units, spread equally throughout the year. It needs to have 1½-month's inventory at the end of each month. If opening inventory is 12,000 units, the number of units to be produced in the first month of the budget year is

a. 10,000

b. 12,000

c. 6,000

d. 13,000

S14.2 Carton Captain manufactures cartons. It expects to sell 350,000 cartons in 2012. The company has enough beginning inventory of direct materials on hand to make 50,000 cartons. The company has 40,000 finished cartons in its beginning inventory and a target ending inventory of 60,000 cartons. Each carton uses 5 grams of direct materials. How many grams of direct materials does Carton Captain need to purchase in 2012?

a. 1,600,000 g

b. 350,000 g

c. 360,000 g

d. 1,800,000 g

S14.3 The standard costs for a manufacturing business are $12 per unit for direct materials, $8 per unit for direct labour, and $5 per unit for manufacturing overhead. The sales projection is for 5,000 units: 3,500 units need to be in inventory at the end of the period and 1,500 units are in inventory at the beginning of the period. The production budget will show costs for that period of

a. $175,000

b. $150,000

c. $140,000

d. $125,000

S14.4 Bobby Jones Inc. is planning sales of 55,000 units for the next three months. The company has a beginning inventory of 10,000 units and would like to have an ending inventory of 15,000 at the end of the three months. It requires 4 kg of direct materials to make 1 unit of finished product. The opening inventory of direct materials is 50,000 kg and the target ending inventory is 60,000 kg. How many kilograms of direct materials does Bobby Jones need to purchase for the three-month period?

a. 250,000 kg

b. 60,000 kg

c. 110,000 kg

d. 132,000 kg

Use the following data to answer questions S14.5 through S14.7.

Munch Enterprises makes a small toy car that is voice activated. Projected sales for the next four months are

Month	Planned Sales (Units)
April	5,500
May	6,500
June	4,500
July	5,600

The cars sell for $35 each. To produce each car requires $12.50 in direct materials and $6.00 in direct labour. Fixed overhead costs related to manufacturing the car are $10,000 per month, while variable overhead is $4.50 per car. Munch normally produces a month's supply of inventory to ensure that it will not fall short in case sales are unexpectedly high. At the end of March, for instance, the company will have inventory to cover April sales.

S14.5 What is Munch's expected profit for April?

a. $192,500

b. $56,000

c. $66,000

d. $59,000

S14.6 The production budget for cars for May (in units) is

a. 6,500

b. 11,000

c. 4,500

d. 10,100

S14.7 The total cost of goods sold for June is

a. $103,500

b. $128,800

c. $157,500

d. $232,300

S14.8 If accounts receivables increase by $15,000 and accounts payables increase by $11,000, the effect on cash flow is

a. Increase of $26,000

b. Increase of $4,000

c. Decrease of $4,000

d. Decrease of $26,000

S14.9 April Co. receives payment from customers for credit sales as follows:

- 30% in the month of sale

- 60% in the month following sale

- 8% in the second month following the sale

- 2% become bad debts and are never collected

The following sales are expected:

January	$100,000
February	$120,000
March	$110,000

How much will be received in March?

a. $96,000

b. $113,000

c. $30,000

d. $110,000

Use the following data to answer questions S14.10 and S14.11.

Grobots Company prepared the following information for the upcoming four month period:

Month	Budgeted Sales
January	$75,000
February	78,000
March	90,000
April	110,000

Budgeted Expenses per Month

Salaries	$25,000	Selling Costs	$20,000
Depreciation	$ 5,000	Insurance	$ 3,000

Salaries and selling costs are paid during the month they are incurred. Insurance is paid quarterly on March 31, June 30, September 30, and Dec 31.

Sales are collected as follows: 30% in the month of sale, 65% in the month after sale, and 5% are uncollectable. Purchases are 30% of sales of a given month and are paid in full the following month.

S14.10 Calculate the cash disbursements for March.

a. $81,000

b. $71,400

c. $82,400

d. $77,400

S14.11 Calculate the cash receipts for April.

a. $110,000

b. $91,500

c. $96,000

d. $68,400

■ PROBLEMS

P14.1 *(Profit Budget and Cash Forecast)* Creassos Ltd. was formed in July 2012 with $20,000 of capital. $7,500 of this was used to purchase equipment. The owner budgeted for the following:

	Sales	Receipts of Accounts Receivable	Purchases	Payments on Accounts Payable	Wages	Other Expenses
July	$20,000	—	$ 8,000	$ 5,000	$3,000	$2,000
Aug.	30,000	$20,000	15,000	10,000	4,000	2,000
Sept.	40,000	30,000	20,000	20,000	5,000	3,000

Wages and other expenses are paid in cash. In addition to the above, depreciation is $2,400 per year. No inventory is held by the company.

a. Calculate the profit for each of the three months from July through September and the total profit for the three months.

b. Calculate the cash balance at the end of each month.

c. Prepare a statement of financial position at the end of September.

P14.2 *(Profit Budget)* Highjinks Corporation's sales department has estimated revenue of $2,250,000 for your division. 60% of this will be achieved in the first half-year and 40% in the remaining half-year. Variable operating costs are typically 30% of revenue and fixed operating costs are expected to be $35,000 per month for the first six months and $40,000 per month thereafter.

The selling expense allocated to your department from the sales department is $15,000 per month for the first half-year; thereafter, $12,000. Salaries are $25,000 per month, depreciation is $5,000 per month, and rent is $8,000 per month. Light, heat, and power are expected to cost $3,000 per month for the first half-year, falling to $2,000 thereafter.

a. Construct a budget for the year based on the above figures.

b. What can you say about the rate of gross profit?

P14.3 *(Profit Budget and Cash Forecast)* Griffin Metals Co. has provided the following data:

Anticipated volumes (assume production equals sales each quarter):
Quarter 1   100,000 tonnes
Quarter 2   110,000 tonnes
Quarter 3   105,000 tonnes
Quarter 4   120,000 tonnes

The selling price is expected to be $300 per tonne for the first six months and $310 per tonne thereafter. Variable costs per tonne are predicted as $120 in the first quarter, $125 in the second and third quarters, and $130 in the fourth quarter.

Fixed costs (in $'000 per quarter) are estimated as follows:

Salaries and wages	$3,000 for the first half-year, increasing by 10% for the second half-year
Maintenance	$1,500
Rates	$400
Insurance	$120
Electricity	$1,000
Depreciation	$5,400
Other costs	$2,500 in the first and fourth quarters, $1,800 in the second and third quarters
Interest	$600
Capital expenditure	$6,500 in the first quarter, $2,000 in the second quarter, $1,000 in the third quarter, and $9,000 in the fourth quarter
Dividend payment	$10,000 in the third quarter
Debt repayments	$1,000 in the first quarter, $5,000 in the second quarter, $4,000 in the third quarter and $3,000 in the fourth quarter

Griffin has asked you to produce a profit budget and a cash forecast for the year (in four quarters) using the above data.

P14.4 *(Budget Information for Strategic Planning)* Mega Stores is a chain of 125 retail outlets selling clothing under the strong Mega brand. Its sales have increased from $185 million to $586 million over the last five years. The company's gross profit is currently 17% of sales, giving it a little more than 20% mark-up on the cost of goods and retail store running costs. Corporate overhead is $19 million and the operating profit is $81 million.

Mega Stores' finance director has produced a budget, which has been approved by the board of directors, to increase sales by 35% next year and to improve operating profit margin to 15% of sales. Corporate overhead costs will be contained at $22 million.

The marketing director's strategy is to continue expanding the company's sales by winning market share from competitors and by increasing the volume of sales to existing customers. It aims to increase its direct mailing of catalogues to customers and its television advertising. The company also intends to open new stores to extend its geographic coverage.

Mega Stores also plans to improve its cost-effectiveness by continuing its investments in major regional warehouses and distribution facilities servicing its national network of stores, together with upgrading its information systems to reduce inventory and delivery lead times to its retail network.

a. Produce a report for the senior management team identifying the financial information that is required to support the business strategy.

b. Identify any non-financial issues arising from the strategy.

P14.5 *(Interpreting Budget Information and Identifying Errors)* Carson's is a retail store that has given the task of preparing its budget for next year to a trainee accountant. The budget is prepared in quarters. The following is the profit budget report produced by the trainee.

In $thousands	Quarter 1	Quarter 2	Quarter 3	Quarter 4	Year Total
Sales	$100	$110	$110	$120	$440
Cost of sales	40	44	44	48	176
Gross profit	$ 60	$ 66	$ 66	$ 72	$264

(continued)

(*continued*)

Expenses:

Salaries	$10	$ 10	$ 10	$ 10	$ 40
Rent	20	20	20	20	80
Depreciation	5	5	5	5	20
Promotional expenses	10	11	11	12	44
Administration expenses	5	5	5	5	20
Total expenses	$ 50	$ 51	$ 51	$ 52	$204
Net profit	$ 10	$ 15	$ 15	$ 20	$ 60

A cash forecast was also prepared, as follows:

In $thousands	Quarter 1	Quarter 2	Quarter 3	Quarter 4	Year Total
Cash inflow from sales	$100	$110	$110	$120	$440
Purchases		$ 40	$ 44	$ 44	$128
Expenses	$ 50	51	51	52	204
Capital expenditure		20			20
Income tax			20		20
Dividends		15	20	25	60
Cash outflow	$ 50	$126	$135	$121	$432
Net cash flow	$ 50	$(16)	$(25)	$(1)	$ 8
Cumulative cash flow	$ 50	$ 34	$ 9	$ 8	

a. What questions would you want to ask the trainee accountant in order to satisfy yourself that the budget was realistic and achievable?

b. Can you identify any errors that have been made in the budget or cash forecast? If so, make any corrections that you think are necessary and comment on any problems you have identified.

P14.6 (*Budgeted Contribution Margin and Product Mix Decisions*) Jaguar Hotel Corporation has a hotel, dining room, and conference centre facility. The accountant has presented the following budget data:

	Hotel	**Dining Room**	**Conference Centre**
Capacity	100 rooms	100 seats	200 seats
Selling price/unit	$75	$35	$40
Material costs/unit	$5 laundry	$15 food	$5 refreshments
Other variable costs/unit	$5 cleaning	$10 labour	$1 light & heat

a. Produce a budget that shows the contribution for each of the three facilities. Rank the three facilities based on the greatest contributions to profitability. What are the constraints?

b. The marketing manager has asked your advice as to whether to accept *either* 200 people attending a conference and staying for dinner in two sittings but with no hotel accommodation (which will make it very difficult to sell hotel rooms) *or* to refuse the conference booking but to maintain the average 60% hotel occupancy, of which half use the dining room.

P14.7 (*Forecasting Cash Balance*) Jethro Turnbull Ltd. is a privately owned business. It has budgeted for profits of $125,000 (after deducting depreciation of $35,000). Accounts receivable are expected to increase by $20,000, inventory is planned to increase by $5,000, and accounts payable should increase by $8,000. Capital expenditure is planned of $50,000, income tax of $35,000 has to be paid, and loan repayments are due that total $25,000. What is the forecast cash position of Jethro Turnbull at the end of the budget year, assuming a current bank overdraft of $15,000?

P14.8 (*Interpreting Budget Information*) Bridgeport Ltd. has produced the following summary profit budget and cash forecast for the next six months.

Bridgeport Ltd.: Profit Budget ($thousands)

	Jan.	Feb.	Mar.	Apr.	May	June
Sales	$1,000	$1,000	$1,000	$2,000	$2,000	$2,000
Cost of sales	400	400	400	800	800	800
Gross profit	600	600	600	1,200	1,200	1,200
Overheads	350	350	350	350	350	350
Net profit	$ 250	$ 250	$ 250	$ 850	$ 850	$ 850

Cash forecast ($thousands)

	Jan.	Feb.	Mar.	Apr.	May	June
Net profit	$ 250	$ 250	$ 250	$ 850	$ 850	$ 850
Capital expenditure	(100)			(250)		
Loan repayment					(400)	
Cash flow	$ 150	$ 250	$ 250	$ 600	$ 450	$ 850

a. What assumptions can you make about the business based on these figures?

b. What questions would you want to ask in relation to the figures?

P14.9 (*Profit Budget, Cash Forecast, and DCF Analysis*) Phonic Solutions is considering creating a new division, which will require an investment in computer and telecommunications equipment of $10 million. The company has a cost of capital of 12%.

The sales department has forecast sales for each of the next five years for this new division as follows:

Year 1	$4 million
Year 2	$6 million
Year 3	$8 million
Year 4	$6 million
Year 5	$4 million

Operations staff has predicted the cost of sales as 30% of revenue. Rent and office expenses are $300,000 each year. Selling and administration salaries will be $400,000 in the first year, increasing each year by 5%. Repairs & maintenance will be $100,000 in each of Years 1 and 2, $200,000 in each of Years 3 and 4, and $300,000 in Year 5. The company depreciates its equipment over four years.

a. Produce the following:

- Profit budget for each of the five years, showing both gross profit and operating profit
- Cash flow for each of the five years
- Discounted cash flow analysis and use this to recommend whether the new division and capital investment should proceed

b. What does theory tell us about the strengths and limitations of budgeting and the discounted cash flow technique?

P14.10 *(Comprehensive Budgeting for a Manufacturing Company)* The following budget information has been compiled for Julius Jones Jeans, the manufacturer of the JJ Jean, for the year ended December 31, 2012.

2012 Expected sales (pairs of jeans)	50,000
January 2012 Opening finished goods inventory (pairs)	12,000
Target Dec 31, 2012 Finished goods inventory (pairs)	15,000
January 2012 Opening finished goods inventory	$720,000
January 2012 Opening work-in-process inventory	$8,500
December 31 Target Work-in-process inventory	$15,500
Selling price (per pair)	$125

Information related to production of jeans:

	Quantity Required for 1 Pair	Opening Inventory	Closing Inventory	Opening Inventory Cost	2012 Costs
Fabric (metres)	1.6	8,500	15,000	$8/metre	$9/metre
Buttons	6	58,000	75,000	$0.25/button	$0.35/button
Labour hours	2.5				$15/hour

Other costs for 2012 (budgeted amount)

Indirect materials	$52,000
Indirect labour	48,000
Production salaries	125,000
Materials handling	38,000
Utilities	189,000
Rent	198,000
Depreciation	15,000
Selling and administrative costs	155,000

Prepare the following budgets for 2012:

- Production budget
- Direct materials budget
- Direct labour budget
- Overhead budget
- Non-production budget
- Budgeted cost of goods sold
- Budgeted statement of comprehensive income

REFERENCES

Anthony, R. N., and Govindarajan, V. (2000). *Management control systems* (10th international ed.). New York, NY: McGraw-Hill Irwin.

Budgetary Control

LEARNING OBJECTIVES

After reading this chapter, you should be able to answer the following questions:

- What is budgetary control and why it is important in the overall performance management process?

- How is a flexible budget different from a master budget?

- What are the key variances that companies identify when analyzing flexible budget results?

- How are variances interpreted?

- How does a company utilize variance information to provide better cost control?

In this chapter, we describe how budgetary control takes place in organizations through the techniques of flexible budgets and variance analysis. A detailed example of variance analysis is provided that demonstrates the key variances which organizations monitor. The chapter also considers how cost control can be exercised in practice.

What Is Budgetary Control?

Budgetary control is concerned with ensuring that actual financial results are in line with targets. An important part of this feedback process is investigating variations between actual results and budgeted results, and taking appropriate corrective action. Budgetary control provides a yardstick for comparison and isolates problems by focusing on variances, which provide an early warning to managers.

A typical actual versus budget financial report is shown in Exhibit 15.1. In this exhibit, the variances are identified as "F" or "U":

- A **favourable variance** (F) occurs when income exceeds budget and/or expenses are lower than budget.

- An **unfavourable variance** (U) occurs when income is less than budget and/or expenses are greater than budget.

Exhibit 15.1 Actual v. Budget Financial Report

	Actual	Budget	Variance
Materials	$ 96,000	$100,000	$4,000 F
Labour costs	32,000	30,000	2,000 U
Overhead costs	38,000	40,000	2,000 F
Other costs	55,000	50,000	5,000 U
Total	$221,000	$220,000	$1,000 U

The weakness of traditional management reports for the purpose of budgetary control is that the business may not be comparing apples with apples. For example, if the business volume is lower than budgeted, then it follows that any variable costs should (in total) be lower than budgeted. Although this represents a favourable variance, it is not necessarily a favourable situation (i.e., sales income is lower than planned). Conversely, if business volume is higher than budget, variable costs should (in total) be higher than budget. In many management reports, the distinction between variable and fixed costs is not made, and it is very difficult to compare costs incurred at one level of activity with budgeted costs at a different level of activity, and to make judgments about managerial performance.

Flexible Budgeting

In a **flexible budget**, budgeted (or standard) costs per unit are applied to the actual level of business activity. Flexible budgets provide a better basis for investigating variances than the original budget, because the volume of production may differ from that planned. If the actual activity level is different from the budgeted level, comparing revenue and/or costs at different (actual and budget) levels of activity will produce meaningless figures. For example, it makes little sense to compare the budgeted costs of producing 40,000 units with the costs incurred in producing 35,000 units.

Variance analysis is carried out between the flexible budget costs and actual costs. Flexible budgets take into account variations in the volume of activity. For example, assume direct materials are budgeted at $2 per unit for 40,000 units but actual costs are $2.10 for 35,000 units. A standard actual report versus a budget report will show the following:

Actual	Budget	Variance
$73,500	$80,000	$6,500 F
35,000 @ $2.10	40,000 @ $2.00	

The favourable variance disguises the fact that fewer units were produced. A flexible budget, on the other hand, adjusts the original budget to the actual level of activity. The flexible budget variance would be shown as follows:

Actual	Flexible Budget Variance	Flexible Budget	Volume Variance	Master Budget
$73,500	$3,500 U	$70,000	$10,000 F	$80,000
35,000 @ $2.10		35,000 @ $2.00		40,000 @ $2.00

This is a more meaningful comparison since it provides two reasons for the overall variance of $6,500 F. First, the $3,500 unfavourable flexible budget variance shows that the materials purchased were more costly than expected, which may be due to poor purchasing negotiations by the purchasing manager or a market increase in product costs. Second, the $10,000 favourable volume variance was due to the fact that 5,000 fewer units were produced. This is likely due to decisions made by the operations manager, who decides on the quantity of product to manufacture. As you can see, separating the total variance into its components helps identify the cause of the variance and assign responsibility to the appropriate manager.

Variance Analysis

Variance analysis involves comparing actual performance to the budget, investigating the causes of the variance, and taking corrective action to ensure that targets are achieved, or adjusted if they are not appropriate. Not only unfavourable variances need to be investigated. Favourable variances also need to be reviewed as they can provide a learning opportunity that can be repeated, or they can sometimes result in an undesirable outcome in other cost areas, as you will see.

Only significant variations from budget require investigation. However, what is significant can be interpreted differently by different people. Which is more significant, for example, a 5% variation on $10,000 ($500) or a 25% variation on $1,000 ($250)? The significance of the variation may be either an absolute amount or a percentage. Similarly, a one-off variance requires a single corrective action, but a variance that will continue requires more drastic action.

Some key indicators that a variance should be investigated include the following:

- The variance is significant in terms of absolute dollar value and/or percentage.
- The variance will likely occur again.

- The cause of the variance is not easily identifiable.
- The variance can be controlled through changes made to production processes, supplier selection processes, product-mix planning, marketing efforts, or other changes to the organization's operational plans and strategies.

Four main types of variances will be reviewed in this chapter:

1. Sales variances: price and quantity variances
2. Direct material variances: price and efficiency variances
3. Labour variances: rate and efficiency variances
4. Overhead variances: variable spending and efficiency variances, and fixed spending and production volume variances

Consider Wood's Furniture, a company that manufactures household furniture. Woods has produced an actual versus budget report, which is shown in Exhibit 15.2. The difference between actual and budget is an unfavourable variance of $16,200. However, the firm's accountant has also produced a flexible budget to assist in carrying out a more meaningful variance analysis. This is shown in Exhibit 15.3.

Exhibit 15.2 Wood's Furniture: Actual v. Budget Report

	Actual	Budget	Total Variance
Sales units	9,000	10,000	
Selling price	$ 175	$ 170	
Revenue	$1,575,000	$1,700,000	$125,000 U
Variable costs:			
Materials			
Plastic	$ 26,600	$ 30,000	$ 3,400 F
Metal	21,000	20,000	1,000 U
Wood	26,600	30,000	3,400 F
Labour			
Skilled	$ 838,750	$ 900,000	$ 61,250 F
Semi-skilled	195,000	225,000	30,000 F
Variable overhead	283,250	300,000	16,750 F
Total variable costs	$1,391,200	$1,505,000	$113,800 F
Contribution margin	$ 183,800	$ 195,000	$ 11,200 U
Fixed costs	130,000	125,000	5,000 U
Net profit	$ 53,800	$ 70,000	$ 16,200 U

The flexible budget shows a favourable variance of $3,300, compared to the flexible budget. This overall variance is made up of individual variances for sales and costs, which are discussed next.

Exhibit 15.3 **Wood's Furniture: Variance Report with Flexible Budget**

	Actual	Sales Price Variance/ Flexible Budget Variance	Flexible Budget	Sales Quantity Variance/ Volume Variance	Master Budget
Sales units	9,000		9,000		10,000
Revenue	$1,575,000	$45,000 F	$1,530,000	$170,000 U	$1,700,000
Variable costs:					
Materials					
Plastic	$ 26,600	$ 400 F	$ 27,000	$ 3,000 F	$ 30,000
Metal	21,000	3,000 U	18,000	2,000 F	20,000
Wood	26,600	400 F	27,000	3,000 F	30,000
Total direct materials:	$ 74,200	$ 2,200 U	$ 72,000	$ 8,000 F	$ 80,000
Labour					
Skilled	$ 838,750	$28,750 U	$ 810,000	$ 90,000 F	$ 900,000
Semi-skilled	195,000	7,500 F	202,500	22,500 F	225,000
Total labour	$1,033,750	$21,250 U	$1,012,500	$112,500 F	$1,125,000
Variable overhead	283,250	13,250 U	270,000	30,000 F	300,000
Total variable costs	$1,391,200	$36,700 U	$1,354,500	$150,500 F	$1,505,000
Contribution margin	$ 183,800	$ 8,300 U	$ 175,500	$ 19,500 U	$ 195,000
Fixed costs	130,000	5,000 U	125,000	0	125,000
Net profit	$ 53,800	$ 3,300 F	$ 50,500	$ 19,500 U	$ 70,000

Sales Variance

The sales variance is used to evaluate the performance of the sales team. The total **sales variance**—the difference between the budgeted sales and the actual sales, or in this case $125,000—is made up of two variances:

- The **sales price variance** is the difference between the actual price and the standard price for the actual quantity sold. This variance identifies the portion of the total variance that is related to changes in selling price.

- The **sales quantity variance** is the difference between the budget and actual quantity sold at the budgeted selling price. This variance shows the portion of the total variance that is due to selling more or less than planned.

Exhibit 15.3 shows the sales price variance as the difference between the flexible budget and the actual sales revenue: that is, $45,000. The variance is favourable because the business has sold 9,000 units at an additional $5 each. The sales quantity variance shown in Exhibit 15.3 is $170,000 U. The variance is unfavourable because the budgeted 1,000 units have not been sold, resulting in lost sales of $170,000.

We have now accounted for the variance between the original budget and the flexible budget (that is, due to volume of units sold), and between the revenue in the flexible budget and the actual (that is, due to the difference in selling price). We now have to look at the variances between the costs in the flexible budget and the actual costs incurred.

Cost Variances

Each cost variance—for materials, labour, and overhead—can be split into two types: a flexible budget variance and a volume variance, as shown in Exhibit 15.4. The **flexible budget variance** is the difference between the actual costs and the costs determined by the flexible budget. The **volume variance** is the difference between the flexible budget and the master budget, as this variance is attributable to a difference in the volume of product produced and sold.

Exhibit 15.4 **Flexible Budget and Volume Variances**

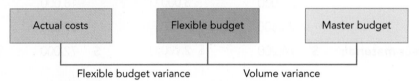

Flexible budget and volume variances for Wood's Furniture are shown in Exhibit 15.3. For example, the direct materials flexible budget variance for plastic is $400 F and the direct materials volume variance for plastic is $3,000 F. To provide more meaning to these variances and to assign responsibility for the variance more specifically within the organization, the flexible budget variance can be broken down further into price and efficiency variances. This is necessary since each type of variance may be the responsibility of a different manager.

Price variances (also called *rate* or *spending variances*) occur because the cost per unit of resources is higher or lower than the standard cost. **Efficiency variances** (also called *usage variances*) occur because the actual quantity of materials, labour, or machine hours used is higher or lower than a company planned to use in the production process. The flexible budget variance is broken down into its price and efficiency variances, as shown in Exhibit 15.5.

Exhibit 15.5 **Price and Efficiency Variances**

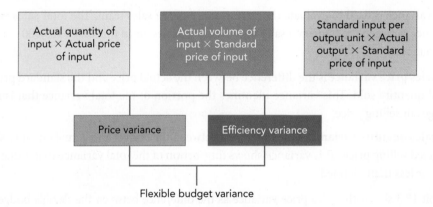

In looking at Exhibit 15.5, it is important to note the difference between inputs and outputs. **Inputs** are the quantity of materials, machine hours, and/or labour used to make the actual output. Inputs are measures, such as kilograms of direct materials, metres of direct materials, machine hours, and/or labour hours. **Outputs** are the final product of the manufacturing process.

The price and efficiency variances that are normally calculated for a manufacturing company are as follows:

1. **Direct materials (DM) price variance** occurs when the actual price of an input is less or more than the standard price of the input.

$$\text{DM price variance} = [\text{Actual inputs} \times \text{Actual price per input}]$$
$$- [\text{Actual inputs} \times \text{Standard price per input}]$$

2. **Direct materials (DM) efficiency variance** occurs when there is a difference between the actual inputs used and what is expected, as outlined in a standard cost card. For example, if a company should use only 1.5 metres of fabric to make a shirt as per a cost card but actually uses 1.8 metres in the product, an unfavourable efficiency variance would result.

$$\text{DM efficiency variance} = [\text{Actual inputs} \times \text{Standard price per input}]$$
$$- [\text{Standard inputs allowed for actual output}$$
$$\times \text{Standard price per input}]$$

3. **Direct labour (DL) rate variance** occurs when the labour rate paid to staff is more or less than planned.

$$\text{DL rate variance} = [\text{Actual labour hours} \times \text{Actual labour rate}]$$
$$- [\text{Actual labour hours} \times \text{Standard labour rate per hour}]$$

4. **Direct labour (DL) efficiency variance** occurs when the actual labour hours used to make a product are less or more than was expected on the standard cost card for a product.

$$\text{DL efficiency variance} = [\text{Actual labour hours} \times \text{Standard labour rate/hour}]$$
$$- [\text{Actual standard labour hours allowed for actual output}$$
$$\times \text{Standard labour rate/hour}]$$

5. **Variable overhead spending variance** occurs if the actual overhead costs are more or less than the standard overhead rate multiplied by the actual volume of the overhead allocation base. For instance, if a company applies overhead on the basis of direct labour hours at a rate of $2 per direct labour hour, it will record $2 for every actual labour hour that is worked. If the actual overhead costs are less or more than this assigned value, a variance will occur.

$$\text{Variable overhead spending variance} = \text{Actual overhead}$$
$$- [\text{Actual overhead allocation base}$$
$$\times \text{Standard overhead rate}]$$

6. **Variable overhead efficiency variance** occurs if the actual allocation base is more or less than the standard allocation base allowed on the cost card for a product. For instance, if the cost card states that each product produced would take two direct labour hours, but the company used three direct labour hours per unit, this would result in an unfavourable variable overhead efficiency variance.

$$\text{Variable overhead efficiency variance} = [\text{Actual allocation base} \times \text{Standard overhead rate}]$$
$$- [\text{Standard allocation base allowed for actual output}$$
$$\times \text{Standard overhead rate}]$$

7. **Fixed overhead spending variance** occurs due to a difference in the actual fixed overhead as compared to the budgeted overhead.

$$\text{Fixed overhead spending variance} = \text{Actual Fixed Overhead} - \text{Budgeted Fixed Overhead}$$

8. **Fixed production volume variance** occurs due to a difference in the volume of product that is produced as compared to budget. Fixed overhead costs are fixed and do not change with changes in units sold or produced. However, overhead is normally applied to units produced each period based on a standard fixed overhead rate. The production volume variance is the difference between the budgeted total fixed overhead costs and the overhead that is applied. The overhead applied is the standard fixed overhead rate × actual production. A favourable variance occurs if the company produces more units than planned. An unfavourable variance occurs if the company makes fewer units than planned.

$$\begin{aligned} \text{Fixed production volume variance} = {}& \text{Budgeted fixed overhead} \\ &- \big[\text{Actual units produced} \\ &\quad \times \text{Standard fixed overhead rate}\big] \end{aligned}$$

To undertake a detailed variance analysis for Wood's Furniture, we need some additional information regarding the materials, labour, and overhead costs, which the accountant has produced in Exhibit 15.6.

Exhibit 15.6 Variance Information

	Standard Usage and Cost per Input Unit	Actual Cost per Input Unit	Actual Quantity of Input Unit used to Make 9,000 Units
Materials			
Plastic	2 kg @ $1.50	$ 1.40	19,000
Metal	1 kg @ $2.00	$ 2.10	10,000
Wood	4 kg @ $0.75	$ 0.70	38,000
Labour			
Skilled	6 hours @ $15.00	$15.25	55,000
Semi-skilled	3 hours@ $7.50	$ 7.50	26,000
Variable overhead	6 labour hours @ $5.00	$ 5.15	55,000

Materials Variances

The total flexible budget variance for materials is $2,200 U, as shown in Exhibit 15.3. However, we need to consider the price and usage variances for each type of material, because the reasons for the variance and the corrective action may be different for each.

MATERIALS PRICE VARIANCE

Using the format of Exhibit 15.5, the price variance for each of the three materials is shown in Exhibit 15.7. While holding the (actual) quantity constant, we can see the effect of price fluctuations. Both plastic and wood have been bought below the standard price, while metal has cost more than standard.

Exhibit 15.7 **Direct Materials Price Variances**

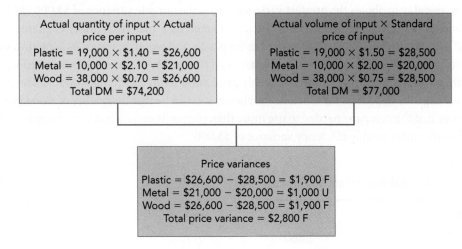

Materials price variances, in general, may be the result of

- Changes in supplier prices not yet reflected in the bill of materials
- Poor or more effective purchasing activities

MATERIALS EFFICIENCY VARIANCE

Again using the format of Exhibit 15.5, we can calculate the efficiency variance for each of the three materials. This is shown in Exhibit 15.8. In each case, while holding the (standard) price constant, there has been a higher than expected usage of materials, resulting in unfavourable variances for all three materials. These efficiency variances may be the result of

- Poor productivity
- Out-of-date bill of materials
- Poor-quality materials

Exhibit 15.8 **Direct Materials Efficiency Variances**

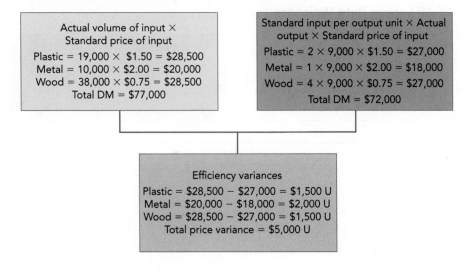

In total, the materials variance is $2,200 U, as shown in Exhibit 15.9. We can see that, of the three materials, metal contributes the greatest variance—an unfavourable variance of $3,000 ($2,000 efficiency and $1,000 price), which needs to be investigated as a matter of priority. There may be a trade-off between the price and usage variances for plastic and wood, however, as sometimes quality and price can conflict with each other. For instance, if the quality of the wood purchased was lower than planned, this might result in the favourable price variance of $1,900 for wood. However, it also can have a negative impact on the efficiency variance. It could be that the quality of wood purchased was so poor that the company needed to use more than planned (some wood was scrapped), and this resulted in the unfavourable efficiency variance of $5,000.

Exhibit 15.9 **Total Materials Variance**

Efficiency	$5,000 U
Price	2,800 F
Total	$2,200 U

Labour Variances

The total flexible budget variance for labour is an unfavourable $21,250, as shown in Exhibit 15.3. Similar to materials, we need to look at the efficiency variance (which may indicate productivity) and the rate variance for each of the two types of labour.

LABOUR RATE VARIANCE

The labour rate variance is shown in Exhibit 15.10. Skilled labour costs an additional 25 cents for each hour worked, while unskilled labour was paid the standard rate. The change in skilled labour costs may be the result of

- Unplanned overtime payments
- A negotiated wage increase that has not been included in the master budget

Exhibit 15.10 **Labour Rate Variances**

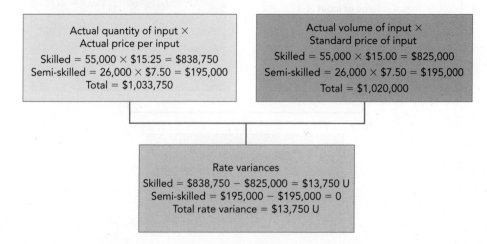

LABOUR EFFICIENCY VARIANCE

The efficiency variance for labour is shown in Exhibit 15.11. The unfavourable variance is a result of 1,000 additional hours being worked by skilled labourers and 1,000 hours less being worked by unskilled labourers.

Exhibit 15.11 **Labour Efficiency Variances**

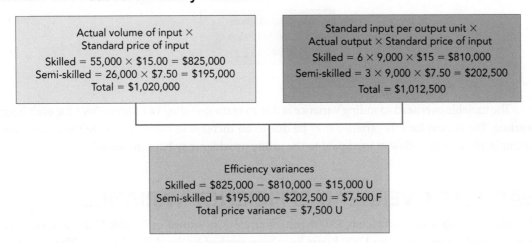

The efficiency variance for skilled labour was unfavourable while the efficiency variance for semi-skilled labour was favourable. This may have been the result of

- Poor-quality material that required greater skill to work
- The lack of unskilled labour that was replaced by skilled labour
- Poor production planning

The total labour variance is an unfavourable $21,250 which is shown in Exhibit 15.12. This is a combination of efficiency and rate variances, but it is mainly due to variations in skilled labour rates and usage, which may need to be investigated by the company.

Exhibit 15.12 **Total Labour Variance**

Efficiency	$7,500 U
Rate	13,750 U
Total	$21,250 U

Overhead Variances

VARIABLE OVERHEAD SPENDING VARIANCE

The variable overhead spending variance is shown in Exhibit 15.13 as $8,250 (unfavourable). The input used by Wood's Furniture in measuring variable overhead is skilled labour hours. The company charges a standard rate of $5 per skilled labour hour for variable overhead. The allocation basis for variable overhead can vary from company to company. Common allocation bases of variable overhead include direct labour hours, machine hours, and square footage.

Exhibit 15.13 **Variable Overhead Spending Variance**

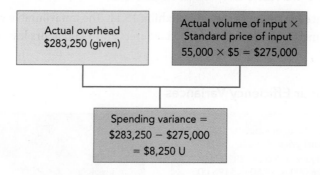

The variable overhead spending variance is due to extra spending in indirect costs for each hour worked. The reason for this variance may be due to an increase in costs to operate the facility. For example, the rate per kilowatt used paid to the utility provider may have increased.

VARIABLE OVERHEAD EFFICIENCY VARIANCE

The overhead efficiency variance is $5,000 (unfavourable), as shown in Exhibit 15.14. The variance has occurred because an extra 1,000 hours have been worked by the skilled laborers. The efficiency variance is typically related to production hours and often follows from variances in labour. The reason may be that as more hours have been worked, more variable costs have been incurred; for example, more machines had to be run and more electricity was consumed.

Exhibit 15.14 **Variable Overhead Efficiency Variance**

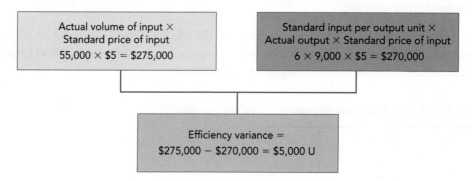

The total variable overhead variance is an unfavourable $13,250, which is a combination of both efficiency and rate variances. The total variable overhead variance is shown in Exhibit 15.15.

Exhibit 15.15 **Total Variable Overhead Variance**

Efficiency	$5,000 U
Spending	8,250 U
Total	$13,250 U

FIXED OVERHEAD SPENDING VARIANCE

The fixed cost spending variance is straightforward. Changes in quantity cannot influence fixed costs (which by definition are constant over different levels of production), so any variance must be the result of a spending variance. In this case, the variance is an adverse $5,000, because costs of $130,000 exceed the budget cost of $125,000, as shown in Exhibit 15.16.

Exhibit 15.16 Fixed Overhead Spending Variance

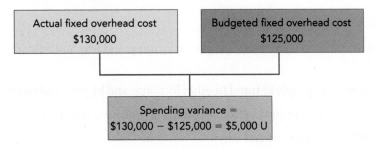

FIXED OVERHEAD PRODUCTION VOLUME VARIANCE

The fixed cost production volume variance is due, in this case, to producing fewer units than planned. Since the company did not use as much capacity as planned, the variance is unfavourable. The fixed overhead rate is based on the budgeted fixed overhead costs divided by the budgeted production ($125,000/10,000 = $12.50 per unit). The production volume variance is shown in Exhibit 15.17.

Exhibit 15.17 Fixed Overhead Production Volume Variance

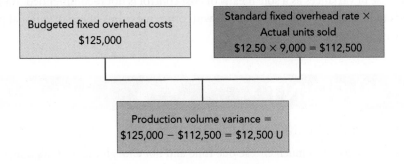

Cost Control

Cost control is a process of either reducing costs while maintaining the same levels of productivity, or maintaining costs while increasing levels of productivity through economies of scale or improved efficiencies in producing goods or services. For this reason, cost control is more accurately considered as *cost improvement*. Cost improvement needs to be exercised by all budget holders to ensure that limited resources are effectively utilized and budgets are not overspent. This is best achieved by understanding the causes of costs—the cost drivers.

For example, the cost of purchasing as an activity can be traced to the number of suppliers and the number of purchase orders that are required for different activities. The more suppliers and purchase orders (the drivers), the higher will be the cost of purchasing. Cost control over the administration of purchasing can be exercised by reducing the number of suppliers and/or reducing the number of purchase orders.

Cost control can also be exercised by undertaking a review of horizontal business process—that is, as the processes cross organizational boundaries—rather than within the conventional hierarchical structure displayed on an organization chart. Such a review aims to find out what activities people are carrying out, why they are carrying out those activities, whether they need to be carried out at all, and whether there is a more efficient method of achieving the desired output.

The questions that can be asked in relation to most costs are as follows: What is being done? Why is it being done? When is it being done? Where is it being done? How is it being done? The following are some examples.

- Projects: Why are they being undertaken?
- Salaries and overtime: What tasks are people performing, and why and how are they performing those tasks?
- Travel: What requires people to travel to other locations and by what methods?
- IT and telecommunication costs: What data is being processed and why?
- Stationery: What is being used and why?

We have already described approaches to total quality management (TQM) and continuous improvement in Chapter 9, and discussed the implications of these processes for cost management and control. It is important to recognize that achieving cost control by reducing variances based on standard costs can be an overly restrictive approach in a TQM or continuous improvement environment. This is because there will be a tendency to aim at the more obvious cost reductions (cheaper labour and materials) rather than issues of quality, reliability, on-time delivery, and flexibility in the purchase of goods and services. It will also tend to emphasize following standard work instructions rather than encouraging employees to adopt an innovative approach to re-engineering processes. Therefore, the use of variances as a sole means of cost control is not recommended. Rather, variance analysis needs to be considered in conjunction with other measures of organizational performance, such as balanced scorecards.

CASE IN POINT

Cost Control in the Restaurant Industry

When a pizza place uses too much cheese one time and not enough the next, it's doing more than annoying and confusing customers—it's losing control of its costs. Not knowing how much to order and keep on hand of such an expensive and perishable item as cheese can take a bite out of profit.

To help with ingredient ordering, quality control, and cost control, many establishments in the restaurant industry use standardized recipes. The recipes show employees how much of each ingredient to use, specifying amounts before cooking. In the case of pizza, grated cheese has less volume than melted cheese. Employees who don't realize this can put too much or too little cheese on top. Following standardized recipes results in more consistent amounts of ingredients used, which reduces waste and allows managers to order more precisely, all of which saves money. Standardized recipes also allow managers to know almost the precise cost of ingredients in any dish, which translates into knowing how to price an item on the menu to maximize profit. Since food costs equal roughly one-third of total restaurant food sales, keeping them under control makes good business sense.

Sources: Cushman, J. W. Who stole 17.46% of my cheese? How to differentiate between food cost and margin in retail, foodservice formats, *CSP Magazine*, June 2010; McGinty, J., Recipe costing: Where do I begin? *FohBoh: The Restaurant Network*, blog posting; *Restaurant benchmarks: How does your restaurant compare to the industry standard?* Baker Tilly Consultants, n.d.

CONCLUSION

In this chapter, we described budgetary control through flexible budgets, variance analysis, and cost control. We explored the types of variances that an organization can calculate and analyze in order to isolate the area which may be causing a cost or revenue to increase or decrease. We discussed how variance analysis can be used to help control costs within an organization, although it must be used in conjunction with other forms of control to ensure that the company continues to emphasize quality, continuous improvement, and employee empowerment.

KEY TERMS

Budgetary control, 378
Cost control, 389
Direct labour (DL) efficiency variance, 383
Direct labour (DL) rate variance, 383
Direct materials (DM) efficiency variance, 383
Direct materials (DM) price variance, 383
Efficiency variances, 382
Favourable variance, 378
Fixed overhead spending variance, 383
Fixed production volume variance, 384
Flexible budget, 378
Flexible budget variance, 382

Inputs, 382
Outputs, 382
Price variances, 382
Sales price variance, 381
Sales quantity variance, 381
Sales variance, 381
Unfavourable variance, 378
Variable overhead efficiency variance, 383
Variable overhead spending variance, 383
Variance analysis, 379
Volume variance, 382

CASE STUDY 15.1: WHITE COLD EQUIPMENT

White Cold Equipment (WCE) makes refrigeration equipment for the domestic market. It sells all of its production wholesale to a large retail chain. WCE's actual versus budget report for a recent month is shown in Exhibit 15.18.

Exhibit 15.18 White Cold Equipment: Actual v. Budget Report

	Actual	Budget	Variance
Sales units	1,000	1,050	(50)
Price	$ 700	$ 700	
Revenue	$700,000	$735,000	$(35,000)
Cost of Production			
Materials per unit		$ 250	
Total materials cost	$245,700	$262,500	$16,800
Labour per unit		$ 150	
Total labour cost	152,250	157,500	$5,250
Manufacturing overhead per unit		$ 70	
Total manufacturing overhead cost	75,600	73,500	(2,100)
Total manufacturing cost	$473,550	$493,500	$19,950
Gross margin	$226,450	$241,500	$(15,050)
Selling and admin. expense	183,500	190,000	6,500
Net operating profit	$ 42,950	$ 51,500	$(8,550)

Management was concerned about the significant shortfall in profits of $8,550 and asked the finance director for more information. The finance director produced a revised report (Exhibit 15.19) based on a flexible budget.

The director's revised report showed that by adjusting the budget to the actual volume of production/sales, the profit was $2,950 higher than expected.

The finance director also produced a variance analysis (Exhibit 15.20). This showed that the gross margin was lower by $3,550 than expected for the 1,000 units actually produced, but that selling and administration expenses were below budget by $6,500. Therefore, profits were higher than expected for the 1,000 units actually produced.

Exhibit 15.19 White Cold Equipment: Flexible Budget Report

	Actual	Flexible Budget	Variance
Sales units	1,000	1,000	0
Price	$ 700	$ 700	
Revenue	$700,000	$700,000	0
Cost of production			
Materials per input	$ 270	$ 250	
Materials consumed	910	1,000	
Materials cost	$245,700	$250,000	$4,300
Per labour hour	$ 145	$ 150	
Labour consumed	1,050	1,000	
Labour cost	$152,250	$150,000	$(2,250)
Manufacturing overhead per labour hour	$ 72	$ 70	
Manufacturing overhead cost	$ 75,600	$ 70,000	$(5,600)
Total manufacturing cost	$473,550	$470,000	$(3,550)
Gross margin	$226,450	$230,000	$(3,550)
Selling and admin expense	183,500	190,000	6,500
Net operating profit	$ 42,950	$ 40,000	$2,950

Exhibit 15.20 White Cold Equipment: Variance Analysis

Materials price variance	$18,200 U
Materials efficiency variance	22,500 F
Net materials variance	4,300 F
Labour rate variance	5,250 F
Labour efficiency variance	7,500 U
Net labour variance	(2,250) U
Overhead rate variance	2,100 U
Overhead efficiency variance	3,500 U
Net overhead variance	(5,600) U
Total manufacturing expense variance	(3,550)
Favourable selling and admin. variance	6,500
Total variance	$2,950 F

■ SELF-TEST QUESTIONS

S15.1 The method of adjusting the budget to reflect the actual volume of sales is called

a. Flexible budgeting

b. Activity-based budgeting

c. Program budgeting

d. Incremental budgeting

S15.2 A company budgeted $170,000 for materials, but the actual costs amounted to $164,000. The company also budgeted $130,000 for labour, but the actual cost was $133,000. The total expense variance is

a. $3,000 U

b. $3,000 F

c. $6,000 U

d. $6,000 F

S15.3 Higher prices from material suppliers will be reflected in the

a. Material usage variance

b. Labour rate variance

c. Material price variance

d. Labour efficiency variance

S15.4 Poor-quality materials that require greater skill to work will be reflected in the

a. Material price variance

b. Material usage variance

c. Labour efficiency variance

d. Labour rate variance

S15.5 If the actual labour rate is higher than the standard labour rate and the actual labour hours are lower than the standard hours allowed, the labour variances will be as follows:

a. Labour rate variance is unfavourable; labour efficiency variance is favourable

b. Labour rate variance is favourable; labour efficiency variance is favourable

c. Labour rate variance is unfavourable; labour efficiency variance is unfavourable

d. Labour rate variance is favourable; labour efficiency variance is unfavourable

S15.6 Harlem Dance Company had budgeted for 4,000 hours of dance instruction for the month of September. Its standard rate for instruction is $6 per hour. Actual revenues for the month of September were $23,600, and actual hours of instruction totalled 3,850. What were the sales price variance and sales quantity variance, respectively, for September?

a. 500 U; 900 F

b. 500 F; 900 U

c. 400 F; 600 F

d. 400 F; 600 U

S15.7 Conrad Corporation has a budget to produce 2,000 units at a variable cost of $3 per unit, but actual production is 1,800 units with an actual cost of $3.20 per unit. What is the flexible budget variance for variable costs for Conrad Corporation?

a. $360 F

b. $360 U

c. $240 F

d. $240 U

S15.8 Calculate the material price variance for Jumpin' Jiminy based on the following information:

	Standard	Actual
Quantity of input purchased (kg)	5,000	5,200
Price per kg	$3.10	$3.05

a. $260 F

b. $260 U

c. $360 F

d. $360 U

Use the following information to answer questions S15.9 and S15.10.

A company makes bulk cookies sold in restaurants. The following standards have been developed:

	Standard Inputs for Each Batch of Cookies	Standard Price per Input
Direct materials	25 kilograms	$2 per kilogram
Direct labour	4 hours	$15 per hour

Each batch of cookies contains 1,000 cookies. During January, production of 100,000 cookies was planned, but 105,000 cookies were actually made. At an actual price of $2.15 per kilogram, 2,250 kilograms of direct materials were purchased and used. The total direct labour cost for the month was $5,600, and the actual pay per hour was $14.00.

S15.9 The direct materials efficiency variance for January is

a. $500 U

b. $500 F

c. $750 F

d. $750 U

S15.10 The direct labour rate variance for January is

a. $300 F

b. $300 U

c. $400 F

d. $400 U

S15.11 During November, 35,000 direct labour hours were worked by the employees of Allied Industries. The direct labour rate variance for November was $26,250 U, and the standard direct labour rate was $12.50. What was the actual cost of direct labour during November?

a. $11.75

b. $13.25

c. $12.50

d. $14.00

S15.12 Granddad's Sauce Company's costing system shows the following information for the month of October:

Actual price per kg of direct material	$3.50
Standard price per kg of direct material	$4.00
Direct material efficiency variance	$800 F
Actual # of units produced	2,600
Standard inputs used to produce	
Actual output of 2,600 units	5,200

What quantity of direct materials was purchased and used in October?

a. 5,200 kg

b. 4,350 kg

c. 5,714 kg

d. 5,000 kg

■ PROBLEMS

P15.1 *(Material Variances)* Creature Comforts makes beds for cat and dogs. The beds are made from flannel fabric and cotton stuffing. In June, the company purchased 1,000 metres of flannel at a price of $5 per metre and 700 kg of cotton stuffing at a price of $2 per kg. During June, 750 kg of cotton and 975 metres of flannel were used in the production of 390 beds (190 dog beds and 200 cat beds). Each type of bed requires the following:

	Dog Bed	Cat Bed
Metres of flannel	3	1.5
Kg of cotton	2	1.5
Price of flannel	$5	$5
Price of cotton	$2	$2

Determine the materials price and efficiency variances for the company.

P15.2 *(Labour Variances)* Connors Custom Kitchens manufactures a standard-sized kitchen island that is used in many of its custom kitchens. The island is a 1.5 metre by 1 metre cabinet. Standard hours to produce the cabinet are 8 direct labour hours at a standard rate of $22 per hour. During the month of January, Connors made 500 cabinets and paid its carpenters $92,000 (using an average pay rate of $23 per hour).

a. Calculate the labour variances.

b. Cite potential reasons for these variances.

P15.3 *(Overhead Variances)* Abby's Fine Meats manufactures packaged meats that are sold in grocery stores. The company uses a standard costing system and applies variable manufacturing overhead to each product based on the kilograms of raw meat used in production. The standard variable overhead rate for the company is $0.35 per kg of raw meat. Each product uses an average of 0.50 kg of raw meat. For the year ended December 31, 2012, the actual variable overhead was $258,000. During 2012, a total of 860,000 kg of raw meat was used in the production of 1,800,000 packages of processed meat.

a. Determine the variable overhead variances for 2012.

b. What are the potential causes of these variances?

P15.4 *(Flexible Budget Variances)* Golly Girls Clothing is a small retailer of clothing for girls ages 6–12. Golly Girls differentiates itself from its competitors by providing custom tailoring. The company budget and actual results for the month of July are shown below:

	Budget	Actual
Revenues		
Units sold	240	250
Retail sales	$6,000	$6,100
Custom tailoring	1,200	400
Total revenues	$7,200	$6,500
Expenses		
Cost of goods purchased	$1,800	$1,850
Retail clerk wages	1,200	1,450
Tailor salary	1,500	1,500
Selling and admin. expenses	800	825
Total expenses	$5,300	$5,625
Net profit	$1,900	$ 875

The manager of the store is concerned about the profit earned in July, which is less than half of the budgeted profit. She has asked you to analyze the variances and identify areas that should be investigated further to determine why profits are not as high as expected. For the budget, Golly Girls assumes that all units sold will require custom tailoring at a cost of $5 per item; however, customer tailoring was provided on only 30% of the items actually sold.

a. Prepare a flexible budget for Golly Girls and identify key variances that should be investigated.

b. Provide potential reasons for the variances and suggestions that will help the company improve its profitability.

P15.5 *(Flexible Budget Variances)* Providore Contractors shows the following actual versus budget report:

	Budget	Actual
Units	25,000	23,000
Selling price per unit	$4	$4.10
Revenue	$100,000	$94,300
Variable costs	@ $2.50/unit	@ $2.35/unit
	$62,500	$54,050
Contribution margin	$37,500	$40,250
Fixed expenses	$30,000	$31,500
Operating profit	$7,500	$8,750

a. Prepare a variance report and reconcile the budget and actual result.

b. Prepare a flexible budget that explains the variances.

P15.6 *(Flexible Budget Variances)* Goodrow Corporation makes mattresses and has prepared the following information related to its standards for making one mattress:

	Standard Inputs	Standard Rates
Direct materials	30 kg	$3.50 per kg
Direct labour	5 hours	$14.00 per hour

Actual results for the first quarter of the year are as follows:

Actual units made/sold	5,000
Direct materials cost	$560,000
Kg used in production	165,000

Direct labour

Labour costs	$360,000
Labour hours of input	24,000

a. What is the total flexible budget variance for direct materials? For direct labour?

b. What is the price variance of the direct materials? Of direct labour?

c. What is the efficiency variance for direct materials? For direct labour?

d. Provide an interpretation of the variances. What might have been the causes for the variances?

P15.7 *(Flexible and Master Budget)* Jones Hardware Division estimated that it would sell 125,000 units this past year. The division planned to ship 1,000 shipments to customers and to utilize 280 m^2 of the corporate warehouse during the year. Its estimated overhead costs for the current year were as follows:

Materials handling	$10.50 per 100 units
Inventory storage	$20.00 per m^2
Shipping	$15.00 per shipment

During the year, the division sold 112,000 units in 980 shipments. It utilized 260 m^2 of the corporate warehouse. The actual costs for the year were

Materials handling	$12,040
Inventory storage	$5,460
Shipping	$14,896

a. Prepare a static and flexible budget for Jones Hardware Division.

b. Calculate the price and efficiency variance for each type of overhead cost.

P15.8 *(Flexible Budget Analysis)* Ny-eve Consulting Group's accountant has produced the following budget, actual, and variance report, showing that profits were behind expectations by almost $18,000.

Ny-eve Consulting Group: Variance Report

	Budget	Actual	Variance
Hours sold	1,200	1,100	
Average price/hour	$100	$90	
Revenue	$120,000	$99,000	$(21,000)
Direct labour hours	1,200	1,150	
Average salary cost	$40	$38.50	
Direct labour cost	$48,000	$44,275	$3,725
Variable overhead costs			
Travel: 5% of revenue	$6,000	$5,200	$800
Fixed overhead costs	$35,000	$36,500	$(1,500)
Total costs	$89,000	$85,975	$3,025
Operating profit	$31,000	$13,025	$(17,975)

a. What does the report tell the reader? What is its limitation?

b. Construct a flexible budget and determine the variances. How does that provide more information to users?

P15.9 *(Variance Analysis)* Hunter–Gatherer Ltd. produces wibbits. The table below shows the budget and actual units sold, together with standard costs and actual costs for materials and labour used in the manufacture of wibbits.

Hunter–Gatherer Ltd.: Data for July

	Budget	Actual
Units of finished wibbits sold	5,000	4,500
Material required (kg per wibbit)	1.5	1.7
Material costs per kg	$12.50	$13.00
Labour hours required (hours per wibbit)	1.2	1.3
Labour costs per hour	$14.00	$13.90

Assume that the quantity of materials purchased and the quantity used are identical.

a. Produce a report that compares the original budget with actual costs for materials and labour in July.

b. Produce a actual versus budget variance report using a flexible budget and calculate the variances on that basis.

c. Calculate both usage and price variances for both materials and labour.

d. Explain why variance analysis using a flexible budget may be helpful for management control.

P15.10 *(Flexible Budget and Variance Analysis)* Gargantua Ltd. has produced the following budget and actual information.

Gargantua Ltd.: Actual and Budget

	Actual	Budget
Sales units	11,000	10,000
Price per unit	$36.00	$37.10
Direct materials		
Magna	46,500 kg: Cost $67,425	4 kg per unit @ $1.50/kg
Carta	11,500 kg: Cost $58,650	1 kg per unit @ $5/kg
Labour	26,400 hours: Cost $187,440	2.5 hours per unit @ $7
Fixed costs	$68,000	$75,000

a. Prepare a traditional actual versus budget report using the above figures.

b. Prepare a flexible budget for Gargantua.

c. Calculate all sales and cost price and efficiency variances.

d. Reconcile the original budget and actual profit figures using the variance analysis.

P15.11 *(Variance Analysis)* John Crow Industries makes trailers that are used for general-purpose towing. The following standard cost card shows the standard inputs and costs for making one trailer:

Standard Cost Card *Trailer Model 100*	
20 metres of timber (at $1.25 per metre)	$25
6 metres of metal (at $5 per metre)	$30
2 tires ($15 each)	$30
7 direct labour hours (at $15 per hour)	$105
Variable overhead (at $10 per labour hour)	$70
Fixed overhead (at $5 per labour hour)	$35
Total standard cost	$295

During the year, the following actual data was reported:

Total sales of trailers	2,000
Timber used	39,500 metres
Timber cost	$1.30 per metre
Metal used	13,100 metres
Metal cost	$4.90 per metre
Tires used	4,020 tires
Tire cost	$15.25 per tire
Direct labour hours	14,500
Total payroll	$220,000
Actual variable overhead	$160,000
Actual fixed overhead	$68,000

a. Calculate the materials, labour, variable overhead, and fixed overhead variances.

b. Which variances need further investigation?

c. Provide a possible explanation for each significant variance.

P15.12 *(Flexible Budget: Fill in the Unknowns)* Complete the following variance analysis worksheet for Serif Industries.

	Actual Results	Flexible Budget Variance	Flexible Budget	Volume Variance	Master Budget
Units sold	50,000				60,000
Revenues	$725,000				$900,000
Variable costs	275,000				300,000
Contribution margin		$(50,000)		$(100,000)	600,000
Fixed costs	175,000	$(10,000)		—	185,000
Profit					

P15.13 *(Solving Unknowns)* The following labour variance information is provided below for the five divisions of the Yolander Company.

	Division 1	Division 2	Division 3	Division 4	Division 5
Units	500	d	600	700	m
Standard labour hours per unit	1	1.5	g	j	2.5
Total standard hours per unit × actual units	a	1,500	1,200	k	2,000
Standard rate per hour	$8.50	$9.50	$10.00	$9.50	$11.00
Actual labour hours	b	1,600	h	2,900	1,800
Actual labour cost	$4,050	$14,400	$12,350	$29,000	$18,900
Labour rate variance	c	e	$650 F	l	n
Labour efficiency variance	$425 F	f	i	$950 U	o

Solve for the unknown variables in the above chart.

P15.14 *(Behavioural Implications of Variances)* Dhariwal Industries is currently reviewing its variance analysis process. Over the years, the company has used variance analysis to help control and manage costs and activities within the company. Suzi Sanchez, the management accountant at Dhariwal, has been feeling a bit unsure of the accuracy of the variances that are being reported each year. Since managers in both sales and production are paid bonuses based on their ability to control and report positive variances, she is suspicious that there may be errors in the budgeting process. The following is a summary of the variances reported for the last four years:

	2009 $	2010 $	2011 $	2012 $
Total sales variance	$3,000 F	$2,000 F	$3,700 F	$4,200 F
Sales price variance	1,000 U	500 U	1,800 F	1,400 U
Sales quantity variance	4,000 F	2,500 F	5,500 U	5,600 F
Total materials variance	400 F	1,200 F	900 F	1,700 F
Materials price variance	800 U	200 U	700 U	500 U
Materials efficiency variance	1,200 F	1,400 F	1,600 F	2,200 F
Total labour variance	1,000 F	1,300 F	2,000 F	1,700 F
Labour rate variance	200 U	500 U	300 U	400 U
Labour efficiency variance	1,200 F	1,800 F	2,300 F	2,100 F

a. What trends in the above data indicate that there could be false information in the budgets for Dhariwal?

b. How could Dhariwal control manipulation of budgets to ensure that the variances reported are meaningful?

P15.15 *(Variance Analysis)* Elsie's Muffins makes two types of muffin that are sold to grocery stores: the standard muffin (which comes in various flavours such as carrot, chocolate chip, bran, and apple spice) and the gourmet muffin (which is injected with homemade jelly and topped with a nut crumble). The direct materials and labour used to make a package of 24 of both the standard and the deluxe brand muffins and their standard costs are shown in the following table:

	Standard Muffins		Deluxe Muffin	
	Quantity	**Cost**	**Quantity**	**Cost**
Baking mix	1 kg	$2 per kg	1.1 kg	$2 per kg
Paper cups	24	$0.005 per cup	24	$0.006 per cup
Jelly and nut crumble	n/a	n/a	350 g	$0.005 per gram
Direct labour	7 minutes	$20 per hour	9 minutes	$20 per hour

Variable overhead is assigned to each package based on direct labour dollars at a rate of 40% of direct labour costs. The factory has total fixed overhead costs budgeted at $50,000 for the year, based on a total production volume of 50,000 packages of muffins per year.

During 2012, Elsie's sold 54,000 packages of muffins: 42,000 standard and 12,000 deluxe. The company used 51,500 kg of baking mix; 1,325,000 paper cups; 3,800 kg of jelly and nut crumble; and 6,800 direct labour hours. Elsie's spent a total of $100,000 on baking mix; $7500 on paper cups; $22,500 for jelly and nut crumble; and $147,000 on direct labour. For 2012, actual fixed overhead costs were $48,500 and variable overhead costs were $52,000.

a. Calculate the materials, labour, variable overhead, and fixed overhead variances.

b. Which variances need further investigation?

c. Provide a possible explanation for each significant variance.

CHAPTER 16

Strategic Management Accounting

LEARNING OBJECTIVES

After reading this chapter, you should be able to answer the following questions:

- What is strategic management accounting and how does it differ from traditional management accounting?

- When developing strategies for a company, why is it important to identify external factors (such as Porter's five forces: threat of new entrants, power of buyers, power of suppliers, threat of substitutes, and competitive rivalry)?

- How can value chain analysis be used to identify areas of strategic opportunity for a company?

- How can a company assess which customers are the most profitable?

- In what ways is activity-based management (ABM) a strategic management accounting approach?

- Why does life-cycle costing provide a more accurate picture of a product's profitability than traditional costing techniques?

- How can cost-reduction tools such as target costing and Kaizen costing be used to create cost advantages for a company?

In this final chapter, we take the traditional concept of management accounting further and explore the area of strategic management accounting. **Strategic management accounting (SMA)** focuses on analyzing information (both internal and external) in a company's environment and utilizing the information to make strategic choices. In this chapter, after discussing further what strategic management accounting entails, we look some of its key accounting techniques.

Strategic Management Accounting Defined

Strategic management accounting (SMA) is linked with business strategy and maintaining or increasing competitive advantage. SMA is defined by the Chartered Institute of Management Accountants as a

> . . . form of management accounting in which emphasis is placed on information which relates to factors external to the entity, as well as non-financial information and internally generated information. (2005, p 54.)

SMA is outward looking, and helps the firm evaluate its position relative to its competitors by collecting and analyzing data on costs, prices, sales volumes and market share, cash flows, and resources for its main competitors (Drury, 2000). Bromwich (1990) suggests that SMA should also consider product benefits and how the cost of providing these benefits relates to the price the customer is willing to pay. SMA advocates also suggest that the time horizon of management accounting reports should be lengthened over the entire life cycle of a product, rather than just focus on yearly results.

In Chapter 6, we looked at management control, in which management accounting plays a considerable role. In the strategic management accounting perspective, the definition of management control systems has evolved from a focus on formal, financially quantifiable information and now includes external information relating to markets, customers, and competitors; non-financial information about production processes; predictive information; and a broad array of decision support mechanisms and informal personal and social controls (Chenhall, 2003).

SMA encompasses the following key areas of analysis within a company:

- Collection and assessment of **competitor and supplier information** on pricing, costs, volumes, and market share.

- Collection and analysis of **customer information**, including the costs involved in serving customers, customer buying patterns, and customer value.

- Identification of **cost-reduction opportunities** and a focus on **continuous improvement** and on **non-financial measures of performance**.

The following are types of analysis that can be used in SMA:

- **External analysis**, which looks at the external environment in which the firm operates (using tools such as Porter's **five forces analysis**).

- **Value chain analysis**, which compares the price customers are willing to pay for features with the costs associated with providing them, and explores the external value chain and assesses linkages between companies in the chain.

- **Customer profitability analysis**, which considers the profitability of serving a company's customers.

- **Strategic costing methods**, such as activity-based management, target costing, and life-cycle costing, which aim to reduce manufacturing costs or focus on optimizing the use of productive capacity within organizations.

Each of the above areas will be further explored in this chapter. Exhibit 16.1 shows a representation of strategic management accounting and how these SMA tools provide a basis for guiding strategy within the firm.

Exhibit 16.1 **Representation of Strategic Management Accounting**

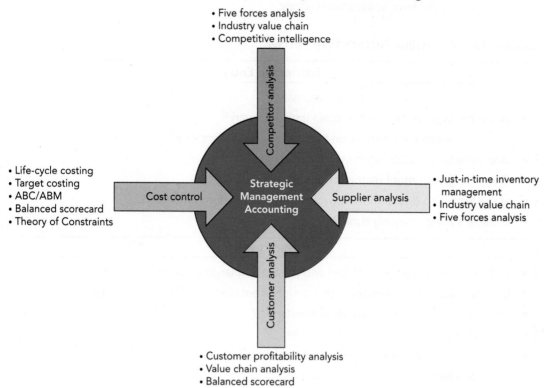

Accounting Techniques to Support SMA

Tools used in the area of strategic management accounting are varied, as shown in Exhibit 16.1 and as we have already discussed in this textbook. In Chapter 6, for example, we showed how accounting has extended measurement tools to include non-financial performance measurement through techniques such as the balanced scorecard. In Chapter 9, we discussed how the Theory of Constraints can help a company identify bottlenecks that, if eliminated, can increase efficiency and improve costs. In Chapter 11, we discussed how activity-based costing techniques can improve overall cost control and maximize profitability through optimal product mix decisions. These are all tools used in strategic management accounting.

In this chapter, we will cover five additional tools or expand on ones that we have discussed briefly in previous chapters. These tools include five forces analysis, value chain analysis, activity-based management, customer profitability analysis, life-cycle costing, target costing, and kaizen costing (*kaizen* is Japanese for *continuous improvement*).

Five Forces Analysis

Michael Porter (1980) developed five forces analysis, which assesses five areas of an industry in which a firm operates. These five areas include threat of new entrants, power of buyers, power of suppliers, threat of substitutes, and competitive rivalry. Porter stressed that "The collective strength of these forces determines the ultimate profit potential of an industry." So the performance of a company depends largely on its ability to create competitive advantage through knowledge and understanding of the forces in its external environment. Exhibit 16.2 shows the five forces and questions that a company can ask to determine the strength of each force. Answering "yes" to most of the questions suggests that the force in question is strong.

Exhibit 16.2 Assessing Porter's Five Forces

Barriers to Entry
• Are there high costs to enter the industry?
• Are there large economies of scale in the industry?
• Is there a limited differentiation from company to company?
• Are there large switching costs for consumers?
• Does the government restrict or control the industry?
• Is the access to distribution networks or retail locations limited?
• Is there a steep learning curve?
Buyer Power
• Is the buyer group concentrated and purchasing large volumes?
• Do the buyer's purchases represent a significant portion of his or her income?
• Are the products or services undifferentiated?
• Does the buyer face few switching costs?
• Does the buyer pose a credible threat of backward integration?
• Is the product or service unimportant to the buyer?
• Is the buyer very knowledgeable about the product, service, and industry?
Supplier Power
• Is the industry dominated by few suppliers?
• Is there a lack of substitute raw materials in the industry?
• Is the industry not important to the supplier group?
• Is the supplier's product or service an important input into the buyer's industry?
• Are the supplier's products or services highly differentiated?
• Does the supplier pose a credible threat of forward integration?
Power of Substitution
• Are there a large number of substitute products or services for the industry?
• Is the relative price/performance trade-off of substitutes higher than the industry in question?
• Are the switching costs of moving to a substitute product or service very low?
Competitive Rivalry
• Are there numerous or equally balanced competitors?
• Is there slow market growth?
• Are fixed costs and exit barriers high?
• Are companies in the industry undifferentiated?
• Are there high strategic stakes?

Source: Adapted from Porter, M. E. (1980). *Competitive strategy: Techniques for analyzing industries and competitors.* New York, NY: Free Press. Reprinted with permission.

THREAT OF NEW ENTRANTS. New entrants into an industry bring new competition and can potentially decrease the market share of existing companies. The threat of new entrants is low, meaning that the barriers to entry are high, if the capital costs required to enter an industry are large, if there are high economies of scale experienced by existing companies in the industry, if there is a high degree of differentiation between companies, if the switching costs for customers to move from one company to another are high, and if other factors exist that make the industry more difficult to enter. If an industry has high entry barriers, incumbent firms have a competitive advantage. Firms operating in industries where there are low entry barriers need to ensure that they create protection of their markets by differentiating their products through learning and innovation, and by improving economies of scale through strategic cost management.

BUYER POWER. Buyers are the customers of a company. Buyers can impact the strategic choices made by a company by exerting pressure to lower prices, provide more services, or provide more value than competitors. Buyer power is high in an industry if the buyers are concentrated and purchase large volumes of a product or service, where a single buyer's purchases represent a large portion of the company's overall sales. Buyers gain power if the switching costs to move from company to company are low and if the buyer is very knowledgeable about the industry's pricing, policies, and practices.

According to Porter (1980), "a company can improve its strategic posture by finding buyers who possess the least power to influence it adversely—in other words, *buyer selection.*" It is important for a company to research and understand its customers so that it can choose customers that will increase the company's competitive position and reduce overall costs. Later in this chapter, we discuss customer profitability analysis, which is a key component of the buyer selection process.

SUPPLIER POWER. Companies that operate in an industry with high supplier power risk experiencing price increases for materials, service-level changes, or changes to the quality of the goods that they purchase. Suppliers with high levels of power have the ability to dictate the price, quality, and terms for their products. Supplier power is high if there are only a few suppliers in the industry that provide a needed product. Suppliers are also powerful if there are few substitutes for their product or if the product is highly differentiated. Supplier power is also high if the industry in which a company operates is not of particular importance to the supplier, as the supplier is not reliant on sales to the company in question.

Companies can offset supplier power by designing or redesigning their products in a strategic manner so that they use inputs that are available from many suppliers in the marketplace. A company is in the best position if suppliers need their business. The more likely it is that a supplier wants a company's business, the more likely the company will be able to negotiate terms and conditions that are in its favour.

THREAT OF SUBSTITUTES. Substitutes are products or services that satisfy the same need or function in the marketplace as a company's product or service. For instance, in the car rental market, substitutes include taxis, public transportation, and even videoconferencing (as a substitute for business travel). Substitute products can reduce market share for a company if the substitute is seen as having better value versus its price. In industries where the threat of substitutes is high, companies need to competitively price their products and services to ensure they are in line with the price and performance of substitutes.

Companies need to look at these competing products and services carefully. For example, according to Besanko, Dranove, Shanley, and Schaefer (2010), hospitals in the United States experienced an increase in the threat of substitutes when technological improvements enabled many procedures to be performed on an outpatient basis, thus reducing the need for hospital stays.

Identifying this threat allowed some hospitals to modify their strategy to provide outpatient services. In the end, they were able to take advantage of this threat by offering a similar substitute service.

COMPETITIVE RIVALRY. The level of competitive rivalry in an industry impacts the strategies of the industry's participants. When rivalry is high, there tends to be an increase in the use of competitive tactics, such as price wars, advertising battles, and new-product introductions as companies fight to maintain market share. Understanding the level of competitive rivalry in an industry is important for companies in order for them to strategically plan the design, pricing, and marketing of their products or services. Rivalry tends to be high if fixed costs are large and industry growth is slow. Rivalry is also high if firms face large exit barriers. Consider the telecommunications industry, which is characterized by high, fixed infrastructure costs. These companies invest heavily in marketing campaigns and offer value-based pricing to be able compete to effectively.

Porter (1980) suggests that the impacts of rivalry, such as lost market share, can be mitigated by increasing buyer switching costs or increasing product differentiation. Telecommunications firms, for instance, increase switching costs to buyers by using fixed-term contracts. Firms must understand the level of rivalry they are facing to be able to strategize plans to control this risk.

Overall, analysis of the five forces helps companies to identify the strategic issues facing their industry and enables them to plan and strategize to ensure they are positioned in the best possible way. Failure to do so can lead to disastrous results. For example, Greyhound Canada, a successful ground transportation company, entered the airline industry in 1996 and then shut down its airline operations in 1997 due to high start-up costs and delays caused by government regulation (Heritage Community Foundation, 2004). This makes one wonder if Greyhound fully analyzed the five forces before it decided to go into this new line of business.

Value Chain Analysis

Chapter 9 introduced the concept of value chain analysis and differentiated upstream value-adding activities (research and development, product design, and purchasing) from production and distribution, and downstream activities (such as marketing and after-sales service). Also discussed in Chapter 9 is how the value chain can be extended from the focus on a single organization to a focus upstream and downstream to suppliers and customers.

Strategic management accounting can be used to help assess the costs and value of activities in the internal value chain for a company to determine if the activities are adding value for the customer. A 1999 publication of the Certified Management Accountants (CMA Canada) organization, *Value Chain Analysis for Assessing Competitive Advantage*, identifies the following five steps for performing an internal cost analysis of a firm's value chain:

1. **Identify the firm's value-creating processes.** Processes are sets of activities that produce a particular output. A company must de-emphasize functional structures to be able to identify these processes. For example, the purchasing activity often starts with the recognition by the employees in the retail store that inventory must be replenished. This information is then passed on to the purchasing department, which sources the needed product and completes a requisition. The activity then continues on to the warehousing department, which receives the goods. The purchasing function, therefore, spans several functional departments, including retailing, purchasing, and warehousing.

2. **Determine the portion of the total cost of the product or service attributable to each value-creating process.** It is often necessary in this step to reclassify the financial information that is produced by a company's costing system so that costs are allocated to activities, not to functional areas like cost centres, profit centres, or other responsibility centres.

3. **Identify the cost drivers for each process.** As was covered in the Chapter 11 discussion on activity-based costing, activity costs can be traced to specific cost drivers within organizations. For the purchasing example above, the number of purchase orders drive the total cost for the purchasing activity. By identifying cost drivers for a particular activity, a company can control the level of the cost driver to ensure that the most value is derived. For example, a company can combine purchase orders to decrease shipping and ordering costs.

4. **Identify the links between processes.** Most activities in a value chain are interdependent. For example, a well-designed product with stringent materials specifications can help reduce service costs. Linkages between activities in a firm or between stakeholders in an industry value chain can create competitive advantage for a company. For example, consider a company that uses supply chain technologies. When a product is purchased from retail stores and scanned at the till, the main warehouse and suppliers are automatically notified of the sale of this item and the need to replenish the inventory. Supply chain technologies such as these enable companies to maintain minimal inventories and save considerable investment in warehousing and storage costs. This type of linkage can be very difficult for competitors to imitate as it is a complex system across multiple departments, stores, suppliers, and raw material manufacturers.

5. **Evaluate the opportunities for achieving relative cost advantage.** At this point, the company can look at the cost drivers and linkages in the value chain to identify cost-improvement opportunities. Can cost drivers be reduced? Can linkages be formed? Can activities be eliminated?

In addition to looking internally at the company's value chain, strategic management accounting information can be used to analyze the costs of suppliers and distributors to determine if tighter controls could be implemented to improve overall costs or if excess profits are being earned by parts of the supply chain. For example, in the automotive industry, large vehicle assemblers collect vast quantities of information about their suppliers' costs: the cost of labour, the cost of manufacturing equipment and its capacity, and the cost of raw materials. This information supports negotiations between the purchasing department and suppliers because the assembler knows the range of costs the supplier will have and adds a reasonable profit margin. This is powerful information during the buying process.

Customer Profitability Analysis

Just as some products/services are more profitable than others, so are particular customers, industry groups, or geographic territories. **Customer profitability analysis** is essential in enabling an organization to make decisions on how to handle unprofitable customers, such as the following three alternatives:

1. Reduce the costs of servicing unprofitable customers.

2. Increase prices to unprofitable customers to cover those costs.

3. No longer do business with unprofitable customers.

Some customers may make such heavy demands on an organization's resources that the customer is no longer profitable. An example is banking, where corporate banking, mortgage lending, and credit cards are far more profitable for banks than basic personal banking. Many people have numerous bank accounts, often with small amounts of money, and banks provide a very expensive network of branches to support that particular customer type. Banks would most likely be more profitable if they eliminated personal banking, although there would be political and reputational consequences. However, banks have encouraged the use of automatic teller machines for cash withdrawals and electronic funds transfer at point of sale so that technology has reduced the cost of processing large volumes of small-value customer transactions.

Customer profitability for large multiproduct corporations often follows a whale curve. As shown in the Exhibit 16.3, 20% of a large multiproduct company's customers can generate 250% of its profits. The remaining 80% of customers can result in lost profits. By identifying the customers than do not deliver value to the company, the company can take steps to reduce the number of these customers or utilize technologies to decrease the cost to serve them.

Exhibit 16.3 Customer Profitability Whale Curve for a Large Multiproduct Company

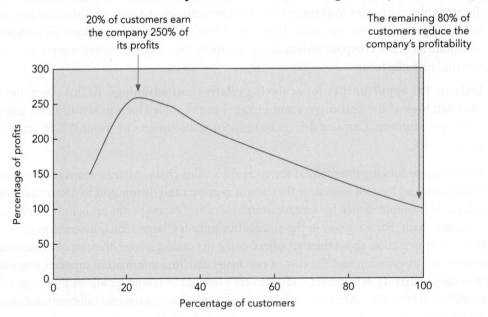

In the following example, as shown in Exhibit 16.4, Customers A and D of Trelally Company are fairly well established, but lower prices are charged to Customers B and C, which have more price competition. While variable production costs are the same, selling and distribution costs are higher for customers B and D than for customers A and C. The company also incurs specific fixed costs for each customer.

Exhibit 16.4 shows that customers B and C are unprofitable. In the short term, it would be better to discontinue serving these customers, but the business needs to consider whether it can increase the selling price, increase the volume, or reduce its variable selling and distribution costs before it makes this decision. Cancelling sales to a customer can impact a company's reputation and future sales potential, so this decision must be carefully assessed.

Exhibit 16.4 **Profitability by Customer**

Customer	A	B	C	D	Total
Sales units	4,000	2,000	1,000	7,000	14,000
Average price per unit	$ 10	$ 7	$ 7	$ 11	
Sales revenue	$40,000	$14,000	$7,000	$77,000	$138,000
Variable production costs ($3 per unit)	12,000	6,000	3,000	21,000	42,000
Variable selling and distribution costs ($2 per unit for A and C; $3 per unit for B and D)	8,000	6,000	2,000	21,000	37,000
Contribution margin	$20,000	$ 2,000	$2,000	$35,000	$59,000
Fixed costs specific to customer	10,000	3,000	3,000	15,000	31,000
Contribution to corporate overhead	$10,000	$(1,000)	$(1,000)	$20,000	$28,000
Corporate overhead					15,000
Net profit					$13,000

Using customer profitability analysis allows organizations to take a strategic view of multiple dimensions of profitability (products/services, customers, and business units) and make strategic decisions about which should be retained, which need further investment, which need price or cost adjustments, and which should be abandoned.

CASE IN POINT

Tracking Consumer Online Habits

Part of assessing customer profitability is knowing which market segments are the most profitable and knowing where to spend your marketing and advertising dollars for the greatest return. The Internet allows companies to target customers with almost laser-like precision. Third-party vendors produce software that collects data when online consumers shop, make restaurant reservations, or visit gambling sites. From this, a "behavioural profile" can emerge of people's presumed age, location, income, shopping and lifestyle preferences, and even their credit rating. Companies using this software can then target which products and services to showcase on their websites, based on the visitor's profile. Some firms, such as Amazon.com, collect their own information based on customer searches and purchases and suggest additional items they might be interested in.

While tracking online habits can benefit businesses, consumers are not always as keen. A recent survey of Americans found that three-quarters knew that their online moves were being watched, and 80% were not willing to tolerate data-tracking programs, even if the programs resulted in bargains. Concerns about online privacy led Canada's Privacy Commissioner Jennifer Stoddart to issue guidelines to businesses to ensure that they follow privacy rules on the Internet. The guidelines include requiring companies to clearly state on their websites how they track consumer behaviour and how the information gathered will be used to target advertising, and easily allow people to opt out of the data tracking before any information is collected.

Sources: Steel, E., & Angwin, J., The Web's cutting edge, anonymity in name only," *The Wall Street Journal*, August 3, 2010; Maag, C., Poll: Americans understand online tracking. And they don't like it, *Credit.com*, March 15, 2011; Advertisers must let consumers skip online tracking: "People's choices must be respected," Says Canada's Privacy Commissioner, *CBC News*, December 6, 2011.

ACTIVITY-BASED MANAGEMENT

Chapter 11 introduced the idea of activity-based costing (ABC). Since ABC focuses on identifying the activities that drive cost within an organization, it is a natural progression that an organization should look at the value of these activities and practise activity-based management. **Activity-based management (ABM)** focuses on controlling activities that consume resources; that is, controlling costs at their source.

Kaplan and Cooper (1998) defined *activity-based management* as

> . . . the entire set of actions that can be taken, on a better informed basis, with activity-based cost information. With ABM, the organization accomplishes its outcomes with fewer demands on organizational resources. . . . (p. 4)

Kaplan and Cooper differentiate between *operational* and *strategic* ABM (see Exhibit 16.5). Operational ABM is concerned with doing things right: increasing efficiency, lowering costs, and enhancing asset utilization. Strategic ABM is about doing the right things, by attempting to alter the demand for activities to increase profitability.

Figure 16.5 Operational and Strategic ABM

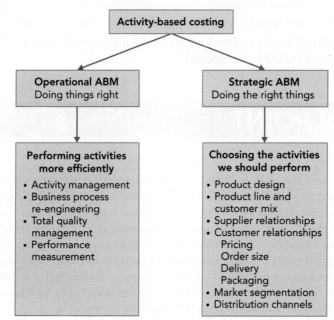

Source: Kaplan, R., & Cooper, R. (1998). *Cost & effect: Using integrated cost systems to drive profitability and performance.* Boston, MA: Harvard Business School Press. Reprinted with permission.

Strategic ABM can be used in relation to product mix and pricing decisions. It works by shifting the mix of activities from unprofitable applications to profitable ones. The demand for activities is a result of decisions about products, services, and customers. Product design changes can reduce the resources required to produce existing products/services. Pricing and product substitution decisions can shift the mix from difficult-to-produce items to simple-to-produce ones. Redesign, process improvement, focused production facilities, and new technology can enable the same products or services to be produced with fewer resources.

Strategic ABM extends the domain of analysis beyond production costs to marketing and selling and administrative expenses, reflecting the belief that the demand for resources arises not only from the production of products/services but from customers, distribution, and delivery channels. Cost information can be used to modify a firm's relationships with its customers, transforming unprofitable customers into profitable ones through negotiations on price, product mix, delivery, and payment arrangements.

Similarly, strategic ABM can be pushed farther back along the value chain to suppliers, designers, and developers. Managing supplier relationships can lower the costs of purchased materials. ABM can also inform product/service design and development decisions, which can result in a lowering of production costs for new products/services *before* they reach the production stage.

Other Costing Approaches

Strategic management accounting also includes other costing approaches. In this chapter we will look at life-cycle costing, target costing, and kaizen costing.

LIFE-CYCLE COSTING

All products and services go through a typical life cycle, from introduction, through growth and maturity, to decline. The life cycle is represented in Exhibit 16.6.

Exhibit 16.6 Typical Product/Service Life Cycle

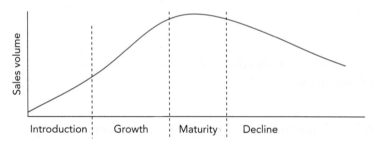

Over time, sales volume increases, then plateaus, and eventually declines. Management accounting has traditionally focused on the period after product design and development, when the product/service is in production for sale to customers. However, the product design phase involves substantial costs that may not be taken into account in product/service costing. These costs may have been capitalized or treated as an expense in earlier years. Similarly, when products/services are discontinued, the costs of discontinuance are rarely identified as part of the product/service cost.

Life-cycle costing estimates and accumulates the costs of a product/service over its entire life cycle, from inception to abandonment. Life-cycle costing considers all costs of researching, designing, manufacturing, selling, and discontinuing a product. This helps to determine whether the profits generated during the production phase cover all of the life-cycle costs. This information helps managers make decisions about future product/service development and the need for cost control during the development phase. Overall, the intention is that the life-cycles costs must be exceeded by the life-cycle revenues.

Consider Yellow Submarine Enterprises, a company that makes high-tech gadgets. Yellow Submarine is considering introducing one of three new gadgets in the market in the upcoming year: Pelorus, Jetsam, or Fathom. The company has estimated life-cycle revenues and costs for each gadget as shown in Exhibit 16.7.

Exhibit 16.7 Yellow Submarine Life-Cycle Revenue and Cost Information

	Pelorus	Jetsam	Fathom
Price per unit	$32	$35	$42.50
Sales quantity in units per year	10,000	8,500	7,800
Number of years in production	2	3	2.5
Costs			
Research and development	$85,000	$60,000	$78,000
Design costs	47,000	55,000	35,000
Production costs (per unit)			
Direct materials	$5	$6	$8
Direct labour	7	9	11
Overhead	5	9	8
Total production costs	$17	$24	$27
Selling and distribution (per unit)	$2	$2	$3

Based on the above information, Yellow Submarine calculated the total life-cycle costs for each product to be as shown in Exhibit 16.8.

Exhibit 16.8 Yellow Submarine Life-Cycle Operating Income

	Pelorus	Jetsam	Fathom
Life-cycle revenues	$640,000	$892,500	$828,750
Life-cycle costs			
Research and development	$ 85,000	$ 60,000	$ 78,000
Design	47,000	55,000	35,000
Production	340,000	612,000	526,500
Selling and distribution	40,000	63,750	58,500
Total life-cycle costs	$512,000	$790,750	$698,000
Life-cycle operating income	$128,000	$101,750	$130,750

The research and development and design costs occur only once in the life of the product, whereas the production and selling costs occur annually. Using life-cycle costing, the company would chose to introduce the Fathom, as it contributes the highest lifetime operating income. Without using life-cycle costing, the company might have chosen to produce the Pelorus or Jetsam. The Pelorus has a higher contribution margin per unit and a larger number of units are sold than the Fathom, but the life of the Pelorus is shorter (2 years as opposed to 2.5 years) and the research and design costs are much higher. The Jetsam might also have been chosen, since it would contribute income for three years as opposed to 2.5 years, but the total lifetime costs of the Jetsam make it less attractive than the Fathom. Life-cycle costing has enabled Yellow Submarine to identify the product that delivers the most lifetime value.

TARGET COSTING

Target costing is concerned with managing whole-of-life costs *during the design phase*. It is most often used when designing products and their related production processes. It has four stages:

1. Determining the target price that customers will be prepared to pay for the product/service.

2. Deducting a target profit margin to determine the target cost, which becomes the cost to which the product/service should be engineered.

3. Estimating the actual cost of the product/service based on the current design.

4. Investigating ways of reducing the estimated cost to the target cost.

$$\text{Target cost} = \text{Target price} - \text{Target profit margin}$$

The technique was developed in the Japanese automotive industry and is customer oriented. Its aim was to build a product at a cost that could be recovered over the product life cycle by setting a price that customers would be willing to pay to obtain the benefits (which in turn drive the product cost).

Target costing is equally applicable to a service. The design of a website where customers can download music or movies involves substantial upfront investment, the benefits of which must be recoverable in the selling price over the expected life cycle of the service.

The investigation of cost reduction is a *cost-to-function* analysis that examines the relationship between how much is spent on the primary functions of the product/service compared with secondary functions. This is consistent with the value chain approach described earlier in this chapter. Such an investigation is usually a team effort involving design, purchasing, production/manufacturing, marketing, and costing staff.

Consider a company that manufactures off-road bikes. A new bicycle is expected to achieve a desired volume and market share at a price of $600, from which the manufacturer wants a 30% margin, leaving a target cost of $420. Current estimates suggest the cost is $450. An investigation is carried out to find which elements of design, manufacture, purchasing, or selling contribute to the costs and how those costs can be reduced, or whether features can be eliminated if they cannot be justified in the target price.

After reviewing these areas, the company identifies that the key features that the customer values are the ability to handle rough roads and trails, disc brakes, and comfort. The company's original cost estimate included an aluminum alloy that provided an extremely lightweight bike. Since weight was not a high priority for its customers, the company discovered it could save approximately $30 per bike by switching to a slightly heavier aluminum alloy. By understanding customers' expectations and reflecting these expectations in the design of the bike, the company was able to achieve the target cost.

This example is very simple. In real life, target costing is an iterative process, but an essential one if the life-cycle costs of the product/service are to be managed and recovered in the (target) selling price. Importantly, this process of estimating costs over the product/service life cycle and establishing a target selling price takes place *before* decisions are finalized about product/service design and the production process to be used.

The reason that target costing must be undertaken prior to design of products is that the design and development phase of a product can basically lock in up to 80% of a product's cost. This is because decisions about the product specifications, production processes, and technological investment to support production are made long before the products/services are actually produced. If you consider the bike example, most of the costs of making the bike are predetermined in the design phase. In the design phase, the company will choose the type of frame, wheels, brakes, and other components that will comprise the final product, and changing the overall product cost by a significant amount is not possible once the product is in production.

Exhibit 16.9 illustrates that at the beginning of a product life cycle when a product is in the design phase, the level of cost commitment is very high but the costs incurred are low. Cost commitment represents the costs that cannot be changed. Once a product enters the production or operations phase, only 20% of the costs can be changed due to the strict design specifications. Consequently, efforts to reduce costs during the operations phase will result in smaller changes to product cost, since most costs are committed or locked in as a result of technology and of process decisions made during the design phase.

Exhibit 16.9 **Cost Commitment**

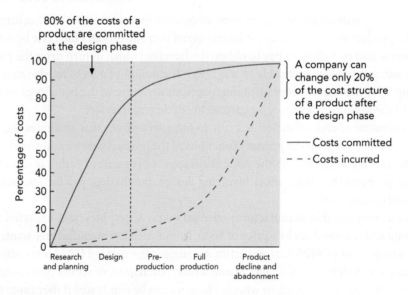

Japanese manufacturers tend to take a long-term perspective on business and aim to achieve the target cost during the life cycle of the product. They recognize that the target cost is rarely achieved from the beginning of the manufacturing phase. Although the achievement of the target cost will mainly be impacted by design changes, even small changes to costs after production has started can have a significant cumulative impact over time.

This idea of cumulative small changes to cost is reflected in the concept of kaizen costing. *Kaizen* is a Japanese word that means *continuous improvement*, so kaizen costing involves making continuous, incremental improvements to the production process. As shown in Exhibit 16.10, while target costing is applied during the design phase, kaizen costing is applied during the production phase of

Exhibit 16.10 Target Costing v. Kaizen Costing

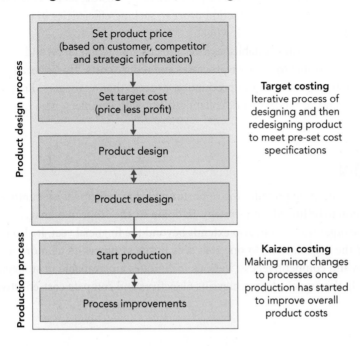

CASE IN POINT

Kaizen Costing in Health Care

Kaizen costing is used by service organizations as well as manufacturers. The health care field is adopting kaizen in a continuing effort to do more with less. Hospitals, for example, are examining every aspect of care—from the flow of patients, supplies, medicine, and information—to uncover wasted steps and movements. Hospitals are encouraging front-line staff to examine everything they do in order to identify inefficiencies, such as walking too far to fetch supplies, filling out forms that no one reads, processing patients at too many stages in their care, or even having too many unused instruments in the operating room.

The Children's Hospital of Saskatchewan in Saskatoon recently embarked on a kaizen exercise to redesign its wards to improve patient flow and care. It hoped to reduce walking distance by 50% and eliminate redundant paperwork.

"We write on 13 different pieces of paper when we admit a mom and a baby from labour and delivery. Thirteen. Could my time be better spent doing something else? I think so," said postpartum nurse Carmen Erickson, who was involved in the exercise of constant improvement.

Hospitals using kaizen costing standardize and document the agreed-on procedures in each process so that staff will work most efficiently all of the time. Standardizing procedures—such as requiring certain medications to be stored separately to prevent mix-ups—can also help minimize errors that can be fatal. Even small improvements—like storing a patient's chart under the patient's mattress where it's more accessible to nurses instead of at the foot of the bed—can free up an extra bed or add one patient to be attended to each day. But experts advise making a lifelong commitment to kaizen costing, to see the maximum benefits.

Sources: Fine, B. A., Golden, B. Hannam, R., and Morra, D., Leading lean: A Canadian healthcare leader's guide, *Healthcare Quarterly, 12/3, 2009; Children's Hospital of Saskatchewan: Getting lean*, 2011 video on the Kaizen Institute website, available at http://us.kaizen.com/success-stories/lean-healthcare-results/lean-hospital-design-using-3p-methodology.html; Region's journey continues with new strategies and lean training, *The Region Reporter*, Saskatoon Health Region, February 8, 2012; Graban, M., A nice kaizen example from the PACU, *LeanBlog*, January 17, 2012, available at www.leanblog.org/2012/01/a-nice-kaizen-example.

the life cycle, when large innovations might not be possible. Target costing focuses on the product or service. Kaizen costing focuses on the production process, seeking efficiencies in production, purchasing, and distribution.

Like target costing, kaizen costing establishes a desired cost-reduction target and relies on teamwork and employee empowerment to improve processes and reduce costs. This is because employees are assumed to have more expertise in the production process than managers. Frequently, cost-reduction targets are set and producers work collaboratively with suppliers, who often have cost-reduction targets passed on to them.

CONCLUSION

Strategic management accounting provides the opportunity for management accounting and other performance information to be linked with strategy. In doing so, the scope of management accounting extends beyond the organization and also extends beyond the financial year. It also moves from a hierarchical view of the organization to one that sees business processes as more important in achieving effectiveness and competitiveness. Various techniques are available in strategic management accounting to help the organization achieve its objectives and compete cost-effectively.

KEY TERMS

Activity-based management (ABM), 412

Customer profitability analysis, 409

Five forces analysis, 405

Kaizen costing, 416

Life-cycle costing, 413

Strategic management accounting (SMA), 403

Target costing, 415

Value chain analysis, 404

CASE STUDY 16.1: ANT

ANT is a multinational packaging equipment supplier to the food industry. ANT developed a computer-numerically controlled (CNC) packaging machine that was more efficient than its competitors'. The cost-benefit ratio of packaging machines is determined by throughput speed, flexibility, and the reject rate. ANT's equipment is two to three times more expensive than the competitors' equipment, but ANT's equipment operates 50–100% faster than conventional packaging machines and has a much lower reject rate.

About 10% of ANT's annual sales revenue has been invested in research and development (R&D), and ANT's machines have worldwide patents. However, two competitors breached the company's patents and substantial sums were spent to defend ANT's intellectual property.

ANT has offices in Canada, the United States, Europe, Australia, and the Middle East. The manufacture of the CNC equipment is outsourced to reduce its capital investment and decrease the risk associated with making a large investment in manufacturing facilities.

ANT's major operating costs are salaries, rent, travel, advertising, and exhibitions. Most of these costs are driven either by export market development or R&D. In particular, international growth has meant rapidly increasing operating expenses. ANT has had a dual focus on growth and cash flow. However, in developing its business, ANT has not relied on traditional accounting-based financial reports.

ANT did not have profit targets. Short-term profit was not meaningful to the owners, as expenditure on R&D, export market development, and patent litigation was incurred a year or more in advance of any income generation. The company instead emphasized sales targets as part of a strategy for market development, along with continual expenditure on R&D. Because there was no attempt to allocate R&D or export marketing costs over products, the direct (subcontracted) manufacturing cost was a relatively small proportion of the selling price. Consequently, product costing did not rely on management accounting data.

As ANT became larger, the owners began to focus more on growth in market share. They developed a sophisticated spreadsheet that contained an industry-level, top–down analysis of markets and competitors. The spreadsheet calculated the installed packaging machine base by market segment, and added a factor for market growth and the anticipated replacement of old machines by customers or potential customers. This was then adjusted by the relative performance of competitors' installed machines to provide a market size at the standard running speed for its own equipment. Using this model, ANT was able to estimate how many machines the company could sell and which of its competitors were likely to lose market share (most had the disadvantage of manufacturing equipment and needed to manage an increasingly underutilized capacity). ANT modified its marketing strategy to target the customers of weaker competitors, in order to force those competitors into losses and thereby secure even more market share from these competitors' failure. Several of ANT's competitors did fail as a result.

ANT's owners developed a network of social contacts, from employees and customers to competitors and suppliers, by attending industry events such as exhibitions and trade fairs, reading the business press, and entertaining. Over time, the owners developed a comprehensive market intelligence that they believed was superior to that of any of their competitors. ANT's spreadsheet model was regularly modified in an iterative fashion after market knowledge was gained through these social events. This knowledge became the driver of ANT's continuous investment in both export market development and R&D.

Market share became a key performance measure. The spreadsheet also led to strategic decisions: first to move to a stainless steel construction and second to develop a low-cost machine. Both met emerging market needs and the desire for increased market share. ANT's strategy and its use of the spreadsheet to inform that strategy were an example of strategic management accounting.

■ SELF-TEST QUESTIONS

S16.1 Which of the following would indicate a high level of supplier power in an industry?

a. Many suppliers in the industry provide similar products.

b. A company's sales represent a high portion of the supplier's overall sales.

c. The supplier could potentially begin selling its products directly to the consumer.

d. A company can use substitute products if the supplier's products are not available.

S16.2 Which of the following industries would be characterized as having low competitive rivalry?

a. Specialty coffee manufacturing

b. Automobile manufacturing

c. Telecommunications

d. Privatized utilities

S16.3 The threat of new entrants into an industry is high if

a. Costs to enter the industry are high.

b. Switching costs are low.

c. Product differentiation is high.

d. Economies of scale are high.

S16.4 Which of the following is the most accurate cost driver for quality costs?

a. Inspection hours

b. Number of units produced

c. Labour hours

d. Machine hours

S16.5 Linkages between activities in a value chain are important to identify because

a. They highlight potential areas of competitive advantage for a company.

b. They may indicate duplication of effort that needs to be eliminated.

c. They should be removed to ensure that cross-subsidization of costs does not occur.

d. They indicate areas where a company may need to control activity costs.

S16.6 When are a product's direct materials cost most likely to be locked in?

a. When the product is designed

b. When the materials are received from the suppliers

c. When the product is manufactured

d. When the company places an order for materials

S16.7 Which of the following formulas is used to calculate target cost?

a. Target cost = Selling price − (Mark-up % × Target cost)

b. Target cost = Selling price − (Mark-up % × Selling price)

c. Target cost = Variable cost per unit + Fixed cost per unit

d. Target cost = Selling price × Mark-up %

S16.8 Life-cycle costing

a. Can involve many accounting periods

b. Involves only the current year's financial data

c. Tracks only costs of producing a product over many years

d. Provides the same costs as traditional costing but is just allocated on a different time period

S16.9 Kaizen costing is different from target costing because target costing focuses on

a. The design specifications of a product

b. Reducing production costs such as direct materials and labour

c. Making small changes that may impact costs overall

d. Identifying the lifetime costs for a product or service

S16.10 The following customers purchase goods from the Abilleet Company on a monthly basis.

	Customer A	**Customer B**	**Customer C**
Units sold	10,000	9,500	20,000
Revenues	$50,000	$45,000	$100,000
Cost of goods sold	$25,000	$22,500	$50,000
Gross margin	$25,000	$22,500	$50,000

In addition to the above costs, Customer A requires 5 deliveries per month at a cost of $1,000 per delivery. Customers B and C each require 10 deliveries a month at a cost of $800 per delivery. Customer C normally requires more customer service support than Customers A and B. Customer C uses 40 hours of customer support, while A and B use 20 hours each. Customer support staff is paid $30 per hour. What is the customer profitability for Customers A, B, and C?

a. $19,400 for A, $13,900 for B, $40,800 for C

b. $25,000 for A, $22,500 for B, $50,000 for C

c. $$44,400 for A, $36,400 for B, $90,800 for C

d. $23,400 for A, $21,100 for B, $48,000 for C

S16.11 Bronry Box Company is evaluating a new product that may be introduced in the upcoming year. The product is a new insulated box that will be used by food distributors. The company is planning to make the new boxes in 12 production runs a year of 1,000 boxes each. Each production run will incur $3,000 in costs to change over the equipment for this new style of box. At this date, the insulated box has incurred $12,000 in research and development costs. The other costs of producing the boxes are $5 for direct materials, $1 for direct labour, and $2 for overhead. Shipping and customer service costs will be $1 per box. The boxes are going to sell for $15 each for Year 1, $15.50 for Year 2, and $16.00 for Year 3. What is the life-cycle operating income for the insulated box?

a. $114,000

b. $126,000

c. $96,000

d. $104,000

S16.12 Sissy Products currently sells purses for $250. Costs of $180 are currently assigned to each handmade purse. The company is introducing a new purse that will be similar in design but they want to price it at $200 per purse. They want to achieve a 25% mark-up on the selling price. The $180 cost for the current purse is made up of

- $50 for direct materials (the company can reduce this to $40 if it chooses a lower-cost supplier)
- $100 for direct labour for 4 labour hours per purse (if the company redesigns the purse, it can reduce the hours to 2.5 hours per purse)
- $30 for overhead (assigned as 30% of direct labour cost)

If the company makes the above changes to design and costs, what will be the target cost for the new purse?

a. $121.25

b. $180

c. $142.50

d. $132.50

■ PROBLEMS

P16.1 *(Five Forces Analysis)* With the popularity of the Apple iPad, the tablet computer market is experiencing high growth rates and record demand levels. Using the Internet as a research tool, complete a five forces analysis for the tablet computer industry. If you were a new company entering this industry, what key facts from the five forces analysis would help you develop a strategy to compete in the marketplace?

P16.2 *(Five Forces Analysis)* Starbucks operates in the high-growth industry of specialty coffee sales. The company has created a large amount of brand equity for its products by focusing on quality and high levels of customer service. Companies like McDonald's and Tim Hortons are competing with Starbucks by providing a lower-priced standardized coffee made from high-quality beans. Prepare a five forces analysis for the specialty coffee market. Suggest two strategic changes that Starbucks might pursue after analyzing the five forces.

P16.3 *(Critical Thinking)* During 2008, the world entered a global recession that resulted in many business failures. Today, companies continue to struggle with a lower degree of consumer confidence and lower levels of consumer spending. What lessons can the global recession teach us about the importance of external factors in strategic planning? Give an example of one company that was able to overcome the recession by changing or adapting its strategies to compensate for the external environment.

P16.4 *(Target Costing)* Skiff Company manufactures sails for small sailboats. Its most popular model, the Aquatic, sells for $3,500. It has variable costs totalling $1,900 per sail and fixed costs of $800 per sail (based on current demand of 4 production runs of 2,000 sails per year). Set-up costs are $50,000 per production run (which are not included in the fixed or variable costs already given). Skiff's current plant capacity is 12,000 sails.

Sky to Sea Inc., Skiff's main competitor, is introducing a new sail similar to the Aquatic that will sell for $2,999. Skiff management feels it must lower the price of the Aquatic in order to compete. The company marketing department believes that the new price will increase demand for the Aquatic by 40% per year.

a. What is the target cost per unit for the new price if the target profit is 25% of sales?

b. Is this target cost achievable with the possible increase in demand?

c. Outline areas of cost reduction that could be investigated by Skiff.

P16.5 *(Target Costing)* Driftwood Industries currently sells coffee tables for $450 each. It has costs per table of $330. A new competitor is opening in the same mall as Driftwood and offers a similar coffee table for $390. The company believes it must lower its price in order to not lose customers to this new company. Bob Jonas, the owner of Driftwood Industries, feels that he may be able to increase his sales of coffee tables by 20% if he lowers his price to $380. He currently sells 1,000 coffee tables per year. Bob was able to compile the following information about the costs of the coffee tables:

Direct materials	$120
Direct labour	$100
Variable overhead	$40
Fixed overhead	$70
Total cost	$330

Fixed overhead is based on production of 1000 tables per year.

Bob feels he can reduce direct labour costs by 15% if he purchases a new saw for $6,000 that will be depreciated over 3 years.

a. What is the target cost if the target operating income is 25% of sales?

b. Is this cost achievable? Show your calculations.

c. By how much would Bob need to increase production to make the purchase of the new saw worthwhile?

P16.6 *(Life-Cycle Costing)* Rocket Fireworks is evaluating a new firework, the Asian Candle, that can be sold for $45 each. The following information pertains to the Asian Candle:

- Design and development costs will total $45,000.
- There will be five production runs of 1,000 units each monthly at a cost of $1,000 per set-up.
- The firework is expected to be in production for four years.
- Direct materials costs will be $10,000 per production run.
- Indirect manufacturing costs will be $24,000 per production run.
- Shipping and customer service costs will be $50 per customer with an average order size of 1,000 fireworks.

a. What are the estimated life-cycle revenues?

b. What is the estimated life-cycle operating income?

P16.7 *(Life-Cycle Costing)* Ages Cosmetics makes an anti-aging line of cosmetic products. It has been developing a new face cream (called the Fountain of Youth) with a breakthrough product called T50, which has shown remarkable improvements in reducing the signs of aging in a large test group. The company has spent $4,500,000 at this point on testing and developing the Fountain of Youth.

The company is expecting to sell 360,000 jars per year for five years. The product is expected to incur the following costs on a monthly basis for production:

Direct materials	$4.25 per jar
Direct labour	$1.00 per jar
Variable overhead	$0.50 per jar
Fixed overhead	$45,000 per month
Selling and admin.	$1.25 per jar

a. What is the life-cycle cost for the Fountain of Youth?

b. What price would you recommend the company charge for this new cream if it wants to achieve a 50% mark-up on life-cycle costs?

P16.8 (*Target Costing*) Great Escapes Company manufactures scooters. The X14 model has total variable costs totalling $4,800 and total fixed costs of $500,000 per month based on annual production of 5,000 scooters. Great Escapes normally has 6 production runs per year, with $280,000 in set-up costs each time. The company currently has plant capacity for 10,000 scooters per year. A competitor's scooter similar to X14 currently sells for $7,500. The marketing department at Great Escapes believes that if the company charges $7,400 there will be an annual demand of 10,000 scooters. An $8,500 price will result in an annual demand of 7,500 scooters. A price of $10,000 will result in an annual demand of 5,000 scooters.

a. What is the annual operating income if the price is set at $7,400? At $8,500? At $10,000?

b. If Great Escapes wants to achieve a target cost of 75% of the target price, at which price should the company set the scooter?

P16.9 (*Customer Profitability Analysis*) Ray's Manufacturing makes electronic components. The company has two main customers. Information related to each customer is shown below:

	Customer A	**Customer B**
Revenues	$300,000	$531,250
Units Sold	60,000	125,000
Units per Order	1,000	900
Price per Unit	$5.00	$4.25
Cost per Unit	$2.50	$2.25
Net Profit	$150,000	$250,000

Customer Specific Costs:

Order taking	$100 per order
Product handling	$0.10 per unit sold
Delivery	$50 per order

a. Prepare a customer profitability analysis.

b. Ray is currently using his full capacity to service Customers A and B. Ray has the option to use his full capacity to serve Customer B, who would to like to purchase more components. Should he consider this option? Why or why not?

P16.10 (*Customer Profitability Analysis*) The following information pertains to lumber sales for the Timber Company for 2012.

	Boards Sold	Demand	Customer-Specific Costs
Customer 1	122,000	140,000	$20,000
Customer 2	135,000	140,000	$20,000
Customer 3	205,000	220,000	$39,000
Customer 4	105,000	120,000	$15,000
Customer 5	150,000	175,000	$28,000

The company also has a discount policy in place. If a customer purchases more than 125,000 boards, a discount of $0.50 per board will apply. If a customer purchases in excess of 200,000 boards, a discount of $1.00 per board will apply. The average price per board is $2.50 and the costs to produce each board are $0.50.

a. Prepare a report showing the customer profitability for each customer.

b. What is the optimal sales mix for the company, considering the demand volumes for each customer?

P16.11 *(SMA)* Good Industries is a large manufacturer of chemicals used in pesticides. The company has been experiencing slow market growth in the last five years and a continued increase in raw materials costs. With a focus on healthier lifestyles, the image of pesticides has deteriorated and people are looking for natural product solutions. The marketplace is now experiencing an increase in the number of producers of natural pesticides.

a. What tools of strategic cost management could help Good to develop new strategies for the company?

b. Describe specifically how Good could use one of these tools.

P16.12 *(Value Chain Analysis)* The following processes were identified by the Bessie Bread Company. Each process is treated as a separate profit centre, and transfer prices are charged in internal transfers between internal processes.

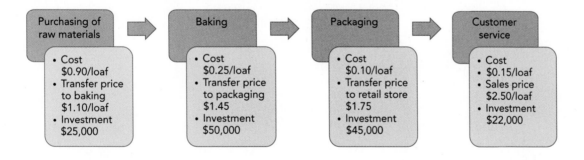

a. Assuming that the company produces and sells 25,000 loaves of bread per year, conduct an analysis of each activity.

1. What are the overall sales, costs (including transferred in costs), and profit made for each activity?

2. What is the ROI for each activity?

3. Which activity contributes the most value for the company?

b. Is there are a specific area of the value chain where the company should seek cost improvements? Suggest areas of cost improvement that could be investigated.

REFERENCES

Besanko, D., Dranove, D., Shanley, M., & Schaefer, S. (2010). *Economics of strategy* (5th ed.). Hoboken, NJ: Wiley.

Bromwich, M. (1990). The case for strategic management accounting: The role of accounting information for strategy in competitive markets. *Accounting, Organizations and Society, 15*(1/2), 27–46.

Chartered Institute of Management Accountants (CIMA). (2005), *CIMA Official Terminology*. Oxford: CIMA Publishing.

Chenhall, R. H. (2003). Management control systems design within its organizational context: Findings from contingency-based research and directions for the future. *Accounting, Organizations and Society, 28,* 127–68.

CMA (Certified Management Accountants) Canada (1999). *Value chain analysis for assessing competitive advantage*. CMA management accounting guideline. MAGs Archive.

Drury, C. (2000). *Management and cost accounting* (5th ed.). London: Thomson Learning.

Heritage Community Foundation (2004). *Alberta's aviation heritage: Greyhound Air*. Retrieved from www.abheritage.ca/aviation/people/beddoe_greyhound_air.html.

Kaplan, R., & Cooper, R. (1998). *Cost & effect: Using integrated cost systems to drive profitability and performance*. Boston, MA: Harvard Business School Press.

Porter, M. E. (1980). *Competitive strategy: Techniques for analyzing industries and competitors*. New York, NY: Free Press.

Porter, M. E. (1985). *Competitive advantage: Creating and sustaining superior performance*. New York, NY: Free Press.

PART **III**

Readings

Part III contains the following supplementary readings:

- Reading 1: Using the Balanced Scorecard as a Strategic Management System

- Reading 2: Teaching Special Decisions in a Lean Accounting Environment

- Reading 3: Intellectual Capital Reporting

- Reading 4: The Strategic Value of Customer Profitability Analysis

- Reading 5: Innovation Killers: How Financial Tools Destroy Your Capacity to Do New Things

Introduction to Readings

USING THE BALANCED SCORECARD AS A STRATEGIC MANAGEMENT SYSTEM

Kaplan, Robert S. and Norton, David P. (2007). Using the Balanced Scorecard as a Strategic Management System. *Harvard Business Review*, July-August, pp. 150–161. Reprinted with permission of Harvard Business Review.

Reading 1 titled "Using the Balanced Scorecard as a Strategic Management System: Building a scorecard can help managers link today's actions with tomorrow's goals" was originally written by Kaplan and Norton (1996) and discusses how organizations can use the balanced scorecard (BSC) as a strategic management system that can link a company's strategic plans with their day-to-day activities. You should read this article and be sure to consider the following advantages of using a BSC in strategic management:

- A BSC approach can help translate high-level mission statements, like "we will be the best in class" or "our customers come first," into concrete plans and actions.

- The process of creating a BSC for an organization integrates the strategic planning and budgeting processes and ensures that budgets support overall strategies.

- A BSC can help top management communicate their vision and plans in a clear manner to the employees within the organization.

- A BSC can link organizational units and align their goals and objectives.

- The BSC process enables strategic learning, where a company can get feedback from the BSC process and make adjustments to strategies as necessary.

TEACHING SPECIAL DECISIONS IN A LEAN ACCOUNTING ENVIRONMENT

Haskin, Daniel (2010). Teaching Special Decisions in a Lean Accounting Environment, *American Journal of Business Education*, June, Vol. 3, No. 6, pp. 91–96. Reprinted with permission.

The idea of lean practices have been common in Japan for almost 50 years, with Toyota Motor Company being the first company to explore lean methods. In North America, we are now seeing a shift to a lean philosophy in many manufacturing companies. Canadian companies like Canada Post and Bombardier have had tremendous improvements in terms of quality, waste management, and efficiency after implementing lean methods. Lean practices are characterized by decreased waste in the production process and increasing customer value. There are five key principles of lean enterprises, as defined by James Womack and Daniel Jones (Lean Enterprise Institute, 2009):

1. Specify the value desired by the customer.

2. Identify the value stream for each product providing that value and challenge all of the wasted steps (generally nine out of ten) currently necessary to provide it.

3. Make the product flow continuously through the remaining value-added steps.

4. Introduce pull between all steps where continuous flow is possible.

5. Manage toward perfection so that the number of steps and the amount of time and information needed to serve the customer continually falls.

Rather than focus on producing mass quantities of a product, lean companies only make what is demanded by customers. The traditional mindset of utilizing capacity through mass production is replaced with a new philosophy of producing what is needed, when it is needed, and with little error. Lean practices are easier to implement with the emergence of technology. Technology has enabled companies to implement a customer driven, value-added approach to production design and accounting through linkages of customers and suppliers along the value chain. In lean companies, traditional accounting methods using standard costs have become less important and new accounting methods focusing on lean methodology are becoming more important.

The reading "Teaching Special Decisions in a Lean Accounting Environment" is written by Daniel Haskin. It describes in detail how lean accounting methods are different from traditional reporting by functional area and how using lean accounting information can be helpful in making decisions related to special orders and outsourcing production.

INTELLECTUAL CAPITAL REPORTING

Holmen, Jay (2005). Intellectual Capital Reporting, *Management Accounting Quarterly*, Summer, Vol. 6, No 4, pp. 1–9. Reproduced with permission of Copyright Clearance Centre, Inc.

It is difficult to measure and quantify human capital and other intellectual capital in an organization. There is a subjective nature to measuring intangible assets. However, intellectual capital is often one of an organization's greatest assets. Intellectual capital comprises information, knowledge, intellectual property (such as copyrights and patents), and relationships. Effectively measuring and reporting intellectual capital can be critical in developing strategies, measuring performance, and communicating performance to both internal and external stakeholders.

The reading titled "Intellectual Capital Reporting" outlines various methods of reporting intellectual capital in a meaningful way that can be used to help an organization develop strategies and make decisions which take advantage of intangible resources. As this article describes, effective intellectual capital reporting can also help improve the understanding of the value of an organization to external stakeholders and enhance an organization's reputation.

THE STRATEGIC VALUE OF CUSTOMER PROFITABILITY ANALYSIS

Van Raaij, Mark M. (2005). The Strategic Value of Customer Profitability Analysis, *Marketing Intelligence & Planning*, Vol. 23, Iss. 4/5; pp. 372–381. Reproduced with permission of Copyright Clearance Centre, Inc.

Customer profitability analysis (CPA), as discussed in Chapter 16, is a tool used by companies to help assess the value of specific customers or customer groups. CPA can help a company improve its shareholder value through optimizing its customer mix and identifying areas where customer costs can be reduced. Often CPA is viewed as a way to identify and reduce unprofitable customers but it is much more than this limited perspective. CPA also helps a company develop a strategic perspective of customer management. As this article suggests, however, CPA needs to be viewed from a prospective viewpoint and customer value should be based on a customer's lifetime value, rather than using only a historical picture of the customers revenues and costs.

INNOVATION KILLERS: HOW FINANCIAL TOOLS DESTROY YOUR CAPACITY TO DO NEW THINGS

Christensen, Clayton M., Kaufman, Stephen P., and Shih, Willy C. (2008). Innovation Killers: How Financial Tools Destroy Your Capacity to Do New Things, Harvard Business Review, January, pp. 98–105. Reprinted with permission of Harvard Business Review.

In today's business environment, companies are continually reinventing themselves or introducing new products or services. In this textbook, we discuss various concepts or tools, including discounted cash flow techniques, relevant costing and performance evaluation methods, that are used in innovation decisions. This article looks in more depth at these concepts and explores some key limitations when we apply these management accounting tools or concepts when making investment (innovation) decisions. Some key assumptions that we tend to make when we use managerial accounting tools in investment decisions are:

- The past accurately predicts the future. We assume that sales volumes will continue if we make an investment or not.

- There is no risk in leveraging older equipment and infrastructures. We assume older outdated equipment or facilities will enable us to keep up with the competition as long as cost control and production efficiencies are maintained.

- An asset's useful life is based on its productive life, rather than its competitive life. An asset's competitive life, the amount of time that it will provide a competitive advantage or at least competitive equality, can be much shorter than an asset's productive life.

- Short term measures of performance are the key focus of decision making. Decisions often tend to have a short-term financial focus, rather than a long-term focus, which dissuades managers from making decisions that don't pay off in the near future.

As this article discusses, these key assumptions can lead to decisions that are not optimal and can prevent a company from competing effectively. The article also provides some recommendations that help to overcome these challenges.

Using the Balanced Scorecard as a Strategic Management System

by Robert S. Kaplan and David P. Norton

Editor's Note: In 1992, Robert S. Kaplan and David P. Norton's concept of the balanced scorecard revolutionized conventional thinking about performance metrics. By going beyond traditional measures of financial performance, the concept has given a generation of managers a better understanding of how their companies are really doing.

These nonfinancial metrics are so valuable mainly because they predict future financial performance rather than simply report what's already happened. This article, first published in 1996, describes how the balanced scorecard can help senior managers systematically link current actions with tomorrow's goals, focusing on that place where, in the words of the authors, "the rubber meets the sky."

As companies around the world transform themselves for competition that is based on information, their ability to exploit intangible assets has become far more decisive than their ability to invest in and manage physical assets. Several years ago, in recognition of this change, we introduced a concept we called the *balanced scorecard*. The balanced scorecard supplemented traditional financial measures with criteria that measured performance from three additional perspectives—those of customers, internal business processes, and learning and growth. (See the exhibit "Translating Vision and Strategy: Four Perspectives.") It therefore enabled companies to track financial results while simultaneously monitoring progress in building the capabilities and acquiring the intangible assets they would need for future growth. The scorecard wasn't a replacement for financial measures; it was their complement.

Recently, we have seen some companies move beyond our early vision for the scorecard to discover its value as the cornerstone of a new strategic management system. Used this way, the scorecard addresses a serious deficiency in traditional management systems: their inability to link a company's long-term strategy with its short-term actions.

Most companies' operational and management control systems are built around financial measures and targets, which bear little relation to the company's progress in achieving long-term strategic objectives.

Thus the emphasis most companies place on short-term financial measures leaves a gap between the development of a strategy and its implementation.

Managers using the balanced scorecard do not have to rely on short-term financial measures as the sole indicators of the company's performance. The scorecard lets them introduce four new management processes that, separately and in combination, contribute to linking long-term strategic objectives with short-term actions. (See the exhibit "Managing Strategy: Four Processes.")

The first new process—*translating the vision*—helps managers build a consensus around the organization's vision and strategy. Despite the best intentions of those at the top, lofty statements about becoming "best in class," "the number one supplier," or an "empowered organization" don't translate easily into operational terms that provide useful guides to action at the local level. For people to act on the words in vision and strategy statements, those statements must be expressed as an integrated set of objectives and measures, agreed upon by all senior executives, that describe the long-term drivers of success.

The second process—*communicating and linking*—lets managers communicate their strategy up and down the organization and link it to departmental and individual objectives. Traditionally, departments are evaluated by their financial performance, and individual incentives are tied to short-term financial goals. The scorecard gives managers a way of ensuring that all levels of the organization understand the long-term strategy and that both departmental and individual objectives are aligned with it.

The third process—*business planning*—enables companies to integrate their business and financial plans. Almost all organizations today are implementing a variety of change programs, each with its own champions, gurus, and consultants, and each competing for senior executives' time, energy, and resources. Managers find it difficult to integrate those diverse initiatives to achieve their strategic goals—a situation that leads to frequent disappointments with the programs' results. But when managers use the ambitious goals set for balanced scorecard measures as the basis for allocating resources and setting priorities, they can undertake and coordinate only those initiatives that move them toward their long-term strategic objectives.

The fourth process—*feedback and learning*—gives companies the capacity for what we call strategic learning. Existing feedback and review processes focus on whether the company, its departments, or its individual employees have met their budgeted financial goals. With the balanced scorecard at the center of its management systems, a company can monitor short-term results from the three additional perspectives—customers, internal business processes, and learning and growth—and evaluate strategy in the light of recent performance. The scorecard thus enables companies to modify strategies to reflect real-time learning.

None of the more than 100 organizations that we have studied or with which we have worked implemented their first balanced scorecard with the intention of developing a new strategic management system. But in each one, the senior executives discovered that the scorecard supplied a framework and thus a focus for many critical management processes: departmental and individual goal setting, business planning, capital allocations, strategic initiatives, and feedback and learning. Previously, those processes were uncoordinated and often directed at short-term operational goals. By building the scorecard, the senior executives started a process of change that has gone well beyond the original idea of simply broadening the company's performance measures.

For example, one insurance company—let's call it National Insurance—developed its first balanced scorecard to create a new vision for itself as an underwriting specialist. But once National started to use it, the scorecard allowed the CEO and the senior management team not only to introduce a new strategy for the organization but also to overhaul the company's management system. The CEO subsequently told employees in a letter addressed to the whole organization that National would thenceforth use the balanced scorecard and the philosophy that it represented to manage the business.

Translating Vision and Strategy: Four Perspectives

National built its new strategic management system step-by-step over 30 months, with each step representing an incremental improvement. (See the exhibit "How One Company Built a Strategic Management System . . . ") The iterative sequence of actions enabled the company to reconsider each of the four new management processes two or three times before the system stabilized and became an established part of National's overall management system. Thus the CEO was able to transform the company so that everyone could focus on achieving long-term strategic objectives—something that no purely financial framework could do.

TRANSLATING THE VISION

The CEO of an engineering construction company, after working with his senior management team for several months to develop a mission statement, got a phone call from a project manager in the field. "I want you to know," the distraught manager said, "that I believe in the mission statement. I want to act in accordance with the mission statement. I'm here with my customer. What am I supposed to do?"

The mission statement, like those of many other organizations, had declared an intention to "use high-quality employees to provide services that surpass customers' needs." But the project manager in the field with his employees and his customer did not know how to translate those words into the appropriate actions. The phone call convinced the CEO that a large gap existed between the mission statement and employees' knowledge of how their day-to-day actions could contribute to realizing the company's vision.

Metro Bank (not its real name), the result of a merger of two competitors, encountered a similar gap while building its balanced scorecard. The senior executive group thought it had reached agreement on the new organization's overall strategy: "to provide superior service to targeted customers." Research had revealed five basic market segments among existing and potential customers, each with different needs. While formulating the measures for the customer-perspective portion of their balanced scorecard, however, it became apparent that although the 25 senior executives agreed on the words of the strategy, each one had a different definition of *superior service* and a different image of the *targeted customers*.

The exercise of developing operational measures for the four perspectives on the bank's scorecard forced the 25 executives to clarify the meaning of the strategy statement. Ultimately, they agreed to stimulate revenue growth through new products and services and also agreed on the three most desirable customer segments. They developed scorecard measures for the specific products and services that should be delivered to customers in the targeted segments as well as for the relationship the bank should build with customers in each segment. The scorecard also highlighted gaps in employees' skills and in information systems that the bank would have to close in order to deliver the selected value propositions to the targeted customers. Thus, creating a balanced scorecard forced the bank's senior managers to arrive at a consensus and then to translate their vision into terms that had meaning to the people who would realize the vision.

COMMUNICATING AND LINKING

"The top ten people in the business now understand the strategy better than ever before. It's too bad," a senior executive of a major oil company complained, "that we can't put this in a bottle so that everyone could share it." With the balanced scorecard, he can.

One company we have worked with deliberately involved three layers of management in the creation of its balanced scorecard. The senior executive group formulated the financial and customer objectives. It then mobilized the talent and information in the next two levels of managers by having them formulate the internal-business-process and learning-and-growth objectives that would drive the achievement of the financial and customer goals. For example, knowing the importance of satisfying customers' expectations of on-time delivery, the broader group identified several internal business processes—such as order processing, scheduling, and fulfillment—in which the company had to excel. To do so, the company would have to retrain frontline employees and improve the information systems available to them. The group developed performance measures for those critical processes and for staff and systems capabilities.

Broad participation in creating a scorecard takes longer, but it offers several advantages: Information from a larger number of managers is incorporated into the internal objectives; the managers gain a better understanding of the company's long-term strategic goals; and such broad participation builds a stronger commitment to achieving those goals. But getting managers to buy into the scorecard is only a first step in linking individual actions to corporate goals.

The balanced scorecard signals to everyone what the organization is trying to achieve for shareholders and customers alike. But to align employees' individual performances with the overall strategy, scorecard users generally engage in three activities: communicating and educating, setting goals, and linking rewards to performance measures.

COMMUNICATING AND EDUCATING. Implementing a strategy begins with educating those who have to execute it. Whereas some organizations opt to hold their strategy close to the vest, most believe that they should disseminate it from top to bottom. A broadbased communication program shares with all employees the strategy and the critical objectives they have to meet if the strategy is to succeed. Onetime events such as the distribution of brochures or newsletters and the holding of "town meetings" might kick off the program. Some organizations post bulletin boards that illustrate and explain the balanced scorecard measures, then update them with monthly results. Others use groupware and electronic bulletin boards to distribute the scorecard to the desktops of all employees and to encourage dialogue about the measures. The same media allow employees to make suggestions for achieving or exceeding the targets.

The balanced scorecard, as the embodiment of business unit strategy, should also be communicated upward in the organization—to corporate headquarters and to the corporate board of directors. With the scorecard, business units can quantify and communicate their long-term strategies to senior executives using a comprehensive set of linked financial and nonfinancial measures. Such communication informs the executives and the board in specific terms that long-term strategies designed for competitive success are in place. The measures also provide the basis for feedback and accountability. Meeting short-term financial targets should not constitute satisfactory performance when other measures indicate that the long-term strategy is either not working or not being implemented well.

Should the balanced scorecard be communicated beyond the boardroom to external shareholders? We believe that as senior executives gain confidence in the ability of the scorecard measures to monitor strategic performance and predict future financial performance, they will find ways to inform outside investors about those measures without disclosing competitively sensitive information.

Skandia, an insurance and financial services company based in Sweden, issues a supplement to its annual report called "The Business Navigator"—"an instrument to help us navigate into the future and thereby stimulate renewal and development." The supplement describes Skandia's strategy and the strategic measures the company uses to communicate and evaluate the strategy. It also provides a report on the company's performance along those measures during the year. The measures are customized for each operating unit and include, for example, market share, customer satisfaction and retention, employee competence, employee empowerment, and technology deployment.

Communicating the balanced scorecard promotes commitment and accountability to the business's long-term strategy. As one executive at Metro Bank declared, "The balanced scorecard is both motivating and obligating."

SETTING GOALS. Mere awareness of corporate goals, however, is not enough to change many people's behavior. Somehow, the organization's high-level strategic objectives and measures must be translated into objectives and measures for operating units and individuals.

The exploration group of a large oil company developed a technique to enable and encourage individuals to set goals for themselves that were consistent with the organization's. It created a small, fold-up, personal scorecard that people could carry in their shirt pockets or wallets. (See the exhibit "The Personal Scorecard.") The scorecard contains three levels of information. The first describes corporate objectives, measures, and targets. The second leaves room for translating corporate targets into targets for each business unit. For the third level, the company asks both individuals and teams to articulate which of their own objectives would be consistent with the business unit and corporate objectives, as well as what initiatives they would take to achieve their objectives. It also asks them to define up to five performance measures for their objectives and to set targets for each measure. The personal scorecard helps to communicate corporate and business unit objectives to the people and teams performing the work, enabling them to translate the objectives into meaningful tasks and targets for themselves. It also lets them keep that information close at hand—in their pockets.

Managing Strategy: Four Processes

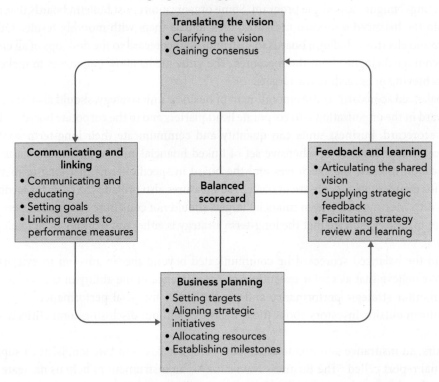

LINKING REWARDS TO PERFORMANCE MEASURES. Should compensation systems be linked to balanced scorecard measures? Some companies, believing that tying financial compensation to performance is a powerful lever, have moved quickly to establish such a linkage. For example, an oil company that we'll call Pioneer Petroleum uses its scorecard as the sole basis for computing incentive compensation. The company ties 60% of its executives' bonuses to their achievement of ambitious targets for a weighted average of four financial indicators: return on capital, profitability, cash flow, and operating cost. It bases the remaining 40% on indicators of customer satisfaction, dealer

How One Company Built a Strategic Management System . . .

2A *Communicate to middle managers.* The top three layers of management (100 people) are brought together to learn about and discuss the new strategy. The balanced scorecard is the communication vehicle. *(months 4–5)*

2B *Develop business unit scorecards.* Using the corporate scorecard as a template, each business unit translates its strategy into its own scorecard. *(months 6–9)*

5 *Refine the vision.* The review of business unit scorecards identifies several cross-business issues not initially included in the corporate strategy. The corporate scorecard is updated. *(month 12)*

Time Frame *(in months)*

0	1	2	3	4	5	6	7	8	9	10	11	12

Actions:

1 *Clarify the vision.* Ten members of a newly formed executive team work together for three months. A balanced scorecard is developed to translate a generic vision into a strategy that is understood and can be communicated. The process helps build consensus and commitment to the strategy.

3A *Eliminate nonstrategic investments.* The corporate scorecard, by clarifying strategic priorities, identifies many active programs that are not contributing to the strategy. *(month 6)*

3B *Launch corporate change programs.* The corporate scorecard identifies the need for cross-business change programs. They are launched while the business units prepare their scorecards. *(month 6)*

4 *Review business unit scorecards.* The CEO and the executive team review the individual business units' scorecards. The review permits the CEO to participate knowledgeably in shaping business unit strategy. *(months 9–11)*

satisfaction, employee satisfaction, and environmental responsibility (such as a percentage change in the level of emissions to water and air). Pioneer's CEO says that linking compensation to the scorecard has helped to align the company with its strategy. "I know of no competitor," he says, "who has this degree of alignment. It is producing results for us."

As attractive and as powerful as such linkage is, it nonetheless carries risks. For instance, does the company have the right measures on the scorecard? Does it have valid and reliable data for the selected measures? Could unintended or unexpected consequences arise from the way the targets for the measures are achieved? Those are questions that companies should ask.

Furthermore, companies traditionally handle multiple objectives in a compensation formula by assigning weights to each objective and calculating incentive compensation by the extent to which each weighted objective was achieved. This practice permits substantial incentive compensation to be paid if the business unit overachieves on a few objectives even if it falls far short on others. A better approach would be to establish minimum threshold levels for a critical subset of the strategic measures. Individuals would earn no incentive compensation if performance in a given period fell short of any threshold. This requirement should motivate people to achieve a more balanced performance across short- and long-term objectives.

Some organizations, however, have reduced their emphasis on short-term, formula-based incentive systems as a result of introducing the balanced scorecard. They have discovered that dialogue among executives and managers about the scorecard—both the formulation of the measures and objectives and the explanation of actual versus targeted results—provides a better opportunity to observe managers' performance and abilities. Increased knowledge of their managers' abilities makes it easier for executives to set incentive rewards subjectively and to defend those subjective evaluations—a process that is less susceptible to the game playing and distortions associated with explicit, formula-based rules.

One company we have studied takes an intermediate position. It bases bonuses for business unit managers on two equally weighted criteria: their achievement of a financial objective—economic value added—over a three-year period and a subjective assessment of their performance on measures drawn from the customer, internal-business process, and learning-and-growth perspectives of the balanced scorecard.

That the balanced scorecard has a role to play in the determination of incentive compensation is not in doubt. Precisely what that role should be will become clearer as more companies experiment with linking rewards to scorecard measures.

7 *Update long-range plan and budget.* Five-year goals are established for each measure. The investments required to meet those goals are identified and funded. The first year of the five-year plan becomes the annual budget. *(months 15–17)*

9 *Conduct annual strategy review.* At the start of the third year, the initial strategy has been achieved and the corporate strategy requires updating. The executive committee lists ten strategic issues. Each business unit is asked to develop a position on each issue as a prelude to updating its strategy and scorecard. *(months 25–26)*

13	14	15	16	17	18	19	20	21	22	23	24	25	26

6A *Communicate the balanced scorecard to the entire company.* At the end of one year, when the management teams are comfortable with the strategic approach, the scorecard is disseminated to the entire organization. *(month 12–ongoing)*

6B *Establish individual performance objectives.* The top three layers of management link their individual objectives and incentive compensation to their scorecards. *(months 13–14)*

8 *Conduct monthly and quarterly reviews.* After corporate approval of the business unit scorecards, a monthly review process, supplemented by quarterly reviews that focus more heavily on strategic issues, begins. *(month 18–ongoing)*

Note: Steps 7, 8, 9, and 10 are performed on a regular schedule. The balanced scorecard is now a routine part of the management process.

10 *Link everyone's performance to the balanced scorecard.* All employees are asked to link their individual objectives to the balanced scorecard. The entire organization's incentive compensation is linked to the scorecard. *(months 25–26)*

BUSINESS PLANNING

"Where the rubber meets the sky": That's how one senior executive describes his company's long-range-planning process. He might have said the same of many other companies because their financially based management systems fail to link change programs and resource allocation to long-term strategic priorities.

The problem is that most organizations have separate procedures and organizational units for strategic planning and for resource allocation and budgeting. To formulate their strategic plans, senior executives go off-site annually and engage for several days in active discussions facilitated by senior planning and development managers or external consultants. The outcome of this exercise is a strategic plan articulating where the company expects (or hopes or prays) to be in three, five, and ten years. Typically, such plans then sit on executives' bookshelves for the next 12 months.

Meanwhile, a separate resource allocation and budgeting process run by the finance staff sets financial targets for revenues, expenses, profits, and investments for the next fiscal year. The budget it produces consists almost entirely of financial numbers that generally bear little relation to the targets in the strategic plan.

Which document do corporate managers discuss in their monthly and quarterly meetings during the following year? Usually only the budget, because the periodic reviews focus on a comparison of actual and budgeted results for every line item. When is the strategic plan next discussed? Probably during the next annual off-site meeting, when the senior managers draw up a new set of three-, five-, and ten-year plans.

The very exercise of creating a balanced scorecard forces companies to integrate their strategic planning and budgeting processes and therefore helps to ensure that their budgets support their strategies. Scorecard users select measures of progress from all four scorecard perspectives and set targets for each of them. Then they determine which actions will drive them toward their targets, identify the measures they will apply to those drivers from the four perspectives, and establish the short-term milestones that will mark their progress along the strategic paths they have selected. Building a scorecard thus enables a company to link its financial budgets with its strategic goals.

For example, one division of the Style Company (not its real name) committed to achieving a seemingly impossible goal articulated by the CEO: to double revenues in five years. The forecasts built into the organization's existing strategic plan fell $1 billion short of this objective. The division's managers, after considering various scenarios, agreed to specific increases in five different performance drivers: the number of new stores opened, the number of new customers attracted into new and existing stores, the percentage of shoppers in each store converted into actual purchasers, the portion of existing customers retained, and average sales per customer.

By helping to define the key drivers of revenue growth and by committing to targets for each of them, the division's managers eventually grew comfortable with the CEO's ambitious goal.

The process of building a balanced scorecard—clarifying the strategic objectives and then identifying the few critical drivers—also creates a framework for managing an organization's various change programs. These initiatives—reengineering, employee empowerment, time-based management, and total quality management, among others—promise to deliver results but also compete with one another for scarce resources, including the scarcest resource of all: senior managers' time and attention.

Shortly after the merger that created it, Metro Bank, for example, launched more than 70 different initiatives. The initiatives were intended to produce a more competitive and successful institution, but they were inadequately integrated into the overall strategy. After building their balanced scorecard, Metro Bank's managers dropped many of those programs—such as a marketing effort directed at individuals with very high net worth—and consolidated others into initiatives that were better aligned with the company's strategic objectives. For example, the managers replaced a program aimed at enhancing existing low-level selling skills with a major initiative aimed at retraining salespersons to become trusted financial advisers, capable of selling a broad range of newly introduced products to the three selected customer segments. The bank made both changes because the scorecard enabled it to gain a better understanding of the programs required to achieve its strategic objectives.

Once the strategy is defined and the drivers are identified, the scorecard influences managers to concentrate on improving or reengineering those processes most critical to the organization's strategic success. That is how the scorecard most clearly links and aligns action with strategy.

The final step in linking strategy to actions is to establish specific short-term targets, or milestones, for the balanced scorecard measures. Milestones are tangible expressions of managers' beliefs about when and to what degree their current programs will affect those measures.

In establishing milestones, managers are expanding the traditional budgeting process to incorporate strategic as well as financial goals. Detailed financial planning remains important, but financial goals taken by themselves ignore the three other balanced scorecard perspectives. In an integrated planning and budgeting process, executives continue to budget for short-term financial performance, but they also introduce short-term targets for measures in the customer, internal-business-process, and learning-and-growth perspectives. With those milestones established, managers can continually test both the theory underlying the strategy and the strategy's implementation.

At the end of the business-planning process, managers should have set targets for the long-term objectives they would like to achieve in all four scorecard perspectives; they should have identified the strategic initiatives required and allocated the necessary resources to those initiatives; and they should have established milestones for the measures that mark progress toward achieving their strategic goals.

FEEDBACK AND LEARNING

"With the balanced scorecard," a CEO of an engineering company told us, "I can continually test my strategy. It's like performing real-time research." That is exactly the capability that the scorecard should give senior managers: the ability to know at any point in its implementation whether the strategy they have formulated is, in fact, working, and if not, why.

. . . Around the Balanced Scorecard

The first three management processes—translating the vision, communicating and linking, and business planning—are vital for implementing strategy, but they are not sufficient in an unpredictable world. Together they form an important single-loop-learning process—single-loop in the sense that the objective remains constant, and any departure from the planned trajectory is seen as a defect to be remedied. This single-loop process does not require or even facilitate reexamination of either the strategy or the techniques used to implement it in light of current conditions.

Most companies today operate in a turbulent environment with complex strategies that, though valid when they were launched, may lose their validity as business conditions change. In this kind of environment, where new threats and opportunities arise constantly, companies must become capable of what Chris Argyris calls *doubleloop learning*—learning that produces a change in people's assumptions and theories about cause-and-effect relationships. (See "Teaching Smart People How to Learn," HBR May–June 1991.)

Budget reviews and other financially based management tools cannot engage senior executives in double-loop learning—first, because these tools address performance from only one perspective, and second, because they don't involve strategic learning. Strategic learning consists of gathering feedback, testing the hypotheses on which strategy was based, and making the necessary adjustments.

The balanced scorecard supplies three elements that are essential to strategic learning. First, it articulates the company's shared vision, defining in clear and operational terms the results that the company, as a team, is trying to achieve. The scorecard communicates a holistic model that links individual efforts and accomplishments to business unit objectives.

The Personal Scorecard

Corporate Objectives

- ☐ Double our corporate value in seven years.
- ☐ Increase our earnings by an average of 20% per year.
- ☐ Achieve an internal rate of return 2% above the cost of capital.
- ☐ Increase both production and reserves by 20% in the next decade.

Corporate Targets					Scorecard Measures	Business Unit Targets					Team/Individual Objectives and Initiatives
1995	1996	1997	1998	1999		1995	1996	1997	1998	1999	1.
					Financial						
100	120	160	180	250	Earnings (in $ millions)						
100	450	200	210	225	Net cash flow						
100	85	80	75	70	Overhead and operating expenses						2.
					Operating						
100	75	73	70	64	Production costs per barrel						
100	97	93	90	82	Development costs per barrel						
100	105	108	108	110	Total annual production						3.
Team/Individual Measures						**Targets**					
1.											
2.											
3.											4.
4.											
5.											
Name:											
											5.
Location:											

Second, the scorecard supplies the essential strategic feedback system. A business strategy can be viewed as a set of hypotheses about cause-and-effect relationships. A strategic feedback system should be able to test, validate, and modify the hypotheses embedded in a business unit's strategy. By establishing short-term goals, or milestones, within the business-planning process, executives are forecasting the relationship between changes in performance drivers and the associated changes in one or more specified goals. For example, executives at Metro Bank estimated the amount of time it would take for improvements in training and in the availability of information systems before employees could sell multiple financial products effectively to existing and new customers. They also estimated how great the effect of that selling capability would be.

Another organization attempted to validate its hypothesized cause-and-effect relationships in the balanced scorecard by measuring the strength of the linkages among measures in the different perspectives. (See the exhibit "How One Company Linked Measures from the Four Perspectives.") The company found significant correlations between employees' morale, a measure in the learning-and-growth perspective, and customer satisfaction, an important customer perspective measure. Customer satisfaction, in turn, was correlated with faster payment of invoices—a relationship that led to a substantial reduction in accounts receivable and hence a higher return on capital employed. The company also found correlations between employees' morale and the number of suggestions made by employees (two learning-and-growth measures) as well as between an increased number of suggestions and lower rework (an internal-business-process measure). Evidence of such strong correlations help to confirm the organization's business strategy. If, however, the expected correlations are not found over time, it should be an indication to executives that the theory underlying the unit's strategy may not be working as they had anticipated.

Especially in large organizations, accumulating sufficient data to document significant correlations and causation among balanced scorecard measures can take a long time—months or years. Over the short term, managers' assessment of strategic impact may have to rest on subjective and qualitative judgments. Eventually, however, as more evidence accumulates, organizations may be able to provide more objectively grounded estimates of cause-and-effect relationships. But just getting managers to think systematically about the assumptions underlying their strategy is an improvement over the current practice of making decisions based on short-term operational results.

Third, the scorecard facilitates the strategy review that is essential to strategic learning. Traditionally, companies use the monthly or quarterly meetings between corporate and division executives to analyze the most recent period's financial results. Discussions focus on past performance and on explanations of why financial objectives were not achieved. The balanced scorecard, with its specification of the causal relationships between performance drivers and objectives, allows corporate and business unit executives to use their periodic review sessions to evaluate the validity of the unit's strategy and the quality of its execution. If the unit's employees and managers have delivered on the performance drivers (retraining of employees, availability of information systems, and new financial products and services, for instance), then their failure to achieve the expected outcomes (higher sales to targeted customers, for example) signals that the theory underlying the strategy may not be valid. The disappointing sales figures are an early warning.

Managers should take such disconfirming evidence seriously and reconsider their shared conclusions about market conditions, customer value propositions, competitors' behavior, and internal capabilities. The result of such a review may be a decision to reaffirm their belief in the current strategy but to adjust the quantitative relationship among the strategic measures on the balanced scorecard. But they also might conclude that the unit needs a different strategy (an example of double-loop learning) in light of new knowledge about market conditions and internal capabilities. In any case, the scorecard will have stimulated key executives to learn about the viability of their strategy. This capacity for enabling organizational learning at the executive level—strategic learning—is what distinguishes the balanced scorecard, making it invaluable for those who wish to create a strategic management system.

How One Company Linked Measures from the Four Perspectives

TOWARD A NEW STRATEGIC MANAGEMENT SYSTEM

Many companies adopted early balanced scorecard concepts to improve their performance measurement systems. They achieved tangible but narrow results. Adopting those concepts provided clarification, consensus, and focus on the desired improvements in performance. More recently, we have seen companies expand their use of the balanced scorecard, employing it as the foundation of an integrated and iterative strategic management system. Companies are using the scorecard to

- clarify and update strategy;
- communicate strategy throughout the company;
- align unit and individual goals with the strategy;
- link strategic objectives to long-term targets and annual budgets;
- identify and align strategic initiatives; and
- conduct periodic performance reviews to learn about and improve strategy.

The balanced scorecard enables a company to align its management processes and focuses the entire organization on implementing long-term strategy. At National Insurance, the scorecard provided the CEO and his managers with a central framework around which they could redesign each piece of the company's management system. And because of the cause-and-effect linkages inherent in the scorecard framework, changes in one component of the system reinforced earlier changes made elsewhere. Therefore, every change made over the 30-month period added to the momentum that kept the organization moving forward in the agreed-upon direction.

Without a balanced scorecard, most organizations are unable to achieve a similar consistency of vision and action as they attempt to change direction and introduce new strategies and processes. The balanced scorecard provides a framework for managing the implementation of strategy while also allowing the strategy itself to evolve in response to changes in the company's competitive, market, and technological environments.

Teaching Special Decisions In a Lean Accounting Environment

Daniel Haskin, University of Central Oklahoma, USA

ABSTRACT

Lean accounting has become increasingly important as more and more companies adopt the lean enterprise model, or some variation of it. Cost and managerial accounting textbooks continue to use, almost exclusively, models based on standard overhead absorption, which, if used in a lean environment, will not accurately reflect the benefits from the movement to a lean enterprise, and may distort the impact of the changes. Because of these developments, accounting students should be exposed to lean accounting models beyond a brief introduction in their basic cost and management accounting courses. This paper presents a model for teaching decision making in a lean company that uses value stream costing for such decisions as special orders and make-or-buy decisions. The use of these models in cost and managerial accounting classes will be of benefit to the future cost/managerial accountants.

INTRODUCTION

As more companies transition from traditional accounting systems to lean accounting systems, the need to focus on particular decision processes under lean accounting becomes more urgent. As discussed below, lean accounting is an entirely different method of collecting information and using information in decision processes than is traditional accounting. A review of cost and managerial accounting textbooks indicates that current textbooks give only a cursory exposure to lean accounting. For example, Horngren (2009) and Garrison (2010) discuss the basic principles of lean accounting along with the related topics of just-in-time inventory and target costing, but no coverage is reserved for the actual application of the lean accounting principles for decision making.

BACKGROUND

Management accountants are, for the most part, trained to collect data and to make decisions based on traditional accounting systems, such as full absorption costing or some modification of full costing such as variable costing. Traditional accounting systems were designed to support management principles like mass production and budgeting, and focused on increasing shareholder value. Principles of lean accounting are very different from those of traditional accounting. Consequently, traditional accounting systems tend to cause behaviours that undermine the principles of lean accounting. To understand these behaviours, we need to review the basics of a lean accounting system.

Lean accounting changes the view that a company has of its customers, because lean organizations seek to maximize the value created for the customer rather than to minimize shareholders' value. Consequently, lean accounting is not just a program to improve the traditional way of doing business, but is a new way of conducting business.

One of the fundamental differences between lean accounting and traditional accounting is that a lean organization is organized by value streams rather than by functions. A value stream is the sequence of processes through which a product is transformed and delivered to the customer. By design, a value stream spans multiple functions, such as production, engineering, maintenance, sales and marketing, accounting, human resources, and shipping (IMA 2006). Value stream organization requires a basic reorganization of accounting information. The process changes from a forecast-driven "push" environment to a customer driven "pull" environment, where production is started only when the customer places an order. With the traditional forecast environment, product will be produced in line with the forecast or budget and stored until an order is received from a customer. Frequently, high inventory levels and even obsolescence may result. Traditional methods of allocating fixed manufacturing costs encourage forecasts for higher levels of production in order to spread the cost over more units and lower the unit cost.

The major differences between push and pull environments require a reassessment of the reports used by the company's decision makers. Departmental expense reports in a push environment are normally used by functional managers who are accounting for the costs that arise in their departments. In a value stream environment, the value stream manager and his/her team are the primary users of the financial information. The information is used for cost control and decision making and is oriented to the value stream and not to functional departments. Unlike traditional full cost accounting, which absorbs all overhead costs into product costs and encourages overproduction, value stream organizations use simple summary direct costing with very little cost allocation. Consequently, lean accounting thinking is contrary to the traditional mindset that producing large batches to absorb overhead is efficient.

The philosophy of lean accounting's pull environment meshes very well with the philosophy of target costing. Target cost is the maximum cost that could be incurred on a product, with the business still earning the desired profit margin at the targeted selling price. Using the traditional costing model, production costs are measured, and the desired profit is added to set the selling price. Target costing considers the entire life cycle of a product, so the planning, development, and design stages of a product's life are important to the cost management process. Efficiency, which is one of the primary goals of lean production, is of prime importance in target costing.

Lean accounting costs the value stream instead of products or other cost objects, so unit product costs are not calculated. Because most of our training and experience is in the role of traditional cost accountants, we may find it difficult to determine how many decisions can be made without standard product costs. Traditional income statements present information on cost of goods sold, applied overhead, and manufacturing variances, while value stream income statements emphasize material purchases, employee and equipment costs, and facility costs. Exhibit 1 (Adapted from IMA 2006) presents a traditional income statement and contrasts it with a value stream statement. Notice that the top and bottom lines are the same on both statements. The difference is the way costs are assigned to value streams and the presentation of these costs. Most costs, especially labour and machine costs, are assigned directly to value streams using some simple cost driver, but such allocations are held to a minimum. Sustaining costs, which are necessary costs that support the entire facility, but cannot be directly associated with particular value streams, are not allocated to value streams, but are shown separately on the statements. Sustaining costs include management and support, facility costs, information technology, and human resource management costs that are not associated directly with a value stream.

One of the primary characteristics of lean accounting is the reduction of inventory to as low a level as possible. Most of us are familiar with tales of profit manipulation under traditional absorption costing created by absorbing fixed manufacturing costs into inventory when the inventory is not sold. This is possible because inventory changes affect profit using traditional accounting methods. The fixed manufacturing costs assigned to inventory will be reported as an asset rather than as an expense, and net income will be increased by the amount of the fixed cost assigned to inventory. With lean accounting, the inventory changes are reported separately as below-the-line adjustments and reported for the entire entity, not the separate value streams. This allows the value stream managers to assess their individual value streams without the complexities of the inventory changes affecting the value stream profit. If the company succeeds in adopting just-in-time inventory methods, the issue would largely disappear. Consequently, the motivation for manipulating inventory values also disappears.

The theory behind just-in-time inventory is to have materials needed in manufacturing at the precise moment they are needed in the manufacturing process. In order to accomplish this goal, a business must continuously seek ways to reduce waste and to enhance value for customers. These ideas are central to both just-in-time inventory and lean manufacturing. Just-in-time makes production operations more efficient and cost effective, and allows better customer response. Because materials are not needed until shortly before they are used in manufacturing, the cost of managing inventory is reduced considerably and may be eliminated entirely. This analysis is based on the assumption that the only relevant costs are the variable costs using the traditional definition. The fixed costs are made irrelevant because of the traditional cost assumption that absorbs all fixed costs into the regular production stream.

Under lean accounting, occupancy costs are actually assigned to value streams according to the amount of space used. Such items as utilities and property taxes are included here. Assignment of these costs provides motivation for the value stream teams to reduce occupancy costs. However, no attempt to absorb all of the occupancy costs is required. Space not used by a value stream is charged to sustaining costs. As a result, occupancy costs are handled in a similar manner to traditional accounting, but they are assigned to value streams instead of other cost objects, such as products or divisions.

Exhibit 1 Functional and Value Stream Income Statements

Techsan Company
Functional Income Statement

Sales	$100,000
Cost of goods sold	70,000
Gross profit	30,000
Operating expenses	28,000
Net operating income	$ 2,000

(continued)

Techsan Company
Value Stream (VS) Income Statement

	VS1	VS2	Sustaining	Total Plant
Sales	$60,000	$40,000		$100,000
Material costs	20,000	15,000		35,000
Employee costs	9,000	8,000	5,000	22,000
Machine costs	10,000	5,000		15,000
Occupancy costs	6,000	4,000	5,000	15,000
Other costs-VS	1,000	1,000		2,000
VS profit	$14,000	$ 7,000	$ (10,000)	$ 11,000
Inventory reduction (Increase)				3,000
Plant profit				14,000
Corporate allocation				12,000
Net operating income				$ 2,000

THE ISSUE-TEXTBOOK COVERAGE OF SPECIAL DECISIONS IN A LEAN ACCOUNTING ENVIRONMENT

Cost and managerial accounting students should be exposed to more coverage of lean accounting than a cursory introduction to this topic. Two areas of coverage that would benefit students are accepting special orders and make-or-buy decisions in a manufacturing environment. These two special decision areas are covered in almost every existing cost or managerial accounting textbook. By placing coverage of lean accounting for these two special decisions close to the traditional coverage in textbooks, students will gain an increased understanding of both traditional accounting and lean accounting, and how the two accounting techniques are similar and different. The following sections make up a presentation that could be used to accomplish these goals.

ACCEPTING SPECIAL ORDERS

Managers often need to evaluate whether one-time orders that are not part of the company's normal ongoing business should be accepted. Using a traditional managerial accounting analysis, the manager would use a short-run, variable-costing-oriented decision format. For instance, Techsan Company receives a request to produce 200 units of a product at $17 each. The normal selling price per unit is $22 each and the unit product cost is $18 as shown below:

Direct materials	$ 8
Direct labour	6
Manufacturing overhead	4
Total unit cost	$18

Based on the full cost analysis above, the company would decline the order because the offered price is below the unit cost. A traditional variable costing analysis would only consider the incremental costs and benefits as relevant. Analysis of the costs reveals that the variable portion of the manufacturing overhead is $1 per unit. The order will have no effect on the fixed manufacturing overhead, but special equipment for the order will cost $200.

	Per Unit	**Total**
Incremental revenue	$17	$3,400
Incremental costs		
Variable costs:		
Direct materials	8	1,600
Direct labour	6	1,200
Variable manufacturing OH	1	200
Total variable costs	15	3,000
Fixed cost		
Special equipment		200
Total incremental cost		$3,200
Incremental net operating income		$ 200

The traditional analysis focuses on relevant costs. The relevant costs are the costs which would be different between the two alternatives: accept the special order or decline the special order. Direct material, direct labour, and variable manufacturing overhead would be seen as relevant costs, and fixed manufacturing overhead would be seen as irrelevant because it would be incurred whether the order was accepted or not. Based on this analysis, the company should accept the special order because net income would be increased by $200.

Analyzing the proposed sale from a value stream costing viewpoint yields an interesting contrast to a traditional analysis although not necessarily a different conclusion. Assume the product desired by Techsan Company would be produced in Value Steam 1 as indicated in Exhibit 1. The following table shows the effect on the value stream:

	Current	**With New Order**	**Change**
Revenue	$60,000	$63,400	$3,400
Material costs	20,000	21,600	1,600
Employee costs	9,000	9,000	
Machine costs	10,000	10,200	200
Occupancy & other	7,000	7,000	
Profit	$14,000	$15,600	$1,600
VS profit %	23.33%	24.61%	1.28%

The changes reflect some new assumptions we make with lean accounting. Direct labour is included in employee costs and is viewed as a fixed cost. The cost of a team of employees in a value stream does not change until additional employees are needed. The existing employees are adequate to cover the increased production in our example, so the increased production does not increase employee costs. Based on this analysis, the order should be accepted because the value stream profit margin is increased 1.28%.

MAKE-OR-BUY DECISIONS

Another important decision concerns whether to produce parts or other products internally or to buy the parts externally from a supplier. A traditional cost accounting analysis would use a short-run, variable costing analysis in much the same manner we illustrated for a special order. Consider the following example. Techsan Company is considering outsourcing a part that is produced and used in Value Stream 1. A traditional analysis reports the following costs of producing the part internally:

	Per Unit	200 Units
Direct materials	$ 7	$1,400
Direct labour	8	1,600
Variable overhead	1	200
Allocated general overhead	3	600
Total costs	$19	$3,800

An outside supplier has offered to sell Techsan 200 units of the product at a price of $19 each. A quick comparison to the full cost analysis above would show no effect on profit as the cost to make is $19 per unit. A traditional variable costing analysis renders the following results:

	Per Unit Differential Costs		Total Differential Costs—200 Units	
	Make	**Buy**	**Make**	**Buy**
Direct materials	$ 7		$1,400	
Direct labour	8		1,600	
Variable overhead	1		200	
Allocated general OH				
Outside purchase price	—	$ 19		$3,800
Total cost	$16	$ 19	$3,200	$3,800
Difference in favour of				
continuing to make	$ 3		$ 600	

The traditional variable costing analysis follows the same line of reasoning as noted earlier for the special order decision. Direct materials, direct labour, and variable manufacturing overhead are seen as relevant costs, while fixed manufacturing overhead is regarded as irrelevant because it would be incurred no matter what decision was made, to make or buy. Based on this analysis, Techsan Co. should continue to make the part instead of contracting with an outside supplier.

In a lean environment, the above cost would be included in Value Stream 1 costs. Direct materials are included in material costs, direct labour is included in employee costs, and variable overhead is included in machine costs. A value stream analysis yields the following results:

	Make	Buy
Revenue	$60,000	$60,000
Material costs	20,000	22,600
Employee costs	9,000	9,000
Machine costs	10,000	10,000
Occupancy & other	7,000	7,000
Profit	$14,000	$11,400
VS profit %	23.33%	19.00%

Note that the buy decision would result in an increase in material costs for the total amount ($3,800) of the contract to purchase, but would cause an offsetting decrease in material costs of $1,200 for a net effect of $2,600. Employee costs would not be affected because they are considered fixed costs under lean accounting.

Techsan should make the product based on the value stream analysis, and the benefit to the company's bottom line is even more apparent than with the traditional analysis. Under the lean accounting analysis, the decision to outsource the part will cost Value Stream 1 over four percent of its profit margin.

CONCLUSION

Lean accounting and the closely related topics of just-in-time inventories and target costing are widely used accounting methods. Coverage of these topics is sparse in current cost and managerial accounting textbooks. This paper proposed a partial solution to the lack of exposure that students get to the application of lean accounting. The type of examples illustrated above would be very useful learning aids. Students would benefit not only from their increased understanding of special decisions and make-or-buy decisions but would also gain a greater understanding of cost assignments, direct costing, and the use of value streams as opposed to traditional segment reporting.

REFERENCES

Garrison, R., Noreen, E., Brewer, P. (2010). *Managerial Accounting*, 13th Edition. McGraw Hill, Irwin.

Horngren C., Datar, M., Foster, F., Rajan, S., Ittner, C. (2009). *Cost Accounting: A Managerial Emphasis*, 13th Edition. Pearson, Prentice Hall.

IMA (2006). Accounting for the Lean Enterprise: Major Changes to the Accounting Paradigm. Institute of Management Accountants.

Intellectual Capital Reporting

By Jay Holmen, Ph.D. , CMA, CFM, CPA

When there is a large disparity between a firm's market value and book value, that difference is often attributed to "intellectual capital." Market value is, of course, the company's total shares outstanding times the stock market price of each. Book value is the excess of total assets over total liabilities. But what is the value of intellectual capital?

Measuring the value of intellectual capital is difficult, but there are methods that can do it. One recent study categorized 12 different approaches to measuring intellectual capital, and another identified more than 30.[1] I will discuss and illustrate several of them, including one developed by Skandia Insurance Company Ltd., and Robert Kaplan and David Norton's balanced scorecard. I will also address how intellectual capital can be included in external financial reporting, and discuss how the accounting rules for reporting intangibles limits the recognition of intellectual capital. Finally, I will outline two proposed approaches for reporting intellectual capital to stakeholders.

First, however, let me define intellectual capital:

"Intellectual capital is intellectual material—knowledge, information, intellectual property, experience—that can be put to use to create wealth."[2]

"It has become standard to say that a company's intellectual capital is the sum of its human capital (talent), structural capital (intellectual property, methodologies, software, documents, and other knowledge artifacts), and customer capital (client relationships)."[3]

"Intellectual capital is a combination of human capital—the brains, skills, insights, and potential of those in an organization—and structural capital—things like the capital wrapped up in customers, processes, databases, brands, and IT systems. It is the ability to transform knowledge and intangible assets into wealth creating resources, by multiplying human capital with structural capital."[4]

Why Measure Intellectual Capital?

Companies may want to measure intellectual capital for a variety of reasons. One study identified five main reasons.[5] First, measuring intellectual capital can help an organization formulate business strategy. By identifying and developing its intellectual capital, an organization may gain a competitive advantage. Second, measuring intellectual capital may lead to the development of key performance indicators that will help evaluate the execution of strategy. Intellectual capital, even if measured properly, has little value unless it can be linked to the firm's strategy.[6] Third, intellectual capital may be measured to assist in evaluating mergers and acquisitions, particularly to determine the prices paid by the acquiring firms. Fourth, using nonfinancial measures of intellectual capital can be linked to an organization's incentive and compensation plan. The first four reasons are all internal to the organization. A fifth reason is external: to communicate to external stakeholders what intellectual property the firm owns.

Daniel Andriessen proposes a much shorter list of the reasons companies may want to measure intellectual capital: to improve internal management, to improve external reporting, and to satisfy statutory and transactional factors.[7]

Intangible resources need to be managed with more attention and differently than other resources, and measuring them helps improve management of them. Effective management of intellectual property also helps measure it. Good measures of intellectual capital will complement financial measures, provide a feedback mechanism for actions, provide information to develop new strategies, assist in weighting different courses of action, and enhance the management of the business as a whole.

Improving external reporting of intellectual capital can (1) close the gap between book value and market value, (2) provide improved information about the "real value" of the organization, (3) reduce information asymmetry, (4) increase the ability to raise capital by providing a valuation on intangibles, and (5) enhance an organization's reputation.

Statutory and transactional reasons for measuring intellectual capital may be either discretionary or mandatory and include setting a transaction price for the sale or license of an intangible or for tax planning, bankruptcy, litigation support, and impairment testing of goodwill.

Andriessen also makes a distinction between valuation and measurement. Valuation attempts to put a monetary number on the value of a resource or liability. Andriessen labels this *financial valuation*. Measurement is a broader term that assigns a number to an observed phenomenon. Sometimes the phenomenon being measured relates to value but is measured in nonmonetary terms; other times the phenomenon does not relate to value. Andriessen labels these *value measurement* and *measurement*.

Internal Reporting of Intellectual Capital

Two of the more noteworthy attempts to measure and report intellectual capital internally are Skandia's Navigator and Kaplan and Norton's balanced scorecard.[8] Both approaches are designed primarily for internal reporting, although Skandia did attempt to report intellectual capital externally using supplements to its interim and annual reports from 1994 to 1998.

SKANDIA NAVIGATOR

Skandia documented its approach to measuring intellectual capital in those supplements, and researchers also have described it.[9] The company's hierarchy of intellectual capital is shown in Figure 1.

The overall market value of the firm can be split into two parts: the financial capital as recorded in the financial reports, and intellectual capital. Skandia breaks intellectual capital into several components of human capital and structural capital. Human capital cannot be owned; it is the value found in employee training, employee competencies, and know-how. Structural capital is what remains after the people have left for the day, and can be split into customer capital and organizational capital. Organizational capital can be broken down further into process capital (how things get accomplished) and innovation capital (protected commercial rights and intellectual property).

Figure 1   Skandia's Hierarchy of Intellectual Capital

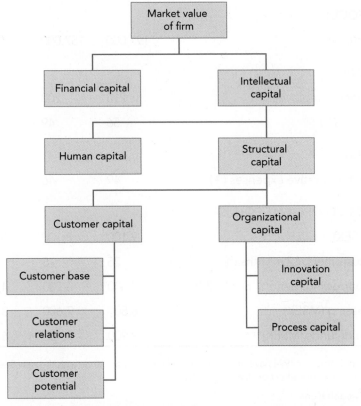

Source: Skandia, *Intellectual Capital—Value Creating Processes*, a supplement to Skandia's 1995 Annual Report.

The Skandia Navigator measurement tool has five main components that are shown in Figure 2: financial, customer, process, human, and renewal and development. A house analogy is used in depicting the Navigator.[10] The financial focus is the roof of the house where the recorded accounts are stored. The foundation of the house, representing the future, is the renewal and development focus. The roof and foundation measure how well the company is preparing for the future. The supporting walls, representing the present, are the customer and process focus. The centre of the house is the human focus because people have a hand in all of the other four focuses. In Table 1, I show one example of how values can be assigned to each of the five components.

BALANCED SCORECARD

Kaplan and Norton's balanced scorecard approach (see Figure 3) is similar to Skandia's Navigator in its use of multiple perspectives. The balanced scorecard uses four perspectives: financial (How do we appear to our stakeholders?), customer (How do we appear to our customers?), internal business

Table 1 Assigning Values to Skandia's Intellectual Capital Measurement Methodology

	1997	1996	1995	1994*
FINANCIAL FOCUS				
Operating income (MSEK)**	104	86	85	75
Total operating income (MSEK)	398	373	351	226
Income/expense ratio after loan losses	1.35	1.30	1.32	1.49
Capital ratio (%)	12.90	14.95	24.48	25
CUSTOMER FOCUS				
Number of customers	197,000	157,000	126,000	38,000
HUMAN FOCUS				
Average number of employees	218	200	163	130
Of whom, women (%)	56	49	45	42
PROCESS FOCUS				
Payroll costs/administrative expenses (%)	49	46	42	38
RENEWAL & DEVELOPMENT FOCUS				
Total assets (MSEK)	9,100	8,100	5,600	3,600
Share of new customers, 12 months (%)	25	25	232	n/a
Deposits and borrowing, general public (MSEK)	7,600	6,200	4,300	1,300
Lending and leasing (MSEK)	8,500	7,600	3,700	3,200
Net asset value of funds (MSEK)***	9,900	7,400	6,300	4,700

*Accounting-based indicators for 1994 have not been recalculated in accordance with the new Swedish Insurance Annual Accounts Act, which took effect on January 1, 1996.

**MSEK = Million Swedish krona.

***Changed calculation methods for 1996 and 1997.

Source: Skandia, "Human Capital in Transformation," *Intellectual Capital Prototype Report*, a supplement to Skandia's 1998 annual report.

Figure 2 Five Components of Skadia's Intellectual Capital Measurement Methodology

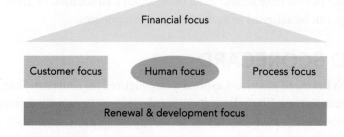

Figure 3 Balanced Scorecard Components

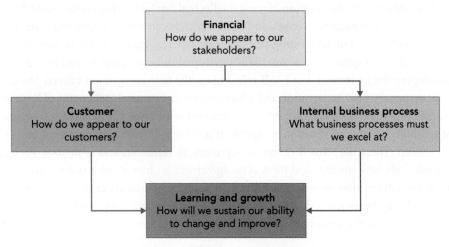

Source: Robert S. Kaplan and David P. Norton, *The Balanced Scorecard: Translating Strategy into Action*, Harvard Business School Press, Cambridge, Mass., 1996, p 9. Reproduced with permission.

process (What business processes must we excel at?), and learning and growth (How will we sustain our ability to change and improve?).[11] The learning and growth perspective includes categories for employee capabilities (human capital), information systems capabilities (information capital), and motivation, empowerment, and alignment (organizational capital).

In their book *Strategy Maps: Converting Intangible Assets into Tangible Outcomes*, Kaplan and Norton attempt to demonstrate how the intangible assets of human, information, and organizational capital can be measured. Human capital includes the skills, training, and know-how of employees. Information capital includes systems, databases, and networks. Organizational capital includes such concepts as culture, leadership, teamwork, and alignment with goals. The value of these assets comes from how well they align with the overall strategic priorities of the organization. Intellectual capital is measured by evaluating how well assets contribute to achieving organizational strategy.

Comparing the definitions of intellectual capital developed by Thomas Stewart and Leif Edvinsson, respectively, with the four perspectives of the balanced scorecard highlights how the balanced scorecard can be used to measure intellectual capital:[12]

> *"Intellectual capital is a combination of human capital—the brains, skills, insights, and potential of those in an organization* [learning and growth perspective: human]*— and structural capital—things like the capital wrapped up in customers* [customer perspective], *processes* [internal business processes perspective], *databases, brands, and IT systems* [learning and growth perspective: information capital]*. It is the ability to transform knowledge* [learning and growth perspective: organizational capital] *an intangible assets into wealth creating resources, by multiplying human capital with structural capital."*[13]

External Reporting of Intellectual Capital

The results of measuring intellectual capital also can be useful to investors. Let's look at three approaches to external reporting of intellectual capital.

SFAS NO. 142

The Financial Accounting Standards Board's (FASB) Statement of Financial Accounting Standards (SFAS) No. 142, "Goodwill and Other Intangible Assets," provides the accounting basis for measuring intangible assets. An intangible asset that is acquired from an external source is initially recognized at its fair value. If an intangible asset is developed internally, it is recognized as an expense when it is incurred. This will limit the recognition of most intellectual capital to what is purchased from outside the organization, such as patents, licenses, and trademarks, because they are the only ones recognized as assets. Generally accepted accounting principles do not recognize a value of human capital nor much of the structural capital, such as internally developed software, patents, and brands.

In developing the Statement, the FASB relied upon the four recognition criteria found in FASB Concepts Statement No. 5, "Recognition and Measurement in Financial Statements of Business Enterprises." These criteria are (1) the item meets the definition of an asset, (2) the item is measurable with sufficient reliability, (3) the information is capable of making a difference in decisions, and (4) the information indeed represents what it claims to represent, is verifiable, and is neutral. As intellectual capital is a relatively new concept and there is no agreement on how to measure it, many intellectual capital items will fail on criterion two (reliability in measurement) and criterion four (verifiable). Until these two criteria can be met, it is doubtful whether many intellectual assets will be included in financial statements. Even so, the amount of intellectual capital a firm has can still be conveyed to investors.

VALUE CHAIN SCORECARD

Baruch Lev has proposed a scorecard approach to provide investors and external decision makers with information relating to an organization's utilization of intellectual capital.[14] In an economy with joint ventures and alliances, outsourcing, built-to-customer ordering, supply chain management, and open source software, many important decisions are now made in consultation with partners in the value chain who are outside the organizational boundaries. Lev's scorecard provides nontransaction and nonfinancial information to support these decisions made with others in the value chain.

The scorecard mirrors three portions of the value chain: discovery and learning, implementation, and commercialization. Each of these three can, in turn, be subdivided into three additional categories for a total of nine categories.

The first phase of the value chain is the discovery of new products or services. These ideas can be generated internally through R&D efforts or employee networks, they can be acquired from outside the entity, and they can be identified through active and formal networks such as joint ventures, alliances, and supply chain integration. The second major phase of the value chain is the transformation of ideas into working products or services. This can be measured through a variety of milestones: patents, trademarks, or other intellectual property; passing formal feasibility hurdles; and, related to Internet technologies, quantitative measures of activity. The third phase of the value chain is the commercialization of the products or services. Customer measures could include brand value, marketing alliances, and customer churn. Performance indicators could include innovation revenues, market share, economic value added, and knowledge earnings. A final category would provide forward-looking information on the product/service pipeline.

A variety of indicators can be chosen for each of the nine portions of the scorecard. The indicators should have three attributes: They should be quantifiable, they should be standardized so comparisons can be made across firms, and there should be statistical evidence to link the indicators to corporate value. Although much of this information is historical, it is not necessarily based on transactions. Thus, little will be found in the existing accounting information.

INTELLECTUAL CAPITAL STATEMENTS

The Danish Ministry of Science, Technology and Innovation has published several reports introducing intellectual capital statements.[15] The Danish Financial Statements Act (June 2001) requires supplementary disclosure of intellectual assets if they are likely to affect future earnings.[16] The disclosures are required for all except the smallest enterprises (fewer than 50 employees) or sole proprietorships.

An intellectual capital statement consists of four elements: a knowledge narrative, a set of management challenges, a set of initiatives, and a set of indicators. (See Table 2 for a sample statement.) The knowledge narrative expresses how the products and services of the organization provide value to the user. It addresses such questions as these: What product or service does the company provide? What makes a difference for the consumer? What knowledge resources are necessary to be able to supply the product or service? What is the relationship between value and knowledge resources?

Management challenges include existing knowledge resources that should be strengthened and new knowledge resources that are needed. Three general types of challenges recognize that a company's knowledge lies in its information systems, the cooperation among employees, and the individual expert or group of experts.

Each management challenge is made up of a number of initiatives, which are actions concerned with how to develop or obtain knowledge resources and how to monitor them. Questions that are addressed include these: What are the existing and potential initiatives and objectives that relate to the company's knowledge management? How do the initiatives and objectives work? What initiatives can be used to boost the company's knowledge management? Indicators are the measures of the initiatives, expressed in effects, activities, and resources. They define the management challenges of the initiatives and make it possible to assess whether initiatives have been implemented and whether they have the desired effect.

Internal and External Reporting

In summary, there are five reasons why organizations may seek to measure intellectual capital: (1) to help formulate business strategy, (2) to develop key performance indicators that will help evaluate the execution of strategy, (3) to assist in evaluating mergers and acquisitions, (4) to link intellectual capital to an incentive and compensation plan, and (5) to communicate a firm's amount of intellectual capital to external stakeholders.

Table 2 Danish Intellectual Capital Statement

Knowledge Narrative	Management Challenge	Initiatives	Indicators
• Product or service: Secure and systematic assess of taxes for businesses	• Deep insight into users' conditions	• Analyze users' expectations and satisfaction • Monitor business activities • Monitor new legislation	• Number of new laws on taxes, excises, and duties • User satisfaction measurement • Number of annual surveys
• Use value: prevention of unfair competition • Knowledge resources: A simple, effective, and correct tax collection system advising users on the administration of often complex statutory rules and regulations	• Hiring and retaining employees	• Plan future need for competencies • Create a family-friendly workplace • Promote Odense Customs and Tax Region, including its role in society* • Develop a relationship between wages and results • Develop assignments characterized by responsibility and independence	• Staff turnover • Age distribution • Number of schemes on part-time work leave and other time off • Number of applicants • Number of employees with new salaries • Number of employees with bonuses • Employee satisfaction survey

(continued)

Table 2 Danish Intellectual Capital Statement (*continued*)

Knowledge Narrative	Management Challenge	Initiatives	Indicators
	• Development of professional and personal competencies among the personnel	• Create an overall understanding of Odense Customs and Tax Region's products • Develop knowledge-sharing across professions • Introduce competency development • Introduce development methods	• Number of job changes in the organization • Number of courses and other knowledge-sharing activities • Number of international exchanges • Training cost size • Competency evaluation
	• Development of new effective processes	• Develop a process and a culture of improvement	• Number of process descriptions • Number of improvement proposals • Benchmarking
	• Electronic accessible rules, practices, processes, and experience	• Anchor rules, practices, processes, and experience electronically • Monitor results of new legislation, user behavior, etc.	• Number of applied process descriptions • Number of decisions • Number of new acts and changed practices
	• Quality assurance with respect to equal treatment	• Prepare quality declarations • Prepare quality assurance guide • Analyse users' expectations and satisfaction • Always behave politely and correctly	• Number of language analyses • Number of quality assurance decisions • Number of appeals • Number of complaints • User satisfaction surveys in this area

*This is an intellectual capital statement from Odense Customs and Tax Region, a private organization located in Odense, Denmark.

Source: Jan Mouritsen, et al., Intellectual Capital Statements—The New Guideline, Danish Ministry of Science, Technology and Innovation, 2003, p. 17.

Skandia's Navigator and the balanced scorecard have been used extensively as measurements of intellectual capital that help develop strategy, assess the effectiveness of corporate strategy, and formulate compensation plans. These are internal uses of intellectual capital. Intellectual capital currently is not being reported to external stakeholders, however, because there is no agreement on acceptable approaches to measuring intellectual capital and because the measures that are used do not yet meet accounting standards for reliability and verifiability.

With the rise of the "knowledge economy" over the past 20 years, however, intellectual capital is becoming more important and should be disclosed. That is why the two newer approaches, Lev's value chain scorecard and the Danish approach for supplemental disclosure of intellectual capital, hold so much promise. I suggest these approaches be given serious consideration.

ENDNOTES

1. Stephen Pike and Göran Roos, "Mathematics and Modern Business Management," *Journal of Intellectual Capital*, February 2004, pp. 243-256; and Daniel, "IC Valuation and Measurement: Classifying the State of the Art," *Journal of Intellectual Capital*, February 2004, pp. 230–242.

2. Thomas Stewart, *Intellectual Capital: The New Wealth of Organizations*, Currency Doubleday, New York, N.Y, 1997, p. 10.

3. Thomas Stewart, *The Wealth of Knowledge: Intellectual Capital and the Twenty-First Century Organization*, Currency Doubleday, New York, N.Y., 2001, p. 13.

4. Leif Edvinsson, *Corporate Longitude: What You Need To Know To Navigate The Knowledge Economy*, Financial Times Prentice Hall, Pearson Education, Inc., Upper Saddle River, N.J., 2002, p. 8.

5. Bernard Marr, Dina Gray, and Andy Neely, "Why Do Firms Measure Their Intellectual Capital?" *Journal of Intellectual Capital*, October 2003, pp. 441–464.

6. Leif Edvinsson and Michael Malone, *Intellectual Capital: Realizing Your Company's True Value By Finding Its Hidden Brainpower*, HarperBusiness, New York, N.Y., 1997.

7. Andriessen, 2004.

8. Skandia, *Visualizing Intellectual Capital in Skandia*, a supplement to Skandia's 1994 Annual Report; Skandia, *Intellectual Capital—Value Creating Processes*, a supplement to Skandia's 1995 Annual Report; Robert S. Kaplan and David P. Norton, *The Balanced Scorecard: Translating Strategy into Action*, Harvard Business School Press, Cambridge, Mass., 1996; Robert S. Kaplan and David P. Norton, *The Strategy-Focused Organization: How Balanced Scorecard Companies Thrive in the New Business Environment*, Harvard Business School Press, Cambridge, Mass., 2001; Robert S. Kaplan and David P. Norton, *Strategy Maps: Converting Intangible Assets into Tangible Outcomes*, Harvard Business School Press, Cambridge, Mass., 2004; and Nick Bontis, Nicola Dargonetti, Kristine Jacobsen, and Göran Roos, "The Knowledge Toolbox: A Review of the Tools Available to Measure and Manage Intangible Resources," *European Management Journal*, August 1999, pp. 391–401.

9. Skandia, 1994; Skandia, 1995; Skandia, *Renewal and Development*, a supplement to Skandia's 1995 Interim Report; Skandia, *Power of Innovation*, a supplement to Skandia's 1996 Interim Report; Skandia, *Customer Value*, a supplement to Skandia's 1996 Annual Report; Skandia, *Intelligent Enterprising*, a supplement to Skandia's 1997 Interim Report; Skandia, "Human Capital in Transformation," *Intellectual Capital Prototype Report*, a supplement to Skandia's 1998 Annual Report; Edvinsson and Malone, 1997; and Edvinsson, 2002.

10. Edvinsson, 2002, p. 84.

11. Kaplan and Norton, 1996, p. 9.

12. Stewart, 2001; and Edvinsson, 2002.

13. Edvinsson, 2002, p. 8 (annotated).

14. Baruch Lev, *Intangibles: Management, Measurement, and Reporting*, Brookings Institution Press, Washington, D.C., 2001.

15. Jan Mouritsen, Per Bukh, Mette Johansen, Heine Larsen, Christian Nielsen, Jens Haisler, Benedikte Stakemann, *Analysing Intellectual Capital Statements*, Danish Ministry of Science, Technology and Innovation, Copenhagen, Denmark, 2003; Jan Mouritsen, Per Bukh, Kirsten Flagstad, Stefan Thorbjørnsen, Mette Johansen, Sita Kotnis, Heine Larsen, Christian Nielsen, Isa Kjærgaard, Lotte Krag, Gustav Jeppesen, Jens Haisler, Benedikte Stakemann, *Intellectual Capital Statements—The New Guideline*, Danish Ministry of Science, Technology and Innovation, Copenhagen, Denmark, 2003. More examples of Danish intellectual-capital statements can be found in *Intellectual Capital Statements in Practice—Inspiration and Good Advice*, Danish Ministry of Science, Technology and Innovation, Copenhagen, Denmark, 2002.

16. KPMG, *The Danish Financial Statements Act*, 2002.

The Strategic Value of Customer Profitability Analysis

Erik M. van Raaij

Introduction

Aided by decreasing costs of computing power and increasingly sophisticated methods of customer data collection, the customer database has become a core asset for organisations of all types and sizes. It is typically used to record and store customer details, such as name and address, and behavioural data, such as purchases made and responses to marketing campaigns. On a tactical level, these data can be used to improve services (for instance, a hotel can offer a personalised service on the basis of the data it has on past customer preferences), or to improve marketing effectiveness (such as when a charity that sends out selective appeals to its most generous donors). In this paper, our focus is on uncovering strategic information—information that has value for top managers—that is hidden within the customer database.

One approach to uncovering such strategic information is performing a customer profitability analysis (CPA). The basics of such an analysis are discussed in the next section. A CPA results in two types of insights: the degree of profitability for each individual customer, and the distribution of profitability among customers within the customer base. These two types of data enable novel analyses related to:

1. costs and revenues;
2. risk; and
3. strategic positioning.

Each of these three areas is discussed in a separate section of this paper. CPA has its limitations, as it is a retrospective analysis, based on historical customer data. We will therefore also look at what is needed to make the shift from retrospective analysis to prospective analysis, and deal with issues like customer lifetime value, and the "strategic value" of customers. The customer base as a network of customer relationships is one of the key market-based assets of the firm underpinning the generation of shareholder value (Srivastava et al., 1998, 2001). CPA provides new strategic insights in the value and the composition of the customer base and it is the aim of this paper to highlight both strategic benefits and limitations of CPA. These insights will benefit account managers, who need to make decisions about marketing expenditure on individual accounts, senior marketing managers, who need to optimize the use of a firm's marketing resources, as well as company directors, who need to evaluate the contribution of marketing to the generation of shareholder value.

Customer Profitability Analysis

"Customer profitability analysis" describes the process of allocating revenues and costs to customer segments or individual customer accounts, such that the profitability of those segments and/or accounts can be calculated. The calculation of customer profitability amounts to an extensive activity-based costing (ABC) exercise (Cooper and Kaplan, 1991; Foster and Gupta, 1994). The first step in ABC is the identification of cost pools – i.e., distinctive sets of activities performed within the organisation (for example, procurement, manufacturing, customer service). For all cost pools, cost drivers are identified: units in which the resource consumption of the cost pool can be expressed (for example, number of purchase orders, number of units produced, number of service calls). Costs are then allocated to cost objects (such as products) based on the extent to which these objects consume cost driver units. ABC as a cost accounting method has revolutionised the way in which costs are allocated to products. Once it became accepted that not every product requires the same type and same level of activities, it was a small step to see that customers, too, differ in their consumption of resources. The size and number of orders, the number of sales visits, the use of helpdesks and various other services can be very different from one customer to another. Consequently, two customers who buy exactly the same product mix for the same prices (thus generating exactly the same profit margins on their purchases) can have different relationship costs, leading to different levels of customer profitability.

Many companies nowadays make use of advanced customer relationship management (CRM) systems, which will compute customer profitability figures on the basis of sales and service data available to the system. But as these figures are only as good as the quality and comprehensiveness of the data put into the system, it is good to review the general process of CPA, such that the accuracy of computed CPA figures can be evaluated. The process starts with scrutinising the list of current customers. Many customer databases contain details of customers who no longer have a relationship with the firm (Mulhern, 1999). The first step in the CPA process therefore deals with the identification of the "active" customers in the customer database, in order to assure that costs are allocated to active customers only. Schmittlein et al. (1987) and Schmittlein and Peterson (1994) have developed quite sophisticated methods to calculate the probability of a customer being an active customer, based on recency and frequency of purchases. A simpler approach would be to define active customers as all customers that have interacted with the company during a specific period, such as the last 12 months, either by placing an order or by receiving sales or service calls.

The next step is the design of the customer profitability model. In this step, the firm's operations have to be analysed to see what activities are performed, and what drives the costs of these activities. For example, the cost driver of sales activities can be the number of sales visits; the driver of order processing activities can be the number of orders. Ultimately, all relevant costs should be assigned to activities, and for each activity, appropriate cost drivers need to be identified.

The actual calculation of customer profitability is done by supplying the model with data. The total cost for a cost pool divided by the total number of cost driver units consumed within a given time period, results in the cost per cost driver unit. Customer relationship costs (for instance, sales costs, service costs, logistics costs) are calculated on the basis of cost driver units consumed by each customer relationship. Customer relationship costs are then subtracted from the individual customer's sales revenues in order to arrive at a customer profitability figure. This will be the most time-consuming step in the CPA process. For instance, if we look at sales activities, we have to gather the costs of all sales activities, the total number of sales visits made by all sales persons, and the number of sales visits paid to each individual customer. The level of detail will be determined by data availability, and by practical considerations. For example, each sales visit could be assigned a standard cost, regardless of visit duration, or the length of visits could be taken into account. The latter is more precise, but it requires more effort to record. Firms who perform this analysis for the first time will find that while many data will be available in various databases, certain data simply is not yet available within the firm (reference suppressed). Some calculations might be very costly to perform, as data in different formats, coming from different databases, may have to be converted record by record.

The information produced by the CPA process is a valuable reward for all these efforts. CPA yields aggregate and individual CPA figures, which together provide novel insights in costs, revenues, risk, and strategic positioning. At the level of individual customers, CPA figures provide a clear picture how buyer behavior (service requests, paying behaviour, and the like) and supplier behaviour (service provision, discounts, marketing efforts, for example) compare with revenues and sales margins. Figure 1 shows a revenue/cost analysis for two customers with identical sales profiles but with different cost profiles. Customer B has higher sales costs (possibly due to a higher number of sales calls and/or as a result of many small orders), has higher service costs (possibly as a result of time-critical operations and/or wrong use of products), and has been assigned high costs for credit (possibly due to lenient credit terms and/or tax paying behaviour). Differences in discount structures could exacerbate the profitability divergence even further.

At the aggregate level, CPA figures provide insights into the distribution and the concentration of profits within the total customer base. The two most common ways in which CPA figures at the aggregate level are depicted are in a customer pyramid (Zeithaml et al., 2001) or as an "inverted Lorentz" (Mulhern, 1999) or "Stobachoff" (Storbacka, 1998) curve. A customer pyramid is used to show tiers of customers within the customer base. Most commonly, the tiers are based on revenues,

Figure 1 **Customer specific relationship costs make the difference between profit and loss for two customers with identical sales**

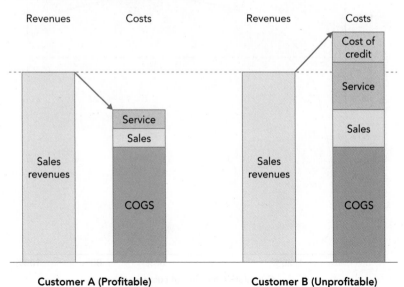

Customer A (Profitable)   Customer B (Unprofitable)

Figure 2 A customer pyramid with four revenue tiers

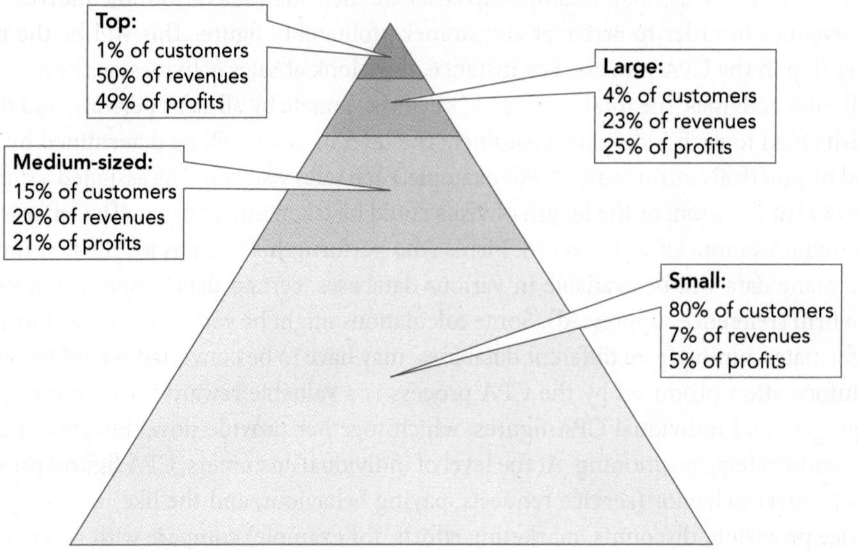

Top:
1% of customers
50% of revenues
49% of profits

Large:
4% of customers
23% of revenues
25% of profits

Medium-sized:
15% of customers
20% of revenues
21% of profits

Small:
80% of customers
7% of revenues
5% of profits

with a large group of low revenue customers at the base of the pyramid and a small group of high revenue customers at the apex. But, when profitability figures are available the customer pyramid can also be drawn along the lines of profitability tiers. Figure 2 shows a customer pyramid based on revenue tiers, but enriched with profitability data. More examples of how customer pyramids can be constructed and used are discussed in Zeithaml et al. (2001).

The inverted Lorentz or Stobachoff curve is drawn by lining up all customers on the horizontal axis from highest absolute profitability to lowest (in many cases negative) profitability, while plotting cumulative profitability on the vertical axis. Figure 3 shows a typical shape of the Stobachoff curve. In this example, the first 60 per cent of customers are profitable, generating about 125 per cent of

Figure 3 The Stobachoff curve depicts how profitability is distributed within the customer base

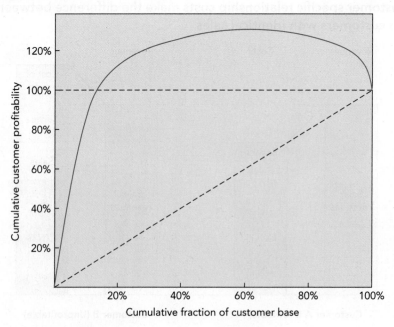

total profits. The remaining 40 per cent of customers are unprofitable and are consuming the profitability surplus generated by the first 60 per cent. More extreme examples have been cited, where the first 20 per cent of customers generate 225 per cent of total profitability (Cooper and Kaplan, 1991). The position of the apex (to the right or to the left) and the size of the area underneath the curve signify the concentration and distribution of profits among customers in the customer base.

In the following three sections, we will show how individual and aggregate CPA figures can be used to make strategic decisions in the areas of cost and revenue management, risk management, and strategic positioning.

MANAGING COSTS AND REVENUES

The first and most obvious use of customer profitability data lies in managing both revenues from individual customers and costs that have to be incurred to secure those revenues. Without the allocation of marketing, sales, and service costs to individual customers, all revenue from customers may seem good revenue, and the investments in marketing, sales, and service to secure those revenues are difficult to justify. CPA enables account managers to bring marketing expenditures per customer in line with current revenues per customer and with future revenue potential.

Customer relationship costs can be reduced by imposing stricter credit terms on customers and by exploring low cost alternatives for marketing, sales and service. New developments in information and communications technologies (ICT), such as the internet and mobile telephony have enabled companies to use low cost approaches such as telesales, self-service kiosks, online ordering, and web-based product support. Strategies for increasing revenues with existing customers include increasing share-of-wallet, cross-selling, up-selling, and helping the customer to grow. Revenues are also managed through pricing. There are three important issues related to pricing: discounts, the pricing of value-added services, and discriminatory pricing. In the absence of customer profitability data, discounts are usually based on sales volume.

This can result in large customers with particularly high service demands receiving discounts that are larger than their customer profitability margin. Such a situation may be sensible in the short run, for instance when a new customer is acquired and a service investment is made in order to build the relationship, but it is untenable in the long run. CPA will also help develop pricing strategies for valued-added services. The analysis may show that certain services depress customer profitability to such an extent, that they can no longer be provided free-of-charge. It can also help to develop discriminatory pricing strategies, where certain customers, such as gold card holders, will continue to receive these services for free, while others, such as blue card holders, will be charged. It must be noted that customer profitability figures may inspire such changes in pricing strategies, but that studies of customer attitudes and value perceptions will need to be carried out in order to make sure that the new pricing strategies are accepted in the market.

MANAGING RISK

CPA also yields information about the vulnerability of future cash flows from customers. The profitability distribution curve (Figure 3) contains information about levels of dependency and subsidisation within the customer base. Subsidisation refers to the extent to which profits generated by profitable customers subsidise losses generated by other customers. Dependency refers to the extent to which profitability depends on a small proportion of customers. The size of the area below the curve and the position of the apex are indicators of subsidisation and dependency. Figure 4 shows the shapes of profitability distribution curves in four situations with different levels of subsidisation and dependency. In a multi-market firm, these profitability distribution curves can be analysed for each

Figure 4 Four possible shapes of customer profitability distribution curves in different situations

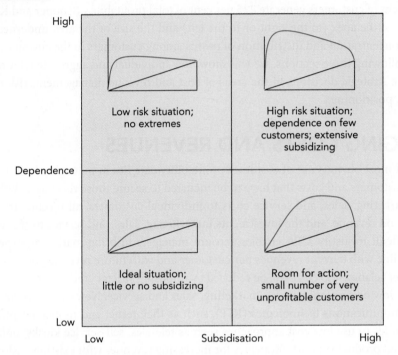

market separately, and while the overall profitability distribution may look low-risk, the curves for individual markets may indicate high-risk situations.

Managers can take various courses of action to mitigate risks related to dependency and subsidisation. In the case of high levels of dependency, two complementary courses of action are recommended. The first course of action would be to focus on the small proportion of profitable customers. It is imperative that these customers are retained, and account managers would do well to review service levels, customer satisfaction, and customer buying behaviour in order to ensure these customers stay with the firm. The second course of action would focus on the loss-making customers. The customer profitability data should show what cost drivers cause these losses of subsidisation and dependency (these may be different cost drivers for different customer groups). Corrective measures could then be implemented to reduce the customer relationship costs and/or to increase revenues for these customer groups.

In situations of high subsidisation, but without high dependence, efforts can concentrate on the loss-making customers. Some loss-making customers may be valuable to the firm for other reasons than immediate profit, but in principle, every loss-making customer represents an opportunity to improve profits. Again, profitability can be improved on the cost side or on the revenue side. On the cost side, service levels can be adjusted, or less costly service concepts (such as self-service) introduced. On the revenue side, pricing and discounting can be adjusted, or cross-selling and up-selling stimulated.

Because dependence within the customer base has a direct impact on the vulnerability of future cash flows, senior management needs to have a good insight in the distribution of customer profitability. In the absence of customer profitability data, such insights usually come from gross margin figures, but our own analysis in an industrial cleaning firm (reference suppressed) has shown that gross margin may explain as little as 12 per cent of customer profitability.

STRATEGIC POSITIONING

The third use of customer profitability data is for segmentation, targeting and positioning. The most common bases for market segmentation are customer needs and customer characteristics, but customer profitability is increasingly used as well (Storbacka, 1997). Based on profitability data, customers can be classified into profitable, break-even, and unprofitable customers. The next step is to describe these groups using descriptor variables or "profilers". In consumer markets, these include socio-demographic, geographic, and psychographic variables; in business markets, others such as company demographics and industry type can be used. Statistical analyses can be used to determine, which combinations of profilers best describe the membership of a particular group.

Armed with this knowledge, organisations can target more customers resembling those in the most profitable segments. This presupposes, however, that managers have a sound understanding of what makes these customers more profitable than others. At the same time, customers that are alike those in the least profitable segments, can be avoided, or at least customer acquisition investments in those segments can be reduced. Current profitability should never be the only parameter for segment attractiveness, however, segment size, segment growth, competitive intensity, and the fit with company objectives and capabilities should also be taken into account.

Whether unprofitable customers should be "fired" (i.e. no further time or effort is to be expended on their account) is an issue that requires special consideration. For many the initial response to negative profitability figures may be to get rid of such a customer. It is important to remember however, that customer profitability iscalculated on the basis of total cost. Even if a customer is not profitable on the basis oftotal cost, the revenues generated by that customer may still outweigh marginal costs.

In that case, the customer still contributes to recouping part of the fixed costs of the organisation. Without such a customer, and with the same level of fixed costs, cumulative profitability would be lower. "Firing" unprofitable customers will have a positive effect on overall profitability only when they are replaced by profitable customers, or when such fixed costs as sales or service infrastructure are cutback.

Once customers have been segmented according to profitability and target segments have been selected, organisations can use profitability data to develop different value propositions for different segments. CPA provides deep insights into the costs associated with various service levels. Combined with insights in customer needs and company capabilities, this can be translated into segment-specific service concepts. The smallest customers (often the least profitable) will be offered self-service or standardised services for a fee, with the degree of customised services increasing for customer groups with higher profitability levels. At the same time, some services that were hitherto free of charge may only be offered for a fee, even for the largest customers.

CUSTOMER LIFETIME VALUE AND THE "STRATEGIC VALUE" OF CUSTOMERS

So far, we have mainly looked at what is called "retrospective customer profitability analysis"—i.e. profitability analysis on the basis of historical revenue and cost data. While retrospective CPA provides valuable insights in current dependence and subsidisation within the customer base, its value for long term customer base management is somewhat limited. In order to move from retrospective CPA to prospective CPA, estimations of future revenues and future costs need to be added to the analysis. The baseline model would be simple extrapolation of current revenues and costs. A more advanced model would take customer life-cycle dynamics intoaccount. Young, growing customers, and customers in growth industries would receive higher estimates of future revenues than customers in mature or declining markets. When an estimate of the duration of the customer relationship is also added to the equation, customer lifetime value can be calculated, as the (discounted) sum of all profits from a customer over the expected duration of the relationship with that customer.

CPA looks only at financial positives and negatives in the relationship with the customer. Account managers are usually quick to add, in defence of any of their accounts with low (or negative) profitability, that non-financial measures should also be included in the assessment of customer worth. This is often described as the "strategic value" of a customer. Senior management should be wary of buying in to the "strategic value" argument, however. A customer is only strategically valuable if having this customer leads to demonstrable additional income with other customers, now or in the near future. Three sources for such indirect revenue streams are as follows.

- *Attraction*. Some customers that are unprofitable by themselves, can serve as reference clients for the acquisition of other, more profitable customers, for instance when entering a new market.

- *Learning*. Some customers can add value as co-development partners, leading to new or improved products or services that can be sold profitably to other customers.

- *Volume*. Some customers can, as a result of their sheer size, absorb large amounts of fixed costs, thus enabling the company to engage in profitable activities with other customers, which would otherwise be financially impossible.

Both prospective CPA and the assessment of the "strategic value" of customers depend heavily upon estimates, assumptions, and forecasts. Retrospective CPA, on the other hand, is more fact-based. All the three methods complement each other in the quest to value one of the most precious assets a firm may have: its customer base.

CONCLUSIONS

CPA is a potent tool for marketing intelligence gatherers and strategic planners to understand how profitability is distributed within the customer base. But apart from their apparent use within the marketing and sales departments, CPA outcomes should also find their ways to the boardroom. The profitability distribution curve shows to what degree profitability depends on a small number of accounts, as well as to what degree profitable accounts subsidise less profitable ones. Even when the curve for the organisation as a whole seems all right, analyses for individual markets may uncover high-risk profitability distributions in certain parts of the customer base.

Shareholder value is created through cash flows from customers. CPA uncovers where these cash flows are generated. In the absence of CPA, CRM strategies are usually based on measures like gross margins and/or volumes. Research has shown that these measures do not necessarily correlate well with customer profitability. CPA provides a more reliable basis for decisions about service level agreements, investments in customer relationships, and strategic targeting and positioning.

Strategic decision-makers should also be aware of the limitations of CPA. First, all customer profitability analyses are based on a cost model, which can have varyingdegrees of sophistication. Within this cost model, assumptions and decisions are built-in, with regard to how fixed and variable costs are assigned to activities, and subsequently, to customers. Users of CPA outcomes should be aware of how the cost model is constructed. Second, CPA, in its retrospective form, analyses past performance, and should be used with an appropriate level of caution, so as not to steer on rear-view mirror information only. Third, low, or negative profitability for a customer should not automatically lead to the conclusion that that customer is to be "fired". More often, it is better to look for opportunities for increasing revenue or reducing cost.

Increasing pressure on shareholder value forces planners to search for opportunities to increase cash flows via cost reductions and revenue increases, and to reduce the volatility and vulnerability of cash flows. CPA provides valuable data for such cash flow enhancements. If improved insights into the distribution of customer profitability can be combined with the increased possibilities of ICT for low cost service delivery, then organisations can plan realistically to develop and implement value-driven differentiated customer service strategies.

REFERENCES

Cooper, R. and Kaplan, R.S. (1991), "Profit priorities from activity-based costing", *Harvard Business Review*, Vol. 69, pp. 130–5.

Foster, G. and Gupta, M. (1994), "Marketing, cost management and management accounting", *Journal of Management Accounting Research*, pp. 43–77.

Mulhern, F.J. (1999), "Customer profitability analysis: measurement, concentration, and research directions", *Journal of Interactive Marketing*, Vol. 13 No. 1, pp. 25–40.

Schmittlein, D.C. and Peterson, R.A. (1994), "Customer base analysis: an industrial purchase process application", *Marketing Science*, Vol. 13 No. 1, pp. 41–67.

Schmittlein, D.C., Morrison, D.G. and Colombo, R. (1987), "Counting your customers: who are they and what will they do next?", *Management Science*, Vol. 33 No. 1, pp. 1–24.

Srivastava, R.K., Fahey, L. and Christensen, H.K. (2001), "The resource-based view and marketing: the role of market-based assets in gaining competitive advantage", *Journal of Management*, Vol. 27, pp. 777–802.

Srivastava, R.K., Shervani, T.A. and Fahey, L. (1998), "Market-based assets and shareholder value: a framework for analysis", *Journal of Marketing*, Vol. 62, pp. 2–18.

Storbacka, K. (1997), "Segmentation based on customer profitability—retrospective analysis of retail bank customer bases", *Journal of Marketing Management*, Vol. 13, pp. 479–92.

Storbacka, K. (1998), "Customer profitability: analysis and design issues", in Brodie, R., Brookes, R., Colgate, M., Collins, B. and Martin, A. (Eds), *Proceedings of the 6th International Colloquium in Relationship Marketing*, University of Auckland, Auckland, pp. 124–44.

Zeithaml, V.A., Rust, R.T. and Lemon, K.N. (2001), "The customer pyramid: creating and serving profitable customers", *California Management Review*, Vol. 43 No. 4, pp. 118–42.

Innovation Killers: *How Financial Tools Destroy Your Capacity to Do New Things*

by Clayton M. Christensen, Stephen P. Kaufman, and Willy C. Shih

For years we've been puzzling about why so many smart, hardworking managers in well-run companies find it impossible to innovate successfully. Our investigations have uncovered a number of culprits, which we've discussed in earlier books and articles. These include paying too much attention to the company's most profitable customers (thereby leaving less-demanding customers at risk) and creating new products that don't help customers do the jobs they want to do. Now we'd like to name the misguided application of three financial-analysis tools as an accomplice in the conspiracy against successful innovation. We allege crimes against these suspects:

- The use of discounted cash flow (DCF) and net present value (NPV) to evaluate investment opportunities causes managers to underestimate the real returns and benefits of proceeding with investments in innovation.

- The way that fixed and sunk costs are considered when evaluating future investments confers an unfair advantage on challengers and shackles incumbent firms that attempt to respond to an attack.

- The emphasis on earnings per share as the primary driver of share price and hence of shareholder value creation, to the exclusion of almost everything else, diverts resources away from investments whose payoff lies beyond the immediate horizon.

These are not bad tools and concepts, we hasten to add. But the way they are commonly wielded in evaluating investments creates a systematic bias against innovation. We will recommend alternative methods that, in our experience, can help managers innovate with a much more astute eye for future value. Our primary aim, though, is simply to bring these concerns to light in the hope that others with deeper expertise may be inspired to examine and resolve them.

Misapplying Discounted Cash Flow and Net Present Value

The first of the misleading and misapplied tools of financial analysis is the method of discounting cash flow to calculate the net present value of an initiative. Discounting a future stream of cash flows into a "present value" assumes that a rational investor would be indifferent to having a dollar today or to receiving some years from now a dollar plus the interest or return that could be earned by investing that dollar for those years. With that as an operating principle, it makes perfect sense to assess investments by dividing the money to be received in future years by $(1 + r)n$, where r is the discount rate—the annual return from investing that money—and n is the number of years during which the investment could be earning that return.

While the mathematics of discounting is logically impeccable, analysts commonly commit two errors that create an anti-innovation bias. The first error is to assume that the base case of not investing in the innovation—the do-nothing scenario against which cash flows from the innovation are compared—is that the present health of the company will persist indefinitely into the future if the investment is not made. As shown in the exhibit "The DCF Trap," the mathematics considers the investment in isolation and compares the present value of the innovation's cash stream less project costs with the cash stream in the absence of the investment, which is assumed to be unchanging. In most situations, however, competitors' sustaining and disruptive investments over time result in price and margin pressure, technology changes, market share losses, sales volume decreases, and a declining stock price. As Eileen Rudden at Boston Consulting Group pointed out, the most likely stream of cash for the company in the do-nothing scenario is not a continuation of the status quo. It is a nonlinear decline in performance.

It's tempting but wrong to assess the value of a proposed investment by measuring whether it will make us better off than we are now. It's wrong because, if things are deteriorating on their own, we might be worse off than we are now after we make the proposed investment but better off than we would have been without it. Philip Bobbitt calls this logic Parmenides' Fallacy, after the ancient Greek logician who claimed to have proved that conditions in the real world must necessarily be unchanging. Analysts who attempt to distill the value of an innovation into one simple number that they can compare with other simple numbers are generally trapped by Parmenides' Fallacy.

It's hard to accurately forecast the stream of cash from an investment in innovation. It is even more difficult to forecast the extent to which a firm's financial performance may deteriorate in the absence of the investment. But this analysis must be done. Remember the response that good economists are taught to offer to the question "How are you?" It is "Relative to what?" This is a crucial question. Answering it entails assessing the projected value of the innovation against a range of scenarios, the most realistic of which is often a deteriorating competitive and financial future.

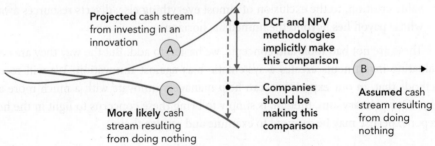

The DCF Trap

Most executives compare the cash flows from innovation against the default scenario of doing nothing, assuming–incorrectly–that the present health of the company will persist indefinitely if the investment is not made. For a better assessment of the innovation's value, the comparison should be between its projected discounted cash flow and the more likely scenario of a decline in performance in the absence of innovation investment.

The second set of problems with discounted cash flow calculations relates to errors of estimation. Future cash flows, especially those generated by disruptive investments, are difficult to predict. Numbers for the "out years" can be a complete shot in the dark. To cope with what cannot be known, analysts often project a year-by-year stream of numbers for three to five years and then "punt" by calculating a terminal value to account for everything thereafter. The logic, of course, is that the year-to-year estimates for distant years are so imprecise as to be no more accurate than a terminal value. To calculate a terminal value, analysts divide the cash to be generated in the last year for which they've done a specific estimate by $(r - g)$, the discount rate minus the projected growth rate in cash flows from that time on. They then discount that single number back to the present. In our experience, assumed terminal values often account for more than half of a project's total NPV.

Terminal value numbers, based as they are on estimates for preceding years, tend to amplify errors contained in early-year assumptions. More worrisome still, terminal value doesn't allow for the scenario testing that we described above—contrasting the result of this investment with the deterioration in performance that is the most likely result of doing nothing. And yet, because of market inertia, competitors' development cycles, and the typical pace of disruption, it is often in the fifth year or beyond—the point at which terminal value factors in—that the decline of the enterprise in the do-nothing scenario begins to accelerate.

Arguably, a root cause of companies' persistent underinvestment in the innovations required to sustain long-term success is the indiscriminate and oversimplified use of NPV as an analytical tool. Still, we understand the desire to quantify streams of cash that defy quantification and then to distill those streams into a single number that can be compared with other single numbers: It is an attempt to translate cacophonous articulations of the future into a language—numbers—that everyone can read and compare. We hope to show that numbers are not the only language into which the value of future investments can be translated—and that there are, in fact, other, better languages that all members of a management team can understand.

USING FIXED AND SUNK COSTS UNWISELY

The second widely misapplied paradigm of financial decision making relates to fixed and sunk costs. When evaluating a future course of action, the argument goes, managers should consider only the future or marginal cash outlays (either capital or expense) that are required for an innovation investment, subtract those outlays from the marginal cash that is likely to flow in, and discount the resulting net flow to the present. As with the paradigm of DCF and NPV, there is nothing wrong with the mathematics of this principle—as long as the capabilities required for yesterday's success are adequate for tomorrow's as well. When new capabilities are required for future success, however, this margining on fixed and sunk costs biases managers toward leveraging assets and capabilities that are likely to become obsolete.

For the purposes of this discussion we'll define fixed costs as those whose level is independent of the level of output. Typical fixed costs include general and administrative costs: salaries and benefits, insurance, taxes, and so on. (Variable costs include things like raw materials, commissions, and pay to temporary workers.) Sunk costs are those portions of fixed costs that are irrevocably committed, typically including investments in buildings and capital equipment and R&D costs.

An example from the steel industry illustrates how fixed and sunk costs make it difficult for companies that can and should invest in new capabilities actually to do so. In the late 1960s, steel minimills such as Nucor and Chaparral began disrupting integrated steelmakers such as U.S. Steel (USX), picking off customers in the least-demanding product tiers of each market and then moving relentlessly upmarket, using their 20% cost advantage to capture first the rebar market and then the bar and rod, angle iron, and structural beam markets. By 1988 the minimills had driven the higher-cost integrated mills out of lower-tier products, and Nucor had begun building its first minimill to roll sheet steel in Crawfordsville, Indiana. Nucor estimated that for an investment of $260 million it could sell 800,000 tons of steel annually at a price of $350 per ton. The cash cost to produce a ton of sheet steel in the Crawfordsville mill would be $270. When the timing of cash flows was taken into account, the internal rate of return to Nucor on this investment was over 20%—substantially higher than Nucor's weighted average cost of capital.

Incumbent USX recognized that the minimills constituted a grave threat. Using a new technology called continuous strip production, Nucor had now entered the sheet steel market, albeit with an inferior-quality product, at a significantly lower cost per ton. And Nucor's track record of vigilant improvement meant that the quality of its sheet steel would improve with production experience. Despite this understanding, USX engineers did not even consider building a greenfield minimill like the one Nucor built. The reason? It seemed more profitable to leverage the old technology than to create the new. USX's existing mills, which used traditional technology, had 30% excess capacity, and the marginal cash cost of producing an extra ton of steel by leveraging that excess capacity was less than $50 per ton. When USX's financial analysts contrasted the marginal cash flow of $300 ($350 revenue minus the $50 marginal cost) with the average cash flow of $80 per ton in a greenfield mill, investment in a new low-cost minimill made no sense. What's more, USX's plants were depreciated, so the marginal cash flow of $300 on a low asset base looked very attractive.

And therein lies the rub. Nucor, the attacker, had no fixed or sunk cost investments on which to do a marginal cost calculation. To Nucor, the full cost was the marginal cost. Crawfordsville was the only choice on its menu—and because the IRR was attractive, the decision was simple. USX, in contrast, had two choices on its menu: It could build a greenfield plant like Nucor's with a lower average cost per ton or it could utilize more fully its existing facility.

So what happened? Nucor has continued to improve its process, move upmarket, and gain market share with more efficient continuous strip production capabilities, while USX has relied on the capabilities that had been built to succeed in the past. USX's strategy to maximize marginal profit, in other words, caused the company not to minimize long-term average costs. As a result, the company is locked into an escalating cycle of commitment to a failing strategy.

The attractiveness of any investment can be completely assessed only when it is compared with the attractiveness of the right alternatives on a menu of investments. When a company is looking at adding capacity that is identical to existing capacity, it makes sense to compare the marginal cost of leveraging the old with the full cost of creating the new. But when new technologies or capabilities are required for future competitiveness, margining on the past will send you down the wrong path. The argument that investment decisions should be based on marginal costs is always correct. But when creating new capabilities is the issue, the relevant marginal cost is actually the full cost of creating the new.

When we look at fixed and sunk costs from this perspective, several anomalies we have observed in our studies of innovation are explained. Executives in established companies bemoan how expensive it is to build new brands and develop new sales and distribution channels—so they seek instead to leverage their existing brands and structures. Entrants, in contrast, simply create new ones. The problem for the incumbent isn't that the challenger can outspend it; it's that the challenger is spared the dilemma of having to choose between full-cost and marginal-cost options. We have repeatedly observed leading, established companies misapply fixed and- sunk-cost doctrine and rely on assets and capabilities that were forged in the past to succeed in the future. In doing so, they fail to make the same investments that entrants and attackers find to be profitable.

A related misused financial practice that biases managers against investment in needed future capabilities is that of using a capital asset's estimated *usable* lifetime as the period over which it should be depreciated. This causes problems when the asset's usable lifetime is longer than its *competitive* lifetime. Managers who depreciate assets according to the more gradual schedule of usable life often face massive write-offs when those assets become competitively obsolete and need to be replaced with newer-technology assets. This was the situation confronting the integrated steelmakers. When building new capabilities entails writing off the old, incumbents face a hit to quarterly earnings that disruptive entrants to the industry do not. Knowing that the equity markets will punish them for a write-off, managers may stall in adopting new technology.

This may be part of the reason for the dramatic increase in private equity buyouts over the past decade and the recent surge of interest in technology oriented industries. As disruptions continue to shorten the competitive lifetime of major investments made only three to five years ago, more companies find themselves needing to take asset writedowns or to significantly restructure their business models. These are wrenching changes that are often made more easily and comfortably outside the glare of the public markets.

What's the solution to this dilemma? Michael Mauboussin at Legg Mason Capital Management suggests it is to value *strategies*, not projects. When an attacker is gaining ground, executives at the incumbent companies need to do their investment analyses in the same way the attackers do—by focusing on the strategies that will ensure long-term competitiveness. This is the only way they can see the world as the attackers see it and the only way they can predict the consequences of not investing.

No manager would consciously decide to destroy a company by leveraging the competencies of the past while ignoring those required for the future. Yet this is precisely what many of them do. They do it because strategy and finance were taught as separate topics in business school. Their professors of financial modeling alluded to the importance of strategy, and their strategy professors occasionally referred to value creation, but little time was spent on a thoughtful integration of the two. This bifurcation persists in most companies, where responsibilities for strategy and finance reside in the realms of different vice presidents. Because a firm's actual strategy is defined by the stream of projects in which it does or doesn't invest, finance and strategy need to be studied and practiced in an integrated way.

Focusing Myopically on Earnings per Share

A third financial paradigm that leads established companies to underinvest in innovation is the emphasis on earnings per share as the primary driver of share price and hence of shareholder value creation. Managers are under so much pressure, from various directions, to focus on short-term stock performance that they pay less attention to the company's long-term health than they might—to the point where they're reluctant to invest in innovations that don't pay off immediately.

Where's the pressure coming from? To answer that question, we need to look briefly at the principal-agent theory—the doctrine that the interests of shareholders (principals) aren't aligned with those of managers (agents). Without powerful financial incentives to focus the interests of principals and agents on maximizing shareholder value, the thinking goes, agents will pursue other agendas—and in the process, may neglect to pay enough attention to efficiencies or squander capital investments on pet projects—at the expense of profits that ought to accrue to the principals.

That conflict of incentives has been taught so aggressively that the compensation of most senior executives in publicly traded companies is now heavily weighted away from salaries and toward packages that reward improvements in share price. That in turn has led to an almost singular focus on earnings per share and EPS growth as *the* metric for corporate performance. While we all recognize the importance of other indicators such as market position, brands, intellectual capital, and long-term competitiveness, the bias is toward using a simple quantitative indicator that is easily compared period to period and across companies. And because EPS growth is an important driver of near-term share price improvement, managers are biased against investments that will compromise near-term EPS. Many decide instead to use the excess cash on the balance sheet to buy back the company's stock under the guise of "returning money to shareholders." But although contracting the number of shares pumps up earnings per share, sometimes quite dramatically, it does nothing to enhance the underlying value of the enterprise and may even damage it by restricting the flow of cash available for investment in potentially disruptive products and business models. Indeed, some have fingered share-price-based incentive compensation packages as a key driver of the share price manipulation that captured so many business headlines in the early 2000s.

The myopic focus on EPS is not just about the money. CEOs and corporate managers who are more concerned with their reputations than with amassing more wealth also focus on stock price and short-term performance measures such as quarterly earnings. They know that, to a large extent, others' perception of their success is tied up in those numbers, leading to a self-reinforcing cycle of obsession. This behavior cycle is amplified when there is an "earnings surprise." Equity prices over the short term respond positively to upside earnings surprises (and negatively to downside surprises), so investors have no incentive to look at rational measures of long-term performance. To the contrary, they are rewarded for going with the market's short-term model.

The active leveraged buyout market has further reinforced the focus on EPS. Companies that are viewed as having failed to maximize value, as evidenced by a lagging share price, are vulnerable to overtures from outsiders, including corporate raiders or hedge funds that seek to increase their near-term stock price by putting a company into play or by replacing the CEO. Thus, while the past two decades have witnessed a dramatic increase in the proportion of CEO compensation tied to stock price—and a breathtaking increase in CEO compensation overall—they have witnessed a concomitant decrease in the average tenure of CEOs. Whether you believe that CEOs are most motivated by the carrot (major increases in compensation and wealth) or the stick (the threat of the company being sold or of being replaced), you should not be surprised to find so many CEOs focused on current earnings per share as the best predictor of stock price, sometimes to the exclusion of anything else. One study even showed that senior executives were routinely willing to sacrifice long-term shareholder value to meet earnings expectations or to smooth reported earnings.

We suspect that the principal-agent theory is misapplied. Most traditional principals—by which we mean shareholders—don't themselves have incentives to watch out for the long-term health of a company. Over 90% of the shares of publicly traded companies in the United States are held in the portfolios of mutual funds, pension funds, and hedge funds. The average holding period for stocks in these portfolios is less than 10 months—leading us to prefer the term "share owner" as a more accurate description than "shareholder." As for agents, we believe that most executives work tirelessly, throwing their hearts and minds into their jobs, not because they are paid an incentive to do so but because they love what they do. Tying executive compensation to stock prices, therefore, does not affect the intensity or energy or intelligence with which executives perform. But it does direct their efforts toward activities whose impact can be felt within the holding horizon of the typical share owner and within the measurement horizon of the incentive—both of which are less than one year.

Ironically, most so-called principals today are themselves agents—agents of other people's mutual funds, investment portfolios, endowments, and retirement programs. For these agents, the enterprise in which they are investing has no inherent interest or value beyond providing a platform for improving the short-term financial metric by which their fund's performance is measured and their own compensation is determined. And, in a final grand but sad irony, the real principals (the people who put their money into mutual funds and pension plans, sometimes through yet another layer of agents) are frequently the very individuals whose long-term employment is jeopardized when the focus on short-term EPS acts to restrict investments in innovative growth opportunities. We suggest that the principal-agent theory is obsolete in this context. What we really have is an *agent-agent* problem, where the desires and goals of the agent for the share owners compete with the desires and goals of the agents running the company. The incentives are still misaligned, but managers should not capitulate on the basis of an obsolete paradigm.

PROCESSES THAT SUPPORT (OR SABOTAGE) INNOVATION

As we have seen, managers in established corporations use analytical methods that make innovation investments extremely difficult to justify. As it happens, the most common system for green-lighting investment projects only reinforces the flaws inherent in the tools and dogmas discussed earlier.

Stage-gate innovation. Most established companies start by considering a broad range of possible innovations; they winnow out the less viable ideas, step by step, until only the most promising ones remain. Most such processes include three stages: feasibility, development, and launch. The stages are separated by stage gates: review meetings at which project teams report to senior managers what they've accomplished. On the basis of this progress and the project's potential, the gatekeepers approve the passage of the initiative into the next phase, return it to the previous stage for more work, or kill it.

Many marketers and engineers regard the stage-gate development process with disdain. Why? Because the key decision criteria at each gate are the size of projected revenues and profits from the product and the associated risks. Revenues from products that incrementally improve upon those the company is currently selling can be credibly quantified. But proposals to create growth by exploiting potentially disruptive technologies, products, or business models can't be bolstered by hard numbers. Their markets are initially small, and substantial revenues generally don't materialize for several years. When these projects are pitted against incremental sustaining innovations in the battle for funding, the incremental ones sail through while the seemingly riskier ones get delayed or die.

The process itself has two serious drawbacks. First, project teams generally know how good the projections (such as NPV) need to look in order to win funding, and it takes only nanoseconds to tweak an assumption and run another full scenario to get a faltering project over the hurdle rate. If, as is often the case, there are eight to 10 assumptions underpinning the financial model, changing only a few of them by a mere 2% or 3% each may do the trick. It is then difficult for the senior managers who sit as gatekeepers to even discern which are the salient assumptions, let alone judge whether they are realistic.

The second drawback is that the stage-gate system assumes that the proposed strategy is the right strategy. Once an innovation has been approved, developed, and launched, all that remains is skillful execution. If, after launch, a product falls seriously short of the projections (and 75% of them do), it is canceled. The problem is that, except in the case of incremental innovations, the right strategy—especially which job the customer wants done—cannot be completely known in advance. It must emerge and then be refined.

The stage-gate system is not suited to the task of assessing innovations whose purpose is to build new growth businesses, but most companies continue to follow it simply because they see no alternative.

Discovery-driven planning. Happily, though, there are alternative systems specifically designed to support intelligent investments in future growth. One such process, which Rita Gunther McGrath and Ian MacMillan call *discovery-driven planning*, has the potential to greatly improve the success rate. Discovery-driven planning essentially reverses the sequence of some of the steps in the stage-gate process. Its logic is elegantly simple. If the project teams all know how good the numbers need to look in order to win funding, why go through the charade of making and revising assumptions in order to fabricate an acceptable set of numbers? Why not just put the minimally acceptable revenue, income, and cash flow statement as the standard first page of the gate documents? The second page can then raise the critical issues: "Okay. So we all know this is how good the numbers need to look. What set of assumptions must prove true in order for these numbers to materialize?" The project team creates from that analysis an assumptions checklist—a list of things that need to prove true for the project to succeed. The items on the checklist are rank ordered, with the deal killers and the assumptions that can be tested with little expense toward the top. McGrath and MacMillan call this a "reverse income statement."

When a project enters a new stage, the assumptions checklist is used as the basis of the project plan for that stage. This is not a plan to execute, however. It is a plan to *learn*—to test as quickly and at as low a cost as possible whether the assumptions upon which success is predicated are actually valid. If a critical assumption proves not to be valid, the project team must revise its strategy until the assumptions upon which it is built are all plausible. If no set of plausible assumptions will support the case for success, the project is killed.

Traditional stage-gate planning obfuscates the assumptions and shines the light on the financial projections. But there is no need to focus the analytical spotlight on the numbers, because the desirability of attractive numbers has never been the question. Discovery-driven planning shines a spotlight on the place where senior management needs illumination—the assumptions that constitute the key uncertainties. More often than not, failure in innovation is rooted in not having asked an important question, rather than in having arrived at an incorrect answer.

Today, processes like discovery-driven planning are more commonly used in entrepreneurial settings than in the large corporations that desperately need them. We hope that by recounting the strengths of one such system we'll persuade established corporations to reassess how they make decisions about investment projects.

We keep rediscovering that the root reason for established companies' failure to innovate is that managers don't have good tools to help them understand markets, build brands, find customers, select employees, organize teams, and develop strategy. Some of the tools typically used for financial analysis, and decision making about investments, distort the value, importance, and likelihood of success of investments in innovation. There's a better way for management teams to grow their companies. But they will need the courage to challenge some of the paradigms of financial analysis and the willingness to develop alternative methodologies.

Glossary of Accounting Terms

Absorption costing A method of costing in which all fixed and variable production costs are charged to products or services using an allocation base.

Accountability The process of satisfying stakeholders in the organization that managers have acted in the best interests of the stakeholders; a result of the stewardship function of managers, which takes place through accounting.

Accounting A collection of systems and processes used to record, report, and interpret business transactions.

Accounting period The period of time for which financial statements are produced—see also *Financial year*.

Accounting rate of return (ARR) A method of investment appraisal that measures the profit generated as a percentage of the investment—see *Return on investment*.

Accounting standards See Generally accepted accounting principles (GAAP) and *International Financial Reporting Standards* (IFRS)

Accounting Standards for Private Entities (ASPE) Standards that set out recognition, measurement, presentation, and disclosure requirements dealing with transactions and events that are important in general-purpose financial statements. Applicable to private companies only.

Accounting system A set of accounts that summarize the transactions of a business which have been recorded on source documents.

Accounts "Buckets" within the ledger, part of the accounting system. Each account contains similar transactions (line items) that are used for the production of financial statements; commonly used as an abbreviation for *financial statements*.

Accounts payable Purchases on credit of goods or services from suppliers who have not yet been paid.

Accounts receivable Sales on credit to customers who have bought goods or services but who have not yet paid their debt.

Accrual An expense for profit purposes even though no payment has been made.

Accrual accounting A method of accounting in which profit is calculated as the difference between income *when it is earned* and expenses *when they are incurred*.

Acid test The ratio of current assets, excluding inventory, to current liabilities.

Activity-based budget	A method of budgeting that develops budgets based on expected activities and cost drivers—see also *Activity-based costing.*
Activity-based costing (ABC)	A method of costing that uses cost pools to accumulate the cost of significant business activities and then assigns the costs from the cost pools to products or services based on cost drivers.
Activity-based management (ABM)	Evaluation of the activities that an organization undertakes to identify areas for improvement in resource usage and overall costs.
Amortization	See *Depreciation,* but usually in relation to assets attached to leased property or intangibles.
Application controls	Controls designed for each individual application, such as payroll, accounting, and inventory control. The aim of application controls is to prevent, detect, and correct transaction processing errors.
Assets	Things that the business owns; resources controlled by an entity as a result of past events and from which future economic benefits are expected to flow to the entity. An entity acquires assets to produce goods or services capable of satisfying customer needs. An asset can be intangible; e.g., a copyright.
Asset turnover ratio	A measure of how efficiently assets are utilized to generate sales.
Attention directing	Specific accounting information intended to draw the attention of managers to, and assisting in the interpretation of, business performance, particularly in terms of the comparison between actual and planned performance.
Audit	A periodic examination of the accounting records of a company, carried out by an independent auditor to ensure that those records have been properly maintained and that the financial statements that are drawn up from those records give a true and fair view.
Audit committee	The governance body that is charged with overseeing the organization's audit, control functions, and financial reporting process.
Average cost	The total of both fixed and variable costs for a product or service, divided by the total number of units produced.
Avoidable costs	Costs that are identifiable with and able to be influenced by decisions made at the business-unit level (e.g., the division level).
Backflush costing	A method of costing that transfers the cost of materials from suppliers, along with conversion costs, to finished goods inventory when production of finished goods is complete (the trigger point).

Balanced scorecard	A system of non-financial performance measurement that links innovation, customer, and process measures to financial performance.
Benefits	Non-salary costs that follow from the payment of salaries or wages. In Canada, benefits include the Canada Pension Plan (CPP) and Employment Insurance (EI) contributions.
Backflush costing	A type of inventory tracking system that uses trigger points, reduces the amount of inventory tracking that is required, and eliminates the need for work-in-progress inventory tracking altogether. Backflush costing is usually associated with a just-in-time manufacturing environment.
Bottleneck resources	Resources that limit the amount of product or service that a company can provide. This can include machine capacity, human resources, or storage capacity.
Bottom–up budgets	Budgets developed by the managers of each department based on current spending and approved plans, which are then aggregated into a total corporate-level budget.
Budgetary slack	A deliberate underestimation of sales in a budget. This often occurs when a division's performance is based on achieving specific sales targets.
Breakeven point	The point at which total costs equal total revenue; i.e., where there is neither a profit nor a loss.
Budget	A plan expressed in monetary terms covering a future period of time and based on a defined level of activity.
Budgetary control	Using financial information to maintain performance as close as possible to the plan, or using the information to modify the plan itself.
Budget cycle	The annual period over which budgets are prepared.
Business entity	A group of people organized for some profitable or charitable purpose. Business entities include organizations such as corporations, partnerships, charities, trusts, and other forms of organizations.
Capital employed	The total of debt and equity; i.e., the total funds in the business.
Capital investment	Investing money in long-term assets, such as plant and equipment, in the hope of getting it back later through future cash flows.
Capitalize	To delay the recognition of the expense for a capital asset until future periods. This recognizes the long-term nature of capital assets and matches the cost of the asset against revenues earned from the asset in future periods.

Capital market	The market in which investors buy and sell shares of companies; normally associated with a stock exchange.
Carrying costs	Costs related to storing inventories, such as depreciation, utilities, insurance, and materials handling.
Cash cost	The amount of cash expended.
Cash forecast	A cash budget that forecasts a company's cash inflows and outflows over a particular period. The purpose of the cash forecast is to ensure that sufficient cash is available to meet the level of activity planned by the sales and production budgets, and to meet all the other cash inflows and outflows of the business.
Cash value added	A method of investment appraisal that calculates the ratio of the net present value of an investment to the initial capital investment.
Centralized business	A business in which most decisions are made at a head-office level, even though the business may be spread over a number of market segments and geographically diverse locations.
Company-wide overhead rate	An overhead rate that is calculated using the total of the overhead costs for the company divided by the total of the allocation base for the company.
Comparability	A qualitative characteristic of financial information. Financial information must be prepared and presented in such a way that users are able to compare the financial reports of an entity through time, and be able to compare the financial reports of different entities in order to evaluate their relative financial position, performance, and changes in financial position.
Conceptual Framework for Financial Reporting	A coherent system of interrelated objectives and fundamentals that can lead to consistent standards, and that prescribes the nature, function, and limits of financial accounting and financial statements.
Confirmatory value	Financial information has confirmatory value if it provides feedback about (confirms or changes) previous evaluations. Together with predictive value, confirmatory value makes financial information relevant—see *Relevance*.
Contingency controls	Controls put in place to safeguard information and systems in case of a critical failure.
Continuous budgets	Budgets that add additional months to the end of the period so that there is always a 12-month budget for the business.
Continuous improvement	A method of total quality management that focuses on achieving customer value, re-engineering business processes, and ensuring that all employees are committed to quality.
Contribution margin	The difference between the selling price and variable costs, which can be expressed either per unit or in total.

Contribution margin ratio	Contribution margin divided by revenues. The contribution ratio is expressed as a percentage.
Controllable profit	The profit made by a division after deducting only those expenses that can be controlled by the divisional manager, and ignoring those expenses that are outside the divisional manager's control.
Corporate governance	The system by which companies are directed and controlled.
Cost behaviour	The idea that fixed costs and variable costs react differently to changes in the volume of products/services produced.
Cost centre	A division or unit of an organization that is responsible for controlling costs.
Cost control	The process of either reducing costs while maintaining the same level of productivity or maintaining costs while increasing productivity.
Cost driver	The most significant cause of the cost of an activity; a measure of the demand for an activity by each product/service, enabling the cost of activities to be assigned from cost pools to products/services.
Cost leadership	A type of competitive strategy in which a company tries to achieve lower costs than its competitors through efficiency, tight cost control, and the avoidance of unprofitable work.
Cost of capital	The costs incurred by an organization to fund all its investments, made up of the risk-adjusted cost of equity and debt weighted by the mix of equity and debt.
Cost of goods sold	See *Cost of sales*.
Cost of labour	The salary or wage paid to the employee, plus any benefits.
Cost of manufacture	The cost of manufacturing goods for subsequent sale.
Costs of quality	The difference between the actual costs of production, selling, and service, and the costs that would be incurred if there were no failures during production or usage of products or services.
Cost of sales	The manufacture or purchase price of goods sold in a period, or the cost of providing a service.
Cost-plus pricing	A method of pricing in which a mark-up is added to the total product/service cost.
Cost pool	The costs of (cross-functional) business processes, irrespective of the organizational structure of the business.
Costs of redundancy	Costs of making staff redundant, including severance payments, legal fees, and outplacement service fees; intangible costs, such as a loss of employee knowledge, skills, and experience; and costs related to low morale on the part of other employees, possibly leading to a decline in employee efficiency.

Cost-plus transfer price	A transfer price between divisions that includes the costs of making the product (either variable or full costs) plus a markup on cost representing profit for the supplying division.
Cost–volume–profit (CVP) analysis	A method for understanding the relationship between revenue, cost, and sales volume.
Current assets	An asset that meets one of the following criteria:

- It is expected to be realized (exchanged for cash, sold, or consumed) in the entity's normal operating cycle or within 12 months after the reporting period.
- It is held primarily for the purpose of trading.
- The asset is cash or a cash equivalent.

  Current assets include bank, accounts receivable, inventory, and prepayments.

Current cost	The cash value that would have to be paid if the same or equivalent assets were acquired currently.
Current liabilities	A liability that meets one of the following criteria:

- It is expected to be settled in its normal operating cycle or within 12 months after the reporting period.
- The entity holds the liability primarily for the purpose of trading.
- The entity does not have an unconditional right to defer settlement of the liability for at least 12 months after the reporting period.

  Current liabilities include bank overdraft, accounts payable, and accruals.

Customer perspective	The perspective of the balanced scorecard that highlights measures related to the company's customers, including customer retention, growth, and satisfaction, among other factors.
Customer profitability analysis	Calculating the specific costs of serving individual customers or customer groups, and determining the overall profit of each customer or customer group, with the intention of maximizing revenues earned from profitable customers and taking steps to reduce the costs of serving unprofitable customers.
Data	Raw forms of information that must be synthesized and summarized into something that is useful and meaningful to a decision maker.
Days' purchase outstanding	Accounts payable expressed in terms of how many days' worth of purchases it represents.
Days' sales outstanding	Accounts receivable expressed in terms of how many days' worth of sales it represents.

Debt	Borrowings from financiers.
Decentralized business	A business in which decentralized division managers are responsible for decision making and control at the business-unit level.
Decision making	Using both financial and non-financial information to make decisions consistent with the goals and strategies of an organization.
Degree of operating leverage	A measure of the extent of long-term debt in comparison with shareholders' equity.
Depreciation	An expense that spreads the cost of an asset over its useful life.
Differentiation	A type of competitive strategy in which a company tries to differentiate its products or services from its competitors' through brand image, technology, or a unique distribution channel.
Direct costs	Costs that are readily traceable to particular products or services.
Direct labour	The labour directly involved in the conversion process of raw materials to finished goods.
Direct labour (DL) efficiency variance	Occurs when the actual labour hours used to make a product are fewer or greater than expected on the standard cost card for a product.
Direct labour (DL) rate variance	Occurs when the labour rate paid to staff is more or less than planned.
Direct materials	Are traceable to particular products, and, for a manufacturer, include the materials bought and used in the manufacture of each unit produced.
Direct materials (DM) efficiency variances	Occurs when there is a difference between the actual inputs used and what is expected, as outlined in a standard cost card.
Direct materials (DM) price variance	Occurs when the actual price of an input is less or more than the standard price of each input.
Discounted cash flow (DCF)	A method of investment appraisal that discounts future cash flows to present value using a discount rate, which is the risk-adjusted cost of capital.
Discount factor	A factor that future cash flows can be multiplied by to determine the cash flow's present value. A discount factor is based on a specific cost of capital and time period.
Dividend	Payment of after-tax profits to shareholders as their share of the profits of the business for an accounting period.
Dividend payout ratio	Measures how much of the available net income was paid out to shareholders in the form of a dividend.
Dividend per share	Dividends declared for each share outstanding.
Dividend yield	A ratio showing how much a company pays out in dividends relative to its share price.

Divisional-based overhead rate	An overhead rate that is calculated for each division within the company by dividing the total overhead costs for the division by the division's allocation base.
Divisional structure	An organizational structure in which divisions are established for major elements of the business. These divisions may be based on geographical territories or different products/services, and each division will typically have responsibility for all of the functional areas: marketing, operations, human resources, and accounting.
Double entry	The system of recording business transactions in two accounts, with a debit in one account and a credit in the other.
Earnings before interest and taxes (EBIT)	The operating profit before deducting interest and tax.
Earnings before interest, taxes, depreciation, and amortization (EBITDA)	The operating profit before deducting interest, taxes, depreciation, and amortization.
Earnings per share (EPS)	Net income divided by the weighted number of shares outstanding during the year.
Economic order quantity (EOQ)	The optimal order quantity for inventory that minimizes overall carrying and ordering costs.
Economic value added (EVA™)	Operating profit, adjusted to remove distortions caused by certain accounting rules, less a charge to cover the cost of capital invested in the business.
Efficiency variances	Variances that occur because the actual quantity of materials, labour, or machine hours are higher or lower than the company planned to use (also called usage variances).
Elastic demand	Exists when a price increase leads to a significant fall in demand because customers are highly sensitive to changes in price and may switch to substitute products.
Employee time record	A detailed list of the time an employee has spent on each job in a factory.
Enterprise resource planning (ERP)	A system that helps to integrate data flow and access to information over the whole range of a company's activities. ERP systems typically capture transaction data for accounting purposes, together with operational, customer, and supplier data, which are then made available through data warehouses from which custom-designed reports can be produced.
Environmental management accounting (*or environmental accounting*)	Collecting, measuring, and reporting costs about the environmental impact of an organization's activities.
Equity	Funds raised from shareholders. The residual interest in the assets of the entity after deducting all its liabilities—see also *Shareholders' equity*.

Equivalent units	In process costing, the resources used in production relative to the resources necessary to complete all units.
Expenses	The costs incurred in buying, making, or providing goods or services.
Faithful representation	A qualitative characteristic of financial information. Financial information must be prepared and presented in such a way that it faithfully represents the events that it purports to represent.
Favourable variance	Occurs if a company's revenues are greater than planned, if a company's costs are less than planned, or if a company uses more productive capacity than planned.
Feedback	The retrospective process of measuring performance, comparing it with the business plan, and taking corrective action if necessary.
Feedback (diagnostic) control	A type of control system in which standards and controls are developed to reduce future occurrences of an error that has been detected in a process. A customer complaint related to poor product quality is an example of feedback control.
Feedforward	The process of determining prospectively whether strategies are likely to achieve the target results that are consistent with organizational goals.
Feedforward control	A type of control system in which predesigned standards and controls are developed to ensure that errors in the process do not occur in the first place. For example, design specifications for a product are an example of feedforward control.
Financial accounting	The production of financial statements, primarily for those interested parties who are external to the business.
Financial perspective	A perspective of the balanced scorecard that represents the financial performance of a company, including measures of profitability, cost control and other financial targets.
Financial report elements	The five classes of items found on the financial statements for a business including assets, liabilities, equity, income, and expenses.
Financial statement	A written document that quantitatively reports on the financial health of an organization. Included in a full financial report are a statement of financial position, statement of comprehensive income, statement of changes in shareholders' equity, statement of cash flows, and notes to the financial statements.
Financial year	The accounting period adopted by a business for the production of its financial statements. This can be a calendar year or another period of time, known as a *fiscal year*. The fiscal year of the Canadian federal government and the provincial and territorial governments in Canada is April 1 to March 31.

Finished goods	Inventory that is ready for sale, either having been purchased as such or the result of a conversion from raw materials through a manufacturing process.
First-in, first-out (FIFO) method	A type of process costing where beginning work-in-process inventory is assumed to be completed first and beginning work-in-process inventory costs are assigned to finished goods and not averaged into the cost per equivalent unit.
Five forces analysis	A strategic analysis tool that assesses the five forces within an industry, including the threat of new entrants, power of buyers, power of suppliers, threat of substitutes, and competitive rivalry.
Fixed production volume variance	A fixed overhead variance that occurs when the volume of units produced by a company is more or less than planned.
Fixed costs	Costs that do not change with increases or decreases in the volume of goods or services produced, within the relevant range.
Fixed overhead spending variance	Occurs if the actual fixed costs are greater or less than the planned fixed costs for a company.
Flexible budget	A method of budgetary control that adjusts the original budget by applying standard prices and costs per unit to the actual production volume.
Flexible budget variance	The variance between the actual results of a company and the flexible budget (that is, the budget based on actual volumes of activity multiplied by budgeted revenues and costs).
Focus	A competitive strategy that emphasizes servicing a particular market segment (whether customer, territory, or product/service) better than competitors that may be competing more broadly.
Full cost	The cost of a product/service that includes an allocation of all the production and non-production costs of the business.
Full-cost transfer price	A transfer price that is made up of the variable and fixed costs of a product or service.
Functional structure	An organizational structure that locates decision making at the top of the corporate hierarchy, with functional responsibilities for marketing, operations, human resources, and finance allocated to departments.
Gains	A form of income not in the ordinary course of business, such as income from the disposal of non-current assets or revaluations of investments.
Generally accepted accounting principles (GAAP)	Standard framework of guidelines for recording financial transactions and preparing financial statements.
Global Reporting Initiative	A multi-stakeholder non-profit organization that works toward a sustainable global economy by providing sustainable reporting guidance.

Going concern	A business that will continue in operation for the foreseeable future.
Gross margin	Gross profit, expressed as a percentage of sales.
Gross profit	The difference between the price at which goods or services are sold and the cost of sales.
Historical cost	The cash or fair value consideration given at the time of an asset's acquisition.
Human resources	The people employed by a company who provide skills, knowledge, and the ability to carry out the functions of the company.
Implementation of strategy	The step in the strategic planning process in which an organization implements its plan and objectives.
Income	The revenue generated from the sale of goods or services, or increases in economic benefits.
Incremental budget	A budget that takes the previous year as a base and adds (or deducts) a percentage to arrive at the budget for the current year.
Indirect costs	Costs that are necessary to produce a product/service but are not readily traceable to particular products or services—see *Overhead*.
Indirect labour	Manufacturing employees who do not directly produce goods or provide services including factory supervisors, maintenance staff, and quality inspectors.
Indirect materials	Materials of little value that are used in production (such as screws, adhesives, and cleaning materials) and are not assigned directly to a product, because the cost of recording their use would be higher than the value achieved.
Industry value chain	Connections of activities between suppliers, the organization, distribution channels, and customers.
Inelastic demand	Exists when small price increases/decreases cause only a small change in demand, because customers value the product more than the price or because no substitute is available.
Information	Synthesized and purposefully summarized data.
Information management strategy	Strategy concerned with ensuring that the necessary information is being provided to users. This includes databases, data warehousing, and reporting systems.
Information systems strategy (ISS)	Provides an umbrella for different information technologies to help ensure that appropriate information is acquired, retained, shared, and available for use in strategy implementation.
Information technology strategy (ITS)	An organization's strategy relating to the technologies that it uses and the people who directly manage those technologies.
Inputs	The quantity of materials, machine hours, and/or labour hours used to make the actual output. Inputs are measures, such as kilograms of direct materials, metres of direct materials, machine hours, and/or labour hours.

Institutional theory	The study of the process by which structures such as rules, regulations, schemas, and norms are formed.
Intangible assets	An identifiable non-monetary asset without physical substance, such as intellectual property (patents and trademarks).
Intellectual capital	The collective abilities of an entity's management, employees, and systems to add value to the company.
Interest	The cost of money, received on investments or paid on borrowings.
Interest cover ratio	An indication of the company's ability to pay interest on borrowed funds.
Internal and external assessment	A step in the strategic planning process in which both the internal and external environments of the company are reviewed to ensure that strategic advantages are being optimized and strategic disadvantages are being minimized. This many include an assessment of a company's internal value chain as well as an external analysis of the social, technological, economic, environmental, and political environments in which the company operates.
Internal business process perspective	A perspective of the balanced scorecard that includes measures of the internal operations of a company. Measures can be related to quality, operational efficiency, and activity management.
Internal control	The whole system of internal controls, financial and otherwise, established to provide reasonable assurance of effective and efficient operation, internal financial control, and compliance with laws and regulations.
Internal rate of return	A discounted cash flow technique used for investment appraisal that calculates the effective cost of capital which produces a net present value of zero from a series of future cash flows and an initial capital investment.
International Financial Reporting Standards (IFRS)	Standards that set out recognition, measurement, presentation, and disclosure requirements dealing with transactions and events that are important in general-purpose financial statements. Applicable to public entities, but private companies can choose to use it, too.
Inventory management	Optimizing the levels of inventory in a company to reduce costs associated with ordering and carrying inventories, while at the same time ensuring that enough inventory is on hand to meet consumer demand.
Inventory turnover	Indication of how many times inventory is turned over in a year; i.e., how many times the company sells its amount of inventory in a year.
Investment centre	A division or unit of an organization that is responsible for achieving an adequate return on the capital invested in the division or unit.

Job cost record	A detailed list of all costs for a particular job.
Job order costing	A costing system that accumulates the materials, labour, and overhead costs for each job.
Just-in-time (JIT) inventory management	An inventory management system in which inventory levels are held to minimum levels and materials are bought only when needed or items are produced only when required for sale.
Kaizen costing	A method of costing that involves making continual, incremental improvements to the production process during the manufacturing phase of the product/service life cycle, typically involving setting targets for cost reduction.
Lead time	The time between when an order is placed by a company with a supplier and when it is needed.
Lean accounting	A just-in-time philosophy for the elimination of wasteful accounting practices that contribute little to management decision making.
Learning and growth perspective	A perspective of the balanced scorecard that includes measures of intangible resources in the company, including employee satisfaction, employee development, and innovation.
Ledger	A collection of all of the different accounts of the business that summarize the transactions of the business.
Leveraging	A strategy whereby an entity obtains funds at a lower cost than the return it makes on investing or utilizing the funds.
Liabilities	Debts that the business owes. A present obligation of the entity arising from past events, the settlement of which is expected to result in an outflow from the entity of resources embodying economic benefits.
Life-cycle costing	An approach to costing that estimates and accumulates the costs of a product/service over its entire life cycle, from inception to abandonment.
Line functions	A company's primary functions that provide a source of revenue and support the company's primary objectives. Operations and marketing are both line functions.
Line item	Generic types of assets, liabilities, income, or expense that are common to most businesses and are used as the basis of financial reporting; e.g., rent, salaries, advertising.
Liquidity	A measure of the ability of a business to pay its debts as they fall due—see also *Working capital*.
Losses	A form of expense not arising from the ordinary course of business, such as losses resulting from disasters such as fire and flood.
Make-versus-buy decision	Comparing the cost of purchasing goods or services on the open market to making the product or providing the service in-house. Also called an *outsourcing decision*.

Management accounting	The production of financial and non-financial information used in planning for the future; making decisions about products, services, prices, and what costs to incur; and ensuring that plans are implemented and achieved.
Management control	A step in the strategic planning process in which the organization is measured and monitored to ensure that its objectives and strategies are being achieved. Also, rules or procedures which ensure that the performance of a company is within acceptable parameters. This can include budgets, performance appraisals, feedback systems, and other control systems.
Management control system	A group of rules or procedures used by a company to maintain acceptable levels of performance.
Management's Discussion and Analysis (MD&A)	A narrative discussion and explanation by a company's management on the company's past performance, current status, and future prospects. The MD&A forms part of a public company's annual financial report.
Marginal cost	The cost of producing one extra unit.
Marginal cost-based transfer price	A transfer price that is based on the additional costs incurred (normally, variable costs) of the product or service.
Margin of safety	A measure of the difference between the anticipated and breakeven levels of activity.
Market pricing	When a company bases the price for a product or service on the competitive market price.
Market transfer price	A transfer price set at the competitive price the product or service is sold for on the open market.
Mark-up	The percentage added to the cost of a product or service that represents the profit that will be earned.
Matching principle	Revenues earned in a specific period are matched with the expenses incurred to earn those revenues to calculate profit for that specific period—see also *Accrual accounting*.
Materiality	Information is material if its omission or misstatement could influence the economic decisions of users made on the basis of financial reports.
Materials requisition record	A detailed list of all the materials used for a particular job.
Measurement	The process of determining the monetary amounts at which the elements of the financial reports are to be recognized and carried in the statement of financial position and the statement of comprehensive income.
Merchandise inventory	Goods that are purchased by a company and resold.

Mission statement development	As a step in the strategic planning process, the company broadly defines its vision and overall direction to achieve this vision.
Mixed costs	Costs that have both a fixed and a variable component.
Multidimensional performance measurement	A performance measurement system focusing on a broad array of financial, non-financial, competitor, and customer information.
Negotiated transfer price	A transfer price that is negotiated between the supplying and purchasing divisions. It may take into account market conditions, marginal costs, and the need to motivate managers in each division.
Net present value (NPV) method	A discounted cash flow technique used for investment appraisal that calculates the present value of future cash flows and deducts the initial capital investment.
Net profit	See *Operating profit*.
Net realizable value (NRV)	The value at which the inventory could be sold on the open market, less costs of disposal such as shipping or reclamation costs.
Network controls	Controls designed to protect a network of computers.
Non-current assets	Assets that are not current assets—see *Current assets*.
Non-current liabilities	Liabilities that are not current liabilities—see *Current liabilities*.
Non-financial performance measure	A quantitative measure of performance that is not expressed in monetary values. This can include measures such as efficiency, customer satisfaction, quality, and market share. Non-financial performance measures are considered leading indicators of financial performance as they will impact the performance of the company in the future.
One-time special orders	An order received from a customer that is outside a company's normal operations, normally at a discounted price. Companies will accept special orders if they have excess capacity in their production process and the special order price covers all incremental costs of the special order.
Operating leverage	The mix of fixed and variable costs in a business. A high operating leverage means that there are high fixed costs, low variable costs, and a high contribution margin per unit sold, and vice versa.
Operating margin	Operating profit, expressed as a percentage of sales.
Operating profit	The profit made by the business for an accounting period, equal to gross profit less selling, finance, administration, and other expenses, but before deducting interest or taxes.
Operations	The business function that produces the goods and services to satisfy customer demand.
Opportunity cost	The cost of not taking advantage of an opportunity, either financial or non-financial.

Optimum selling price	The price at which profit is maximized, which takes into account the cost behaviour of fixed and variable costs and the relationship between price and demand for a product/service.
Ordering costs	Costs associated with ordering inventory, including costs to prepare and pay for purchase orders and costs associated with receiving and inspecting goods that are delivered to the factory.
Outputs	The final product of the manufacturing process; often called *units of production*.
Overhead	Any production costs other than a direct cost; may refer to an indirect production cost and/or to a non-production expense.
Overhead costs	Indirect costs of producing a product or providing a service. Can include factory rent, utilities, indirect labour, indirect materials, and other indirect costs.
Payback method	A method of investment appraisal that calculates the number of years taken for the cash flows from an investment to cover the initial capital outlay.
Percentage of completion method	A costing method used with long-term contracts when revenues and gross profit are recognized in the applicable periods of production, not when production has been completed.
Period costs	The costs that relate to a period of time.
Personnel management	A function concerned with job design; recruitment, training, and motivation; performance appraisal; industrial relations, employee participation and teamwork; remuneration; redundancy; health and safety; and employment policies and practices.
Planning	Using financial information to help establish goals and strategies to achieve those goals, including preparing a budget to communicate the plans and goals to the organization.
Predictive value	Financial information has predictive value if it can be used to predict future outcomes. Together with confirmatory value, it makes financial information relevant—see *Relevance*.
Prepayment	A payment made in advance of when it is treated as an expense for profit purposes.
Present value	The present discounted value of the future net cash inflows that assets are expected to generate.
Price/earnings (P/E) ratio	The share price of a company's shares divided by the earnings per share.
Price-maker	A firm that is a market leader and sets the price in the market for a product or service.
Price-taker	A firm that is not a market leader and sets its prices based on the competitive market prices.

Price variances	Variances that arise when the cost of resources is higher or lower than the standard cost (also called rate or spending variances).
Priority-based budget	A budget that allocates funds in line with strategies.
Problem solving	Using accounting information to help identify the best choice from a range of alternative actions.
Process costing	A method of costing for continuous manufacture in which costs for an accounting period are compared with production for the same period to determine a cost per unit produced.
Product costs	The cost of goods or services produced.
Production budget	Relates to the production of a product or service, including materials, labour, and overhead.
Profit before interest and taxes (PBIT)	See Earnings before interest and taxes (EBIT).
Profit centre	A division or unit of an organization that is responsible for achieving profit targets.
Profit margin	The percentage of the selling price that represents profit.
Profitability index	See *Cash value added*.
Provision	Estimates of possible future liabilities or asset reductions that may arise, but where there is uncertainty as to timing or the amount of money.
Quality management	Measuring and controlling quality within a company in order to improve customer value, overall financial performance, and the efficiency of the operations process.
Raw materials	Unprocessed goods bought for manufacture; part of inventory.
Realizable value	The cash value that could currently be obtained by selling an asset.
Recognition	The process of incorporating into the statement of financial position or statement of comprehensive income an item that meets the definition of an element.
Relevant costs	The cost that is relevant to a particular decision; future, incremental cash flows.
Relevant cost of labour	The costs of labour that will change if a particular course of action is chosen. Any costs of labour that will stay the same regardless of the action are irrelevant.
Relevant range	The upper and lower levels of activity in which the business expects to be operating in the short-term planning horizon (the budget period).
Residual income (RI)	The profit remaining after deducting from profit a notional cost of capital on the investment in a business or division of a business.

Responsibility centre	A division or unit of an organization for which a manager is held responsible; may be a cost centre, profit centre, or investment centre.
Return on capital employed (ROCE)	The operating profit before interest and taxes as a percentage of the total shareholders' equity plus the long-term debt of the business.
Return on investment (ROI)	The net profit after tax as a percentage of the shareholders' investment in the business.
Revenue	A form of income that arises in the ordinary course of business; typically, income earned from the sale of goods and services, including fees, interest, dividends, royalties, and rent.
Risk	The potential that a chosen action (including the choice of inaction) could negatively influence the achievement of the organization's strategic, operational, and/or financial objectives.
Risk mitigation strategies	Strategies used to reduce or avoid risk in investment decisions. Strategies include risk transference, risk reduction, or risk acceptance.
Safety stock	Extra stock that is kept on hand to cover any unexpected increases in demand.
Sales growth	Percentage increase in sales, year over year.
Sales mix	The mix of products/services offered by the business, each of which may be aimed at different customers, with each product/service having different prices and costs.
Sales price variance	The difference between the actual price and the standard price for the actual quantity sold. Identifies the portion of the total variance that is related to changes in selling price.
Sales quantity variance	The difference between the budget and actual quantity at the budgeted selling price. Shows the portion of the total variance that is due to selling more or less than planned.
Sales variance	The difference between the budgeted sales and the actual sales.
Salvage	The residual value of an investment at the end of its useful life.
Scarce resources	Resources that are limited within a company, including space, equipment, materials, and staff.
Scorekeeping	Gathering accounting information with the purpose of capturing, recording, summarizing, and reporting financial performance.
Security controls	Controls to prevent unauthorized access, modification, or destruction of stored data.
Sensitivity analysis	An approach to understanding how changes in one variable of cost–volume–profit analysis are affected by changes in the other variables.
Shareholder return	The ratio of net profit to shareholders' equity.
Shareholders' equity	The capital invested in a business by the shareholders, including retained profits—see also *Equity*.

Shareholder value analysis	The process of increasing shareholder value through new or redesigned products/services, cost management, performance management systems, and improved decision making.
Six Sigma	A quality management approach that aims to improve quality by removing defects and the causes of defects.
Source document	A document that records a transaction and forms the basis for recording in a business's accounting system.
Staff functions	Functions that indirectly support the primary operations of a company but do not provide a source of revenue; can include accounting, information technology, and human resources.
Statement of comprehensive income	A financial statement measuring the profit or loss of a business—income less expenses—for an accounting period. Previously known as an *income statement*.
Statement of financial position	A financial statement showing the financial position of a business—its assets, liabilities, and capital—at the end of an accounting period. Previously known as the *balance sheet*.
Step costs	Costs that are constant within a particular level of activity, but can increase when activity reaches a critical level.
Stewardship	The act of managing a business on behalf of owners that are not actively involved in the management of the company. In publically held businesses, the management of a company provides stewardship to the company's shareholders.
Stockout costs	Costs that occur when a company has an inventory shortage, includes express delivery charges and the opportunity cost of lost sales.
Strategic management accounting	The provision and analysis of management accounting data about a business and its competitors, which is of use in the development and monitoring of strategy.
Strategy development	A step in the strategic planning process in which an organization clearly defines its strategy based on its overall mission and the internal and external environments in which it operates.
Sunk costs	Costs that have been incurred in the past and cannot be recovered.
Sustainability	Meeting current needs without jeopardizing the ability to meet future needs.
Target costing	A method of costing that is concerned with managing whole-of-life costs of a product/service during the product design phase; the difference between target price (to achieve market share) and the target profit margin.
Target rate of return pricing	A method of pricing that estimates the desired return on investment to be achieved from the fixed and working capital investment and includes that return in the price of a product/service.
Theory of Constraints	A capacity management approach that focuses on bottlenecks in production and the need to maximize volume through the bottleneck operations.

Throughput contribution   Sales revenue less the cost of materials.

Total employment cost   The total cost of labour to the employer, including an employee's salary; the employer's share of EI and CPP payments; bonuses, profit shares, and non-cash remuneration such as stock options; health benefits, such as dental and medical insurance; pension contributions; expense allowances; and business-provided motor vehicles.

Timeliness   A qualitative characteristic of financial information; having information available to decision makers in time to be capable of influencing their decisions.

Time value of money   The concept that states that one dollar is worth more now than it will be in a year's time, because it can be invested now at a rate of interest that will increase its value.

Top–down budgets   Spending limits are first developed by senior management, and department managers must then establish their individual budgets within these limits.

Total quality management   A comprehensive measurement system focused on design, purchasing, operations, distribution, marketing, and administration functions aimed at improving performance and efficiencies by improving quality.

Transaction   An exchange or transfer of goods, services, or funds.

Transaction processing system   A product of financial accounting activities in which data are collected about each business transaction.

Transfer price   The price at which goods or services are bought and sold within divisions of the same organization, as opposed to an arm's-length price at which sales may be made to an external customer.

Triple bottom line   A term referring to a company not only reporting on its financial results, but also on its social and environmental impact.

Unavoidable cost   A cost that cannot be influenced at the business-unit level but is controllable at the corporate level.

Understandability   A qualitative characteristic of financial information. Financial information is understandable if it is classified, characterized, and presented in a clear format.

Unfavourable variance   Occurs if a company's revenues are less than planned, if a company's costs are more than planned, or if a company uses less productive capacity than planned.

Value-based management   A variety of approaches (see Chapter 2) that emphasize increasing shareholder value as the primary goal of every business.

Value chain   Design, production, marketing, distribution, and customer support activities carried out by an organization, and the relationships among these activities.

Value chain analysis	A strategic management accounting tool that helps assess the costs of activities in the internal value chain for a company and the value of those activities to determine if the activities are adding value for the customer.
Variable cost	A cost that increases or decreases in proportion with increases or decreases in the volume of production of goods or services.
Variable costing	A method of costing in which only variable production costs are treated as product costs and in which all fixed (production and non-production) costs are treated as period costs.
Variable overhead efficiency variance	Occurs if the actual allocation base for overhead is more or less than the standard allocation base allowed on the cost card for a product.
Variable overhead spending variance	Occurs if the actual overhead costs are more or less than the standard overhead rate multiplied by the actual volume of the overhead allocation base.
Variance analysis	A method of budgetary control that compares actual performance against the business plan, investigates the causes of the variance, and takes corrective action to ensure that targets are achieved.
Verifiability	A qualitative characteristic of financial information. Different knowledgeable and independent observers could reach consensus, although not necessarily complete agreement, that a particular depiction is a faithful representation.
Volume variance	Fixed cost spending variance that is due to producing more or fewer units than planned.
Weighted average cost of capital	See *Cost of capital*.
Weighted average method	A type of process costing system in which all costs (beginning work-in-process and costs from the current period) are averaged together to determine the cost per equivalent unit.
Working capital	Current assets less current liabilities; money that revolves in the business as part of the process of buying, making, and selling goods and services, particularly in relation to accounts receivable, accounts payable, inventory, and bank.
Working capital ratio	The ratio of current assets to current liabilities.
Work in progress	Goods or services that have commenced the production process but are incomplete and unable to be sold.
Zero-based budgeting	A method of budgeting that ignores historical budgetary allocations and identifies the costs that are necessary to implement agreed strategies.

Answer Key for Self-Test Questions

Chapter 1

S1.1 d
S1.2 c
S1.3 e
S1.4 b
S1.5 e
S1.6 c
S1.7 c
S1.8 c
S1.9 b

Chapter 2

S2.1 a
S2.2 b
S2.3 b
S2.4 d
S2.5 d
S2.6 a

Chapter 3

S3.1 c
S3.2 d
S3.3 d
S3.4 c
S3.5 a
S3.6 b
S3.7 c
S3.8 c
S3.9 d
S3.10 b
S3.11 b
S3.12 c

Chapter 4

S4.1 b
S4.2 d
S4.3 d
S4.4 d
S4.5 b
S4.6 d
S4.7 d
S4.8 b
S4.9 b
S4.10 a
S4.11 d

Chapter 5

S5.1 d
S5.2 b
S5.3 c
S5.4 a
S5.5 d
S5.6 b
S5.7 d
S5.8 d
S5.9 a
S5.10 c
S5.11 d
S5.12 d

Chapter 6

S6.1 e
S6.2 a
S6.3 e
S6.4 a
S6.5 a

S6.6 c
S6.7 a
S6.8 c
S6.9 a
S6.10 b
S6.11 c
S6.12 b

Chapter 7

S7.1 c
S7.2 b
S7.3 d
S7.4 b
S7.5 b
S7.6 d
S7.7 b
S7.8 a
S7.9 b
S7.10 b
S7.11 d
S7.12 a
S7.13 c

Chapter 8

S8.1 a
S8.2 a
S8.3 c
S8.4 c
S8.5 c
S8.6 a
S8.7 b
S8.8 a
S8.9 d

S8.10   c

S8.11   a

S8.12   b

S8.13   a

S8.14   d

S8.15   b

Chapter 9

S9.1   b

S9.2   a

S9.3   d

S9.4   b

S9.5   b

S9.6   a

S9.7   c

S9.8   d

S9.9   d

S9.10   b

S9.11   c

S9.12   a

Chapter 10

S10.1   c

S10.2   a

S10.3   c

S10.4   b

S10.5   a

S10.6   b

S10.7   b

S10.8   d

S10.9   a

Chapter 11

S11.1   a

S11.2   a

S11.3   a

S11.4   d

S11.5   c

S11.6   c

S11.7   a

S11.8   a

S11.9   d

S11.10   b

S11.11   c

S11.12   a

Chapter 12

S12.1   c

S12.2   a

S12.3   c

S12.4   b

S12.5   d

S12.6   d

S12.7   a

S12.8   d

S12.9   b

S12.10   a

S12.11   c

S12.12   c

Chapter 13

S13.1   b

S13.2   b

S13.3   c

S13.4   b

S13.5   a

S13.6   d

S13.7   d

S13.8   a

S13.9   a

S13.10   c

S13.11   b

S13.12   b

Chapter 14

S14.1   d

S14.2   a

S14.3   a

S14.4   a

S14.5   b

S14.6   c

S14.7   a

S14.8   c

S14.9   b

S14.10   d

S14.11   b

Chapter 15

S15.1   a

S15.2   b

S15.3   c

S15.4   d

S15.5   a

S15.6   b

S15.7   b

S15.8   a

S15.9   c

S15.10   c

S15.11   b

S15.12   d

Chapter 16

S16.1   c

S16.2   a

S16.3   b

S16.4   a

S16.5   a

S16.6   a

S16.7   b

S16.8   a

S16.9   a

S16.10   a

S16.11   a

S16.12   a

Index